Parenting Life Now

This book is dedicated to Nolan and Laura Henderson, to other parents who face unimaginable challenges as they raise their children, and to all parents who are just trying to make it through the day. You are not alone.

"Embrace the challenge to create a new tomorrow."

St. Jude Children's Research Hospital

Donate by phone: (800) 805-5856

Donate online: https://www.stjude.org/donate/donate-to-st-jude.html

Sara Miller McCune founded SAGE Publishing in 1965 to support the dissemination of usable knowledge and educate a global community. SAGE publishes more than 1,000 journals and over 600 new books each year, spanning a wide range of subject areas. Our growing selection of library products includes archives, data, case studies, and video. SAGE remains majority owned by our founder and after her lifetime will become owned by a charitable trust that secures the company's continued independence.

Los Angeles | London | New Delhi | Singapore | Washington DC | Melbourne

Parenting Life Now

Kelly Jean Welch

Kansas State University

Victor Harris

The University of Florida

Los Angeles | London | New Delhi
Singapore | Washington DC | Melbourne

FOR INFORMATION:

SAGE Publications, Inc.
2455 Teller Road
Thousand Oaks, California 91320
E-mail: order@sagepub.com

SAGE Publications Ltd.
1 Oliver's Yard
55 City Road
London, EC1Y 1SP
United Kingdom

SAGE Publications India Pvt. Ltd.
Unit No 323–333, Third Floor, F-Block
International Trade Tower Nehru Place
New Delhi – 110 019
India

SAGE Publications Asia-Pacific Pte. Ltd.
18 Cross Street #10-10/11/12
China Square Central
Singapore 048423

Printed in the United States of America

Library of Congress Control Number: 2023906407

ISBN: 978-1-0718-1695-0

Acquisitions Editor: Erica DeLuca

Product Associate: Avren Keating

Production Editor: Laureen Gleason

Copy Editor: Christobel Colleen Hopman

Typesetter: diacriTech

Cover Designer: Scott Van Atta

Marketing Manager: Jennifer Haldeman

This book is printed on acid-free paper.

23 24 25 26 27 10 9 8 7 6 5 4 3 2 1

BRIEF CONTENTS

DETAILED CONTENTS

Chapter 2 The Varied Experiences of Parenting 43

PREFACE

When high school teachers Laura and Nolan took their infant son to the hospital with flu-like symptoms, they didn't know that their world was about to be forever changed. After a thorough evaluation, barely three months old, Grit was diagnosed with an exceedingly rare Stage 4 soft-tissue cancer. Paralyzed in fear and not able to make sense of anything, they relied on the exceptional team of medical, human service, child, and parenting professionals to walk them through every step of their uncertain journey.

Today, countless parents sometimes find themselves with nowhere else to turn for help as they try to navigate out-of-the-blue parenting challenges, such as that faced by Nolan and Laura, and emerging difficulties that weren't on parenting radars as recent as five years ago, such as parents seeking information about how to best support their gender nonconforming child. There is no question that parenting in contemporary society is challenging—and the parenting professional must be equipped to help parents successfully navigate the everyday and extraordinary challenges present-day parenting presents. *Parenting Life Now* is just the tool to effectively and sufficiently equip today's parenting professional.

With its conversational tone, *Parenting Life Now* is a core text for upper level postsecondary students as it describes and promotes the ways in which parents and those professionals who work with parents (such as teachers, healthcare providers, social workers, therapists, child life specialists, sociologists, psychologists, and child care providers) can employ strengths-oriented, best practices to deliver effective, quality education and care. Comprehensive, contemporary, and relevant to today's complex societal issues and changes, *Parenting Life Now* engages students through a balanced, integrated approach of *early childhood education, human development, and family science* disciplines.

This text is a carefully crafted synthesis of theory and application. As well as being academic family practitioners and researchers, much of our work is applied in nature. For example, we have strong ties to education, each having taught in public schools in the United States. Kelly, a Certified Family Life Educator (CFLE), has created a number of psychoeducation programs for women, and for mothers and their infants and children, for both the United States and Caribbean countries; she has also developed sexuality education programs for high school and college students. Vic, also a CFLE, currently directs the Healthy Marriage and Responsible Father SMART Couples Project in Florida. This program is aimed at helping people to form and maintain strong relationships.

It is important to note that we also emphasize theory in our work with individuals, couples, parents, and families because theories provide the foundation of evidence-based practice, and they are the underpinning of a holistic approach to parenting and parenting education. Our goal with *Parenting Life Now* is to guide readers to an understanding of the importance and implications of theory for practitioners, while providing robust applied coverage throughout the book. We begin the book with an overview of classical social and family models that organize different contexts of society and encapsulate family development over time. Subsequent chapters address postmodern thought, such as *intersectionality, African Heritage theory*, and *Critical Disability theory*. Throughout the text, we fuse application and theory to better equip readers for real-world practice.

Students who are preparing to work with parents and their children, and those who are or will be parents themselves, will discover the ways in which infants, children, adolescents, and adults develop across the lifespan while they simultaneously experience the changing nature of family systems and parent–child relationships over time. In the first parenting professional text of its kind to do so, the intersectionality of complex, multifaceted societal issues is synthesized into our traditional understandings of child and adolescent development.

Parenting Life Now Is a Standout Experience

Parenting Life Now provides students with a fresh, engaging, realistic, and academically informative introduction to the study of parenting, rearing, and educating children. While parenting books traditionally emphasize individual development of children and adults, they fall short of providing an in-depth understanding of how family experiences and family systems affect parenting practices. By using a **family science** lens to understand today's parenting experiences and child outcomes, *Parenting Life Now* meets the needs of today's professionals by employing the scientific study of children, families, and close interpersonal relationships to gain a comprehensive understanding of the diversity of family living and parenting. In addition to child development research and theories, *Parenting Life Now* implements the pillars of family science:

- **Relationship focused:** An emphasis is placed on forming, strengthening, and maintaining healthy interpersonal relationships across the lifespan. Throughout the text, myriad couple and family experiences and processes are discussed at length, and attention is given to how the parent–child relationship changes across time.
- **Multidisciplinary:** There are many theoretical strengths and concepts found in other disciplines. All key aspects of the social sciences are drawn upon in a family science approach, and each chapter provides an exploration and investigation of major theoretical concepts.
- **Evidence based:** When working with families and parents, family science professionals access research findings to develop and implement effective programs and policies that serve children and families. *Parenting Life Now* provides substantially more attention to diversity, sexual orientation, and identity experiences than any similar text, as well as enhanced coverage of multicultural issues. Hundreds of current, relevant empirical studies and demographic trends are reported.
- **Strengths oriented:** The core belief of family science is that all parents and families have strengths. With this belief at the forefront, programs are designed and

implemented that enable individuals and families to become self-sufficient. This text provides students with the understanding that *all* parents have strengths, *all* parents experience struggles, and that *all* parents can learn to struggle well and to "do" parenting to their best capabilities.

- **Preventive:** Rather than intervene after problems and difficulties crop up, the family science approach seeks to prevent problems through educational programs with individuals, couples, parents, and families. Students are given an in-depth look at family science career opportunities, such as Family Life Educator (FLE), child life specialists, child therapists, Parents as Teachers, Child Development Associate, Early Childhood Educator, and couple and family therapist (CFT). This book also provides a robust discussion about government policies that affect family living.
- **Applied:** Professionals trained in the early childhood, human development, and family science paradigms possess the knowledge and skills to apply research findings to effectively serve all couples, parents, and families in today's diverse and global society.

To this end, by synthesizing the chapter subject matter with Family Life Educators' practice guidelines, each chapter concludes with a *Parenting Life Education* discussion that applies chapter content to the real world:

- **Chapter 1:** Parenting Life Education: Fostering Healthy Family Formation
- **Chapter 2:** Parenting Life Education: Embracing Differences and Ending Division
- **Chapter 3:** Parenting Life Education: Influencing Parents and Parent Education From Contemporary and Historical Perspectives
- **Chapter 4:** Parenting Life Education: Discussing Childbirth and Pregnancy From a Values-Respective Position
- **Chapter 5:** Parenting Life Education: Addressing Family Needs and Achieving Family Goals
- **Chapter 6:** Parenting Life Education: Fostering Roots and Nurturing Wings
- **Chapter 7:** Parenting Life Education: Promoting Identity and Self-Governing While Providing a Safe Place to Fall
- **Chapter 8:** Parenting Life Education: Removing Barriers and Assisting in Transitions
- **Chapter 9:** Parenting Life Education: Protecting Children's and Adults' Well-Being
- **Chapter 10:** Parenting Life Education: Helping Families to Help Themselves
- **Chapter 11:** Parenting Life Education: #TEAMGRIT
- **Chapter 12:** Parenting Life Education: Affirming Identities, Advocating for Rights and Services, and Promoting Healthy Developmental Outcomes

Distinguishing Coverage

One of the things that makes the study of contemporary parenting so challenging is the rapidly changing nature of these experiences and the diversity that accompanies it. The changes in the experiences of children and parents in our culture are happening so swiftly that there is often a lag between people's experiences and research. Every effort has been made to bring you the most relevant, current information, and we think that you will find that this book provides the most thorough, comprehensive, significant coverage available today, including the newest available research and the most recent trends and demographics. *Parenting Life Now* provides inclusive coverage that affects parenting experiences today:

- **Chapter 1:** In this chapter, we describe the experiences of individuals and couples who decide to have children, and we provide a thorough discussion regarding LGBTQ+ individuals and couples. We also provide newer evidence that addresses *lesbian comotherhood*, gay fatherhood, and gay/lesbian adoption. The primary emphasis of this chapter is to provide readers an understanding of today's parents in the United States.
- **Chapter 2:** In this chapter, we describe portraits of American families and their racial, ethnic, and cultural experiences, as well as the unique parent–child interactions that occur in different racial/ethnic groups. Throughout the text, we use the term *Latinx* as a gender-neutral alternative to Latino or Latina. We address *undocumented and immigrant families* with children, and provide a rare discussion about contemporary Indigenous family patterns and parent–child interactions. *Intersectionality* and *African Heritage* theory are introduced before students read in-depth coverage about how children learn about their racial and ethnic identities (*racial and ethnic socialization*), the effects of racism on children's health, and the importance of *antidiscrimination education for children*.
- **Chapter 3:** This chapter provides thorough coverage about the family as a system of interconnected members, and the tenets of *Family Systems* theory. We build upon this theory and its principles as we examine the ways in which diversity affects family communication strategies and experiences. An evidence-based discussion about *adolescent and parent views about social media* ties this contemporary parenting issue to the *Symbolic Interaction framework*, and helps readers to make the connection between application and theory. We also discuss how theory is applied when creating and implementing children and family policies at the federal and local levels.
- **Chapter 4:** A *nonherteronormative* approach is used to describe pregnancy, childbearing, and early days parenting to validate sexual and gender minorities as a part of childbearing practices in contemporary America. *Transgender men and nonbinary people (TGNB)* who have a functioning vagina, ovaries, and uterus are capable of becoming pregnant, carrying a pregnancy to term, and giving birth; thus, pregnancy is possible for transgender men and queers. We use the term *gestational*

parent to refer to the pregnant person, the individual who is carrying and birthing human life.

- **Chapter 5:** Distinctive coverage includes a comprehensive discussion about the whole child and holistic development, and the parents' roles in the healthy development of the infant's brain, and coverage about self-regulation in early childhood. Ethnic group differences in parenting infants and toddlers are also described.

- **Chapter 6:** Distinguishing coverage in this robust chapter includes discussions about topics that present challenges to today's parents, including *children's mental health* (pre- and post-COVID-19), *inadequate and inequitable education, and the interplay between technology, social media, and children's mental health.* Because too-many-to-count parents face obstacles in finding accurate information about how best to support their *sexual and gender minority children*, we are proud to introduce a first-of-its-kind discussion about child sexual development in a parenting textbook. Thorough coverage about *Adverse Child Experiences (ACEs)* is provided.

- **Chapter 7:** This data-rich chapter helps the parenting professional to understand adolescent experiences in the United States. Two contemporary parenting practices, *emotion-related parenting* and *emotion coaching*, describe ways in which parents can help their teens to self-regulate and to teach them about emotions. Distinguishing coverage includes sexual and gender minority adolescents and friendships; hooking up experiences; teen dating violence; teenage pregnancy; sexually transmitted infections; and adolescent substance use and abuse. Anxiety, depression, and suicidality are also addressed.

- **Chapter 8:** Coverage in this chapter discusses the ways in which the parent–adult child relationship changes over time. We discuss in detail the growing phenomenon of adult children living at home, and the challenges this living arrangement present to aging adults, as well as reciprocal losses that are experienced when children become caregivers for their parents.

- **Chapter 9:** This chapter describes parenting in single-parent families and stepfamilies, and focuses on the aftermath of divorce. Distinctive coverage includes the relationship between the *custodial parent and the child*, and the *noncustodial parent and the child*.

- **Chapter 10:** In this chapter, we address common pre-COVID-19 challenges that dual-career couples experienced as parents, as well as those challenges encountered by single-parent mothers and fathers. Because of the nation-wide innumerable financial crises caused by the COVID-19 pandemic, we examine the fallout as today's families try to regain their economic footing after losing their jobs, and, in many cases, their life savings to the pandemic.

- **Chapter 11:** Family violence (intimate partner, domestic, and violence perpetrated against children) is discussed in this chapter. We discuss *gender-based violence*

(GBV), violence that is experienced because of a person's gender/gender identity, and consider the intersectionality of GBV, single-parent mothers, SES, and race. We also address another rapidly increasing, threatening crisis for American parents, that of homelessness, and its effect on parenting and child development. We describe ways in which parenting professionals can support homeless parents and their children.

- **Chapter 12:** In this chapter we introduce *critical disability theory (CDT)*, a framework that is aimed at shifting paradigms about disabled children. CDT provides the understanding that disability is a multifaceted experience that is not necessarily limited to a person's health, but that it is a cultural, social, and political oppression experience as well. To this end, we do away with euphemisms (such as special needs, differently abled, exceptional children, person with a disability, etc.) and instead use the term *disabled*; we adopt identity-affirming language to value and recognize children's strengths, rather than their "limitations." We also include a discussion about parent–child relationships.

We are so pleased with this text, and believe that its relevant, distinguishing coverage embodies Laura and Nolan's parenting experiences with their son, Grit, and speaks to the challenges facing today's parents. As Nolan says, "You just fight another day. That's how he did it. That's how we're doing it." *Grit* means courage, resolve, strength of character, perseverance, determination, tenacity. These are the characteristics that so well describe this child's personality.

And, without question, these are the characteristics that propel determined parents and families to do whatever it takes to raise children in the face of unprecedented challenges and changes in the world today. Thank you for joining us in our efforts to promote healthy child, parent, and family relationship development, and to educate parenting professionals and practitioners who are informed, equipped, and empowered to work with parents in diverse, inclusive, and equitable ways.

ABOUT THE AUTHORS

Long-time colleagues and friends, Dr. Welch and Dr. Harris, together provide readers a holistic, all-encompassing, culturally sensitive, inclusive, and relevant text that speaks to the rewards and challenges of parenting today: *Parenting Life Now.*

Kelly Jean Welch, PhD, CFLE, has vast experience as a human development and family science professor, author, program developer, and practitioner. Dr. Welch's primary areas of research, writing, and practice include lifespan development, the formation and maintenance of interpersonal relationships, family processes across the lifespan, family crisis and change, and human sexuality across the life course. She has developed programming for individuals and families who are navigating medical crises, as well as programming for sexual and reproductive health, and spends her summers working with HIV+ mothers and their babies in the Caribbean. After twenty years at Kansas State University as an Associate Professor of Teaching in Human Development and Family Science, Dr. Welch recently transitioned to teaching Early Childhood Education courses in impoverished, diverse, at-risk public schools in Kansas. Through creative, innovative programming, Dr. Welch has established a sustainable education model where high school students earn Child Development Associate (CDA) certifications through hands-on experiences in early childhood education centers, giving high school graduates a solid footing to earn livable wages, breaking the cycle of intergenerational poverty. This programming also shows promise in closing the ever-widening child care supply gaps in the state of Kansas. Dr. Welch hopes to replicate this model in other states where there are prolific child care deserts. Dr. Welch is the mother of four adult sons, and is Emaw to eight grandchildren.

Victor Harris, PhD, CFLE, is currently an Associate Professor and Extension Specialist at the University of Florida in the Department of Family, Youth and Community Sciences. He has authored and coauthored over 300 books, publications, and creative works for youth and adults reaching readers in more than 100 countries. His research interests include close relationships with a focus on healthy communication, conflict resolution, couple and parenting education, and balancing work and family. Dr. Harris directs the Healthy Marriage and Responsible Fatherhood SMART Couples Project, designed to help youth, singles, couples, parents, and coparents better understand how to form and maintain strong, healthy, long-lasting relationships. To date, more than 7,500 youth and adults have successfully completed SMART Couples programming. Dr. Harris's studies, research, teaching, and outreach has taken him to nearly all 50 of the United States and to more than 35 countries. He and his wife, Heidi, reside in Florida and have also directed multiple travel study groups to Europe. They enjoy studying different cultures and peoples and how they form and maintain close relationships. He and Heidi have three children and four grandchildren they love spending time with.

1 PARENTING LIFE NOW

LEARNING OBJECTIVES

1.1 Explain the childbearing trends in the United States, including why birth to unmarried parents is becoming more common.

1.2 Describe the emerging trends of teenage pregnancy and same-sex couples who raise children.

1.3 Discuss why parents today choose to have children, to delay childbearing, or to remain childfree by choice.

1.4 Outline the processes of adoption and the experiences of LGBTQ+ individuals who adopt.

1.5 Describe the concepts of motherhood and fatherhood, paying particular attention to the experiences of lesbian mothers and gay fathers.

1.6 Demonstrate knowledge of the pillars of the Family Science paradigm.

grit—noun: courage, bravery, determination, tenacity, fortitude, toughness, endurance, perseverance.

High school teachers, Nolan and Laura, named their son Grit because they believed in the power of perseverance. They didn't know at the time that their son would need each and every one of these characteristics—and more—to make it to his first birthday. Shortly before Christmas, the parents took their 3-month-old son, Grit, to the hospital due to dehydration and flu-like symptoms. After a battery of painful tests, Grit was diagnosed with embryonal rhabdomyosarcoma, a cancer of the soft tissue. Grit was only the second 3-month-old on record to ever be diagnosed with this tissue mass on the prostate, and he began 52 weeks of intensive chemotherapy treatments. At 22 months of age, a tumor was found in his lung, and despite surgery and chemotherapy treatments to destroy the new tumor, the mass continued to grow. Grit then began 20 rounds of radiation treatments. By the time he was two years old, Grit had been under anesthesia 25 to 30 times. Today, Grit is a spunky, eager, mischievous, chatty 3-year-old who is in remission. And while chemotherapy treatments are a routine part of his life, and his bald head is as much a part of his personality as is his name, you would never know that this little guy has had to embody the meanings of his name to make it this far.

But Grit isn't the only one who has fought this horrific battle: His parents are every bit as much the warriors as their son. As Nolan's former professor and now colleague, I marvel at he and Laura's tenacity. Their endurance. Their toughness. Their perseverance. I am amazed at their ability to parent their older daughter while simultaneously confronting head-on their son's deadly cancer. When I watch Grit play and laugh and explore and question and wonder, I am awed at his healthy development, despite the tremendous obstacles he has encountered and overcome. I shake my head in disbelief. I cry in thankfulness and gratitude. How did they do it?

Source: Author's files.

Parenthood is fraught with ups and downs, choices and challenges, and elation and disappointment. But today parenting is more daunting and demanding than it ever has been before, with every day, common stressors such as single parents and couples meeting the financial demands in a flailing economy and unprecedented job loss in the United States, crisis home schooling amid the COVID-19 pandemic in 2020, concern for the well-being of older loved ones, working remotely from home while simultaneously engaging children in activities and maintaining their routines, and doing the best they can to meet the emotional needs of their children. Even without the unusual circumstances in 2020, for parents, a "good day" may have hinged on whether a child passed a spelling test or won a blue ribbon at the science fair, or whether a son or a daughter received a university scholarship. A bad day may have been one in which parents discovered that their child was victim of a school bully. Add to the common stressors the sudden hit from the unexpected: We have seen the hopeless, helpless, and lost looks on the faces of our friends as they confronted the sudden death of their 14-year-old son in a skiing accident. We have seen our friends confront and struggle with their young adult son's opioid addiction—and we were there holding and comforting them when he succumbed to that war. And for nearly three years, we witnessed the physical, emotional, mental, spiritual, and financial suffering of Nolan and Laura as they faced head-on Grit's illness, and the unfolding of his young life that they could never have imagined or prepared for. To be sure, with all of its joys and triumphs, parenting can be an intimidating task—and sometimes a frightening experience. Certainly, parenting requires *grit*.

Children have always been a part of the family structure. Across the pages of time and history, children were considered a vital, necessary segment of society because they were needed to ensure the survival of the culture or race—they were viewed as necessary economic assets for society's continuation and as the manual labor needed to bring about that continuation (Humphries, 2010). My husband's family is a prime example of this. When his grandfather was nine years old, he made passage by himself from the then Czechoslovakia to the United States where he labored in the fields until he earned enough money to bring his parents and siblings to this country. My husband's mother was one of nine children. Before the age of seven, every child had chores (which required strenuous physical labor) to do on the family farm. In the

Children have always been a part of a family's structure because there was a practical benefit to having children as free manual labor.

Source: Photo Courtesy of Kelly Welch.

19th and much of the 20th centuries, whether children worked on family farms or were used as indentured servants or apprentices, their presence in society was essential because they helped to bring about the society's future (Gunnarsson et al., 2006). Today, children the world over still represent their culture's future, and because of this, society expects parents to do a good job and create healthy, productive citizens (Lerner et al., 2004). Parenting a child in the 21st century is a monumental responsibility!

Throughout our course of study together, we'll explore what it means to be a mother or a father, or a parent, and what the parenting role requires at different stages of infant, child, and adolescent development. We also look at contemporary issues that today's parents face, such as teaching children about their racial/ethnic identities, high-risk families, and parenting sexual minority children and adolescents. As with any other human service field, knowing what to expect and equipping ourselves with knowledge and expertise prepares us to rise to the challenges. This book provides people in, or desiring to enter, the helping professions with information about effectively working with parents, be it in an early childhood setting, in healthcare, or in a therapeutic setting. It also assists prospective parents and those who are already parents in exploring the concepts of parenting so that they might develop the skills necessary for effectiveness in their roles.

People can grow their families in a number of ways. In this chapter, we begin our study of parenting life today by taking a look at current childbearing trends in the United States, which includes examining teen pregnancy and parenthood, as well as pathways to gay and lesbian parenting. We look at how people decide to have children and how they determine their family sizes, and the distinctions between parenthood and parenting. We'll then explore the concept of parenting education by looking at past education efforts, assess the present, and look briefly at the challenges for the future. We'll conclude our discussion with gaining an understanding of how parenting and early childhood practitioners can foster healthy family formation.

CHILDBEARING TRENDS: WHO'S HAVING BABIES?

Parents and family life are the foundations that influence a child's development and well-being from birth into early adulthood; both play instrumental roles in stimulating and shaping a child's cognitive, social, and emotional development (Solomon-Fears, 2008). Because of the tremendous influences parents and the home environment exert on a child's development, we begin our study of the pathways to parenting by gaining an understanding of the childbearing trends in the United States today: Who's having babies, and how old are America's parents?

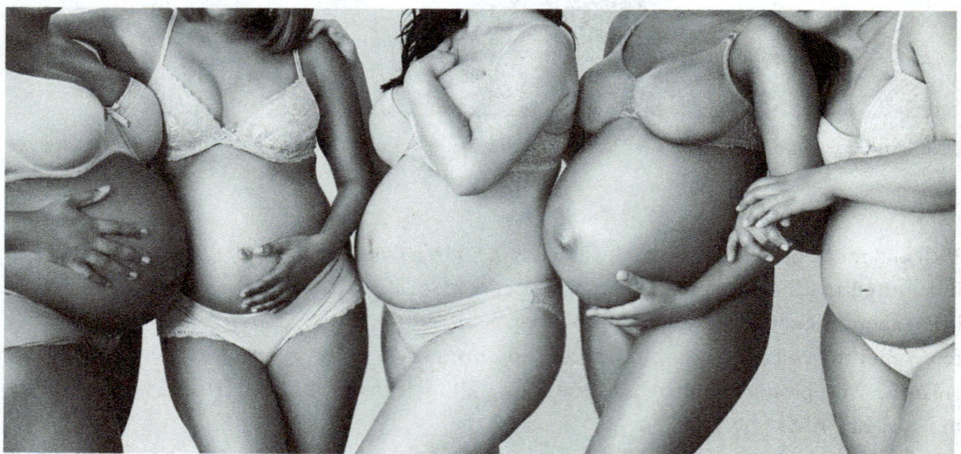

Each year in the United States, nearly four million babies are born. Today, about 40 percent of births are nonmarital, and the average age of childbearing has increased from a person's 20s to their 30s.

Source: iStock.com/DelmainDonsonPhotography.

Who Are America's Parents?

Each year, the population in the United States increases by the addition of slightly less than four million babies (CDC, 2019a). The **crude birth rate** is the number of childbirths per 1,000 women, per year. These figures are tracked worldwide; in general, the crude birth rate in economically disadvantaged countries is higher than in more economically advantaged countries. In less economically developed countries, such as Niger, Uganda, Kenya, and Pakistan, the crude birth rate is significantly higher than in richer countries. In 2018, the crude birth rate in the United States was 11.8 (per 1,000 women); this is in comparison with 14.2 in 2007 and 24 in 1960 (National Vital Statistics Reports, 2019).

The **total fertility rate** is the average number of live births per woman, in a given population, per year. The U.S. fertility rate in 2018 was 1.72, down from 1.76 in 2017 (National Vital Statistics Reports, 2019). Countries that are less economically advantaged tend to have higher fertility rates, just as they have higher crude birth rates. It is important to note, however, that fertility rates are also a reflection of a region's religious, cultural, and ethnic norms. For example, because of their collectivist cultural beliefs and their strong ties to families, Latinx cultures tend to have more children than individualistic cultures such as the United States and the United Kingdom. The one-child policy in China—a practice that encouraged late marriages and late childbirths, and mandated only one child per couples in urban areas—was a cultural norm that today accounts for China's and Taiwan's low fertility rates. In 2015, this policy was relaxed; under a new policy, families today are permitted to have two children. For any given country, a fertility rate of 2.1 is considered to be the **replacement fertility rate**. As you can see, the United States is currently below this replacement rate. By tracking the crude birth rate from year to year, as well as the fertility rates, demographers are able to see certain childbearing trends, such as the age of birth mother.

What is the current teen birth rate? Are women waiting until they are older to have children? Are there more babies born to single women than there are to married women? Answers to these questions can be found by looking at birth certificate data—the registered births. How many teens are giving birth?

Trends Among Teenagers

In 2004, the birth rates for teenaged mothers reached a historic low, with a birth rate of 41.2 births per 1,000 women aged 15 to 19 (CDC, 2005). At the time, these trends were quite encouraging because in 1991 the birth rate for teen moms was nearly 62 per 1,000 women. In 2018, the birth rate for women aged 15 to 19 was 17.4 births per 1,000—an all-time low and a 55 percent decline since 2007 (National Vital Statistics Reports, 2019). It's still too early to know if this downward trend is permanent, but one thing is for certain: Today, teenaged sexual partners are either abstaining from sexual intercourse or they are practicing safer methods of sex and contraception. As you can see in Figure 1.1, the numbers of births among teen moms vary between races and ethnicities. Encouragingly, the birth rates have declined for all groups.

Trends Among Unmarried Parents

Nonmarital births are widespread, and they touch families of all different races and ethnicities, income class, religious groups, and demographic areas. In 2018, slightly over 40 percent of all births in the United States were nonmarital births; this rate has remained relatively steady since 2014 (Centers for Disease Control and Prevention, 2019). Births to unmarried partners can be first births or subsequent births; they can occur to a person who has never been married, as well as to divorced or widowed individuals. Further, a woman with children may have had one or more within a marriage and other births outside of marriage. And, because prior to 2016, U.S. demographers did not consider gay or lesbian partnerships to be

FIGURE 1.1 ■ Birth Rates (per 1,000 Women) for Females Aged 15–19, by Race and Hispanic Origin of Mother: 2016 and 2017

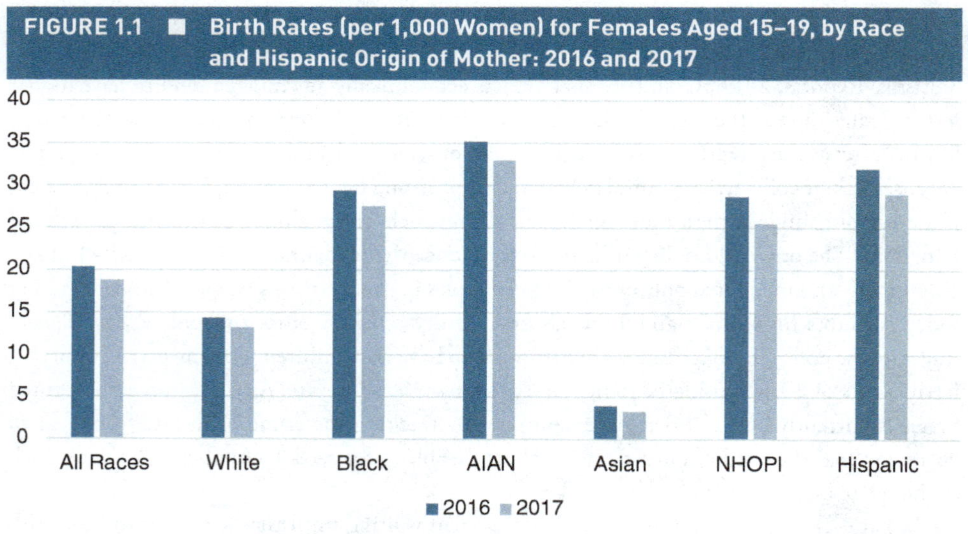

Source: National Vital Statistics Reports (2021).

"marriages," births to these couple were considered to be "nonmarital" births. Today, Black/Black Caribbean families are typically formed when an unmarried mother gives birth to a child; the recent data confirm that more than two-thirds (67 percent) of African American births were nonmarital births (National Vital Statistics Reports, 2017). By way of comparison, slightly more than one-half of births among American Indians/Native Alaskans were to unmarried women, and about one-fourth were to nonmarried white women (National Vital Statistics Reports, 2017).

A number of factors are associated with the unprecedented rates of births that occur outside of marriage (Solomon-Fears, 2008):

- Marriage postponement—there is an increase in the median age at first marriage
- Childfree movement—there is decreased childbearing among married couples
- Increased divorce rates
- Increased numbers of cohabiting couples
- Increased sexual activity outside of marriage
- Improper use/lack of use of contraceptive methods
- Participation in risky behaviors that often lead to sex, such as alcohol and drug use

When considering all of these factors, the trend of births to unmarried partners may very well continue and may even further increase. Certainly, these trends will continue to reshape the landscape of American family life and parenting experiences.

Pregnancy at Different Ages

In the past, women in their 20s were thought to be at the peak of their childbearing years and have historically accounted for the most births. What are today's trends? In 2017, among women aged 20 to 24, the birth rate was 71.0—down from 85.1 in 2008 (National Vital Statistics Reports, 2018; see Figure 1.2). In contemporary America, the primary childbearing years are now a person's early 30s. These data may reflect the overall trends of people who delay childbearing to pursue educational and professional endeavors, as well as an increase in cohabitation. Today, Millennial women account for the vast majority of births in the United States—82 percent (Pew Research Center, 2018a). However, they are delaying childbearing in comparison to Generation X people. For example, while today 48 percent of Millennial women are parents, when Gen X women were the same age, 57 percent of them were already moms (Pew Research Center, 2018b). These data support the idea that people are delaying childbearing today.

The United States is also seeing an increase in births among older women not traditionally thought of as in their "childbearing years." As you can see in Table 1.1, birth rates are increasing among women between the ages of 40 and 49.

Childbearing trends evolved throughout the 20th and into the 21st centuries. As the data show, many people are delaying childbearing—perhaps due to education and career opportunities or perhaps due to relationship circumstances. Later we'll explore in depth why some individuals and couples delay—or defer all together—childbearing.

EMERGENT PARENTING TYPES

Now that you have a good understanding of the birth trends in the United States, let's take a more in-depth look at two groups of parents that have become an increasing focus of family and social scientists: Teenage mothers and gay and lesbian parents. Although we extensively

FIGURE 1.2 ■ Birth Rates Among All Age Groups, 2017

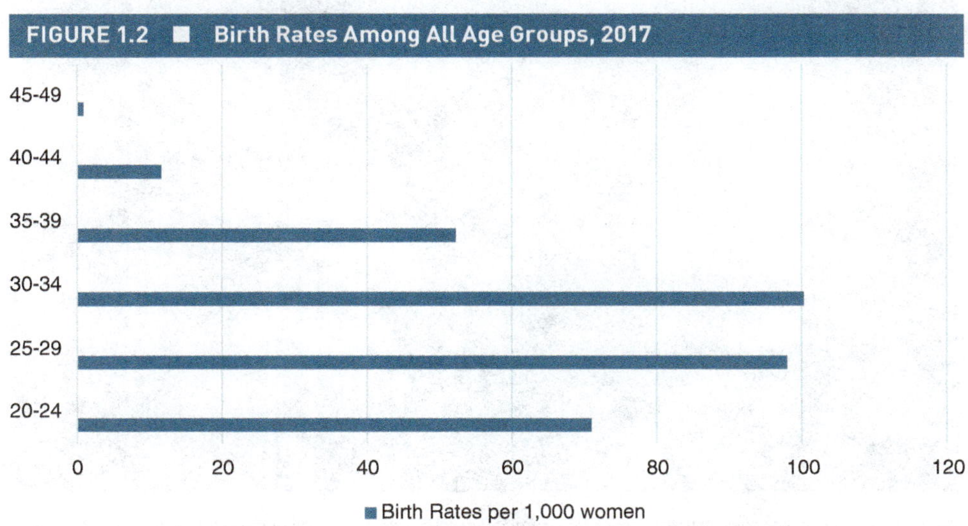

Source: National Vital Statistics Reports (2021).

TABLE 1.1 ■ Birth Rates Among Older Women, Ages 40–49: 2010–2017

Year	Age of Person Giving Birth	
	40–44	45–49
2010	10.2	0.7
2011	10.3	0.7
2012	10.4	0.7
2013	10.4	0.8
2014	10.6	0.8
2015	11.0	0.8
2016	11.4	0.9
2017	11.6	0.9

Source: National Vital Statistics Reports (2021).

explore these parenting groups in Chapters 2 and 7, here it's important to understand that these two, emerging parent–child structures are altering the ways in which parenting is understood. Indeed, there is no one-size-fits-all parent structure in our contemporary society.

Although teenage pregnancy carries with it many medical, psychological, and developmental obstacles, with educational, informational, and emotional support, young parents can overcome these difficulties.

Source: Tina Stallard via Getty Images.

Teenage Parents

During the next 12 months, more than half a million teenagers will become pregnant and nearly 195,000 will give birth (The Alan Guttmacher Institute, 2018). In spite of the recent declines in teen birth rates to U.S. adolescent girls and young women, the teen pregnancy rate in the United States is substantially higher than in other Western industrialized nations. For example, in America, the teen pregnancy rate is 17.4, while Canada has a teen pregnancy rate of 12.8 (The Alan Guttmacher Institute, 2018). The Guttmacher Institute, a nonprofit organization that focuses on sexual and reproductive health research, notes that although the United States has seen substantial declines in teen pregnancy rates over the past 10 years, adolescent birth rates remain more than twice as high as those found in other countries. Figure 1.3 presents the birth rates of other Western countries.

In our study of parenting and working with parents, it is important to understand the incidence of teen pregnancy because births to teen moms are linked to a host of critical issues in our society today: Poverty, overall child health and well-being, births to unmarried women, responsible fatherhood, sexuality and health concerns, education/school failure, child abuse and neglect, and other risky behaviors, such as drug and alcohol use and abuse and crime (Power to Decide, 2019). There is no doubt that teen pregnancy and childbearing carry both social and economic impacts on the teen moms and their children. Without question, teen mothers face a range of developmental risks.

The National Organization on Adolescent Pregnancy, Parenting, and Prevention (2008) has stated, "[Given that] all children need healthy, nurturing, stable relationships and to experience the protective factors during early childhood...[and] given the competing dynamics of adolescence and the demands of parenthood, it is incumbent upon families, communities, and

FIGURE 1.3 ■ Birth Rates, by Country: 2018

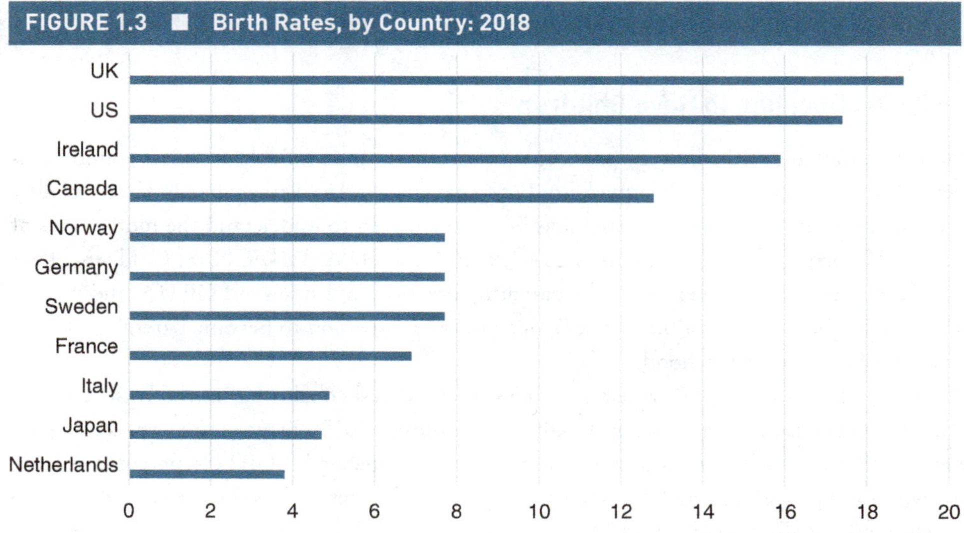

Source: The Alan Guttmacher Institute (2018).

society to provide supportive [structures] to teen parents to ensure their children grow health and safe and reach school ready to learn." To this end, a national campaign to reduce teen pregnancy should include the following:

- *Comprehensive school-based programs* designed to keep the pregnant and/or parenting adolescent in school and on track to complete her degree.
- *Comprehensive family support services* designed to help parents of the pregnant and/or parenting teen to develop parenting skills and coping skills.
- *Expansion of government programs* designed to improve the medical and psychosocial health and well-being of pregnant and parenting teens and their offspring. Youth-friendly contraceptive and reproduce health services should be included.
- *Comprehensive community programs* designed to enhance adolescents' parenting skills and support the unique needs of teen mothers and fathers and to provide early education for at-risk infants and children.

In 2007, then-U.S. presidential candidate Senator Barack Obama (D-IL) introduced a bill to reduce teen pregnancies in minority communities. The Communities of Color Teen Pregnancy Prevention Act of 2007 sought to strengthen community-based intervention efforts for teen pregnancy services and to establish a comprehensive national database to provide culturally and linguistically sensitive information on teen pregnancy reduction. Senator Obama noted:

Teen pregnancy can derail the plans of students with dreams of achieving professional success, and it's hitting minority communities particularly hard. Pregnancies in Black and Latino communities remain inexcusably high. We must develop innovative approaches to strengthen our community support networks and services to educate our teens about pregnancy and provide them with every chance to succeed in school and beyond (Congress, 2008).

LGBTQ+: Deciding to Have Children

How do sexual minorities become parents? What are the routes available to them to build families? Although the number of planned families by gay men and lesbian women has been steadily growing in recent years, little research has been undertaken to understand the motivations of gays and lesbians to become parents (Bos et al., 2004; Costa & Tasker, 2018; Goldberg et al., 2014). In Chapter 2, we'll examine the parenting practices and styles of LGBTQ+ individuals and couples; here we take a brief look at this group's motivation to become parents and their traditional routes to parenthood.

Today there are 705,000 same-sex couples (married and cohabiting) in the United States, and 68 percent are raising children (Goldberg & Conron, 2018). Female same-sex couples are more likely than male gay couples to parent children. In general, LGBTQ+ parents are more likely than opposite-sex couples to choose adoption and foster care as their preferred route to parenthood (Goldberg et al., 2009, 2012).

While only 2 percent of different-sex couples adopt children, 21 percent of LGBTQ+ parents adopt their children (Goldberg & Conron, 2018). Of course, some LGBTQ+ parents raise their biological children. Figure 1.4 shows us the percentages of U.S. coupled households in which there are children and the relationship of the child to the parent.

In a study of 366 prospective LGBTQ+ adopters of children, the researcher wanted to determine the reasons why same-sex couples wanted children, specifically, their motivations for adoption (Costa & Tasker, 2018). The study found these overarching themes among LGBTQ+ parents:

- **Seeking permanency:** "We wanted a forever family" (p. 4165).
- **Altruistic/moral motivation:** Couples wanted to provide a permanent home for a child in need.
- **Individualistic/intrinsic motivation:** "I thought that sharing the adoptive experience with my trans partner would be more equitable than being the biological parent in our partnership" (p. 4168).
- **Motivated reasoning:** Although some potential parents had hoped to have a biological child, ultimately their desire for being a parent was more important than how the child came to their family.

The emergence of planned gay fatherhood and lesbian motherhood is indicative of broad social change that is taking place in our society and societies around the world. Regardless of

FIGURE 1.4 ■ Households Raising Children Among Coupled Households With Children by Couple Type and Relationship to Child

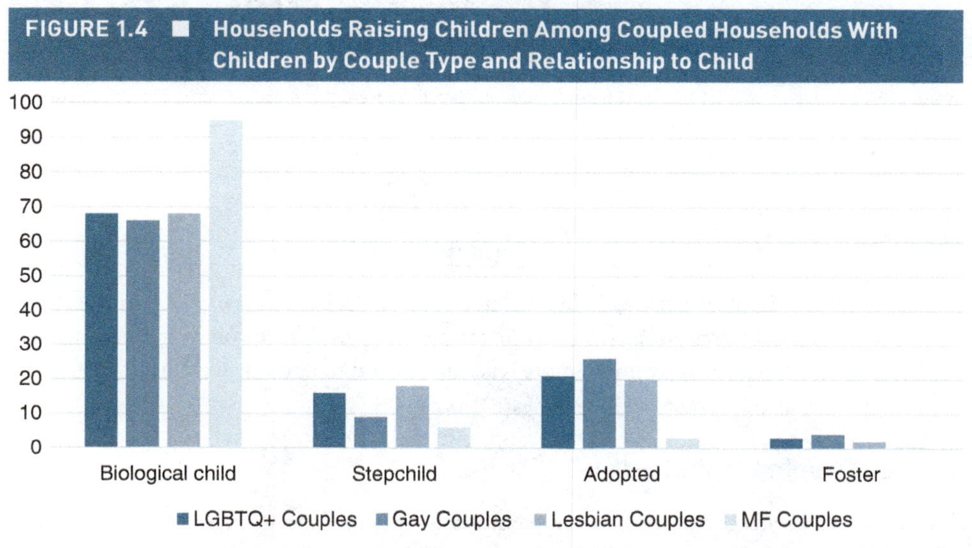

Source: Goldberg, S. K., & Conron, K. J. (2018). *How many same-sex couples are raising children in the United States?* Williams Institute. https://williamsinstitute.law.ucla.edu/publications/same-sex-parents-us/

their sexual orientation, people are questioning existing parenting norms and are finding ways to create families (Berkowitz & Marsiglio, 2007). Examining the experiences of gay men and lesbians gives us an important opportunity to accept them into the parenting mainstream. In Chapter 4, we'll take an extensive look at the parenting experiences of LGBTQ+ people, as well as their experiences with the transition to parenthood.

While LGBTQ+ couples may go the "traditional" route of having children, these couples are far more likely than straight couples to foster and adopt children.

Source: FatCamera via Getty Images.

HAVING CHILDREN: NOW, LATER, OR NEVER?

Do you want children? At what age did you come to your decision—have you wanted to have children/not have children for as long as you can remember, or have you only recently come to this decision, as you have acquired more relationship and life experiences? And when is the "right time" to have children?

Why Do People Want Children?

The decision to become a parent is a very complex issue because it includes a number of interrelated components. For instance, do we have a child because of the subjective value societies place on them or because of personal, intrinsic reasons—or both? Do we have children because society *expects* us to?

Since the 1970s, researchers have attempted to document the various needs that children fulfill for adults; they have also tried to better understand how adults perceive the value of children (see Hoffman & Hoffman, 1973). Over the past four decades, researchers have discovered that people most often desire to have children because of the psychological and emotional satisfaction they offer to parents, the social ties children offer as adults age, and their economic value (such as tax breaks; for a complete review, see Lawson, 2004). On the other hand, the lack of desire to become a parent has been associated with adults who place a greater importance on self-fulfillment, leisure time, relationship quality, career advancement, and greater financial freedom (Seccombe, 1991).

Two main approaches have been taken by social science researchers to understand the attitudes and motivations associated with becoming a parent: The perceived value of children and the appeal of parenthood.

The Perceived Value of Children

Most studies and theories about the motivation to become a parent center on the perspective that there are perceived rewards and costs associated with parenthood (Lawson, 2004). Many of us engage in a cost–benefit analysis when we choose our life partners; we also do the same when we decide whether to have children. For example, some research suggests that one of the rewards of having children is that they meet some of our basic psychological needs (such as love and affection), and this is what motivates peoples' desires to have children (Al-Fadhli & Smith, 1996; Yamaguchi & Fergusson, 1995). Some adults may evaluate the costs (such as substantial decreases in personal time and freedom and substantial increases in financial responsibilities) and decide against having children. If prospective parents believe that the net value of having children is greater than the costs associated with having children, they will be motivated to have children (Lawson, 2004). On the other hand, if they judge that the costs outweigh the benefits, they will forgo the Mommy/Daddy track and seek other sources to meet their needs, such as turning to nieces and nephews for psychological need fulfillment not met by having their own children.

Table 1.2 shows the Perceptions of Parenting Inventory, which helps people determine the rewards and costs they associate with having children (Lawson, 2004). As you can see, this inventory assesses the rewards of parenting, which include *enrichment* and *continuity*, as well as the costs, which include *isolation, instrumental costs*, and *commitment*. As you look through the table, with which items do you most strongly agree? Most strongly disagree with? It's important to note that your answers may change over time. For example, you may not want to have a child at this time because of the financial and emotional costs; however, when your circumstances change, you might decide that the benefits of having children outweigh these particular costs.

The Appeal of Parenthood

Probably all of us have seen children having a temper tantrum at the grocery store or Target and go limp as a wet noodle when an exasperated parent tries to pick the child up to get him or her out of the store as fast as possible. And under our breath (or out loud), we have probably said, "I will *never* have children!" Certainly, there are times when having children doesn't seem like a

TABLE 1.2 ■ Perceptions of Parenting Inventory: Factors People Consider Before Becoming Parents

Enrichment
Caring for the child would bring me happiness.
Parenting the child would be rewarding.
My spouse/partner and I would grow closer together through the experience.
Parenting the child would make me a better person.
Isolation
I would have less time to spend doing what I enjoy.
Caring for the child would interfere with the time I want to spend with my spouse.
Commitment
Parenting the child would be a never-ending responsibility.
The child would be dependent on me.
Instrumental Costs
Raising the child would be financially expensive.
Parenting the child would be emotionally exhausting.
Caring for the child would be physically exhausting.
Continuity
I would look forward to being a grandparent in the future.
Our relationship would change over the years from parent to friend.
The child would carry on my family name.
Perceived Support
My friends and family would help me care for the child.
My family and friends would provide social support.

Source: Based on Lawson (2004).

very appealing thought—even after we've had them! Despite the fact that all of us have probably not wanted children at one time or another, there is some evidence that there are certain psychological factors that are related to the appeal of parenting, particularly that of early childhood experiences.

A number of studies have attempted to show that our early experiences with our parents, such as parental nurturance, discipline, and attention, are significantly related to the motivation to parent. For example, some research has demonstrated that bad memories of our childhood experiences have accounted for unique variances in why some people choose to have children and others do not (Gerson, 1980, 1985, 1986). These experiences underlie what is known as the **family projection process** (Bowen, 1966). This process stresses that the appeal of having children is the result of finding a way to satisfy our individual unmet needs from childhood. Stated another way, people who become parents do so because they feel that they were not given enough love, attention, or support as a child. Their own children, then, serve to enact their internalized unsatisfactory childhood experiences—parents have children to give them what they themselves never had as a child. It's important to note, however, that other research has shown that as individuals enter their 30s, they feel less dependent on childhood memories in making important life choices, such as having children (Gerson et al., 1991).

The decision to have a child or forgo childbearing is a crucial—and irrevocable—decision that warrants careful and thoughtful attention. And, although many of you may know that you desire to have children, the timing of parenthood is also an issue that needs to be considered. Just when is the "right time" to have children in the lifespan of a couple's relationship?

Ready or Not? The "Right Time" to Have Children

Families experience a common lifecourse pattern, referred to as the *Family Life Cycle*, and for many families, this lifecourse includes having children (Duvall, 1977; McGoldrick & Carter, 1982; Rankin, 2000; Rodgers & White, 1993; Russell, 1993). Within psychology and family studies/family sciences, a *life transition* (such as the decision to become a parent) is considered to be a point at which people take on new roles and obligations (Hagestad & Call, 2007). A **turning point** is a transition that entails a permanent, lasting shift in the direction of the lifecourse of a person's relationship. Often, this term is used in connection with the transition to parenthood (Hagestad & Call, 2007). **Timing** refers to the age at which a transition takes place. Thus, when considering the decision to become a parent, the timing of parenthood is given much attention because it speaks to the significance of this transition/turning point in a person's life.

Across life, the majority of individuals follow and relatively adhere to socially approved and shaped pathways, such as the "right" time to get married and the "right" time to have children. These proper times are referred to as **age-related norms**—and these norms are culturally specific. In the United States, for example, the age-related norm of a woman giving birth for the first time is 26 years old, and for fathers, it's 31 (CDC, 2018). By way of comparison, in Switzerland, Japan, Spain, Italy, and South Korea, the age-related norm for women to give birth for the first time is 31. As sociologists Gunhild Hagestad and Vaughn Call (2007) observe, unlike men who can produce children well into old age, "biology presents a woman with nonnegotiable deadlines [for becoming pregnant]," because after a certain point in her lifespan, she no longer has the ability to produce eggs (p. 1342). Thus, a woman's "window of opportunity" to become pregnant is essentially limited to her teens, 20s, and 30s. Women who pass these age norms are often subjected to informal chastising with comments such as, "Having a baby at *your* age?" (Hagestad & Call, 2007). Society also structures the sequence of life transitions. For instance, may societies condone childbearing only after a couple is married. However, as you saw earlier, a significant number of childbirths in this country are to unmarried women; it is clear the childbearing sequence is undergoing change in our society and in other Western societies, as well.

So, when is the "right" time to have children? There is no research that helps us to understand parenthood timing from a practical viewpoint, but there are a number of questions a woman, birthing person, or a couple might ask themselves before becoming pregnant or deciding to bring a child into the relationship through adoption:

- **Do I have the parenting skills necessary to raise a child?** Parenting skills include things such as patience; being able to stay calm in the midst of turmoil; being able to control your anger; understanding how to effectively discipline a child in age-appropriate ways; being able to communicate expectations, warmth, and nurturance; and being an effective role model.
- **How strong is your relationship?** The way a couple treats each other teaches children about love, intimacy, communication, relationships, trust, and respect. Do you have a solid foundation on which to raise a family?

- **Do you and your partner have similar beliefs?** It is imperative that parents in relationships share similar beliefs about discipline, education, child care, and what child behaviors are or are not acceptable. This is especially important if you have an interracial or interfaith relationship.
- **Where are you financially?** Not only must you be able to provide for your child's basic needs (food, shelter, and clothing) but you also need to consider saving for their future education needs, as well as your own.
- **When do you want children?** Rarely does a child bring a couple closer together? Be sure to examine the true motivations for wanting a child.

As most parents will attest, children are wonderful and worth the sleep deprivation, arguments how to/not to raise them, and overdue credit card bills. But in each family, there are many personal factors involved in deciding when to have children. It's not a simple decision because having children *will* change your life. Are you up to the challenge?

The "no kids, no thanks" movement is rapidly growing in the United States. Many couples in their 30s, like Laura and Kyle, decided that they would rather travel the world than have the costs and responsibilities associated with raising children. Where do you stand on the kids/no kids issue? Is there anything that would change your mind?

Source: The Good Brigade via Getty Images.

Childfree by Choice

Never married, Ricky Gervais, the co-creator of the television series *The Office*, has been with his partner, Jane Fallon, for more than 30 years, and they remain childless. As Gervais said,

"We never wanted to be parents, with all that entails: The loss of freedom, total dependency." The **childfree-by-choice** trend is certainly nothing new as a number of A-list celebrities, such as Oprah Winfrey, have opted to remain childfree. Even Dr. Seuss, the infamous children's book author, was childfree by choice. But the "no kids, no thanks" trend is moving beyond the borders of Hollywood and extending to mainstream United States. Today, 4 in 10 (37 percent) of adults over the age of 50 say they don't ever expect to become parents; among adults under age 50, about one-fourth say they just don't want kids (Pew Research Center, 2018a).

Voluntarily childlessness is an emerging field of empirical research in family studies, sociology, and psychology; however, there are studies that help us understand why people opt to remain childfree. For example, one landmark study found that there are certain categories or groups among those who elect not to become parents. These groups include those who are certain they do not want children, those who are certain they do not want children at this point in their lives, those who are ambivalent about having children, and those who feel the decision was made for them due to health reasons or lack of a partner (Cartwright, 1999). In a 2019 study of 322 that examined attitudes toward voluntary childlessness, the researchers discovered that study participants with higher education levels and lower levels of sexism (i.e., adherence to "traditional" gender roles and norms) held positive attitudes toward childlessness; study participants in their 20s and 30s were also more likely to endorse childlessness (Bahtiyar-Saygan & Sakalli-Ugurly, 2019). Conversely, those who possessed traditional gender roles and norms perceived children as necessary to form a family, and as such, provided less support for childlessness.

The reasons people remain childfree are as many and varying as the reasons people opt to become parents. Rathus and Nevid (1992) found in their landmark study of hundreds of couples that there are various reasons why individuals and couples opt for the no-kids track: More time with one another, freedom from the responsibility of raising children, financial freedom, able to devote more time to careers, and concerns about worldwide overpopulation. More recent research seems to confirm these findings. For example, one study posits that there is a value shift taking place in Western cultures, and because of this, people place higher priority on individualization and secularization, a disconnection from the eras-old importance placed on religious and spiritual concerns (Lesthaeghe, 2014).

This newer field of research has also revealed some contributing individual factors—*microfactors*—to the childfree-by-choice patterns seen today:

- **Urbanization:** There are few economic rewards for parents to have many children (Brewster & Rindfuss, 2000; Longman, 2004; van Doorne-Huiskes & Doorten, 2011).
- **Women's professional opportunities:** Increasingly, women have more opportunities to pursue professional and career opportunities (Abma & Martinez, 2006; Agrillo & Nelini, 2008; Koropeckj-Cox & Pendell, 2007; Tanturri & Mencarini, 2008). Some women do not have a longing to have children (Morison, 2013; Peterson & Engwall, 2013).
- **Lack of maternal feelings:** Some people indicate that they lacked a "maternal instinct" or they are generally uninterested in children. Men, more than women, believe that parenting

required too many sacrifices, including great financial expense. Both men and women indicate that they felt their personalities are not suited to parenting (Park, 2005).

- **Economic downturn:** The perceived ability to provide for children is a significant influencer of childbearing decisions, particularly for women (Brewster & Rindfuss, 2000; Longman, 2004; van Doorne-Huiskes & Doorten, 2011).
- **Stable partner relationship:** Those who have stable relationships (and thus, the presence of a co-parent) are more likely to have children than those who do not (Tanturri & Mencarini, 2008).

Macrofactors—those influencers seen at the societal level—also affect childbearing decisions. Changing social values, decreasing importance of religion, access to legal abortion, and effective contraceptives also alter childbearing. Those who choose to be childless do so because of their dislike of children, choice of lifestyle, lack of interest in children and parenting, or a belief that the world is too dangerous for children. For instance, in 2019, American politician Alexandria Ocasio-Cortez (D-NY) raised the issue of whether adults should continue to have children, given the environmental impact of doing so and given the impact of climate change. Although no empirical studies to date have addressed this topic, an online poll of Business Insider (2019) readers found that 38 percent of Americans aged 18 to 29 who responded to the survey believe that climate change should be considered when deciding to have children (Irfan, 2019).

Although to some it may appear that people remain childfree for selfish reasons, this is not necessarily the case. Couples must be honest when assessing whether or not to become parents. Some people feel that their lives are complete and full without children. Others choose to be childfree because of unfortunate circumstances, and in these instances, the decision can be a painful one. For example, a close friend of mine desperately desired to be a mother but because she is a genetic carrier of an always-fatal type of muscular dystrophy, she opted to remain childless. Other couples may not consciously decide not to have children—they simply fall into childlessness.

Delayed Childbearing

While some couples remain childfree by choice and other couples are childless for medical or physiological reasons that prohibit them from becoming pregnant, some couples have perhaps every intention of becoming parents but for one reason or another parenthood eludes them. As Megan, a colleague of mine, explains:

> Before we became engaged, Kale and I knew we wanted children—it was something we held in common. He comes from a very large family, and I come from a family with three other siblings. Our plan was to have our first child by the age of 35, but our business was really taking off and we thought we had plenty of time. We began trying to conceive at about the age of 35 or so and found out we had infertility problems. We tried fertility treatments for a few years with no success…so now we find ourselves in our mid-40s without children. Totally not planned. Or wanted. But even though it's

not what we planned, after the grief passed for the family we had hoped for, we're very content with our lives right now.

Sociology professor Jean Veevers (1980) wanted to better understand how couples like Megan and Kale become a childless couple. This study defined four specific stages involved in delayed childbearing decision-making:

1. **Postponing childbearing for a definite period of time:** Couples in this first stage intentionally delay childbearing in order to achieve certain goals they have set for themselves, such as meeting educational goals. Like Megan and Kale, perhaps they want to devote their attention to their careers or give their new business time to get established.
2. **Postponing childbearing for an indefinite period of time:** "We'll eventually get around to having children." In this stage of decision-making, couples' reasons for not having children become more and more unclear and perhaps indefinable even to themselves. For whatever reasons, they feel that the timing is "just not right."
3. **Weighing the pros and cons of being parents:** During this stage of decision-making, couples deliberate the costs and benefits associated with parenthood.
4. **Coming to terms with being childless:** It is at this point that couples realize they have become childless by default. Like Megan and Kale, many couples may have intended to become parents, but numerous postponements in their decision-making essentially made the decision for them.

The reasons women delay childbearing are similar to the reasons they choose to be child-free: educational, professional, and career opportunities and stressors; economic considerations; and the stability of an interpersonal relationship (Fitzpatrick et al., 2017; Mills et al., 2011). A study in 2019 of 326 women determined some common reasons women delay childbearing (Molina-Garcia et al., 2019). The study's findings are presented in Table 1.3.

TABLE 1.3 ■ Reasons Reported by Women for Delaying Childbearing and Motherhood

Reasons for Delaying Parenthood	Percentage (%)
Personal	64
Employment (balancing work and family)	15
Medical/health concerns	9.8
Financial considerations	3
Other	4.6

Source: Molina-Garcia et al. (2019).

Even though subsequent infertility and significantly increased risks of negative outcomes for the baby are associated with delayed childbearing in biological women, there are several bodies of empirical evidence that suggest childbearing among older parents is advantageous to children. For example, University of Maryland sociology professor Steve Martin (2002) found through his review of the literature that both economic and psychosocial (social and emotional) benefits for the child are associated with delayed childbearing. He cites a number of studies that indicate that the older a woman is when she has her first child, the greater the economic benefit to both herself and her baby. Findings further indicate that women who postpone childbearing are more likely to stay in the workforce throughout retirement eligibility, and, as a result, they have distinctively higher earning potential than early child bearers. Women who postpone childbearing are also better able to find quality child care because of their earnings. Quality child care, in turn, increases the woman's work productivity, and her earnings potential greatly reduces "lost career time." In addition to being born into a higher income bracket, children born to older parents have better access to education opportunities. Children of older parents also suffer fewer financial consequences if their parents divorce.

Children of older parents also experience psychosocial benefits. For instance, older parents have stronger and more reliable social support networks than younger parents, providing more stability for the entire family to cope with the inevitable stressors that accompany childrearing (Martin, 2002). The quality of the mother–child relationship is higher compared with mother–child relationships of younger mothers. For example, older mothers tend to be more positive about parenting and show less anger and frustration in parenting, while older fathers tend to be very involved in their children's lives, although they are not as physically active in play as are younger fathers. Older fathers are also more likely than younger fathers to share household tasks following the birth of a baby. And finally, because they have already experienced many significant life experiences, older parents are less likely than younger parents to experience depression, loss of self-esteem, or feelings of incompetence in parenting. Martin concludes that although older parents may experience fatigue and a lack of energy, their increased maturity seems to outweigh these negative psychosocial outcomes.

Family Size: Lots of Tots?

So, you've made the decision to have children. The next question is, how many children do you desire to have? A Gallup Poll (2018) of 1,000 U.S. adults revealed that slightly less than one-half of those surveyed indicated that two children are the "ideal" family size; about one-fourth said that three children were ideal (see Figure 1.5). The ideal family size trends change over time and reflect cultural and societal changes. For instance, there is a sharp decline in the perceptions of ideal family size between the 1960s and 1970s. This trend may reflect the advent of the birth control pill in the 1960s, which gave women more control over their fertility; this increased control may have, in turn, shaped attitudes about ideal family size.

In many ways, the United States is considered to be a pronatalist society. **Pronatalism, or natalism**, is an ideology that embraces childbearing. Pronatalist attitudes and beliefs are prevalent in the United States (Watkins, 2008). For instance, when a woman or a couple gives birth to just one child and says, "no more," or when she or they decide to forgo having children

FIGURE 1.5 ■ "Ideal" Family Size

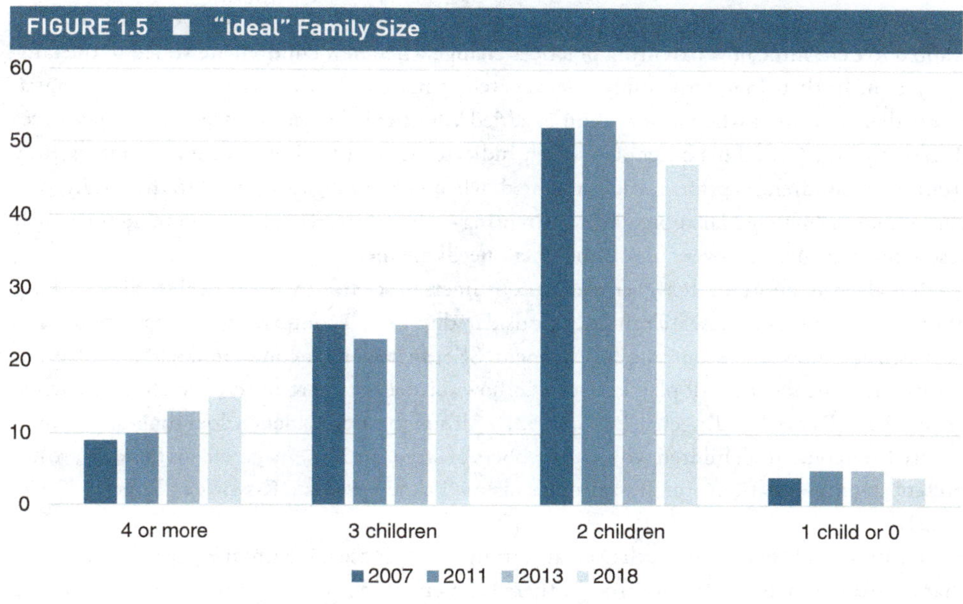

Source: Gallup (2018).

altogether, sometimes people aren't sure how to respond. Is she infertile? Do they feel overwhelmed as parents? Are they selfish? **Antinatalist** countries discourage childbearing. China's recently abolished one-child-per-family policy is an example of this.

Do parents have only so much to give to their kids? One theory maintains that some parents' resources are limited and become depleted when additional children are added to the family.

Draining Mom and Dad: The Resource Dilution Hypothesis

Parental time, energy, and resources are limited, and the **resource dilution hypothesis** contends that parents' finite resources become diluted when spread over a larger number of children (Blake, 1981). A number of studies in the 1980s and 1990s seemed to support this theory when the researchers discovered that a child in a large household receives less attention than a child in a smaller household, and this lack of attention later affected the educational level the child attained (see Strohschein et al., 2008, for a complete review). Other studies have similarly shown that maternal attention is greatest for firstborn children and less for subsequent siblings, and that mothers reduce positive interactions with their older children following the birth of another. With these results in mind, you may be thinking, "Wow, family size *does* matter—I'm only going to have one child!" But newer research may contradict these prior findings.

Researchers from Canada surveyed more than 13,000 parents and found that, because the relationship of a parent to each child is unique, effects of family size need to be studied differently than they were in the past (Strohschein et al., 2008). In their study, the investigators looked at two different areas of parenting: positive interaction (the extent to which parents are responsive to their children's needs) and consistent parenting (the frequency with which parents set boundaries and establish standards for appropriate behavior). Using these two factors, they wanted to determine how parenting practices change when new children are added to the family system. In their long-term study, the researchers discovered that "parents do not so much *dilute* their resources when a new child is added…[rather,] they act to deploy their resources differently" (p. 681). This body of research indicates that instead of draining resources away from other children, as prior studies suggested, when new siblings are added to the family, parents employ a "managerial approach" to parenting—they shift, reallocate, and reorganize their resources to ensure that every family member's needs are met.

It is always important, however, that as consumers of science and empirical studies, we keep at the forefront that all research must be considered in its full context. In this case, we need to fully consider how the "economic development, SES, increasing incomes [today]" as well as our abilities to time fertility, all play key roles in how our parenting resources are allocated across generations (Riswick & Engelen, 2018, p. 521). Although prior evidence does suggest potential negative outcomes for children who are members of large families, "negative [outcomes] are not present in all populations, for all outcomes or in all time periods" (Riswick & Engelen, 2018, p. 521).

It's impossible to determine the "ideal" family size because it is a uniquely personal decision that is affected by many factors. Today, there is an emerging trend that needs to be addressed when discussing family size: the Quiverfull movement.

Although some may disagree with couples' choices to have large numbers of children, these families are yet another type of diverse family form in the United States.

Source: Dennis MacDonald / Alamy Stock Photo.

The Quiverfull Movement: "Don't You Know What Causes That?"

Large families are considered unusual in the United States (Arnold, 2005). Although rather common in the past, families with more than six children are so rare today that the census no longer tracks these data (Hartill, 2001). But with the Quiverfull movement, today an increasing number of parents are having as many as 20 children.

The **Quiverfull (QF) movement**, which began in the 1980s, is a pronatalist belief that is practiced among some evangelical Protestant Christian couples in the United States, as well as some Catholics and Mormons, and also has some adherents in Canada, Australia, New Zealand, and England. Forgoing all forms of birth control as a matter of principle and personal choice, a "Quiverfull" couple is motivated to have many children because of a desire to be obedient to what they believe are spiritual commands and mandates. Citing biblical passages such as "be fruitful and multiply" and "blessed is the person who has a quiver full of children," adherents to the Quiverfull movement maintain an "open willingness" to joyfully receive and not thwart however many children are bestowed upon them (Campbell, 2003).

But how does religion affect a person's fertility? Some earlier research suggested that there are three conditions that produce religious effects on fertility: (1) the religion promotes norms about fertility-related behaviors, such as the use of birth control; (2) the organization is able to enforce conformity to these norms (either through social influence or through sanctions); and (3) the religion is a very important part of a person's individual identity (McQuillan, 2004). A study of 7,600 nationally representative subjects to identify what determines differences in rates of fertility among some religious groups confirms the earlier research (Hayford & Morgan, 2008). The researchers found that women for whom religion is an important facet in daily life have higher fertility intentions, compared with nonreligious women. As sociologists Jennifer McMorris and Jennifer Glass (2018) observe, "religious messages, mores [norms], and laws profoundly shape the gendered lives of men and women." (p. 433). The Pew Research Center's (2017) investigation into the relationship between religiosity and fertility supports the idea that women who practice their religious beliefs have more children than those who state they are unaffiliated with a religion. This demographic examination looked specifically at Christian and Muslim fertility:

- **Globally:** On average, women who are affiliated with religiosity have 2.5 children; those who are not have 1.6.
- **Christian:** Between 2010 and 2015, 33 percent of all births worldwide were to Christians.
- **Muslim:** Between 2010 and 2015, 31 percent of all births worldwide were to Muslims.
- **Unaffiliated:** Between 2010 and 2015, 10 percent of all births worldwide were to those unaffiliated with a religious belief or practice.

It is projected that by 2060, 36 percent of all births globally will be to Muslims, and 35 percent will be to Christians; 9 percent of births will be to the religiously unaffiliated. This information is important because it helps us to see that for some people and their partners, religious affiliation appears to impact childbearing attitudes, beliefs, and behaviors. Without question, further study needs to be undertaken to better understand this intersection of gender expectations and religion.

Although some may disagree with couples' choices to have large numbers of children, it is important to consider whether they—just as other diverse family forms—should be afforded the same social support as other families are.

ADOPTION: BY CIRCUMSTANCE OR CHOICE

Having a baby is something that seems so easy. But each year, more than six million couples in the United States face difficulties becoming pregnant; hundreds of others desire to become parents, but for numerous reasons, they wish to adopt rather than to become pregnant. In general, there are three main types of adoption (Davenport, 2018):

1. **Domestic infant adoptions:** Annually, there are about 18,000 such adoptions in the United States. This type of adoption comprises only about 0.5 percent of all live births in the United States and only about 1 percent of births to single parents.
2. **International adoptions to the United States:** There are roughly 20,000 international adoptions each year in the United States. The countries children are adopted from include China, Ukraine, India, Haiti, Ethiopia, Uganda, and the Philippines.
3. **Foster care adoptions:** Annually, about 57,000 children are adopted from foster care. On average, about one-fourth of children who enter foster care are adopted, and about one-half go back to their families. The remaining children remain in foster care.

Once a family decides to growth their family through adoption, a standard process is put into place.

The Adoption Process

Each adoption agency may have its own policies and procedures, but generally there are five steps to adoption. The process may take months, or a few years, depending on whether the couple or individual desires to adopt a newborn baby or if they are waiting for a specific race/ethnicity.

Step 1—Initial Information: To begin, each prospective adoptive parent must select an agency or a private organization through which to adopt. Couples may choose to adopt domestically (from the United States) or internationally (from abroad). Many people believe that international adoptions cost far less than domestic adoptions, but this is not the case. For example, the average cost to adopt a baby within the United States is $38,000; the average cost to adopt a child from China is $36,000 (Davenport, 2018). Wait times also vary, depending on the country from which a couple adopts. In the United States, the average wait time is about one to two years; the average wait time for a child from China is six months to a year (Davenport, 2018).

Step 2—Preparation: To be eligible for adoption, prospective parents must undergo a home study. The home study helps to ensure that the child is going to be placed in a loving, caring, nurturing home. During the study, an adoption specialist social worker interviews the couple and assesses such things as their relationship stability, their feelings about and readiness for becoming parents, and aspects about their daily lives. The social worker also checks the parents' health and income status; parents undergo a background check as well. Many adoption agencies and placement agencies assign an adoption specialist social worker to parents who helps them through each stage of the adoption process.

Step 3—The family in waiting: After the adoptive family has successfully completed all required documentation and the home study, they are considered to be a family in waiting—they enter a waiting period of somewhat unknown length, until a match occurs that results in a successful adoptive placement. This time frame varies for every adoptive family.

Step 4—The placement: After the couple is matched with a birth mother/couple, the adoptive couple works with the specialist until the baby is born; if a birth mother is not located, adoptive parents may choose to work with the adoption specialist until an older child is found. Placement typically occurs immediately after all the paperwork is completed and filed. Perhaps one of the most intensely felt fears of adopt parents is that the birth mother will change her mind; in reality, however, very few birth mothers decide to raise their babies after initiating the adoption process, but it is their right to do so. It is very important that a birth mom is not forced into her decision by others. Women who do change their minds about relinquishing their children for adoption are typically under the age of 17, have no plans for the future, live with their parents, and have mothers who oppose the adoption (Adamec, 2004).

Step 5—It's final! After the specified time frame has passed (this varies from state to state), and all of the documentation has been completed and filed with the court, a final court hearing is held and the adoption decree is awarded to the parents.

Gay and Lesbian Adoption

As we previously discussed, same-sex couples are much more likely than different-sex couples to rear adopted children, and the number of available children who need to be adopted far exceeds the number of heterosexual adoptive parents (Gates, 2013). The landscape of gay and lesbian adoption continues to undergo rapid change. As of this writing in 2020, rampant discrimination in adoption policies exists in the United States: Five states prohibit adoption discrimination based on sexual orientation and gender identity; four states prohibit discrimination based on

Sexual orientation and/or identity have nothing to do with the quality of parenting, caregiving, nurturing, and love provided to children.

Source: Adam Hester via Getty Images.

sexual orientation only; and 41 states remain silent on the issue altogether. It's important to note that 10 states permit state-licensed child welfare agencies to refuse to place children with LGBTQ+ people and same-sex couples, if doing so goes against their religious beliefs. These states are primarily situated in the Midwest and the South (i.e., Texas and Florida).

Generally, when considering any gay/lesbian adoption, today's courts are primarily focused on the "best interest of the child," and beliefs that lesbian and gay adults are not fit parents have no empirical foundation (among many others, Anderssen et al., 2002; Patterson, 2000; Perrin, 2002). As such, a person's sexual orientation should not be used as a factor in determining whether an LGBTQ+ individual or couple can adopt or foster parent a child. The American Civil Liberties Union, a nonprofit, nonpartisan group that monitors the individual civil liberties of Americans spelled out in the Constitution, maintains that where same-sex parenting is prohibited, it is because these states adhere to "stereotypical" views that gays and lesbians are unfit to be parents.

Those opposed to the concept of same-sex adoption may believe that a female role model and a male role model are necessary in children's lives. Others claim that children who are reared by gay or lesbian parents might themselves grow up to be LGBTQ+. Others are concerned that children of gay and lesbian parents will be teased ruthlessly and relentlessly by their classmates. Issues at the forefront of this discussion address gender identify and sexual orientation, as well as children's overall well-being:

- **Gender identity:** In response to whether children need both a mother and a father in order to establish a solid gender identity, studies show that few differences in gender identity exist between children reared by same-sex parents and heterosexual parents (for a review, see Bos et al., 2018).
- **Sexual orientation:** Empirical studies reveal that being raised by LGBTQ+ parents does not increase the likelihood that the child will be gay or lesbian. Notes one body of research, "sexual identities (including gender identity, gender role behavior, and sexual orientation) develop in much the same ways among children of lesbian mothers as they do among children of heterosexual parents" (American Psychological Association, 2004).
- **Children's well-being:** Having gay or lesbian parents is less an indicator of the quality of the parent–child relationship than are parenting styles. Ultimately, it is the quality of parenting, not sexual orientation, that determines how children of same-sex parents fare (Bos et al., 2016, 2018; Gartrell et al., 2018).
- **Shared parenting:** Lesbian and gay parents tend to divide child care tasks and responsibilities relatively evenly, and they report higher levels of satisfaction in their couple relationship than heterosexual couples do (Bos et al., 2004; Ciano-Boyce & Shelley-Sireci, 2002; Johnson & O'Conner, 2002).
- **Parenting:** Gay and lesbian parents possess strong parenting skills; this is reportedly due to greater levels of parent–child interaction and lower levels of physical punishment (Goldberg et al., 2014; Goldberg & Smith, 2014). Perhaps Sara Bonkowski (2003) best sums up the experience of same-sex adoption when she explains:

> Remember that a child needs the love and support of both parents. If [parents are] gay or lesbian, in time the child will know and come to understand. Many of the concerns and worries that may be raised about LGBTQ+ individuals are concerns of adults; the concerns of a child are much simpler. If a gay or lesbian parent forms a caring paternal or maternal bond with his or her young child, by the time the child is old enough to understand LGBTQ+ relationships, the child will know the parent and appreciate that Mom or Dad is, in every respect, a good parent.

In other words, if states are truly making decisions in the best interest of the children, the verdict is in: Children don't care. And they thrive.

CHANGE OVER TIME: PARENTING IS A PROCESS

For those who are to become parents, there are no words to convey the excitement they will feel the first time they hear the baby's heartbeat or hear their baby's first cries and first words. When a parent sees a baby's first smile, the sense of love, responsibility, and commitment is palpable. But the thrills move beyond infancy. Watching children grow, learn, and discover and uncover this world at every stage of their development is both entertaining and exciting (except for driver's education and dating—those fall into the "frightening and scary" category!). To watch them move from the rambunctious, rough-and-tumble years of childhood to the young adults they become fills parents with a sense of pride, and at times apprehension, as they enter the real world on their own. But that growth from infancy to manhood or womanhood involves a tremendous process of not only individual growth and change but also growth and change in the parents and in their relationship.

Today, most parents in the United States state that being a mother or a father is central to their overall identity (Pew Research Center, 2015). Interestingly, parenting being an important contributor to identity doesn't vary much by generation. The percentages of respondents who indicated being a mother/father is important to their identity were as follows:

- Aged 56–76: 51 percent
- Aged 22–38: 60 percent
- Under aged 22: 58 percent

Also, 9 in 10 parents today say that being a parent is a rewarding experience for them (Pew Research Center, 2015). Of course, the age of the children influences parents' satisfaction with raising children: Those who have younger children (under age six) are more likely to indicate that parenting is rewarding than parents who have older children. Both mothers (54 percent) and fathers (56 percent) say that at times, parenting is tiring (Pew Research Center, 2015).

Richard Lerner and his colleagues (1995) suggest that parenting is a *process*, a course of events that evolve and change over time. As you saw in the previous chapter, the early days of parenting bring new challenges, experiences, and trials into the family system. As children grow, parents grow, too. This parenting process meets both the biological needs of the children and, at the same time, the needs of the society in which children are socialized. Indeed, two of the base goals of parenting are to meet the **survival needs** of infants, which include the provision of food, shelter, safety, security, and love, and to meet the **socialization needs** of children, which encompasses ensuring they become productive, contributing members to society. Parent educator and author Chris Theisen (2004) notes that there are eight essential parenting responsibilities:

1. Providing a safe environment
2. Providing basic needs
3. Providing self-esteem
4. Teaching children morals and values
5. Developing mutual respect
6. Providing effective and age-appropriate discipline
7. Being involved in the child's education
8. Knowing the child by communicating with him or her

Given the sheer importance of parenting, there is little wonder that so much attention has been focused on this area of family life and intimate relationships. Family practitioner Virginia Satir (1972) once observed, "Parents teach in the toughest school in the world—*the school for making people*."

What is motherhood? In the four years since I've been a mom, I have become a rock holder: My pockets are heavy with rocks. Rocks sag in my backpack. They clunk in my coat. My son finds rocks and urges me to have them, and sweetens the deal with crumbling leaves, an array of sticks, and wildflowers. He is giving me the world. Or tries to.

Source: Maggie Downs (2019); iStock.com/AmazingNaturePhotography.

Motherhood

In societies across the globe, women are expected to become mothers by certain culturally determined ages, and this expectation creates pressures for them to bear children. Thus, becoming a mother is considered to be a normative developmental stage for women in all cultures. In the broadest sense, **mothering** is defined as a process whereby someone performs the relational and logistical work of caring for others (Arendell, 2000). With this definition, we can see how someone—a woman or a man—could "mother" someone who is not a child, such as an aging parent or a sibling who has a disability; we can also "mother" a friend or a loved one who is in need. However, in most societies, women are expected not only to be the bearers of children but also to nurture, care for, and socialize them as well—mothers are expected to "mother" the children in society (Arendell, 2000).

Girls and boys are socialized to fulfill roles that are determined and defined by their cultures; although each society's roles are unique, motherhood is one of the few roles assigned to women that appears to be universal, and the experience of motherhood today remains a central part of many women's identities (Arendell, 2000). For example, in a study of 1,200 parents, women identified themselves as mothers more often than they identified themselves by their occupation or career or their marital status; on the other hand, fathers identified themselves by their occupation and not by their status as fathers (Rogers & White, 1998). Even though today women fill multiple roles, such as provider and caregiver to aging parents, they are also expected to simultaneously "nurture, schedule, taxi, and feed their families"—and to do it all well (Medina & Magnuson, 2009). Because of these multiple demands and expectations, some researchers believe that the standards for "good mothering" are escalating (Douglas & Michaels, 2004, cited in Medina & Magnuson, 2009). Today, 60 percent of full-time working moms indicate that they have little free time to engage with hobbies and friends, in comparison with mothers who work part-time (48 percent) and mothers who are not employed outside of the home (47 percent; Pew Research Center, 2015).

Professor of sociology and women's and gender studies Sharon Hays (1996) examined the social construction of motherhood in the latter part of the 20th century. From her scholarly works, she coined the term *intensive mothering* to reflect the mothering roles and expectations that have been evolving since the 1980s, when women flooded the workplace. **Intensive mothering ideology** is the Western cultural belief that a mother should give of herself unconditionally and focus all of her time, energy, money, love, support, and every other resource she has on raising her children. If she works outside of the home, she is expected to make up the time with her children that is "lost" at work. Furthermore, intensive mothering is expected of mothers even if a father is present in the home, if he is employed, and if they share equally in household and childrearing tasks. As this ideology shows us, the cultural expectation of mothers today is clear: The well-being of children is the responsibility of the mother, and she is to respond to their needs before those of her own or of her husband or partner. Of course, this means that women who fall short of this cultural ideal do not fit today's social construction of "good mothers" (Medina & Magnuson, 2009).

The transition to motherhood is a major developmental life event for most women because it requires women to restructure their goals, behaviors, and responsibilities (Mercer, 2004). The theory of **Maternal Role Attainment (MRA)** speaks to the fluid, continual, fluctuating processes associated with becoming a mother (Rubin, 1967). According to this theory, women actually begin adopting roles associated with motherhood during their pregnancies, such as bonding emotionally with the growing fetus. While pregnant, a woman also begins to observe the behaviors of mother models she has in her environment (such as her own mother, grandmothers, and friends); as her pregnancy continues, she adopts those behaviors she believes would be ideal for her and her child, and she rejects behaviors she judges as inappropriate for herself. Through pregnancy, and after the birth of her child, she continues to construct an "ideal" image of herself as mother; she then adopts roles that support this ideal image.

There are a number of factors that influence MRA (Mercer, 1986):

- Age of the mother
- Socioeconomic background
- Social stress and support
- Temperament
- Self-concept
- Childrearing beliefs and attitudes
- Role strain
- Perception of the infant

Particularly important to MRA is the woman's relationship with her own mother. For example, one body of research demonstrated that young mothers' current relationships with their mothers were recreated in their relationships with their infants (Kretchmar & Jacobvitz, 2002). Other research found that pregnant mothers' attitudes and memories about their mothers influenced their prenatal attachment to their babies, and that young mothers' memories of how accepting or rejecting their own mothers were also influenced their ability to adopt motherhood roles (Crockenberg & Leerkes, 2003; Priel & Besser, 2001).

"Motherhood" is a developmental process that is influenced by many factors and is one that unfolds over time—the new mother affects and is affected by her child, by her spouse or partner, by her past experiences in her own childhood, and by her relationship with her mother.

"Remember that a child needs the love and support of both parents..." Empirical evidence suggests that, as long as parents are warm, responsive, and communicative, parents' sexual orientations are not a factor in the healthy development of children.

Lesbian Co-motherhood

In 2018, nearly 90,000 lesbian mothers were raising children in the United States (Goldberg & Conron, 2018). Like their heterosexual counterparts, most lesbian-mother couples were raising their biological children (68 percent), but today, lesbian couples are significantly more likely to adopt or foster children than different-sex couples (Goldberg & Conron, 2018). Do lesbian mothers attain motherhood roles differently than heterosexual mothers? A substantial body of research suggests that regardless of sexual orientation, becoming parents for the first time is challenging for most couples because of the renegotiation of roles and identities that must take place to incorporate the role of "parent" (Cao et al., 2016). But sexual minority female parents encounter additional role/identity stressors in the transition to parenthood because they are required to balance the heteronormative ideals of "mother" (Cao et al., 2016). It is indisputable that when it comes to mothering, our culture "often fails to acknowledge that there are families with other types of arrangements" (Walker, 2017, p. 2).

Photograph courtesy of Nancy L. Forsyth and Eli Ingraham.

Perhaps the greatest difference between heterosexual and lesbian motherhood is the uniqueness of the couple relationship. With heterosexual couples, each partner enters parenthood with clearly defined "mother" and "father" templates (Walker, 2017). Conversely, with same-sex mothers, the mothering role is shared—this is referred to as **lesbian co-mothering (LCM)**. Birth nurse practitioner Katherine Walker (2017) works closely with LCM couples and describes the specific challenges these mothers face:

Ambiguous roles—beyond the mother/father binary: What is the role of the mother who does not give birth? As Walker has discovered in working with LCMs, lesbian co-mothers often find it difficult to identify with the role of mother or father. As one of her clients stated, "[When we went to our childbirth classes] I dreaded the prospect of potentially being the only woman in a group of 'dads'. It felt strange at times to be part of this group because there was an assumption that I would simply take on the role of a 'dad' during my partner's pregnancy [and birth experience]." Walker's research also discovered that the nonbirth LCM often feels invisible and insecure due to the maternal gatekeeping of the birth LCM.

Bonding and breastfeeding: A common fear among lesbian co-mothers is that a baby will form a stronger emotional and physical bond with the breastfeeding birth mother than with the co-mother, particularly because breastfeeding is known to enhance the development of maternal identity (Zizzo, 2009). It is not uncommon for LCMs to experience jealousy; this is also common among heterosexual fathers. Walker notes that some lesbian mothers have successfully established co-breastfeeding or shared feeding. Other lesbian mothers enjoy nonnutritive breastfeeding, where babies suckle at the breast without receiving milk.

Emotional support: Lack of emotional support following birth is known to increase the likelihood of postnatal depression (PND; Hatloy, 2013). Today, scant literature exists that addresses PND among lesbian co-mothers, but Walker's (2017) review of the literature suggests that LCMs are at greater risk because they do not have the cultural and community support that heterosexual couples do following the birth of a baby.

As with every other area of couple relationships and family life, it's important to understand that there is great diversity in the experiences of motherhood. As Walker (2017) concludes, "LCMs are not fathers! [In childbirth and parenting classes] LCM may not want to be grouped with fathers...and they may not feel like mothers yet either."

Fatherhood

Like motherhood, the social construction of fatherhood continues to change over time. Among America's first families in Colonial Williamsburg in the 17th century, for example, British immigrants brought the traditional patriarchal family structure to Virginia. The **patriarchal family structure** included the father figure, who was considered to be the authority over his entire household—wife, children, dependent kin, servants, slaves, and apprentices. This family structure served to preserve the wealth and power of the patriarch's household and the family's lineage. When fathers died, they willed their land and property to their sons, ensuring that the family's wealth remained within the family. Daughters typically inherited servants and livestock, rather than land or money. Within this family structure, fathers were all-powerful and served as the unquestioned, oftentimes uncaring, ruler (Lamb, 1987). In this era, men were charged with the responsibility of their children's moral and spiritual development, and because of this, discipline was their responsibility. The early father–child relationship was typically emotionally distant and correctional; it also lacked warmth, nurturing, and affection because these behaviors were associated with parental indulgence that was thought to ruin the character of the children (Pleck & Pleck, 1997). Patriarchal parenting continued in the United States until the mid-18th century.

With the rise of industrialism and urbanization in Western cultures, the social construction of fatherhood began to change. As fathers moved their work into factories and away from the home, mothers' roles expanded to include moral teacher and disciplinarian (Pleck & Pleck, 1997).

Historians note that the separation of the workplace from the home life created two opposing trends that are still in existence today: *father-absence* and *father-involvement* (Rotundo, 1993). Some men, for instance, withdraw emotionally, psychologically, and physically from their children because their work requires that they are absent from their families; on the other hand, the decline of patriarchy has given men "permission" to display more warmth, nurturing, and intimacy with their children, allowing them to be more involved.

Today, modern fathers tend to fall somewhere between these two opposing fatherhood types, and researchers are suggesting that a "new fatherhood" is emerging in our culture (Yogman & Garfield, 2016). **Father involvement** is defined as the time a father and his child(ren) spend together (Gauthier et al., 2004). With this new model of father involvement, fathers are expected to be both the provider of the family's needs and also actively engage in the everyday caring of their children (Barbeta & Cano, 2017). The importance of fathers' involvement in the lives of their children cannot be overstated. One newer body of research suggests that father involvement is essential for two primary reasons (for a complete review, see Cano et al., 2018):

1. Father involvement increases gender equality within families.
2. Father involvement is associated with positive child development.

Among contemporary parenting, involved fathering is a distinguishing feature of parents from fathers in the historical past. There are racial and ethnic differences in fathering experiences, and we'll discuss those in just a bit. Still today, however, the vast majority of mothers are more involved in the daily care and routines of their children than fathers are (Cano et al., 2018; Craig, 2006).

Whether people are discussing divorce laws in suburbia or crime rates in the inner city, the issue of fathering takes an active, often political, role in the ongoing dialogue over the status of the American family. There is a wide spectrum of thought concerning the importance of fathers in the United States. For some, fathers are merely a perk for children, adding interesting yet nonessential elements to a child's development. To others, the mere presence of a father is enough to cure all of society's ills. Politics aside, the research does seem to suggest that fathers are a valuable part of a child's healthy upbringing (we explore the consequences of absent fathers at length in Chapter 9).

Dads as Playmates

In one study of cognitive development in children, the intellectual and social development a child gains through the mother's verbal expressions and educational activities are also learned and reinforced through physical play with the father. Mothers do play with their kids, but children generally respond more to play with their fathers. Fathers are usually more lenient with children when it comes to exploration and adventure, which helps develop cognitive skills and encourages independence.

The importance of quality, involved fathering cannot be overstated. An abundance of research suggests that children experience better physical, educational, and social-emotional outcomes.

Source: iStock.com/nensuria.

Decreased Behavioral Problems

As fathers take a more active role in the lives of their children, behavioral issues are positively affected. Eating meals at the table, helping with homework, working on projects together, and informal, spontaneous moments are linked to fewer behavioral issues with children. Children show greater prowess at school when both parents are actively involved, but the level of *fatherly* involvement has been shown to be a more important predictor of scholarly success.

If we use a family systems approach to understanding parenting, we can see that mothers and fathers together create a subsystem in the family—the parent subsystem. Every day, parents are faced with decisions and challenges about how to bring up their children and how to most effectively parent them. When fathers and mothers share parenting responsibilities and when they agree on parenting decisions—when they co-parent—all family members benefit.

Gay Fatherhood

We discuss LGBTQ+ parenting and family experiences at length in Chapter 9. Here, it is important to understand sexual minorities' desires to become parents. Within the last decade, substantial progress has been made toward better understanding parenthood aspirations among gay men. **Parenthood aspirations**—the desire, hope, or want to become a parent—include three factors (Gato et al., 2016; Tate & Patterson, 2019):

1. *Parenthood desires:* How strongly a person wants to become a parent
2. *Parenthood expectations:* A person's realistic belief about the probability of becoming a parent
3. *Parenthood intentions:* How likely a person is to pursue parenthood options

Empirical science has well established that gay men report lower desires to become parents than do straight men (among many, Jeffries et al., 2019; Leal et al., 2019; Shenkman et al., 2019; Tate et al., 2019), and they also report lower parental aspirations (desires, expectations, and intentions) than do heterosexual men (Tate & Patterson, 2019). It's important to note, however, that lower parenthood aspirations may be because that, still today, LGBTQ+ persons face more obstacles to the routes to parenthood than do heterosexuals, such as socioeconomic barriers that prevent them from accessing adoption resources or using the assistance of an unrelated pregnancy carrier (Blake et al., 2017; Leal et al., 2019; Perrin et al., 2019; Scandurra et al., 2019). There also appear to be inconsistencies in the desire to become a parent and actually pursuing parenthood. For example, one study found that while 20 percent of gay study participants wanted to become parents, they had no intentions of pursuing fatherhood; 5 percent of heterosexual men reported the same (Riskin & Tornello, 2017). A similar study of gay men in Israel found that over two-thirds (68 percent) of the study respondents reported a strong desire for parenthood, but only about one-third (31 percent) expected to fulfill their parenthood aspirations (Shenkman, 2012).

In what ways does sexual orientation affect expectations for family formation for gay men? In a study that included 156 gays and 60 cisgender heterosexual men, the researchers discovered a stark finding: Sexual minority men were more likely than their straight counterparts to want a family and children, but they did not expect that their desires and aspirations would be achieved—gay men "[envisioned] a hoped-for future that is out of reach" (Tate & Patterson, 2019, p. 2679).

When gay men do become parents, though, they face societal stigma in several aspects of their lives. In a study of 732 men in 47 states, the researchers found (Perrin et al., 2019):

- 40 percent of gay men faced social barriers when they attempted to adopt a child
- 63 percent of survey respondents reported that they faced stigma (particularly fewer legal and societal protections) because of their gay fatherhood status
- 50 percent of gay fathers avoided social situations out of fear of stigma for themselves and their children
- Nearly one-third (over 30 percent) reported stigma in religious environments
- One-fourth experienced stigma from family members, neighbors, gay friends, and people in the community (i.e., waiters, salespeople, teachers, and physicians)

What is particularly disconcerting about these study findings is that the very sources that are to be supportive and nurturing—families, friends, teachers, religious institutions, and physicians—are those that hold belief patterns that present barriers to gay fathers. The implications of this study are clear: Parent educators and others who work with and care for these families must understand the unique challenges and obstacles LGBTQ+ parents face so that their needs can be met and their families better served. Regardless of family structure, the ultimate goal should be helping children to grow into healthy, mentally/emotionally strong adults.

Consider the interaction and relational patterns between you and your parent(s) or primary caregiver. Did these experiences allow you to feel that you were worthy of affection and love? Or instead, did your early parent–child experiences cause you to feel shame, guilt, and doubt, resulting in fear of intimacy, fear of abandonment, betrayal, and rejection in your adult relationships? As we are growing up, our parent and family interactions convey to us our worth—our purpose—as individuals, and this perception influences our ability to relate to others on an intimate level the remainder of our lifespan.

Given the ups and downs of parenting and the inherent adjustments that must be made as a result of children's demands, given its uncertainty, given the fact that no two children are alike, and given the fact that no two people (or parent) experience parenting in the same way, is it really possible to prepare for what one developmentalist (Carter & McGoldrick, 1999) describes as "one of the most definitive stages of life"? Probably not. Nevertheless, we can address those contemporary issues that affect parenting and the stressors associated with the transition into parenthood and parenting. Although the experience of parenthood is without a doubt unpredictable, many parents (though not all) find it to be the most rewarding life experience.

PARENT EDUCATION: THE STUDY OF PARENTING THROUGH AN APPLIED LENS

The central concept of this book is to examine parenting and working with parents by utilizing the Family Life Education (FLE) approach as a central theme. Borrowing and adapting theoretical frameworks from the fields of sociology and psychology, the **Family Life Education** perspective unveils the inadequacies families feel when they are faced with change, and then provides organized, programmatic education to help strengthen families. Some approaches (such as family therapy) first look to *intervention* instead of education; however, this text's approach acknowledges that intervention often comes too late to be effective in fully developing the potential of individuals and families. FLE is a tool used to explore parenting, but it is not a "theory." Instead, it is a *lens* through which we can study and understand parenting and parent–child relationships.

Understanding Families' Needs and Developing Their Potentials

The concept of parent education has existed in this country as early as the 1920s. The term **parent education** is used to include a variety of experiences to assist persons who are already parents to be more effective in their roles, as well as to educate individuals who desire to work as a helping professional with parents and their families. In the 1960s, when U.S. culture experienced much social upheaval, people who had concerns for the "staggering list of social ills" that had an impact on family life began to conceive and organize education for family living (Smith, 1968). With young adults' newfound emphasis on sex, drugs, and rock and roll, the country was ripe for a family education concept. These early efforts to educate families centered on a **dealing-with-problems focus** (Arcus et al., 1993). Society was rapidly changing. The Vietnam War provoked cries from young adults against the "establishment"—those who promoted long-held, established societal beliefs and norms about marriage, sexuality, gender roles, childbearing, childrearing, and politics.

A concept that went hand in hand with the dealing-with-problems focus to educate parents and families was the **preventing-the-problems focus**. FLE professor and parent educator Richard Kerckhoff (1964) maintained that families faced with radical societal changes only needed to be shown how to do the correct things. According to Kerckhoff, if families could somehow be pointed in the right direction, then "the divorce rate would drop, children would be reared properly, and the institution of family would be saved" (p. 898). Problem prevention remains a prevalent theme in FLE today. As renowned family life educator and professor of human sciences Carol Darling noted, efforts to educate families in family living is "the foremost preventive measure for the avoidance of family problems" (1987, p. 816). The **developing-family-potentials focus** also arose out of the societal turmoil of the 1960s. Promoting goals ranging from building on family strengths to developing healthy, fulfilling, and responsible interpersonal relationships, FLE efforts were—and still are today—intended to build on positive aspects of family life and bring about human capabilities that improve and enhance personal life and family living (Arcus et al., 1993).

The definitions of **parent education** have changed and progressed over time (Arcus, 1993):

Early 1960s: Education was primarily found in public schools, where educators taught students to be effective present and future family members. Traditional gender and parenting roles were reinforced.

Mid-1960s: Coinciding with the Civil Rights Movement in 1964, parent and family education efforts involved teaching students and parents facts, attitudes, and skills associated with relationships. Relationships between parent–child and husband–wife were emphasized.

Late 1960s: Scholars began to study parents' and family members' behaviors, functioning, values, and attitudes. Education was a planned and programmed learning within the community, geared toward developing people's parenting potentials.

Early 1970s: Programs centered on interactions between family members, individual characteristics, and imparting information about parenting and family relationships so that people gained a greater understanding of how they affect and are affected by their families. Programming is taught in schools, religious settings, colleges, and within the community.

Mid-1970s: Educational programming centered its focus on providing instruction for parents and families so they could understand the physical, mental, emotional, social, and economic aspects of parenting life.

Early 1980s: Planned and programmatic information about parenting and other relationship issues was offered to individuals of all ages.

Late 1980s: Parenting and FLE became concerned with preserving and improving the quality of human life by studying individuals and families as they interacted with their many environments.

1990s–Current: Education efforts enable adults to reach their full personal potentials in daily living, relating to others, parenting, and coping with life's events.

While the focus of parent and FLE has changed over time in response to the needs of society, what remains today in educational programming is the emphasis of considering both *individual development* and the *environment of the family*, and how children's development, health, and well-being are impacted and shaped within the context of family living. Of significant importance to the developing child is the parent–child relationship (Bornstein, 2002). So, as we work our way through our course of study, we will focus on individual development as we examine the parenting experience. This *applied* framework provides us an understanding of how parent education positively impacts parent–child interactions and how these experiences, in turn, lead to healthier child outcomes, such as is the case with Nolan and Laura in the opening vignette of this chapter (Brooks-Gunn & Markman, 2005; Karoly et al., 2005; Knitzer & Lefkowitz, 2006; Powell, 2005). Finally, this applied parent education perspective provides to helping professionals an understanding of family-oriented services and government policies that strengthen families and family living, and as such (Arcus et al., 1993; Weiss, 1990).

Nolan, Laura, Ella, and the mighty warrior, Grit. "We can overcome because we were given the tools as parents to not only fight for our son, but also for our marriage and family...I'll never stop fighting."

Source: Photo courtesy of Nolan and Laura Henderson.

The Pillars of Parent Education

Traditionally, parenting education textbooks and courses adopt a developmental approach, a lens that emphasizes a child's development from birth through adolescence. While knowledge and understanding of child and adolescent development is an integral part of being an effective parent educator, this approach falls short of educating and training helping professionals to apply and use this knowledge while working with parents. Traditional textbooks also often neglect the study of how development is influenced by the multiple processes that occur within the family system. By using a **family science** lens to understand today's couples and families, *Parenting Life Now* meets the needs of today's professionals by employing the scientific study of children, families, and parenting to gain a comprehensive understanding of the diversity of parenting life today. In addition to social science research and theories, we will explore and apply the pillars of family science. The family science parenting education approach is:

Relationship-focused: An emphasis is placed on forming, strengthening, and maintaining healthy interpersonal relationships across the lifespan.

Multidisciplinary: There are many theoretical strengths and concepts found in other disciplines. All key aspects of the social sciences are drawn upon in a family science approach, and our study provides an exploration and investigation of major theoretical concepts.

Evidence-based: Family science professionals access research findings to develop and implement effective programs aimed at educating and working with parents.

Strengths-oriented: The core belief of family science is that all families have strengths. All parents have strengths. With this belief at the forefront, programs are designed and implemented that enable individuals, parents, and families to become self-sufficient. During our study together, you will come to understand that *all* families have strengths, *all* families experience struggles, and that *all* families can learn to struggle well and to "do" family living to their best capabilities.

Preventive: Rather than intervene after problems and difficulties crop up, the family science approach seeks to prevent problems, through educational programs, with individuals, couples, parents, and families before they occur. We will engage in a robust discussion about government policies that affect parents and their children.

Applied: Professionals trained in the family science paradigm possess the knowledge and skills to apply research findings to effectively service all couples, parents, and families in today's diverse and global society.

Now, armed with an understanding of the landscape of who's having children, it's time to roll up our sleeves and begin our exploration of contemporary parenting life. Although each of us accomplishes many milestones in our individual lifespan development, we do so within the context of family living. Every phase of our individual development across our human life cycle

TABLE 1.4 ■ Key Content Areas in Family Life Education

- **Families in society** includes varying family forms; cross-cultural and diverse families and family values; and social and cultural variations (ethnicity, rage, and religion).
- **Family processes** focuses on family communication patterns, conflict resolution, coping strategies, families in crisis/stress and distress/and families with special needs (military, step-foster, adoptive families, etc.).
- **Human growth and development** explores human development across our lifespan.
- **Human sexuality** presents sexual anatomy and physiology, reproduction, the emotional aspects of sexuality, sexual response and dysfunction, and our sexual values.
- **Interpersonal relationships** focuses on love, human intimacy, and relational skills, such as communication.
- **Family resource management** focuses on family financial goals and planning, and money decisions.
- **Parent education** looks at the choice and challenges of parenthood, including the rights and responsibilities of parents, parental roles, and variations in parenting practices, and styles.
- **Family law and public policy** focuses on laws relating to marriage, divorce, cohabitation, child custody, child protection and the rights of children, and public policy (civil rights, social security) as it affects the family.
- **Ethics** concerns the diversity of human values and the complexity of how values are shaped in contemporary society.

Source S.R. Czaplewski and S.R. Jorgensen, Copyright 1993 by SAGE Publications Inc Books.

intersects with the development of the family throughout its developmental cycle, ultimately shaping who we are as relational people. The next step, then, is to help you gain an appreciation of America's family living arrangements and the cultural contexts, influences, and differences that affect parenting and parenting life.

PARENTING LIFE EDUCATION: FOSTERING HEALTHY FAMILY FORMATION

We've covered a lot in this introductory chapter, from gaining an understanding of the current trends in childbearing to the factors that go into the decision to have children and to the concepts of "motherhood" and "fatherhood" in our culture today. All of these are critically important to a fundamental understanding of the choices and challenges people encounter as they begin their journey into parenthood, and as parent educators and helping professionals, it is of the utmost importance that this transition to parenthood is used to enhance, nurture, and fortify couple and family relationships so individuals are better equipped to handle the stressors associated with parenthood.

In our study of parenting life today, you will come to learn that, through quality educational programming, parent educators' efforts for individuals and couples considering parenthood or who are transitioning to parenthood are centered on fostering healthy family formation and maintaining healthy families. By promoting strong communication skills and other interpersonal relationship skills, as well as empirically based best parenting practices, this preventive approach helps individuals and couples to "do" parenting to their best abilities and capabilities.

It's been said before that you can't really understand the changes in your life that children will bring until you've actually become a parent. Expectant and adoptive parents spend many months preparing for the arrival of their baby or the child they've adopted. By the time they bring their child home, they've probably taken birth classes, attended a few parenting classes, and read articles about what to expect. But even with all of this preparation, the reality is, many parents don't know just how much their day-to-day lives are about to change: The transition to parenthood is one of the greatest stressors a couple or an individual will encounter. To survive and to thrive, preparation needs to go beyond welcoming the baby or the child home. As parent educators, it is our responsibility—and *privilege*—to guide, encourage, and support parents in their endeavors to "make people" (Satir, 1972), no matter the challenges they encounter along the way.

At the beginning of this chapter, we posed the question: How did Nolan and Laura transverse that jagged, unpredictable, uncertain path of their son's cancer? How did they make it? Nolan, a human growth and development high school teacher, explains:

> We can overcome because we were given the tools as parents to not only fight for our son, but also for our marriage and for our family. This is why what we teach is so important. This is why we do what we do. And I'll never stop.

That's grit.

2 THE VARIED EXPERIENCES OF PARENTING

LEARNING OBJECTIVES

2.1 Explain the ways in which societies and cultures influence the experiences of parenting and family life.

2.2 Describe the landscape and trends of various family structures in the United States today.

2.3 Summarize the process of racial and ethnic identity formation in children.

2.4 Using Bronfenbrenner's Ecological Model and each of its ecosystems, discuss the ways in which systemic racism is perpetuated in the United States today.

- In Norway and many other Scandinavian countries, parents have their children (as young as two weeks old) nap in the outdoors, regardless of how cold it is. It is commonplace for parents to park their infants' baby strollers for up to three hours on busy sidewalks while they go inside to stores and restaurants. Parents believe that frigid infant/child napping promotes better sleep and that it increases the duration of sleep.

Without question, parenting is a cultural experience. In Norway, parents leave their infants and toddlers outside to nap because of the cultural belief that frigid air is healthy for children.

Source: iStock.com/AlexPnferov.

They also believe the cold temperatures (as cold as 4° below 0) promote health in their infants (Coleman, 2015).

- In Japan, children as young as the age of six (oftentimes with their younger siblings as young as three or four) run various errands for their parents (such as shopping for groceries) and children as young as four take subways—with no guardian (Doi et al., 2018). The purpose of these practices is to indoctrinate children early into **group reliance**, the cultural belief that children can count on anyone in the community to help them (Dixon, 2020). **Free-range parenting** is a newly emerging parenting style that promotes the idea of raising children to function as independently as possible, as young as possible (Skenazy, 2010).
- French parenting is described as kind—but no nonsense (Andersen, 2020). For example, babies are allowed to cry for longer periods than American parents allow their children to cry because French parents believe it teaches babies to comfort themselves. In the French culture, parents praise their children sparingly (everyone does *not* get a trophy), children eat on a strict schedule with no in-between meal snacks, and "no" means "no." Put simply, French children learn about delayed gratification early on. The French firmly believe that parenting doesn't mean that adults are at the constant service of their children (Druckerman, 2020).
- In the Polynesian Islands, independence is encouraged early on: Children, as young as three years of age assume a caretaking role for younger toddlers and babies—and most are not their own siblings. This type of independence and responsibility encourages *community responsibility* (Ritchie & Ritchie, 1983).

While certainly some of these parenting practices may seem unusual to us according to our American standards, what strikes you most about these child-rearing behaviors? What was your initial reaction when you read about these different parenting customs? Is there only one best way to raise a child? Even though some of these parenting practices may be discrepant with your beliefs about parents' responsibilities, the ways in which parents raise their children is quite diverse, but the world over, parents raise their children with one singular goal: Molding their children into effective adults (Bernstein, 2016).

In essence, **diversity** refers to the broad spectrum of demographic and philosophical differences among people groups both within and outside of a culture. When we talk about being **diverse**, or about diversity in the United States and abroad, we are referring to peoples' differences in age, gender, race, ethnicity, culture, sexual orientation, religion, and socioeconomic status (SES); each of these factors are key variables in parenting practices. When we study people from an inclusive and diverse perspective, it not only furthers our knowledge about the variances in parenting experiences but it also helps us to value individuals and groups, free from bias. This then fosters a climate of equity and mutual respect.

Today it is essential that students know the differing arrangements of families because this understanding enables human service providers and other family professionals and educators to work more effectively support, value, and work with diverse families (Banks & McGee-Banks, 2019). Without question, culture ties its members together and significantly impacts how children are raised—child-rearing varies across countries and communities in our global society, and the role culture plays is profound.

Because we do not develop in isolation, and because we very much are influenced by the cultures in which we live, our parenting reflects these societal differences, as evidenced in the examples above. We continue our intriguing study of contemporary parenting life by first turning our attention to the cultural identities that shape parenting experiences. We'll then gain an understanding of the compositions of today's families, examining the different cultural contexts in which parenting occurs; we also address characteristics of parenting and parent–child interactions among diverse cultural groups in the United States. We'll conclude with an exploration of the multiple contexts of society that affect parenting and child development.

PARENTING IN CULTURAL CONTEXTS

As we continue our study of contemporary parenting, it is necessary to embrace the idea that we do not develop in isolation. Who we are as human beings—every emotion, fear, thought, and behavior—is somehow linked, both genetically and environmentally, to the family in which we were raised. It is also important to understand that there are many areas of parenting that are affected and influenced by the broader culture in which we live, by the many facets of society that surround us. Often these influences are overlooked in the study of the processes associated with parenting practices.

Social Identity: Collectivist Cultures

It is important to understand that how people parent is determined in large part by how a culture defines its **social identity**, or whether societal goals emphasize the advancement of the group's interests or individual interests (van Kleef et al., 2015). Particularly important is whether the culture defines itself as a *collectivist* culture or an *individualistic* culture because culturally approved beliefs influence our expectations, experiences, attitudes, and behaviors (Neto, 2007). It profoundly affects the ways we behave and respond to the world.

In **collectivist cultures**, individuals define their identity in terms of the relationships they hold with others. For instance, if asked the question, "Who are you?" a collectivist is likely to respond by giving the family's name or the region from which he or she originates (Triandis & Suh, 2002). The goals of the collective—the whole society—are given priority over individual needs (Myers, 2008). Group membership is important, and society members value social order (Stamkou et al., 2019). In these cultures, members strive to be equal, contributing, beneficial members of the society, and their personal behaviors are driven by a feeling of obligation and duty to the society (Johnson et al., 2005; Triandis & Suh, 2002). Collectivist cultures promote the well-being and goals of the collective *group*, rather than the well-being and goals of the *individual*. Because of the desire to maintain harmony within the group, collectivist cultures stress harmony, cooperation, and promoting feelings of closeness (Kupperbusch et al., 1999).

Latinx, for example, value strong interdependent relationships with their families, and they value the opinions of close friends (who, in many cases, are treated as family members); this, in turn, influences how they experience and practice parenting (Prioste et al., 2015; Stamkou et al., 2019). Asians and Arab Americans, too, accentuate the importance of the collective whole, and they therefore emphasize family bonds in their parenting and family experiences (Liu et al., 2019; Stamkou et al., 2019). A bit later in this chapter we'll take an in-depth look at parent–child relationships in various collectivist cultures.

Social Identity: Individualistic Cultures

In **individualistic cultures**, where individual goals are promoted over group goals, people define their identity or sense of self in terms of personal attributes, such as wealth, social status, education level, and marital status (Myers, 2008). Unlike in collectivist cultures, *individualists* view themselves as truly independent entities from the society in which they live, and their personal needs and rights guide their behavior, rather than the needs of the society (Johnson et al., 2005). Individualistic cultures, such as those of the United States and Europe, promote the idea of autonomy and individuations from the family (Yaman et al., 2010). As one researcher succinctly notes, the fundamental differences observed in individual development are the result of their collectivist or individualistic upbringing because each social identity carries its own distinct values and characteristics (Gallardo, 2019).

While the United States federal government may define "family" as individuals who are related by birth, marriage, or adoption, today's families are not one-size-fits-all. This is reflected in the many different and diverse family forms in the United States.

Source: iStock.com/nd3000.

A culture's social identity shapes and directs the attitudes, norms, and behaviors of its members. But there are other cultural factors that significantly influence and shape parenting and family life experience, such as family structure and race/ethnicity.

WHAT IS FAMILY?

What is "family?" How do you define it? In all likelihood, your definition may be entirely different from the federal government's definition or from ours. The reason for these differences is that our definitions and your definition of family are based on *unique experiences within our own families.* An understanding of family is necessary because variations in parenting attitudes and styles are evident among the diverse cultural groups in the United States, as well as in the diverse family structures in which children are raised today. In nearly all societies the world over, the family is the social unit that is responsible for nurturing, protecting, educating, and socializing children (Barbour et al., 2005).

According to the United States Census Bureau (2019a), a **family** "is a group of two people or more (one of whom is the householder) related by birth, marriage, or adoption and residing together; all such people (including related subfamily members) are considered as members of one family." On the other hand, a **household** "consists of all the people who occupy a housing unit. A household includes the related family members and all of the unrelated people, if any, such as lodgers, foster children, wards, or employees who share the housing unit. A person living alone in a housing unit, or a group of unrelated people sharing a housing unit such as partners or

FIGURE 2.1 ■ Types of Households in the United States

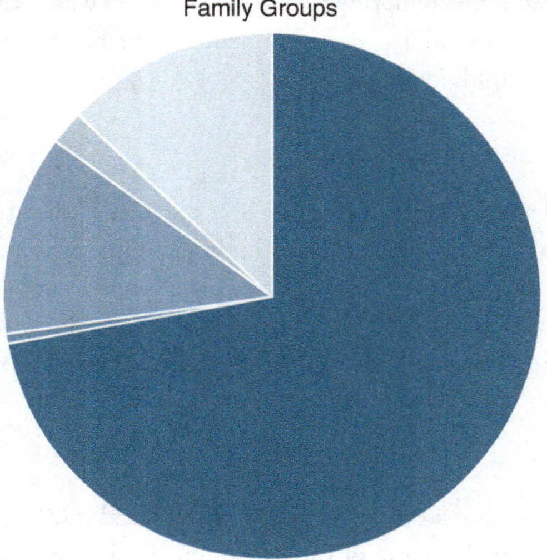

Source: U.S. Census Bureau (2019).

roomers, is also counted as a household" (U.S. Census Bureau, 2019a). Thus, according to the federal government, a married couple and their children are considered to be a family, whereas intimate couples who live together who are not married make up a household. In nearly all societies the world over, the family is the social unit that is responsible for nurturing, protecting, educating, and socializing children (Barbour et al., 2005). Figure 2.1 illustrates for us the types of households in the United States (U.S. Census Bureau, 2019a). As you can see, nearly three-fourths (72 percent) of all households today are married-couple families, but there is great diversity in family forms (U.S. Census Bureau, 2019b). It's interesting to observe that nearly 13 percent of families today classify themselves as "other nonfamily households." A **nonfamily household** comprises a householder living alone, such as a widow, or where the householder shares the home with people to whom she/he is not related, such as a widow sharing her home with two friends. Not only has the distribution of households shifted over time, so too has the size of U.S. households. For example, in 1970, the average household size was 3.14 whereas today it is 2.53.

The question arises, then, is it possible to arrive at a one-size-fits-all definition of "family," as the U.S. Census Bureau describes? Probably not, for there exist as many definitions or descriptions of "family" as there are students who are reading this textbook, and beyond. The concept of family is, indeed, a subjective notion.

Each of us experiences our individual development in our family of origin, or family of orientation. Our **family of origin** is the family into which we are born or brought into by adoption or circumstance (such as being raised by a grandparent). It is the family in which we are raised and socialized to adhere to the customs and norms of the culture in which we live. As we explore the nature of contemporary parenting, we use statistics to help us identify current patterns and trends. Although it is sometimes tempting to skip over statistics when reading, numbers are necessary because they present overall trends and provide us with an instant snapshot of American families in which today's children develop.

Nuclear and Extended Families

Today, it is essential that students of parenting and parenting education know the differing family arrangements of families, because this understanding allows human service providers and other family professionals to more effectively support, value, and work with diverse families (Banks & McGee Banks, 2019). In the sections that follow, we'll first take a look at *nuclear* and *extended* family forms. We'll then examine the expanding family landscape in our culture today.

Nuclear Family

The **nuclear family** consists of a biological father, a biological mother, and their biological or adopted children. In the truest sense of the definition, nuclear families consist of first-time married parents, their biological or adopted children, and no other family members living in the home. In 2018, the "typical" nuclear family form was found in about 65 percent of family households (Pew Research Center, 2018a). Figure 2.2 illustrates the family configurations in which children in the United States live today. Notice that although the majority of children

FIGURE 2.2 ■ Unmarried Parents Living With a Child Over Time

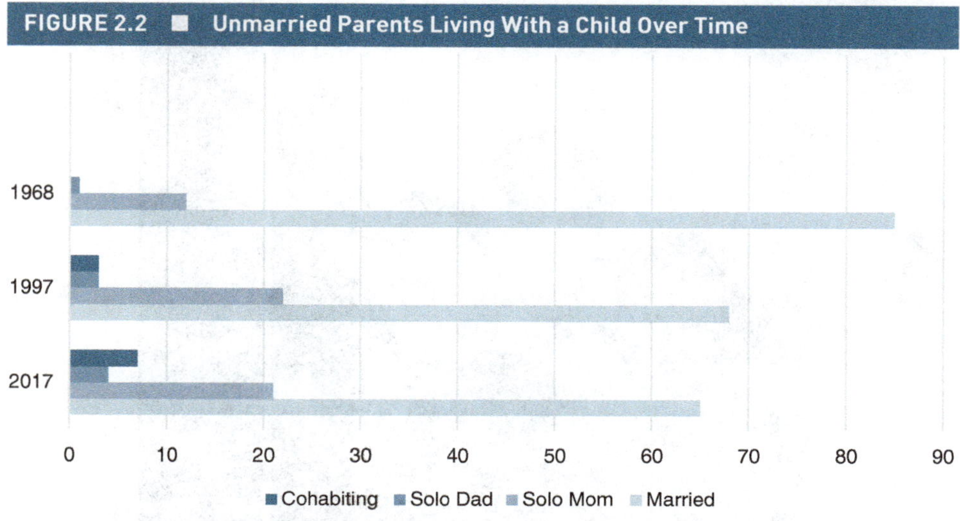

Source: Pew Research Center (2018a).

live in nuclear families, other family forms show the complexity of contemporary family living. For example, among parents living with a child, a growing share of unmarried parents are cohabiting: In 2017, 35 percent of unmarried parents were cohabiting in comparison with 13 percent in 1968 (Pew Research Center, 2018a). We'll discuss cohabiting parents at length later in this chapter.

Often, the nuclear family is referred to as the *traditional* family. This term carries with it a conventional depiction of the family form and the accompanying family values and traditions. *Family values* is a term that is commonly used today by politicians and TV news reports, although it may mean different things to different people. Most often, *family values* refers to a society's paradigm or viewpoint that expects its members to adhere to perceived "proper" social roles, such as marrying and having children, remaining monogamous and faithful to the marriage partner, and opposing same-sex relationships, marriages, and parenting by gay or lesbian partners. The family values viewpoint also frowns on births to women outside of marriage. It evokes a certain set of ascribed gender roles; for example, the women fulfill homemaker and mothering responsibilities (the breadmaker role), and the men fulfill the role of primary wage earner (the breadwinner role). This particular family form is also considered a patriarch, wherein the male is dominant and is in charge of most decision-making in the family.

Historian and author Peter McWilliams (1998) offers insight into the roots of the traditional family. He notes that the modern concept of two adults rearing their children under a single roof grew out of necessity during the Middle Ages, when the minimum number of people required to own and maintain a plot of land was two. In order to multiply their wealth, it was necessary to have others work the land; children were free labor. Thus, in order to have the free labor provided by children, it was economically necessary that one of the adults was a man and the other was a woman—and they were thus paired until death. According to McWilliams, love had nothing to do with the pairing. "Even if a husband and a wife hated each other, all they had to do was wait

Which child abuses substances? Which child has behavioral problems in school? Which child copes with mental health issues? Is this a nuclear family or a stepfamily? In the 1950s, we would never know because these real-life problems were never addressed. The television and media portrayed an idealized image of the American family: The breadwinning dad, the breadmaker mom, and the practically perfect children who all live in their always-perfectly-kept home.

Source: CBS Photo Archive/Contributor.

a little while—with disease, war, childbirth, and an average lifespan of about 25, most marriages lasted less than five years. The departed partner was immediately replaced, and the system continued." Men and older children worked the land and the women tended to the livestock, the crops near the home, and the younger children. Because the system worked so well, the church eventually got involved and, over time, the one-man/one-woman for life theology emerged.

If we were to identify a specific period in American history that the traditional family form was in vogue, we would look at the period of the 1950s in the United States (McWilliams, 1998). The high postwar marriage and birth rates, coupled with a prosperous economy in which a single wage earner could support a family, led to a national perception of the period as a "golden era" for families (McWilliams, 1998).

Through the television and the media, families tuned in to watch the idealized image of the American family: The wise, reassuring father who came home from a hard day at the office; the apron-clad homemaker mother (wearing pearls and heels and lipstick) who offered comfort and support to her hardworking husband and perfect children; the clutter-free, immaculate home; and the homogenous neighborhood. Notes McWilliams (1998), the family life portrayed in the 1950s media was wholesome—there were no single parents (unless the father was a widower, such as with the fathers in *My Three Sons, The Andy Griffith Show*, and *Bonanza*), no infidelities, no divorce, no abuse, no teen runaways, no financial problems, no stress, and no prior marriages or children from prior marriages. There was no discussion about religion, politics, and the economy. No one lost his job. There was no violence in the home or school or neighborhood. There was no drug usage. No racism. No LGBTQ+ relationships. And no babies born out of wedlock.

Despite TV Land's depiction of the American family during this era, like *Leave It to Beaver*, it is questionable whether this idealized image of family really ever existed. Author and professor of comparative family history, Stephanie Coontz, notes the discrepancies of the idealized 1950s "good old days" family form portrayed in the media and the reality of family living during the 1950s (Coontz, 1992, 1999):

- About one-quarter of the population lived below the poverty line.
- The number of pregnant brides more than doubled from the 1940s.
- From 1944 to 1955, the number of babies born outside of marriage and relinquished for adoption rose 80 percent.
- Juvenile delinquency was so prevalent that in 1955 Congress considered nearly 200 bills to address the social problem.

As Coontz notes, the 1950s were a dismal time for women, minorities, gays and lesbians, and any other social group that did not "fit in" with the images typified on the television screen.

The traditional nuclear family is no longer predominant in the United States. In the 21st century, 1950s television shows like *I Love Lucy* have been replaced by shows such as *Family Guy, Modern Family, Black-ish*, and *A Million Little Things*, which better reflect the diversity found in today's families.

Extended Family

The **extended family** is typically defined as a family unit where two or more generations of close family relatives live together in one household. There are three common extended family configurations (Barbour et al., 2005):

1. A mother and father with children (may be married or not), with one or more grandparents
2. A mother and father with children (may be married or not), with at least one unmarried sibling of the parents, another relative, such as a cousin
3. A divorced, separated, or never-married single parent with children, in addition to a grandparent, sibling, or other relative.

This type of extended or *multigenerational* family structure was the basic element of slave life in the 19th century and remains today an integral part of the lives of many families, particularly in families of color (Pittman, 2012a,b). During, and sometime after the era of slavery, upon marriage, African couples were not permitted to form their own households; because of this, the newly married couple joined an already-existing family compound (Sudarkasa, 2007). The African extended families were organized in one of three ways: blood-related relatives and their children (i.e., parents and in-laws); a group of married spouses, where all men were referred to as "husbands," all women were referred to as "wives," and all children considered themselves as siblings, not cousins; extended family and **fictive kin** (unrelated by birth, but emotionally close) (Sudarkasa, 2007). Still today, families with African roots often experience close-knit, multigenerational family groups—in addition to parents and children, family members may be grandparents, aunts, uncles, and cousins (Cross, 2020).

Today, about 57 percent of African American/Black Caribbean children have lived in an extended family home compared with 20 percent of white children (Banerjee, 2019). Similarly, about 35 percent of Hispanic children have lived in an extended family home. Overall, 17 percent of all children in the United States live in an extended family household (Banerjee, 2019). No data exist to determine how many extended family members live nearby (not necessarily with) other family members, but we know that multigenerational family members can provide much emotional and economic support, along with the richness of family legacy and heritage.

The Expanding Family Landscape

In the United States today, there is no such thing as a "traditional" or "typical" family configuration. In order to better serve today's families and to help them reach their full potentials, we need to understand the changing compositions of contemporary families, as well as the racial and ethnic compositions of families.

Single-Parent Families

Today, one in four U.S. parents are unmarried (Cilluffo & Cohn, 2019). **Single-parent** family types can be the result of the choice of the parent or by circumstance; they can result either from divorce, the death of a spouse, or unmarried parenthood. Trends indicate that single-parent households are on the increase in the American family: In the past 10 years, the number of children who live with two married parents has decreased from 68 to 65 percent (Institute of Family Studies, 2019). Table 2.1 illustrates children's living arrangements from 1970 to 2019. While the percentage of children living with no parents has remained relatively stable over the past nearly 50 years, the percentage of children living with unmarried parents has increased, while those living with two parents has decreased. Understanding these trends in single-parenting experiences is important because as our study will show us in just a bit, single parents oftentimes live in poverty—which, in turn, affects their children's development.

TABLE 2.1 ■ Children's Living Arrangements by Presence of Parents in the Home, 1970–2018

Percentage of Children Who Live With...						
	1970	1980	1990	2000	2010	2018
Two parents	85.2	76.7	72.5	69.1	69.4	68.9
Single parents	11.9	19.7	24.7	26.7	26.6	27.0
No parents	2.9	3.7	2.8	4.2	4.1	4.1

Source: Institute for Family Studies (2019).

Childless/Childfree Family

Couples may consider themselves **childless** if they are unable to conceive or bear children of their own or adopt children. Some couples today prefer to remain **childfree** as a conscience choice. And although they're waiting longer to have children, older women today are more likely to have children than a decade ago. Today, 86 percent of women aged 40 to 44 are mothers in comparison with 80 percent in 2006 (Pew Research Center, 2018). The U.S. Census Bureau measures the presence of children primarily by examining the *general fertility rate* (how many children a woman bears). In 2018, there were 59 births for every 1,000 women aged 15 to 44; this is a decrease from 70 births for every 1,000 women aged 15 to 44 in 2010 (Pew Research Center, 2018b). The typical American family today has an average of 1.9 children under 18; this is a decrease from the average number of 2.44 children per family in 1970 (Pew Research Center, 2018b).

It is important to note, however, that this is not the first generation of people who are deciding not to have children. Notes Philip Morgan, professor of sociology at Duke University, "Childlessness is not new, [but] in the past it was more closely connected with non-marriage than now. During the depression, many Americans also chose not to have children because they could not afford them. Childlessness levels now are not higher than those in the 1930s" (Taylor, 2005). Morgan adds that there are many factors involved in couples' decisions to remain childfree today.

Stepfamily

A **stepfamily** (or reconstituted family) is formed when, after death or divorce, a parent marries again. A stepfamily is also formed when a never-married parent marries and children from different biological families end up living within the new marriage for part of the time. In short, the presence of a stepparent, stepsibling, or half-sibling designates a family as a stepfamily (U.S. Census Bureau, 2019a).

The U.S. Census Bureau no longer provides stepfamily data, so it is difficult to obtain accurate statistics about stepfamilies. But Census experts today estimate that one of three

Americans—about 33 percent—is now either a stepparent, a stepchild, a stepsibling, or some other member of a stepfamily (Gaille, 2017). Although the popular sitcom 1970s television show *The Brady Bunch* portrayed stepfamily living as an emotionally cohesive, trouble-free, happily adjusted family, this idealized concept of the stepfamily form is simply not the norm. (Because of the complexities of stepfamily living, an entire segment of a chapter is devoted to this family form in Chapter 9.)

Cohabiting Family

Unmarried partners who live together in a single household are referred to as **cohabiting couples**. Although once considered a scandalous, uncommon alternative lifestyle, cohabiting before marriage (or instead of marriage) is now *the* prevailing living arrangement of intimate partners—the next step following serious dating. The U.S. Census Bureau today estimates that 35 percent of couples in the United States are cohabiting (U.S. Census Bureau, 2019b). In 2018, cohabitation was a more common living arrangement of children than living with a single parent. For example, while 3.5 percent of children lived with an unmarried parent, 4.2 percent lived with a parent and the parent's unmarried partner (Institute of Family Studies, 2019). This is a significant increase from 2007, where the percentage of children living with unmarried single parents and cohabiting parents was nearly identical (2.6 percent and 2.9 percent, respectively). Today, an estimated 5.8 million American children live with cohabiting parents (Institute of Family Studies, 2019). In 2018, there were 8.5 million unmarried opposite-sex couples living together (U.S. Census Bureau, 2019b). Many of these couples have no plans for eventual marriage. Indeed, 51 percent of women's first marriages are preceded by cohabitation (Institute of Family Studies, 2019). The rates of cohabiting parents vary by race; these data are presented in Figure 2.3.

FIGURE 2.3 ■ Children's Living Arrangements by Race/Ethnicity

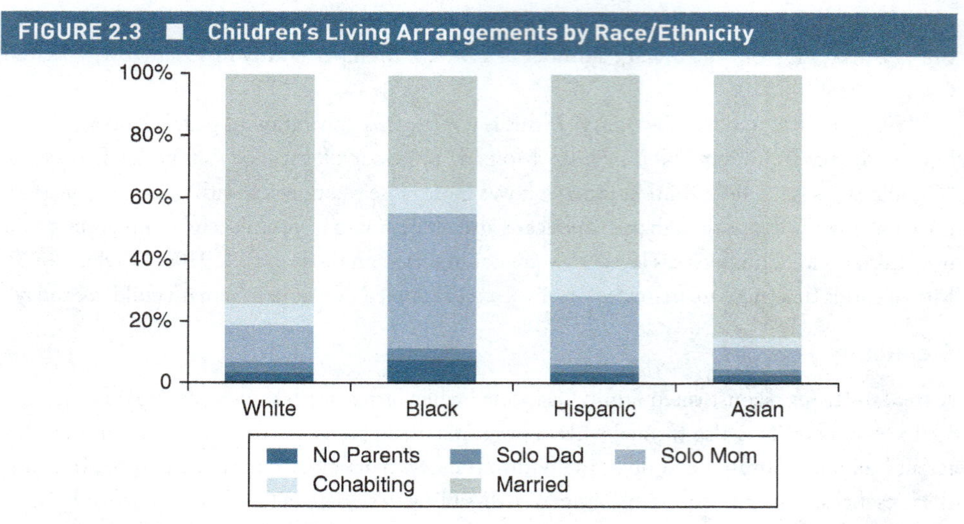

Source: Institute for Family Studies (2019).

Gay and Lesbian Families

Lesbian and gay families consist of same-sex partners who live together in the same household, and may include either natural-born or adopted children. As you saw in Chapter 1, in the United States today there are 935,000 same-sex households, up from 780,000 same-sex households in 2011 (U.S. Census Bureau, 2019c). Census Bureau statisticians point out, however, that this increase reflects the fact that same-sex families were previously uncounted, undercounted, or underreported, and not that the numbers of gay or lesbian families have increased significantly (U.S. Census Bureau, 2019c). Same-sex family forms may or may not resemble traditional marriage roles, such as in the division of household chores; today, same-sex couples tend to share more equally household and child care tasks than different-sex couples (Goldberg et al., 2012). Interestingly, when one partner earns less than the other, the lower earner contributed to more traditional feminine tasks, including a greater contribution to child care.

In the LGBTQ+ community, **chosen family**—nonbiological kinship bonds—replace blood families and become the bedrock of trust, support, and love; sometimes, LGBTQ+ individuals live with their chosen family (Carlson & Dermer, 2017; Hull, 2018). Kathleen Hull, professor of sociology and gender, women, and sexuality studies, notes that many LGBTQ+ individuals do not receive support and acceptance from their blood relatives, and because of this, they have formed nonbiological families with people who do love and support them (Hull, 2018). Another social scientist observes, "Until the world is a more inclusive place, [chosen family] will continue to exist within the LGBT community" (Mitchell, 2008).

Immigrant Families With Children

Immigrants are people who reside in the United States who were not U.S. citizens at birth. **Immigrant families with children** are those with at least one parent who was born outside of the United States. From 1994 to 2017, the population of immigrant children in the United States grew by 51 percent to 19.6 million. This number represents one-fourth of all U.S. children (Child Trends, 2018a). *First-generation* immigrant children are those who were born outside of the United States; *second-generation* immigrant children are those who were born within the United States to immigrant parents. The growth we've seen in immigrant children are due to second-generation immigrants. In 2017, more than one-half (54 percent) of all immigrant children were of Hispanic origin (Child Trends, 2018a). Non-Hispanic Asian children comprised 17 percent of immigrant children. About 25 percent of first- and second-generation immigrant children live below the federal poverty level (Child Trends, 2018a).

Our study so far has shown us that in the 21st century, it is hard to encapsulate or sum up the "typical" American family—it simply doesn't exist today in our complex, multifaceted, ever-changing, global society. To get the full grasp of parenting, we now need to examine the racial and ethnic characteristics of contemporary families.

CONTEMPORARY FAMILIES

As the United States moved into the second half of the 20th century, a number of social and cultural, economic, and political changes occurred that continue to have an impact on today's 21st century families and family living: *social and cultural forces*, such as lowered birth rates and an increase in nonmarital cohabitation; *economic factors* that include the influx of women into the workforce; and *political factors*, such as legalized abortion in 1973 and the Civil Rights legislation of 1965 which bans racial, ethnic, sexual, and sexual orientation discrimination.

All of these factors worked in tandem to change the traditional family in this century. Experts in the field of marriage and family living, however, view the changes occurring during the last half of the 20th century differently. Those with more conventional, conservative, or religious outlooks are concerned about what they perceived to be a moral decline in family life—that is, the increase in nonmarital cohabitation and same-sex relationships and in the number of births outside of marriage. These groups prescribe a return to more conventional, long-held family values as a way to reverse the trends (Popenoe & Whitehead, 2005). Those with a more contemporary outlook hold that these trends represent both flexibility and adaptability in today's families and in the society at large (Solot & Miller, 2004). In spite of increasing relational and economic stresses faced by today's families, marriage represents the most frequently chosen family form, with approximately 93 percent of the population choosing marriage at least once (U.S. Census Bureau, 2019a).

In the United States, there is more diversity now than ever before. Families today are complex and diverse, ranging from traditional two-biological-parent family structures, to single-parent homes, to extended family forms, to married gay or lesbian couples. There is also greater diversity of racial, ethnic, economic, and religious composition, and so social workers, family life educators, psychologists, sociologists, and health and mental health professionals must be aware of the full range of diversity in families today (see Figure 2.4).

It is incumbent upon parenting professionals to know the racial and ethnic composition of U.S. families because this knowledge aids in our understanding of the complex, changing nature of family living and parenting. When discussing contemporary parenting in the United States—particularly among African American/Black Caribbean and Latina mothers—it is important to introduce the concept of intersectionality. **Intersectionality** refers to the interconnected nature of social categorizations—such as race, social economic class, sexual orientation, and gender—regarded as creating overlapping and interdependent systems of discrimination or disadvantage (Oxford Learner's Dictionary, 2019). Put another way, intersectionality is a theoretical perspective that helps to explain the complex and cumulative ways in which the effects of multiple types of discrimination combine or overlap, further marginalizing an individual or a people group. As a theoretical framework, intersectionality "encourages scholars to examine individual subjectivities and behaviors as unique but also shaped by and in conversation with broader sociocultural and historical processes and inequalities" (Elliott & Aseltine, 2013, p. 722).

Conceptualized by Kimberlé Crenshaw (1991), law professor and social theorist, the basic premise of intersectionality maintains that people are often disadvantaged in multiple ways by

FIGURE 2.4 ■ Racial and Ethnic Composition of American Families: Projected Population by Race, 2016–2060

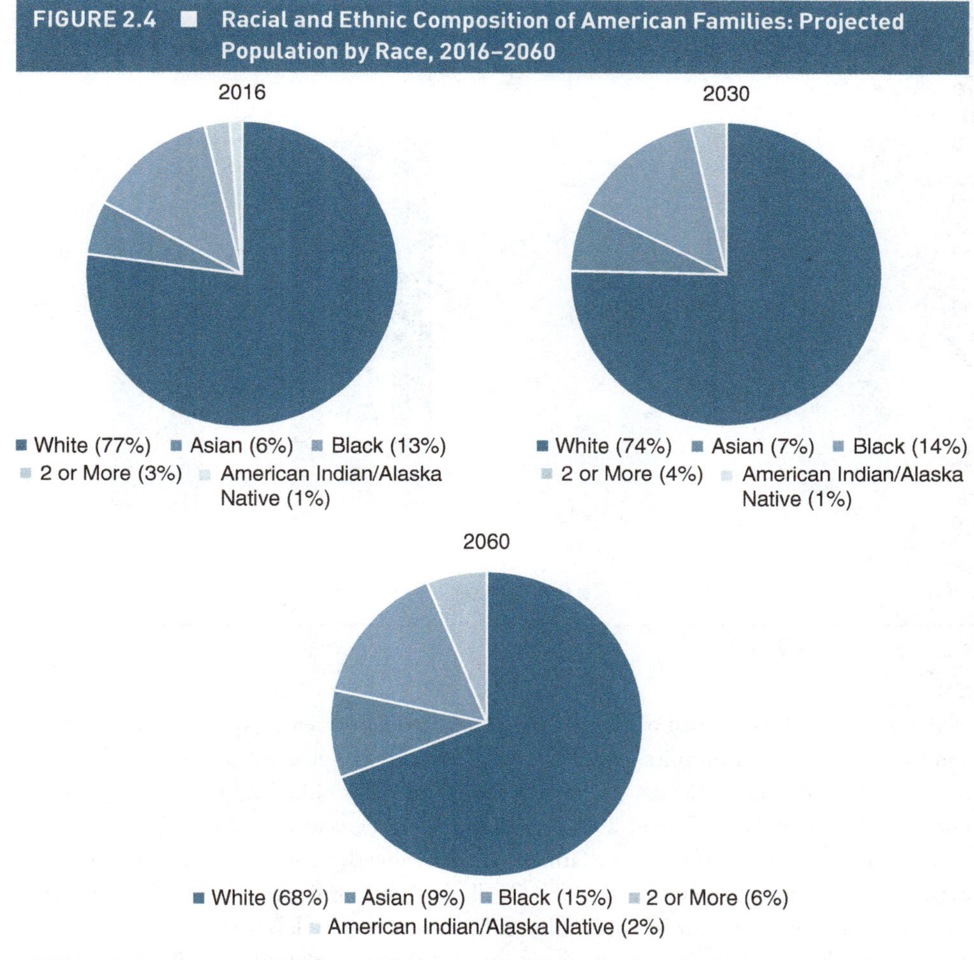

Source: U.S. Census Bureau (2018b).

multiple sources of oppression. Identity markers, such as race, SES, gender, gender identity, and religion, do not exist independently of each other. Indeed, each informs and impacts the other, which in turn affect the others; this creates a complex coming together, merging, of oppression. We'll take a closer look at this concept in the section that follows. Now, we briefly examine the racial and ethnic compositions of families so that you have a firm understanding of the diversity within the United States.

African American/Black Caribbean Families

Historically, African American/Black Caribbean families assumed the traditional married-couple family structure, with children born inside the marital union. Today, it is common for Black children to be born to a single mother. As Figure 2.5 illustrates, nearly 70 percent

FIGURE 2.5 ■ Percentage of All Births That Were to Unmarried Women, by Race and Hispanic Origin

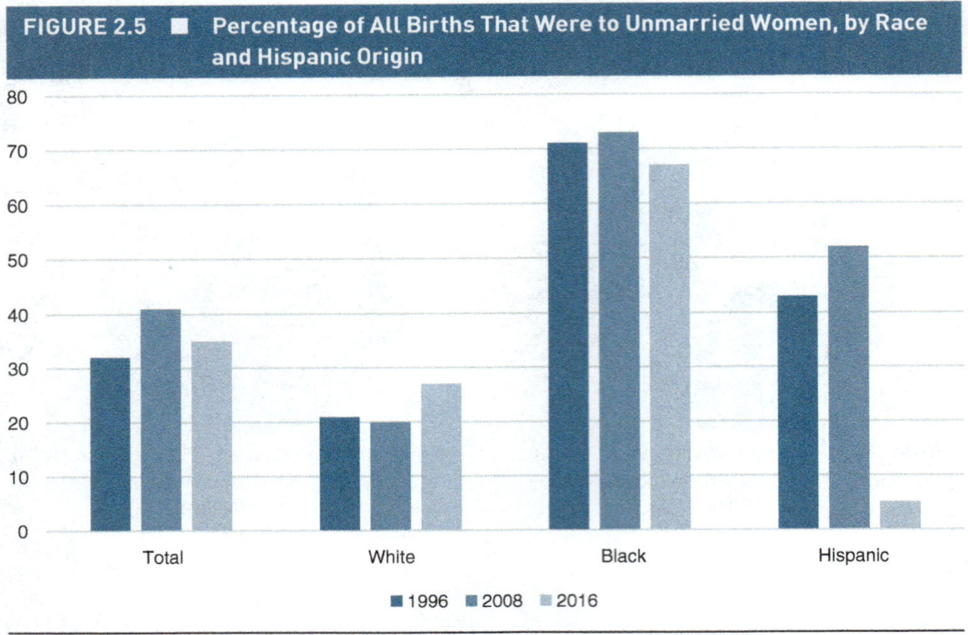

Source: Child Trends (2018b).

of the births to Black women of all ages are to unmarried women (Child Trends, 2018b). In comparison with white families, where nearly one-fourth (24 percent) live in a single-parent home (Kids Count Data Center, 2019a), 65 percent of Black children live in a single-parent home (Kids Count Data Center, 2019a). Eventually, 37 percent of Black children reside in two-parent homes, but many of these families are formed with a child who was born outside of marriage (Kids Count Data Center, 2019b). Of all racial and ethnic groups in the United States, African American/Black Caribbean families suffer one of highest levels of unemployment and poverty and the lowest median family income—slightly over $40,000 annually (U.S. Census Bureau, 2018a).

Multigenerational, extended family ties are common among Black families (Cross, 2020). Census bureau data estimate that about 26 percent of African American/Black Caribbean children live in some type of extended family (Pew Research Center, 2018c). **Multiple mothering,** a practice that involves aunts, cousins, close friends, and fictive kin who provide mothers with a range of modeling and tangible support, is commonplace (Greene, 1995). According to a study by Noelle St. Vil et al. (2018), characteristics of African American/Black Caribbean extended family networks include:

- Strong commitment to family and family obligation
- Availability of and willingness to provide child care
- Reinforcement of social skills and family values in children

- Willingness to allow relatives and close nonrelatives to move into the family home
- Strong network of emotional support
- Strengthen marriages by protecting against the inability to meet responsibilities of multiple roles
- Close system of mutual aid and support.

Because of the large numbers of female-headed households among African American/Black Caribbeans, some research suggests that the child-rearing and economic support of extended kin is necessary; it is within the extended family networks of grandmothers, grandfathers, aunts, uncles, and cousins that children are cared for, socialized, educated, and have their emotional needs met (Cengage, 2020; Sarkisian & Gerstel, 2004; Taylor, 2000). Why are extended family forms so prevalent among Black families today? The history of Black Africans and Caribbeans helps us to better understand the present.

Before being ripped from their homelands, West African slaves embraced clans as their normative family experience. Clans were similar to extended family forms seen among African American families today.

Source: iStock.com/monkeybusinessimages.

Pre-slavery Influences

Between 1525 and 1866, over 12 million Africans were shipped to the New World (Transatlantic Slave Trade Database, 2020); of these, 388,000 were brought to the United States, and 4.8 million were brought to the Caribbean. While in their homeland, the West African family—referred to as a *clan*—very much resembled the extended family forms commonly seen among African American families today: It was the primary base for social relationships, connections, emotional attachment, and membership (Cengage, 2020). It was also the hub of economic activity. This clan structure served as the model for "family" life during slavery (Hallam, 2004).

How slaves experienced "family" was very much dependent upon the type of farming and agricultural activities they were expected to carry out (Hallam, 2004). For example, while cotton plantations required a great deal of slave labor to harvest the crops, tobacco farming did not (Hallam, 2004). Often, slave families were broken up and spread across many different plantations in a given region; when husband and wives were separated, they *married abroad*—a term that describe spouses who had different owners and lived apart from each other. Separation of family members was a constant threat. Notes Dr. Jennifer Hallam, a scholar in the History of Art, "When a master died, his slaves might be indiscriminately distributed among his heirs or sold off to multiple buyers. When a planter's child was born or married, he or she might receive the gift of a Black attendant. Mothers were taken from their own children to nurse the offspring of their masters. And slave children were torn from mothers and brought into the house to be raised alongside the master's sons and daughters" (Hallam, 2004, p. 2). Because of the large numbers of single mothers and orphaned children, *communal parenting* evolved, and children were often cared for by older women who could no longer be used for hard, physical field labor; these women were referred to as "aunties" or "grannies" (Hallam, 2004). These communal families became the substitute for the extended family that was central to African cultures and provided both physical and emotional support for enslaved women and children (Franklin & Moss, 1988; Gutman, 1977).

Without question, regardless of the unimaginable experiences and conditions of slavery, African men and women made every effort to create and maintain a family that was "an incomparable source of solace and strength and a primary means of survival" (Hallam, 2004, p. 2).

Contemporary African American/Black Caribbean Family Patterns

There are a number of theories that speak to the diversity and rich cultural heritages of Black families. For example, the **cultural variation approach** refers to the range of social practices (i.e., gender roles, economic systems, and social hierarchy) observed in different cultures around the world and the maintenance of these ways of life (Wan, 2017). The **African Heritage theory** views African American/Black Caribbean cultures as distinctly different from white, European American cultures; this theory takes into consideration the unique characteristics and elements of West African culture (from where most slaves were captured) that were preserved while they were enslaved in America and the Caribbean, such as the value of extended families, kinship patterns, marriage, sexuality, and child-rearing (Hale-Benson, 1988). There are three primary tenets of African Heritage theory:

1. The cultural elements and practices are not commonly characteristic of white culture.
2. They are found among nearly all Afrocentric communities (especially in the Caribbean).
3. The characteristics still today embody West African culture (Hale-Benson, 1988).

This theory contends that language, development, interactions, and behavioral patterns of African American/Black Caribbean children differ as a result of growing up in a distinct African culture.

Central to the cultural variation approach is the idea that African culture has survived and has been subtly transmitted through multiple generations, without conscious effort. **Bicultural socialization, or biculturalism**, is a process wherein both the aspects of African and/or Caribbean heritages and Western culture are integrated (Okere, 2017). **Acculturation** refers to the transfer of societal values and customs from one group to another—it is a cultural shift where individuals or people groups adopt the predominant behaviors and traits of a different culture. Conversely, biculturalism is a distinct cultural orientation in which there is a blending of both cultures and a preservation of the original culture (Schwartz & Unger, 2010).

As an example of biculturalism, Black parents are more likely to socialize their children without strict differences determined by the gender of the child and to share in instrumental support (such as child care and in decision-making about child-rearing), housework, and financial assistance (Amos, 2013; Hill, 2001; Sarkisian & Gerstel, 2004; White-Johnson et al., 2010). Emotional support from the family is also important to Black families. For example, in a large study that sought to determine the racial differences in family support, the researchers found that nearly 70 percent of African Americans reported offering emotional support to family (including extended family and fictive kin) members; nearly 100 percent reported that they offered instrumental support (Sarkisian & Gerstel, 2004).

Afro parents also place more value on raising their children to be hardworking, ambitious, and financially independent than white parents do (Amos, 2013; Pew Research Center, 2015), and Black parents believe their children's behaviors and attitudes are a reflection of their parenting. All of these parenting practices are a reflection of parenting in African communities (Amos, 2013). It's important to keep in mind that when we use the word "parenting," we are referring not only to the Black child's parents but also to the extended family members/fictive kin who participate in child-rearing (Amos, 2013). It is vitally important for parenting professionals and teachers to fully acknowledge and embrace the importance of extended and fictive kin in Black children's lives, as well as the critical roles these family members play in children's well-being and academic success (Amos, 2013).

We'll explore the various parenting styles in Chapter 5; in the next sections, we examine the general ways in which ethnic parents interact with their children. There are three reasons why we observe different relational patterns among different races and ethnicities: differing cultural norms, differing perceptions, and differing interpretations (Chao, 1994; Gonzales et al., 1996; Rudy & Grusec, 2001).

African American/Black Caribbean Parent–Child Interactions

Black parents play a crucial role in socializing their children into African culture and to participate successfully in school and society. Overall, African American parents self-rate their parenting interactions with their children as high in measures of control and harshness and low in measures of sensitivity (Berlin et al., 1995; McLoyd & Smith, 2002). Interestingly, these parenting behaviors closely resemble acceptable parenting styles in other Afrocentric cultures (Shumow et al., 1998). Recall that differing interpretations are important when observing behaviors in other cultures. In the case of African American parent–child interactions, white, Euro-Americans view some behaviors as harsh (Gonzales et al., 1996); however, Black children report that their parents' behaviors are expressions of love and care (Brown & Johnson, 2008).

This isn't to say that Afro parents are uninvolved or ineffective. A substantial body of evidence supports that strict parenting observed in African American families is associated with positive effects in children:

- More independence and social maturity in preschool girls (Baumrind, 1972).
- More favorable self-regulation in three-year-old children (Chen & French, 2008; LeCuyer et al., 2011).
- More respect for parenting authority in school-aged children (Dixon et al., 2008).

In a study of 161 parents and 270 school-aged children, the investigators discovered that Black parents' involvement at home regarding school-related matters and racial education/racism awareness had positive influences on their children's academic success, whereas the lack of

Latinx families enjoy the rich, multigenerational relationships of extended family members and nonrelated kin who become as close as blood relatives. Latinx families embrace *familism*: The best interests of the family are placed ahead of the interests of the individual family member.
Source: istock.com/aldomurillo.

racism education/awareness and cultural pride in the school system negatively influenced children's school success (McKay et al., 2003).

Over the last two decades, a more balanced depiction of African American/Black Caribbean family life has emerged, with growing appreciation of the rich cultural diversity in these families, both in form and functioning.

Latinx Families

Latinx are people of Latin American origin or descent. This term is used as a gender-neutral alternative to Latino or Latina. Today, Latinx Americans account for slightly over 18 percent of the total U.S. population; this figure does not include the three million residents of the U.S. territory, Puerto Rico (U.S. Census Bureau, 2018b). This population traces their roots to Spain, Mexico, and the Spanish-speaking nations of Central America, South America, and the Caribbean. The fastest-growing population in the United States because of the large proportion of Latina women of childbearing age, the Hispanic population of the United States is nearly 59 million, making people of the Hispanic origin the nation's largest ethnic or racial minority (U.S. Census Bureau, 2018b; U.S. Census Bureau, 2019d).

About 76 percent of Latinx children live within two-parent families (U.S. Census Bureau, 2019d). Similar to the experiences of African American/Black Caribbean women, births to unmarried Latina women have increased since the 1970s. Nearly 40 percent of all Hispanic origin births are to unmarried women (Child Trends, 2018a,b). Currently, nearly 20 percent of Latinx children live in a household with their mothers and have no father present; 27 percent live in an extended, multigenerational family household with grandparents, and one-fourth live with their grandparents (Pew Research Center, 2018c; U.S. Census Bureau, 2019c).

Educational attainment varies among this population, as Figure 2.6 illustrates. In the United States today, Latinx families earn, on average, about $50,000 per year (U.S. Census Bureau, 2019d). It's important to keep in mind that many Hispanic immigrants may have successful businesses in other countries or professional degrees from other countries, but because of the language barrier when they arrive in the United States, they are unable to secure high-paying jobs.

Contemporary Latinx American Family Patterns

Latinx are highly group- and community-oriented and value strong interdependent relationships with their families; a high value is placed on family as the primary source of one's identity (among many, Carteret, 2011; Constante et al., 2019; Stein et al., 2019). This collectivist family type is an extended family, including grandparents, aunts, uncles, and cousins. But this intense sense of family belonging isn't just limited to family—Latinx value the opinions of close friends who are considered to be part of the immediate family (who, in many cases, are treated as family members). **Familismo or familism** is the term used by Latinx to describe their loyalty to their collective family, and it refers to the mutual support and obligation shared between family members (Calzada et al., 2014; Carteret, 2011). Within this family dynamic, family members are provided clothing, shelter, food, education, and emotional support. People of Hispanic origin further extend family relationships to fictive, or nonrelated, kin, such as godparents and

FIGURE 2.6 ■ Educational Attainment of Latinx Residing in the United States

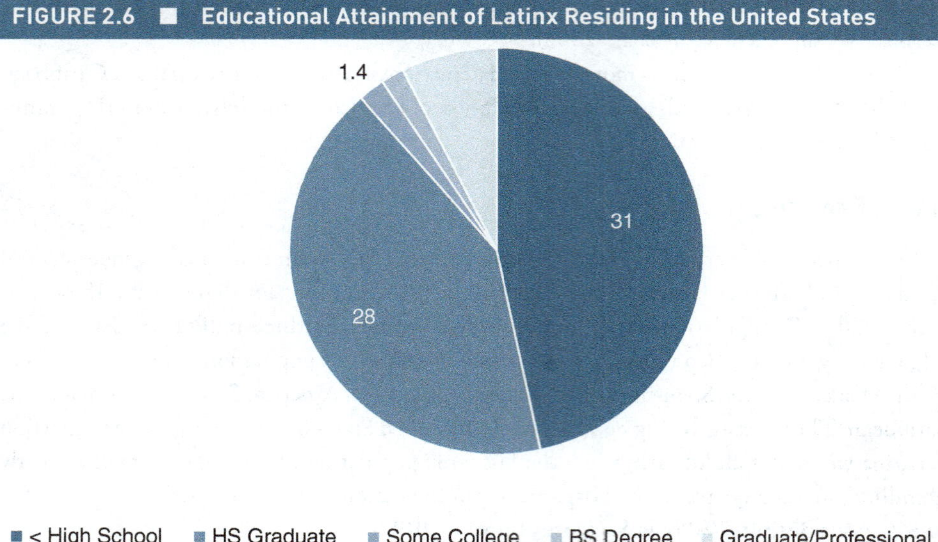

Source: Untied States Census Bureau (2019d).

close friends. Within Latinx communities, the well-being of the family takes precedence over the well-being of the individual.

A 1987 landmark study discovered there are three interrelated facets of familism values (Sabogal et al., 1987):

- **Familial obligations:** The family members' responsibilities to provide economic and emotional support.
- **Perceived support and emotional closeness:** Family members' perceptions that each family member is dependable; because of this interdependency, family members are to be unified and maintain close relationships.
- **Family as referent:** All behaviors should meet with the family's expectations.

Furthermore, a substantial body of research exists that speaks to the protective effects of familismo with Latinx youth. For example, because they put family needs before their own, they develop empathy and sensitivity for the needs of others (Calderon et al., 2011). The highly supportive family structure prevents or reduces depressive symptoms in Latino-descent adolescents (Piña-Watson et al., 2019), and low-income, Latinx urban youth experience lower levels of violence exposure (Kennedy & Ceballo, 2013). Familismo is also associated with a higher attachment to school and greater academic success (Stein et al., 2013). To gain the trust of the parent(s) and other family members, it is essential that early childhood educators, teachers, child life specialists, social workers, therapists, and other helping professionals, understand, appreciate, and recognize the collective loyalty Latinx families embrace (Calzada et al., 2014). Failure to do so can lead to conflicts with Latinx parents.

Respeto—respect—is another important trait found in Latinx culture (Cardona & Softas-Nall, 2010; Paniagua, 2005). It involves a "highly emotionalized dependence and dutifulness" to hierarchical relationships (Folicov, 2007, p. 48). Latinx children are taught from the earliest age to be obedient and respectful to parents, elders, and people in positions of authority (i.e., teachers, law enforcement); children value this authority and perceive it to be parental love (Bain, 2006; Delgado-Gaitan, 1994; Santiago-Rivera et al., 2002; Vazquez, 2004).

Personalismo refers to the warmth and familiarity expressed in family and extended kin relationships, and it is central to Latinx interpersonal relationships (Paniagua, 2005; Smith & Montilla, 2006). One of the primary goals of Latinx parents is to raise well-educated children, which means instilling in their children proper social skills and the *respeto* needed for quality relationships (Santiago-Rivera et al., 2002).

It is necessary that those working with parents have an understanding of all of these unique expectations—*familismo, respeto*, and *personalismo*—because it promotes the cultural competence required to effectively engage and work with Latinx children and parents. These rich cultural beliefs require that that helping professionals take time to build trust and rapport with these families (Cardona & Softas-Nall, 2010).

Latinx children often reside within families in which at least one parent is an immigrant—foreign-born—or who are themselves foreign-born. Today, one out of four U.S. children is living in an immigrant family (Zong et al., 2019); Latinx immigrants and their children commonly live within extended family forms during the first 10 years following immigration (Carranza et al., 2002). Even as immigrants establish their own households, they do so nearby their families' homes. Second- and third-generation Hispanic Americans have even larger extended kin networks than do immigrants (Carranza et al., 2002).

Latinx Parent–Child Interactions

Parenting is central in the lives of Latinx adults, and their cultural values are infused in their daily interactions with their children, as you saw earlier with the concept of *familismo/familism* (Domenech Rodriguez et al., 2009; Guilamo-Ramos et al., 2007; Parra-Cardona et al., 2008). One writer (Ramirez, 1989) noted that *el amor de madre* (motherly love) is a greater force in Latinx families than wifely love; that is, the parent–child relationship is more important than the spousal relationship.

Although a number of studies have been conducted on the attitudes and practices of Latinx parents, the studies have failed to provide consistent conclusions (Allen et al., 2008). For example, some researchers found that Latinx parents are nurturing and egalitarian, but other studies have found that they are permissive (Hill et al., 2003). However, other research maintains that immigrant Latinx parents adapt their parenting behaviors to the environment/location in which they live in order to manage and cope with the stressors of the new environment (Reese, 2002).

Because Latinx families are a rapidly growing ethnic group in this country, careful research still needs to be undertaken to give keener insight into these family relationships and parenting styles. Especially important to understand are the ways in which traditional cultural values and intergenerational relationships influence contemporary family relationships and parenting.

Asian American Families

Asian American families come to the United States from countries including Korea, Japan, China, Taiwan, Vietnam, Cambodia, Sri Lanka, and Indonesia. Each Asian country has a unique culture unto itself, which accounts for the vast cultural and ethnic differences within this racial group. Like Latinx families, Asian American families place great emphasis on extended kinship ties and the needs of the entire family, rather than on the needs of the individual. About 61 percent of all Asian American children live with both biological parents; only 9 percent live in mother-only families, and about 4 percent live in father-only families (U.S. Census Bureau, 2019e). Today, approximately 13 percent of Asian women give birth outside of marriage (Child Trends, 2018b). With an annual income of over $80,000 per year, Asian American families have the highest median household income of all racial groups in the United States (U.S. Census Bureau, 2019e). This is perhaps because Asian Americans have the highest educational attainment and qualifications of all ethnic groups in the United States—nearly 54 percent have earned at least a bachelor's degree (U.S. Census Bureau, 2019e).

Contemporary Asian American Family Patterns

The literature on Asian American families is not as robust in comparison with the research on other cultural and ethnic groups; however, we do know that the time of immigration to the United States seems to affect the degree of acculturation into mainstream culture, with third- and fourth-generation families demonstrating more similarity to U.S. culture than first- and second-generation immigrants (Choi et al., 2005). Similar to Latinx families, Asian American families are child-centric. Within the Asian family structure, a greater emphasis is placed on the parent–child relationship than on the husband–wife relationship (Fong, 2002). In exchange for the undivided loyalty and for sacrifices parents make for their children, Asian American parents expect respect and obedience from their children (Fong, 2002). Figure 2.7 presents the priorities of Asian American adults; as you can see, being a good parent is at the top of their priorities.

Asian American Parent–Child Interactions

Filial piety has governed intergenerational Asian families for over 3,000 years (Mack, 2019). This complex system involves a series of obligations of child to parent—most centrally to provide aid to, comfort to, affection to, and contact with the parent. This child-to-parent devotion also brings glory and honor to the parent by doing well in educational and occupational areas, that is, achieving success in the outside world (Mack, 2019). It means that children are expected to satisfy their parents, and to respect and to show deference and reverence for elders in all situations (Kelley & Tseng, 1992; Lin & Liu, 1993). This concept is deeply ingrained in Chinese and other Asian cultures and has served as the moral foundation of interpersonal relationships for centuries (Lin & Liu, 1993).

Overall, Asian parents tend to be warm, affectionate, and lenient toward infants and young children, but once they reach the "age of understanding," discipline becomes much stricter

FIGURE 2.7 ■ Percentage of Asian Americans and the General U.S. Public Life Goals and Priorities

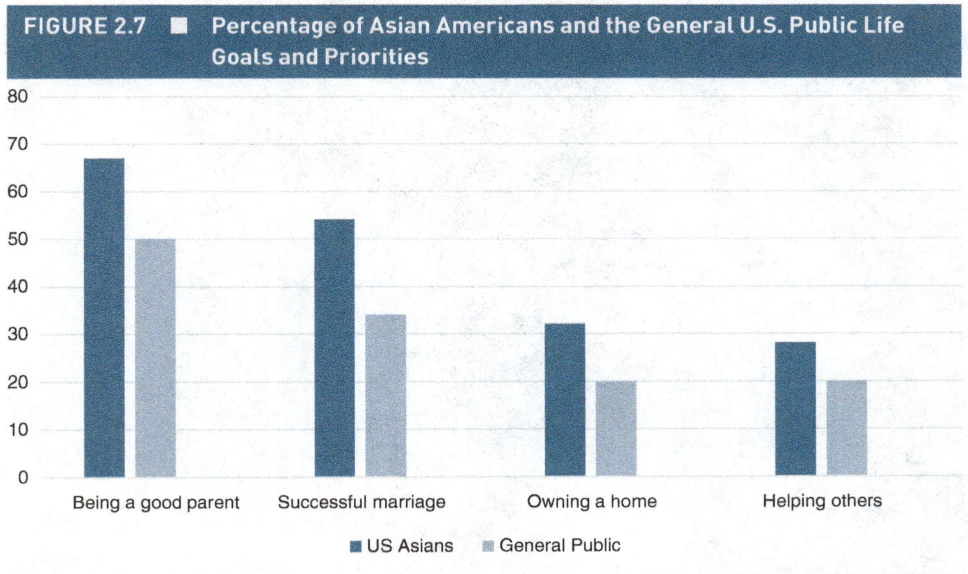

Source: Pew Research Center (2012).

(Kelley & Tseng, 1992; Kim et al., 2013). Children are taught mutual dependence, group identification, self-discipline, and good manners, as well as the importance of education. Departure from parental goals is seen as a reflection on the parents; therefore, parents take complete responsibility for the development of their children and are very involved in child-rearing (Li & Hein, 2019; Zhao, 2007; Zhao & Qiu, 2009). Asian Americans view the parenting role mainly as one of teacher (Kim et al., 2013).

Even though Asian parenting historically has been seen as more demanding and rigid than mainstream American parenting (Kim et al., 2013; Leung & Kwon, 1998; Li & Hein, 2019), some research suggests that Asian parenting styles may be a Western concept that does not accurately depict Asian socialization (Gorman, 1998). In one study, the author found little rule setting for adolescents among the Chinese mothers, suggesting that these mothers did not characterize their roles as including domination and control (Gorman, 1998). These mothers perceived that they were training their children, giving them guidance, and helping them to make good decisions; that is to say, they provided pertinent information and arguments but left the final decision in their children's hands. This approach is consistent with the Asian cultural value of individual responsibility—expectations for their children's successful adjustment rather than on a need to dominate their children (Kim et al., 2013; Leung & Kwon, 1998; Li & Hein, 2019).

Understanding *filial piety* is important to helping professionals because it helps those of us who work with children and their parents to see that Asian American parenting is characterized by an interaction of expectations and obligations, rather than parental control and child submission.

Native Americans/Alaska Natives embrace rich cultural heritages and an identity that stresses the importance of intergenerational family ties. Native spiritual and religious beliefs are numerous and diverse, and the beliefs often shape their attitudes toward marriage and family life.

Source: Flickr/Grand_Canyon_NPS (2010).

Native American/Alaska Native Families

The terms *Native American, American Indian, Alaska Native, First Americans, First Nations,* and *Indian* are often used interchangeably and are used to describe the Indigenous people of the continental United States (UCLA: Equity, Diversity & Inclusion, 2020). Here, we use the term **Native American/Alaska Native (NA/AN)** to refer to aboriginal peoples of the United States and their descendants, and who maintain tribal affiliation or community attachment. Today, about 2 percent of the total U.S. population reports that they are Indigenous Americans (U.S. Census Bureau, 2019f). About one-third of this population is under the age of 18, making this a young ethnic group (U.S. Census Bureau, 2019f). As with other racial and ethnic groups in the United States, Native American/Alaska Native communities are culturally diverse with 561 federally recognized Native entities, and an additional 365 state-recognized American Indian tribes (U.S. Census Bureau, 2019f). Native Americans prefer to be identified by tribal names, such as *Wampanoag, Lakota,* and *Kickapoo* (Fleming, 2007; Makes Marks, 2007); our discussion here is generalized.

In order for us to accurately understand Native American family experiences, we must be aware of the unique qualities associated with this race. Unfortunately, comparatively little research has been conducted on Native American family life, and especially on Native

American parenting. Despite this gap in the empirical literature, however, the census data do give us insight into some characteristics of Natives. For instance, nearly 67 percent of all Native American households are married couple households. Interestingly, over one-third of households are nonfamily households. This means that a significant number of Native American families are headed by someone other than a parent, such as a grandparent, or even by nonfictive kin; nearly 52 percent of Native grandparents assume responsibility for their grandchildren (U.S. Census Bureau, 2019f). Although nearly 80 percent of this population has at least a high school diploma, the median household income of single-race American Indian and Alaska Native households is slightly over $39,000. This compares with $58,000 for the nation as a whole.

Contemporary Indigenous Family Patterns

The predominance of extended family/nonfictive kin households among Natives is a reflection of the cultural roots of this racial group. Native American/Alaska Natives embrace a social identity that stresses the importance of family ties. For instance, when they introduce themselves to other Natives, they do so by telling them their maternal heritage, clans, and homelands (Makes Marks, 2007). In contrast to patriarchal societies where people's lineage is determined along **patrilineal** lines (the father's heritage), the roots of Indigenous peoples' social and clan relationships are by and large **matrilineal**; that is to say, these societies trace their heritage form a female ancestor to a descendant of either sex. This is also referred to as **uterine descent**. Within these societies, women are not given power per se because they are women—they are given power because of their status of mother, the power of female as mother (Makes Marks, 2007).

Indigenous peoples' spiritual traditions and religious beliefs are also numerous and diverse, and as such, the depth and dynamics of Native Americans' religious experiences are difficult to categorize or classify. Even so, there is an underlying or essential principal belief that informs most Natives' spiritual practices: The belief in the existence of unseen powers, and that something exists beyond them that is sacred and mysterious (Makes Marks, 2007). Within this belief are family attitudes, norms, and behaviors which are unknown because Native Americans are among the most misunderstood and understudied ethnic group in our culture; this is because they are commonly culturally isolated (Hellerstedt et al., 2006).

The Native American family system is vastly different from other extended families in this country. These networks are structurally open, assume a village-type characteristic, and are usually composed of *clans*, which include several households of relatives (Carson et al., 1990). The roles of family members and the structure of the extended family vary across tribes. Traditionally, they live in relational networks that serve to support and nurture strong bonds of mutual assistance and affection (Atkinson et al., 1998; LaFromboise & Low, 1989). Guidance and wisdom received from elders facilitate family cohesion and resiliency, and the personal support from extended family members and the community, especially during times of crisis, contributes immensely to family strengths (Carson et al., 1990).

Indigenous Parent–Child Interactions

Perhaps because of the diverse nature of Indigenous people groups, there is little systematic knowledge about parenting styles and how they vary from tribe to tribe. However, child-rearing practices are shaped largely by the worldviews of Native American populations, which regard children as beloved gifts and the center of Native community (BigFoot & Funderburk, 2006). Pregnant Indigenous women actively engage with their unborn children, singing to them and talking to them, so the infants know they are wanted and welcomed (BigFoot & Funderburk, 2006). From pregnancy, the growing baby is viewed as:

- an eager learner;
- a worthwhile human being;
- a willing seeker of the traits necessary to be a kind, caring, and empathic person to self and others;
- accepted by all relatives;
- a group member with the clan or band, rather than an individual (BigFoot & Funderburk, 2006).

The most striking difference in child-rearing and socialization is the exposure of children to a wide array of persons to whom they can become attached—parents, siblings, aunts, uncles, cousins, and grandparents—thus protecting children and providing them with the assurances of love (Dykeman & Nelson, 1995). The extended family plays as much a role in child-rearing, supervision of children, and the transgenerational transmission of teachings and customs as do parents, and parenting is very much a communal effort (BigFoot et al., 2007; Carson et al., 1990; Forehand & Kotchick, 1996; LaFromboise & Low, 1989). Notes one Native family practitioner, "Because a child is considered a gift from the Creator, caretakers have the responsibility to return to the Creator a person who respects him/herself [and others]." (BigFoot & Funderburk, 2006, p. 10).

As Indigenous children enter school, they often feel stranded between two cultures. Many speak a first language other than English, practice an entirely different religion, and hold different cultural values, yet they are expected to perform successfully according to conventional Western criteria (Brayboy et al., 2012; Little Soldier, 1992). These children also use their Native culture as their "anchor" when at school (Huffman, 2008, p. 187). Since these children have grown up with a group-oriented philosophy, striving for individual achievement is foreign to their world outside of school (Little Soldier, 1992). Because children are likely to feel marginal in both cultures, biculturalism must become an educational priority (Waterman, 2019).

Arab American Families

Very little empirical information exists about Arab American families, although their population is increasing in the United States. Coming from countries such as Afghanistan, Israel, Iran, Iraq, Kuwait, Palestine, Saudi Arabia, Syria, and Turkey, the term *Arab American* does not refer necessarily to a racial group as much as it does geographic location and religion, which among Middle Eastern families is very diverse. There are no U.S. government demographics on the number of Arab Americans. This is because the U.S. Census Bureau does not track information and trends on the religious practices of those who reside in the United States. According to the Pew Research Center (2017a), there are 3.45 million Muslims living in the United States; they account for about 1 percent of the total U.S. population. They are the fastest growing immigrant population today; three in ten have immigrated to the United States since 2010 (Pew Research Center, 2017b). Nearly 42 percent of Arab Americans are American citizens. Of those who were foreign-born, nearly 70 percent have become naturalized U.S. citizens (Pew Research Center, 2017b).

Contemporary Arab American Family Patterns

The most common living situation among U.S. Arab families is a multigenerational household; 57 percent live in this type of home configuration (Pew Research Center, 2017b). Nearly 20 percent live in a home with non-Muslims (such as a spouse). As a result of these tenets of the Muslim faith, heterosexual marriages and nuclear families are expected of devout Muslims (Boellstorff, 2005). Table 2.2 denotes the living arrangements of Muslim Americans today in the United States.

It's very important to understand that Arab Americans differ widely in their religious beliefs and practices of religion (Arab American Institute, 2019). This is essential to know because cultural typecasts of Islamic/Arab American women tend to lump religion (Islam) and ethnicity (Arab) into one-and-the-same components of culture, portraying them as veiled Islamic traditionalists who are submissive, secluded in the home, and uneducated (Zahedi, 2007). However, the majority of Arabs adhere to the Islamic faith because the religion is viewed as a lifestyle "guide" (Abudabbeh, 2005). Arab American families embrace a strong collectivist belief (Henry et al., 2008).

As sociology professor and researcher Jen'nan Ghazel Read of the University of California points out, understanding Arab American culture is complicated (2003). On the one hand, as a group, Arab Americans are more highly educated and are more likely to earn $100,000 or more per year than any other ethnic or racial group in the United States (Arab American

TABLE 2.2 ■ Household Configurations of Muslim Americans

	All U.S. Muslims %	Foreign Born %
One-person household	23	22
Multiple-person household	75	75
Households with children	50	55
No children	46	43

Source: Pew Research Center (2017b).

Arab American parents stress conformity to the collective and require obedience from their children. Although little is known about this people group, it is known that family and children are highly valued.

Source: istock.com/FatCamera.

Institute, 2019; Pew Research Center, 2017). On the other hand, Arab religious and cultural customs and rituals reinforce traditional gender roles wherein women raise and nurture the children, and men protect and provide for the family (Mourad & Carolan, 2010). Indeed, male dominance is the cultural norm in most Arab countries; thus, in the United States, it is common for fathers to assume the role as head of household (Haboush, 2007). As a result, many Arab Americans' marital and family experiences are strongly shaped by traditional Arab views of honor, modesty, dignity, shame, and gender, as well as by the historical values of Islam (Arab American Institute, 2019; Smith et al., 2021). A predominant characteristic of Arab families is the cultural practice of keeping emotions to oneself and to guard the privacy of the family (Al-Darmaki & Sayed, 2009; Kobeisy, 2004). This is important to know because it prevents them from seeking help from others—going outside of the family for assistance is viewed as unacceptable and shameful behavior (Al-Darmaki & Sayed, 2009; Kobeisy, 2004).

Arab American Parent–Child Interactions

Arab American parents keep a traditionally strict, demanding, rigid, and undemocratic household (for a full review, see Binghalib, 2007, 2011). Similar to Asian families, parents believe that their children's behaviors are a reflection of them, and because of this, shame and honor are stressed (Haboush, 2007; Mourad & Carolan, 2010, as cited in Binghalib, 2007, 2011). Parents stress conformity to the collective whole and use shame to control children's behaviors (Haboush, 2007; Mourad & Carolan, 2010). And, similar to the Asian culture, children strive to carry out their lives in such a way to not disappoint their parents (Haboush, 2007; Mourad & Carolan, 2010); they are taught at an early age that obedience to their parents is second only to the obedience to Allah (Haneef, 1997). The paucity of research impedes our understanding of this rich culture and people group, but what we do know from empirical science is that family and children are important (Binghalib, 2007, 2011).

It's important to stress, however, that because Arab Americans come from a vast number of countries, parenting styles vary greatly. For instance, those from Lebanon use the authoritative Western approach to parenting, and families from Egypt, Algeria, and Palestine equally use permissive parenting and authoritarian parenting styles (see Dwalry et al., 2006). Love shown by Arab parents may be expressed in symbolic ways (i.e., providing protection, housing, food, and education), not in explicit ways (such as saying "I love you" repeatedly to a child). Indeed, country of origin significantly influences parenting styles and practices.

Without a doubt, there is great variation and diversity in our upbringing and our individual experiences with family and family living. It is virtually impossible in contemporary society to rely on the U.S. Census Bureau's rigid definition of *family* consisting of "two or more persons living together and related by blood, marriage, and adoption."

HOW DO CHILDREN LEARN ABOUT THEIR RACIAL/ETHNIC IDENTITIES?

As our study so far has shown us, there are racial/ethnic differences in the ways in which parents interact with their children. Emerging research is beginning to shed even more light on these differences, especially in the distinct parenting challenges with which people of color are faced.

Racial and Ethnic Socialization

African American/Black Caribbeans, Hispanics, Native Americans, Asian Americans, and Arab Americans in this country often experience racism. **Racism** is a belief system which holds that race accounts for differences in human character and/or ability; it results in discrimination and prejudice based on someone's skin color or ethnic background. Because of the historical disparaging and marginalizing views of people of color, and because of historical racial barriers in equal opportunities, racial and ethnic minority parents are faced with the challenges of insulating their children from the negative consequences of racism. They deal with these challenges by teaching their children how to "navigate and negotiate" the racism terrain through a process referred to as racial/ethnic socialization (Coard et al., 2007). And today, many adults have negative feelings about racial relations in the United States, as Figure 2.8 shows us.

Furthermore, most Americans across all racial and ethnic groups say that today, more and more people in the United States express racist and/or racially insensitive views, as illustrated in Figures 2.9 and 2.10 (Pew Research Center, 2019).

FIGURE 2.8 ■ Race Relations in the United States: 2019

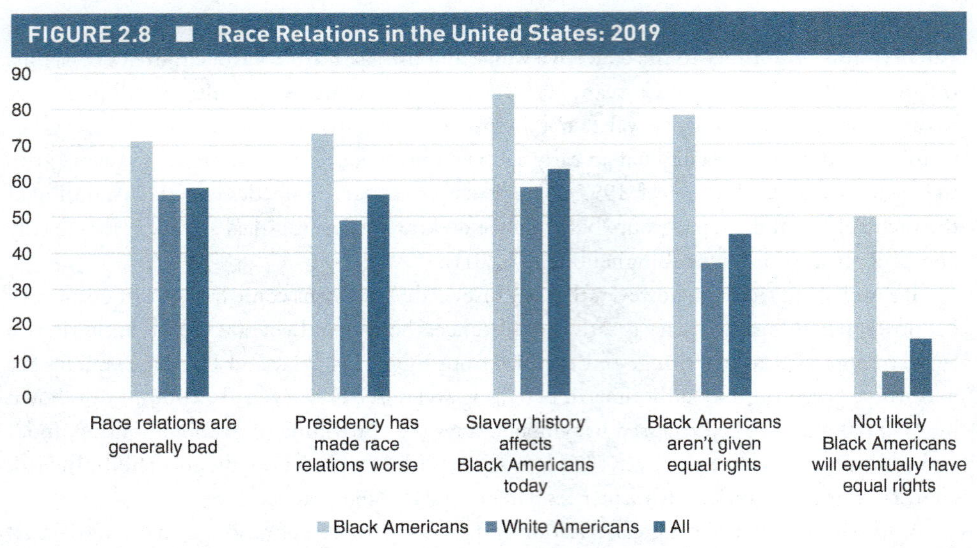

Source: Pew Research Center (2019).

FIGURE 2.9 ■ How Common Is It for People to Express Racist Views?

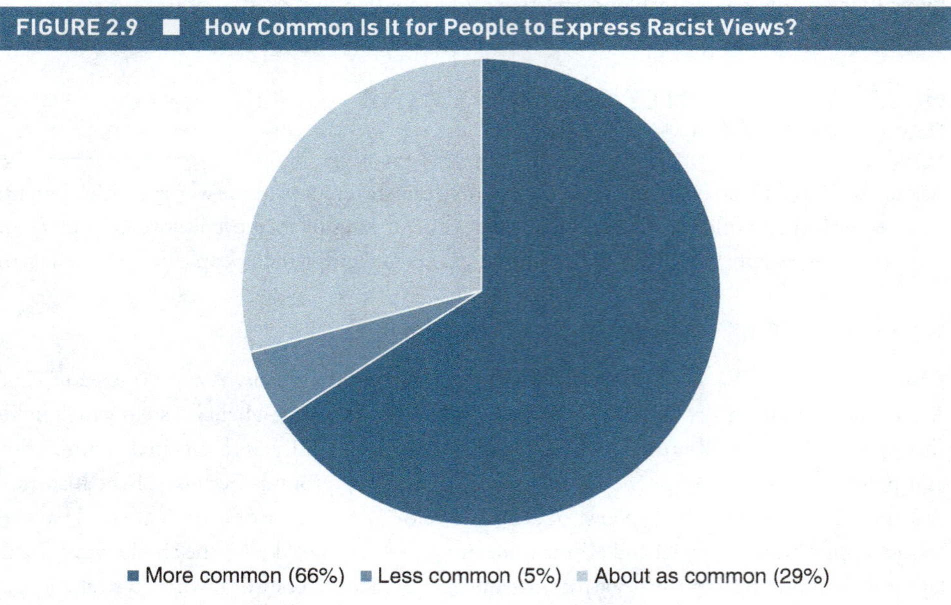

Source: Pew Research Center (2019).

Racial/ethnic socialization is the way in which families teach children about the social meanings of their race/ethnicity: What does it mean to "be" Black, Hispanic, Asian, Native American, or of Arab descent? Oftentimes, this socialization also includes teaching children the consequences of ethnicity and race, such as racism (Brown et al., 2007). Throughout the

FIGURE 2.10 ■ How Acceptable Is It for People to Express Racist Views?

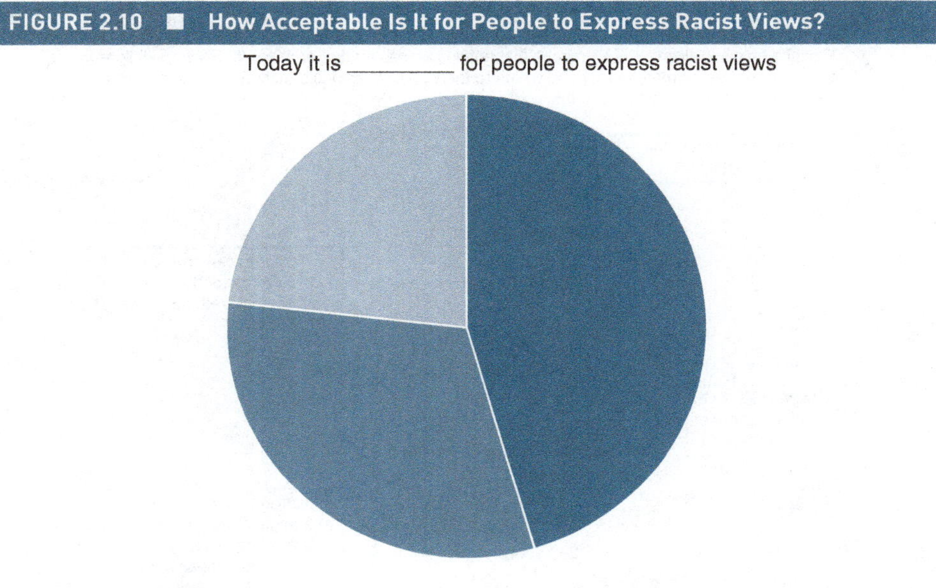

Source: Pew Research Center (2019).

socialization process, which is presented in Figure 2.11, children learn about the similarities and differences between races/ethnicities, as well as prejudice and discrimination that some people face. Through intergenerational discussions (which often include story-telling of ancestors' histories), conversations with parents, observations, and modeling, cultural knowledge is transmitted and children learn to "perform" race (Brown et al., 2007). Racial socialization not only teaches children the values and norms associated with their race/ethnicity, but it also shapes attitudes that help them to cope with race-related barriers (Coard et al., 2007). Typically, many white parents don't place importance on discussing racial or ethnic differences with their children (Brown et al., 2007). But given that racism and racial insensitivity appears to be increasing in prevalence in the United States, teaching children to be empathic about race, ethnicity, and racial identity is of critical importance (Markus & Moya, 2010). As African American former school principal and student advocate Paul Richards (2018) notes:

> Empathy is a critical disposition to possess in today's context. Developing *cultural* empathy can come from exploring the practice of arranged marriages, or the central importance of family hierarchy in certain cultures, or what it is like to have dark skin in a white environment. There are countless examples that are appropriate [to educate children about]. The exploration should culminate in the [child] developing a strong sense of his or her own ethnic identity, and how this identity is interdependent with how other people and society view it. It is with this cultural toolkit that our youth will be ready to thrive in the global world.

FIGURE 2.11 ■ Time Line of the Development of Racial and Ethnic Identity

Racial/ethnic socialization is a process that unfolds across a number of years. How are children taught to "be" their race/ethnicity and what are the social meanings attached to being a member of a racial or ethnic group?

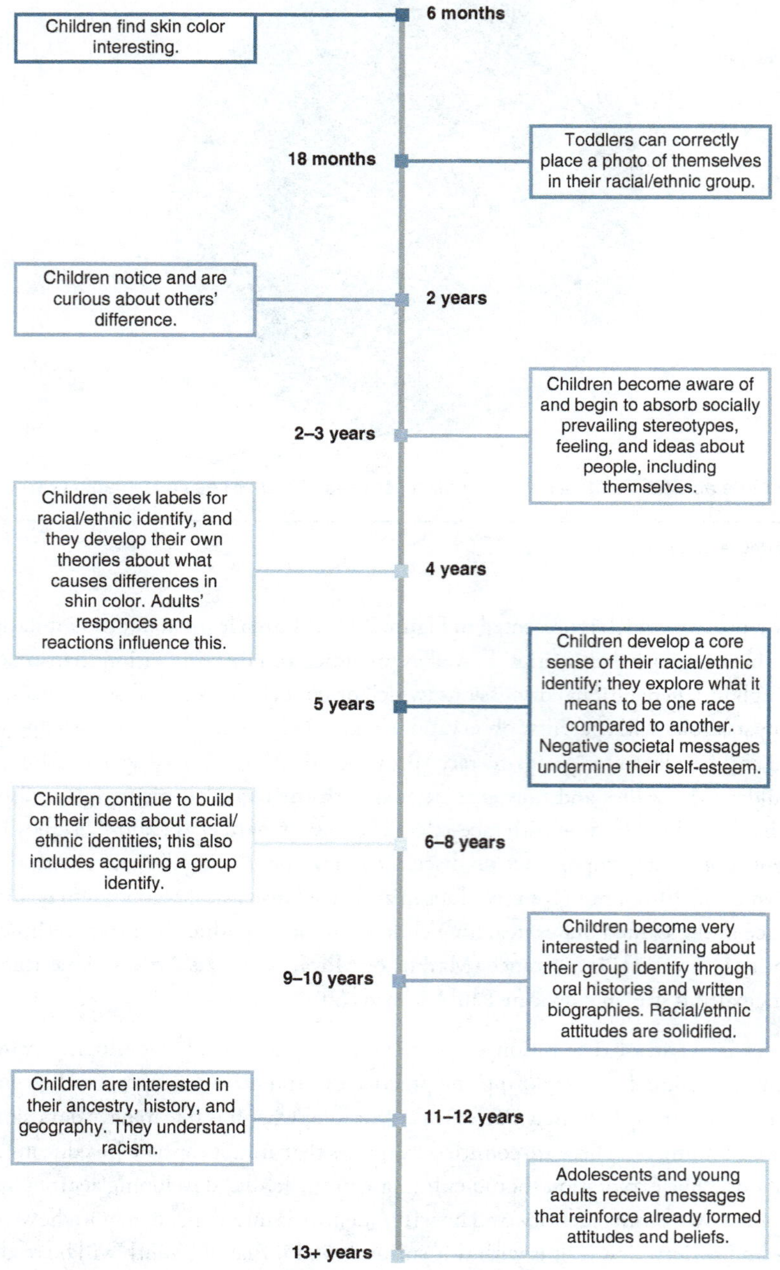

Sources: Coard et al. (2007) and Stein et al. (2018).

Racial/ethnic socialization practices have been linked to a number of positive outcomes in minority children and adolescents, as shown here. For a comprehensive review of the literature, see Coard et al. (2007), Hughes et al. (2006), and Huynh and Fuligni (2008).

- **Well-developed racial identity:** Children embrace racial and ethnic pride, history, and cultural traditions.
- **Heightened self-esteem:** Children's and adolescents' self-esteem is sensitive to the racial/ethnic messages they receive from their parents. Children who are taught to "blend" with mainstream culture have lower levels of self-esteem because they in some ways deny their heritage.
- **Higher academic functioning:** Positive ethnic identity and high self-esteem are associated with better academic outcomes and higher levels of motivation among children and adolescents.
- **Decreased levels of depression and anger:** The practice of cultural socialization is protective against racial discrimination because children and adolescents develop coping and problem-solving strategies to help buffer racism and deal with prejudice.

Racial/ethnic socialization among minority families is an emerging field of family and social science studies. It is a very complex issue, and we have much to learn about the multiple processes associated with this type of socialization, as well as how what children are taught about race influences their lives.

Hate Hurts: Antidiscrimination and Inclusivity Education for Children

We live in a world that is not free from bias and discrimination, and because of this, parents, guardians, and teachers, must impart to our children that *everyone* has the right to feel included. It is important to teach children that *hate hurts* and leaves emotional scars that can affect not only a person's self-worth but also every aspect of a person's life. Because a child develops his or her self-concept and beliefs about others well before entering kindergarten, antibias and antidiscrimination education must begin early in the home and in the early years of school. Parents, guardians, and teachers need to model attitudes and behaviors that help young children appreciate and value the differences in others. To avoid prejudice and discrimination, we must:

- Model the values, attitudes, and behaviors we want our children to develop. This requires being aware of our own conscious and unconscious stereotypes and behaviors.
- Expose children to people and experiences from other cultures and belief systems.
- Encourage children to see that relationships with people who are different from themselves can be rich and rewarding experiences.
- Talk with children about the similarities and differences between themselves et al. Help them to see that being "different" from someone does not mean the person is "worse" than someone else.

- Integrate diversity, equity, and inclusion information and communication into conversations and activities.
- Teach children to be sensitive, critical thinkers, so that through examining and questioning they can better understand any issue.
- Adopt a "zero tolerance" policy about racism, prejudice, bias, and discrimination. Teach them that words *do hurt.*

Despite the fact that today's parents and families are diverse in structure, income level, and racial and ethnic composition, and despite the fact that today's families experience family living in diverse ways, one particular theorist has been able to organize the different cultural contexts of family life so we can see the level of influence each context has on us. With this in mind, in the section that follows we'll take a look at Bronfenbrenner's Ecological Model, a model noted for grouping the various contexts that surround us and influence our individual and parenting/family development.

CULTURALLY SPECIFIC INFLUENCES THAT AFFECT FAMILY LIFE

To understand the multiple areas of individual and parenting development, we turn our attention to the *Ecological Model* developed by Uri Bronfenbrenner (1979). Central to this model is the concept that people develop in a variety of interacting contexts. **Contexts** refer to areas of individual and family development that play a role in the relationship between people and their environments; these multiple contexts make up a person's "culture" (Bronfenbrenner, 1979).

These multiple environments surround individuals from birth and play a significant interactive role in development. In order to truly understand parenting life today and parent-child interactions, we must first understand the interactive relationships *between* and *among* the different factors within the various contexts of development (Huitt, 2003). If we want to study the effects of divorce on a child's development, for example, we can study the child separately, but we can also introduce or take away various factors within a certain context to better determine which has the greatest impact on a child's development. And, to better understand the influences and impacts of these contexts, we need to consider the concept of *intersectionality*, introduced earlier.

So far in our study of contemporary parenting, we have paid considerable attention to the racial and ethnic composition of the United States. We have stressed the importance of understanding these differences because each diverse family culture is "characterized and distinguished from other cultures, by deep-rooted and widely acknowledged ideas about how one needs to feel, think, and act as a functioning member of the culture" (Bornstein, 2012, p. 212). Thus, our cross-cultural study of the differing groups establishes the base of working with parents: We affirm that each cultural group embodies certain traits and characteristics that are unique to them, and that are vitally necessary to their members. And, because of this uniqueness, we expect that there are cultural variations in the experiences of parenting (Bornstein, 2012).

Bronfenbrenner's Ecological Model

Figure 2.12 presents the Ecological Model. Notice that the person is located in the center of five concentric, nested circles that expand outward, similar to ripples on the surface of water. Each of those circles represents a different layer of societal interactions and influences external to the individual, which affects his or her development. The circles nearest the individual have more immediate impacts on us, and those farther out are more distant. Perhaps what makes this model so useful is that Bronfenbrenner recognized that the impact on relationships is *bidirectional*: Not only does the environment influence the individual but also the individual influences the environment. For example, a new baby in a family has an impact on the parents just as much as the parents have an impact on the baby. When a couple goes through a divorce, both spouses are affected, but their children and other extended family members and friends are also affected. And, even though the individual or the family may not directly interact with various levels of society (such as the different levels

FIGURE 2.12 ■ Bronfenbrenner's Ecological Model

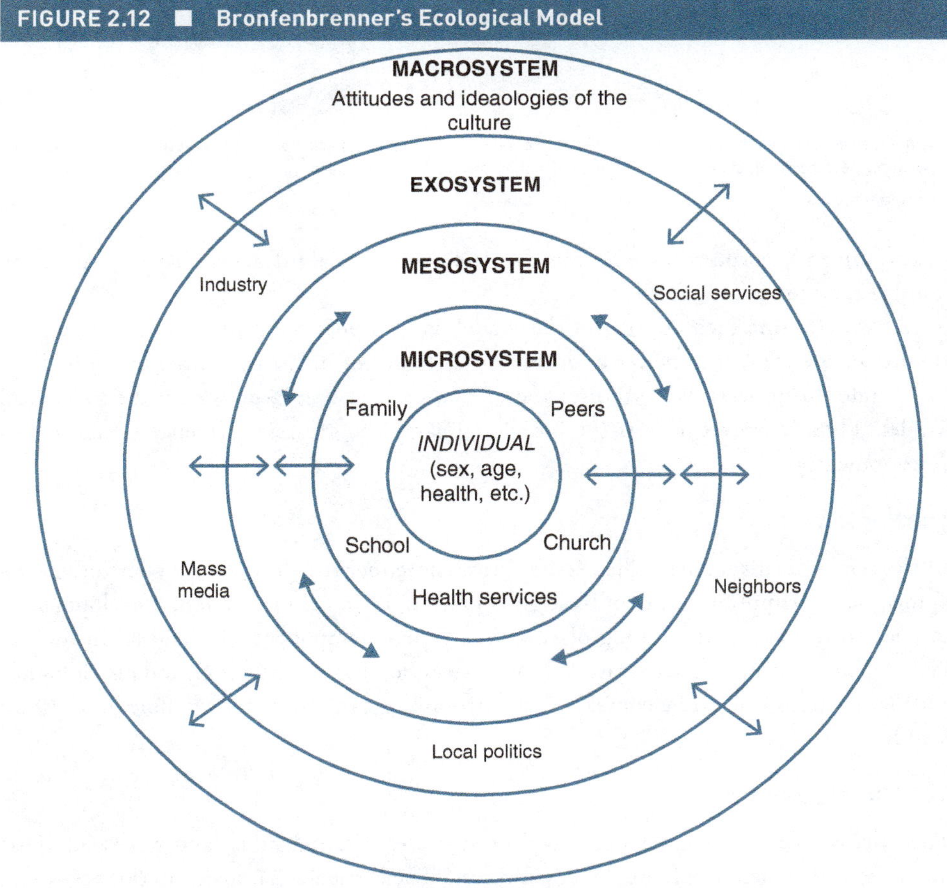

Source: Based on Bronfenbrenner, *The Ecology of Human Development* (1979).

The *microsystem* is the developmental context nearest the individual, and its components exert the most influence on a person's development, such as the influence of a child's school and teachers.

Source: istock.com/FatCamera.

of government), as you will see later in our study, these social influences have an impact on family functioning and health.

As we examine each context in the model, it is important to bear in mind the positioning of the context to better understand the degree of influence on the individual. To help guide this process, we will discuss each **context, or ecosystem**, within the Ecological Model. Those contexts nearest the individual carry the greatest influence on her or his development.

The Person

At the center of this model is the person. Bronfenbrenner recognized that a person's development is not simply a matter of biology, cognition, or social interaction. Development is instead an intricate intertwining of *all three* of these components. Individual influences include, but are not limited to, race, ethnicity, genetics, health, nutrition, and physiological abilities or disabilities. The contexts that surround us can affect, for example, our overall health.

The Microsystem

The **microsystem** is the developmental context nearest the individual and represents those interactions in which people are directly involved. The elements that make up this ecosystem are the individuals, groups, and agencies that have the earliest and most immediate influences on the individual. These include:

- **The family of origin:** The family in which we are raised is the most influential on our development. The family structure (single-parent or two-parent family), SES (wealthy, middle class, or low income), race and ethnicity (strong influences on family educational and income levels), parenting styles (Are the parents warm and supportive? Do they abuse or use substances?), and parental involvement all play important roles in who children become.
- **Daycare/schools:** Because children spend an average of seven hours a day in daycare or in a classroom, Bronfenbrenner believed them to be a key influence on development. For example, the location of the school is important; students in small or rural communities or small suburbs tend to score higher on standardized tests than children from larger schools (Huitt, 2003).
- **The community:** Many of us have heard the saying, "It takes a village to raise a child." Neighbors, neighborhoods, peer groups, and workplaces make up a community. The greater the community's involvement in the child's life, the greater the child's success and achievement throughout life (Sikorski et al., 1999). Community involvement may include literacy programs, nutritional programs, recreational opportunities, or teen mentoring programs.
- **The church, synagogue, mosque, or temple:** Religious institutions influence the development of a person's character and ethical and moral development (Nord & Haynes, 1998).

We individuals also have an impact on our environment: As we comply or rebel, agree or disagree, or express our views, hopes, and ambitions, we exert influence on the elements with which we interact.

The Mesosystem

In the **mesosystem**, Bronfenbrenner retains all of the elements that are present in the microsystem, but now focuses on the interaction *between* the various elements rather than on the individual. For instance, how does the school affect the family? How does the church or temple affect the family? In what ways does the school impact the neighborhood? Consider a school district that tries to establish a sex education program that offers free condom distribution and referrals to health clinics for abortion in a community that has a strong fundamental religious belief system. Is it likely that a conservative community would endorse these practices? Likewise, consider the influence of a neighborhood organization that creates an after-school athletic and academic program for children located in a neighborhood that has a large gang presence, or a neighborhood watch organization that creates a network of "safe" houses that children can run to if a stranger attempts to approach them on the way home from school. These scenarios illustrate how elements within the microsystem interact with each other rather than directly with an individual and his or her family.

Although further away from the individual than the micro- and mesosystems, the *exosystem* is the societal context in which policies are made that impact individuals and families, such as fertility legislation..

Source: istock.com/Jcarillet.

The Exosystem

The **exosystem** consists of the fabrics of society in which policies are made and influenced that ultimately have an impact on the elements of the microsystem and the individual. Social policies are beneficial to families when they foster and support the major functions of a family, such as child-rearing, economic support, and caring for family members (Alberts, 2002). As Figure 2.12 shows us, the exosystem serves as an umbrella for all of the "systems" in a society.

Consider the state board of education, which establishes policies and selects curricula that are used in each of the local school districts. At the same time, the hierarchies of various religious denominations determine the central tenets of their faith, which include and determine what behaviors are deemed to be appropriate or inappropriate according to those tenets. In turn, those religious beliefs in large part determine what is taught in the public schools. As a result of this influence, a public school education may be vastly different in one state compared with another, depending on the components of the exosystem. In Kansas public schools, for example, teachers are permitted to teach the tenets of evolution, but they are also required to teach creation by intelligent design. The theory of *intelligent design (ID)* maintains that the universe is best explained by creation by an intelligent cause, rather than by evolution of species. Further, in 2016, battles raged in the Kansas legislature over a bill under consideration in the House that would prevent school boards from using national sexual education curriculum to give more control to local educators. Also up for debate was the issue as to whether Kansas schools should continue to provide sex education in public schools. These issues remain undecided. The broader point here is that because Kansas is in the center of the "Bible belt" in the United States, many curricula decisions are centered on the religious hierarchy of the state.

The media are another element within the exosystem. Some news outlets are thought to have either liberal or conservative bias in the way that they report news information, consequently influencing how certain policies and perspectives are viewed. In movies and through television programming, we also see changes in how families and family life are portrayed. Whether these changes are simply representations of historical changes in families over time, or are attempts to change perceptions about what family life should be, is not always clear. How these movies and TV shows are perceived may depend, to some extent, on a person' life experiences and the influences that have shaped their development to this point.

The Macrosystem

The **macrosystem** represents the next layer in Bronfenbrenner's model. It recognizes that a society has a set of overarching cultural values and beliefs that affect individual development by establishing either implicit or explicit rules about what is or is not acceptable behavior. In a population as diverse as that of the United States, there are hundreds of different religious, racial, and ethnic groups. Each may have specific cultural norms that do not conform to a broader set of values. Additionally, not all groups that fall within a general ethnic category will be the same. For instance, not all Hispanics share the same belief system. Mexican Americans may have cultural values and expectations different from those of Cuban Americans. Jews have different values than do Islamics or Buddhists. And liberals have different values than do conservatives. The cultural values of parents who are first-generation immigrants to the United States may be vastly different from those of their children who have been acculturated in American values through their interactions with peers at school and the media.

The Chronosystem

The **chronosystem**, the next, and outermost layer, reflects changes that happen over time. It accounts for the collective historical precursors of current social debates over, for example, social and economic discrimination, women's rights to reproductive choice, and the long-held definition of marriage, such as who can marry whom (Dutton, 1998).

Bronfenbrenner's framework allows us to grasp both the nature of the main interacting influences on our lives and to examine the role that each play. With the Ecological Model, we can explore and better understand parenting and parent–child relationships. Throughout our study together, we'll explore certain areas of Bronfenbrenner's model, such as the *economic, religious*, and *government contexts*, and how they shape and affect the experiences of intimate partners and families today. In the section that follows, we'll use the concepts of Bronfenbrenner's Model to help us understand the roots of *systemic racism* in the United States.

Systemic Racism

In 2020, protests erupted in the United States over the unequal, brutal, and fatal treatment of African Americans by law enforcement. Compounding the tragic, unnecessary death of George Floyd, a Black man killed by police in Minnesota, Black Americans were simultaneously disproportionately affected by pandemic-induced historic unemployment, permanent job loss, and COVID-19 infections and fatalities. Not since the Civil Rights Movement in the 1960s had America seen such an outcry for racial justice and equality. Many in the United States had difficulties understanding the newly emerged outcries of racism—while, individually, a person may have adhered to antiracist viewpoints and beliefs, many white Americans didn't understand the concept of systemic or institutional racism.

At its base, racism is "an ideology of racial domination in which the presumed biological or cultural superiority of one or more racial groups is used to justify or prescribe the inferior treatment or social position(s) of other racial groups" (Clair & Denis, 2015, p. 12720). Typically, when we think of racism, we think of individual beliefs and attitudes. But a different type of racism also exists: **Systemic, or institutional racism**, is a type of subtle, less overt form of racism that is deeply embedded and commonly practiced in a society (Carmichael & Hamilton, 1967). The term was first introduced in 1967, and it speaks to the prevailing discrimination found in the criminal justice system, employment, housing, healthcare, and education in the United States (Clair & Denis, 2015). The Urban Institute provides us an understanding of systemic racism when they write:

> Throughout this country's history, the hallmarks of American democracy—opportunity, freedom, and prosperity—have been largely reserved for white people through the intentional exclusion and oppression of people of color. [What we see today] is a direct result of the historical and contemporary policies, practices, and norms that create and maintain [institutional racism]. (Urban Institute, 2020)

Bronfenbrenner's Ecological Model helps us to understand the ways in which racism is deeply engrained in U.S. culture.

The chronosystem: Recall that the chronosystem accounts for the whole of historical precursors that shape current ideas and beliefs; it also shapes Black identities (Bronfenbrenner & Morris, 1998). Without question, the origins of systemic racism accompany the formation of America as early as 1619, when it is believed that the first slaves were purchased by English colonists (Austin, 2019). From this point and onward in U.S. history, people of color experienced oppression and segregation from whites (Brown et al., 2013).

The macrosystem: This context comprises the overarching cultural values and beliefs that affect individuals and govern behaviors. Because slavery created an historical system of control over Blacks, a racial hierarchy evolved (Brown et al., 2013; Hamilton & Roy, 2020; Rothstein, 2017; Trask-Tate et al., 2014).

The exosystem: Quality education, employment, housing, healthcare, treatment by law enforcement: All of these elements in this context are shaped by both the ideologies, values, and beliefs within the macrosystem and the chronosystem, and have an impact on an individual and they/his/hers' microsystems. Social policies that affect parenting and families are also made at this level. The disparity in the quality of life and upward mobility seen between Blacks and whites, established early on in the history of America, is underscored and expressed in this context still today (Hamilton & Roy, 2020; Urban Institute, 2020).

The microsystem: This context comprises an individual's immediate cultural environment. Some researchers today have referred to the influences in this ecosystem (i.e., family, friends, and teachers) as "social capital" (Hamilton & Roy, 2020, p. 104). **Social capital** can be thought of as the different relationship networks people have. Because of the historical, hierarchical beliefs about whites and Blacks, and because of the inequality experienced by Blacks set into place because of these hierarchical beliefs, a system of oppression and control still exists today in the microsystems of many African Americans; this is known as a lack of social capital (Brown et al., 2013; Hamilton & Roy, 2020; Rothstein, 2017; Trask-Tate et al., 2014). When we work with parents of color, we need to be very much aware and understanding of how "parents of color are silenced by fear, lack access [to many services], and are required to work within a [historical] system that perpetuates racial order" (Hamilton & Roy, 2020, p. 105).

Native Americans have also been, and continue to be, subjected to the cruelty of systemic racism. In 1830, the **Indian Removal Act,** fueled by racism, allowed the U.S. government to relocate Indigenous people. Known as the **Trail of Tears,** Cherokee First Americans were brutally forced at gunpoint to leave their homelands to allow white settlers access to their land; the Natives were classified as "noncitizens" (Watson, 1990). "Civilizing" Native children became a priority of the U.S. government (as well as Canada and Australia), and between 1870 and 1900, 307 boarding and day schools were established with three goals in mind:

- To teach Native children individuality and wean them from the collectivist, tribal families
- To learn English to function within the dominant white European American culture
- To teach Christianity (Montgomery & Colwell, 2019).

This forced cultural assimilation required children to leave their families, change their names to American names, cut their hair, wear school uniforms, speak English, and pray Christian prayers. Children in the boarding schools lived in abhorrent conditions, with poor housing. They suffered physical abuse, malnourishment, and contracted diseases from Euro-Americans (Montgomery & Colwell, 2019). Today, these actions and practices would be known as *ethnic cleansing* and *genocide* (Mench-Tum, 2001).

By using Bronfenbrenner's Ecological Model of cultural and historical contexts, we can see how systemic or institutional racism was established and continues to be perpetuated against people of color. Moving forward as a country requires that we examine and abolish paradigms and policies at all societal levels that reinforce hierarchical and divisive beliefs and practices (Hamilton & Roy, 2020).

One of the greatest responsibilities parent professionals and educators have today is helping to end the division in our society. This can only be accomplished by acknowledging and embracing differences.

Source: iStock.com/rawpixel.

PARENTING LIFE EDUCATION: EMBRACING DIFFERENCES AND ENDING DIVISION

Up to this point, our study has highlighted the fact that the United States is a blend of races, ethnicities, and religions from all over the world. Often, though, we tend to focus on our own experiences, failing to realize the vastness of the human race. Many of us fall into the trap of thinking that how *we* experience family and parenting is the *only* way to experience these aspects of life. After all, we are each experts in our individual understandings. In order to gain a truer insight into the workings of parenting, we must step back from our cultural norms and stereotypes and enlarge our scope, so that we may see and take in more—and so far, our study has given us this opportunity.

Tragically, this wonderful medley of race, ethnicity, culture, and ways of life are not embraced by all. With this in mind, Dorian Solot and Marshall Miller (2004) put forth the following affirmation of family diversity:

> We believe that all families should be valued, that the well-being of children is critical to our nation's future, and that people who care for one another should be supported in their efforts to build happy, healthy relationships. One of America's strengths is its diversity, which includes not only a wide range of races, ethnicities, creeds, abilities, genders, and sexual orientations but also a range of family forms.

All of the diversity seen today in the United States contributes to a unique, distinct social fabric that adds a deep richness to our culture. But along with diversity comes substantial differences in family structure, family living, and family experiences. Although the "traditional" family has long been held as the "ideal" standard in childrearing and family life, we are no longer a society composed primarily of married couples raising their biological or adopted children. Today, there really is no such thing as a homogenized American family. Throughout our course of study together, you will gain not only a deeper understanding of parenting life today but also a deeper appreciation for these differences.

As diverse and distinct as U.S. families are today, though, they are all a part of the whole. We do not develop in isolation! Just as important, we do not experience family living and parenting life separately from our surrounding environments—and we do not experience family life in isolation from other families, no matter how different they may be from our own.

Because "parenting" transcends race, religion, ethnicity, sexual orientation, and sexual identity, you will see yourself somewhere among the pages of this book. *Together*—you the student, your classmates, we the authors/teachers, and your professor/instructor—using this text as our guide, we will examine and understand the complexities and intricacies of parenting life. We hope that this book will help you gain a solid, practical understanding of parenting and the importance of family life on children's development, and equip you and empower you with the education to help you develop your full potential in your professional, personal, and family life. In this pursuit, we hope to engage your entire essence—your intellect, your emotions, and your heart.

3 UNDERSTANDING PARENTING THROUGH THEORY

LEARNING OBJECTIVES

3.1 Delineate between the key concepts of Family Systems theory and Symbolic Interaction theory.

3.2 Characterize the differences between the ways in which biological men and biological women communicate.

3.3 Summarize the characteristics of verbal and nonverbal communication, and the ways in which nonverbal communication impacts couple and family relationships.

3.4 List the cornerstones of communication.

3.5 Describe the sources of conflict in interpersonal relationships, and how constructive and destructive conflict differ.

3.6 Explain the ways in which a parenting professional can synthesize the *Human Life Cycle* and the *Family Life Cycle* to better develop parenting education programs and to work with parents and families.

My mother's sister was only in her 30s when she learned that her cancer had metastasized to her rib cage. Her condition was considered terminal, and other than medical treatment to ease her pain, there was nothing that could be done. Although we lived in the Midwest and she and her family lived in California, my mom and my aunt talked almost daily until about two or three days before Aunt Jean died. My aunt was honest with my mother about her illness, and my parents were, in turn, honest with my siblings and me. We knew our aunt was dying. We began our mourning and began to say our goodbyes to this person who would be so greatly missed.

But there was a secret: Aunt Jean's children did not know she was ill. They did not know that she had had surgery for her cancer about four years earlier. They did not know she was dying. Her children, aged 12 and 15, were not told of their mother's imminent death. They were brought to the hospital only as she approached the last hours of her life, and only then were they able to express their love and say goodbye.

Although I was only in the eighth grade when these events unfolded, I couldn't believe how unfair it was to the children that they did not know their mother was dying. How could anyone keep this devastating and life-altering news from someone they loved? Why all the secrecy?

In my frustration with the situation, I yelled at my parents, *"Who makes up these rules about when we can say things in our families and when we can't?"*

The "mother" of family therapy, Virginia Satir, infamously observed that it is impossible for family members to "not communicate," because every action—spoken or unspoken—is communication. Each family makes up their own rules as to what can and cannot be communicated.

Source: iStock.com/GPointStudio.

At one time or another in our families, we have probably either said or heard:

"That's not what I said!"

"You never listen to me!"

"That's not what I mean."

"Let me finish!"

Our parents or guardians spend the first two years of our lives teaching us to walk and to talk—and the next 16 years teaching us to sit down and be quiet. We all have been "communicating" in one form or another since the moment of birth and have been using words to convey our needs, wants, hopes, and feelings since about the first year of life, so why is it that so many of us have such difficulty conveying what we *mean?* Why is it that family members have such difficulty in *accurately receiving* the messages we send? And who *does* make up the rules for when and what we can or cannot say in our families?

Effective parenting requires effective communication, both between the parents and between the parents and their children. When there is strong communication between parents—whether they are married, cohabiting, or divorced—there is a greater likelihood that children will develop in healthy ways. But what exactly is "communication"? As professionals who work with parents and their children, it is incumbent upon us to evaluate family processes, such as communication, from a systems perspective, and to use this theoretical perspective to understand family interactions. With this in mind, we begin this chapter with a discussion about the interrelated, interactive nature of parenting and family relationships. We'll then use this foundation, and other family and social science theories, to inform our understanding of conflict and conflict management. We'll then discus the processes associated with individual and family development and conclude by exploring the roles that federal and state/local governments play in healthy child and family development.

PARENTING AND THE COMMUNICATION PROCESS

Communication is best thought of as a process. Process implies progression, development, and change over time. All interpersonal relationships involve change, and communication is no exception. As our intimate relationships grow, change, and develop over time, so too do our communication patterns and behaviors. The communication process is such a critical aspect of our lives that it shapes the family and gives it its distinct identity (Galvin et al., 2019).

Communication is a transactional process, in which we affect and are affected by others. Although this baby is incapable of speech, the infant is both giving and receiving communication in this interaction.

Source: istock.com/prostockstudio.

When we communicate, whether in interpersonal or social interactions, we have a joint or reciprocal impact on each other in our exchanges. This dynamic is a **transactional** process in which we simultaneously affect and are affected by our intimate relations. When we discuss communication in this context, the focus of the interaction is not on the *words* individual family members speak but instead on the *interconnectedness* of the relationship. To fully understand the communication process, we first need to explore two theoretical frameworks that are a foundation of family studies: the Family Systems theory and the Symbolic Interaction theory.

Family Systems Theory: The Family as an Interconnected System

The family as a system of interrelated components is a contemporary framework for examining family interactions. Developed by psychiatrist and theorist Murray Bowen (1913–1990), the **Family Systems theory (FST)** views families as a whole entity made up of interconnected parts that seek to maintain balance. In recent years, this theoretical approach has become so popular among family researchers and family practitioners that an expanding array of family topics has been examined through this lens, including youth suicide, cancer treatments, family grief, and spiritual development. The popularity of its use is due, in part, to a central concept that all of us maintain interdependent relationships with others on a day-to-day basis. Within family life, FST acknowledges that the family is made of interconnected parts that affect each other.

The Family as a System

Encompassing areas of study from economics to biology to the intricacies of family life, **General Systems theory (GST)** is a world view or a paradigm that puts forth the notion that objects do not exist in isolation, but instead are interconnected to parts of a larger whole (Boss et al., 1993). The term *system* means "to place together" or to connect one entity to another (Rosenblatt, 1994).

Consider the human body—a whole, living, breathing, ever-changing organism. As a system, it consists of numerous interdependent yet separate entities, such as the nervous system, the circulatory system, the digestive system, the reproductive system, and so forth. In short, the human body is a complex network of many subsystems that are organized into a single whole. Just as the human body illustrates how a system works, a **family system** is also a living, ever-changing, dynamic entity that consists of various individuals and their interconnected, intergenerational patterns of interactions. In this context, a system's primary function is to bring together and arrange the various interrelated parts into a whole, organized entity (Rosenblatt, 1994).

Family Systems theory provides a framework for those who work with families and allows them to gain insight into the relational patterns and interactions among the separate individuals or **subsystems**. Prior to the 1950s, the treatment of psychological and behavioral problems and emotional distress focused on the internal world—the internal dysfunction—of the individual patient. However, that treatment model failed to take into consideration the reciprocal, interactive nature of interpersonal relationships (Nichols & Schwartz, 2009). As the concepts of the General Systems theory gained widespread acceptance across disciplines, family practitioners, social workers, and family therapists began to view and understand individual psychological problems in a new way—that these problems *were developed and maintained within the context of the family.*

Key Concepts: Applying the Systems Framework to the Family

There are several key concepts and metaphors used to convey the thoughts and ideas central to Family Systems theory. The core assumptions of this family framework hold that every part of the system is interconnected and that we can understand only by viewing the whole (White et al., 2014).

Interconnecting To get a better handle on these assumptions, let's return to the example of the human body. Suppose that through laboratory diagnosis you are found to have diabetes; if left untreated, will the disease remain in its initial state or will it eventually spread to and affect other systems in the body? You probably assumed correctly that, indeed, if left untreated, the diabetes would eventually spread throughout the multiple body systems, causing blindness and even loss of a limb because of the interrelated, interdependent relationship between the various body systems.

The family as a system of interconnected subsystems is no different. Family members affect and are affected by each other—what happens to one family member eventually affects (or happens to) others within the family unit. Thus, the Family Systems theory is concerned with the *interactions* and *interrelations* between the various pieces of the whole and their effect on each other.

Consider what happens to a mobile or wind chime when anything disrupts it or causes it to move. What disrupts one piece of the mobile, for example, disrupts and affects all of the other pieces on the mobile. The same holds true in family life (see Figure 3.1). Expected or not, joyous or tragic, such events impact and have an effect on every family member (subsystem) within the family system.

Looking at the Whole A second key assumption of Family Systems theory is the idea that the only way we can understand an individual family member's behavior and communication patterns is by looking not just at the individual member but also by *looking at the whole*, the entire family system. Because we affect and are affected by each member in our families, it is impossible for us to understand each other's behavior and communication patterns without knowing more about the families in which we were reared—our family of origin.

In your family, have you ever been able to finish another family member's sentence? Have you ever been able to predict, almost to the minute, how long your parents' argument will last, and what it is about? Most of us know what behavior or communication pattern will elicit certain responses from our siblings or parents in many situations. Similarly, we recognize patterns in our family members such as what might lead to an argument or praise. The communication patterns that exist in our families come about as a result of this concept of wholeness. As interconnected pieces, we create our family's own reality, and that reality is distinct and separate from any other family (Galvin et al., 2019).

Establishing Boundaries Every system, whether it is an educational system, political system, or family system, has some type of border or **boundary** between it and its environment.

FIGURE 3.1 ■ Virginia Satir's Concept of the Family as a Mobile

Source: Satir.

In a family—and particularly in a discussion about family communication—boundaries serve the purpose of affecting the flow of information within the system. Boundaries are essential because they are what separate and make us distinct from our environment or from other family members.

Boundaries fall along a continuum. On one end are *closed boundaries,* where no information comes in or goes out; on the other end, there are *open boundaries* where the transfer of information is so unobstructed that family members within the systems lose their identity. A family system's health is categorized by the degree to which the boundaries are permeable (White et al., 2014). In Figure 3.2, note how in the closed boundary system the borders are so tightly closed that little or no information is allowed in or out of the family system. This type of a closed boundary is often seen in families where abuse occurs. The amount of information that leaves the family system is quite limited (such as family members not discussing publicly what takes place privately in the home). In the same way, information or interference from outside of the

FIGURE 3.2 ■ Types of Boundaries

Boundaries affect the flow of information within a family system and make us distinct from other family members. A family's health and well-being is categorized by how open or closed the coundaries are.

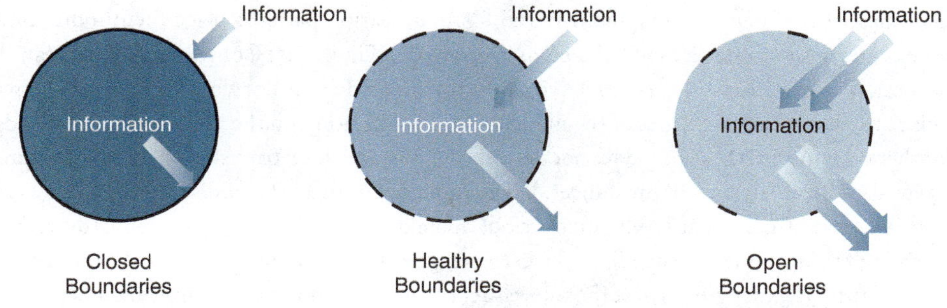

Source: Sage.

family system is limited or prohibited (such as the abusive partner dictating who can visit or phone family members).

Conversely, notice in open systems that information is allowed to freely come in and exit the family system. A certain level of open boundaries is necessary for the health and well-being of families. However, when boundaries are too open—when too much information flows between the subsystems—members in the family system lose their distinct identity. For example, if parents continually share pieces of their parental subsystem with their children (such as their marital problems, their financial problems, or their work-related problems), the boundaries become blurred and the children lose their distinct identity as children.

Maintaining Balance When an infection enters your body, various systems work together to bring your body back into **balance** or **homeostasis**. According to FST, every family has the same goal, which is to maintain its balance or homeostasis when it experiences any departure from its usual state of balance (the family's state of "normal"). Regardless of the system type, it will act to reduce any source of disruption or disturbance (Boss et al., 1993). The disruption can be of internal origin, such as a teenager who suffers from an eating disorder, or it can be of external origin, such as a parent who loses his or her job. Whether from within the family or outside the family, the system will do whatever it takes to bring it back to balance—and this includes arguing, disagreeing, and family conflict.

To restore equilibrium in a family system, we most often use established, habitual communication interactions and behaviors. Sometimes our communication strategies are healthy and adaptive; sometimes they are dysfunctional, unhealthy, and maladaptive. The Circumplex Model is a tool family therapists and family practitioners use to understand the boundaries of families and hence to better understand families' health and level of functioning.

The Circumplex Model Those who study and work with family systems are particularly interested in what constitutes behavioral, relational, and communication interaction patterns. In an effort to provide a means by which to assess a family's level of functioning and health, the **Circumplex Model of Marital and Family Systems** was created to address family cohesion, adaptability, and communication (Olson et al., 1979).

David Olson, an influential family scientist, family therapist, and professor, posited that families whose cohesion, adaptability, and communication patterns place them more toward the center of the model exhibit balance, as illustrated in Figure 3.3. Consequently, these families function more sufficiently and effectively over time than do families whose interaction patterns place them on the outer edges of the model. A family's position on the model on the outer edges rather than toward the center does not necessarily indicate a level of dysfunction; this placement may just reflect current circumstances. For example, a family in the midst of crisis or stress may exhibit lower than usual levels of cohesion, adaptability, and communication. Additionally, although some families may fall on the extreme outer levels on the model, satisfactory levels of family function may still exist if those levels represent usual, normative family members' expectations (Boss et al., 1993).

Creating Rules This chapter's opening vignette reminds us that some families have secrets. These secrets may range anywhere from a college student's substance abuse to Aunt Betty's eating disorder to child maltreatment or financial difficulties. In many cases, families with secrets

FIGURE 3.3 ■ Olson's Circumplex Model of Family Functioning

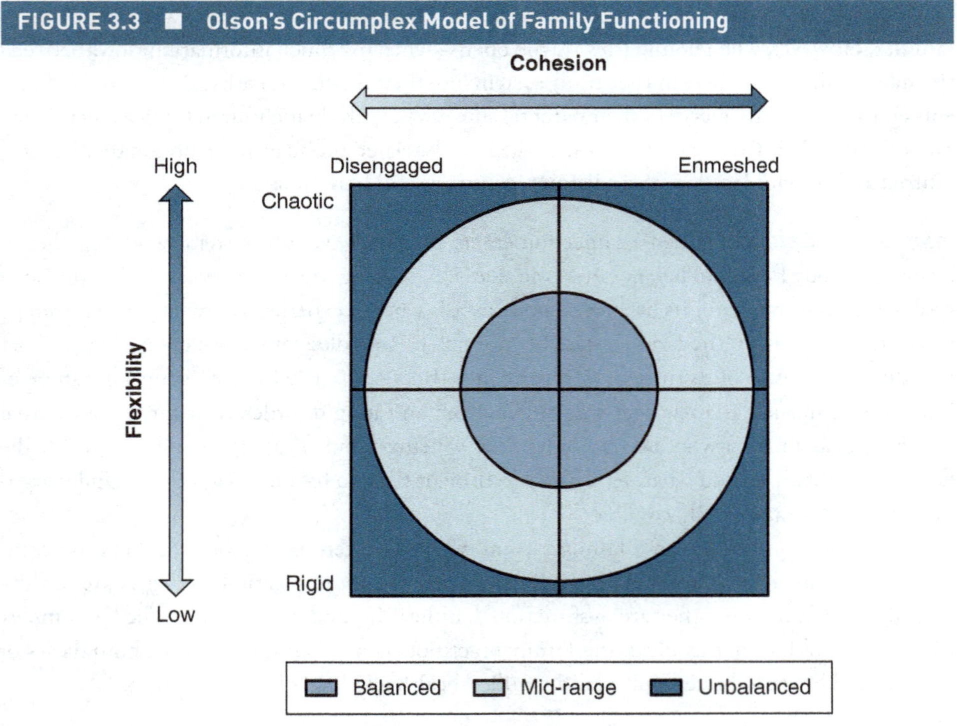

Source: Olson et al. (1979).

appear fully functional, cohesive, and adaptable, but perhaps within these families, the family members recognize that this is far from the truth. All families have rules for how they communicate with each other and how and what information is shared (or not shared) with those outside of the family system. There are **communication rules** that govern what family members can and cannot discuss or share and how they are to interact with their own family members.

Who *does* make the rules concerning what family members can and cannot say within their families, and how do these rules come about? The family of origin—with its cultural, ethnic, and multigenerational influences—creates an individual family's rules of communication. For example, you may have only been "shsssh'd" once or twice before you learned that it was not okay to talk with your friends or other relatives about how your parents seem to constantly argue about money. You may have discovered after an attempt or two or three that your parents were not comfortable talking about sex with you. Through repeated interactions such as these, over time you learned what is acceptable to talk about, either within or outside of the home.

Professor of communication studies Kathleen Galvin and her colleagues (2019) provide some categories of rules for communication:

What we can and cannot talk about: Every family has different values and contexts that dictate how they communicate about sex, health issues, salaries, bills, or a family member who is deceased.

Feelings that are allowed to be shared: In some family cultures, feelings are masked by accepted behaviors. In other family settings, expressing anger, fear, sadness, and rage is encouraged. Culture, ethnicity, values, and family history come into play when establishing rules for dealing with feelings and emotions.

Decision-making: Each family has its own set of rules for decision-making. Are decision-making responsibilities shared? Divided? Dictated by the head of household? Can decisions be challenged? Families may run the gamut on how decisions are made.

How we can talk about it? Can you talk about a situation openly, or do you have to somehow dance around the real issue? Is Mom really just "under the weather" with a cold or the flu, or does she have a more serious illness?

Communication strategy: Each family has rules that govern its communication strategies. Do you talk about a situation only when everyone has calmed down? For example, in some families, there is the timing-is-everything strategy. Family members learn *when* they can approach a parent for advice or ask for something special. Some families also strategize *with whom* they can share certain information (such as, Don't tell Dad, he'll get upset!).

Such communication rules are not easily broken. Even if we know that our family's communication rules do not work or are not effective, we tend to remain loyal to them (Kellogg, 1990). We are less likely to try to challenge or change the rules if our family is not flexible or adaptable to change. Well-adjusted families allow some rules to be renegotiated as the family passes through the various developmental stages in the family's life cycle (Galvin et al., 2019).

What affects one family member affects the entire family, as is the case when a teen girl deals with an eating disorder. Have you ever experienced a situation in your personal life that affected your whole family? Has someone in your family experienced a situation that affected or impacted you?

Source: iStock.com/fizkes.

Putting Family Systems Theory Into Action: Family Wholeness and Interconnection

To continue our examination of the interconnectedness of families and the concept of wholeness in family communication, let's take a look at a hypothetical family situation (Natenshon, 1999).

It was quite obvious to Amybeth's parents that some sort of medical intervention was needed for their daughter. She was becoming dangerously thinner, and her eating disorder was now all consuming. But Amybeth wasn't the only one suffering—everyone in the family home was suffering along with her.

Because Amybeth only picked at her food, family meals had become a battleground with tempers flaring and emotions running high. Her brother often retreated to his bedroom in the heat of the arguments. Her mother, Terri, usually ended up in tears, and her father, Peter, usually ended up yelling at no one in particular. Even though her parents did not feel that they were the cause of their daughter's disordered eating, they did experience feelings of confusion, inadequacy, and overwhelming guilt—and they transferred their feelings to everyone in the family. They knew their reactions to Amybeth's disordered eating were contributing to the deterioration of the family.

Peter explored the treatment options for Amybeth by speaking with their family doctor and by searching the Internet. He found that most eating disorder treatment plans excluded the parents and siblings, relying instead on psychoanalysis for the individual patient. This puzzled him because not only was it obvious that the entire family was affected by Amybeth's illness but the entire family would also be instrumental in her recovery process. The family doctor referred him to a licensed family therapist who specialized in the treatment of eating disorders in children and adolescents.

During the initial consultation with Amybeth and her parents, the therapist noted that family therapy would be a very effective way to treat not just Amybeth's individual needs but also to treat every family member's needs. The therapist outlined a treatment program of facilitated changes that would aid her recovery. The treatment plan also allowed the family to make its own parallel changes that would accommodate Amybeth's changing needs, as well as the needs of their family system.

In our hypothetical example, Amybeth's parents came to understand through family therapy their daughter's patterns of disordered eating and learned how to help her. They also understood that they must lead a joint effort between the various components of the family system so the family could work together to help Amybeth—and in doing so, help the entire family. The family-centered therapeutic treatment they selected recognized and respected the power of the family system to help eradicate the disease Amybeth was fighting (Natenshon, 1999). The family system had the potential to either bring about a positive, healing change or continue family behaviors and communication/interaction patterns that sustained Amybeth's eating disorder.

Unlike conventional psychological theories (such as psychoanalysis) that focus on the individual person and his or her behavioral problems or emotional distress, Family Systems theory encourages the examination and the inclusion of the entire family system in the medical or psychological treatment of one family member. Understanding the interconnection of family members is important because it is within the family system that communication patterns and behaviors are acquired (from the family of origin), and it is within the family system that *every* family member plays a part in the family's health and functioning.

And herein lies the dilemma that each new couple faces: Each partner brings to the relationship the established and familiar boundary types, balance, and rules from his or her own family of origin. Each member of the couple acts on his or her own subjective meanings of what family and parenting life is and what it is not. In our everyday interactions with one another, then, how do we communicate these meanings? How do we understand one another? What determines whether our communication efforts are successful? Symbolic Interaction theory, a foundation of family studies, seeks to answer these questions.

Meanings: The Symbolic Interaction Framework

We all have probably viewed a play or movie when we had to stifle laughter because the acting was so awful. And we all have been brought to sobs and tears or side-splitting laughter because the actors on stage were *so* believable, so realistic, and authentic in their character portrayal. Why is it that some actors are able to convey their meanings and their messages—their *roles*—so skillfully and credibly that we are drawn into the very center of their agony or humor, whereas others clearly didn't pay attention in acting class? The ability to effectively communicate meanings between actors is essential not just in the theater but in family and parenting life, too.

In our daily interactions, most of us have said, often in frustration, "That's not what I mean!" The **Symbolic Interaction theory** revolves around the notion that human behavior is a continuous dialogue in which people watch the behaviors of other people and then react to those behaviors. All human behavior is social behavior in which there is an exchange of messages and symbolic meanings between actors. This is much more complex than it appears at first glance because in order to understand the exchange of these messages/meanings, we also have to gain an understanding of *how* we acquire the meaning in the first place.

There are countless cultural symbols that convey such things as welcome, respect, and affection. Knowing and understanding different cultural communication practices, such as a young child not making eye contact with a teacher or a respected elder, is vitally important for the parent professional.

Source: iStock.com/RichLegg.

Key Concepts: Conveyors and Interpreters of Meaning

Fundamental to Symbolic Interaction theory is that people react based on the meanings they find in any situation. According to Symbolic Interaction theory, the goal of human interaction is to create shared meanings and to understand the meanings that are communicated between people.

Symbols: In an attempt to share meanings, each culture uses **symbols** or codes. Some symbols are universal behaviors, such as the kiss, which represents affection, love, or a greeting. All cultures use language as a means to anchor meanings to each symbol.

We live in a world that is full of symbols, and knowingly or not, we communicate using these shared codes or shared meanings. From the moment a newborn baby takes its first breath, communication between the baby and its caregivers is based on the sharing of symbols; from birth and throughout life, we attach meanings to symbols, define symbols, and interpret symbols in our individual environments. For example, a smile can be a symbol of reassurance, compassion, understanding, or greeting. Or it can be a symbol of contempt or condescension.

Our socialization within our culture and how we socially interact aid in our acquisition and interpretation of the meanings of symbols. For example, children in the United States are taught to maintain eye contact with adults while they are spoken to, but children from Hispanic and Asian cultures avoid eye contact with authority figures as a symbol of respect (Adetunji & Sze, 2012; Akechi et al., 2013). Similarly, Native American children are taught that direct eye contact with a teacher is "showing off" (Adetunji & Sze, 2012; Richardson, 2012).

Culture also affects attitudes about symbols of affection, such as a hug or a handshake. In European and Asian cultures, hand-holding or casual embraces by members of the same sex is culturally acceptable (Sorokowska et al., 2017). Americans, however, may not share these symbols of friendship and may feel uncomfortable with this display (Sorokowska et al., 2017). Physical distance during a conversation is a symbol of respect in some cultures. For instance, in the Middle East and South America, people stand closely while conversing, whereas European Americans and African Americans prefer more distance. Being sensitive to cultural communication practices enhances our communication skills (Sorokowska et al., 2017).

Cultural competence refers to accepting and respecting cultural differences, being aware of the dynamics of these differences, and continually expanding cultural knowledge (Torres, 1993). Being sensitive to cultural beliefs and practices not only conveys respect for the diverse people in contemporary U.S. society but it also minimizes cultural stereotyping. It's important to note, however, that while it's our responsibility as helping professionals to understand cultural differences, it is equally as important that we not adopt a one-size-fits-all view of each people group. As one group of researchers observe, cultural competency requires ongoing education: "Cultural competence is about continually developing and refining a skill set and worldview that are useful across different situations, not about acquiring discrete bits of knowledge that are results of overgeneralization" (Povenmire-Kirk et al., 2015).

There are guidelines to consider when communicating among diverse cultures (Torres, 1993):

1. *Cultural awareness* refers to the process of becoming sensitive to another culture's beliefs, practices, and lifestyles. It also includes appreciating our own culture and becoming aware of biases or prejudices we may hold toward others.
2. *Cultural knowledge* refers to understanding the worldviews from which others operate.
3. *Cultural skill* involves being able to accurately interpret others' cultural ways of interacting.
4. *Cultural encounter* refers to directly engaging in cross-cultural interactions in order to gain a culture-specific understanding of someone.

Although we spend a lifetime sharing and interpreting symbols, we run into difficulty in our interpersonal and family relationships when we operate on the assumption that we all are on "the same page" that we all share the exact, precise meanings of symbols.

As an example of this, when walking across campus one day with an emeritus professor much older than I am, a student passed by and called out, "Hey, Dr. Dawg, wassup?" Knowing the student, I stopped and engaged in conversation for a moment or two. As the professor and I continued our walk, she was visibly shaken and upset, "Dog? What does he mean, *dog?* Dog? Students are now calling professors *dog?*" I spent several minutes trying to convince her that when the student used the term, it really was a term of endearment and affection. This example illustrates that all social and intimate relationships depend on our ability to nurture a culture of shared *meanings* (White et al., 2014). We must, as individual actors, ensure that we are on common ground—or be able to recognize when we are not on common ground—and share the same connotation in our communication efforts.

Roles: Another key concept in Symbolic Interaction theory is the idea of **role**, which Boss and colleagues (1993) call a "system of meanings" (p. 147). We all have different roles in our families and in our circles outside our families. Sometimes one role takes priority over another, but that does not negate or minimize the other roles we have either taken on or have been assigned. For example, I simultaneously have the roles of mother, mother-in-law, grandmother, sister, aunt, friend, professor, volunteer, researcher, patient, and author. In each of my roles, I take on the role of actor and I follow the rules—the *expectations*—assigned to that role (like it or not). As audience members during a play or a movie, we have certain expectations of the actors on stage or on screen. This is different from being a theatrical actor; taking on or being assigned a role carries with it certain expectations, not just from oneself but from others as well (Mead, 1934). These role expectations enable us to anticipate the behavior of others (Boss et al., 1993). When a person takes on or is assigned too many roles, role strain and role conflict may result. *Role strain* occurs when there are competing demands from multiple roles. *Role conflict* is the psychological stress and tension that result when people undertake multiple roles that are incompatible.

The Symbolic Interaction framework has been used to examine a number of family issues. These issues include father involvement following divorce, the study of the cultural influences of ethnicity, shared grief work following the death of a loved one, the shared meanings associated with sexuality, and gender role attitudes between mothers and daughters. Family and interpersonal communication interactions lend themselves to the use of Symbolic Interaction theory because the central themes of this theory are concerned with how meanings are formed, assessed, sustained, and transformed through culturally and socially defined processes (Blumer, 1969). When thinking about the central themes of Symbolic Interaction theory and the theory's significance of understanding meanings, how does the use of technology and social media impact interpersonal communication?

Makers of Meanings: Adolescent and Parent Views About Social Media

There's no doubt about it: The ways in which individuals, couples, families, and peers communicate today has changed significantly, even within the last 10 years (Procentese et al., 2019).

For example, in early 2020, many of you had your college or high school experiences come to an abrupt halt due to the novel Coronavirus, COVID-19—you were learning in a traditional brick-and-mortar setting, and within a matter of hours your learning was transitioned to online formats. So, although digital technology can serve a society very well, such as when it was needed to bridge the gap in teaching and learning, not everyone shares the same meanings about it and social media. There is a particular difference of meaning between adolescents and their parents.

One researcher accurately describes what the day looks like for most of us:

> Every morning, almost every individual's first instinct is to reach for their phone and check through their notifications and social media accounts. They wake up scrolling through them, liking pictures, commenting, sharing, tweeting, etcetera. There is never a moment where an individual is not connected through a social media platform somehow. Social media has become a big part of our lives, and most of us cannot live without it. We spend every waking second engaging with it, learning and receiving new information, ideas, and concepts through it. This has shaped our culture, our society, and, perhaps, even our general view of life. And in the moments where we are not attached to it, we react in ways that are similar to the symptoms of withdrawal. People hardly consider or ponder about why we feel that way, and how heavily social media impacts us as a society. (Phoon, 2017, p. 1)

In the United States, over three-fourths (77 percent) of adults aged 18 and over own a cell phone (Ictech, 2018). Given that 88 percent of U.S. teens have either a desktop or laptop computer at home, and 95 percent have a smartphone (Pew Research Center, 2018), just how often are today's youth and teens connected to their friends through texting and/or social media? On average, teens (aged 13 to 17) send 67 texts per day (Pew Research Center, 2016). Another study found that nearly one-fourth (22 percent) of teenagers log on to a social media site at least 10 times per day, and more than 50 percent log on to social media at least once per day (O'Keeffe & Clark-Pearson, 2011). Teens in the United States say they use the following platforms (Pew Research Center, 2018):

• YouTube	85%
• Instagram	75%
• Snapchat	69%
• Facebook	51%
• Twitter	32%
• Tumblr	9%
• Reddit	7%
• None	3%

There's no question about it: Smartphones and social media impact our daily lives. But is this impact negative or positive? What *meanings* do teens assign to the use of technology to communicate with others—is it a positive experience or a negative experience? Among those teens surveyed, 45 percent stated that technology had neither a positive or negative impact on their lives. The survey also found:

> **Positive:** About one-third (31 percent) of teens say that social media and texting have mostly a positive effect on their lives. Those surveyed reported that technology helps them to connect with family and friends; meet others with the same interests; helps them to get support from others; and helps with their self-expression.
>
> **Negative:** Nearly one-fourth (24 percent) of teens report that technology has mostly a negative effect on their lives. The main reasons teens say it has a negative impact on their lives are bullying; rumor spreading; lack of in-person contact; harms relationships; and peer pressure (Pew Research Center, 2018).

Overall, the teens' meanings assigned to digital technology and social media are mixed. But how do their parents feel? As you have seen in our study of couples and families so far in this chapter, the effectiveness of families relies on how families handle daily interactions and communication within the family system (Procentese et al., 2019). In a study of 227 parents and their teens (ages 13 to 18), the researchers wanted to determine the parents' positive and negative interpretations of their teens' use of cell phones and social media:

> **Positive:** Parents said that technology improves healthy family communication and cohesion; it helps in bringing different generations together (i.e., teens, parents, and grandparents); it helps families to navigate developmental transitions; digital technology strengthens family resilience—the ability to positively face difficulties.
>
> **Negative:** Parents said that cell phones and social media interfere with family rules and boundaries; they expose families to privacy risks; they risk deteriorating family intimacy (i.e., the emotional connections between family members); they make the relationships within the family more vulnerable (Procentese et al., 2019).

The researchers conclude their work with this impactful insight: "It is not the real impact of social media on family systems that matters, but it is how family members *perceive it*"—it is the meaning they assign to its use (Procentese et al., 2019).

One of the central themes of Symbolic Interaction theory is that meanings are changed through culturally and socially defined processes (Blumer, 1969), and we can see from our own daily lives and our dependence on our devices how culture has influenced/is influencing our interpersonal interactions. Given this, helping professionals, such as Certified Family Life Educators, are in a unique position to educate parents and families about the ways in which digital technology can be both a positive and a negative influence on relationships (O'Keeffe & Clarke-Pearson, 2011). As helpers, we can educate and advise families, schools, and communities about healthy online use, as well as those things that may have adverse effects on individuals.

This lack of shared meanings and inaccurate interpretations causes frustrations and misunderstandings in all forms of human interactions—especially between parents.

Family Diversity and Communication

Because our first experiences with interpersonal relationships occur within our families of origin, our understanding of how families communicate and of family life is often narrow (Turner & West, 2006); we thus need to widen our knowledge of communication behaviors within a broad range of family types. Do family structures differ in the issues that challenge them?

Communication within nuclear families: Issues important in today's contemporary families center on communicating about the division of household chores, the effects of work life on family life, and the involvement of men in their children's lives. Men in contemporary nuclear families have increased the amount of time they spend with their children as well as doing household chores. But spillover—when the stresses associated with work affect home life—tends to increase levels of conflict at home.

Communication in LGBTQ+ families: LGBTQ+ partners and parents struggle with relationship issues (such as conflict) and parenting issues (such as child care) just as heterosexual parents do. But gay fathers tend to receive more support from their families of origin than do lesbian mothers, although self-disclosure of their sexual identity is a difficult communication subject for many.

Communication within stepfamilies: Family communication within stepfamily structures most often centers on negotiating roles, communication rules, and the unique family subsystems that are formed when two families merge to form a stepfamily. Families who understand that it takes time for families to "blend" see less family conflict than those families who challenge or resist the process of merging the two families.

Communication within single-parent families: In families in which *collectivism* is endorsed (as in Asian American families and Hispanic or Mexican American families), single parents receive a great deal of support, protection, and emotional reinforcement. In cultures in which *individualism* is embraced, as in white families, the family of origin may communicate blame and guilt to the single parent.

Communication within heterosexual cohabiting families: Unique to cohabiting couples is a lack of communication role models for this specific family configuration. Cohabiting couples face greater demands in the areas of roles and support of their family structure.

Now that you have a firm understanding of communication as a transactional process, a knowledge base about how we acquire/share meanings, and the significance of these meanings in gendered and family form communication, it is time to explore another fundamental topic of communication, *conflict*.

PARENTING COMMUNICATION AND CONFLICT

Any interpersonal or social interaction provides us with a wealth of information. But why is it that today's divorce courts commonly hear that marital partners are "failing" to communicate (Gottman, 1999; Gottman & Porterfield, 1981; Gottman et al., 2002; Stanley, 2017)?

How we communicate in our families influences the quality and the content of our relationships, including parenting relationships and parent–child relationships (Kapetanovic et al., 2019). Because we develop all of our interpersonal (social and relational) communication skills within our family of origin, this is where we build our foundation (whether in healthy ways or unhealthy ways) for communicating to resolve conflict; share intimacy; and express our needs, wants, fears, hopes, frustrations, anger, or desires. When we discuss parenting communication, we are referring not just to the talk that takes place among couples but also to the entire array of communication transactions.

Broadly stated, **communication** is the process of making and sharing meanings. Professors and researchers of communication studies Lynn Turner and Richard West (2018) summarize the general concepts of communication that we have learned so far:

Communication is a transaction: Communication is a transactional process in which parties act simultaneously as senders or receivers of messages. All human behavior is a continuous dialogue.

Communication is a process: Communication is dynamic and ever-changing. Viewed in this way, emphasis is placed on the *process* of meaning-making, rather than on the *outcome* of the exchanges. Each family undertakes the process of meaning-making differently; culture and ethnicity are key in the process of meaning-making.

Communication involves co-construction of meanings: Each person in a relationship speaks a unique language that was acquired from his or her family of origin. The process of communication thus consists of learning the meaning of things—*constructing definitions*—between family members.

Communication involves symbols: In order to construct meanings or definitions of things, people rely on *symbols* or *codes*. Across cultures, the codes that are used for communication are *verbal* and *nonverbal*. These two broad categories are used to describe how we convey meanings to one another, both in our interpersonal and social relationships.

Conflict in Relationships

Every couple fights. Every family fights. Due to the complex, interrelated nature of interpersonal relationships, conflict is inevitable. In all facets of intimacy, love, sexual encounters, parenting, childrearing, communication, and communication patterns, there are opportunities for quarrels and differences of opinion that may lead to arguments, conflict, and all-out shouting matches. Because of the interactive, systemic nature of family and intimate relationships,

To understand communication and conflict, it is first important to understand that all communication is dependent on the context in which it is taking place and how we were taught to communicate with others.

Source: iStock.com/wundervisuals.

conflict can quickly spill into every area of family life. When this occurs, strained relationships lead to a stressful living environment.

Although the experience of conflict is unique to each family, in empirical studies that examine conflict, there appear to be common themes of marital and family conflict. Family interaction authors Stephen Anderson and Robert Sabatelli (2011) provide an overview of the current scientific studies as they relate to these areas of marital conflict.

- **Money matters:** Who makes it? Who spends it and how? Who manages the family finances? (see Chapter 10)
- **Division of household labor:** Who does what and when and how often? Is there role equity within the home? Is equality important in this context? Who decides? (see Chapter 10)
- **Sex:** How frequently does each partner want to have sex? How long should it last? Who does what and when? What are each partner's sexual scripts and are these scripts flexible enough to accommodate the partner's desires?
- **"Tremendous trifles":** This category is a catch-all for a wide array of disputes that emerge over personal habits such as snoring, not picking up after oneself, and consistently being late; personal preferences, such as preferring to watch television reruns and figure skating competitions over golf, baseball, and action adventure movies; and day-to-day

> living, such as who picks up the kids from school, who takes the kids to soccer, who picks up the dry cleaning, and who does the grocery shopping. (see Chapter 10)

The issue at hand, then, is not whether conflict will erupt—it will. The question is what kind of conflict will it be? Just because conflict exists does not mean that there is a problem with the relationship. John Gottman (1994b), the most influential researcher in the areas of marital happiness/marital satisfaction and conflict management, points out that the basic difference between functional and dysfunctional families is the way in which families process—or *use*—conflict.

Next, we will have a look at the process of conflict and the factors associated with family conflict, as well as the nuances of destructive, constructive, and unresolved conflict.

What's All the Fuss? The Sources of Conflict

Conflict typically occurs when family members believe that their desires and goals are not compatible with those of one or more members in the family (Galvin et al., 2019). Many newly formed couples or families try to avoid conflict, but if they manage it properly, conflict can actually be quite beneficial to the relationship and foster growth within the family system. As with any other aspect of marriage and family life, learning about the sources of conflict allows us to better navigate our personal relationships and helps us help others to use conflict to foster stronger relationships.

There are so many things we can argue about when it comes to family living and parenting: where to go to eat, whether a once-used towel is clean or not and needs to be thrown into the laundry hamper, what time the children should be home—the list is virtually endless! Anderson and Sabatelli (2011) provide a comprehensive discussion concerning marital and family conflict and the underlying sources of conflict in marriage: conflicting role expectations, conflicting needs for connection and autonomy, and conflicts in fairness and equity.

When Role Expectations Conflict

We establish relationships, and when we marry or partner with someone, we bring with us a ready set of expectations based on how each of us has been socialized. When our expectations are not met, conflict results. For example, women who have been socialized to accept more traditional gender roles may expect to be the primary caretakers and disciplinarians for the children. They may also expect to be primarily responsible for household tasks and expect their husbands to manage the household finances. These women may also expect their husbands to initiate sexual activities. Conversely, men who have been reared according to more contemporary gender roles may expect to be equal partners and have equal say in how the children are reared. They may also assume that household tasks and household finances will be divided equally between the spouses. They may expect sex to be initiated by either partner. When expectations such as those just described are not fulfilled, conflict erupts.

Anderson and Sabatelli (2011) note an impressive body of research that speaks to role conflict and differences in role expectations as major sources of marital strain, friction, opposition, and hostility (among others, Bagarozzi & Anderson, 1989; Sabatelli, 1988). When spouses have opposing expectations, and when couples do not discuss their expectations or periodically align them, fertile ground exists for discontent to take root.

When Connection and Autonomy Conflict

The interdependent nature of marital and family relationships essentially guarantees that conflict is inevitable due to a human need to be intimately connected and yet separate (autonomous) at the same time. According to Anderson and Sabatelli (2011), as long as one partner's needs do not conflict with the other's, the couple peacefully coexists. But when one partner's need to be alone competes with the other partner's need to be together, the potential for conflict arises.

When Fairness and Equity Are in Question

When we enter into a marital partnership, we do so with our own unique perceptions of what constitutes a fair and equitable relationship. For instance, many people enter into committed partnerships and marital relationships expecting that the relationship will always be 50/50. Perhaps the relationship would remain relatively conflict-free if these expectations were consistently met. But how realistic are these expectations? Anderson and Sabatelli (2011) point out that any infringement, breach, or abuse of these norms—our perceptions—becomes the underlying source of conflict in our interpersonal relationships.

In assessing the concepts of equity and fairness, we tend to believe that the relationship is fair if the benefits we receive are comparative to the costs. In other words, if we get as much out of the relationship as we put into it, then it is fair. An equitable relationship exists when each partner gains similar benefits for being in the relationship. When there is perceived unfairness or perceived inequity, conflict results (Anderson & Sabatelli, 2011). When couples work at resolving the conflict, the result is a change in how the couple interacts.

Types of Conflict

Relationship conflict usually occurs because of miscommunication, poor communication, or misperception. Sometimes it is the result of negative behaviors. We generally think of conflict as something we need to avoid because the term implies that conflict is harmful to a relationship. But conflict can be beneficial and strengthen the relationship and initiate growth if dealt with properly. Conflict can be either constructive or destructive to the marital relationship. Additionally, couples vary in their conflict styles.

Constructive Conflict

While in the midst of a heated argument, it might be difficult to think that any good can come out of it; however, **constructive conflict** serves to build relationships and foster loyalty, commitment, and intimacy.

John Gottman has consistently found that the manner in which couples handle conflict ultimately determines whether they divorce. In a study that sought to determine the differences in communication patterns of those couples who sought marital counseling and those who did not, Gottman and his colleagues (1977) found that the more happily married couples avoided negative comments (such as hurling insults at one another during a disagreement or a heated battle) and instead affirmed the value and worth of the other partner, in spite of their disagreements.

In a landmark empirical study, Gottman (1994b) found that how couples communicated about their differences determined marital longevity: Even though some of the arguments the couples experienced were all-out shouting matches or openly verbally combative, couples with high marital satisfaction maintained a ratio of *five* positive comments to every *one* negative comment. In his work *Why Marriages Succeed or Fail* (1994b), Gottman explored his idea that conflict management styles distinguish troubled from nontroubled couples. Through his study, he found there are two specific marriage types: regulated and nonregulated.

Regulated couples use communication patterns and interpersonal behaviors that promote closeness and intimacy, such as using more positive comments than negative comments during times of tension. According to Gottman (1994b), there are three types of regulated couples: the validating couple, the volatile couple, and the conflict-minimizing couple.

> **The validating couple:** This type of couple uses a constructive conflict management style. They tend to be empathic and supportive of one another and try to gauge each other's emotions. These couples listen actively and respectfully and validate that what their partner is feeling is important. Validating couples seldom express negative emotions toward one another. They tend to be happy but not necessarily passionate.
>
> **The volatile couple:** Unlike the validating couple, the volatile couple type is charged with intense emotion, passion, and romance, and it is this emotion and passion that spills over into every area of marital and family life, including conflict. But despite the intense, emotional disputes, fights, and shouting matches that take place, these couples remain genuinely and intimately connected to one another.
>
> **The conflict-minimizing couple:** These couples ignore or avoid conflict or minimize the significance of the trouble. Despite the fact that the conflict-minimizing couple reduces or lessens the conflict that exists—and hence, lives with unresolved issues just below the surface—these couples manage to keep the discontentment and unresolved problems from spilling over into other areas of their relationship, According to Gottman (1994b), they still manage to use positive language rather than negative, distancing language, which ultimately promotes a deeper level of intimacy.

How can a volatile couple with explosive emotions or a couple who totally ignores or avoids the conflict be considered constructive in their conflict management? When Gottman proposed that successful, satisfied married couples maintain a five-to-one ratio of positive comments to negative comments, he illustrated the importance of balance and affirmation. When couples are able to balance positives and negatives constructively, the end result is an effective relationship that withstands and grows from conflict.

Destructive Conflict

We have all had our share of disputes and arguments with family members. The dispute or conflict may have been successfully resolved so that the relationship was able to change, adjust to the stress, and subsequently deepen loyalty, commitment, and intimacy levels. At other times, however, many of us have experienced conflict that resulted in greater hurt, anger, confusion, and pain. **Destructive conflict** can be either overt, which refers to obvious conflict, or covert, which is subtler but nonetheless hurtful. Whether it is overt or covert, destructive conflict is unhelpful, and at its very worst, deadly (as in the case of physical violence that escalates).

According to Galvin and her colleagues (2019), covert destructive conflict falls within five specific categories:

1. *Denial* is exhibited when a person's words do not align with his or her nonverbal behavior, for example, when someone shouts, "Nothing is wrong!" as he storms out the room.
2. *Disqualification* occurs when a person attempts to cover up an expressed emotion; for example, she might say, "I'm sorry I'm so upset with you, but it's been a horrible day at work."
3. *Displacement* refers to a situation in which someone takes out his or her frustration on someone who is not the original object of anger. An example of this displacement is **scapegoating**, which occurs when anger and hostility are directed at one family member, in particular, who always bears the brunt of everyone's frustration. A child who is always blamed for instigating trouble in the family, for example, is known as the family's scapegoat.
4. *Disengaged* couples or family members have little or no emotional closeness. These family members act out their anger or hostility through their lack of interaction with one another.
5. *Pseudomutuality* refers to pseudo (fake or false) mutuality (getting along). Pseudomutual families may appear to be close with no indication that conflict exists, yet anger and hostility are always just beneath the surface.

Overt destructive conflict is often verbal and is characterized by the use of negative, hurtful language, such as "idiot," "stupid," or "jerk." Verbal assaults may or may not involve screaming or yelling (Galvin et al., 2019). When couples and families engage in this type of destructive conflict, they often resort to language that will inflict the most harm possible.

Another type of verbal conflict is **gunnysacking**, which is also destructive. This describes when a spouse or a family member holds in resentment, hurt, anger, frustration, and bitter feelings until that "last straw," finally unloading all of the pent-up feelings in the midst of an argument.

According to Gottman (1994b), **nonregulated couples** are those who have a difficult time bouncing back from arguments and disputes because the way they handle the conflict only compounds the issues at hand, even day-to-day disagreements erupt into full-fledged arguments. Nonregulated couples are distinguished from regulated couples in that their interactions tend to be far more negative than regulated couples, and they have a substantially lower ratio of positive-to-negative exchanges. According to Gottman, there are four ways in which nonregulated couples handle conflict. He characterized these as the "Four Horsemen of the Apocalypse":

1. **Criticism:** Criticism almost always involves the word *you*. *You* never... *You* always... *You* are so... *You* are such a.... Almost without exception, criticism involves an attack on the *person*, rather than a complaint against the family member's *behavior*. In other words, the comments are meant to hurt, and usually they do.

2. **Defensiveness:** It is human nature to defend ourselves if we perceive that we are being attacked, be it physically, verbally, or emotionally. Recall from our previous discussion that often the way we perceive a message is not the way that the sender intended it to be received; however, often someone speaks words deliberately aimed to hurt. The criticism/defense/criticism/defense interaction pattern becomes a vicious cycle of negativity.

3. **Contempt:** Contempt can be characterized as disrespect, scorn, or all-out hatred for one another, and it is most often the result of constant critical interactions. This pattern of criticisms and defensiveness breeds deeper levels of disdain in a marriage. Over time, the mutual contempt becomes so pervasive and all-encompassing that it erodes all other areas of the marriage to the point where the couple eventually focuses only on the negative behaviors of the other spouse.

4. **Stonewalling:** According to Gottman (1994a), **stonewalling** takes place when communication between partners completely shuts down. In these instances, either one or both spouses distance themselves by refusing to communicate, ignoring and becoming remote from the other. Marital separation or dissolution is a likely outcome when this negativity process becomes the standard.

Nonregulated couples' inability to constructively manage their conflict ultimately causes a downward spiral in the marriage. As the negativity increases and intensifies, over time nonregulated couples eventually reframe their perception of their marriage and *focus only on the negative aspects of one another's behavior and the relationship.*

UNDERSTANDING PARENTING THROUGH THEORY

Because we all consider ourselves knowledgeable about family life, it can be quite tempting to make assertions about a form of family behavior we consider to be "right" or "wrong" based on our personal experience. But "family life" extends well beyond our personal worlds. One way to understand and envision "family" beyond our own worlds is to expand our knowledge through theories.

Strongly held beliefs about what constitutes "family" have molded, and at times, dominated, services available to families and family policy. Yet, in order to move beyond these commonly held assumptions and common beliefs about family, family scientists and theorists cannot rely on widely held suppositions about family; rather, they must study the family empirically.

A solid, foundational knowledge base in *Family theory* is essential for students of and professionals interested in the fields of couple and family life. Throughout our study, we will examine several *theories and frameworks* that are fundamental to the understanding of human behavior and family relationship patterns. In the family sciences, a **theory** is a general principle that is used to understand or to explain certain events or family experiences, such as family communication or family crisis. A **framework** is a systematic structure for classifying families, their behaviors, or their experiences. Theories profoundly affect what we know about families because they provide structure for how we think about families, what we observe, how we interpret what we observe, and how we use this information to create programs and introduce policies that affect and enhance family life (Smith, 1995). In short, a theory allows us to move beyond our everyday, common beliefs about family and move toward an objective, scientific understanding of family and family processes.

An Introduction to Family Theories

We do not develop in a vacuum. The most significant influence on both our individual development and our ability to relate to others, by far, is our *family of origin*. Our family is the base from which we venture out and learn to share ourselves in close and intimate relationships. The ability to share ourselves is a complicated, elaborate mixture of our own individual development and our family experiences (whatever they might be). Our family history also plays a significant role, as generations before produced our grandparents and parents—those who have influenced us the most.

Today, many theories exist that attempt to explain the workings of family, and each have made numerous contributions to the field of family studies. James White, David Klein, and Todd Martin, authors of *Family Theories: An Introduction* (2014), describe today's prevailing family theories.

1. *Ecological theory* is concerned with the many social and cultural contexts that affect family living. As you learned in Chapter 1, these contexts include factors that exert immediate influences on the family, such as schools, churches or temples, and neighborhoods. Other contexts include the government, educational systems, the political system, and the overarching value system of a given society.
2. *Family Development theory* divides the experiences of family into phases, or stages, of normative changes associated with family growth and development, such as the birth of children and the launching of these children into early adulthood. This theory is concerned with understanding the changes in family structures and the roles of family members across each stage of family development. According to this theory, healthy families are able to adapt to these changes across time.
3. *Conflict theory* maintains that society shapes individual and family behavior. At the core of this theory is the notion that conflict is normal and expected in families and in society. Thus, to understand families, Conflict theory maintains that we need to understand the sources of conflict and the sources of power.

4. *Family Systems theory* concentrates on the interactions between family members, and it views the family as an interconnected group of individual members whose behaviors affect and are affected by other family members' behaviors. What happens to one family member, such as an illness or a loss of a job, affects every family member.

5. *Symbolic Interaction theory* concerns itself with how people form and share meanings in their communication efforts. Its primary focus is the use of symbols to convey meaning through verbal and nonverbal communication.

6. *Social Exchange theory* (discussed in Chapter 7) focuses on the costs and rewards associated with our human behaviors. In short, this theory maintains that people weigh costs and rewards before they decide to act—we engage in behavior that brings us maximum rewards and minimum costs. According to this theory, we form relationships with other people if we expect that the relationship will be rewarding. It is human nature to avoid relationships that we perceive will be costly to us.

Because of the family life education approach of this textbook, and because of this book's topical nature, as we work our way through our study, we will focus on the foundations of various family theories and how they help us understand the intricacies of our interpersonal relationships. We will examine the theories throughout the coming chapters as they relate to certain

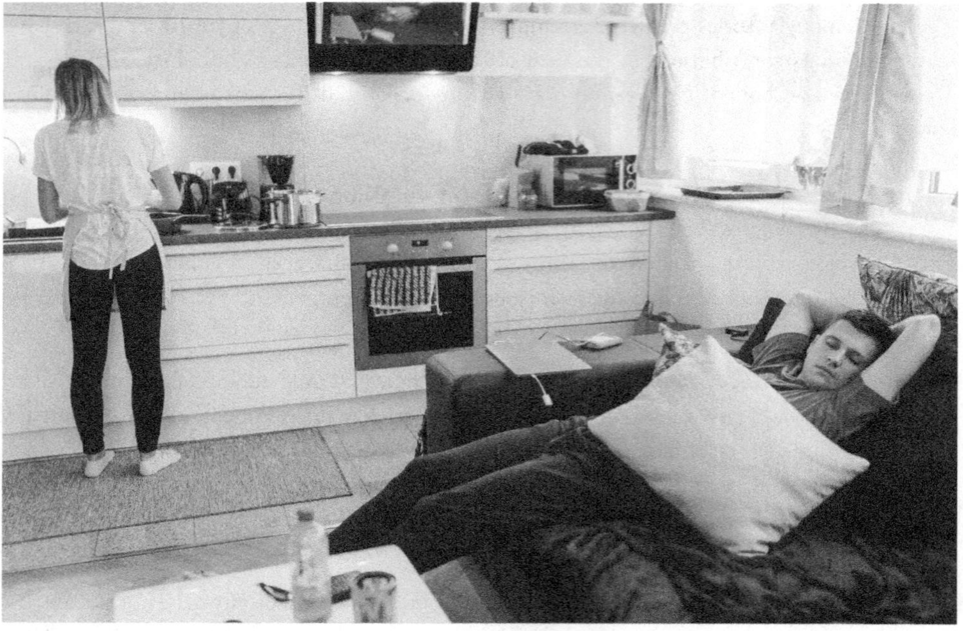

According to Structural-Functionalist theory, males adopt instrumental roles such as providing for the family, while females adopt expressive roles, such as keeping the home and nurturing the husband and children.

Source: iStock.com/bojanstory.

topics. We begin by looking at what is recognized by many family specialists and sociologists as the "grandfather of Family theory": Structural Functionalism.

Structural Functionalism

Perhaps the most influential contributor to the study of parenting and family life is Talcott Parsons (1902–1979). Out of his passion to investigate the wide range of problems concerning American values, social structure, social problems, and patterns of institutional change, Parsons devised the **Structural-Functionalist perspective** of the family (Fox et al., 2005). This theory has continued to influence Family theory for 30 years.

Parsons's functionalist view of the family maintained that gender-based role specialization was necessary in order to promote family (and hence, societal) equilibrium. **Instrumental roles** were assigned to the husband-father, who, as the task-oriented mate, was assigned responsibility for being the primary breadwinner and protector against imbalance or disequilibrium. To complement the male, the wife-mother was assigned **expressive roles**, the people-oriented mate responsible for enhancing emotional relationships among the members of the family (Boss et al., 1993). According to Parsons, then, the 1950s heterosexual, nuclear breadwinner-homemaker family represented the most functional of all family forms (Parsons, 1951). To be sure, Parsonian thought heralded the belief that if men and women abided by their gender-specific roles, not only would the family unit be ensured stability and solidity but also society at large would similarly benefit.

Although some of the original ideas of this theory have been discarded because of their patriarchal nature (such as the belief that the "correct" family form is that of a man, woman, and child), many of the theory's assumptions are still in use today. Much of what you will see in other family theories in this text are clear descendants of functionalism.

Key Concepts of Structural Functionalism

At the heart of Structural Functionalism rests the notion that society is considered to be a whole that is made up of separate, interconnected parts, and that this whole (*social system*) seeks maintenance and stability in order for it to persist and endure. Functionalism also holds that each subsystem (or social unit) seeks balance or *homeostasis*; a change in one unit affects a change in the other units in order for balance to be maintained. The core of Structural Functionalism is that each member of the social system conforms to a certain set of clearly defined rules or beliefs that exist for the sole purpose of advancing the greater good and continued existence of the society to which the individual belongs. In other words, the whole social system must survive, and it cannot survive without individual members working together toward its continued existence by way of *certain functional requirements* (Boss & others, 1993, p. 196), such as sexual reproduction, economic reproduction, education, and religion (Bernardes, 2000). This theory derives its name in part because of the function of each subsystem—the contribution—to the survival of the whole societal system. A subsystem's function can contribute either in a positive fashion (functional) or a negative fashion [dysfunctional) to the society.

In order for functions to contribute to the overall good of the society, they must adhere to *structures* or patterns of role arrangement. For example, the family is thought to be a key subsystem because it promotes the survival of the societal system by providing new members through procreation, and by socializing children to conform to societal beliefs, norms, and ways of life (Boss & others, 1993). According to structural functionalists, the traditional nuclear family has historically been thought to best promote the needs of the larger society. A *nuclear family* is defined as the "socially sanctioned cohabitation [marriage] of a man and a woman who have preferential or exclusive enjoyment of economic and sexual rights over one another and are committed to raise the children brought to life by the woman" (Pitts, 1964). This definition clearly delineates social organization and properties of the family system, as the following conditions illustrate:

1. The marital couple assumes the responsibility of childrearing, and such specialized roles increase the functionality of the system.
2. The man and the woman have exclusive economic and sexual rights over one another. According to Boss and colleagues, such clearly outlined marital roles establish well-defined rights and obligations to one another—and thus, to the society at large.
3. With the clearly specified roles that foster exclusive economic and sexual rights over one another, in addition to bearing and rearing children within the socially sanctioned form of cohabitation, these types of role specialization underscore the most significant property of a system—its ability to maintain homeostasis or balance. When family balance is enhanced, the overall equilibrium of the society is reinforced, as well (Boss & others, 1993).

Structural Functionalism dominated sociological theory from the early 1940s through the 1960s, then fell out of the theoretical limelight; however, despite being considered obsolete by some scholars, particularly feminist scholars, other academics believe that Structural Functionalism still governs much study of family sociology and family life (Boss & others, 1993; Smith, 1993).

Structural Functionalism and the Family

Structural Functionalism emphasizes the traditional, heterosexual nuclear family and highlights two primary functions of the family in society: the socialization of children to society's culture and norms, and the stabilization of adult personalities. This view revolves around the idea that the family is organized and governed by unchangeable, fixed, irreversible role configurations—and that these gender-specific family functions operate in order to benefit the family itself as well as to promote the greater good of the society. With these functions and family structures in mind, let's take a look at research that addresses the increasing occurrence of same-sex couples bearing or adopting children.

In 2002, the American Academy of Pediatrics supported legislation permitting lesbian partners to co-parent children born to one partner or adopted by the couple. The Academy maintained that children reared in lesbian families "can have the same advantages and the same expectations... for adjustment, and development" as those children reared in heterosexual families (p. 339). And, as you will see in our study together throughout this course, a number of contemporary researching findings suggest that no substantial differences exist between lesbian and heterosexual parents in affective development or areas of self-concept, happiness, and overall adjustment. Dr. Susan Golombok (1983, 1999), founder of the Family and Child Psychology Research Centre at City University, London, further maintains that children of lesbian mother families do not appear to demonstrate greater instances of psychological disorders, difficulties in peer relationships, or atypical gender development. As for sexual orientation, Golombok notes that most children reared in lesbian families identified with heterosexuality.

If we were to apply Parsons's Structural-Functionalist theoretical framework to this research, the *male* husband-(always)father and the *female* wife-(always)mother, we see the theory calls into question the function of same-sex couples. Recall, too, that these specialized gender roles allow the family to successfully carry out its chief function of socializing the children to the predominant beliefs and norms of the culture.

If we compare Parsons's assigned roles to roles depicted in contemporary research on lesbian parenting, where there exist two family members—*both female* wife-mothers—what happens to family stability? When two women rear children and do not abide by clearly outlined, specialized gender roles, what happens to the family structure? By Parsonian assumption, the lesbian parenting family form deviates from the ideal family form, and as such should turn out children who are nonconforming to societal norms. But is this what studies of lesbian parenting

Structural Functionalism asserts that because gay parents do not conform to the approved gender roles of society, their children will similarly reject cultural gender norms (and will thus not develop well). Research suggests, though, that children raised by LGBTQ+ parents do well because the only important parenting factor is providing nurturing, attentive care.

Source: iStock.com/FluxFactory.

suggest? On the contrary, the studies indicate that children born into and/or reared by lesbian parents show no significant negative or harmful effects in the children's emotional development, self-concepts, or overall adjustment (Baiocco & others, 2015, 2019; Bos et al., 2016; Farr, 2017). In fact, there appear to be no differences between children of lesbian parents and children of heterosexual parents. According to current research, then, the gender of the parents doesn't affect children's sexual orientation. The only parenting factor that is important is that the children are being cared for in a nurturing environment. One could perhaps argue, however, that one lesbian parent assumed the instrumental role and the other assumed the expressive role, and that as long as each of the roles were filled, one's gender doesn't matter.

Throughout your course of study, you will see discussed at length in subsequent chapters a number of social conflicts that some sociologists and family scientists would argue are a direct result of the inequalities of power in family structures: family violence, the feminization of poverty, divorce, single motherhood, and violence against the elderly.

Now that you have a knowledge base in the forms and functions of marriage and family and the basic concepts of Family theory, it is necessary that you understand how you affect and are affected by the intimate relationships in your life. Next, we build on our knowledge base as we explore individual and family development.

FAMILY INTERACTIONS

Each of us accomplishes many developmental milestones in our individual lifespan development, and we do so within the context of family living. Every phase of our individual development across our Human Life Cycle intersects with the development of the family throughout its developmental cycle, ultimately shaping who we are as relational people. In this section, we take a close look at the *Human Life Cycle* and the *Family Life Cycle* (Figure 3.4).

The Human Life Cycle

All human development is a complex, dynamic, and multifaceted process. As we grow and change, we accomplish what developmentalists, psychologists, and therapists term **developmental tasks**. These entail achieving certain biological, physical, cognitive/intellectual, social, emotional, and spiritual tasks across the lifecourse. It is important to be aware of these developmental milestones because every point in our life cycle interconnects with the developmental stages of the family (Carter & McGoldrick, 2005). A son who becomes chronically ill during his college experience, for example, may disrupt a parent's plans to retire early because of the added health expenses. Conversely, a dying parent might delay a student's college experience because she feels she needs to be with her family through her parent's illness.

The developmental tasks that most of us experience are considered to be **normative**—they come at relatively predictable points in our lives and are generally expected. These events are often referred to as **on-time events** because of their relative predictability across the lifespan. For example, we expect an adolescent to undergo physical changes somewhere between 10 and

FIGURE 3.4 ■ Time Line of the Human Life Cycle

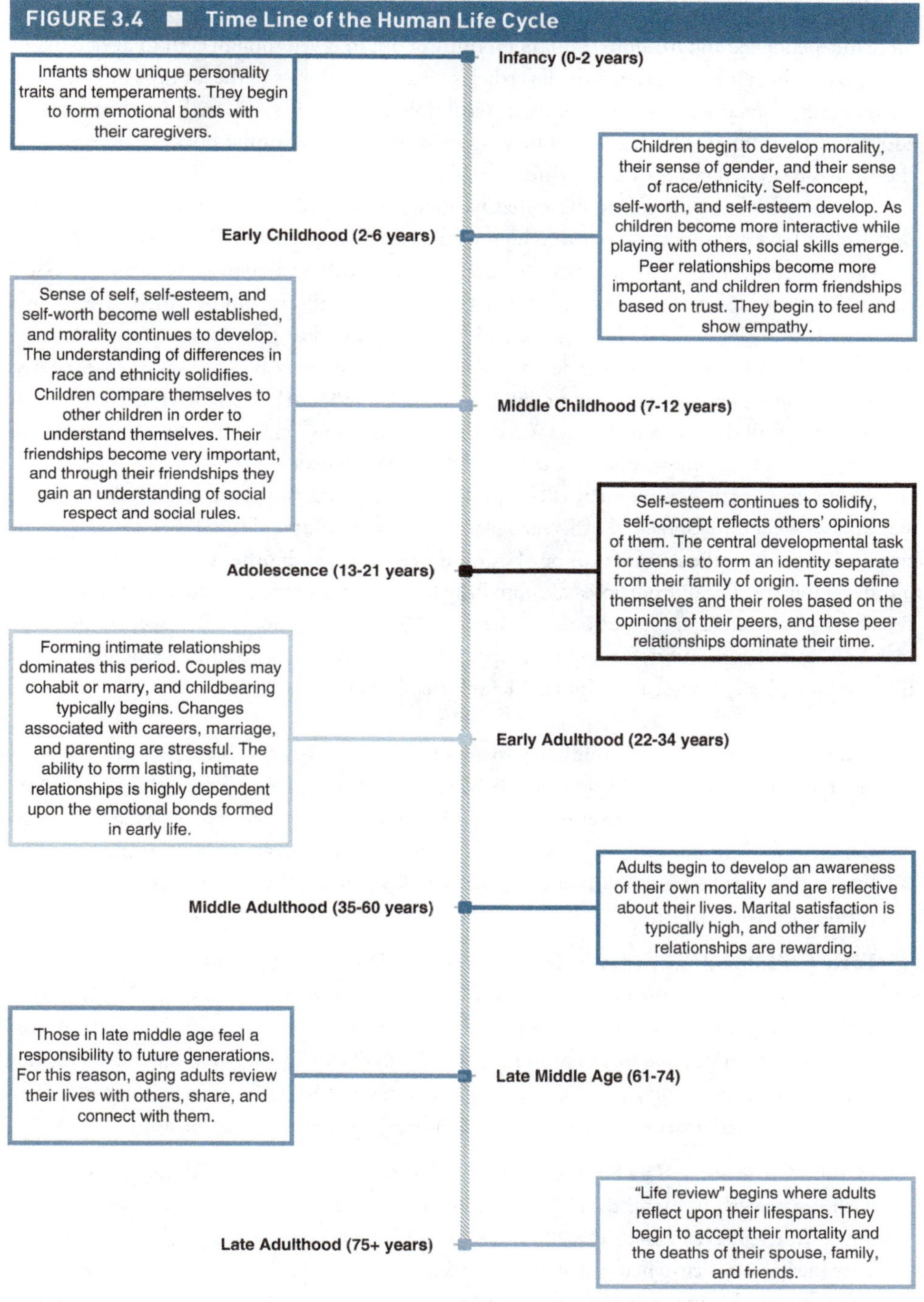

16 years of age. Along with these physical changes, we expect them to begin to desire more and more independence and freedom from their family of origin. Even though certain developmental tasks may be normative, they may nevertheless cause disruptions in the family's interactions. Additionally, sometimes events occur at atypical points in the lifespan, such as when a young adolescent gives birth. This is referred to as an **off-time event** because it does not take place at the more typical point in the person's life.

Nonnormative life events are those that we do not anticipate, and that we cannot predict, but that do have an impact on our developmental lifecourse, such as Grit's story in the opening vignette of this book. It is not expected that an infant will be diagnosed with an aggressive cancer. It is not expected that both parents who are in the military will be called to serve in a war oceans away, for example, leaving the children to be reared by grandparents, aunts, uncles, or friends. We don't anticipate or expect that our son or daughter will have a severe reading disability. Nor do we expect that a parent will lose his or her job, or that a natural disaster such as fire or floods will destroy our homes. Whatever the situation or circumstance, the nuances of our individual development affect the family and its development.

Although human development is complex, it is important to gain a fundamental understanding of what developmental tasks take place over the lifecourse. This allows us to grasp the significance of how the members of our family affect us and each other through each stage of our development. For our purposes of more fully understanding the intricacies of human relationships, our discussion focuses on the *psychosocial* (social and emotional) aspects of development. What follows is a brief synopsis, adapted in part from renowned and influential family life educators, Betty Carter and Monica McGoldrick (2005).

Infancy (0–2 years)—From infancy to about two years of age, babies learn to walk, talk, and trust their caregivers. Every time a baby cries, the baby is sending out a signal of distress or need. Every time a caregiver responds to the baby's signals of distress or need and meets those needs with comfort and love, the baby learns that the world is a secure place and begins to form the foundation of trust that will be central—in fact crucial—to his or her future intimate relations.

Early Childhood: The Play Years (2–6 years)—During this period of growth, children are eager and able to learn new skills—including social and emotional skills. In this phase, children begin to learn empathy and show concern for others' feelings; they will comfort someone who appears to be sad or in need. Children of this age begin to form relationships with peers, learn to obey rules, control their emotions, and delay the need for immediate gratification—all essential stepping stones to future, "grown-up" relationships.

Middle Childhood: The School Years (7–12 years)—This phase of development brings with it a growth in moral development and what is termed by some researchers as "heart logic" (Carter & McGoldrick, 2005). As friendships become increasingly important, so does the importance of being able to express feelings and emotions in an appropriate fashion and of being able to respect the rights and needs of others. As children's capacity for empathy and understanding develops, so too does their tolerance for diversity, such as differences in gender, race, and ethnicity, unless parents and those in authority over them instruct them differently. During the school years, a child's sexual development and sexual identity also begin to intensify. All of these developmental leaps add to "who" the child will be someday in her or his intimate partnerships.

Adolescence (13–21 years)—With rapid body changes also comes an increase in the adolescent's capacity for moral understanding; an increase in the understanding of self in relation to peers, family, and the community; and an increased awareness of his or her sexual identity (Carter & McGoldrick, 2005). As their ability to understand the world and relationships increases, adolescents become better equipped to tackle intimate social relationships.

Early Adulthood (22–34 years)—As young adults, men and women during this developmental phase develop the ability—based on the relational foundations laid throughout all of infancy and childhood—to form and engage in emotionally mature intimate relationships. Throughout this phase of life, they continue to master their abilities to negotiate the complexities of marriage, family, and intimate relationships. At this phase, they learn to steer the course in interdependence, mutuality, and reciprocity in relationships, and open themselves up to those they trust (see more about this in Chapter 5). At this juncture, they seek someone to share their lives with.

Middle Adulthood (35–60 years)—Adults in their middle adulthood years are typically actively involved in raising and caring for their children. Adults look beyond themselves and focus their energies and attentions on the next generation and on others, such as their aging parents.

Late Middle Age (60–74 years)—Although adults at this age deal with and manage declines in their physical and intellectual abilities, they begin to take steps to "pass the torch" to the next generation (Carter & McGoldrick, 2005). They feel a responsibility to future generations and will reach out in an attempt to make connections with them. My father, for example, a veteran of the Vietnam War, faced and endured such difficulties during his year in combat that he never shared them with his family. As he began to near the end of his own lifecourse, he is beginning to share his experiences with his children and grandchildren; in doing so, he is connecting us to his past.

Late Adulthood (75 and older)—Grief, loss, retrospection, and growth are the benchmarks of this developmental phase (Carter & McGoldrick, 2005). As adults age and start to think about the end of life, they begin to reflect on their lives and come to grips with the legacy they will leave to future generations. At the same time, they must accept the deaths of family and friends and their spouse or life partner—and they must accept the inevitability of their own mortality and death's eventuality. Not only do they need to accept death and dying but they must also accept the lives that they lived.

As you can see, our early life experiences—from the moment of birth—have an impact on our development of our relational skills and abilities.

The Family Life Cycle

What perhaps best distinguishes a family life education approach in the study of marriage, family, and intimate relations from other disciplines is the focus on and application of the Family Life Cycle. Although some fields such as psychology, sociology, and feminist studies might disagree with the tenets of the Family Life Cycle, Carter and McGoldrick perhaps best sum up the efficacy of its inclusion in the examination of family and parenting when they note, "We strongly believe that individual development takes place only in the context of significant emotional relationships and that most significant emotional relationships are family relationships, whether by blood, adoption, marriage, or commitment" (1999, p. 5).

There are experiences throughout our lives that establish a foundation for our ability to love and relate to others. Integral to these experiences is our family of origin. As you have learned throughout our study so far, we do not develop in isolation! Every phase of our development is affected by, intersected by, and overlapped with the developmental cycle of our family, and our family development is influenced by the multiple cultural contexts that surround it, as Bronfenbrenner's model illustrated for us in Chapter 2. The **Family Life Cycle** comprises multiple entrances and exits from the family of origin. For example, a young adult leaving for college is an exit, whereas the formation of a new family of origin as children marry is an entry. Families with young children experience multiple entries with their new family members, but families in later life experience multiple exits, such as when family members die. Along with the changes in the *structure* of the family come certain *emotional transitions* and *related changes* in the family status that are needed to move on developmentally.

This cycle of family growth and transition is depicted for us in Table 3.1. As you can see, in each stage, there are challenges in family life that cause us to develop or gain certain relational skills. Developing these skills helps us work through the changes associated with family life; at the same time, we develop relational skills we will someday carry into our own intimate relationships. Of course, few make these transitions seamlessly; sometimes families' relationships are painfully stretched as they experience job loss or financial problems, severe illness, or the death of a loved one.

Whether you are a parent or child, brother or sister, bonded by blood or love, your experiences through the Family Life Cycle affect who you are and who you become.

It is important to note, however, that there are criticisms of the Family Life Cycle. Specifically, the Family Life Cycle has been criticized because it ignores the varying family constellations we discussed in Chapters 1 and 2 (such as families of color, gay/lesbian families, or intergenerational/extended families). In short, any deviations or differences from a "traditional" family is ignored by the Family Life Cycle. It also assumes that *all* families of origin share a common group identity, ignoring the fact that many today have departed from the previously common progression of family life. Finally, the model has been criticized because it is child-centric—it assumes that all families have children.

Prominent family life educators Betty Carter and Monica McGoldrick address these inadequacies of the Family Life Cycle in their book, *The Expanded Family Life Cycle* (2005). They note that today students of family and intimate life need to think about human development and the life cycle in a way that reflects society's shifts to a more diverse and inclusive definition

TABLE 3.1 ■ The Family Life Cycle: Phases, Tasks, and Issues

Phase	Task	Issue
Pairing/marriage	Fusion as couple	Leaving family of origin Readiness for intimacy Establishing goals, roles, and values as new couple
Childbearing	Creation	Sharing each other with children Role ambiguity—wife, woman, mother?
School-age children	Nurturing	Providing security (emotional and environmental) Learning how to parent Simultaneously spouse and parent Increasing parenting demands Increasing work demands
Family with adolescent children	Boundary-testing	Control versus freedom Power struggle and rebellion Separation from family of origin Social and sexual exploration
Family as "launching ground"	Leaving/letting go	Changing roles of children still at home The empty nest—loss or opportunity? Parents rediscover each other Latent marital conflict may surface
Middle years	Reviewing/reappraising	Mid-life crisis? Fulfilment/disappointment Accepting limitations Changing self-image Death of parents Anticipating retirement
Aging	Facing mortality	Aging, illness, death Religion and philosophy Isolation/dependency Bereavement

Source: Neighbour (1985).

of the family. Without question, as Chapter 1 showed us, today there is no prototype of an American family, and Chapter 2 described the rich diversity seen in contemporary America.

An understanding of family theories—theories that are specific to the experiences of parents, children, and families—is imperative for those who work with parents and their children because these theories lay the groundwork for the development and implementation of effective family policies (Moen & Coltrane, 2005). As effective parenting professionals, in our everyday work we apply the tenets of theories and evidence gathered from research studies to work with parents and children. We create and deliver family-based programming and interventions with the singular goal of enhancing children's development (Cowan & Cowan, 2018). In the section that follows, we'll begin our study of federal and state/local family policies that support parents and children. This discussion of historical and contemporary government policies is the prerequisite for understanding appropriate courses of action when working with parents and children (Moen & Coltrane, 2005).

POLICIES SUPPORTING PARENTS AND CHILDREN

The United States government has a 100+-year history of designing and implementing programs and services for parents to help them create safe, nurturing environments in which to raise their children (National Academies of Sciences, Engineering, and Medicine, 2016). As seen in Table 3.2, as early as 1909, the federal government began to put into place policies and

TABLE 3.2 ■ Timeline of the U.S. Government's Support of Children: The Children's Bureau

- **1912:** The Children's Bureau is founded. The Bureau was tasked with gaining an understanding of infant mortality, the birth rate, orphanages, the types and causes of accidents of children, childhood diseases, and juvenile delinquency.
- **1923:** The Bureau shifted its focus to preserving families and keeping children with their families, rather than institutionalizing them.
- **1930:** The Children's Bureau included children's welfare and education as priority needs.
- **1940s:** The development of standards for daycare was the focus of the Bureau.
- **1950s:** Child development experts began to study the social and emotional well-being of children and began to focus on children's healthy personality development.
- **1965:** The Head Start program was created by the federal government.
- **1968:** Early Childhood became the focus, and efforts were made to coordinate various programs.
- **1974:** The Child Abuse Prevention and Treatment Act was passed, and emphasis was placed on efforts to report child abuse and neglect; evidence-based services for abused children began to emerge.
- **1980s:** The Bureau's priorities continued to focus on child abuse and neglect, as well as improving the adoption and foster care systems.
- **1990s:** The adoption and Safe Families Act was passed, and it highlighted the three charges for child health: safety, permanency, and well-being.
- **2000s-current:** The Children's Bureau emphasizes the need for and continuation of quality research for use in creating evidence-based programs and practice.

Source: Children's Bureau Timeline (2020).

programs to support and benefit vulnerable children in the United States. Over time, the government's efforts have included focusing on child maltreatment (i.e., abandonment, neglect, and abuse), poverty, infant mortality, juvenile delinquency, health and wellness, education, early childhood education and experiences, daycare, adoption, and foster care (Child Welfare Information Gateway, 2019). As experts note, however, most of the policies in the United States that support parents and children have been reactionary, rather than preventive (National Academies of Sciences, Engineering, and Medicine, 2016).

As our study has shown us so far, parents and families are instrumental in providing for their children's needs; however, as we saw earlier, broader society—the *ecosystems* that surround a child—also plays a vital, necessary role in children's healthy development. The federal government's economic investments made in children today include food, shelter, health, and well-being, early childhood development, and education (Urban Institute, 2019). The importance of these federal children programs cannot be overlooked because "[these investments] made in children today have far-reaching consequences for society in the future, affecting the quality and strength of tomorrow's workforce, economy, and educational, criminal justice, and health systems" (Urban Institute, 2019, p. 1). As the Urban Institute accurately observes, the ways in which a government invests in its members, and who benefits from that investment, speaks to the priorities of that society. As Table 3.2 illustrates, the priorities, and thus the government's expenditures, have evolved over time. In the sections that follow, we'll explore federal and local policies that support and invest in children.

Federal Policies and Expenditures, and Children's Well-Being

Employment and poverty are two indicators of child well-being in the United States (Annie E. Casey Foundation, 2020). Prior to the COVID-19 pandemic that forced the closure of a substantial number of businesses in the United States, 18 percent of children under the age of 18 lived in poverty, and slightly over one-fourth (27 percent) of children lived in homes where their parents did not have stable employment (Annie E. Casey Foundation, 2020); we address poverty at length in Chapter 11. Tragically, the COVID outbreak amplified the ranks of the unemployed in the United States by more than 14 million—before the outbreak, 6.2 million were unemployed, and after government mandated business and school closures more than 20 million Americans were unemployed (Pew Research Center, 2020). Prior to the pandemic, U.S. unemployment was at its lowest since the World War II era. Women and people of color were the hardest hit by COVID-19 closures, as seen in Figure 3.5. Recall from the previous chapter the concept of *intersectionality*, the cumulative effects of different types of oppression, such as sex and race. When viewing unemployment through the lens of intersectionality, we can see that white men and women were least affected by the pandemic economic shutdown, while women of color were most significantly impacted. Understanding unemployment and poverty is important because it provides a context for us to view the necessity of the government's assistance for children.

FIGURE 3.5 ■ COVID-19 Unemployment Impact: Percentage of Women and Men, by Race, Who Became Unemployed

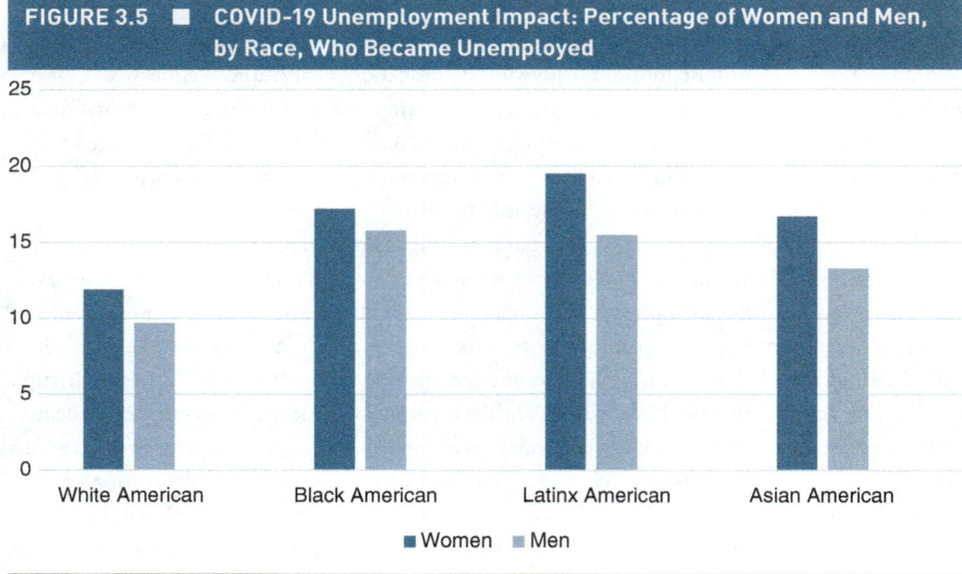

Source: Pew Research Center (2020).

Before the pandemic, nationally representative surveys of parents with children indicated that:

- 44 percent had difficulties in paying for food, medical care, housing, or utilities (Sandstrom et al., 2019).
- 25 percent of all U.S. parents and 50 percent of low-income parents experienced food insecurity, and had limited access to well-balanced, nutritious food (Waxman et al., 2019). During the pandemic, across the country, the U.S. Department of Agriculture (USDA), National School Lunch Program, School Breakfast Program, and Child and Adult Care Food Program fed nearly 35 million children daily (Dunn et al., 2020).

In 2018, the U.S. federal government spent approximately $6,200 per child under the age of 19; this figure has been steadily declining for the last decade and is the lowest amount since 2010, when the government invested about $6,700 per child (Urban Institute, 2019). This lower investment reflects a reduction in federal spending on education and nutrition programs. In general, there are nine areas of government funding provided for children:

- **Tax reductions:** Child tax credits; dependent exemption; dependent care credit; earned income tax credit
- **Health:** Medicaid; Children's Health Insurance Program (low-cost health coverage); vaccines for children

- **Nutrition:** Supplemental Nutrition Assistance Program (SNAP, formerly food stamps); Child Nutrition; Supplemental food for women and children (WIC)
- **Income security:** Social security; Temporary Assistance for Needy Families (TANF); Supplemental Security Income (SSI); Veterans benefits; child support enforcement
- **Education:** Education for the disadvantaged (Title I); special education; school improvement; Indian education; dependents' schools abroad; innovation and improvement
- **Early education and care:** Head Start; Child Care and Development Fund
- **Social services:** Foster care; adoption assistance; Unaccompanied Alien Children
- **Housing:** Section 8 low-income housing assistance; low-rent public housing
- **Training:** Training and education for working with federal programs (Urban Institute, 2019).

Figure 3.6 presents the presents the breakdown of these annual expenditures. It's important to note that less than 10 percent of the budget is spent on early education and care, social services, housing, and training (Urban Institute, 2019).

It is impossible to predict the economic impact of COVID-19, and even before these unprecedented challenges, the state of future children's programs supported by the federal government was grim: Over the next 10 years, with the exception of health, every category of spending on children is projected to decline, with only three cents of every dollar of the 1.5 trillion in federal spending going to children (Urban Institute, 2019). Of greatest concern is the reduction in spending to support education for children of all ages.

FIGURE 3.6 ■ Breakdown of Annual Government Funding for Children in the United States

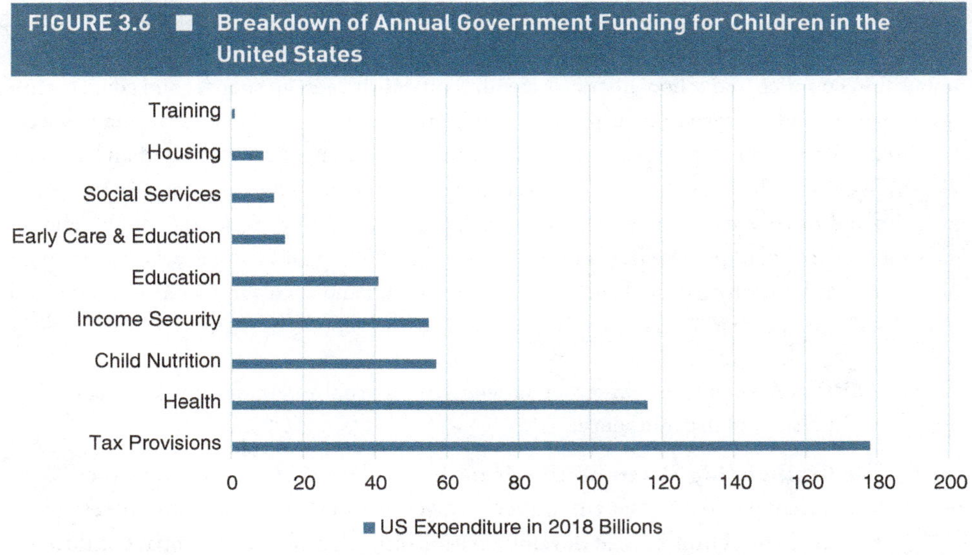

Source: Urban Institute (2019).

The importance and value of parent educators and professionals in today's stressful society cannot be overstated. Parents and families are hurting—and the need has never been greater for qualified parent professionals to aid and support them.

Source: iStock.com/fizkes.

State and Local Policies, and Expenditures, and Children's Well-Being

In general, state and local child agencies provide four main types of services: child protection and investigation; family-centered services, foster care, and adoption. State and local (cities, townships, counties, and school districts) spend significantly more to support and educate children than the federal government does. In 2017, 40 percent of state and local budgets were allocated to education, and 42 percent of expenditures went to public welfare (Urban Institute, 2018). Of course, there are differences in spending, and these are the result of varying demographics and other ecosystem contexts. For example, Alaska, New York, and the District of Columbia spent more per capita (from $14,000 to $19,000) than Georgia, who spent about $6,700 per child. Many national agencies service children and their families at the state level (Child Welfare Information Gateway, 2020):

- **ASPIRA Association:** This group provides educational and leadership resources exclusively for Hispanic youth.
- **Big Brothers/Big Sisters of America:** This organization operates with the belief that every child has the ability to succeed and thrive. Adult volunteers are matched with children and develop relationships that positively impact children and youth.

- **GLSEN:** The Gay, Lesbian, and Straight Education Network is an organization that is devoted to ensuring safe schools for all students by promoting school climates where differences are valued.
- **Head Start:** This nonpartisan, not-for-profit organization promotes school readiness of children under age five from low-income families; they provide education, health, and other social services.
- **Child Abuse Prevention and Treatment Act (CAPTA):** State and community-based grants help to improve child protective service systems.
- **Title IV-E Programs:** Funds are available for states and tribes to provide foster care, guardianship assistance, and adoption assistance for children with special needs.
- **Home Visiting Programs:** These family-focused services are offered to expectant parents and their new babies and young children. The primary focus of these programs is to provide maternal and child health education, positive parenting practices, and safe home environments.
- **Parent Education Programs:** Programs such as *Parents as Teachers, The Nurturing Parent, Compassionate Child Rearing*, and *The Circle of Security* are popular programs that enhance parenting practices and behaviors. They reinforce parenting skills as understanding developmentally and age-appropriate child development, positive interactions and play between parents and children, and using positive, effective discipline; all of these improve children's emotional and behavioral outcomes (Barlow & Coren, 2018).

There is no question that federal and state/local agencies and innovative educational programming are effective in contributing to successful outcomes for children (Barlow & Coren, 2018). Just as importantly, parent's social and emotional well-being is supported as well (for a complete review, see Barlow & Coren, 2018).

Although federal and state/local investments in children and families are vitally important for their health, we cannot overlook the essential role of helping professionals. Oftentimes, students ask about the differences in the roles of human service providers and other social service roles, such as social workers and child life specialists when working with parents and children. In brief, social workers and child life specialists work directly with individuals and meet their needs by connecting them with social programs (federal, state, and local), and they sometimes counsel their clients. Rather than working one-on-one with people, human service professionals commonly work with the entire perspective in mind, including programs' goals and objectives, to support needy and underserved populations and communities. For example, these professionals may design and implement parent educational programming, or they may provide supervision to people who work closely with clients, or they may be fundraisers or grant writers. No human service career is more important than another because each profession helps people to live to their fullest potentials. Throughout our study together, we will further explore the roles of both the helping professional and the government.

PARENTING LIFE EDUCATION: INFLUENCING PARENTS AND PARENT EDUCATION FROM CONTEMPORARY AND HISTORICAL PERSPECTIVES

One of the key responsibilities of helping professionals is to help parents maintain strong, healthy, well-functioning interpersonal relationships and to improve how they relate to one another and their children (National Council on Family Relations, 2020). To this end, human service providers and other care professionals are required to gain a knowledge and an understanding of how parents and families communicate (patterns seen in the couple's relationship and parent–child relationships), as well as the sources of conflict and how they manage it. Parenting practitioners are skilled professionals who can assess these internal family processes from a Family Systems perspective.

If we reflect on the opening story of this chapter, we can begin to recognize the destructive and potentially damaging long-term effects certain communication patterns can have on us. When my family members involved in keeping "the secret" were doing what they felt was best, they did not anticipate that eventually this very secret would significantly damage people's abilities to trust, self-disclose, and form their own relational cultures. The story should remind us that although we all need to communicate—to give or receive information—the communication process involves much more than the sharing or withholding of information.

With divorce courts backed up with marriages that failed because couples believe they are not communicating, communication is not in fact the reason for the dissolution of the marriages. Couples *are* communicating—by every spoken word, every form of nonverbal or emotional behavior. The trouble is that they are not communicating effectively. As we discussed, effective, healthy communication means listening and hearing *beyond the words.* Sometimes it means hearing with our hearts—listening compassionately—and not with our ears. Productive and healthy communication also involves a basic understanding that everything we say or do in a family affects us, as we simultaneously affect others.

Who makes the rules about what we can or cannot say in a family? *We* make the communication rules. *We* enforce these communication rules over time, through repeated interactions, even if they prove to be ineffective or destructive. To create a relational culture that is rich and rewarding to each family member, confirming your family members and/or your partners by recognizing and accepting their messages is essential. One of the greatest gifts parents can give their children is to create an environment where each child is valued as a contributing member to the family system and as a contributor to family communication, and an environment where family members communicate often.

The study of parenting and working with children is fascinating. By using reliable scholarship, we can look beyond our own family experiences, intuition, logic, and instinct to examine and understand the impact of parenting on the lives of children. By using the many theoretical frameworks provided by sociological studies and Family Science, we have a lens through which we can view and better understand parenting processes. In essence, we can "know" parenting and parenting life, and with this knowledge, we can inform the attitudes and practices of parents through the creation and dissemination of quality parent education and programming. In doing so, we enhance the well-being of children in this country.

4 BECOMING PARENTS: CHOICES AND CHALLENGES

LEARNING OBJECTIVES

4.1 Characterize the processes of fertilization and conception, and the reproductive organs that support pregnancy.

4.2 Outline the changes that occur in the developing baby month by month, and describe the four stages of labor and birth.

4.3 Describe the emotional and relationship changes that occur throughout pregnancy and in the transition to parenthood.

4.4 Explain the options birthing parents have today.

4.5 Identify the issues associated with unexpected outcomes, including infertility, birth defects, and pregnancy loss.

After four years of marriage, my husband and I were in a place in our lives where we decided it was time to start a family. A year and a half later, I was nowhere near being pregnant. So began the journey for answers and help in becoming parents as we began infertility testing and treatment.

At first it was difficult, the not knowing. During this time of trying, hoping, and praying, many friends around me began to start their families, too. And with each phone call to tell me of their pregnancies, I found myself there again, trying to hold back my sadness and tears as I congratulated them on their happiness. ... Why me?

A year of testing and treatment began for us. Then month after month, the hope of becoming pregnant started to fade. And with each failed attempt to get pregnant with all the technology and medical assistance, I again could not stop the tears. ... Why me?

But at some point, after living with an exhausted heart for so long, a shift in our thoughts began. What is it you want? What is it you really want? The answer: To become PARENTS. Then we realized that for us, the way to become parents was not through pregnancy, but through adoption. HOPE! So began the second leg of our journey, our journey to *make a family*.

Many months went by as we went through the process of getting on the adoption list … selecting an agency, doing the home study, and preparing our home for that someone. And then came *The Wait*.

Two and a half years go by, and then one October morning it happened—The CALL! "You have a son!" For years I question, "Why me?" But then suddenly I knew why … Our son was always supposed to be ours, but we just had to wait on him to get here. And oh, he was so worth the wait!

Pregnancy always intrigued me, and newborns always took me captive. So it did not come as a surprise to anyone who knew me when I became a childbirth educator and a **doula**—a professional provider of labor support (emotional, physical, and informational) to women and their companions. Many years and countless births later, I am still intrigued with the mystery of how a single cell zygote is knit together in the secrecy of the mother's womb into a 10-trillion-celled person.

The birth of a baby is life-altering. Each time a child is born, or added to a family through adoption or fostering, a family is born as well. People can grow their families in a number of ways, as you learned in Chapter 1. In this chapter, we begin our study of becoming parents by taking a look at being pregnant, pregnancy, and childbirth. We then explore the emotional and relationship challenges and changes many birth parents experience. We'll conclude our discussion by looking at the difficult topics of unexpected pregnancy outcomes, pregnancy loss, and stillbirth. As you begin your study about the intriguing aspects of prenatal development, it's important to keep at the forefront of your thinking that, while there are some things that parents cannot control during pregnancy (such as the genetic influences), there are many lifestyle choices and behaviors they can adopt prenatally that positively influence their baby's development.

BEING PREGNANT

Just as with other events associated with family and parenting life, pregnancy and childbirth are processes that change over time, and the experiences encompass a number of sequential stages (conception, pregnancy, childbirth, and caring for the baby). In this section, we'll explore the processes of fertilization and conception, and we'll examine the physical and emotional changes that take place throughout pregnancy.

To begin our study of pregnancy and childbirth, we first need to understand that the term "parent" means different things to different people. To some, parent may mean to be a mother or a father, while to others, the term is defined as to give life or raise children. Traditionally, pregnancy and childbirth have been discussed from a **heteronormative** perspective, the belief that *heterosexuality* is the norm. The heteronormative paradigm asserts that a **gender binary** exists—that there are two opposite and distinct genders, male *or* female. In most societies, sex, sexual orientation, gender, and sexuality align with the binary archetype (Farmer & Byrd, 2015; Hill & Willoughby, 2005). So, when discussing pregnancy and childbirth, more often than not the person giving birth is referred to as the "woman" or the "mom," while the birth partner is referred to as the "dad."

When working with parents, it's important to approach pregnancy and childbirth from a *nonheteronormative*, inclusive perspective.

Source: Chichicko, Wikimedia Commons.

Nonheteronormative refers to individuals who do not adhere to the heteronormative gender binary expectation (Hahn et al., 2019). In the discussion that follows, we adopt a nonheteronormative pregnancy and birth paradigm to include sexual and gender minorities as a part of the norm. *Transgender men and nonbinary people (TGNB)* who have a functioning vagina, ovaries, and uterus are capable of becoming pregnant, carrying a pregnancy to term, and giving birth; thus, pregnancy is possible for transgender men and queers, and pregnancy and birth typically progress the same as the experiences of cisgender women (Berger et al., 2015; Hahn et al., 2019; Hudak, 2019; Light et al., 2018; Obedin-Maliver & Makadon, 2016; Reis, 2020). TGNB who give birth can choose if they want to be referred to as mom, dad, or parent.

To be inclusive of all pregnant and childbearing individuals, here we use the term *gestational parent* to refer to the pregnant person. **Gestation** is the process of carrying human life in the womb; the **gestational parent** is the individual who is carrying and birthing life. Let's now turn our attention to exploring the physical and emotional changes associated with pregnancy. Unless otherwise noted, all discussions related to the physiological changes associated with pregnancy are supported by the science of Elaine Marieb and Katja Hoehn, Mount Royal University (2019).

How We Reproduce

The dynamic process of human life begins with the union of the sperm (provided by the biological male) and an ovum (provided by the biological female). Fertilization of the ovum is a complex process that involves a delicate balance of sex hormones, excellent timing, and a little bit of luck.

Fertilization

During sexual intercourse, millions of mature sperm are ejaculated into the vagina. In the subsequent 24 to 72 hours, sperm begin their remarkable journey through the cervix, through the uterus, and into each of the fallopian tubes. Only about 200 of the original 100 million-plus sperm reach the ovum, which is usually located in the upper third of the fallopian tube after it is released from the ovary during the process of ovulation.

Once the sperm reach the mature ovum, they connect themselves to its outer layer. As this occurs, the egg has a series of contractions that pull the sperm into it. Once a sperm penetrates the egg, **fertilization** has occurred. The outer layer of the egg hardens, making it impossible for another sperm to enter it. The product of fertilization is the single cell *zygote*.

Conception

There are three phases of prenatal development: The germinal period, the embryonic period, and the fetal period. The **germinal period** (weeks 0 through 2 of pregnancy) begins with the fusion of the sperm and the ovum in the fallopian tube and ends after the **conceptus** (the fertilized ovum) has successfully implanted in the blood- and nutrient-rich lining of the uterus; this is **conception**. As the zygote undergoes cellular changes, it makes its way through the fallopian tube to the uterus. This five- to seven-inch journey takes approximately 10 to 14 days, during which time the zygote develops into a ball of cells, known as the **blastocyst**. Once the blastocyst reaches the uterus, it implants in the endometrium, the lining that was prepared to nourish the product of fertilization. Implantation signifies that conception has occurred. The **embryonic period** occurs weeks 3 through 8, and the **fetal period** comprises weeks 9 through 40.

The Changes Through Pregnancy

From the moment the egg is fertilized, throughout the approximate 260 to 280 days of pregnancy, a gestational parent's body is in a continuous state of change and growth. The changes are so dramatic that an obstetrician colleague of mine once noted, "The pregnant body is so different, and the physical demands with which it manages are so complex that being pregnant almost constitutes a third sex" (Welch, 2004). Although everyone recognizes the enlarged, expanded abdomen of childbearing, other physiological changes take place that are not visible or as obvious.

The *uterus* is a pear-shaped organ that houses the fetus; fetus is a Latin term that means "young one." During pregnancy, muscle fibers of the uterus become thicker and lengthen to accommodate the growing fetus, and it becomes capable of holding 500 to 1,000 times the volume of its nonpregnant state. The ligaments that support the weight of the uterus stretch, causing much of the discomfort associated with pregnancy.

The *placenta* and the *umbilical cord* are the life-support systems between the fetus and the pregnancy carrier. Typically attached to the upper portion of pregnant person's uterus, the placenta weighs about two pounds by the time the baby has reached full term. The placenta provides critical functions, such as transporting oxygen between the pregnant parent and baby, and passing the birth parent's immunities to the baby (Welch, 2004).

With the exception of the parent's blood and the baby's blood (which never mix), oxygen and nutrients travel back and forth between the gestational parent and the baby via the umbilical cord. About three feet long, the cord is composed of two arteries and one vein; the arteries are longer than the vein, which causes the cord to twist (Welch, 2004). The two arteries carry the blood from the baby to the placenta, which rids it of carbon dioxide and other waste products and provides oxygen, returning the blood back to the baby. The cord is without nerves, so there is no pain caused for either the pregnancy carrier or the baby when the cord is cut.

Inside the uterus, the *amniotic sac* is a tough membrane that holds the fetus, placenta, umbilical cord, and amniotic fluid (the "water" surrounding the baby in the uterus). About the thickness of the skin between the thumb and forefinger (Welch, 2004), the membrane often ruptures or tears, either initiating labor or occurring after labor has begun. This is referred to as the birth person's "water breaking." The amniotic fluid is composed of the baby's urine, amniotic cells, secretions from the baby's lungs, and the baby's sloughed-off skin cells (Welch, 2004). Replaced every three to four hours, the baby swallows the fluid and excretes it as urine, and it is this process that sustains the volume of amniotic fluid.

Over the course of approximately nine months, many changes take place physically and emotionally within the gestational parent; if this parent is in a relationship, relationship changes also take place with the partner. In the following section, we'll study the changes in the gestational parent and the baby.

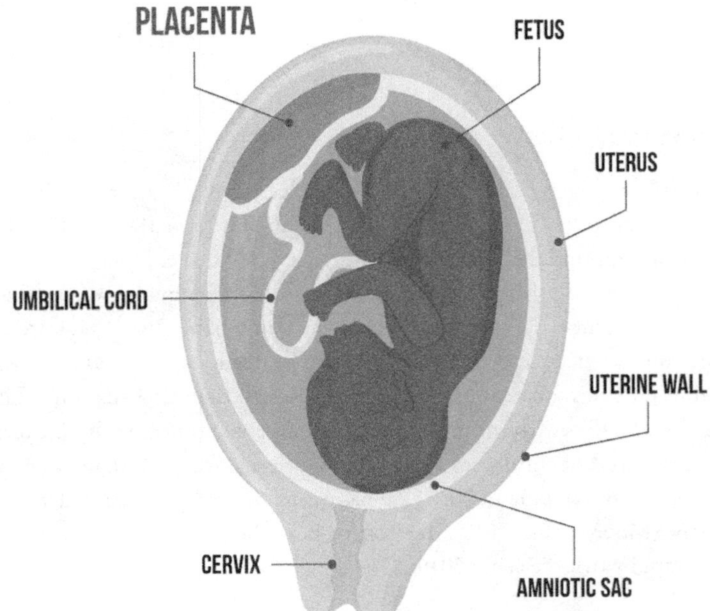

The uterus houses and protects the growing baby. The placenta and umbilical cord are the baby's life-support system, transferring oxygen and nutrition, and carrying away wastes, such as carbon dioxide.

Source: istock.com/Anastasiia Krasavina.

PREGNANCY AND BIRTH

The **first trimester** covers the first 12 weeks of pregnancy, the **second trimester** covers weeks 13 through 26, and the **third trimester** covers weeks 27 through 40. A pregnancy that is carried from 37 to 40 weeks is considered **full term**; any baby born before the 37th week of pregnancy is considered **preterm** and may be prone to respiratory and other difficulties. Throughout each trimester, both the gestational parent and the growing baby undergo specific week-by-week changes. For our purposes in our study of parenting, we discuss the growth and development taking place in the baby, and the implications of this period of development across the lifespan.

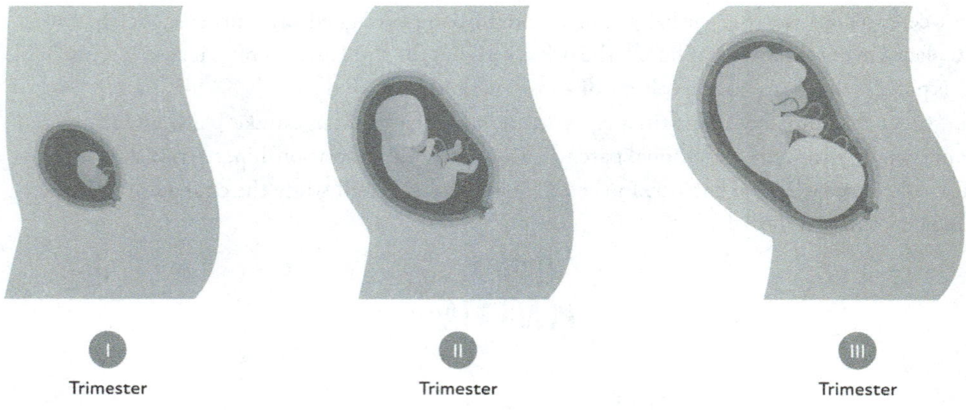

The developing person.

Source: iStock.com/AnastasiaUsenko.

The First Trimester (0–12 Weeks)

The first trimester of pregnancy is characterized by rapid cell multiplication and differentiation, and growth of the conceptus. The genetically programmed differentiation of all anatomical structures is completed around the 12th week of pregnancy (Marieb & Hoehn, 2019). Although we certainly can't control everything in our environments, there are many things parents can do to create a safe environment—the womb—for the developing baby. **Teratogens** are substances (such as over the counter medications, alcohol, vaping, or cigarettes) or environmental factors (such as lead paint, tainted water, or gestational parent stress) that can cause prenatal damage, leading to **congenital birth defects**, or those anomalies present at birth (we discuss birth defects a bit later in this chapter). The third week through about the eighth or ninth weeks of pregnancy is the **critical period of development**, when the baby's organs and physical structures undergo rapid development (Moore et al., 2019). Teratogens pose the most risk to the structures that develop the most rapidly (Moore et al., 2019).

The Critical Period of Development

Figure 4.1 illustrates the critical and sensitive periods of development; the weeks of gestation are presented across the top of the illustration. As you can see, the bar denotes *the critical period*

FIGURE 4.1 ■ Critical Periods in Human Development

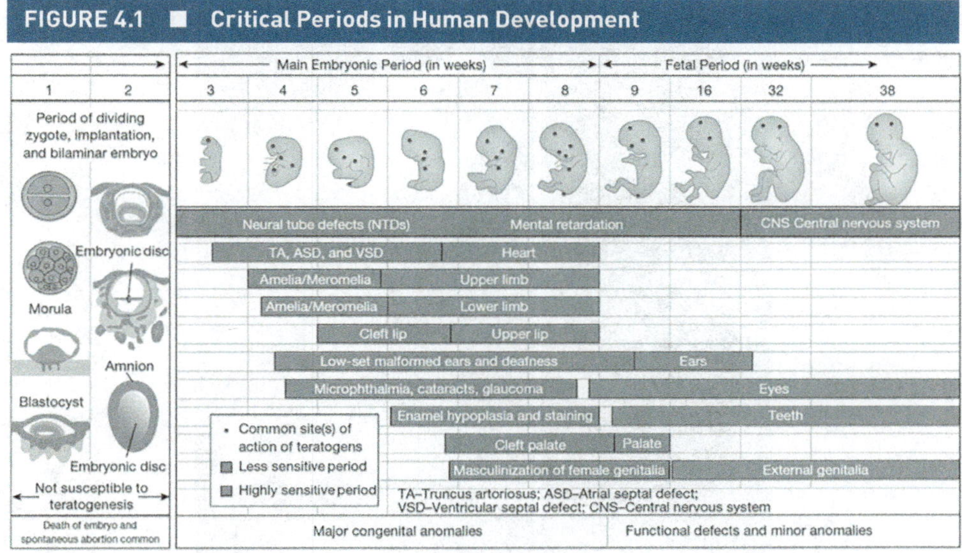

Source: Levine. (2021). *Child development* (4th ed.). SAGE. Originally adapted from Moore et al. (2019).

where, if encountered, the teratogen has its greatest impact. For example, the baby's central nervous system (the brain and spinal cord) undergoes its most significant development weeks 3 through 16 of pregnancy. If a pregnant person consumes alcohol (a teratogen) during this period in pregnancy, it is likely that the development of the central nervous system will be negatively affected. After the critical period, other weeks are the *sensitive period* of development. If the baby is exposed to a teratogen, there may still be a negative impact on the developing baby, but the effect may not be as severe as during the critical period (Moore et al., 2019). It is of the utmost importance, then, that pregnant parents (and their partners) accept their responsibility of making health and lifestyle choices that are beneficial to the optimal growth and development of their children.

Typically, during weeks 1 and 2 of pregnancy, the conceptus is not at risk to teratogens—exposure to a substance is survived by the zygote (Marieb & Hoehn, 2019). Major anatomical defects and minor anatomical structural abnormalities that can occur throughout pregnancy include the following impacts:

Week 3: The heart begins beating at day 21; the heart and central nervous system are highly susceptible to teratogens.

Week 4: Eyes, ears, arms, and legs are forming from the 4th to about the 8th weeks of pregnancy.

Week 6: The teeth and palate (the roof of the mouth) develop until early week 9.

Week 7: The external genitalia are most impacted from the middle of week 7 until the end of week 9.

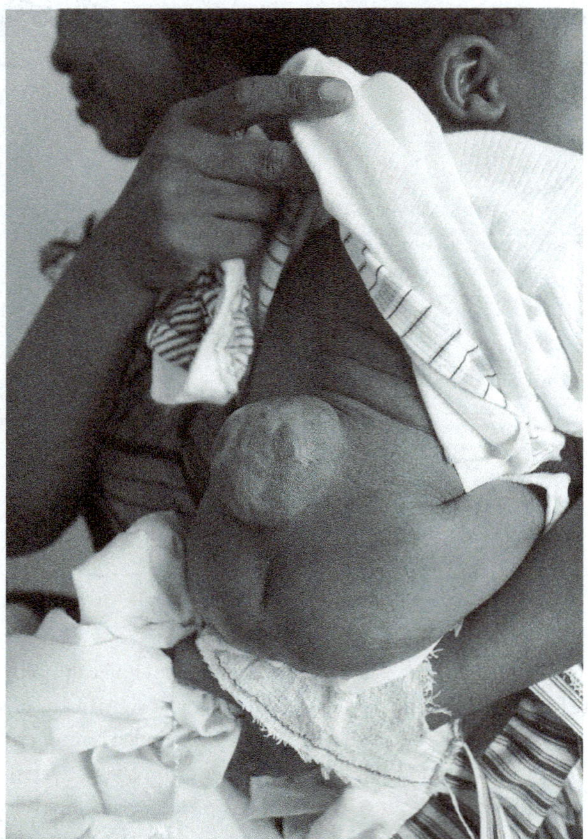

Spina bifida is a *neural tube defect* that occurs during pregnancy. Gestational parents can greatly reduce the risk of this birth defect by regularly taking a prenatal vitamin that contains folic acid.

Source: BSIP via Getty Images.

The central nervous system and primitive brain development begin during the third week of prenatal development, and they are significantly influenced in structure and function by the gestational parent's nutrition and other wellness factors. For example, if the pregnant parent routinely takes a prenatal vitamin that contains *folic acid*, birth defects of the brain and spinal cord are reduced by more than 70 percent (Mayo Clinic, 2020a). **Neural tube defects (NTDs)** occur when the spinal cord fails to develop properly during pregnancy, and the associated defects include (March of Dimes, 2020):

- **Spina bifida**: The spine, or backbone, is the protective cage that encases the spinal cord. Spina bifida, referred to as "open spine," happens when the bones in the spine or the spinal cord do not close correctly; this leaves an opening in the back, and usually occurs at about day 28 of pregnancy. Spina bifida causes many health issues for the baby, including bowel and/or bladder problems, intellectual disabilities, paralysis, muscle weakness, or joint pain. About 1,645 babies are born with spina bifida each year in the United States; Latinx gestational parents are more likely to have a baby with NTDs than white or African American are (March of Dimes, 2020).

- **Hydrocephalus**: In this condition, there is a buildup of fluid inside of the developing baby's brain; it is sometimes referred to as "water on the brain." Typically, brain fluid drains away from the brain down through the spine, but if there is an NTD, the fluid is prevented from draining properly. The fluid causes pressure on the child's brain and can result in developmental and learning disabilities, intellectual disabilities, and slowed growth. In the United States, hydrocephalus occurs about 1 in 4,000 births (March of Dimes, 2020).
- **Anencephaly**: This serious birth defect results in the baby having missing parts of its brain and/or skull. It occurs when the upper part of the neural tube does not fuse closed all the way. About 1 in every 4,600 babies in the United States are born with this defect (March of Dimes, 2020).

Prenatal Brain Development

Brain development becomes quite rapid from the ninth week of pregnancy until birth, generating as many as 250,000 brains cell per minute, and the baby's brain nearly doubles in size between the 16th and 28th weeks of pregnancy (Tierney & Nelson, 2009). As you can see, the rapid development and proliferation of cells makes the fetus especially vulnerable to toxic exposures, particularly its brain. Lead paint, for example, can alter the connections in the prenatal brain, causing the brain to develop abnormal signaling and communication networks (Tierney & Nelson, 2009).

The importance of the proliferation of brain cells during the prenatal period cannot be overstated because brain development during this part of the lifespan lays the foundation for the child's future cognitive capabilities and learning (Tierney & Nelson, 2009). In Chapter 5, we will discuss how these brain cells further mature and begin the process of *synaptogenesis*, the process of brain cells connecting to one another.

The more developed the unborn baby's brain becomes, the more its behaviors will change in the womb (Moore et al., 2019). For example, as the brain develops and matures, the communication between brain cells develops and the baby becomes capable of coordinating physical movements; rolling from side to side is added to its movements, and the baby will begin to suck its thumb. As the baby's brain matures, its hearing becomes more fully developed and the baby is able to recognize familiar sounds. Driven largely by input from the environment, the baby's brain continues to grow in an explosive way during the first two years of life.

The Second Trimester (13–27 Weeks)

The second trimester begins in the fourth month of pregnancy or at about 13 weeks. The growth of the fetus causes the gestational parent's uterus to expand, giving the appearance of being pregnant. Although the fetus has been moving for quite some time, the gestational parent has not yet felt the movements because of the fetus' size. Fetal movement, referred to as **quickening**, is most often felt around the 20th week of pregnancy (Marieb & Hoehn, 2019). By about the end of the fourth month of pregnancy, the larger fetus makes its presence known by jabbing, poking, kicking, stretching, and hiccupping. The fetus also begins to develop hair and eyebrows, and on its body appears a soft, downy hair called **lanugo**. The fetus begins to suck and swallow. If born now, it is unlikely the baby will survive. During the fifth month, the baby begins to respond to the birthing parent's voice, and its lungs begin to develop a smooth coating that allows the air sacs in the lungs to inflate. The baby is about 9 inches long and weighs about 1.5 pounds; fat begins to accumulate under the baby's skin.

By the sixth month of pregnancy, the fetus is about 12 to 14 inches long and weighs about 2 pounds. The skeleton begins to harden, and toenails and fingernails are visible. The skin is covered with a white, waxy coating called **vernix**. This coating provides a lubricant for the baby's skin and will slough off as the baby approaches the 37th week of pregnancy. If the baby is born before the 24th week of pregnancy, the chances of survival are slim. Although some babies do survive, there is a strong possibility that development will be impaired or delayed.

The Third Trimester (28–40 Weeks)

The third trimester begins in the seventh month of pregnancy. This is characteristically the period of the most rapid fetal growth. During the seventh month, the baby continues to develop fatty tissue under its skin, and at a length of about 16 inches, it weighs close to 3 pounds. If born now, the baby has a chance at survival, although it is unlikely that a baby would be able to maintain an adequate oxygen supply or body temperature on its own. Babies born before the 36th week typically lack enough of the smooth coating of the lungs that allow them to freely expand and fill with air. If the gestational parent enters into labor prematurely, every effort will be made by the healthcare team to stop labor (this is done through various medications). Every day that can be added to life inside the womb increases the baby's chances of survival and allows the respiratory system to develop more fully.

At 32 weeks, the baby is about 17 inches long and weighs about 4 pounds. By about week 36, the baby will gain one to two pounds per week, and at full term will weigh 6 to 10 pounds (or more!), and reach a length of 20 to 23 inches. By the eighth month, the baby's eyes, which have been sealed closed early in the pregnancy, are now open. Its living quarters are becoming too cramped for sweeping movements or side-to-side rolls, but its jabs, pokes, and kicks continue to reassure the birth parent that the baby is okay. The fine, downy hair on the baby's skin begins to slough off, as does the vernix.

After 260 to 280 days, the once single-celled zygote has matured into a 10-trillion-celled baby and has developed sufficiently to survive outside the confines of the pregnant parent's protective womb. By the end of pregnancy, breathing becomes increasingly difficult for the gestational parent—the expanding uterus interferes with the movement of the diaphragm, and lung function changes because of hormonal influences. With a 25 to 40-pound weight gain and the demands of the growing baby, increasing fatigue is common. The weight of the growing uterus and the added weight of the baby cause pressure on the birth parent's bladder, resulting in frequent trips to the bathroom. Physiological changes take place in the ligaments that support the uterus in preparation for labor and birth, which causes achiness in the pelvic area. **Braxton-Hicks contractions**, often referred to as *practice contractions*, result when the uterus begins to contract and relax. They are often a precursor to labor and birth.

LABOR AND BIRTH

Several theories exist that explain what may trigger the onset of **labor**, the rhythmic uterine contractions that help expel the baby, but no one knows for certain why a gestational parent enters labor. Does the fetus somehow transmit a hormonal signal that it is ready for birth? Does the placenta emit a signal that it can no longer sustain the growing baby? Does the birth parent's pituitary gland play the central role? What medical science does tell us is that the body produces chemicals called **prostaglandins** (usually at the end of pregnancy) that aid in the softening of the cervix (Marieb & Hoehn, 2019). Although the exact reason may remain a mystery in medical science, a birth parent's body does provide clues that birth is approaching.

Understanding Labor

The questions students always have is, "How will I know when labor is really real?" and "How do you know when to head to the hospital or the birth center?" The simple answer is this: With true labor (labor that's going to get the job done and the baby here), the uterine contractions always become *longer, stronger,* and *closer together*; with "false" or practice labor, the frequency and intensity of the contractions don't noticeably change. Labor is divided into four stages, and each stage has one or more phases (see Welch, 2011).

Stage 1: Labor. The cervix **effaces** (becomes thinner) and it **dilates** (opens). Before a gestational parent can begin to push, the cervix must dilate to 10 centimeters, or about 4 inches. Typically about the thickness of the space between your eyebrows, and about as firm as the tip of your nose, the cervix thins to about the thickness of the small piece of skin between your thumb and forefinger; by the time the baby is born, the cervix is as soft as the inside of your cheek. Stage 1 is divided into three phases (Welch, 2011):

- **Phase 1: Early (Pre) Labor (0–3 centimeters).** *Pre-labor* is often referred to as early labor and is commonly not only the longest phase of labor, but the easiest phase, as well. During this phase, the gestational parent may be happy and chatty, excited and fearful. Relaxation and rest are key. During this phase, labor contractions are about 5 to 15 minutes apart and last about 20 to 40 seconds. For a first-time birth parent, pre-labor can last up to a few days prior to the coordination of the uterine contractions. Once contractions become more regular, this phase lasts anywhere from 6 to 10 hours.

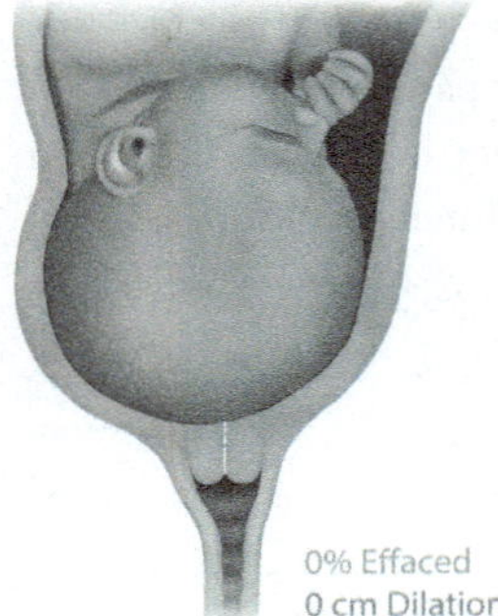

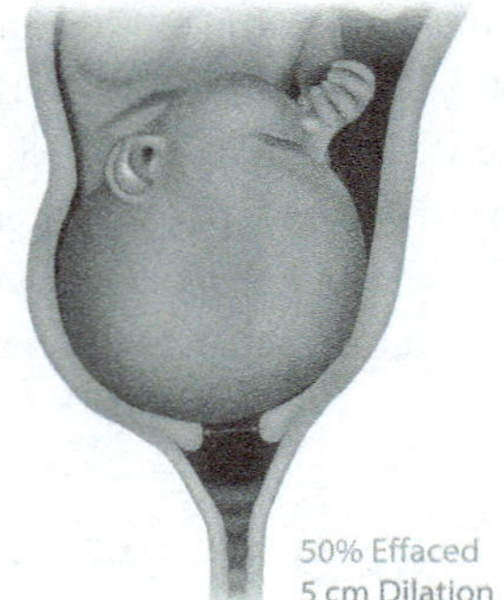

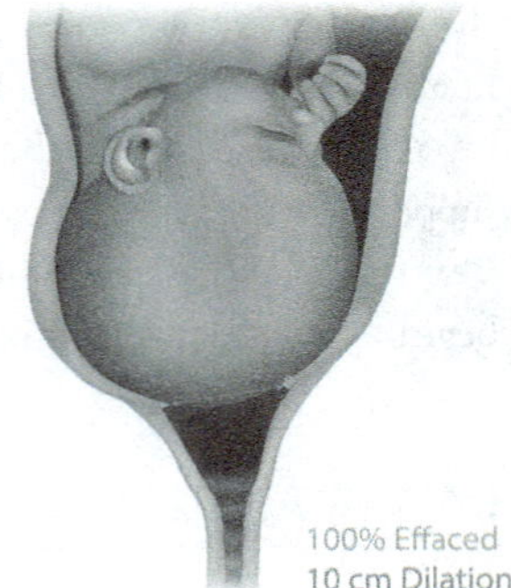

Phase 1: *Early (Pre) labor* is typically the longest and easiest phase of labor and birth, lasting about 6 to 10 hours in first-time childbearers. The cervix dilates 0 to 3 cm.
Source: iStock.com/Sakurra.

- **Phase 2: Active Labor (4–7 centimeters).** *Active labor* is characteristically the most difficult and challenging part of labor—not just because of the intensity of pain but because of the emotional commitment required for labor and birth. During this phase, the laboring parent becomes very serious and draws inward to focus on the tasks at hand. The parent is less talkative, selectively attentive, and has more difficulty comprehending conversation (partly because more and more oxygen is being sent away from the brain to meet the demands of the uterus and the baby). Labor contractions intensify, occurring 3 to 4 minutes apart and lasting for a minute at a time. As the cervix continues to thin out, the baby continues to descend further into the pelvic cavity, causing more pressure on the birth parent's back. The laboring parent may have more difficulty relaxing and may request pain medications. Active labor lasts from 2 to 5 hours.
- **Phase 3: Transition (8–10 centimeters).** With contractions about every 2 minutes and lasting from 60 to 90 seconds, *transition* presents the most physically and emotionally challenging phase of childbearing. The birthing person becomes irritable, hypersensitive, and emotionally overwrought. Needs may change quite suddenly. Many laboring people feel out of control during transition and need tremendous emotional and physical support from their birth partner. As the person labors, focus continues to turn inward and because of the intensity of concentration required to manage the contractions, the laboring parent becomes unaware of the surroundings and conversations. The descent of the baby causes the birthing parent to feel a strong, irresistible urge to bear down. Many laboring parents experience uncontrollable shaking of their legs and become flushed and sleepy. The good news is that this phase only lasts from about 5 to 25 contractions.

In early labor, the uterus is as hard as the tip of your nose; in active labor, it becomes as hard as your chin; by transition, the uterus feels as hard as your forehead. Stage 1 is complete when a gestational parent is dilated to 10 centimeters, and at this time, the birth parent begins to push.

Stage 2: Pushing and Delivery. Although the journey through the vagina is only about 5 inches, it may take a first-time gestational parent approximately two hours to push the baby out. During a uterine contraction, as the laboring parent bears down, the force of the contraction holds the baby down, helping the perineum to stretch (this force is what causes the burning sensation when pushing). As the intensity of the contraction lessens, the baby retreats upward. Because of this, pushing is somewhat of a one-step-forward-two-steps-backward process. Once pushing efforts become coordinated, most gestational parents feel as though they are now active participants in the birth, rather than engaging in act of passive surrender to the contractions (Welch, 2011). When the baby's head *crowns*, or is visible, the baby will no longer retract after a contraction. The second stage of labor ends with the delivery of the baby.

Stage 3: Delivery of the Placenta. The birth of the placenta usually occurs within 5 to 30 minutes after the delivery of the baby. Immediately after the baby's birth, the placenta begins to separate from the uterine wall. Some healthcare providers allow the placenta to deliver on its own timetable; however, in the United States, it is common for some physicians to tug on the umbilical cord to expedite the process. To aid expulsion of the placenta (and to help minimize the risk of postpartum bleeding), birth parents are encouraged to breastfeed as soon as possible. If a gestational parent chooses not to breastfeed, or is incapable of breastfeeding (such as in the case of some trans men who had surgery to remove their breasts), a medication is given intravenously that causes the uterus to contract.

Stage 4: Recovery. This stage is probably the least mentioned process of labor and birth, but by no means less important. The stage encompasses the first 2 to 3 hours after birth through the first 24 months after labor and delivery. Because of the tremendous fluctuations that a gestational parent's hormones undergo during the nine months of pregnancy, labor, and birth, it takes time for the body to return to its prepregnancy status. During this time, the birth parent may experience **postpartum depression** due to hormonal fluctuations after giving birth, which may include a loss of appetite, crying, feelings of helplessness and hopelessness, inability to sleep, or fear of going near the baby. Any or all of these symptoms signify the immediate need to contact the healthcare provider.

Although the hours of labor and birth are challenging, many couples experience great closeness and intimacy as they work together to bring their child into the world.

PARTNER RELATIONSHIPS DURING PREGNANCY

Just as with other events associated with parenting, pregnancy and childbirth are processes that change over time, and the experiences encompass a number of sequential stages (conception, pregnancy, childbirth, and caring for the baby). These emotional and physical changes in the gestational parent are associated with changes in couple well-being and relationship satisfaction (Cowan & Cowan, 2000).

In the sections that follow, we'll explore the common emotional changes that occur during pregnancy, and how these changes affect a couple's relationship. We'll also look at the early days of transitioning to parenthood and the difficulties that incorporating another member into the family system brings. Having realistic expectations when you are about to become a parent can make the transition to parenthood much smoother because there's a lot to consider—and to worry about—when expecting a baby.

For example, having a baby and raising it to the age of 18 is a costly endeavor! Table 4.1 shows the estimated annual costs of raising a child. The data are based on a survey by the U.S.

TABLE 4.1 ■ The Cost of Raising a Child to the Age of 18: 2019

	Housing	Food	Transport	Clothing	Health	Child Care/ Education	Misc.	Total
Dual-parent Up to $59,410 annual income	53,820	31,050	24,630	11,130	14,070	23,640	10,740	**169,080**
Dual-parent Up to $102,870 annual income	70,560	37,620	33,900	13,500	18,990	41,100	19,230	**234,900**
Dual-parent Over $102,870 annual income	127,800	47,640	49,500	19,080	21,810	88,440	35,400	**389,670**
Single-parent Up to $40,410 annual income	51,120	33,090	17,850	7,080	12840	22,980	12,450	**157,410**
Single-parent Over $59,410 annual income	105,840	48,390	40,140	10,830	22,410	72,910	33,000	**333,420**

Source: U.S. Department of Agriculture (2019).

Department of Agriculture (2019) and show costs based on a family with two children, on a per-child basis. These figures do not include any estimates for sending a child to college, or any costs associated with a child who lives in the home after the age of 18 (which, as you have learned, is common today in America). Each baby brought into a family system (through birth or adoption) is anywhere from a 100-thousand-dollar to a quarter of a million-dollar investment. As soon as pregnancy is confirmed or the adoption is finalized, parents should sit down together and work out a *realistic* budget—from pregnancy clothes, baby gear, the baby's nursery, and medical costs associated with having a baby, to perhaps going from two incomes to one—it all adds up quickly! Talking about these anticipated changes early on helps parents better manage their finances, and it also helps reduce conflicts that arise because of money issues.

Aside from the money concerns, couples have other things they must negotiate as they start their journeys to become parents. As you saw earlier, gestational parents experience physical changes, and these changes affect the couple's relationship. Emotional changes are also common during pregnancy.

Pregnancy: Emotional and Relationship Changes

The birth of a child is a demanding couple and family life situation, and the transition to parenthood is a very difficult adjustment for most couples (Parfitt & Ayers, 2014;

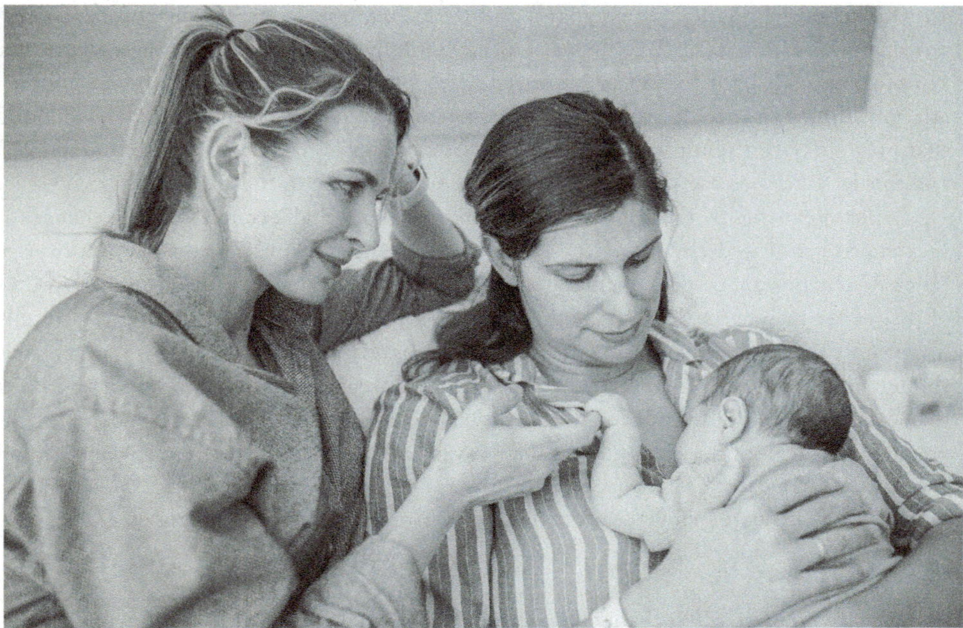

Decades of research shows that the transition to parenthood is difficult for most parents. This is thought to be due to the systemic nature of family life—adding a person to the family system introduces many challenges.

Source: iStock.com/svetkid.

Salmela-Aro et al., 2006). What follows are the emotional and relationship changes associated with the stages in pregnancy.

The First Three Months

Due mostly to the hormonal changes that occur in pregnancy, in the early weeks, a pregnant person's emotions are often unstable, resulting in mood swings, and it is not uncommon for the gestational parent to feel depressed. Even if the pregnancy was planned and hoped for, the pregnant person may cry—often for no apparent reason. Frequently, these emotional changes are unsettling for the partner, wife, or husband, and the partner may feel inadequate or incapable of meeting the pregnant partner's needs. It is not uncommon for both partners to be concerned about the family's finances, and the additional costs associated with rearing a child.

To date, no studies examine the emotional and relationship challenges of pregnant trans men or queers; for this reason, when discussing these studies, the birth parent will be referred to as "her" or "she" because the studies explored the experiences of pregnant and postpartum biological women. Studies that explore couple relationships during pregnancy are rare, but in one study, the researcher found that couple relationships are more stable than unstable during pregnancy, despite the hormonal changes that take place in the pregnant person (Richardson, 1981). The researcher found that, overall, women rate their relationships with their partners as more satisfactory than unsatisfactory during pregnancy. Other studies have shown that women are particularly sensitive to their partner's negative attitude/mood while they are pregnant, and these emotions from men may cause depressive symptoms in women (Buehlman et al., 1992; Notarius et al., 1989); these depressive symptoms are thought to lead to increased levels of conflict and jealousy in the couple's relationship (Massar & Buunk, 2019; Salmela-Aro et al., 2006). Other studies have found that pregnancy can result in decreased levels of closeness and communication in couples, and this leads to increased conflict between the two (Florsheim et al., 2003).

Human sexuality is reactive to our daily circumstances, and a couple's sex life changes as they encounter altered circumstances (Welch, 2011). And, certainly, pregnancy is a time of "altered" circumstances! Couples are often concerned that having sex during the early weeks of pregnancy may harm the baby or the gestational parent, but these concerns are typically unwarranted. Unless the physician or midwife indicates otherwise, sexual activity is permissible throughout pregnancy. However, both the gestational parent and the partner should remember that, because of the early changes associated with pregnancy (such as breast tenderness), the pregnant partner may not be in the mood for any kind of touch. Couples need to keep in mind that the pregnant parent is not rejecting the *partner*—just the *thought of/act of sex* (Welch, 2011). It's best for a partner to follow the pregnant partner's lead about sex throughout pregnancy.

The Next Three Months

The second trimester brings changes in the gestational parent's emotions, too. Most gestational parents understand that weight gain is a normal and necessary part of pregnancy, but some individuals—particularly those who struggle with eating disorders—may become dismayed at their ever-increasing weight. Some pregnant persons may feel overwhelmed with the responsibilities of parenting or frustrated because their expanding abdomen prevents them from performing job tasks; some may even find that pregnancy interferes with educational or career plans. Worries about finances may affect decisions regarding if and when to return to work after the baby's birth, and, in turn, may affect the couple's relationship. While many pregnant people feel attractive and sexy during pregnancy, some feel awkward and unappealing. Most, however, indicate this as a time of great sexual pleasure (Welch, 2011). A lot of partners worry that they will "hit" the baby during sexual intercourse, but this concern is unwarranted. The baby is way out of reach, tucked securely in the uterus. Some positions can be uncomfortable, though, so couples often have to get creative in finding sexual positions, such as side-lying positions. The key to sexuality in pregnancy is the same as during any other point in a couple's communication—open and honest communication. It's also important the couple continues to nurture their relationship by going out on dates together or having special nights at home with no interruptions from family and friends. The best parents are parents who make their relationship a priority and foster intimacy.

The Last Three Months

Coupled with the physiological changes that occur as the big day nears are multiple relational and emotional changes. By the ninth month, many gestational parents feel overwhelmed and, quite frankly, tired of being pregnant! Many pregnant people (and their partners) may lose interest in sex, not only because of exhaustion but also because finding a comfortable sexual position is at times an exercise of futility and hilarity. With baby showers being given for the parents-to-be and final preparations being made in anticipation of bringing the baby home, fears, anxieties, and worries about labor and birth become very real and very intense for birthing parents and their partners. Some may worry that they will not be able to tolerate the pain or that they will appear foolish, and the birth partners may worry that they will not be able to meet their partner's physical and emotional needs during the birth process. It is not uncommon for birth partners to worry that the expectant parent will turn to someone else for support; they worry that they will be inadequate. Sometimes a gestational parent may feel that the baby is taking over their entire being. Sometimes a birth partner feels that the parent-to-be is no longer interested in them, him, or her—that the gestational parent will turn all attention to the baby. Financial worries may escalate during this time, as well.

The Transition to Parenthood: Pregnancy and Postpartum Relationship Quality

The transition to parenthood is difficult for most people. In the past, researchers have concentrated on the *individual* factors that may lead to conflict in relationships during pregnancy and have ignored the importance of the *relational dynamics* of relationship dissatisfaction and symptoms of depression (Salmela-Aro et al., 2006). Thus, results of such studies concluded that the changes in the couple's relationship following pregnancy and during the transition to parenthood were due to such things as a gestational parent's depressed mood, rather than due to the systems nature of their relationship (for example, see Campbell et al., 1992).

To illustrate the importance of examining the couple's relationship, and not just the individual, researchers from Finland studied the experiences of 320 women and their partners through pregnancy and into the early months of parenthood (Salmela-Aro et al., 2006). They discovered that, in those couples who reported high levels of conflict, the struggles and disagreements that were present during the transition to becoming parents were already a part of the couple's relationship. In other words, depressive symptoms and marital satisfaction during pregnancy were common to the couple's relationship during pregnancy—these characteristics didn't suddenly appear as the couple became parents, as earlier studies suggested.

The researchers also found a decrease in marital satisfaction during the transition to parenthood among couples who reported high levels of marital satisfaction during early pregnancy. The investigators speculated that this is because pre-pregnancy "happy" couples have taken time to nurture their relationships, and that as pregnancy/parenting demands increase over time, their attention shifts from their relationship to the baby.

Other research that examined 293 Dutch couples explored relationship quality during pregnancy and the early months of pregnancy (Kluwer & Johnson, 2007). Based on the assumption that adding a new member to the family system is accompanied by drastic and dramatic changes in a couple's relationship, this study looked at conflict frequency during pregnancy. This study found:

- More frequent conflict during pregnancy was related to lower levels of relationship quality across the transition to parenthood.

- Lower levels of relationship quality during pregnancy were linked with more conflict during pregnancy.
- Frequent conflict is likely to determine declines in relationship quality during the early months of parenthood.

These findings are very important to our understanding of parenting life because they show us that couples' relationship discord and distress stemmed from problems that *existed during pregnancy*, not necessarily because of the *transition to parenthood*. It may very well be that the first childbirth isn't what elicits troubles, but instead, that the troubles have always been there and are just highlighted once the baby arrives. Some couples may be more vulnerable to a difficult transition to parenthood than others (Kluwer & Johnson, 2007).

Finally, other evidence suggests that couples who do not live together, who are unhappy with their partner, or who perceive their relationship to be a negative one, experience increased anxiety and depression during pregnancy and the early months of parenting (Figueiredo et al., 2008). All of the empirical findings are important, for they suggest that *both* members of the couple need to be supported during pregnancy in order to prevent or decrease the stressors associated with the transition to parenting.

Sexual and Relationship Satisfaction After Childbirth

As a childbirth educator and sexuality professor, one of the most common questions I am asked by my students in this unit is: "How soon after childbirth can we have sex?" According to the American College of Obstetrics and Gynecology (ACOG), couples are encouraged to wait for six weeks before resuming intercourse (2019). This waiting period allows the birth parent's body to heal after birth and labor experiences. Primarily, it is important to wait because it gives time for the vaginal area to heal, and time for the cervix to close and regain its barrier to infection. A general rule of thumb is to wait to resume sexual intercourse until after the initial postpartum checkup; at this point, couples can also discuss birth control options available to them. Nevertheless, most couples resume sexual activity when they feel comfortable doing so. One study indicates that while most couples resume sexual activity within six weeks of delivery, women may not experience an orgasm until about three months after delivery (Connolly et al., 2005). Another body of research confirmed that if both partners enjoy a rich sex life throughout pregnancy, they tend to evaluate their levels of tenderness and communication higher in the first six months after delivery (von Sydow, 1999).

Generally, couples' sex lives undergo change after they become parents. In particular, sexual desire appears to be lower for the birthing parent than it is for partners in the first year after giving birth (Ahlborg et al., 2000, 2005). Apart from lower sexual desire, there are also physical changes in the experiences of sex after childbirth. A study that examined 480 postpartum women found among new mothers that more than 50 percent experienced pain during first intercourse after delivery; this pain continued somewhat for six months (Barrett et al., 2000). Another examined more than 500 women and their partners to evaluate which factors determined sexual activity and sexual relationship satisfaction one year after a first birth (Brummen et al., 2006). By three months after the birth of their babies, more than 80 percent of couples had had sex; by one year after birth, about 94 percent had. The most significant finding was that there was a predictive factor for no sexual intercourse one year following birth: Women who were not sexually active when they were three months pregnant had an 11 times higher chance of not being sexually active one year after giving birth (Brummen et al., 2006).

These changes, in turn, cause stress and tension between the couple and compound the transition to assume the new roles of parents. If new parents are able to communicate openly about their sexual desires and the stressors associated with becoming parents, and if they confirm each other emotionally and sexually, they experience better adjustment (Ahlborg et al., 2000, 2005). Indeed, an investigation of 820 postpartum couples found that, by the time the babies were about six months old, most of the parents indicated that they were "very happy" in their relationships (Ahlborg et al., 2005). Factors contributing to their relationship happiness were a strong social support network and having someone to provide relief so the couple could spend some time away from the baby. Among those who indicated that they were unhappy, factors included economic problems, having a partner who was away from home too much (which led to less emotional and physical intimacy), and frustration with the partner's lack of help or sharing responsibility.

FROM PARTNERS TO PARENTS

When a new baby or child joins a couple, thus creating a new family system, all of the couple's established ways of interacting and relating, their patterns of behavior, and their marital/relationship and gender roles have to be adjusted to accommodate the addition to the family system. Whether it's baby number one or baby number seven, transitioning to life with the new family member presents challenges.

Most new parents expect a period of transition after the birth of a baby, but they tend to underestimate the demands and changes that accompany parenting. While the adjustment to parenthood is considered by most people as a life event filled with delight and happiness (Hansen, 2012), scientific study reveals otherwise (Meeussen & Van Laar, 2018). Part of new parents' disillusionment comes from the unrealistic beliefs stemming from cultural myths that paint an idyllic, cozy picture of parenting (Gilliam & Coleman, 1981; Harwood et al., 2007); instead, parents learn all too quickly that parenting is exhausting (Roskam et al., 2017). Another prominent myth in contemporary Western culture is that new mothers are capable of doing it all, of being a superwoman (Lazarus & Rossouw, 2015; Staneva & Wittkowski, 2013), but when these expectations confront reality, some feel overwhelmed and unprepared to effectively parent (Lazarus & Rossouw, 2015).

While there are special, tender, and precious times when parenting seems pleasant and tranquil, there are more times that dispel these myths, such as when the baby cries through the night, fusses all day, or won't stop crying no matter the myriad ways the exasperated parent tries to soothe and comfort the infant. There is always something to attend to. And it is the new parents' responsibility to learn how to care for, respond to, nurture, and love the baby.

Simultaneously, parents still have to figure out who they are in their new roles and who their partner is in their new family system. No longer is the couple simply a couple—they are also a mother or a father and all that goes along with this redefined, multifaceted position. Suddenly, the parent becomes a child development specialist, behavior expert, communications director, therapist, financial wizard/estate planner, nurse, head of safety and health administration, dispute and arbitration authority, labor boss, teacher, sex educator, spiritual advisor, and zoo keeper/funeral director/grief counselor (to date, my family has buried two dogs, three cats, three hamsters, one bunny, one squirrel, and about 100 goldfish; there is still a gerbil on the loose somewhere in the house).

To understand the transition and stressors associated with bringing a baby or a child into the family, we need to recall our study of Family Systems theory from Chapter 3. Remember that the family can be likened to a mobile—any time we add or take away a member from the mobile (the family system), an imbalance is temporarily created (see Figure 4.2). This imbalance

FIGURE 4.2 ■ Revisiting Virginia Satir's Mobile from Chapter 3

Source: iStock.

is felt and experienced as stress and conflict. Even though bringing home a new baby or adopting a child is a joyous occasion for most couples, the happy nature of the event doesn't minimize the fact that a new subsystem has been added to the family system, calling for a shifting of family roles, family balance, and family boundaries; all of these factors are what account for the stressful transition when baby makes three (or four, or five, or...).

The Changes Associated With Parenthood

In general, research has looked at the transition to parenthood in two different ways. In the first, new parents are seen as making an abrupt shift that results in persistent change, and this transition to parenthood is thought to cause negative changes in a couple's relationship processes (Lawrence et al., 2008). The second predominant perspective views the transition to parenthood as a significant—yet temporary—stage in a couple's relationship and family development. According to this paradigm, the changes associated with new parenting roles are anticipated, short-lived, small in magnitude, normative changes, and different couple types adapt to these challenges in varying ways (Lawrence et al., 2008).

Over many years, research into the changes associated with parenthood, be it through birth, adoption, or the formation of stepfamilies, has centered on four primary areas (for a comprehensive review, see Ceballo et al., 2004):

1. **Psychological well-being:** Among biological parents, the transition to parenthood has been associated with increased levels of depression for both mothers and fathers, and these in turn affect marital satisfaction. Because of the stressors associated with adopting a child (such as the drawn-out adoption process and perhaps prolonged periods of infertility), the transition to parenthood for adoptive parents is typically associated with overall positive quality of life and high marital satisfaction. Among stepfamilies who are gaining a stepchild, the transition to stepparenthood has been associated with increased levels of depression.
2. **Marital quality:** Following the birth of a child, marital relationships are often characterized by negative interactions, declines in marital satisfaction and sexual intimacy, increased levels of conflict, and drops in leisure time spent as a couple. Most research, however, indicates that these declines persist for only about one year, and that they are modest. In a majority of the studies, parents indicated that the rewards of parenting outweighed the initial negative experiences. Adoptive parents may experience these same declines, but to a lesser extent than biological parents do; creating a stepfamily with children creates a difficult transition for most couples.
3. **Family relations and social support:** For some families, the birth of a child enhances family relationships, and oftentimes relatives help new parents adjust to their roles of mother and father by providing practical and emotional support; some parents experience higher levels of depression and distress if their extended family does not offer such support. Among adoptive parents, studies to date show that the emotional

and practical support from family members exceeded their expectations, and this support was related to positive family experiences.

4. **Roles:** After the birth or adoption of a child, roles significantly change for mothers and fathers. Some research suggests that adults indicate that the "parent" role is greater than the "partner" role. Among some, the "worker" role remains stable, but others report sharp declines in that role and relate more to the "mother" role.

As you can see, for several decades parent educators and family practitioners have characterized the transition to parenthood as a challenging, and often difficult, lifecourse stage where couples are faced with unanticipated realities of limited time, energy, and resources. But as research shows us, if prospective parents hold realistic expectations going into parenting, becoming parents is less stressful to them and to their relationship (Harwood et al., 2007). Of course, just when parents believe they have figured out the ins and outs of parenting, the child passes into a new phase of growth and development (with its own uncharted territory) or another baby is added to the family.

Co-parenting

How parents negotiate their childrearing beliefs and share in everyday parenting responsibilities is referred to as *co-parenting*; in essence, it is the support parents provide to one another in the raising of their children (Gable et al., 1994). Joint parenting is important to children's well-being because it creates a home environment that fosters their growth and development. Although most research concentrates on heterosexual parents who are married or divorced, co-parenting also applies to others who are jointly raising children, such as grandparents and LGBTQ+ parents.

Co-parenting can best be thought of as an alliance between parents (Gable et al., 1994). It is a significant component of parenthood because partners can turn to one another for support when they are faced with the stressors and demands of raising children. In a very real way, co-parenting is an extension of the couple's relationship, and it is just as important a process in family living as is communication, love, intimacy, or sex. That's not to say that co-parenting is easy to achieve, however. When a new baby or a child arrives on the scene, partners have to find ways to expand their interactions to include the new addition—but at the same time, they have to set limits on these interactions so as to maintain a healthy couple relationship. In other words, they have to remember that their role as a couple is just as important (if not more so) as their roles of parents. This is sometimes easier said than done! In general, there are three types of co-parenting: supportive, unsupportive, and mixed (Belsky, 1990). There is a wide range in ways in which parents work to raise their children:

Supportive co-parenting: Parents directly or indirectly agree with each other by promoting the same general message to the child (such as sticking to the agreed-on curfew and not changing it without consent of the other parent). It also occurs when one parent directly asks the other for assistance with an issue that involves the child (such as helping with discipline).

Unsupportive co-parenting: This occurs when one parent subtly—or not so subtly—undermines the other parent's efforts (such as changing curfew without consulting with the other parent). It also takes place when one parent interrupts the interactions of the other parent and child (such as following a divorce), when one parent is openly critical of the other's parenting styles or parenting activity, or when a parent ignores the other parent's request for assistance with a child's needs.

Mixed co-parenting: In this type of co-parenting, one or both parents' responses are mixed—sometimes they support one another, sometimes they don't.

Co-parenting strategies are important to a child's overall development and well-being because they provide predictability and stability in family rules, practices, and discipline for children. For example, numerous studies have linked positive co-parenting to children's emotional well-being and academic success (among many others, Latham et al., 2018; Lunkenheimer et al., 2017; Parkes et al., 2019).

Supportive co-parenting has also been associated with older children's well-developed self-regulatory abilities (Cowan & Pape Cowan, 2019). Although many of the studies of co-parenting in the United States have focused on white, middle-class samples, research on urban Chinese families and Japanese families has demonstrated that both parents' involvement in daily, meaningful caregiving was linked to academic success and greater child empathy (McHale et al., 2000; Ogata & Miyashita, 2000); when parents have conflict in their co-parenting, children are more likely to act out and to display anxious behaviors (Becher et al., 2019; Gibler et al., 2018).

Despite what family and social scientists currently understand about co-parenting, much still needs to be learned about the relationship between effective and ineffective shared parenting and its impact on children. There are also other factors that have been found to be strong predictors of children's overall well-being: parenting styles. We explore parenting styles at length in the next chapter.

It is indisputable that the manner in which parents interact with and guide their children influences their development in more ways than are immediately visible (such as behavior and school performance). Children's abilities to love, to be loved by another, to feel secure and accepted, and to form attachment bonds with others—the very bonds that will later allow children to enter into love relationships of their own—are also shaped by their parents.

UNEXPECTED OUTCOMES

During each of my four pregnancies, I experienced the common fears and worries about the health and well-being of my babies. I went through all of the "what ifs" I could possibly think of, yet there were admittedly some things I dared not think about, such as delivering an unhealthy, physically impaired or physically challenged baby, or even the death of the baby. Many couples experience unexpected outcomes when they are unable to become pregnant, such as the voice of the woman in the opening vignette of this chapter. For most couples, the process of fertilization and conception works as it is supposed to. But for other couples, becoming pregnant represents grueling work and becomes a difficult and heart-wrenching challenge.

When Conception Fails: Infertility

In the United States today, approximately 6 million women, or about 10 percent of women aged 15 to 44, have an impaired ability to become pregnant (CDC, 2019). **Sterility** refers to the absolute inability to reproduce, either because the gestational parent has no uterus or ovaries, or the male has no testes or sperm production. No amount of medical intervention can help a sterile person reproduce. **Infertility** is the inability to conceive a baby after trying for a period of one year. Infertile women are also those who have no difficulties conceiving but are unable to sustain the pregnancy.

Women and Infertility

Approximately one-third of the problems associated with infertility are due to women's reproductive systems (American Society of Reproductive Medicine, 2019). Specifically, problems with the monthly release of an ovum from the ovary (ovulation) are responsible for most female infertility. Lack of ovulation may be due to hormonal imbalances, which refers to a decline in or an absence of the hormones estrogen and progesterone, which are necessary for pregnancy. Other causes of infertility may be a pituitary gland tumor (quite rare), or lifestyle habits such as poor nutrition (as in the case of anorexia or bulimia), stress, or even intense athletic training (U.S. Department of Health and Human Services, 2003). Once a gestational parent reaches the age of 35, the ovaries' ability to produce eggs diminishes.

Even when women successfully ovulate, the fertilized ovum may have difficulty reaching the uterus due to blocked or scarred fallopian tubes. This disorder, known as **pelvic inflammatory disease (PID),** is primarily caused by untreated sexually transmitted infections. PID renders one-in-ten women per year infertile, making it the leading cause of infertility in young women (ACOG, 2019). Endometriosis may also prevent the fertilized ovum from traveling through the fallopian tube to the uterus or may prevent the fertilized ovum from becoming embedded in the uterine lining.

Men and Infertility

About one-third of fertility difficulties are due to male reproductive problems (U.S. Department of Health and Human Services, 2019). Healthy, robust sperm are necessary in order for fertilization of the ovum to take place. There are two primary forms of infertility in men: **azoospermia**, which means that no sperm cells are produced; and **oligospermia**, which means that few sperm cells are produced. Sometimes, these conditions are the result of a genetic disease, such as cystic fibrosis, and sometimes, they are the result of poor reproductive health. To produce an adequate number (at least 20 million sperm per milliliter of semen), the male must be healthy and lead a healthy lifestyle.

The American Society of Reproductive Medicine (ASRM) is an internationally recognized nonprofit medical organization that disseminates information, education, and standards in the field of reproductive health. According to the ASRM (2019), to improve fertility, men should consult with a physician about the proper vitamins and minerals that improve sperm function. In addition, men should limit alcohol intake and stop smoking, as alcohol lowers testosterone levels and smoking may cause the production of malformed, slow-moving sperm. Finally, men should keep their cool. For healthy sperm production, the testes must be cooler than the rest of the body—this is why nature designed the male's testicles to hang outside of the body. Males considering parenthood may want to avoid hot tubs, saunas, steam rooms, very hot baths, and placing laptop computers on their laps. And yes, men should wear boxers instead of briefs.

Treating Infertility

There are a variety of treatment options available, ranging from medication (fertility drugs to enhance ovulation) to surgery. Less invasive medical treatments include fertility drugs and donor insemination, often referred to as **artificial insemination**. In biological women, fertility drugs increase egg production. When fertility drugs are used, sometimes more than one egg is produced, leading to multiple births. Artificial insemination, a popular fertility treatment used by both heterosexual and LGBTQ+ couples, is the medical process in which donor sperm is placed into the gestational parent's vagina, cervix, or uterus by a syringe. Sperm are collected (through masturbation of the donor) and stored by medical facilities called **sperm banks**, and sperm can be donated by someone known to a prospective parent or can be donated anonymously. Compensation varies, but someone who donates twice per month can earn about $1,500 a month; a vial of sperm from a sperm bank costs anywhere from $150 to $3,000 (Mayo Clinic, 2019). If these treatment options fail, there are other more invasive (and more costly) treatment options. Today, people have available to them various routes of **Assisted Reproductive Technology (ART)**, which are treatments that involve fertilization through the hands-on manipulation of ova and the sperm. To date, 17 states in the United States require that health insurance companies cover these medical procedures (although the extent of coverage varies state to state). Although it is not clear, some states offer infertility insurance coverage, but it is not a state mandate that they do so.

- For infertile couples in which a person has blocked or absent fallopian tubes, or where a biological man has a low sperm count, **in vitro fertilization (IVF)** is typically used to help the couple conceive. IVF is a process whereby a gestational parent's eggs are surgically removed from the ovary and mixed with sperm in a laboratory culture dish. After about 40 hours in the culture dish, the eggs are examined to see if they were fertilized, and if they were, to see if cell division is taking place. If the balls of cells appear to be growing at a normal rate, the fertilized eggs (embryos) are placed within the uterus. This process bypasses the fallopian tubes. The average cost of IVF is $12,400 per attempt (Penn Medicine, 2019).
- **Gamete intrafallopian transfer (GIFT)** involves manually manipulating the sperm and eggs, but instead of fertilizing the eggs in a dish, the unfertilized eggs and the sperm are placed in the gestational parent's fallopian tubes. This is designed to foster natural fertilization within the birth parent's fallopian tubes. The average cost of GIFT is about $10,000 to $15,000 per attempt (ASRM, 2019).

- In **zygote intrafallopian transfer (ZIFT)**, the sperm fertilizes the gestational parent's eggs in a laboratory. The fertilized eggs are placed immediately in the fallopian tubes, rather than in the uterus (as in IVF), allowing the conceptus to travel naturally to the uterus and implant. The average cost of ZIFT is $10,000 per attempt (ASRM, 2019).

Surrogacy is an option when people may desire to have a biological child, but for medical or other reasons (as in the case of gay men or trans individuals who have undergone sex confirmation surgery), they may not be able to do so. IVF is performed, but the embryos are implanted into a surrogate mother who carries the pregnancy to term—the surrogate is the baby's biological mother. Upon birth, the baby is given to the biological parents. In some instances, a surrogate mother is artificially inseminated with the father's sperm. She carries the baby through delivery and gives the baby to the biological father and his partner to raise. Since 1987, there have been 1 million babies born in the United States as a result of ART (Penn Medicine, 2019).

Traditionally, gay men have experienced barriers to becoming fathers, but with the increase of society's acceptance of gay parenting, and with the legal changes that have granted gay men the option of fatherhood, more gay men are turning to surrogacy as an option to becoming a parent (Berkowitz, 2013; Gato et al., 2016). According to some bodies of research, gay men prefer surrogacy over adoption or fostering because it allows for genetic fatherhood; gay couples prefer surrogacy because it allows for the genetic expression of at least one of the partners (Berkowitz, 2013; Blake et al., 2017; Goldberg & Scheib, 2015; Golombok & others, 2018). IVF and surrogacy are the most common route of biological parenthood for gay men in the United States (Perkins et al., 2016). Although every case is different and unique, the cost of surrogacy ranges from $90,000 to $130,000 in the United States; India, Thailand, Russia, and Mexico only allow surrogacy to heterosexual parents.

According to the American Society for Reproductive Medicine (ASRM, 2015), only one-fourth (24 percent) of the ART needs in the United States are being met, and this involuntary childlessness as the result of infertility profoundly impacts the physical, social, economic, and psychological well-being of women and men. The Society's ethics committee believes that the creation of a family is a basic human right, and the lack of insurance coverage for infertility—which creates treatment gaps among underserved populations—creates racial, ethnic, geographic, and economic disparities in childbearing (2015).

The Psychological Impact of Infertility

Infertility is often distressing, frustrating, and depressing. Hoping, longing, and wishing month after month after month for a positive pregnancy test only to find out that the efforts failed again constitutes a real-life crisis for couples. The stress on finances and on the marriage or partnership can lead to a breakdown of the couple's relationship. Fortunately, many support groups and infertility counseling organizations exist to help infertile women and couples navigate through the physical and emotional challenges infertility brings. Groups such as the National Infertility Association and the International Council on Infertility Information Dissemination offer psychological, psychosocial, and informational support for those experiencing infertility.

The Physically Challenged Baby

Although we all long for a healthy baby, not all of us will have the perfect baby. Birth defects and anomalies can range from barely noticeable to life-threatening to fatal. No matter how severe the defect, parents of infants with birth defects and physically challenged babies mourn the loss of the healthy child they imagined they'd deliver.

As you learned earlier, a *birth defect* is a physical anomaly that is present at birth; it may be inherited, or it may be the result of environmental influences during pregnancy and/or birth (March of Dimes, 2020). Major birth defects can have serious effects on a child's health and development and may impact the functional ability of the child (CDC, 2019). Today, one in every 33 babies—about 3 percent of all babies—born in the United States have a birth defect (CDC, 2019). These defects account for 20 percent of infant deaths and are the leading cause of deaths in infants. Birth defects include (CDC, 2019):

- Brain/spine: 2,600 per year
- Eye: 751 per year
- Heart: 16,282 per year
- Mouth/face: 6,253 per year
- Stomach/intestine: 2,706 per year
- Muscle/bone: 17,723 per year
- Chromosome (genetic): 7,286 per year

At the Parents Encouraging Parents Conference, Roger and Ann Figard (1992), personal communication, presented the *Loss and Grief Cycle* (see Figure 4.3) that parents of physically challenged babies experience. As you can see, parents don't experience the loss just one time, such as when discovering the baby has a birth defect. Rather, the loss is experienced at various ages and stages of the child's development, throughout the child's life. In Chapter 12, we'll explore children with exceptionalities, and the processes associated with parenting these children.

Fetal Alcohol Spectrum Disorders

Fetal alcohol spectrum disorders (FASDs) is an umbrella term that includes a group of anatomical and intellectual conditions that affect a developing baby in the womb when a gestational parent drinks alcohol during pregnancy. FASDs are the leading cause of preventable birth defects in the United States (CDC, 2020a) and occur because alcohol in the mother's blood passes to the baby through the placenta and the umbilical cord. The alcohol is a toxic teratogen and causes lifelong damage to the developing baby's brain, organs, limbs, and facial features (Society for the Study of Addiction, 2019). Fetal alcohol syndrome (FAS) was first understood in 1973 when physicians noted a specific cluster of birth defects in infants, and since that time,

FIGURE 4.3 ■ Loss and Grief Cycle for Parents of Physically Challenged Children

When parents lose a child to death, or when they have a baby born with birth defects, they experience a cycle of grief and loss.

Pregnancy In pregnancy, the unknowns about the baby encourage a parent to hope and dream and fantasize about what the baby will be like.

The Fantasized, Hoped-For Child Often, the parents develop an idea or mental picture of the perfect child-to-be. This can include the sex of the child, talents, or other characteristics important to the parents.

Birth of a Challenged Child The parent is faced with the reality that the hoped-for child and the real child are not the same child.

Ideational Object Loss Unconsciously, the parent's mind recognizes the death of the dream of the hoped-for child and this moves the parent into a cycle of grief . . . letting go of the hoped-for child and accepting the real child.

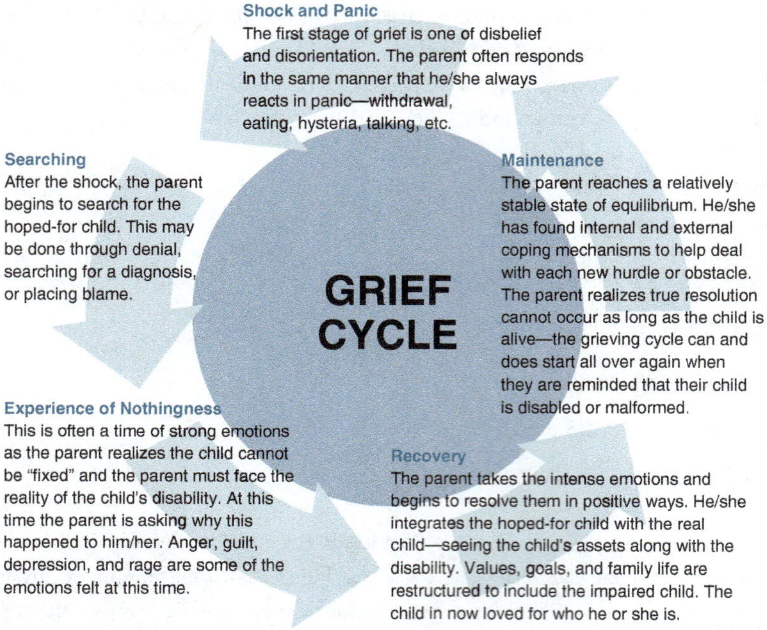

Source: Ann Figard and Roger Figard (1992, personal communication).

copious research studies have confirmed that exposure to alcohol in the womb causes adverse developmental impacts on the baby (Williams & Smith, 2015).

FASDs are permanent, disabling physiological and intellectual conditions that affect children of every racial, ethnic, and socioeconomic status group, both in this country and across the world. In the United States, it is estimated that 1 in 13 embryos/fetuses exposed to *any* level of alcohol will develop FASD, and globally, 630,000 are born with the disorder each year (Society for the Study of Addiction, 2019). There are four FASD diagnoses. Physicians determine what type of FASD a child has based on the child's physiological anomalies and symptoms (CDC, 2020b):

- **Fetal Alcohol Syndrome (FAS)**: This is the most serious of the FASD conditions. *Physical defects* include distinctive facial features, such as small, wide-set eyes, a very thin upper lip, and no dent in the skin between the nose and upper lip; defects in the joints, arms, legs, and fingers; vision and/or hearing difficulties; heart defects and defects in the kidneys; small head and brain size; and slow physical growth. *Brain and nervous system difficulties* include problems with memory, attention span, communicating with others, learning disorders, delayed cognitive development, and intellectual disability. Some FAS children also have difficulties identifying consequences of choices and problem-solving, and establishing and maintaining relationships.

- **Alcohol-Related Neurodevelopmental Disorder (ARND)**: People with ARND do not typically have the physical defects seen in FAS, but they do experience difficulties in their cognitive functioning, such as with learning. They often do poorly in school, have problems concentrating and staying on task, and have intellectual disabilities. Poor impulse control is commonly experienced by those with ARND. In essence, ARND affects children's cognitive and socioemotional development.
- **Alcohol-Related Birth Defects (ARBD)**: Children with ARBD primarily experience defects of the internal organs, such as the heart and kidneys. They may also experience defects in their skeleton or with their hearing.
- **Neurobehavioral Disorder Associated with Prenatal Alcohol Exposure (ND-PAE)**: For children to receive this diagnosis, the gestational parent's alcohol consumption is surveyed. The birth parent had to have consumed 13 or more alcoholic drinks per month of pregnancy, or more than two alcoholic drinks at one time (CDC, 2020a). This condition causes problems for children in three distinct areas:

    1. *Thinking/memory*: The child may have problems planning and keeping due dates for assignments straight, remembering to bring school work home for homework or forget to bring homework or assignments to school; the child may also forget what has already been learned.
    2. *Behavior problems*: These are manifest in severe tantrums or episodes of rage, irritability, mood swings (sometimes drastic), and anger when asked to shift from one task to another.
    3. *Life skills*: Children struggle with day-to-day life skills, such as bathing, brushing teeth, dressing, making the bed, and getting along with others.

Perhaps the greatest tragedy of FASDs is that they *do not need to happen*. Students consistently ask, how much alcohol is safe? The answer is simple:

- *There is no safe amount of alcohol when a gestational parent is trying to get pregnant.*
- *There is no safe amount of alcohol when pregnant.*
- *There is no safe time to drink alcohol during pregnancy.*

As you think about your fertility and whether you desire to have children someday, it is of the utmost importance that you adopt a healthy lifestyle *now*—a lifestyle that assures optimal development of your child.

GIVING BIRTH: TYPES OF BIRTH SETTINGS

Where we give birth and who cares for us during pregnancy, labor, and delivery significantly affects the overall birth experience. Today, there are a number of birth setting options available. Gestational parents and their partners are encouraged to seek a provider that offers consistent, safe, and effective care, and to select an environment that enhances individual wishes for birth experiences (Welch, 2011). Care providers and birth settings should provide abundant support, comfort, and information.

In 2018, nearly 3.8 million people gave birth in the United States (CDC, 2020c). The ACOG asserts that medically supervised births in a hospital or accredited birth center are the safest options for both the gestational parent and the baby (ACOG, 2019). Nearly 98 percent of expectant parents in the United States deliver their babies in a clinical setting (MacDorman & Declercq, 2019). The infant mortality rate supports this claim: In 1900, when the majority of childbirths occurred in the home, 100 babies died for every 1,000 born; today, about six babies die for every 1,000 born (CDC, 2020c). Even so, nearly 2 percent of gestational parents and their partners opt to have their babies at home (MacDorman & Declercq, 2019). In the sections that follow, we'll discuss contemporary birth settings in the United States.

Hospital Births

The most common setting in the United States, hospital births are typically supervised by obstetric nurses or midwives, and/or physicians (OB/GYN or family physician). Interventions, such as IV for hydration, fetal monitoring, episiotomy, bed confinement during labor and birth, and limited food intake may be used routinely. Today, hospital rooms often resemble comfortable bedrooms or birth centers—but this does not mean that the *hospital birth model* (often referred to as the *medical birth model*) supports an intervention-free birth. Hospital birthing models vary widely, however, and pregnant people and their partners are encouraged to choose a hospital that best suits their needs and wishes. Hospital birth settings are best for high-risk pregnancies or newborns who are at risk for developing complications. If the baby is healthy and the birth was without complications, most gestational parents and their babies leave the hospital within 48 hours following birth.

Birthing Center

Free-standing birthing centers are not widely available in the United States. These facilities are not within a hospital and are typically not associated with a hospital. Prenatal care and care throughout labor and birth are usually provided by a nurse midwife; often, there is a physician available if complications arise. Care is reflective of the *midwifery model*, which adheres to the belief that birth is a natural, physiological process. Continuous physical, emotional, and informational support is provided throughout labor and birth. Medical interventions, such as IV fluids, constant fetal monitoring, and episiotomies are not routinely used. Women are encouraged to listen to their bodies, to move freely, to use a number of labor and birth positions, and to eat if they feel hungry. However, birth centers are not equipped to provide certain types of pain management. If an emergency arises, ambulance transport to a hospital is required. If all is well, parents and their babies are typically discharged within 12 hours of birth.

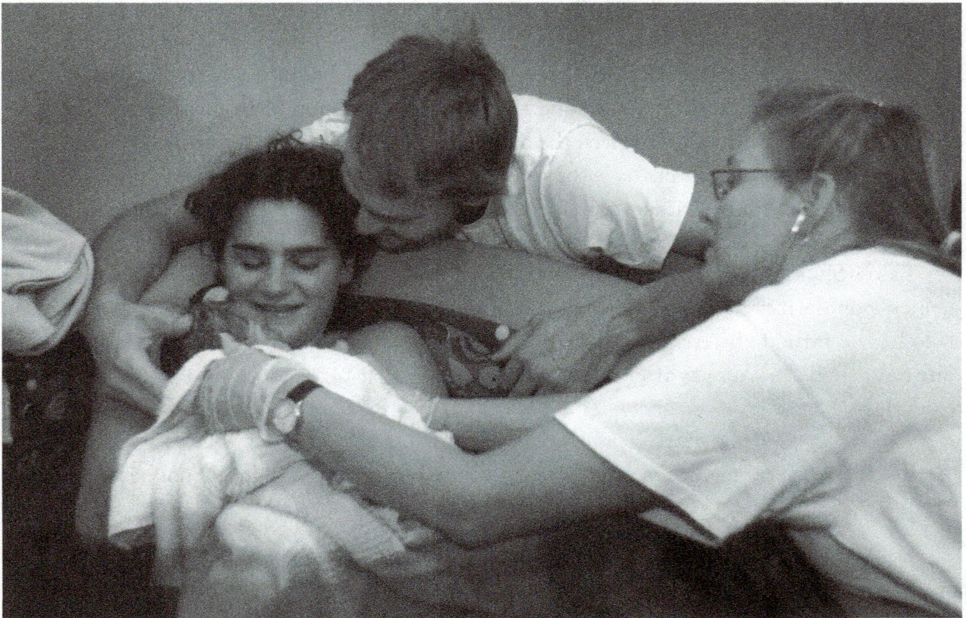

Free-standing birthing centers are not widely available in the United States. These facilities are not within a hospital and typically are not associated with a hospital. Prenatal care and care throughout labor and birth are provided by nurse midwives; if a complication arises, there is a physician available. Care is reflective of the *midwifery model*, which adheres to the belief that birth is a natural process that proceeds best without intervention. Continuous physical, emotional, and informational support is provided.

Source: Star Tribune via Getty Images.

Home Births

Home births are quite similar to birthing center births, except, as the name implies, parents choose to give birth in their home. Individuals and couples who choose this birth setting often do so because of the individualized, personal birth experience. As with birth centers, home births do not provide pain medication options; if there is an emergency, transport to a hospital is necessary.

Where individual couples give birth is an intimately personal decision, and expectant parents are encouraged to fully research all of their options and choose the birth setting that most closely aligns with their beliefs and birth experience expectations. A new trend is sweeping the Unites States, *freebirthing*.

Freebirthing: Freedom of Choice? or Dangerous Consequences?

As you can see, there are a number of birth setting options in the United States, but **freebirthing**, or **unassisted childbirth (UC)**, refers to the process of intentionally giving birth (typically in the home) without the guidance of a midwife, physician, or other medical professional. Freebirth is also referred to as *DIY (do-it-yourself) birth, unhindered birth*, and *couple's birth*. Many parents-to-be also forgo prenatal care. It is difficult to ascertain the numbers of those who freebirth because many of these individuals and couples choose to live "off grid." It is estimated that about 1 percent of homebirths are intentional freebirths (Wells, 2019).

Those who opt for freebirth often adhere to the beliefs that birth is a natural function of the human body, not a medical one, and that women have given birth for thousands of years without medical assistance. But given the possibility of complications with any labor and delivery, should gestational parents have the right to give birth (and potentially risk the health and well-being of the infant) without medical assistance? As with many other issues in the human service and family science discipline, the evidence is conflicting.

Laura Shanley, MD, is the author of the book, *Unassisted Childbirth* (2016), and has helped popularize the freebirthing underground movement in Western cultures. Shanley, who has no formal obstetrics training, gave birth to five of her children at home, unassisted; one baby died a few hours after birth. Shanley notes that births options are a pregnant person's right, because:

- Birth is not a medical condition or a medical emergency and should not be treated as such.
- Most common medical interventions (such as IV or an epidural for pain relief) cause more harm than good and often result in unnecessary C-sections.
- Birth parents have the right to experience the intuitive, natural progression of their individual birth and the right to give birth in an undisturbed, natural setting.
- Birth is an intimate, sexual, and orgasmic experience; privacy is of the utmost important to allow the erotic dimensions of birth.
- Freebirth increases the gestational parent's ability to bond with the newborn because it is the parents' responsibility to take full care of the baby and ensure its welfare.

Because of the increase in the number of unassisted childbirths and the growth of this underground movement, several national medical societies have issued strong statements opposing the practice, indicating that unassisted childbirth is courting danger (Society of Obstetricians and Gynaecologists of Canada, 2007). To date, the Society of Obstetricians and Gynaecologists of Canada (SGOC), the ACOG, the Royal Australian and New Zealand College of Obstetricians and Gynaecologists, the Royal College of Midwives, and the American College of Nurse-Midwives urge pregnant parents to avoid freebirth because of the risks associated with the practice:

- UC is linked to substantially higher rates of maternal and neonatal deaths.
- When a complication occurs during childbearing (such as the sudden decrease of available oxygen to the baby or cardiac problems in the birth parent), death of the person giving birth or fetus can occur within a matter of minutes without the expertise of trained medical professionals.

In the United States and the United Kingdom, those who engage in unassisted childbirth may face legal repercussions; if something happens to the parent who gave birth or the baby in a planned freebirth, the gestational parent, partner, family members, or friends may face criminal charges. In some instances, social services or Child Protective Services become involved because of the perceived disregard for the baby's safety.

PREGNANCY LOSS

Most pregnancies proceed without many complications. Even when complications do occur, Western medical science provides pregnant people with treatment for nearly every complication related to pregnancy. Complications can range from skin rashes to excessive vomiting, to high blood pressure, to anemia, to vaginal bleeding or cramping, and to the loss of the pregnancy.

Miscarriage

The most common loss in the first month of pregnancy is miscarriage. Any loss of a fetus or embryo before the 20th week of pregnancy (the fourth month of pregnancy) is termed a **spontaneous abortion** or **miscarriage** (Merck Manual, 2020). *Early miscarriage* occurs with the loss of a fetus before the 12th week of pregnancy, and *late miscarriage* occurs with the loss of a fetus between the 12th and 20th weeks of pregnancy. Approximately one-fourth to one-third of pregnant people experience some type of bleeding or cramping during the first 20 weeks of pregnancy; of those, about half of the pregnancies result in pregnancy loss. About 85 percent of all miscarriages take place before the first 12 weeks of pregnancy; these pregnancy losses usually take place because of abnormalities in the embryo or fetus (Merck Manual, 2020). In two-thirds of these miscarriages, the pregnancy loss can be linked to the pregnant person's health or lifestyle, and in one-third, no cause is known (Merck Manual, 2020). Known causes of miscarriage include abnormalities in the embryo or fetus resulting from a pregnant person's illnesses or disorders such as diabetes, infections, injury, hypothyroidism, or from lifestyle choices such as using cocaine, especially crack (Merck Manual, 2020).

Stillbirth

Even though society at large may not recognize the emotional and physical impact of any pregnancy loss, the impact on the parents is life-altering. **Stillbirth** refers to the death of a fetus after the 20th week (four months) of pregnancy and occurs in approximately one in every 115 births or about 26,000 per year (March of Dimes, 2022). Only about 14 percent of the fetuses die during the labor and birth process; the remaining 86 percent die before labor has begun (March of Dimes, 2022). In developing countries or less economically advantaged countries, the stillbirth rates are much higher because medical care is not as readily available. In up to half of all cases, tests cannot determine the cause of the stillbirth (March of Dimes, 2022). However, because of ongoing research in the United States and a commitment to children's health and well-being, we do know some causes of stillbirth today (March of Dimes, 2022):

- **Birth defects:** About 15 to 20 percent have one or more birth defects due to chromosomal disorders or environmental causes (such as the effects of teratogens).
- **Placenta problems:** About 25 percent are caused by *placental abruption*, where the placenta peels partly or completely away from the uterus. This results in heavy bleeding; the baby will die from lack of oxygen.
- **Poor fetal growth:** About 40 percent have poor growth patterns in the womb and are too small to survive within the womb. Women who smoke and/or have high blood pressure are at increased risk for stillbirth.
- **Infections:** In about 10 to 25 percent, infections involving the gestational parent, the fetus, or the placenta cause fetal death.
- **Chronic health conditions:** About 10 percent are related to chronic health conditions of the pregnant person, such as high blood pressure, diabetes, and kidney disease.

The loss of an embryo or fetus at any stage in the pregnancy is devastating. A stillbirth is particularly crushing, however, because most often the pregnant parent has experienced fetal movement, and many pregnant people indicate the emotional and physical bond with the baby intensifies once fetal movement takes place. When pregnant, a person is keenly aware of every flutter, poke, kick, and jab the baby makes, and when the fetal movement stops, the pregnant person becomes almost immediately aware that something is wrong. When a gestational parent reports the cessation of movement to their/his/her physician, an ultrasound is performed to detect cardiac movement or a heartbeat. If there is no cardiac movement, the baby is no longer alive.

Some people will choose to carry the baby and let labor begin naturally; most prefer to have labor *induced* or started by artificial methods. Although at first glance it may seem cruel to allow a birth parent to endure the pain of labor to deliver a stillborn baby, it is essential for the parent to preserve its capacity for future childbearing and to minimize any possible complications (ACOG, 2019). The other alternative is to have the fetus delivered by cesarean birth. As with any surgical procedure, a cesarean birth carries with it added risk to the gestational parent's health such as complications from the anesthesia, postoperative infection, and permanent scar tissue that forms near their/her/his reproductive organs. Even though cesarean birth rates are soaring, vaginal birth is still the safest method of delivery with the shortest and least painful physical recovery.

Many parents find the labor and birth experiences of stillborns to be rewarding and satisfying. Despite the fact that the birth parent and partner did not receive the outcome they had hoped for, the birth process is a time of quiet reflection and recognition that the baby was, is, and will always be a significant part of their lives and in the lives of their family. Although it may seem morbid to some, after the birth of the baby, physicians, midwives, and nurses encourage parents and family to hold, bathe, dress, cuddle, and sing to their infant to bond with the baby. Parents and families of stillborn babies are typically given several hours to bond with the baby because this bonding experience is crucial in their grieving and mourning. In other countries, such as the United Kingdom, parents and families are given days to be with their deceased baby.

In instances of stillbirth, greeting the baby also means saying goodbye. Although parting with anyone we love is devastating, parents who suffer the prenatal or postnatal loss of a baby carry the loss for the rest of their lives. Whether or not the baby ever took a breath—the life had meaning and significance to the parents and their families. The intense, overwhelming feelings of grief are simply an affirmation that the baby's life was real and significant. Moving through the grief and mourning to a place of healing takes time. Sometimes outside resources are necessary to help parents cope with their devastating loss. In time, the loss is integrated into their marriage, their relationship, and their lives.

When the Unexpected Happens

Unexpected outcomes are just that—something we do not anticipate. When preparing for childbirth, most books and childbirth preparation classes skim over—or ignore altogether—the possibility that a baby may be born with a birth defect. But when parents have a baby born with a birth defect, they are often, understandably, overwhelmed by fears and emotions. Family Life Educators, human service providers, social workers, healthcare providers, and clergy encourage parents to:

- **Acknowledge their emotions:** As you learned in this chapter, expectant parents have an image of a hoped-for child. When a baby is born with birth defects, parents need time to mourn the loss of this hoped-for child. Shock, denial, and grief are common emotions.
- **Seek support:** Joining support groups or talking with someone who has had similar experiences, or seeking help from a psychologist, clergy member, or social worker is helpful for parents.
- **Seek information:** Parents should educate themselves about their child's condition. Sources of information include the baby's physician, online resources, books, the March of Dimes, the National Information Center for Children and Youth with Disabilities, and various support groups. There are also resources (state and local) that assist parents in paying for costs associated with certain birth defects. Hospital social workers can help direct parents to appropriate information resources.

- **Use a team approach:** For the most part, children born with birth defects need a team made up of doctors, child life specialists, or developmentalists, and social workers to treat them. Some children's hospitals have such teams already in place. Parents need to play an active role in their child's treatment plan.

When educating expectant parents, we encourage them to create their personalized "what if" list. What if I don't want to be a parent or I'm not ready to be a parent? What if my partner doesn't find me attractive? What if I wanted a nonmedicated birth and I have to use pain medications? What if I have a premature baby? What if my baby has birth defects? What if I can't look at my baby because of the defect? What if my baby is stillborn? What if my baby dies? While we certainly cannot anticipate every possible result associated with pregnancy and childbirth, coming to terms with the fact that sometimes the pregnancy and childbirth experience doesn't yield our desired outcomes is an essential and necessary step in becoming a parent.

PARENTING LIFE EDUCATION: DISCUSSING CHILDBIRTH AND PREGNANCY FROM A VALUES-RESPECTIVE POSITION

As parent educators, one of our greatest responsibilities is to educate parents about prenatal development and what to expect regarding the transition to parenthood (Deave et al., 2008). As our study has shown us in this chapter, optimal prenatal lifestyle choices significantly impact the baby's development in the womb, and this early development sets the stage for the baby's lifespan growth and development. Helping professionals, be they healthcare providers, doulas, home visit practitioners, child life specialists, or social workers, play a crucial part in helping parents to establish healthy, well-functioning roles and responsibilities, and in creating and maintaining healthy pre- and postnatal environments for their children. As we continue our study in the next chapter, you'll come to understand that the child's environment and their experiences are the engines that drive brain development and other aspects of development, such as cognition and psychosocial well-being (Nelson et al., 2019). There is no question about it: Parental knowledge about child development and parents' individual well-being impact a child's holistic development.

Decades of research has shown us that transitioning to parenthood is one of the greatest stressors a family faces, and although parenthood—a central role for many—oftentimes provides intrinsic rewards for adults (such as having a sense of purpose), today's parents shoulder tremendous responsibilities (Musick et al., 2016; Nomaguchi & Milkie, 2017, 2020). And more often than not, these responsibilities conflict, creating even more stress. It's important for the helping professional and parent educators to understand that the emphasis in empirical research changes across time. For example, in the 1980s and 1990s, research sought to better understand *responsive parenting*, and in the 2010s, much of the parenting research focused on economic insecurity and its impact on child development (Nomaguchi & Milkie 2020). And as you saw in this chapter, cultural changes often dictate what needs to be examined and parenting issues that need to be better understood, such as the pregnancy, childbirth, and parenting experiences of transgender, nonbinary individuals, and their partners.

Regardless of the research emphasis in a particular decade, though, as parent educators, we have one central goal and purpose: How we can best support parents of all ages, of all races and ethnicities, of all socioeconomic backgrounds, of all religious beliefs, and of all sexual and gender identities in relation to childbearing experiences, the transition to parenthood, and parenting skills. No matter how daunting the task, however, the rewards gained in advocating for parents in one of their most important roles are many.

In the next chapter, we begin our fascinating exploration of holistic infant and child development. We will take what we've learned from these first chapters and synthesize—*weave together*—the theoretical and informational foundations with an understanding of the biological, cognitive, and psychosocial growth of children. The ability to synthesize these concepts is the hallmark of the applied professional.

5 THE CHANGING NATURE OF PARENTING: INFANCY AND EARLY CHILDHOOD

LEARNING OBJECTIVES

5.1 Describe the concept of the whole child and relate it to the importance of the parent–child relationship.

5.2 Summarize the theories of child development as they relate to the biophysical, cognitive, and socioemotional domains of development.

5.3 Explain Erikson's basic concept of *trust versus mistrust*, and how this concept directly relates to attachment in early childhood; provide an explanation as to why letting an infant "cry it out" may have negative effects on a baby's attachment.

5.4 Explain infant and toddler brain development, and the ways in which parents/caregivers are responsible for growing a child's brain.

5.5 Discuss the shift that occurs in parents as nurturers to parents as protectors through the first two years of life.

5.6 Define and describe the four primary parenting styles.

5.7 Identify the ways in which parents help their toddlers to develop a strong self-concept.

A voluminous amount of empirical science has determined that how parents parent is fundamental to optimal developmental and health outcomes for the infant and the child (among many, Altenburger & Schoppe-Sullivan, 2020; Fosco & Lydon-Stale, 2019; Khaleque & Ali, 2017; Murphy et al., 2017). The **parent–child relationship** refers to the emotional and physical connections between a parent and the child, and it includes attributes such as emotional cohesion (closeness), parental influence on the child's development, attachment, and parental investment in the child's well-being (Brauner-Otto et al., 2020; Lutz et al., 2009; Nomaguchi & Milkie, 2020). Through their parenting styles and behaviors, parents also serve as important social influences for their children and contribute to children's positive well-being and a positive worldview (Cassidy & Conroy, 2006; Fosco & Lydon-Stale, 2019; Khaleque & Ali, 2017; Malik & Marwaha, 2020). The formation of the parent–child relationship appears to occur in one of two ways: *biologically*, through the reproduction of genetic offspring, or *legally*, through the court system (Mihalec-Adkins & Cooley 2020; Miller et al., 2022).

In this chapter we explore the different theories of child development and examine in-depth the significance of infants' and toddlers' abilities to develop trust and attachment with their parents or caregivers, and the importance of infant stimulation in the development of trust. We then examine brain development across the first two years of life, and the roles that experiences and the environment play in shaping a child's brain. We'll then turn our attention to parents' responsibilities as protectors and nurturers as they adjust to the child's growing autonomy through toddlerhood and provide an environment rich for social and intellectual learning. We conclude our study in this chapter by taking a look at programs for parents of infants, toddlers, and preschool children.

PARENTING INFANTS AND TODDLERS

The term **caregiver** has been used in the literature to refer to the person or persons responsible for providing primary care of the infant or young child. At the very minimum, the caregiver's role is to provide for the child's basic needs for food, safety, shelter, and warmth, but it is also the caregiver's responsibility to support the healthy physical, intellectual, and social/emotional health of the child. Thus, the parent–child relationship encompasses the interactive processes in which parents and children engage, from the neonate's first minutes, through the early years of the child's life, through adolescence, and into adulthood.

The Parent–Infant Relationship

Every aspect of the child's growth and development, and every facet of the child's health and personality, is dependent upon the parenting skills and capabilities of the adult(s) who rear the child (World Health Organization, 2004). This isn't as easy as it seems because it requires that the caregiver(s) not only recognizes the child's needs but that they can also appropriately respond to the child's needs. At least three major factors appear to influence relationships between parents and their babies (Eiden et al., 1995; Fox, 1995):

1. *The past*—the quality of the parents' own early experiences. What type of care did each parent receive as babies or toddlers? Those who had warm, responsive, involved parents and who continue to have current adult–adult relationships with their parents tend to exhibit more confidence (and thus, more involvement) in their parenting (Bert et al., 2009; Cox & Paley, 2003; Kershaw et al., 2014). Conversely, those new parents who experienced ill-functioning families tend to exhibit these same, negative parenting behaviors with their own children (Bert et al., 2009).
2. *The present*—the parents' present condition, such as the parents' relationship stability, presence of relationship and/or family conflict, job security, health, daily stressors, and so on (among many, Goldberg & Carlson, 2014; Hannapi & Lipps, 2019; Murphey et al., 2018; Ponnet, 2014).

3. *The infant*—temperament of the infant. Every baby is born with unique characteristics. For example, is the infant calm or is the baby generally fussy? Parents who recognize their children's temperament patterns are better able to anticipate and respond to their baby's needs (Micalizzi et al., 2017; Sanson et al., 2018).

But how do these three factors interact to affect a baby's development and parenting practices? Dr. William J. Doherty is a professor of Family Social Science at the University of Minnesota. He and his colleagues put forth the Ecosystem Model of parental involvement which describes the ways in which present parenting beliefs and practices are shaped from past experiences in a person's family of origin and current interpersonal relationships (i.e., marriage, cohabitation, divorced, and remarried) (Doherty et al., 1998). A more recent study by W. Kim Halford and associates expands upon Doherty's Ecosystem Model. As seen in Figure 5.1, this investigation team's interpretation of Doherty's earlier work presents an ecological model that illustrates the interactions between each parent's individual characteristics and experiences, the couple's interaction patterns, the individual characteristics of each child, life events, and social and other contexts in which those life events are experienced (Kim Halford et al., 2018). In essence, there are three broad classifications of influences on the parent–child relationship.

FIGURE 5.1 ■ Ecological Model of Parental Relationships

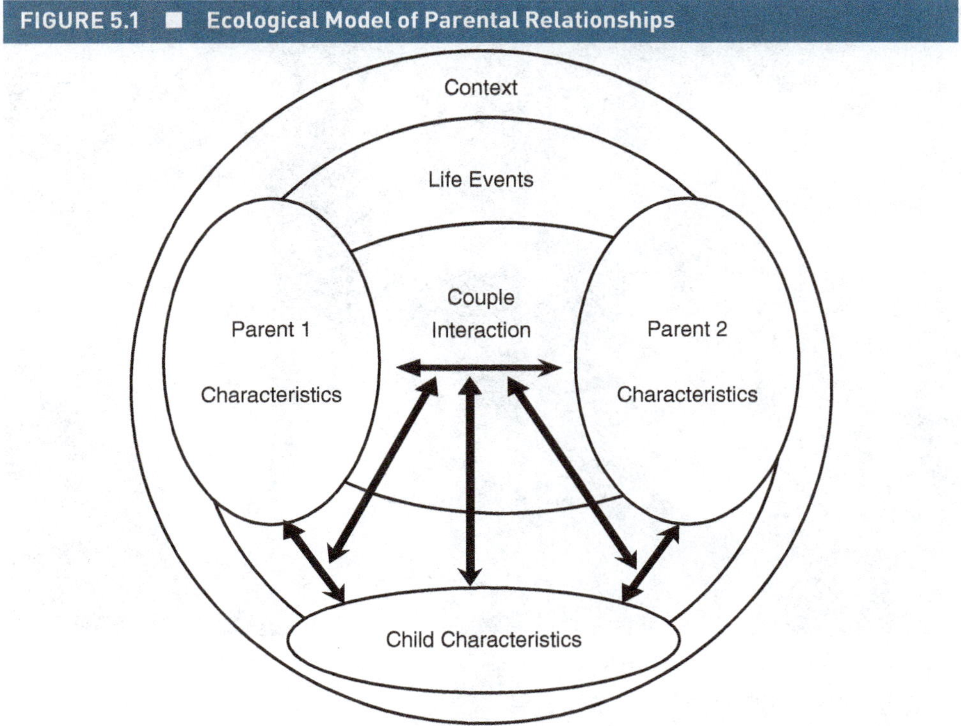

Source: Kim Halford et al. (2018), based on Doherty et al. (1998).

Context

This refers to the environments in which families live, as well as to family law and policies, healthcare, and parenting education (among other things) that are available to parents (Kim Halford et al., 2018). As you saw in Chapter 2, a person's social identity largely shapes relationship and family expectations (such as extended family support for the parenting individual or couple) (Halford & Pepping, 2017).

Life Events

According to Kim Halford and associates (2018), *life events* refer to circumstances and situations that impact all family members. Recall from Chapter 3 that a family comprises individual family members that make up a whole, interacting, interrelated system. Because of the systemic nature of families, what happens to one family member impinges upon all family members. For example, decades of research amply documents that highly conflictual couple interactions are associated with more frequent negative parent–child relationships and poorer child outcomes (for an expansive review, see Brock & Kochanska, 2016). This is why it is vitally important for parenting professionals to understand not only individual development, but also family development and the ways in which family members affect and are affected by one another.

"Parents have the toughest job in the world—raising people." Virginia Satir

Source: iStock.com/monzenmachi.

Individual Characteristics

This dimension refers to long-term traits and attributes in each parent and in each child (Kim Halford et al., 2018). Previous bodies of research explored the effects of maternal postpartum depression, parent–infant interaction, and child development, and found that maternal depression and anxiety have a bearing on the parent–infant relationship (Feldman et al., 2009; Field, 2010; Parfitt et al., 2013). Specifically, depressed mothers do not talk with and touch their infants as frequently as nondepressed mothers, and they have greater difficulty attuning to their baby's communication; they also display more hostile and less responsive parenting (Kingston et al., 2012; Tronick & Reck, 2009). It is important to note the interplay that occurs between parent and infant: The characteristics of the parent(s) and the characteristics of the infant additively and interactively determine the parent–infant relationship, and this relationship largely affects a child's development (cognitive, behavioral, and emotional), school adjustment, and social competence (see Høifødt et al., 2011 for a comprehensive review).

Infant Temperament

Other research has shown that the more difficult the child is temperamentally, the less responsive the mother is likely to be. A classic longitudinal study described *easy babies, difficult babies*, and *slow-to-warm-up babies*, and these are presented in Table 5.1 (Thomas & Chess, 1977). A description of the different temperaments of babies is based on nine traits, which are thought to be largely innate/inborn. For example, difficult babies tend to cry a lot and have irregular schedules. It is tough to soothe them, and they do not adapt easily to new people and situations. These babies do not fare well with impatient, unresponsive mothers, and may, in fact, contribute to their mothers' impatience and unresponsiveness. Goodness of fit does not occur between mother and baby, and **synchrony**—reciprocal, mutually rewarding interactions—is difficult to achieve.

TABLE 5.1 ■ Infant Temperaments
Easy babies: These infants are generally happy, cheerful, quickly establish routines, and easily adapt to changes in routine, and they are typically easy to soothe and calm (Pluess & Belsky, 2010).
Difficult babies: As the name implies, difficult babies tend to react intensely and negatively to stimuli, people, events, and places. Their eating and sleeping routines are irregular; they cry frequently and are difficult to soothe. These infants do not like change and do not adjust well to it. Parenting difficult babies is exhausting (Kiff et al., 2011).
Slow-to-warm-up babies: These infants are best described as being uneasy or cautious when presented with new people, situations, stimuli, and events—they are sometimes referred to as having a *wait and see* personality (Stephens, 2007).

Sources: Kiff et al. (2011), Pluess and Belsky (2010), and Stephens (2007).

Goodness of fit refers to how well the baby and the parent's temperaments fit or work together. Difficult babies do not settle well if the parent is overly reactive or dismissive.

Source: iStock.com/martinedoucet.

Goodness of fit—the center of parent/infant relationships—refers to how well the parent and the infant's temperaments "fit" together (Srvanti, 2017). There are two types of goodness of fit: how a particular personality trait interacts with the environment; and how the personality trait interacts with the people in the environment (McClowry et al., 2008). For example, difficult babies tend to cry a lot and have irregular schedules. It is tough to soothe them, and they do not adapt easily to new people and situations. These babies do not fare well with impatient, unresponsive mothers, and may, in fact, contribute to their mothers' impatience and unresponsiveness. *Synchrony*, reciprocal, mutually rewarding interactions, refers to the compatibility of the baby's temperament and the parents' temperaments. It is difficult to achieve when there is a mismatch between the infant's capacities and the environment (Chess & Thomas, 1999).

Of course, while an infant's temperament influences parent–child interactions and relationships, temperament alone is not the overall determinant in children's outcomes because of the interactive nature of a child's environment (Pluess & Belsky, 2010). *Differential susceptibility* is equally important in child development, and it refers to how infants and children with a difficult temperament are *disproportionately* affected by parent–child interactions (Pluess et al., 2010). Difficult babies and children are more sensitive, more reactive, and more susceptible to parenting quality than easy babies are. This susceptibility goes both ways—difficult infants and children are more susceptible to *both* low-quality and high-quality parenting (Pluess & Belsky, 2010).

It seems obvious, then, that the infant is no mere passive recipient of stimulation who is controlled by the adults in his/her/their environment. Rather, babies are active participants in their own development, and their unique manners of participation are a critical factor in the kind of parenting they receive.

Competent caregiving lays the foundation for social interaction, reciprocal communication and signaling, and the development of special skills during the period of infancy. Of course, just when parents believe they have figured out the ins and outs of parenting, the child passes into a new phase of growth and development (with its own uncharted territory)! An understanding of infant and toddler development is essential for parents, so they can parent their child in the most effective ways possible.

The Whole Child

When examining infant, toddler, and child development, it is important to adopt a *whole child* approach, regardless of the theory (or lens) through which a child's behavior is viewed and understood. A **whole child, or holistic**, paradigm acknowledges and supports a child's development in all four domains, and it also adopts an educational approach that embraces "policies, practices, and relationships that ensure each child, in each school, in each community, is healthy, safe, engaged, supported, and challenged" (National Association for the Education of Young Children, 2020). Not only does whole child parenting education aspire to promote the greatest possible growth in the domains of development, it also promotes the highest possible levels of respect for the environment and a sense of social justice (Miller, 2010). One of the hallmarks of holistic education is that parenting and educational experiences are adapted to meet the needs of the child, rather than making the child adapt to the environment (Miller, 2010).

Parent professionals, early care providers, and early childhood educators embrace the concept that when working with children, all four aspects of the child (biological, cognitive, socioemotional, and learning competencies) must be nurtured.

Source: iStock.com/sturti.

When conceptualizing the concept of the whole child, developmentalists typically include four specific, unique domains of development: biological, cognitive, socioemotional, and general learning competencies (Allen & Kelly, 2015). As seen in Figure 5.2, these domains are interrelated and interconnected—what happens in one domain of development impacts all of the other domains. The domains are characterized as (Allen & Kelly, 2015; National Research Council, 2015):

- **Biological:** This developmental domain emphasizes the physical development and health of the child. It includes important contributing factors to a child's well-being, such as nutrition, safety, sensory development, fine and gross motor development, brain development, rest, exercise, and self-help skills (such as feeding, dressing, washing hands, and brushing teeth). Growth in this domain is the most rapid between the ages of 0 and 2.

FIGURE 5.2 ■ The Domains of Child Development

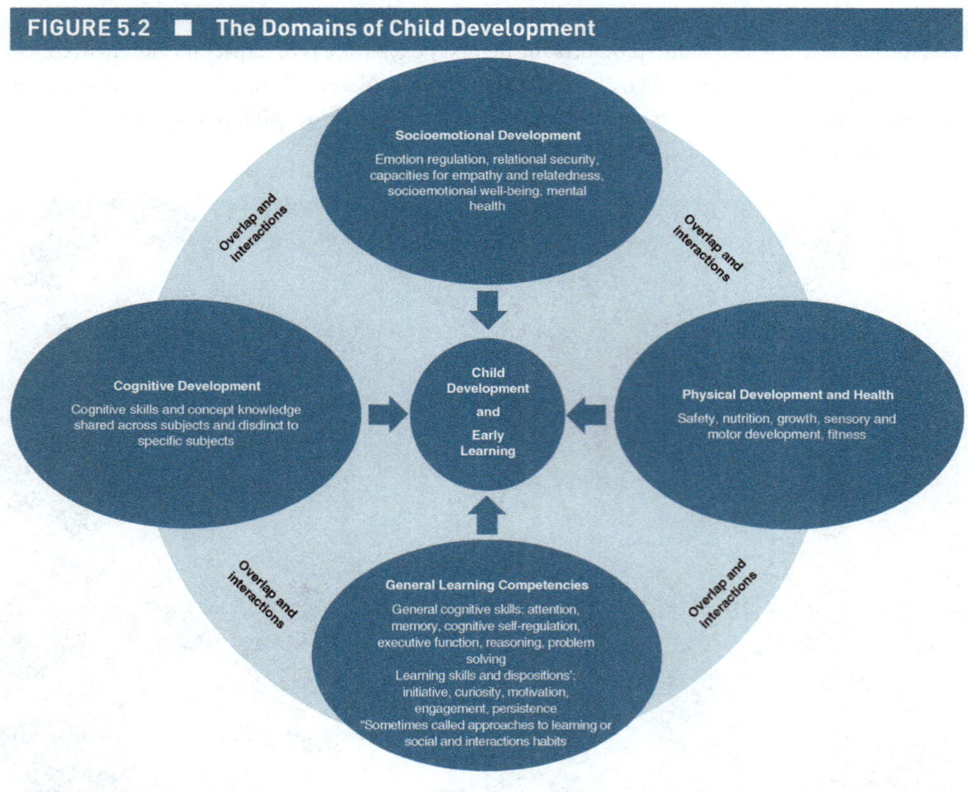

Source: Institute of Medicine (IOM) and National Research Council (NRC). (2015). *Transforming the workforce for children birth through age 8: A unifying foundation*. The National Academies Press.

- **Cognitive:** Cognitive development includes how children think, learn, understand, experiment, explore, and figure things out. It also includes language development, creativity, and imagination. As children grow, it includes the skills and knowledge they acquire in different subjects. Parents and caregivers of infants and toddlers can help to develop this domain by reading both fiction (children's books) and nonfiction books (such as informational books about plants and animals) to their children, and allow them to explore their environments through their senses. In daily interactions with children, parents can help children's curiosity to develop by asking questions. For example, when seeing a turtle in the yard, a caregiver can ask the child, "How do you think the turtle eats? What do you think is its favorite thing to eat? Why do you think it's that color?" It is important for parents to remember that *repetition* for children is vitally important in shaping the child's brain connections and providing predictability in the environment—even though adults may tire of reading the same book over and over and over, or even if they threaten to smash the radio if they hear "Baby Shark" one more time!
- **Socioemotional:** This domain encompasses both intra- and interpersonal processes. Socioemotional development refers to the child's ability to relate to the feelings of others, to identify their own feelings, and to self-regulate (control their own feelings and behaviors); it also includes being able to establish and maintain relationships with others.
- **General learning competencies:** This domain is sometimes referred to as *approaches to learning* (Allen & Kelly, 2015; National Research Council, 2015). It includes initiative, motivation, persistence, and engagement.

As we think about the whole child, we need to recall what we learned in Chapter 2 regarding Bronfenbrenner's Ecological Model: Remember, no child develops in isolation, and as parent educators, we are called to work with the whole child and with those in their microsystems (their parents, teachers, schools, churches/temples/mosques, and the communities)—these are the closest, most caring people in their worlds. As the World Health Organization observes, "[Working with children's environments] presents a solid foundation to integrate interventions to promote better caregiver–child interactions into the design of primary healthcare programs for mothers, other caregivers, and children...and are appropriate for community-based nutrition, early child care, violence prevention, orphan and foster care, and parent education programs" (National Research Council, 2015, p. 1).

This brief review of the whole child lays the groundwork for our need to recognize the importance of the child's relationship(s) to parents or other caregivers and leads us to our discussion about the theories that seek to explain and understand child development.

Examining children's development is a fascinating field of study. In the next section, we'll continue our study of child development theories as we examine Erik Erikson's theory of socioemotional development.

TRUST, ATTACHMENT, AND RECIPROCITY

The degree to which a child comes to trust the world, other people, and himself depends to a considerable extent on the quality of care an infant receives. The baby whose needs are met when they arise, whose discomforts are quickly removed, and who is cuddled, touched, played with, and talked to develops a sense of the world as a safe place to be and of people as helpful, dependable, and trustworthy.

Similar to the foundation of a house that is built, floor by floor, so too is the foundation of our ability to trust others and to relate to one another built on developmental stage by developmental stage. In the 1950s, psychologist Erik Erikson provided a lifespan approach for **psychosocial development**, which is the social and emotional development of an individual. Essentially, Erikson's *Eight Stages of Man* were formulated to put forth the notion that our social and emotional development is a lifelong process; that what happens or does not happen at one stage will eventually affect our psychosocial development during later stages of life (Erikson, 1958, 1963). Erikson's theory asserts that if each stage is completed successfully, the child develops a healthy personality and acquires basic virtues. **Basic virtues** are described as personality strengths and characteristics that can be used to resolve developmental crises (McLeod, 2018). Table 5.2 outlines Erikson's eight developmental stages, which encompass what developmentalists refer to as a *cradle-to-grave* approach to understanding individual psychosocial development. We begin our study of psychosocial development by examining the early experiences in life, from infancy through the school years.

Establishing Basic Trust: Erikson's Theory of Psychosocial Development

Trust Versus Mistrust

The fundamental developmental task of infancy (0 to 2 years) is learning to *trust* primary caregivers. During Stage 1 (**trust vs. mistrust**), if the child is nurtured, loved, and receives affection, the infant will develop a sense of trust and security (Erikson, 1958, 1963). When care is consistent and accepting, trust is fostered in the baby. Every time a parent or caregiver responds to a baby's cries of distress or needs for attention, the adult sends resounding signals to the baby that the world is a safe place in which to live. This trust carries through to every subsequent stage of development. Erikson did not believe, though, that the problem of basic trust versus mistrust was resolved once and for all during the first year of life; rather, it arises again at each successive stage of development.

If, on the other hand, a parent or primary caregiver does not respond to the needs of the baby, or if the baby's distress signals are ignored or neglected, the baby will become insecure and mistrustful of others. Inconsistent, inadequate, and rejecting care leads to mistrust, an attitude of fear and suspicion on the part of the infant toward the world in general and toward people in particular. If basic physical and emotional needs are not met, the child feels somehow empty, cheated, at a loss, and ill at ease, with others and with themself.

TABLE 5.2 ■ Erikson's Developmental Stages

Influential psychologist Erik Erikson formulated the Eight Stages of Man developmental theory. According to Erikson, a person is in a continuous state of development from the cradle to the grave.

Erikson's Theory of Psychosocial Development

Stage	Age and Basic Virtue	Developmental Task
Trust versus Mistrust	Infancy, 0–24 months Hope	Child develops a belief that caregivers will provide a secure and trustful environment.
Autonomy versus Shame and Doubt	Toddlerhood, 2–4 years Will	Child develops a sense of independence and free will; feels shame if the free will isn't used appropriately.
Initiative versus Guilt	Early Childhood, 4–6 years Purpose	"The Age of Acquiring": Child learns to explore his/her/their environment and acquires a newfound set of skills; feels a sense of initiative and accomplishment.
Industry versus Inferiority	Middle Childhood, 7–12 years Competency	"The Age of Mastery": Child masters the skills acquired during early childhood.
Identity versus Role Confusion	Adolescence, 13–21 years Fidelity	Teen develops a sense of who they/he/she is in comparison to others (sense of "self"); develops a keen sense of role expectations.
Intimacy versus Isolation	Young Adult, 22–35 years Love	Develops ability to give and receive love; begins to consider long-term relationships, marriage, and parenting as realistic options.
Generativity versus Stagnation	Middle Adulthood, 36–65 years Care	Develops interest in giving of oneself to younger generations by helping them lead meaningful lives and by caring for them.
Integrity versus Despair	Older Adulthood, 65+ years Wisdom	Desires to find meaningful and personal gratification with the life one has lived.

Source: Welch (2010).

It is during Stage 1 that the child's initial capacity for intimate and loving relationships begins to take shape—and the foundation for *current and future intimacy* and loving relationships is laid. Consider the following scenario. When my sons were younger, I took them to the city swimming pool one afternoon. While there, I saw a friend who had recently adopted a son. The child was about three years old at the time of his adoption; he had been removed from his birth mother's home because of neglect and physical abuse. The adoptive father and I engaged in conversation while his son played in the "kiddie" pool. He relayed to me how the child appeared to be withdrawn. He explained that his son would not snuggle or cuddle with them and would not respond to any displays of affection. A woman approached us and said, "Excuse me, but is that your little boy?" My friend looked up to see that his child had fallen and seriously cut his forehead. We might expect a three-year-old who has banged his head to scream and cry or run over to a parent for emotional and physical comfort, but this little boy, cut and bleeding, did not cry. He did not come to his father for help. Instead, he got out of the swimming pool, lay down on the concrete, and put his head in his arms. Quiet. Not seeking help.

This story illustrates the significance of early relationships and their significance to relational intimacy in later life stages. Because this child received little or no nurturing and affection from his first intimate relationship—the mother–child relationship—he did not develop a sense of trust in his caregivers, as most children do. And because of this lack of trust, he did not turn to his father when he was hurt. Without a doubt, having security and comfort needs met in the early years of life plays a significant role in shaping intimate relationships (McAdams, 1989). In a very real sense, early intimate relationships provide a "crystal ball" that allows us to look into the future of a child's relational and intimacy abilities. This child's early experiences don't necessarily spell relational doom for him, however, because there are many opportunities for him to form healthy attachments in his lifespan.

Crying: Baby's Communication

The newborn comes equipped with one major means of communicating with others in the environment—crying. And, although crying is a normative, expected neonate and infant behavior (Moller et al., 2019), it is associated with parental exhaustion (Kurth et al., 2011), parental depression (Wake, 2006), and shaken baby syndrome (Barr et al., 2006). It is quite common for babies to cry for about one to three hours per day, and it's also common for babies to have a fussy period in the evening (Penn State Hershey, 2020). However, some babies cry excessively and despite their best efforts, parents are unable to soothe their babies. This is known as **excessive infant crying**, and is defined as crying for at least three hours per day, for at least three days per week, and for at least three weeks in a row (Penn State Hershey, 2020). It is estimated that about 20 percent of newborns cry excessively and are unable to be soothed (Lucassen, 2001).

One recent study sought to understand which soothing methods evoked a **calming response (CR)** in the baby (Moller et al., 2019). In a study of 69 infants (0 to 6 months in age), the researchers studied which soothing method had the most immediate CR on the baby—swaddling (wrapping a baby securely in a blanket so only its head is peaking out), sound (quietly shushing or talking to the baby), or movement (patting the baby's back or bottom, rocking, gently bouncing the baby up and down); the study also examined whether the parent or a smartcrib (a mechanical crib with movement) had the greatest CR. The researchers found that infant crying and fussiness decreased much more quickly when parents used active calming methods (i.e., swaddling, sound, or movement), in comparison to when parents sat still with the baby and cuddled the child. The study also discovered that babies exhibit a stronger CR when parents soothe the baby in comparison with mechanical soothing (such as a baby swing). This study is important for parents and parent educators alike because it shows us that parental behaviors and parent–infant interactions used to reduce infant crying are effective.

The swiftness with which parents attend to a crying baby is also important. A landmark study found that infants who have an early history of delay on the part of the mother in responding to crying tend later to cry for longer periods than do infants with a history of less delay (Ainsworth, 1979; Bell & Ainsworth, 1979); the consistency and promptness of maternal response during the first three months (or its absence) affects the pattern of later infant crying. Furthermore, the researchers discovered that infants whose cries had been neither ignored or responded to with undue delay developed modes of communication other than crying. So, a baby whose experience has been that its mother responds to its signals with consistency and promptness learns to expect that *signaling*—and, later, communication—is potentially successful in producing a desired or intended result, and not merely that there will be a response to crying. It is important to note that although fathers and other caregivers were not involved in this classic study, it is reasonable to assume that the study's conclusions would apply to them as well.

Purple crying refers to a normative growth and developmental period that is characterized by the baby's persistent, unconsolable crying. It usually starts when a newborn is about two weeks old and lasts until the baby is about three months old. It is important and necessary that the infant's cries are tended to, even though a parent or caregiver's nurturing and care will not quiet the cries.

Source: istock.com/atstockproductions.

Letting Babies "Cry It Out"

One of the most common questions we hear from our students is, "Should parents let their babies cry it out?" The **cry it out** approach is a method some parents use to let their infants cry themselves to sleep, rather than employing soothing skills; this is also sometimes referred to as **sleep training** (Bilgin & Wolke, 2020; Gradisar et al., 2016). Before we go any further, it is imperative to understand that, as discussed here, the cry it out approach only refers to infant sleep routines—it *does not* imply that neonates and infants should be left to cry without soothing if they are hungry or have any other need, such as a diaper change. And, as with many other aspects related to parenting, there are conflicting opinions: Some studies have established that there are long-term negative effects of under-responding or need-neglect in babies (Blunt Bugental et al., 2003; Bremner & Narayan, 1998; Dawson et al., 2000; Heim et al., 2008; Heim & Binder, 2012), but although scant, emerging evidence suggests that this is not necessarily the case, and that allowing babies to cry teaches babies to self-sooth.

One study of 178 infants and their caregivers assessed babies at ages 3, 6, and 18 months (Bilgin & Wolke, 2020). The researchers wanted to determine if babies left to cry themselves to sleep and to self-regulate experienced lower levels of attachment (discussed at length below) when they were 18 months old; the research method consisted of parents/caregivers assessing the frequency of their baby's cries while using the cry it out approach. The results of this study found that leaving infants to cry was rarely practiced in the early weeks and months after the baby's birth, but it increased over 18 months. However, allowing babies to cry it out from birth was associated with decreased crying frequency at three months, six months, and 18 months. The authors claim that "no adverse impacts of leaving infants to cry it out in the first 6 months on infant-mother attachment and behavioral development at 18 months were found" (Bilgin & Wolkie, 2020, p. 1). The researchers emphasized that letting a baby cry it out had no negative impact on a warm infant–mother relationship.

Another study included 43 sets of parents, with babies between six and 16 months of age (Gradisar et al., 2016). The parents were divided into three groups:

- *Graduated extinction*: This group of parents was asked to leave the child alone and wait longer periods of time before comforting the baby.
- *Bedtime fading*: These parents stayed in the baby's room (without holding or rocking the baby) until the baby fell asleep.
- *Control group*: This group let the baby cry it out with no interventions.

Babies' cortisol (the stress hormone) was tested to determine the level of stress associated with not being immediately soothed. The researchers discovered that babies over three months in age in the *graduated extinction* group and the *bedtime fading* group fell asleep more quickly and stayed asleep longer. The babies in the first two groups experienced lower levels of stress than babies who were left to cry it out. The researchers concluded that there was no evidence to support that gradually allowing babies to cry at longer intervals at bedtime until they learned to self-regulate posed any behavioral problems later on (Gradisar et al., 2016).

The La Leche League, an international group whose mission is to provide breastfeeding mothers support, encouragement, information, and education (La Leche League, 2022), asserts that "While babies may indeed stop crying if left unattended long enough, they are not learning to self-soothe—they are simply giving up on the hope that comfort will come." Professor James McKenna (University of Notre Dame) makes the point that, all primate infants—including humans—need to experience close contact and proximity with their caregivers, and that because human neonates are born developmentally immature and have immature brains, they require optimal human care and touch (McKenna, 2020).

The La Leche League (2022) accurately points out that Gradisar and his colleagues' study (2016) makes the assumption that it is "normal" for babies to fall asleep by themselves and sleep through the night at a certain age; however, as you saw earlier, each baby has its own temperament, its own needs for sleep, and its own needs for closeness with a parent or caregiver. While the studies discussed here provide an emerging parenting practice, it's important that parents listen to their baby's signals and respond accordingly.

Maintaining a Predictable Environment

Equally important as prompt, consistent attention to the infant's needs is the maintenance of an orderly, predictable environment. The infant at birth does not view herself as a separate entity from others in the environment. In fact, at first, everything and everyone is an extension of the baby (Piaget, 1952). A critical task of infancy, then, is to develop a sense of self and of others as separate from self (Erikson, 1963). This task is related in a complex way to establishing a sense of basic trust.

In the beginning, much of the infant's world is centered on physiological needs. If fed when hungry, changed when wet, helped to sleep or rest when tired, and cared for by the same few people the baby recognizes as significant, then the infant's day-to-day environment becomes predictable, stable, and consistent, free of chaos. The baby comes to know that certain things happen at certain times and that familiar people come when a cry is elicited. The baby also learns to recognize, too, the particular patterns of responses of special caregivers—their tones of voice, their scents, and the way their bodies feel when held closely. All of these consistent, predictable subtleties help the baby learn that she can depend on others.

Trust is also built from the child's own behavior; that is, a baby begins to view herself as competent by her ability to act on her environment and her success in eliciting certain responses from her caregivers. If, however, the infant is cared for by a number of people, if there is no routine or predictability in feeding, sleeping, or being played with, and especially if there is neglect or abuse, then the baby's sense of basic trust in herself as competent and others as dependable is impeded.

Profoundly related to a sense of trust during the first year is the security of attachment the infant develops for his parent(s) and other primary caregivers.

In most cultures around the world, babies are worn and held almost constantly. Babies who are worn or carried in a sling are calmer and cry less. They also remain in a quiet state of alertness longer than babies who are not worn.

Source: iStock.com/ranplett.

Attachment: An Emotional Bond

Attachment refers to the special bond that the infant forms with significant adults in his life; more specifically, attachment is the feelings of safety and security when a child is with an adult (Wittmer, 2011). It is best described as an emotional or affectional bond that ties or binds the child to the parent or primary caregiver (among many, Bowlby, 1958, 1969, 1980, 1988, 2005; Rees, 2007; Shemmings, 2011; Simpson & Rhodes, 2017).

Some experts regard attachment as encompassing the totality of the infant–parent relationship, expressed in a range of interactive contexts (Pederson & Moran, 1996). In order to encapsulate the enduring, lasting patterns of interpersonal relationships from the cradle to the grave, John Bowlby (1980) developed the **attachment theory** based on his observations of parent–child interactions. With the premise that all babies need nurturance in order to survive, Bowlby asserted that in the process of providing for these survival needs, newborns form a type of bond—an emotional attachment—with their caregivers (typically the mother and/or father).

Bowlby's attachment theory advances the idea that it is from this close affectional emotional bond that children derive a sense of security, a trusting sense that the world, and the interpersonal relationships we encounter along the way, is a safe place to be. So influential is Bowlby's attachment theory, it has shaped early childhood education, child care, and child psychology and psychiatry, and has been the cornerstone of understanding child and adolescent development for decades (Fitzgerald, 2020; Wells, 2018). More recently, emotional attachment has also been linked to physical health and wellness (Pierrehumbert et al., 2012; Pietromonaco & Collins, 2017; Pietromonaco et al., 2013).

Because of the importance of these early human relationships, Bowlby, along with prominent researcher Mary Ainsworth and her associates, asserted that the attachment behaviors that take place throughout infancy ultimately direct, shape, and mold our personality (Ainsworth et al., 1978). Consequently, these behaviors in turn significantly direct, shape, and mold the interpersonal attachment relationships we experience later on as children, adolescents, and adults (Ainsworth et al., 1978).

Some researchers believe that attachment may begin even earlier than infancy and toddlerhood. They suggest that the emotional and affectional bonds actually begin during pregnancy, well before birth takes place (Gurol & Palot, 2012; Klaus et al., 1995; Ossa et al., 2012; Sadeghi & Mazaheri, 2007; Salehi et al., 2019; Salehi & Kohan, 2017; Sedgmen et al., 2006). Although researchers may not agree on the exact time attachment occurs, they do agree that the ability to form and experience an emotional attachment to a parent(s) or caregiver in the earliest days and months of life, is, in effect, a predictor of an individual's ability to form meaningful, successful interpersonal (and love) relationships in the future.

Biological and environmental factors work together to facilitate the infant's attachment to significant others. Maternal sensitivity and responsivity are the central features that appear to foster secure attachment:

- **Maternal sensitivity:** Sensitivity is the mother's ability to perceive the infant's signals accurately and the ability to respond to them promptly and appropriately (Aarestrup et al., 2020; DeWolff & van Ijzendoorn, 1997).
- **Maternal responsivity:** Responsivity refers to the degree to which mothers respond to their baby's cries, how affectionate and tender they are, how positive their behaviors are, and how often they interfere in their baby's ongoing behaviors (Black et al., 2017; Eshel et al., 2006; Isabella & Belsky, 1991; Landry et al., 2012).

Other variables that seem to affect security of attachment are mutuality and synchrony, stimulation, positive attitude, and emotional support (DeWolff & van Ijzendoorn, 1997; Leclère et al., 2014; McFarland et al., 2019). The child's temperament and gender also affect attachment; insecure attachment is a greater likelihood in boys (Fox, 1995).

Attachment Types

There are three major categories or classifications of attachment: secure, secure-avoidant, and insecure-resistant. Researchers determine a baby's attachment type by using a laboratory setting referred to as the **Strange Situation.** The infant's response to the stress induced by being separated from his parent is used to assess the security of attachment (Ainsworth et al., 1978).

Infants rated as **secure** (about 55 percent of the population) use their parents as a secure, safe base (i.e., returning to them periodically when exploring a new situation) from which to explore the novel environment, and the parent's response to the infant's signals is appropriate and predictable—the parent and the child's behaviors are in harmony (Brown & Ward, 2013; Shemmings, 2011). Secure infants seek comfort from their parents when distressed, such as upon the parent's return after separation in the Strange Situation (Brown & Ward, 2013; Pederson & Moran, 1996; Shemmings, 2011). Secure attachment occurs when the child is cared for by warm, responsive parents or caregivers. These children typically develop healthily, both cognitively and emotionally, and they feel comfortable expressing their needs (Brown & Ward, 2013; Shemmings, 2011).

Insecure-avoidant infants (about 23 percent of the population) tend to be relatively independent of their parents and display little proximity seeking (the tendency to reduce distance from the attachment figure in times of distress) (Brown & Ward, 2013; Shemmings, 2011). Typically, parents display inconsistent behavior, being at times attentive to their infants' signals and at other times inattentive; this may be because they have difficulty responding in sensitive ways to the child's needs (Brown & Ward, 2013; Shemmings, 2011). Infants may actively seek comfort from their parents, but when they are successful at gaining attention, they become fussy and hostile (Pederson & Moran, 1996). Overinvolved and intrusive parents also foster insecure ambivalence by leading their infants to develop defenses whereby they shut down from within. Insecure-avoidant behavior, then, is a *self-protecting* strategy for parental insensitivity and intrusiveness. This attachment style may be associated with poor social development later on. For example, it is not uncommon for children with this attachment style to hide their feelings because they fear that any show of need may drive someone away, and they feel that they are not worthy of love (Brown & Ward, 2013; Shemmings, 2011).

Infants classified as **insecure-resistant** (8 percent of the population) have parents who are underinvolved (Brown & Ward, 2013; Shemmings, 2011). The parent's behavior is unresponsive, such as delaying in responding to the infant's cries. These infants tend to be distressed by separation from the parents in the Strange Situation and to seek contact during reunion, but appear to be inconsolable (Steele et al., 1996).

Disorganized attachment (15 percent of the population) describes infants who do not fit into any of the three major classifications (it is believed that nearly 80 percent of children who experience neglect or abuse have this attachment style), and some children who are on the autism spectrum develop disorganized attachment (Brown & Ward, 2013; Shemmings, 2011). This type of attachment is considered to be a risk factor for aggressive behavior, and for concurrent and subsequent psychopathology, because they are raised by parents or caregivers who are frightening to be with (van Ijzendoorn & Bakermans-Kranenburg, 2003).

Attachment Across Generations

A different line of research investigated the attachment transmission patterns across generations. Using the *Adult Attachment Inventory (AAI)*, mothers' or fathers' relationships with their own parents or primary caregivers during their early childhood years are assessed. Parents are then asked to describe their relationship with their parents and to provide specific memories, such as experiences of rejection, distress, hurt, loss, abuse, and separation. Parents are classified into the secure or one of the insecure groups, depending on the clarity, coherence, and completeness of their narratives.

One study found a significant relationship between both mothers' and fathers' attachment and their infants' attachment classifications (between secure and autonomous and between insecure-avoidant and dismissing) (Steele et al., 1996). This study's results also demonstrated an apparently greater influence of the mother as opposed to the father upon infant–parent attachment. Another study found similar results. In nearly three-fourths of the dyads, there was a match between mother–child attachment classifications of secure/insecure (Eiden et al., 1995). These data lend support to the notion of the intergenerational transmission of attachment patterns.

The importance of secure attachment cannot be overstated. As the infant's first primary socioemotional relationship, our secure attachment with our parent(s) and caregivers lays the foundation for future positive relationships with peers, siblings, romantic partners, spouses, and ultimately, our own children. The quality of the parent–child relationship during the first year plays the primary role in this important process.

Developing Reciprocity

The parent–infant system is reciprocal in nature, with the behavior and characteristics of one influencing the behavior and characteristics of the other. Much more has been written about mother–infant reciprocity than father–infant; however, the same sort of reciprocity can be developed between a father and the infant and between any caregiver and an infant.

Reciprocity is the degree of positive or negative involvement at given points during interaction (Brazelton et al., 1974). Similar concepts are those of synchrony and mutuality. As you saw earlier, *synchrony* refers to the extent to which the parent–infant interaction is reciprocal and mutually rewarding (Leclère et al., 2014; Planalp et al., 2013). On the other hand, asynchronous interactions are those that are represented by one-sided, unresponsive, or intrusive behavioral exchanges (Leclère et al., 2014). *Mutuality* includes positive exchanges in which parent and infant attend to the same thing, mutual gazing, parents' skillful modulation of babies' arousal, and active maintenance of the interaction (Kerr et al., 2020). Reciprocity appears to be brought about by a process of mutual adaptation between parent and child—both learn to recognize cues, signals, or patterns of specific behaviors and characteristics of each other in numerous situations (Bornstein et al., 2012; Planalp et al., 2013). This sort of mutual adaptation begins in the prelinguistic phase and, in time, allows each partner to communicate to the other their involvement in the interaction.

Both mother [and father] and infant contribute to the maintenance of an optimal level of reciprocity (Planalp et al., 2013; Vaish et al., 2018). For example, sensitive mothers provide appropriately timed stimulation for their infants. That is to say, they take cues from the infant—whether the baby is alert or drowsy, what stimuli the baby is attending to, and what signals the infant is sending. These mothers are neither intrusive nor unresponsive. They respond contingently to the baby's behavior. They reduce or stop stimulation when appropriate, to allow the infant a brief period to withdraw and reestablish equilibrium. By the same token, babies seek stimulation when they desire it, they create or prolong pleasant situations, and they avert their gaze or turn their heads when stimulation is too overwhelming. Thus, the two partners work together to regulate the reciprocal interaction (Bornstein et al., 2012; Planalp et al., 2013).

The development of reciprocity and the goodness of fit during the first six months of life facilitate the infant's learning to separate himself from others in his environment. The infant learns which behavior patterns represent "Mommy" and thereby can distinguish her from others in the environment. Reciprocity fosters a sense of competence in that the child learns that he can influence how others behave toward him (Planalp et al., 2017). During the last half of the first year, the infant's behaviors signal a preference for particular types of responsiveness instead of generalized responsiveness. The child begins to anticipate his parent's actions in response to his own and initiates interactive sequences or alters interaction the parent has initiated in order to better suit his own needs and devices. The development of a system of communication is determined to a large extent by the manner in which the parent responds to the infant's signals in the earlier months (Planalp et al., 2017).

It appears that the development of reciprocity in the early months and the maintenance of reciprocal relationships in the later months are both critical to healthy development. It is clear that both mother (or father) and infant either facilitate or impede this progress. Either an unresponsive baby or an unresponsive parent can interfere with the development of reciprocity, as can an overly intrusive mother who seldom gives her infant opportunity to initiate interaction. Along with establishing basic trust, developing secure attachments as well as reciprocity, to give babies the best start in life parents and caregivers must also effectively stimulate their infants.

Along with establishing basic trust, developing secure attachments as well as reciprocity, to give babies the best start in life parents and caregivers must also effectively stimulate their infants.

BRAIN DEVELOPMENT AND INFANT STIMULATION

Only within the later part of the 20th century was significant attention given to any aspect of infant care other than caring for physical needs. But with the influence of Piaget, the development of infant child care centers, and bodies of research concerning the importance of the first two or three years of life, today more emphasis is placed on optimal experiences during the infancy period. The most exciting and revealing research has been conducted by neuroscientists and focuses on brain development of fetuses, infants, and children.

Brain Development: Wiring the Brain

The electrical activity of young brain cells actually changes the physical structure of the brain. Over the first few months of life, the connections between brain cells take place at a rapid rate.

FIGURE 5.3 ■ Illustration of Connections of Brain Neurons at Birth, 3 Months, 6 Months, 12 Months, and 24 Months

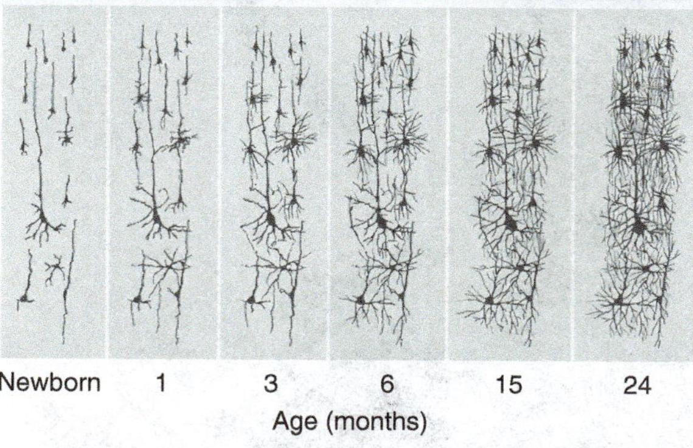

Experience by experience, the connections between brain cells are built. These connections change the physical structure of the brain, and literally wire the brain for a child's future learning.

Source: Kolb and Fantie (2008).

These connections reach their peak at about age two and remain at that level until about age 10 (see Figure 5.3). Spontaneous bursts of electrical activity strengthen some connections, and those not reinforced by activity become weak and atrophy.

What triggers these bursts of electrical activity? Sensory experiences and stimulation (National Research Council, 2015). Children who experience these bursts have brains that thrive, while those who are deprived of stimulating environments have brains that suffer (Blair & Raver, 2016; Takeuchi et al., 2015). For example, children who do not play much or who are seldom touched by their parents or caregivers have been found to develop brains as much as 30 percent smaller than normal for their age (Nash & Schaefer, 2011). It is repeated positive experiences that wire a child's brain—for vision, for emotions, for language, for movement—by providing a variety of experiences, including interesting things to look at; loving and responsive care; talking, singing, and reading; and space and objects to explore (National Research Council, 2015; Takeuchi et al., 2015; Tierney & Nelson, 2009).

Beginning at about age 10, the brain discards or prunes its weakest connections, preserving those that have been strengthened by repeated experiences, either positive or negative. For example, early experiences of stress form some sort of template around which later brain development is organized (National Research Council, 2015). Additionally, infants reared by depressed mothers show significantly reduced activity in the area of the brain that serves as a center for happiness and joy—sad experiences produce sad brains (National Research Council, 2015). These findings emphasize the importance of early experiences and their impact on later development. It places an enormous responsibility on parents

Providing stimulating environments with age-appropriate toys and books helps to grow a healthy, robust brain in the child.

Source: iStock.com/FGTrade.

and other primary caregivers of infants to provide appropriate, timely, and reciprocal stimulation.

Parents provide stimulation in two ways: by structuring the environment to facilitate sensorimotor activities, and by interacting directly with their infants. Babies are born with sensory equipment that helps them to attend to every stimulus.

Vision

It is now known that infants can see from the moment of birth, but their focus and coordination are immature. Visual stimulation should consist of bright colors, light-and-dark contrasts (stripes, bull's eye patterns, and geometric shapes), objects that move, and contoured surfaces (Hyvarinen et al., 2014). Although familiarity is important in the early months, within five or six months, infants seem to prefer attending to moderately complex stimuli (Hyvarinen et al., 2014).

The human face is a favorite object for attention: It is contoured, it moves, and it talks. Close face-to-face gazing and vocalizing provide opportunities for significant visual, auditory, and even tactile stimulation. Frequent changes in position—from back to stomach, from crib to blanket on the floor, and from infant swing to a parent's lap—provide infants with different vantages points of vision and the variation they seek. The infant's room should have pictures, mobiles, collages, and other items that can be moved and changed frequently as the infant seeks novelty and variation.

Hearing

For auditory stimulation, vocalizing (such as imitating coos and babbles, talking, and singing) is of utmost importance (National Institute on Deafness and Other Communication Disorders (NIDCD), 2017). The amount and the type of language used in the home during the period of infancy is a critical factor in the child's later intellectual development. Exposure to music (all types), daily sounds in and out of the house, and reading regularly to the baby, all help to provide auditory stimulation. It should be emphasized, however, that control of noise and distraction is important. Infants who are bombarded with noise (constant TV, radio, shouting, and general commotion) learn to tune out the distractions and may have difficulty later in auditory discrimination (NIDCD, 2017).

Touching

Of all the types of sensory stimulation, tactile (touch) stimulation seems to be the most important for healthy development (Barnett, 2005). The sense of touch is the most highly developed sense at birth, having functioning prenatally longer than the other senses. Holding, cuddling, stroking, rocking, and movement are essential to the infant. Caregivers can provide tactile stimulation while feeding and changing the baby, as well as in other routine activities. Adults who prop bottles or who put their babies to bed with a bottle not only deprive the baby of a sense of warmth and closeness but also deprive them of critical visual, auditory, and tactile stimulation. Toys that have varied textures (soft, slick, fuzzy, flexible, and rigid) also provide diverse tactile experiences.

Providing Infant Stimulation: The Parents' Roles

Throughout infancy, much of the parents' role centers on providing an interesting, stimulating environment for their baby. If parents provide such an environment, the infant's learning will be self-initiated.

On examining Piaget's description of the growth of intelligence during the period of infancy, it becomes even more clear that the environment does not mold the child's behavior by simply imposing itself on a passive infant. Rather, the infant seeks contact with her environment—the baby searches for environmental events to happen and seeks increased levels of stimulation and excitation. The infant interprets events in her environment and gives them meaning, and consequently produces specific behaviors (Piaget, 1952).

The sensitive caregiver encourages action cycles with the infant by observing her moods, knowing what is interesting to the baby and learning what her skills are, giving the infant a chance to practice the familiar, and then challenging her to extend her skills in new directions with moderately novel materials and behaviors.

It is important, then, to balance the infant's day with self-initiated, independent activities for which the parent has set the stage, and with interactive exchanges. An effort should be made to keep these interactions spontaneous, fun, and consistent with the needs of both parent and child, striving for high mutuality. Remembering always that quality of stimulation if more important than quality, infant stimulation should be varied, appropriately timed, linked to the infant's actions, and presented in a context of basic trust.

Each phase of the parent–child interaction can alter the status of a child, so that during the subsequent phase of interaction, the child stimulates the parent in a different way or reacts different to parent behavior. In turn, parents discover that previous behaviors are no longer appropriate, and they are faced with finding new ways of guiding and interacting with the child.

PARENTS AS PROTECTORS

As a child becomes mobile, the role of parents gradually takes on the new dimension of protector. The once dependent, "helpless" child is transformed into an active, tireless, curious toddler. Suddenly, the child can see the top of the table, reach the magazines, flush toys down the toilet, drink from the pet's bowl, eat the dog's or cat's food, and perform a host of other activities that are fascinating to their growing curiosity. These behaviors are related to the fact that the toddler no longer needs hands to assist with getting around—the child is now free to feel and touch and explore things that are attractive. Of course, this means that as protectors, parents must provide the safest environment possible for toddlers to exercise their growing independence and increased capacity for learning.

Coping With Autonomy: "Me Do It!"

The years from one to three constitute for the child a declaration of independence (Brazelton et al., 1974). Stage 2 in Erikson's theory of psychosocial development is described as **autonomy versus shame and doubt**. The child takes pride in their new accomplishments of walking and climbing, opening and closing, dropping, pushing and pulling, and holding on and letting go. The toddler now wants to do everything for themself. This sense of autonomy or independence is thought to be one of the most important psychological skills for children to develop optimally and to flourish (Ryan & Deci, 2017). So, when we think about autonomy in children, we must encourage the people with whom they most frequently interact (i.e., parents and teachers), to be actively supportive of this independence (Barrable, 2019).

Striving for Independence

If parents recognize the young child's need to do what the toddler is capable of doing at his own pace and in his own time, the child develops a sense that he can control his muscles, his impulses, himself, and, not insignificantly, his environment. The phrase, "Me do it!" is familiar to most parents who have developed the endless patience required to let the child dress himself in the morning, pour his own milk, or put away his toys. Erikson believed, however, that if caregivers are impatient and do for the child what the child is capable of doing himself, parents reinforce a sense of shame and doubt. When caregiving is consistently overprotecting, critical, harsh, or unthinking, the child develops an excessive sense of doubt about his abilities to control his world and himself, and develops shame with respect to other people.

Evidence shows that resistant and angry child behavior peaks during the second year and then begins its decline thereafter. In fact, mothers and fathers have been shown to react more positively to 12-month-olds than to 18-month-olds, and parents' self-rated enjoyment of parenting declines from 18 to 24 months. Many parents resist their toddlers' strivings for autonomy, and/or they have limited skill in managing effective the child's emerging developmental advances (Belsky et al., 1996). Studies show that about 65 percent of parent–child interactions at age 2 are parental prohibitions, and parents interrupt their toddlers every six to eight minutes to induce them to change their behavior (Baumrind, 1996).

This striving for autonomy in toddlers is often coupled with open negativism toward the parents. With toddlers' "No's!" they establish themselves as separate from their parents. They learn what parents expect of them and how parents will act in response to them. Parents can minimize setting themselves up for a "no" from the child by phrasing statements in the form of expectations rather than choices when choices are not intended. For example, if a parent expects the toddler to go to bed, he/she/they should not say, "Do you want to go to bed?" Instead, the parent should say, "It's bedtime."

Self-Regulation

There is no question that once children become mobile, parents must set firm limits and enforce them consistently in a loving manner. Either extreme in the setting of limits at this stage interferes with healthy development. The most important limits have to do with the child's own safety and well-being. The newfound freedom of the toddler carries with it potential danger, making the setting and maintenance of limits necessary. The other purpose of parental control at this point is to make it possible for the child to know how and when to control themself. Erikson (1963) believed that a lasting sense of goodwill and pride derives from a sense of self-control without loss of self-esteem.

It is during toddlerhood that children need to begin to learn self-regulation. **Self-regulation** refers to a child's ability to manage or direct his or her thoughts, emotions, and actions, and this skill grows quite rapidly in early childhood (McClelland & Cameron, 2012). In essence, when children have the ability to self-regulate, they are better able to calm themselves when upset. Further, when children are confronted with a new situation that is difficult to handle (such as going to preschool or kindergarten), children who possess self-regulation skills can better control their emotions and behaviors. A substantial body of evidence indicates that self-regulation is predictive of school success, from before kindergarten, throughout school, into adulthood (Blair & Razza, 2007; Liew et al., 2008; McClelland et al., 2010; Valiente et al., 2008).

How does self-regulation develop in children? Just as with Bronfenbrenner's Ecological Model (see Chapter 2), there are multiple contexts that contribute to self-regulation: One's biological predisposition; relational skills developed with adults and caregivers; internal (intrinsic) and external (extrinsic) motivations; caregiver support; and environmental factors (such as chronic stress, poverty, or trauma) (Rosanbalm & Murray, 2017). As you can see, the development of self-regulation occurs in the same way almost all of child development occurs: As an interaction between the child and her environment. It is the environment that enhances the development of self-regulation, and the environment that can impede its development.

Just as with the development of attachment, parents or caregivers contribute to a child's self-regulation development by:

- providing a warm, responsive parent–child relationship;
- providing and structuring a stress-free, physically and emotionally safe environment;
- providing consistent, predictable routines and expectations;
- teaching self-regulation skills through modeling (Rosanbalm & Murray, 2017).

Table 5.3 presents the ways in which self-regulation is observable in infancy, toddlerhood, and the pre-K years. As you can see, as the child's brain and body develop, so, too, does the toddler's capacity to develop self-regulation.

Temper Tantrums

More severe forms of negativism are manifested by toddlers in their frequent temper tantrums. These occur normally because toddlers' wishes and desires for independence are

TABLE 5.3 ■ Self-Regulation in Early Childhood
Infancy
• When overwhelmed, infants shift their attention or avert their gaze
• To reduce emotions, babies will self-soothe by sucking (a pacifier, fingers)
Toddlerhood
• Able to focus attention for first shorter, then longer periods of time
• Adjusting behavior to achieve goals (i.e., stop crying to receive the toy)
• Can label a few feelings in accordance with vocabulary growth ("I happy!")
• Turning to a secure base when overwhelmed
Preschool
• Demonstrates empathy
• With guided support, can use calming strategies such as taking deep breaths
• Recognize that self and others have feelings
• Identify solutions when experiencing unexpected outcomes

Source: Adapted from Rosanbalm and Murray (2017).

thwarted. They are perpetuated by the parents who either force a contest of wills or give in to toddlers' desires. Neither technique is appropriate. Contests of wills may be avoided by making expectations simple, clear, and consistent. When children test these expectations (and they will—often!), parents can assist cooperation by reinforcing verbal requests by physical contact (such as, taking the child by the hand and leading the toddler in the desired direction), modeling the expected behavior for the child, and offering realistic choices so that she can exercise independence—what kind of juice is wanted, which book she wants to read, or which shirt is the favorite one to wear that day. If all this fails and a tantrum ensues anyway, then the worst possible behavior is for the parent to give in to the child's wishes, if it is clear that those wishes are inconsistent with the limits the parent has already set. Consistent failure to pay attention to tantrum behaviors usually serves to reduce its occurrence. Parents fail to reinforce it not only by not giving in but also by withdrawing attention from the tantrum and refusing to allow the child to harm herself, others, or property. It may be necessary to remove the child from the immediate environment in order to remove reinforcing agents.

Belsky and his associates (1996), in their research with families and their first-born male toddlers, identified a group of families who seemed to have more difficulty than others managing their children. The families in the "most troubled" group were more likely to rely on basic control techniques (directives and prohibitions) and least likely to couple these control efforts with guidance (simple declaratives accompanied by reasons or explanations). Their children were found the most defiant and subsequently experienced the most escalation of negative affect by parents. Further, these children demonstrated more aggression and acting out, and their parents reported more daily hassles.

These investigators found that, in addition to low socioeconomic status (SES), families likely to be "most troubled" were characterized by more support for and less interference with the fathers' work; had both mothers and fathers who were less social, more negative, and less friendly; and had both mothers and fathers who were least satisfied with the social support they were receiving.

The authors raised the important question of whether trouble in the second year forecasts further trouble in childrearing. Some experts speculate that the parent–child interaction during toddlerhood represents a critical period for patterns that persist in the future. If such is the case, it seems that parents with toddlers should be targeted for family support and parent education programs that might offset future problems.

Although autonomy is a necessary stage of healthy development, it can sometimes be frustrating—for both parent and child. Even though parents can feel threatened and ill equipped to handle their toddler's negativism and lack of compliance, they should recognize that this is expected, healthy development. By finding an appropriate balance between too little and too much independence, they can facilitate their toddler's self-control without causing the child to lose self-esteem.

Providing toddlers the opportunity to engage with other children helps to encourage and develop necessary social and emotional skills, such as sharing, cooperation, and empathy.

Source: Photo Courtesy of Abbigail George.

Social and Intellectual Learning

There are four areas of learning that are critical during this period: the acquisition of social skills, language, the development of curiosity, and the formation of the roots of intelligence.

In the first area, toddlers need exposure to interactions with other children their own age. Frequently, parents choose to place toddlers in a play group or a child care center at this time so children can learn basic social skills, such as waiting one's turn, sharing toys and equipment, delaying gratification, and getting along well in groups.

Children who do not have playgroup or child care experiences during toddlerhood need the opportunity to interact with their peers. Oftentimes, however, children treat their peers as objects, not people, especially in the beginning stages of association. The "No, mine!" protest that is familiar to all of us further emphasizes the immaturity of the toddler's understandings of social interactions. The child's grabbing, pulling, biting, and hitting are in part due to egocentricity and in part due to lack of language skills that older children use when cooperating in play.

The learning of appropriate social skills requires a patient adult who recognizes the child's immature level of development and therefore does not place too many demands on the toddler to "be nice" or to "share the toys." Parents and educators in the know duplicate toys and activities to minimize conflict over any special one. They also use distraction and offer alternatives, and most importantly, model appropriate social behavior for the child.

An extremely important event in the life of the toddler is the rapid development of language. From 18 months to 3 years, the average vocabulary of a child leaps from approximately 20 to 22 words to 900 words! Naturally, the child understands far more words than are used. The parent's role in language development includes

- labeling familiar objects and events;
- expanding on the child's telegraphic speech;
- reinforcing language attempts;
- modeling.

Numerous studies indicate that a child's development is correlated closely with the quality and quantity of language used in the home. Further, children learn early language from adults, not from other children. The degree to which parents talk *with* the child, ask/answer questions, read to the child, and consider language as a valued tool for intellectual development relates to early language facilitation in the child.

The development of curiosity and the formation of the roots of intelligence during the toddler stage are related closely to language development. Even before the toddler has the language to ask questions, the child demonstrates curiosity by using the senses of touch, taste, smell, vision, and hearing. These senses, coupled with the ability for independent locomotion, provide important cues about the toddler's expanded world and assist in the formation of basic concepts related to color, shape, size, weight, distance, and causality. As the child acquires greater language facility, he is able to expand his concepts by attaching labels to them. For example, a toddler with a basket full of objects from around the house can learn something about size, shape, and cause-and-effect relationships. With the parent's verbal interaction, the child is also learning that a particular word stands for a particular object. Besides, he is probably having a lot more fun than a toddler whose mother tries to teach her the alphabet or how to use the computer.

As in earlier infancy, there should be a balance between self-initiated and self-sustained activities by the child, in addition to parent–child interactions. In this way, the child controls much of his own learning within a framework provided by the parent.

PARENTS ARE NURTURERS

Nurturance is affectionate care and attention. This definition aptly describes the chief role that parents assume as their children move into the preschool period. Although the child's environment still must remain safe and protective, preschool children do not need the constant watchful eye of parents that was so necessary for infants and toddlers. To discover the optimal amount of supervision without interference, assistance without indulgence, and warmth and love without suffocation is difficult for many parents. They find that their need to be needed is still very strong, and some find it difficult to meet that need in a way that is healthy for both themselves and their children.

Warmth refers to a parent's emotional expressions of love. Children of parents with warmth and empathy are more motivated to participate in cooperative strategies, and these parental characteristics are associated with children's internalization of moral values. On the other hand, a predominance of parental negative mood and facial expressions is associated with defiance and hostile aggression in children (Baumrind, 1996).

It is likely that a child's perception of the emotional climate that exists within the home is of far greater consequence in healthy development than the specific behaviors of the parent. Furthermore, consistency in the kind of discipline used by parents, how it is administered, and in what context seem to be more influential in facilitating healthy development than the specific type of discipline used (Baumrind, 1996). If parents have not agreed already on the goals and values they have for their children, it is critical that some agreement be reached at this point. Belsky and his associates (1995) reported that spousal disagreements about childrearing attitudes and values when children were three years old predicted both child behavior problems two years later and marital dissolution seven years after that. Other research shows that such disagreements forecast psychological and behavioral development when children are as old as 18.

Each parent is different and interacts with the child in ways that are unique to their own style, but consistency in making and enforcing rules, as well as a common agreement as to whether discipline will be permissive, authoritative (democratic), or authoritarian offers the young child the consistency that is vital to her growing sense of competence. In essence, children need to know that behavior approved by one parent is approved by the other parent. They need the comfort that parents respond with consistency—both within the individual parent and between the parents.

A strong love relationship between parents at this time further facilitates their roles as nurturers of their children. Respect for each other and respect for their children as individuals creates a positive emotional climate in the home. Additionally, the love and respect parents have for one another is an effective tool for facilitation of the identification process in the late preschool period.

One major consideration in providing nurturance is knowing how to establish limits and achieve responsible behavior in young children without threatening their sense of autonomy and initiative.

The Styles of Parenting

Parenting or parenthood is not a single behavior. Professor of Family Studies and Family Life Educator Carol Darling and her colleague (1993) describe parenting as multiple behaviors that, together, shape children's outcomes. Research psychologist Diana Baumrind asserts that normal parenting centers on the issue of control and that parents' primary roles are to influence, teach, and control their children. Based on her observations of parent–child interactions, Baumrind believes that there are two specific dimensions of childrearing: parental warmth or responsiveness/affection/supportiveness toward the child, and parental control or how demanding or restrictive the parents are toward their child (also referred to as *behavioral control*). In examining these two dimensions, Baumrind (1991) identifies four parenting styles, which we discuss here. Each of these parenting styles reflects different patterns of parental values, practices, and behaviors.

Uninvolved Parenting

Uninvolved parents are typically low in responsiveness, warmth, and affection, and they are low in parental control or demands (Sanders, 2008). Parents may both reject and neglect their children. Not all parents who are uninvolved are neglectful or rejecting; some are simply detached and uninterested in their children's lives. For example, some parents, although they may meet their child's basic needs (shelter, clothing, education, and food), may not offer praise for a child's efforts or compliment the child's accomplishments. In essence, there are few meaningful and inclusive family interactions.

There are a number of negative consequences of uninvolved or disengaged parenting for child and adolescent well-being (for a thorough review, see Kuppens & Ceulemans, 2019). Across all racial and ethnic groups, for example, there are reports of increased substance use and abuse, higher rates of delinquency, poorer school performance, and negative psychological well-being (Pittman & Chase-Landsdale, 2001; Samaniego & Gonzales, 1999; Steinberg et al., 1991, 1994). Today, we know that there are certain outcomes associated with uninvolved parenting (Cherry, 2018):

- Children must learn to provide for themselves.
- Children and adolescents may become fearful of depending on others.
- Kids are often emotionally withdrawn.
- Adolescents tend to exhibit more delinquency.
- Children and adolescents experience fear, anxiety, or stress because of lack of family support.
- Adolescents are at greater risk for substance abuse.

Other research further suggests that disengaged parenting styles, when combined with families who live in dangerous or socially disorganized neighborhoods, are linked with increased adolescent delinquency in African American and Latino boys (Roche et al., 2007). There is also an association of uninvolved/disengaged parenting with increased school problem behavior and depression among African American youth, particularly when mothers are not involved in their children's parenting. This evidence is clear and convincing: The stakes of uninvolved or detached parenting are profound among Black, particularly among adolescent males.

Permissive Parenting

Also referred to as *indulgent* and *careless* parents, **permissive parents** demonstrate high levels of warmth, affection, and responsiveness toward their children, and also show adequate to high levels of parent–child communication (Odame-Mensah & Gyimah, 2018). This parenting style does not place high demands on children nor do parents attempt to control their children's behavior; children's behavior is mostly self-regulated. Baumrind (1991) refers to these parents as *lenient* and *nontraditional*. Permissive parents rarely invoke the use of punishment, and very often children are given great latitude in making decisions for their lives (Kang & Moore, 2011; Odame-Mensah & Gyimah, 2018).

Similar to uninvolved or disengaged parenting, children and adolescents of parents who set no boundaries and who do not provide behavioral regulations experience higher levels of depression, poorer school performance, poorer psychological adjustment and well-being, and greater use of substances (Pittman & Chase-Landsdale, 2001; Samaniego & Gonzales, 1999; Steinberg et al., 1991, 1994). Parents who engage in *autonomy granting* might allow their children to set their own curfews and do not monitor the children's free time (Kang & Moore, 2011). This can evolve into putting their children at risk for elevated depression; this is particularly true for Asian females and Black males (Radziszewska et al., 1996). In high-risk (low income/low education), dangerous neighborhoods and communities, permissive parenting is associated with increased adolescent delinquency, school problem behavior, and poor school performance, particularly among adolescent African American males (Roche et al., 2007).

Authoritarian Parenting

According to Baumrind, **authoritarian parents** are "obedience- and status-oriented, and expect their orders to be obeyed without explanation" (1991, p. 62). To put it another way, authoritarian parents are very demanding and controlling with their children, but at the same time not very responsive, warm, or affectionate toward their children. This type of parenting style is characterized by rigid rules of behavior, which children are expected to follow with no questions asked, and it is often referred to as *punitive* parenting (Hosokawa & Katsura, 2019). Parent–child communication is very low, and there is no room for compromise. Power is the key player.

Across all racial and ethnic groups, this type of restrictive, punitive parenting is associated with increased emotional problems (such as anxiety), psychological problems (such as depression), and increased behavioral problems (Eamon & Mulder, 2005; Grogan-Kaylor, 2005; McLeod & Nonnemaker, 2000). When parents use corporal punishment (spanking or hitting), children and adolescents exhibit more incidences of problem behaviors; however, this is found more among whites and Latinos than it is among Blacks (Lansford et al., 2004). Corporal punishment also appears to be more strongly associated with behavior problems in boys than it is in girls (Grogan-Kaylor, 2005). Interestingly, punitive/restrictive parenting is associated with *increases* in depression, delinquencies, and problem behaviors for African American males who live in safe neighborhoods/communities, but it is linked with *decreases* in these maladies for Blacks who live in dangerous neighborhoods. We'll discuss the possible reasons for these findings a bit later.

Authoritative Parenting

With this parenting style, parents are responsive while demanding certain behavioral standards. This style of parenting does not use shame, withdrawal of love, or guilt (as might authoritarian parents) to control behavior. **Authoritative parents** set clear boundaries for their children's behavior, but they are flexible and will change these boundaries if the situation warrants. For example, a teen's regular curfew may be at midnight, but on prom night, the teen may be allowed to stay out much later. Authoritative parents are warm and responsive, and they encourage parent–child communication. Children are expected to follow the rules of the house but are still allowed to be autonomous. With this style, parents use a balance of power and reason.

Of all of Baumrind's parenting styles, authoritative parenting provides children with a balance of control and warmth, which yields the best outcome for children's health and well-being in the areas of social competence and psychosocial development. A number of research studies consistently demonstrate that children reared by authoritative parents exhibit more social competence than do other children (Amato & Fowler, 2002; McClunn & Merrell, 1998; Steinberg & Morris, 2001).

- Both boys and girls reared by authoritative parents exhibit lower levels of problem behavior across all stages of the lifespan, across all ethnic groups (Jackson et al., 1998; Kim et al., 1999).
- Children reared by authoritative parents are better able to balance the demands of conforming to others' expectations with their own needs for uniqueness and autonomy (Durbin et al., 1993; Shucksmith et al., 1995).
- Both boys and girls tend to perform better in school if they are reared by authoritative parents—this higher level of performance is seen from preschool throughout early adulthood (Brooks-Gunn & Markman, 2005; Chen & Kaplan, 2001).
- Effective parenting skills further the growth of children's social and communication skills, as well as their ability to concentrate on tasks and at school (Connell & Prinz, 2002; Lamb-Parker et al., 1999).
- Authoritative parents of adolescents allow their teens to have autonomy, but they simultaneously define clear boundaries and articulate their concerns about safety and well-being (Smetana, 1995).

When parents are warm, sensitive, and responsive to their child's needs, they foster a wide range of interpersonal development in children, from the development of a healthy sense of self, to a sense of belonging and well-being, to high levels of self-esteem (Harvard Family Research Project, 2006).

Ethnic Group Differences in Parenting

In Chapters 1 and 2, we saw that in America today, there is vast racial and ethnic diversity. When examining contemporary parenting, an understanding of ethnic identity and how it influences parenting is of profound interest because "racial and ethnic background, country of residence, immigration status, and socioeconomic status influence the manner in which parents parent their children" (Clark et al., 2015, p. 697). As we have previously discussed, *individualistic* and *collectivist* cultures influence the goals of parenting differently, as well as parents' views about parenting (Clark et al., 2015). And, as we've also learned, different racial and ethnic groups vary as to whether they identify as an individualistic or collectivist culture.

In a landmark, large-scale study of approximately 10,000 adolescents representing four ethnic groups (African American, white, Hispanic, and Asian American), the researchers found that the *authoritative* parenting style was the most common among white families and least common among Asian Americans; it was also more common among married biological parents than it was among single-parent or stepfamilies (Steinberg et al., 1991). The study also showed that parenting styles differ by social class. Authoritative parenting was more common among middle class parents than among working class parents, with the exception of Asian American parents, who demonstrated authoritarian parenting styles.

Other parenting practices, such as spanking for discipline, vary in frequency by race and ethnicity.

Subsequent research has found that *parenting goals*, (i.e., raising children so they will succeed in college and in their careers), are tied to parenting styles (Cheah & Rubin, 2004). Parenting goals are influenced by the parents' cultural values. For example, Asian American parents may raise their children with the *authoritarian* parenting style because they believe it helps to maintain their cultural identity, while Black parents may do so because they are "keenly aware of the degree to which social forces such as racism may impede their children's achievement of educational, economic, and social success … they [believe] that adopting an authoritarian parenting style will enhance their children's potential for success" (Boyd & Bee, 2009, p. 224). The link between this parenting style and child outcome variables such as self-control suggests that it is effective for Blacks (Broman et al., 2006). It is important to note, however, that not *all* African American parents adopt this parenting style—parenting styles are as unique as each individual.

These studies show us that there are *culturally specific* processes that underlie parents' behaviors and communication. The reality of parenting is that it is an experience which comprises interconnected, multiple processes that are affected by the parents' race/ethnicity, cultural beliefs, income level, and living environment. Much more work needs to be done to fully understand the interplay of cultural contexts and parenting because these studies can serve as a launching pad for Family Life Education programs and public policies to strengthen family life (Cebalo et al., 2008).

There is a difference between discipline and punishment. When a parent disciplines a child, it is through firm instruction—the aim is to change the child's behavior. On the other hand, punishment is used to stop or change the behavior by using physical methods.

Source: iStock.com/fizkes.

Discipline and Punishment: One and the Same?

One of the major concerns that parents of young children face is how much or how little to discipline their children. In our society, the terms *discipline* and *punishment* are often used interchangeably. **Discipline** refers to one who receives *instruction* from another. When the term is used correctly, then, a system of discipline should imply a broad positive system of guidance of the young child, with particular methods of **punishment**—most often physical in nature—being only a minor aspect (if any) of that total discipline system.

Inductive discipline focuses on encouraging the young child to take into account the potential effects of their behavior on other people and on themself when making decisions about what they will and will not do. This approach is most often combined with an authoritative parenting style. The inductive parent emphasizes process goals, stressing the "how" rather than the "what" of behavior. This is in contrast to a parent telling a child that certain behaviors are good and others are bad, which is more likely to produce unnecessary feelings of guilt and shame. It is important to show children why their present behavior pattern is inappropriate, show them how to act instead, and demonstrate the expectation that they will change their behavior in the desired direction. Parents who use inductive disciplinary techniques often have children who are less likely to violate prohibitions than other children are.

Natural and Logical Consequences

Ruydolf Dreikurs was noted for his approach to discipline through the use of natural and logical consequences (Dreikurs & Grey, 1968), and this approach is still widely used today. **Natural consequences** are those that occur naturally from the behavior, such as the child who refuses to eat goes hungry. **Logical consequences** are those that are assigned by the parent to express the reality of the social order, not of the person. For example, a child who disturbs the rest of the family at mealtime is given the choice to settle down or to leave the table.

There are advantages of using natural and logical consequences (Dinkmeyer et al., 1997):

- It holds children (not parents) responsible for behavior.
- It allows children to make their own decisions about what courses of action are appropriate.
- It permits children to learn from the natural or social order of events, rather than forcing them to comply with the wishes of people.

When using this type of discipline, a parent must separate the deeds from the doer—the parent's actions must be based on respect for the child as a person separate from the child's actions. The parent should also be firm in following through with the consequences, yet kind in the tone of voice used to discipline the child. Encouragement is implicit in this approach. Children eventually learn to accept responsibility for their own behavior in a way that conveys mutual respect and avoids power struggles.

Spanking

Spanking is a common occurrence in families with young children, and fathers typically spank less than mothers do (Day et al., 1998). Well over 61 percent of mothers of preschool children report spanking their children, with a mean of about three spankings per week (Giles-Sims et al., 1995).

The strongest and most consistent predictors of parental spanking are the personal characteristics of the parents (i.e., young age and conservative religious ideology) and perceived characteristics of the child (such as whether the child was difficult) (Day et al., 1998). Other characteristics lead to wide variations in the incidence and intensity of spanking behaviors. Black mothers, for instance, spank more than other mothers (Giles-Sims et al., 1995). Rural mothers, young mothers, and Protestant mothers spank more than urban, older, and Catholic mothers.

Figure 5.4 presents the racial differences in using spanking as a discipline technique. In a representative study of 4,000 participants, the researchers found that Black parents (59 percent) are more likely than white (46 percent) or Latinx (48 percent) parents to say they sometimes spank their children (Finkelhor et al., 2019). As you can see, parents of all races are more likely to spank children under the age of 9 than they are to spank children ages 10 to 17. Overall, 37 percent of parents in the United States spank their children; this represents a decline in spanking, and as the authors of the study observe, this decline in "other forms of violence against children and in society" (Finkelhor et al., 2019, p. 5). Interestingly, two-parent families and single-parent families are no more or less likely to spank than the other—50 percent of two-parents use corporal punishment, and 50 percent of single-parent families likewise discipline their children.

FIGURE 5.4 ■ Percentage of Parents Who Spank by Race and by Age of Child

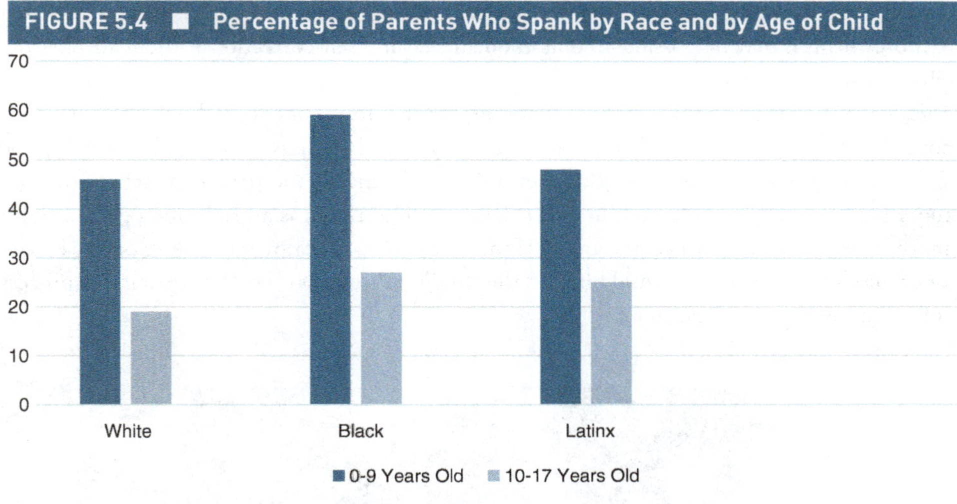

Source: Finkelhor et al. (2019).

TABLE 5.4 ■ Administering Physical Punishment

When a parent or caregiver decides to administer physical punishment (spanking), several conditions must first be met.

1. **The punishment should immediately follow the act.** Spanking is effective at suppressing rule-breaking behaviors when it is administered without delay. Waiting until Dad or Mom get home from work actually punishes the child all day.
2. **The punishment must be deserved and understood.** When deciding to spank, a parent must take into consideration the contexts of the child's misbehavior. For example, did he miss his nap because Mom continues to shop? Children need to know exactly what they are being punished for—especially preschool children, who have short memories. An explanation of the misbehavior and punishment works well to result in effective discipline.
3. **The punishment must be related to the act.** The punishment must fit the crime. If a child, for example, colors on the wall, an appropriate punishment is having her help to clean the wall. This way, she associates the punishment with the act and is less likely to repeat it.
4. **The punishment should be administered in a loving way.** Parents should be loving, calm, and understanding when administering discipline. This sends the message that the child isn't bad, but that the behaviors were unacceptable.

Source: Adapted from Giles-Sims et al. (1995).

These findings are important for us to understand because spanking can pose a serious threat to the well-being of children: It increases the chances of both physical aggression and delinquency and is associated with depression, spouse abuse, and reduced occupational achievement in adulthood (Giles-Sims et al., 1995). Thus, when a parent deems it necessary to administer physical punishment (spanking), several conditions should be met. These are summarized for us in Table 5.4. As you can see, if parents use spanking judiciously and concentrate on achieving compliance with their standards by using explanations, reason, and external reinforcement, it may be possible to obtain obedience and self-correction without stimulating self-punitive reactions.

One of the major disadvantages of spanking or other forms of corporal punishment is that normally they serve as a vehicle for the release of parental feelings as opposed to helping the child learn appropriate behavior. But even more problematic, the parent models aggressive, angry behavior for the child and, in effect, tells the child that it is all right for a person to hit another person when they become angry. If the parent remains calm and focuses on the behavior of the child instead of the child himself, the child's self-respect is not damaged in the process of facilitating acceptable behavior.

The pride of accomplishing a great task! Providing children the opportunities to create and solve problems strengthens the development of their self-concept and self-esteem.
Source: Photo courtesy of Brittany Wessling.

BUILDING SELF-CONCEPT, INITIATIVE, AND LEARNING

One of the most significant results of nurturance during the preschool period is the building of a healthy self-concept in young children. Self-concept is believed to be intimately related to the individual's interactions with significant others in her social world.

Developing a Self-Concept

Traditionally, the two aspects of the child's self-concept that have been emphasized are a sense of belonging and a feeling of worth. Although these are no doubt critical to the child's overall feeling of self-esteem, the more recent examination of the child's perceived behavioral competencies is consistent with the view of the child as an active participant in her overall development. It appears that the young child's ability to interact successfully with her environment is a vital aspect of her development of a positive self-worth. As you saw earlier, the characteristics of authoritative parents contribute to young children's self-concept.

Abundant evidence also suggests that a child's self-concept is a powerful determinant of their behavior. A correlation exists between self-concept and achievement as early as kindergarten, though this relationship becomes more prominent during the school-age period. In fact, a person's chances for success increase as her self-esteem increases. Preschool children with poor self-concepts may be overly cautious when attempting new tasks, fearing failure. They may appear anxious, defensive, and withdrawn. Although self-concept changes over the course of development—for better or for worse—the preschool period is a crucial time for observing behaviors that might suggest a poorly emerging self-concept.

Developing a Sense of Initiative

Erikson (1963) described his third stage of psychosocial development as **initiative versus guilt.** This stage has its beginning in the latter part of the third year after the child has attained proficiency in walking and feeding himself. The child's attention, no longer needed to develop and control basic activities (such as in toilet learning), is now free to add a new dimension to his newly achieved muscular autonomy. He now directs his attention toward increasing participation in his social environment, largely his family, but also to other adults and peers.

Whether a child leaves this stage with a sense of **initiative**—a sense that he can accomplish anything before him—depends to a considerable extent on how her parents respond to his self-initiated activities. Children who are given freedom, opportunity, and encouragement to initiate play, to ask questions, and to engage in fantasy play have their sense of initiative reinforced. But at the same time, conscience is beginning to develop, and the child begins to understand the difference between right and wrong and pleasing and displeasing his parents. If he thinks that his play is bad or dangerous or that his questions are a nuisance, he may develop a sense of guilt over self-initiated activities. This guilt may persist through later life stages.

Children who successfully resolve the conflict between initiative and guilt learn to control their behavior and respect social conventions and moral responsibilities. At the same time, they do not lose their psychological freedom to assume initiatives and the responsibilities that come with them. Conversely, children who fail to resolve this conflict successfully tend to emerge with overly strong and inflexible consciences that inhibit them from taking initiative in ambiguous situations in which they are not sure that they are safe from disapproval.

Providing Learning Experiences

Much of what we have discussed—methods of discipline, the building of a healthy self-concept, and developing initiative—can hardly be separated from providing optimal learning experiences. A child who is nurtured, who is given freedom to initiate, and who feels good about herself as a person and a family member is inspired to learn. A young child learns from every event in which she participates, from her peers, her play, and her everyday interactions with her environment. Warmth, nurturance, and responsiveness are prerequisites for effective learning experiences during the preschool years.

Through play, young children learn in a way that no one can teach them. Play is the major vehicle for learning during the early childhood years, and preschoolers like to "mess and manipulate." They learn about their physical world by touching, examining, testing, exploring, evaluating, and imagining. Perhaps the most important ingredient for learning experiences is people. A loving, caring adult who is available to the child to answer his questions, to engage him in imagination and fantasy, to introduce him to new words and ideas, and to pick up on his cues of curiosity cannot be replaced by dozens of toys. The adult who structures the environment so that learning occurs, who allows the child freedom and encouragement for exploration, and who interacts with him in a warm, accepting manner provides the most important learning experiences of all.

PARENTING LIFE EDUCATION: ADDRESSING FAMILY NEEDS AND ACHIEVING FAMILY GOALS

There is no consensus about the most effective form or timing of parent education. It seems, however, that parent education programs for the parents of very young children are particularly important for two reasons. First, it is assumed that a person is most motivated when they are a parent or they are about to become a parent. Also, parents have a more realistic orientation to some of the problems of parenthood than potential parents have and will reap more benefits from a program that is directed toward their current needs. Second, the emphasis that has been placed on the importance of the environmental experiences for brain development in the early years and their implications for the child's further development suggests the need for early intervention and support for parents. In fact, when it comes to education programs, the earlier the better, the longer the better, and the more consistent the better.

Recently there has been renewed interest in home-visiting programs for new parents, which currently serve a variety of populations and achieve many different goals. Home visitation is not a single, specific, uniformly defined service; rather, it is a strategy for service delivery—it brings various services to a family rather than requiring the family to come to the service provider(s). Programs primarily target pregnant people and/or families with young children up to three years of age.

In addition to home visitation programs, each year, *Head Start* state programs enroll 1.1 million preschoolers, and Head Start professionals provide 4.6 million home visits; since its founding, Head Start has served 37 million children (National Head Start Association, 2022). Today, educational services, such as high-quality language, literacy, and prereading activities, are offered to low-income families, prisons that house women and children, and migrants. Also, childhood education, adult education, parenting education, and literacy programs are becoming integrated. The goal is "family literacy" programs that service both parents and children.

Because the early childhood years are so important for laying the foundation for later development, and because parenting today is so complex, careful, well-planned programs that support and enhance parents' roles are essential. The goals of the programs range from a single goal, such a preventing low birth weights, to multiple goals, such as promoting a child's physical health and cognitive development. Still others take an even more comprehensive approach, seeking to address the needs of other family members. Some programs target specific populations, such as pregnant teens or families at risk for child abuse and neglect, whereas other programs are universal, or open to any family who wishes to participate (Gomby et al., 1993). One such example of a universal program is *Parents as Teachers*, which is widely used across the country. Though not empirical, evaluations of the Parents as Teacher program indicate that both parents and children benefit—children, by demonstrating advanced academic skills once they are in school when compared with nonparticipants, and parents, by being involved more than nonparticipant parents in their children's schooling. We'll discuss this program at length in the next chapter.

In order for programs to be effective, then, several factors need to be considered in developing and implementing programs for parents of infants and toddlers; both short- and long-term planning are necessary in order for home service programs to be effective and have lasting impact. The following issues need to be considered when developing programs for parents of infants and toddlers.

1. Training professionals that are sensitive to and skillful in counseling about the daily issues and adjustments of parents and young infants.
2. Designing long-term programs that emphasize the psychological aspects of parenting children during the first three years of life.
3. Considering the particular needs of parents of different racial, ethnic, and SES backgrounds in developing program content.
4. Designing programs that have immediate relevance for age-related development.
5. Using delivery methods that reach a broader range of parents, particularly those who are in the most need.

When choosing a career to work with parents and their children, it is essential to understand that parent educators and other helping professionals work collaboratively with parents, their children, and other community partners with one singular, common goal: To ensure that the needs of the whole child are met, and that parents and caregivers are supported in ways that help them to reach their potentials and to achieve their goals. The work is demanding, indeed—particularly now as our nation faces tremendous health and economic challenges in the aftermath of the COVID-19 pandemic. However, generations before us have confronted and overcome the challenges of their time, and working together, committed helping professionals will do the same today.

6 THE CHANGING NATURE OF PARENTING: MIDDLE CHILDHOOD

LEARNING OBJECTIVES

6.1 Summarize a preteen/adolescent's brain growth, both in architecture and functions.

6.2 Explain the concept "Parents are children's first and best sex educators."

6.3 Discuss common sexual behaviors expressed in middle childhood, and why it is important for parent educators to understand healthy childhood sexual development.

6.4 Contrast healthy and productive ways in which supportive parents communicate with their sexual and gender minority children with unsupportive parents.

6.5 Describe parent–child attachment in middle childhood, and how this attachment process aids or hinders the child's development of self-concept and self-regulation.

6.6 Identify the factors that influence children's mental health.

6.7 Summarize the importance of friendships to school-aged children, and the ways in which the parent's influence diminishes.

6.8 Describe Adverse Childhood Experiences and their importance to children's development.

6.9 Discuss children's use of technology and social media, and their impacts on children's mental health.

6.10 Provide examples of qualities that ensure equitable access to and participation in an afterschool program.

Middle childhood, ages about 6 to 12, is a critical, although often overlooked and understudied, period of development (DelGiudice, 2018; Mah & Ford-Jones, 2012). Because of the tremendous growth and transformations that take place in early childhood and adolescence, significant scholarly attention is given to these developmental periods, but historically, middle childhood has received far less empirical investigation. Although development slows somewhat during middle childhood, or the *school years*, there are a number of advances in a child's cognitive abilities, social and emotional characteristics, and physical growth. Indeed, the growth and experiences during middle childhood have wide-ranging implications for an individual's adulthood and are heavily dependent upon the child's environment, particularly the parent–child relationship (DelGiudice, 2018).

Before we continue, it is important to note that middle childhood and family experiences vary between cultures. For example, as we saw in the previous chapter, parenting children through the early years in Western cultures is hands-on—it is protective, instructive, and nurturing, and these societies embrace distinct child developmental stages; these parenting characteristics only change somewhat as children get older (Lancy, 2010, 2015, 2017). In some non-Western cultures, however, independence and resilience are encouraged, and in some civilizations (e.g., the Igbo of Nigeria, the San in Southern Africa, and the Semai from Malaysia), children as young as three years are left to meet their own needs, and parents are not expected to protect their children nor interactively guide their development (Ember & Cunnar, 2015). Nevertheless, Western cultures adopt the paradigm that middle childhood is a distinct, noteworthy period of human development, and while parenting does change in middle childhood, parents continue to very much influence their child's development.

Although some cultures encourage early independence, in Western cultures such as the United States, middle childhood—the *school years*—are thought to be a distinct developmental period where children still need their parents' protection and guidance.

Source: istock.com./Fstop123.

The middle childhood years are accompanied by a number of transitions in the child's physical maturity, cognitive capacity and capabilities, changes in relationships with parents and peers, exposure to new experiences, and responsibility demands from home and school (Collins & Madsen, 2019). Table 6.1 presents a brief overview of the developmental changes during this brief—but momentous—period of growth. Especially important to the holistic development of the child is the maturation of the brain and how these changes affect all aspects of a child's development, including relationships with self and others.

TABLE 6.1 ■ Middle Childhood Development

Body Growth	Growth is slower than in early childhood Variations in growth patterns due to biological sex, ethnic origin, genetics, hormones, nutrition, and environment Biological female increased body fat Biological male increased muscle mass Emergence of sex differences in late middle childhood About 2–3 inches increase in height each year Increased gross motor skills (coordinated walking, running, etc.) Increased fine motor skills
Brain Growth	By age 8–9, the brain is 90%–95% of its adult size Ongoing increase in white matter growth Frontal lobe growth (responsible for planning, reasoning, social judgment, and ethical decision-making) Brain circuity and pathways increase
Cognitive Growth	Master the use of logic in concrete ways Vocabulary increases to over 40,000 words, classification skills improve Reversibility and conservation emerge Selective attention increases Working memory increases and improves
Social/Emotional Growth	Development of industry Social cognition (experiential knowledge) improves Growth in peer relationships and increase in time spent with peers Increased independence from parents Shift from inward view of the world to outward view Development of self Self-esteem, self-worth, self-regulation, and self-confidence form a child's self-concept

Source: Collins and Madsen (2019).

CHILD BRAIN MATURATION AND THE ENVIRONMENT

From pregnancy through emerging adulthood, an individual's brain rapidly develops and matures, with the most impressive, dynamic growth occurring the first two years of life (Gilmore et al., 2018). Optimal brain development requires direction from experiences in the environment, and the parent–child relationship/family relationships are central to the architecture and function of the child's developing brain (Knudsen, 2004).

Dr. Eric Knudsen is a professor of neurobiology at Stanford University, Stanford, California. His work demonstrates that during certain periods of development, environmental influences affect the developing person in profound ways (Knudsen, 2004). The term **sensitive period** refers to the idea that experiences and environmental stimuli exert disproportionate influence on long-term developmental outcomes (Colombo et al., 2019). This concept is especially important to understand because during a sensitive period of brain development, certain experiences shape the connectivity of brain cells in precise ways; thus, the effects of these experiences are irreversible (Knudsen, 2004). It is this fundamental principle that guides our understanding of the importance of healthy parent–child and family relationships throughout all of childhood and adolescence.

Preadolescent Brain Development

The brain reaches its adult size by about age 7 or 8 (Paris, 2019), and throughout childhood, the cortical regions of the brain thicken and undergo tremendous transformation. In the prefrontal cortex, neural connections flourish, and gray matter peaks at about age 11 in genetic females and about age 12 in genetic males (Johnson et al., 2009). Dendritic overproduction is subsequently pruned, cutting back rarely used connections. Although maturation of the prefrontal cortex is not complete until an individual is in their early- to mid-20s, the structural changes in the child's brain affect every area of their middle childhood development, from physical abilities such as increases in coordination and reaction time, to gains in memory functioning, logic, and attention span, to decision-making, planning, problem-solving, and impulse control. Johnson and colleagues rightly conclude that preadolescent brain changes allow the brain to respond to the demands of its environment and the child's growth (Johnson et al., 2009). Given the enormity of the impact of brain changes on a child's lifespan development, middle childhood is, indeed, a sensitive period as Knudsen theorized (Mah & Ford-Jones, 2012). As Mah & Ford-Jones conclude, "The degree to which [brain changes occur] is modulated by the experiences a child has. As such, children have a greater chance of reaching their potential when they have access and opportunity to engage in stimulating environments, experiences, and interactions that support and promote their individual capacities and capabilities" (Mah & Ford-Jones, 2012, p. 81).

The Adolescent Brain Cognitive Development (ABCD) Consortium began a pioneering study in 2016. This study seeks to understand the cognitive processes and brain functions that bring about adolescent development and that are possible contributors to mental health challenges in adulthood and other experiences later in life (Chaarani et al., 2021). This 10-year, long-term study follows nearly 12,000 children and their families, and tracks children's physical, emotional, and mental development beginning at age 9 or 10. Using magnetic resonance imaging brain scans of the children, the investigators hope to determine how childhood experiences affect brain, cognitive, and emotional maturation. Dr. Deborah Yurgelun-Todd, a principal investigator in the study, notes that the first data revealed which parts of the brain are activated when children engage in cognitive control, reward processing, working memory, social-emotional function, and inhibitory control—all operations that are situated in the brain's executive function system, the prefrontal cortex (Chaarani et al., 2021).

This research is a vital first step in providing psychologists, social workers, physicians, educators, and other helping professionals an understanding of both protective and risk factors in children's environments, and how these factors affect mental health and well-being.

Parenting and the Preadolescent/Adolescent Brain Structure

There is great interest in the effects of parenting, childhood experiences, and childhood environments on structural brain changes during preadolescence and adolescence (Whittle et al., 2014). It is well established that adverse experiences and events during sensitive periods of brain development affect brain structures and functions in the following ways:

- There is an association between child abuse and deficits in memory, executive functions, and IQ (Hart & Rubia, 2012).
- Abused children have deficits in cognition and impairments in academic and emotional functioning (Letkiewicz et al., 2021).
- Child neglect is associated with learning difficulties, memory deficits, and cognitive delays (Pechtel & Pizzagalli, 2011; Pollak et al., 2010).
- Atypical emotional development (stress, sensitivity, behavioral regulation, and interpersonal problems) (see Bick & Nelson, 2016, for a full review).
- Attention and behavior difficulties are observed in children who have had adverse experiences (Pollak et al., 2010).

For nearly every executive function, experience—negative or positive—shapes brain development by being incorporated into the brain's connective network, and this brain connectivity lasts the remainder of the lifespan (Whittle et al., 2014). Other bodies of research show that *positive* parent–child interactions are just as important in determining brain structures and their functions as do negative interactions. For example, warm, responsive, supportive parenting is linked to positive cognitive, behavioral, and psychological growth and development that remains throughout the individual's life (Eshel et al., 2006; Landry et al., 2008, as presented in Whittle et al., 2014). Collins and colleague, too, note that attentive, warm, responsive parent–child relationships in middle childhood are associated with the development in the child of positive executive functions, such as a strong self-esteem and feelings of confidence (Collins & Madsen, 2019).

The brain is a highly sophisticated organ that relies on the interaction of biological forces (genetics) and experiences for its development. A major factor in the holistic child developmental process is the parent–child relationship, and this interaction between children and their caregivers contributes to the architecture and function of the brain in monumental ways. To be sure, biology and experience merge and form the foundation for adolescence and adulthood.

CHILD SEXUAL DEVELOPMENT

The physical changes that take place in middle childhood, between the ages of seven and 11, are perhaps not visible to others, but during middle childhood, or **prepubescence**, significant physical changes begin to occur. In the United States, **puberty**—a time of muscular, skeletal, and reproductive growth—usually begins in genetic girls between ages 8 and 13, and in genetic males between 9 and 14; it is a gradual process that takes years to complete (Backes & Bonnie, 2019; National Institutes of Health, 2020). Although puberty is a universal transition, some children mature more quickly than others due to the interactive result of social forces (such as being bullied) and biological forces (such as childhood obesity) (Backes & Bonnie, 2019; Downing & Bellis, 2009). A number of studies, for example, indicate that Black genetic females go through physical pubertal changes earlier than white, Latino, and Asian American girls (Biro & Wien 2010; Ge & Natsuaki, 2009; Keenan et al., 2014).

Biological females tend to mature more quickly than biological males, which is why girls are oftentimes much taller than boys during the elementary school years.

Source: iStock.com/ozgurdonmaz.

Gonadarche, the initial production of sex hormones by the testis (genetic male) or ovary (genetic female), typically occurs between ages 9 and 11 (see Backes & Bonnie, 2019). Outward signs of the sexual maturation process are evidenced as early as second or third grade, about the ages of 9 or 10. For instance, breast buds are visible in girls, and sparse pubic and underarm hair develop about six months later. These **secondary sexual characteristics** may appear as early as second grade in girls and are often accompanied by growth spurts in height and weight. Boys, too, undergo the development of secondary sexual characteristics, although they are typically about two years behind girls. Some girls will have their first menstruation during the middle childhood years. By about age 11, most children have a basic understanding of the human reproduction process, and they also know the proper terminology for their sex parts (Welch, 2010). It's important to note that although most children do know the proper names for their sexual anatomy, they more often use slang words when discussing their body parts.

Parents as Sex Educators

Middle childhood and adolescence are vitally important developmental periods when many youth and teens experience their first amorous relationships and develop their sexual identities (Lantos et al., 2019). Just as importantly, they are learning how to be responsible, respectful intimate partners, and are developing relationship skills that will be foundational for later adult relationships. Today, mothers more so than fathers, communicate with their kids about sex and sexual behaviors (Wikkeling-Scott, 2011). Although parents typically do not provide the type and accuracy of sexuality information and education that school health programs do, they still influence their children in critical ways in the communication of parental expectations and role modeling (Flores & Barroso, 2017; Lantos et al., 2019). Parent–child/teen discussions about **sexual and reproductive health (SRH)** have several protective factors:

- Youth and teens delay sex and use contraceptives more frequently than those who do not communicate with their parents about sexuality and health (Lantos et al., 2019).
- Several bodies of research suggest that adolescent sexual initiation is delayed if parents monitor and supervise their activities; there is also a decrease in sexual risk behavior (see Grossman et al., 2018).
- Warm and responsive parenting styles are also associated with delayed sexual initiation in adolescents, as well as a decrease in the likelihood that teens will engage in frequent sexual intercourse when they do become sexually active (Rodgers & McGuire, 2012).
- When parents disapprove of adolescent sexual activity, teens are less likely to engage in sexual behaviors, and if they do become sexually active, they tend to have fewer sex partners (Saewyc et al., 2008).
- Girls are more likely to practice safer sexual behaviors (including abstinence), use contraception and/or condoms, and delay first sexual intercourse when they have high levels of communication with their parents (Commendador, 2010; Hicks et al., 2013; Widman et al., 2016, as reported by Lantos et al., 2019).

Lantos and colleagues conducted an extensive analysis of National Survey of Family Growth data and examined sexual and reproductive health discussions among parents and their children (Lantos et al., 2019). The investigators were particularly interested in the racial/ethnic differences in the frequency and content of SRH discussions parents had with their children. Their work discovered that race and ethnicity factor into the frequency and types of parent–child SRH conversations. Figures 6.1 and 6.2 present the study's findings. As you can see, there are racial and ethnic differences in the types of SRH conversations parents have with their children. This is a very important finding because it may help explain to some degree why the teen pregnancy rate and sexually transmitted infection rates are disproportionately higher among Latinx youth and teens. Interestingly, Lantos's work also suggests that country of origin may contribute to parent–child SRH discussions: Foreign-born children and teens are more likely to engage in discussions about sex-related topics with their parents than are American-born teens (88.5 percent and 84.2 percent, respectively) (Lantos et al., 2019).

To be sure, parents are their children's first and best sexuality and sexual health educators. Perhaps one of Lantos's most important findings is that, while Latinx parents did not talk about sexual matters with their kids, the parents *believed* that they were communicating their values and beliefs clearly with their children. Among other parent cohorts, barriers to effective conversations included:

- Teens' beliefs that their parents were not well-informed about sexual matters in today's world.
- Parents' inability to acknowledge that their child was having sex.
- Cultural mores, norms, values, and beliefs.
- Parents' beliefs that their kids were getting the information they needed from school.
- Parents' beliefs that their children were too young and that the conversation could wait.

FIGURE 6.1 ■ Female Prevalence of Talking to Parents About SRH by Race/Ethnicity

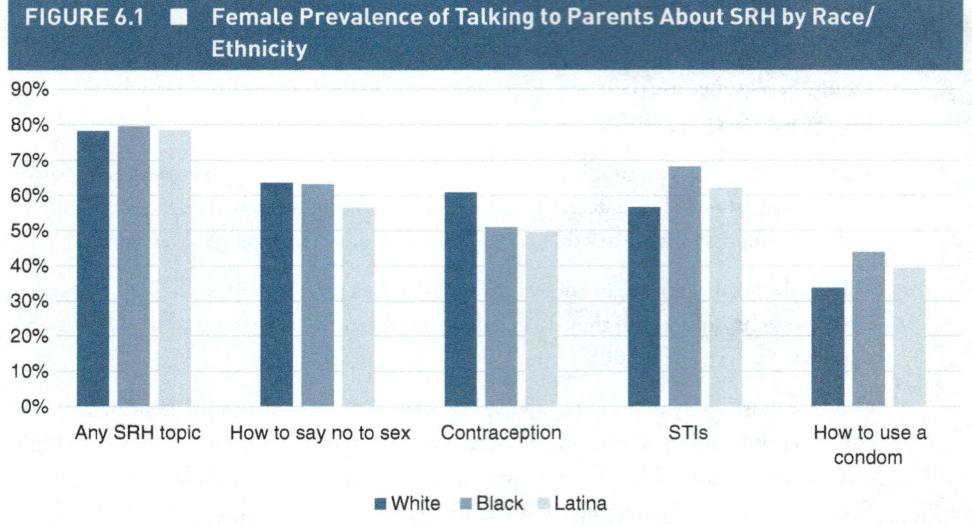

Source: Lantos et al. (2019).

FIGURE 6.2 ■ Male Prevalence of Talking to Parents About SRH by Race/Ethnicity

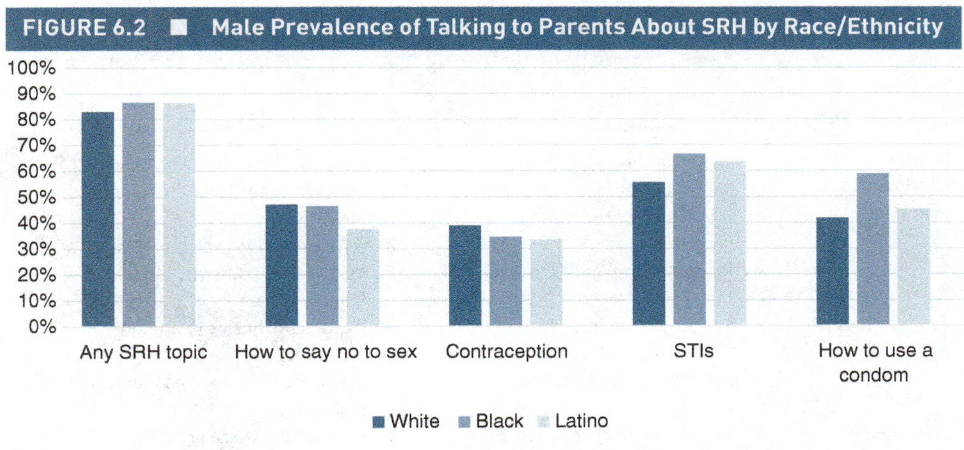

Source: Lantos et al. (2019).

Lantos aptly summarizes the study by highlighting the importance of parents and children having an open, trusting, communicative relationship, where daily communication about even the mundane things in life often occurs. A supportive parent–child relationship sets the stage for the child's healthy relationship and sexual future. Advocates for Youth, a nonprofit organization, works to provide sexuality education and equality for LGBTQ+ youth. They also suggest a number of ways in which sexual health can be improved for youth of color; these are presented in Table 6.2.

Children's Sexual Behaviors

As a child's body begins to sexually mature, they now have different ways in which to experience sexuality, and Table 6.3 presents these common behaviors. Not surprisingly, sexual behaviors increase in children as they mature physically. Although children begin to experiment more

TABLE 6.2 ■ Effective Ways to Serve Youth of Color

Programs are more effective when they	• Use comprehensive sexuality education, including information on *both* contraception and abstinence • Provide easily accessible contraceptive services and methods • Offer community service and leadership opportunities to help youth develop life skills
Prevention programs for youth of color are more effective when they	• Are culturally relevant and competent, using the language of the target population • Consider the social and cultural factors that influence behaviors • Provide peer support to change peer norms • Aim at building life skills • Focus on the needs of the whole person

Source: Based on Advocates for Youth (2004).

TABLE 6.3 ■ Healthy Childhood Sexual Development

Developmental Stage	Common Behaviors	Healthy Development
Middle childhood (5–8 years)	• Potty humor • Jokes to describe body parts • Slang for body parts and functions • May act along "gendered" lines of the society • Sex play/sex games with same-aged children may occur (usually involves touching and looking) • Private masturbation for the purpose of pleasure • Becomes aware of different sexual orientations • Asks about genitals, breasts, babies • Limited understanding of adult sexual behavior • Single or infrequent occurrences of peeping • Affectionate behaviors with peers	• Promote understanding of how children experience their gender identity • Support gender nonconforming children or those who identify as transgender • Explain the basics of human reproduction • Talk about the changes that will occur in puberty • Explain that there are different sexual orientations, and call them by appropriate terms (heterosexual, gay, lesbian, bisexual, transgender, etc.) • Teach that masturbation occurs in private • Educate about personal body rights (your body is your body only) • Educate about responsibility (treat all people equally and with respect)
Late middle childhood (9–12 years)	• Asks questions about sex • Begins dating/hanging out in groups • Draws sexual parts, uses sexual words, looks at nude photos • Menstruation and nocturnal emissions • Masturbates in private for pleasure and orgasm • Experiences of sexual attraction • Puberty begins or continues • Sexual fantasies about a celebrity • Seeks out sexual information from Internet • Needs more privacy	• Provide accurate sexual health education • Educate about reproduction, pregnancy, STIs, even if a child doesn't ask for it • Respect child's need for privacy • Discuss family values and expectations about dating and sex • Educate about appropriate and safe boundaries • Discuss expectations about social media use • Communicate openness about availability for all questions and situations • Help normalize children's feelings and uncertainties • Encourage children to understand they have rights and responsibilities in friendships and relationships • *Keep the conversation going*

Sources: Based on National Sexual Violence Center (2013).

with masturbation during the school years, few parents want to discuss the issue (Strachan & Staples, 2012). Boys touch their genitals more frequently than do girls, but masturbation is a common sexual behavior in boys and girls during this developmental period.

Privacy becomes a major issue to children in grade school (National Sexual Violence Center, 2013; Wurtele & Kenny, 2012). Although their sexual curiosity begins to grow, they simultaneously become less likely to undress in front of others, touch their sex parts in public, or even kiss nonfamily adults. Although this shift to privacy may be due to the desire for autonomy during this developmental stage, some researchers believe that children in Western societies become more private in their sexual expressions because they have begun to internalize the social mores and sexual scripts of a sexually repressive culture (Okami & Shackelford, 2001; Tice et al., 2001; Wiederman, 2005).

Today it is estimated that about 1.3 million children identify as LGBTQ+, but only about one-fourth of parents are supportive of their sexual and gender minority children.

Source: iStock.com/FG Trade.

As children grow, their sexual behaviors further develop. So, too, do their gender and sexual identities begin to form. We address sexual orientation development at greater length in Chapter 7 as we study adolescent identity formation; here, it is essential to understand that gender is one of the primary ways in which children organize their social worlds, and that gender-nonconforming and transgender children may identify as such early on.

Parenting Sexual and Gender Minority Children

In contemporary society, parents face challenges as they navigate unchartered territory when parenting their sexual/gender minority child. **Sexual and gender minority youth (SGMY)** are individuals who identify as gay, lesbian, bisexual, or transgender (CDC, 2021). **Sexual minority youth (SMY)** are people who identify as gay, lesbian, or bisexual, who are romantically attracted to or enjoy sexual contact with people of the same sex (CDC, 2021). **Gender identity** refers to a person's concept of male, female, both, or neither (CDC, 2021). A person's gender identity can be different from the genetic sex assigned at fertilization, when the egg and sperm fuse together and join parents' DNA. In Chapter 7, we'll discuss at length the parenting experiences of LGBTQ+ adolescents, but because of the centrality of gender to a developing child's sense of self, we first explore aspects of gender:

- **Gender expression**: How a person chooses to present their gender to their social world through appearance and behaviors
- **Gender minority**: A person's gender identity is not in alignment with their genetically assigned sex
- **Gender nonbinary**: Individuals who do not define themselves as male or female
- **Gender nonconforming**: A person's physical appearance and behaviors do not align with societal norms and mores of "male" or "female"

About 2 percent of American youth and adolescents identify as transgender, or about 1.3 million (Johns et al., 2019). Only 27 percent of trans youth say their family is very supportive, and only 43 percent indicate they have a trusted adult in their family they can turn to for support (Human Rights Campaign, 2021). Today, few bodies of evidence exist that help to broaden our understanding of gender identities, and SGMY experiences and issues are only recently being investigated by researchers (Kuhar et al., 2018). But one thing is for certain: The experiences of gender minority children not only affect their social and emotional development but they also impact the child's family (Hafford-Letchfield et al., 2019, 2020).

An analysis of 42 peer-reviewed studies about the links between family support and the health and well-being of SGMY youth was undertaken by Cornell University (2017). In general, the analysis yielded several findings that speak to the importance of parent and family support for SGMY youth (for a complete bibliography of the studies reviewed, see Cornell University, 2017).

1. Increased risk of physical and mental health dangers, to include depression, suicidality, substance abuse, psychological distress, and low self-esteem. Rejecting parents further heighten the risks for these experiences in their children.
2. Parents and families with harmful, rejecting behaviors have been shown to modify their behaviors to promote their children's mental and physical health.

3. Protective parenting and family factors include *sexuality-specific* acceptance (not general, overall support): affirming children's sexual orientation and expressions of gender; openly talking to children about their LGBTQ+ identity; defending and protecting them when they experience bullying; and welcoming their LGBTQ+ peers into parents' and families' lives.

4. If parents and family respond in a supportive way when an LGBTQ+ youth comes out, it contributes in positive ways to the child's healthy development. Children are coming out at younger ages, and as such, family awareness must begin during the child's school years, not when a child enters adolescence.

Finally, it is important to recognize the myriad factors that impact and shape the ways in which parents and families respond to a child's sexual identity and expressions of gender: race, ethnicity, religiosity, socioeconomic class, nativity, and regional origin all interact in complex ways to influence sexuality and "gender" (Cornell University, 2017). It is the responsibility of adults—from parents to practitioners to educators to policymakers—to protect and nurture the health and well-being of children and to provide them the support that they need to flourish.

MIDDLE CHILDHOOD: FOSTERING SOCIAL AND EMOTIONAL GROWTH

With growing competencies and an emerging sense of individuality, the school-aged child gradually decreases conformity to parents and increases conformity to peers. As a child develops from infant to toddler to preschooler to middle childhood, the parent's role also changes in significant ways, as do the importance and types of interactions between parent and child (Collins & Madsen, 2019; DelGiudice, 2014). The parenting role shifts to two primary tasks: encouraging the child's individuation and identity formation by fostering their involvement with friends and school, and learning to parent from a distance to guide children toward greater autonomy (American Academy of Pediatrics, 2015; Collins & Madsen, 2019). This shift requires that parents become less hands-on, yet still very much involved in their children's lives and serving as strong role models and reinforcing agents for their children's behaviors.

Middle childhood represents a period of change for parents and children. As previously mentioned, the attention given by scholars to this developmental period is significantly less than what is given to early childhood and adolescence. Nevertheless, there is evidence that provides insight into the unique parenting challenges associated with parenting the school-aged child.

This section presents the distinctive features of the changes in parents' child-rearing practices and shifts in the parent–child relationship. We also explore the ways in which parenting affects children's development of self-regulation and coping capacities.

Attachment in Middle Childhood: A Changing Social World

Perhaps one of the greatest changes in school-aged children's experiences is the increased time spent in school, with friends, and away from home. Even as children's social worlds begin to expand, however, their most important, influential relationships continue to be at home. Secure attachment to parents, established during infancy, has long-term effects on children's behavior (Ainsworth, 1989; Bowlby, 1969). Traditionally, though, empirical study into attachment bonds has focused on the first three years of life, then late adolescence into and through adulthood, leaving a sizable gap in the literature regarding attachment bonds and middle childhood (Boldt et al., 2014). In spite of this paucity of research, however, some investigators have provided us insight into this critical developmental period.

Kerns and colleague assessed mother–child attachment in their investigation of 10- to 12-year-olds to determine how attachment is linked to parenting and child depression (Kerns & Brumariu, 2016). Children completed assessments to ascertain security, avoidance, ambivalence, and disorganization, and parents were assessed on warmth/engagement and psychological control. The study found that, while parents continue to be children's primary attachment figures, there are key differences of attachment experiences in early childhood and middle childhood (as described in Abtahi & Kerns, 2017):

- **Proximity versus availability:** In early childhood, the goal of attachment is maintaining proximity to the attachment figure, but in middle childhood, the child needs assurances that the attachment figure is available. Parents shift from closely monitoring their children to supervising behaviors from a distance (Boldt et al., 2016).
- **Nonverbal emotional connection versus collaborative partnership:** In the early years, an emotional bond is formed because of quality, nonverbal emotional connections that take place between parent and child, whereas in middle childhood, both parties engage in mutuality of contact, open communication, and a collaborative partnership (Kamza, 2019).

Both Kerns' (2016) and Abtahi's (2017) work point out another defining characteristic of attachment experiences in middle childhood—the "secure base" established in early childhood becomes even more important to a child's well-being as the child ages because of children's limited experiences in dealing with their social worlds. Another body of research suggests that, similar to the early childhood period, children in middle childhood use their parents as secure bases because these attachment figures support the exploration that occurs as social worlds enlarge, similar to an infant who is learning to crawl and walk (Kamza, 2019). Kamza, however, observes that during middle childhood, the *intensity* of attachment behaviors (e.g., seeking the secure base) decreases (Kamza, 2019). Waters and associates note that more research is needed to identify the circumstances in which children reach out to their secure base in middle childhood or signal that they need parental intervention (Waters et al., 2015).

As children age, the attachment bond evolves to a mechanism that helps children to self-govern and to regulate their emotions. To be sure, middle childhood represents an important period of change for emotion regulation.

Attachment and Self-Regulation Development

One of the most fundamental skills that children develop is the ability to self-regulate (Vohs & Baumeister, 2011). **Self-regulation** refers to an individual's ability to modulate emotional, cognitive, and behavioral arousal in the context of environmental demands (Perry, 2019). Other authors add that self-regulation involves conscious, deliberate inhibitory actions (Ziv et al., 2017). In essence, self-regulation is self-control. A subset of self-regulation includes **emotion regulation (ER),** which refers to a person's ability to change the intensity of emotional experiences, and **inhibitory control (IC),** which involves withholding responses that may not be appropriate (Perry, 2019). A child's ability to control their emotions is a vital, necessary skill for developing and maintaining social relationships (Láng, 2010), and throughout childhood, children become increasingly self-reliant in regulating their emotions (Skinner & Zimmer-Gembeck, 2007). Children with secure attachment enter middle childhood with a number of psychological strengths, including emotion understanding, a healthy developing self-concept, strong peer relationships, and better social problem-solving skills (Thompson, 2008). All of these require emotional regulation.

Not surprisingly, attachment figures throughout early and middle childhood appear to facilitate the development of a child's ER abilities, and securely attached children are better able to regulate their emotions (Brumariu, 2015; Parrigon et al., 2015; Zimmer-Gembeck et al., 2015). Throughout early childhood, warm, responsive parents guide and assist children when they experience negative emotions or struggle to manage their negative feelings (Cassidy, 1994). Other researchers further suggest that authoritative parents, because they are more keenly attuned to their children, tend to more accurately and insightfully assess and evaluate their children's feelings (Waters et al., 2010).

In a study of ninety-nine 9- to 11-year-olds, researchers sought to determine children's emotional reactions/regulation after being exposed to a social stressor task—children were exposed to a story stem in which the child and mother were in the story's narrative (Abtahi & Kerns, 2017). In each story, the child is presented with an emotional dilemma; after the reader finished the story stem, children were asked to describe what happened next in the narrative. The researchers found that securely attached children recovered their positivity after the stress event. Conversely, avoidant children experienced a suppression and lack of awareness of negative emotions and emotional distress. The researchers put forth the idea that, when stressed, securely attached children focus on the challenges, whereas insecurely attached children concentrate on minimizing the emotions they are feeling. The authors of the study go on to observe that because avoidantly attached children have a history of rejection from their attachment figure, these children develop suppression as a way to avoid rejection (see Abtahi & Kerns, 2017, for a review). This is an important concept to underscore because the ways in which children learn to regulate their emotions within the parent–child relationship generalize to other contexts and situations—particularly in the realm of peers and chumships (see Kerns et al., 2007).

Children's Mental Health

Prior to the COVID-19 pandemic that began in 2020, as many as one in five children had a mental health diagnosis (Child Trends, 2021). Most mental health disorders have an onset in childhood or adolescence (Kessler et al., 2005), and six months into the pandemic, parents began to report a surge in their children's anxiety and depression, in part due to the mandated home confinement of children (Singh et al., 2020). One body of research indicates that nearly three-fourths (72 percent) of parents said they saw a decline in their children's well-being; 40 percent of these parents sought help for their children's anxiety, and 37 percent sought help for their child's depression (Child Mind Institute, 2021). Additionally, 30 percent desired treatment for their children's problem behaviors, and nearly one-fourth (23 percent) were concerned about their children's learning challenges.

As our study has shown us so far, children's individual development is very much a product of family, societal, and cultural interactions. The social and emotional health and well-being of children are essential to lifespan development, and as you've seen, what happens in one developmental period significantly impacts lifelong trajectories. There is no question that the middle childhood period of development provides a critical window for prevention, early detection, and intervention of mental health disorders (Abramson, 2021). Unfortunately, the pandemic aggravated already-present challenges associated with the environmental risk factors of mental health in American society (Abramson, 2021).

Prior to the COVID-19 global pandemic, 20 percent of American's children had a mental health diagnosis. After the pandemic, nearly three-fourths of parents reported a negative change in their children's mental well-being.

Source: iStock.com/MarioArango.

Low Socioeconomic Status

Children in lower-income households and poverty have a greater risk of developing a mental health disorder (Reiss et al., 2019). Stressors associated with finances, employment, lower educational opportunities, and social interaction with peers more often suffer from mental health illnesses; socioeconomic status (SES) also significantly impacts access to and use of mental health services and healthcare (Austin & Wagner, 2010; Senn et al., 2014). Children from low SES are two to three times more likely to develop a mental health disorder than their peers who have a higher SES (Reiss, 2013).

Intersectionality

In the United States, Latinx and Blacks are disproportionately affected with higher rates and more severe symptoms of mental health disorders than whites (Alegria et al., 2015). In addition to the stressors associated with racism and race-based trauma (discussed a bit later in this chapter), some youth also face considerable assaults on their identities because of limited civil and human rights regarding documentation status, sexual orientation, gender identity, and physical ability (American Psychological Association, Working Group for Addressing Racial and Ethnic Disparities in Youth Mental Health, 2017). Today's young people are also daily confronted with racial inequality images and news stories through media. Parents, educators, and practitioners need to be aware of youths' intersecting identities.

Inadequate and Inequitable Education

Social and educational inequities are known to exacerbate the risk of developing mental health disorders (Singh et al., 2020). Prior to the COVID pandemic, there already existed great inequity in educational opportunities for children, with higher SES and white students having an educational advantage over lower SES, Black, Latinx, and Native students (Dorn et al., 2020). During the pandemic, it was estimated that approximately 60 percent of low-income students logged online for virtual learning as compared with 90 percent of higher income students (Curriculum Associates, 2021; Dorn et al., 2020). Practitioners believe this discrepancy is due to several factors, including lack of an environment conducive to learning, lack of personal devices and high-speed Internet, and lack of parental supervision.

Although studies regarding the effects of school closures due to the pandemic are just now being undertaken, one body of research speculates that learning loss—how much learning students lost during school closures—will be greatest among African American, Latinx, and Native American students (Dorn et al., 2020). Figure 6.3 presents the average loss of learning among racial/ethnic groups and low-income learners. These data estimate that remote learning experiences make worse existing achievement gaps by 15 to 20 percent (Dorn et al., 2020). Although mental health services were embedded within schools prior to the pandemic, there is no question that an integrated care system that nurtures both a child's mental health and equitable educational opportunities is needed now more than ever before to protect the well-being of this country's school children (Fazel et al., 2014).

At this point in our study, you're beginning to understand the ways in which multiple forces in society interact and work together to shape a child's physical, cognitive, and social-emotional

FIGURE 6.3 ■ Average Months of Learning Lost Compared With Typical In-Class Learning

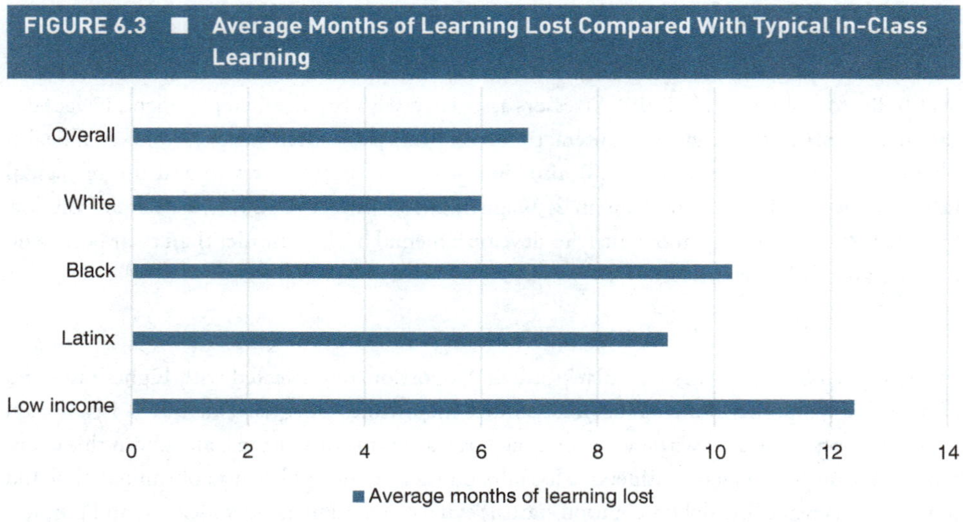

Source: Based on Dorn et al. (2020).

development. Indeed, we do not develop in isolation! To be sure, a healthy parenting style during middle childhood is necessary for children's healthy development and adjustment: Promoting mutual respect while gradually encouraging greater independence and self-regulation are important goals at this time because school-age children enter Erikson's fourth stage of psychosocial development.

MIDDLE CHILDHOOD: DEVELOPING INDUSTRY

At about the age of 6, children enter the fourth stage of Erikson's (1963) theory of psychosocial development—**industry versus inferiority**. This stage ends at about age 11. The child's feelings of competence at this stage is the belief that they are capable and able to do meaningful tasks. It includes taking on projects and tasks because of a basic interest in doing them, and in working to complete them to achieve satisfaction (a sense of industry) from the results. When the child's use of his expanding skills and competencies meets with success, when he receives support and approval form parents, peers, and teachers, then he develops a sense of **industry**.

On the other hand, there is a pull toward an earlier level of lesser production. Children have fears of **inferiority**—a persistent sense of inadequacy or a feeling that they are of lower status than others. Because of this inferiority, a child tries to overcome by diligently engaging in opportunities to learn by doing. If there are repeated experiences of failure and disapproval, feelings of inferiority dominate.

Since children strive to accomplish a sense of industry, they are work-oriented. Attention should be given then, both at home and at school, to the establishment of positive work habits. Erikson believed that many of the attitudes toward work and work habits that are exhibited later in life are formed during this developmental period. It is therefore important that both parents and teachers provide many opportunities for the child to succeed at a variety of work experiences. In doing so, they also further the formation of children's healthy self-concepts.

Building a Healthy Self-Concept

There are three basic dimensions of **self-concept**: a *sense of belonging* (the individual perceives themself as part of a group and is accepted and valued by the other members of that group); a *sense of worth* (the individual perceives themself as a "good" or worthy person); and a *sense of competence* (the individual perceives that they are successful at doing things well). Parenting style and the quality of interactions between parents and children are significantly related to the child's development of a healthy self-concept.

There has been much discussion concerning the relationship between children's self-concept and academic achievement. Parental attitudes and behaviors—as well as the quality of the parent–child relationship—begin early to have a strong impact on how a child views themself. The school-age child's sense of self is very much a reflection of the success of interactions with others, especially their parents (Brown et al., 2009; Rodriques et al., 2012). For example, there is ample evidence to suggest that positive self-concept is related to high academic achievement during the school-age years (Chapman et al., 1990). On the other hand, low self-concept and low academic achievement interact and negatively feedback on each other. Since parental acceptance and support seem to be relevant factors in the child's self-concept, this dimension of parent behavior should be related to the child's academic performance.

In the view of self, a child plays a role, too. Children behave in ways consistent with the ways they see themselves (Brown et al., 2009). If children feel they are worthless, they will expect others to treat them as worthless. Since children cannot be viewed as simply mirror images of external events but as active, striving, learning individuals, self-esteem represents the child's unique organization of their own genetic makeup, the evaluations made of self by significant adults, and the feedback they receive from their world. There seems to be a downward trend in self-concept as children enter school because of the increased sources of evaluations by teachers and peers, but by fifth grade, the trend climbs upward. Because the school-age child is more independent and increasingly in charge of themself, more and more evaluations of behavior are self-evaluation, and a larger percentage of rewards are self-rewards. It seems important, then, for parents to help children identify their strengths and reward themselves for those while minimizing negative evaluations of weaknesses.

To this end, researchers examined the direct and indirect associations among general family relationships, school-focused parent–child interactions, child personal characteristics, and school adjustment with 161 fourth- and seventh-grade children, their parents, and teachers (Ketsetzis et al., 1998). Results indicated that child characteristics (exclusive of self-esteem) are directly associated with school adjustment. However, a variety of parent–child interaction factors and family-life factors also are found to predict adjustment indirectly. Overall, parental pressure decreases self-esteem, but parental support increases it.

The researchers concluded that excessive parental pressure for school success is associated with decreased levels of children's self-esteem, frustration tolerance, and intellectual effectiveness. Another study confirmed that parental support enhances children's self-esteem (Franco & Levitt, 1998). These researchers further found that parental support contributes indirectly to the quality of the child's best friendship, which, in turn, contributes further to self-esteem.

The role of the parent in developing a healthy self-concept in the child during middle childhood, just as in infancy and early childhood, remains crucial. Even though the child has a structured learning environment in school, the home continues to be an important learning laboratory.

Providing Learning Experiences

With a growing sense of industry, children work to expand both their body skills and their perceptual skills. The role that parents play in structuring the home environment to permit these capacities to develop and in assisting and encouraging the child to pursue relevant out-of-home, out-of-school activities is extremely important.

The significance of play during middle childhood cannot be overemphasized, since it provides the child with situations in which he can test himself, work out feelings, experiment with roles, learn rules and expectations, and develop and practice skills that will be important for adult life in society. Many of these goals are achieved by play involving peers or by team efforts.

Learning experiences outside of the home and school classroom are vitally important for a child's healthy development. These activities do not have to be organized activities, such as sports.

Source: iStock.com/SanJeri.

Out-of-Home Learning Experiences

Aside from peer-group interaction within the normal course of a school day, children have an opportunity to achieve group status as well as to broaden their scope of learning through organized out-of-home activities, such as sports, music or dance, scouting troops, and church/temple/mosque activities.

Clearly, there are both advantages and disadvantages to children being involved with such activities. The advantages are relatively obvious, as they allow children to:

- associate and identify with unrelated adults who are important socializing agents for them;
- extend their peer interactions beyond the classroom, making friendships with others from a variety of cultural backgrounds;
- spend time with other children who share their interests;
- develop and practice their growing bodily and perceptual skills within the context of a group setting;
- learn to play by rules and how to be good winners and good losers.

The disadvantages may not be quite so obvious to parents. First, many parents fall into the "more is better" trap or the "my child is busier than your child" syndrome when planning for the child's out-of-home activities. In their desire to develop well-rounded children, some parents over-enroll their children in activities, so that there is little time left for meaningful interaction or for children to pursue other interests.

The second major disadvantage is that parents may actually coerce children to be involved in an activity simply because the parents themselves enjoy it. A typical example is the athletic father who almost literally forces his son into sports. When children are not genuinely interested in an activity, the activity will not provide effective learning experiences for them. Finally, the competitive aspect of organized sports may overshadow their inherent learning potential. Parents need to examine the competitive aspects of such organized groups and identify the potential for positive development that accompanies them.

In-Home Learning Activities

Two types of family activities that provide valuable learning experiences for school-age children are those that are planned and organized (such as camping or going to a museum) and those that are unplanned or spontaneous (going on a picnic, kicking a soccer ball in the yard, reading together). Activities give families opportunities to share common interests, to be together away from a usually hectic home schedule, and to share new experiences.

Parents who make arrangements for their children to be involved in an array of enriching social and cultural experiences during the elementary years have children who perform better on achievement tests and who are rated as more task-oriented and better adjusted by their teachers (U.S. Department of Education, 2021). In addition, parental involvement with children is consistently related to child competence throughout the child's development.

The school-age years continue to be an important stage during which learning experiences outside the school play a crucial role in the child's development. Parents enhance learning by creating a home environment that is conducive to learning, by helping the child select extracurricular activities that promote overall adjustment and development, and by helping the child achieve a mix of peer and family activities that is acceptable to both parents and children.

School Adjustment

It appears that parenting styles and practices during middle childhood have far-reaching impact on children's school experiences. For example, one benchmark study of 585 parent/children pairs sought to determine the impact of supportive parenting on children's school adjustment over a seven-year period; children and parents were assessed when the children were five years old, when they were in kindergarten, and in every grade thereafter through grade 6 (Pettit et al., 1997). Parental proactive teaching, calm discussion in disciplinary encounters, warmth, and interest and involvement in the child's peer activities are parenting aspects that predict children's behavioral, social, and academic adjustment in both kindergarten and grade 6. Each kindergarten adjustment outcome is associated with multiple supportive parenting variables, which then predict changes in children's academic performance from kindergarten to grade 6. These predictive relationships suggest that early positive and supportive parenting qualities might play a distinct role in promoting children's school adjustment.

In this study, supportive parenting also appears to buffer some of the developmental risks associated with early family adversity. Supportive parenting is most strongly related to child adjustment in grade 6 for those children who had been reared in single-parent and/or low SES families in their early years. This finding suggests that supportive parenting may serve as a protective factor against the risks associated with certain types of family adversity.

Parenting style also relates to school adjustment, academic achievement, and self-concepts. Using family reports and observations over a three-year period, researchers examined family factors relating to children's adjustment during the middle-school years (Bronstein et al., 1996). Children and parents were assessed when the children were in the fifth, sixth, and seventh grades. Results showed that supportive and aware parenting (characterized by affection, approval, attentiveness, responsiveness, guidance, and receptivity to emotions), is associated with fifth-grade girls' and boys' more positive self-concept, higher academic achievement, and greater popularity with their peers, as well as with lower incidence of psychological and behavioral problems in the following year. In addition, the relationship between the positive parenting measures and adjustment outcomes appears to be stable over time; that is, parenting a first-grader similarly correlates with the same adjustment measures obtained in the seventh grade.

As predicted, more problematic parental behaviors are associated with negative school adjustment outcomes. Furthermore, parenting practices are related to eventual improvements in girls' and boys' adjustment over the transition to middle school, including better academic performance, decreased incidence of psychological and behavior problems, and increased peer popularity. Aware parenting is particularly salient for boys, in that it appears to be associated with decreased externalizing behavior, whereas for girls, it appears to serve as a buffer against a decline in self-esteem. Problematic parenting behaviors tend to be associated with negative changes in adjustment over time for both boys and girls.

Whether it's a whispered secret in a school hallway or a pickup game of basketball on a Saturday morning, children's friendships provide companionship and support for their budding sense of self-concept and identity.

Source: iStock.com/TomWang112.

MIDDLE CHILDHOOD: EXIT PARENTS, ENTER FRIENDS

The elementary school years present a tremendous opportunity for social and emotional growth. The school-age child shows unceasing energy toward investing all possible efforts in producing. The child works incessantly on expanding bodily, muscular, and perceptive skills as well as on expanding knowledge of the world around themself. Questions such as, "How is this made?" "How does this work?" "Why do things work the way they do?" dominate a child's days. With a sense that they can accomplish anything and everything, children feel a strong need for accomplishment and ward off failure at almost any cost. The child's peers become far more significant, and the child tries to relate to and communicate with peers as frequently as possible. Acceptance by peers is critical for a child's ego development.

Preadolescence represents a transition from the adult code of the parent to the peer code—a transition from dependence to independence, which will ultimately lead the child at adolescence into identity formation. The group phenomenon, or clique formation, during preadolescence is essential to the child's later functioning as a citizen in society. However, the more the "clique" character is subversive of certain adult standards, the more thoroughly it is enjoyed by the child. In many cases, then, the peer code may be diametrically opposed to the adult code. Some examples include the values of good grades in school, obedience to adults, dress codes and hairstyles, and dirty jokes and/or language. What is labeled "good" or "bad" behavior by parents may be labeled exactly the opposite by peers. Often the peer-group behavior or code is unspoken but nevertheless strongly implied.

Perhaps the most difficult adjustment that parents must make when their children are preadolescents is that of understanding and accepting the child's rejection of adult standards and her loyalty to peers. Although most parents *want* their children to be independent, they wish it could be done less painfully. They wish they could impart the wisdom of experience to their children. Parents may feel guilty because they think that they have failed—otherwise the child would not reject them. The child, in turn, may feel guilty because they do love their parents but cannot bear to lose face with friends. The resolution of this crisis is an important factor in parent–child relationships at this time. A satisfactory resolution will determine, to some extent, how parents deal with the so-called midlife crisis.

"Will You Be My Best Friend?" Developing Friendships and Chumships

The elementary school years present a tremendous opportunity for social and emotional growth. For children in about first grade through sixth grade, the initiation and formation of peer groups increase, as does the significance of these relationships to the child's developing sense of self. As children move through elementary school, more and more of their time is spent interacting with same-sex peers. Be it a whispered secret during recess, a quick pickup game of basketball after school, or helping with the drudgeries of long division in a school hallway, childhood friendships provide children great companionship and an opportunity to disclose their innermost secrets, wishes, and fears. In addition, childhood peer relationships afford children a "safely net" that allows them to practice and rehearse their new relational roles.

The formation of peer groups is a multistep process. An academic who studied the formation of friendships, D. C. Dunphy (1963) in a classic study examined adolescent friendship development in urban areas. The earlier stages of friendship development described by Dunphy are found during the school years:

- **Stage One: Pre-Crowd Stage.** From about kindergarten through fifth grade, during this stage of friendship development, isolated unisex peer groups exist in the form of *cliques*, small groups of four to nine members. Spontaneous, shared activities provide the opportunity to relate personally. Boys tend to join larger groups and enjoy doing activities together, whereas girls tend to join smaller, more intimate groups. These peer group types dominate the school years. It is not uncommon to see these types of peer groups on a school playground, where boys are excluding girls from their pickup soccer game at recess, or where girls forbid boys to listen in on their "girl talk." Members are attracted to one another on the basis of similar interests, neighborhoods, schools, or religions. Boys' groups are often larger and more stable than girls' groups (Atwater, 1992).

- **Stage Two: Beginning of the Crowd.** Still same-sex in nature, peer groups toward the end of sixth grade or beginning of seventh grade begin to shift to *crowds*, which consist of 10 or more members. Crowds are essentially a collection of cliques—membership in cliques is required to belong to the crowd (Atwater, 1992). Crowd activities such as after-school dances and sporting events provide preadolescents the chance to "practice" interacting with the opposite sex, alleviating the uneasiness that often comes with opposite-sex relationships. For instance, Katie may have a crush on Danny, yet she flirts with all the other boys in her friendship crowd. In this way, she practices her newfound intimacy skills on others, without the risk of being rejected by Danny if she flirts with only him.
- **Stage Three: Crowd in Transition.** During the end of junior high (eighth or ninth grade) and throughout high school, peer groups are seen as in transition. During this time, smaller cliques are formed within the larger crowd. The pairing off of male and female couples, typically seen sooner in early maturing boys and girls, drives the crowd into transition. While the crowd may still hang out together for certain events, such as going to a movie or to a school basketball game, they more frequently begin to prefer to interact with the smaller group of friends, and begin to exclude others from the emerging smaller clique.
- **Stage Four: Fully Developed Crowd.** The fully developed crowd is composed entirely of opposite-sex cliques; no longer are the same-sex friendship affiliations as dominant as they were throughout elementary school and the early years of junior high. Peer groups during this stage exist only long enough for members to learn or to be socialized into those characteristics needed for adult relationships, such as sharing intimate thoughts and feelings, and interdependence.
- **Stage Five: Crowd Disintegration.** As adolescents mature into adulthood and take on adult responsibilities, such as a job or pursuing a college degree, and as they become involved in serious intimate relationships, crowd-type friendship groups begin to disintegrate. Often the support of friends is replaced by an intimate partner with whom young adults now share and disclose, and with whom they are perhaps sexually involved. Friendship groups consequently become more loosely associated. Over time, many find their spouse or life mate to be their "best" friend, although they still hold on to one or two close friends.

Other researchers have since found peer group formation to be similar to Dunphy's original 1960s study of peer group formation (Atwater, 1992; Paul & White, 1990).

What is it that makes friendship so special or so different from other kinds of relationships in our lives? Research has shown that friendships, unlike family relationships, provide us more feelings of freedom, closeness, and pleasure; we are also able to experience higher levels of self-disclosure with our friends than we do with our families (Mendelson & Kay, 2003; Rybak & McAndrew, 2006). Furthermore, friendships are often quite emotionally rewarding because the sharing that takes place between friends fosters the growth and development of empathy. **Empathy** is the capacity to understand another's circumstances or situation, and the ability to feel or express emotional concern for another person. It is believed that the experiences of empathy are what lead to a greater sensitivity—and emotional bond—to each other, both in friendships and any other intimate relationship (Rybak & McAndrew, 2006).

As you can see from Dunphy's study, as children grow through childhood and enter adolescence, their dependence on their parents for intimacy lessens and they turn to "chumships" for support. It is also interesting to note how the changes in friendships are associated with life transitions. Some researchers have discovered that maintaining and adapting friendships throughout these life changes help buffer the stress associated with major transitions, such as going away

Friendships for LGBTQ+ children and youth are especially important because they buffer against bigotry and discrimination, and help to keep children from isolating. What are some ways in which educators or parent professionals can encourage friendships with gender and sexual minority children?

Source: iStock.com/InesFraile.

to college or getting married (Brooks, 2002; Oswald & Clark, 2003). It is important to understand these developmental changes in peer groups structures and the significance of friendships because each type of friendship group (intimate relationships) throughout life affects a person's psychosocial development in all subsequent stages of life.

LGBTQ+ Friendship Experiences

Even though the importance of friendships on children's mental health and well-being is firmly established, scant literature exists that speaks to the friendship experiences of LGBTQ+ individuals. As you have seen so far, friendships—and the intimacy they provide—positively impact development because of the social and emotional benefits they offer. But given that friendships also help people to learn more about themselves and to develop their unique identities, how do sexual orientation and sexual identity affect friendship experiences? What do we know about friendship experiences of LGBTQ+?

Up to this point, LGBTQ+ friendship research has focused its attention to better understanding how friendships form between LGBTQ+ individuals (Galupo et al., 2014). According to psychologist M. Paz Galupo of Townson University, Maryland, friendships for gender and sexual minorities are especially important because they are critically important for gays, lesbians, bisexual, and transgender individuals because "[these friendships] function as families of choice, and serve to buffer gender and sexual minorities from social isolation or rejection associated with homophobia and transphobia" (Galupo et al., 2014, p. 2). Groundbreaking bodies of science further help to inform our understanding and importance of LGBTQ+ friendships:

- Friendships within the LGBTQ+ community provide emotional support (Hines, 2007).
- Friendships provide opportunities to gain comfort in sharing experiences with coming out (Hines, 2007).
- These friendships provide opportunities for transgender people to share their knowledge and decision-making process with others about transitioning (Galupo, 2007, 2009).
- LGBTQ+ friendships provide the unique benefit of helping one another to emotionally process their orientation and identity minority statuses (Galupo, 2007, 2009).
- LGBTQ+ friendships are seen as providing "needed counseling that [is] unavailable from the traditional healthcare system" (Galupo et al., 2014, p. 2).
- Friendships fill in the gaps of support in society—vitally necessary in a society where LGBTQ+ identities are at odds with established social norms (Galupo et al., 2014).

Galupo and colleagues' (2014) research studied 536 gender-variant individuals. Their results provide us a deeper understanding of the benefits and barriers across gender identity and sexual orientation of a friend. The results are presented in Table 6.4. As you can see, there are specific pros and cons in friendship experiences.

TABLE 6.4 ■ Friendship Benefits Across Gender Identity and Sexual Orientation of a Friend

Benefits of Friendships With Transgender People and Sexual Minorities
Understanding sexual minority and transgender experiences
Knowledgeable on issues of gender, sex, and privilege
Shared experiences
Can talk about transgender issues
Offers support via mentoring and shared resources
Comfortable being myself
Shared community: "Family" and belonging
Nonjudgmental/open-minded
Accepting
Affirmative use of language in reference to identity
Opportunity for dating/sexual partners
Benefits of Friendships With Cisgender and Heterosexual Individuals
Helps me feel "normal"
Transgender/sexuality issues don't dominate the conversation and friendship
Validation more powerful from someone with normative identity
More opportunity for friendships due to larger population
Helps me present as identified gender ("Pass")
Accepting
Affirmative use of language in reference to identity
Offers more diverse perspectives and interactions
Barriers of Friendships With Transgender People and Sexual Minorities
Invalidating gender identity and personal experience
Transgender issues dominate conversation and friendships
Negative emotions, drama, and emotional instability
Fear of being "outed" by association or disclosure
Barriers of Friendships With Cisgender and Heterosexual Individuals
Not knowledgeable on issues of gender, sex, and privilege
Insensitive use to language in reference to identity
Difficult to talk about transgender/sexuality issues
Fosters feelings of discomfort
Not understanding nonnormative experience
Fewer shared experiences

Source: Based on Galupo et al. (2014).

The Effects of Racism on Children's Health

The deleterious effects of racism and racial discrimination are well documented in the scientific literature, and the effects are associated with poor physical and mental health outcomes in all ages across racial and ethnic minorities (for a review, see Polanco-Roman et al., 2016). **Race-based traumatic stress theory** holds that some people who encounter racism and/or discrimination experience it as psychological trauma, provoking physical, social, and emotional responses similar to posttraumatic stress (Bondolo et al., 2009; Carter, 2007).

The effects of racism are observed as early on as childhood, and an analysis of 121 studies confirms that among children, the most prevalent and consistent outcomes are negative mental health outcomes (Priest et al., 2013, as presented in Macedo et al., 2019):

- Lower self-esteem
- Higher anxiety
- Greater amounts of stress
- Higher depression
- More suicide ideation and attempts
- Increased aggression
- Attention-deficit/hyperactivity disorder
- Externalizing behavior problems

Other research additionally finds that children who experience race-based trauma have difficulty focusing in school, feel helpless, and frustrated (Jonson-Reid & Wideman, 2017). Children may also become hypervigilant and be uncertain and fearful of their environments, experience an increased sensitivity to threat, and the inability to perceive a future (Smith, 2010). Nena Hisle, the National Child Traumatic Stress Network (2022) provides guidance for parenting professionals, educators, healthcare providers, social workers, and others who work with **BIPOC (Black, Indigenous People of Color)** children. This is presented in Table 6.5.

There are a number of protective factors that help children of color to become more resilient in the face of structural racism. When children have unwavering networks of predictable, warm, communicative relationships with parents and caregivers, they are better able to cope with threatening racial trauma (Morsy & Rothstein, 2019). Additionally, stable, orderly, and safe neighborhoods, and emotionally supportive and responsive schools with positive teacher–student relationships further protect against racial trauma by promoting children's

TABLE 6.5 ■ Mitigating the Effects of Racism for BIPOC Children
Answer children's questions in developmentally and age-appropriate language.
Create a culturally safe classroom.
Help children increase their feelings and emotions vocabulary.
Integrate youth development approaches to promote resilience and strengths.
Promote routine and schedules, and a stable, predictable environment.
Set boundaries and limits with consistency and patience.
Show unconditional love and acceptance.

Source: NCTSN.

autonomy and self-concept (for a review, see Morsy & Rothstein, 2019). Supportive parenting educational programs, such as home visitations (see Chapter 5), have been shown to counteract the negative effects of threats, such as race-based trauma in children. The aim of in-home programs like the ChildFIRST Initiative is to help parents to establish strong parent–child relationships so that they can help to develop their children's coping skills (see Morsy & Rothstein, 2019).

'TWEENS: CONTEMPORARY CHALLENGES FOR PREADOLESCENTS

As our study has shown us, early life experiences lay the foundation upon which developmental health and wellness are laid, and these experiences—both positive and negative—profoundly influence a person's life course. The first Adverse Childhood Experiences (ACEs) research was completed over 20 years ago (Felitti et al., 1998), and this pioneering work provides us tremendous insight into how childhood experiences impact adult physical and mental health. In the section that follows, we'll explore toxic childhood stress and ACEs, as well as the contemporary issue of social media use and its impact on children's mental health. We'll then discuss a significant challenge in middle childhood, the experiences and outcomes of bullying. Many ACEs are within control of a child's environment, and it is therefore incumbent upon parenting professionals to recognize factors that mediate the effects of adversity.

Adverse Childhood Experiences

Adverse Childhood Experiences (ACEs) refer to three specific environmental kinds of adversity children may face: *household dysfunction* (such as high parental conflict, divorce, substance use/abuse among parents); *neglect* (deprivation of the child's basic needs); and *physical and/or emotional abuse* (Center on the Developing Child, 2021). The effects of ACEs are

FIGURE 6.4 ■ Racial and Ethnic Experiences of at Least One ACE by Race and Ethnicity

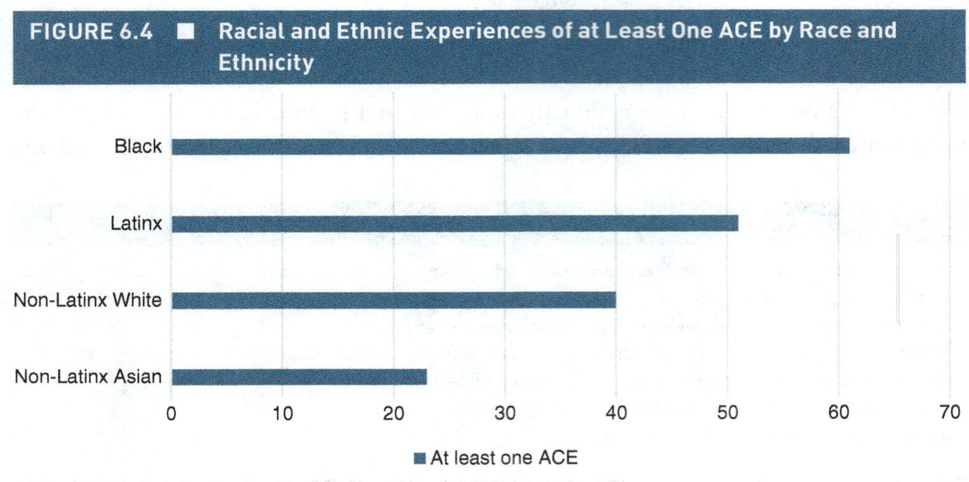

Source: Child Trends (2018).

cumulative—the more adverse experiences a child suffers, the greater the likelihood of poorer lifespan trajectories.

According to data from 2018, 45 percent of children in the United States have experienced at least one ACE (National Conference of State Legislatures, NCSL, 2021), and in 2019, the Centers for Disease Control and Prevention found that 61 percent of adults experienced at least one ACE in childhood (CDC, 2019). Nationally, one in ten children have experience three or more ACEs, making them especially vulnerable to later-life physical and mental health consequences (Child Trends, 2018). Additionally, racial and ethnic groups are disproportionately affected, as Figure 6.4 presents. Sadly, there is no question that ACEs increased for children in 2020–2021 during the COVID-19 pandemic.

There are any number of circumstances and experiences that can trigger a toxic stress response in children. When individuals perceive certain situations or events as threatening, the body responds in certain physical and cognitive ways, or with a *stress response* (Florida State University, 2021). Children tend to respond to stress in one of three distinct ways (Center on the Developing Child, 2021):

- **Positive stress response:** This stress response is mild and temporary, and it is almost always improved with the interaction of a warm, caring, responsive adult. Tender parenting/caregiving serves as a protective factor against children's elevated stress responses. Positive stress can occur in common, everyday, childhood experiences, such as going to a new school or being introduced to a new babysitter. This category of stress response is usually temporary and brief.
- **Tolerable stress response:** In this stress response, the body's reactions are more severe and are the result of uncommon stressors, such as the death of a loved one, or experiencing a serious illness. Even though the responses are more significant than those elicited due to everyday stresses, the stressor is tolerable if a supportive adult helps the child to better cope and regain a sense of control in their environment.
- **Toxic stress response:** The most severe stress response occurs when a child experiences frequent and/or prolonged harsh and/or dangerous living environments and relationships, and other protracted stress that is outside of the child's control. This includes physical, emotional, or sexual abuse; chronic neglect, poverty; bullying; parental/caregiver substance abuse; parental/caregiver mental illness; parental/caregiver incarceration; divorce; racism; homelessness; domestic or intimate partner violence; community disruption; or natural disasters—without consistent adult support and care.

It's important to note that often, children experience multiple sources of toxic stress simultaneously, and this relentless activation of the body's response reactions has

TABLE 6.6 ■ Protective Environmental Factors Against the Impact of Adverse Childhood Experiences

Child	Family	Community
Caring adult relationships, including teachers and mentors	Provide nurturing, safe, consistent, predictable, stable support and care	Access to medical and mental health care
Positive, supportive peer networks	Engage in parental monitoring, supervision, and consistent enforcement of expectations and boundaries	Access to safe, stable, affordable housing
Resiliency and internal locus of control	Warm, responsive, communicative parenting style	Food security
Does well in school	Resolve conflicts in healthy ways	Engaging, empowering after-school programming
Delay onset of sexual activity	Provide concrete support in times of need	Access to safe, dependable, affordable, high-quality child care and preschool

Note: ACEs vary in type and impact, and there is no single cause. Parenting professionals must work at all three levels—the individual, the family, and the community—to provide effective buffers against the effects of toxic stress.

Source: CDC (2021).

Cyberbullying has negative effects on a youth's mental health, from low self-esteem to suicidal ideology and attempts. *Words hurt.*

Source: iStock.com/JTansirimas.

profound effects on a child's brain structures and functions, cognitive development, and body systems; all of these increase a child's lifelong risk for physical and mental health conditions (for a thorough review, see Nelson et al., 2020). Fortunately, there are a number of mitigating factors that can buffer against the consequences of ACEs; these are provided in Table 6.6.

One of the most impactful ACEs in a child's life is bullying and/or cyberbullying. A major risk factor for poor adult outcomes, bullying—peer abuse—is a common experience for many of today's youth (Wolke & Lereya, 2015).

Peer Abuse and Victimization

In January 2010, 15-year-old Irish immigrant Phoebe Prince hanged herself. For nearly three months on a daily basis, the Massachusetts high school student endured verbal assaults, vicious text and email messages, demeaning Facebook posts, and threats of physical harm. The day before her suicide, students threw soda pop cans at her while taunting and yelling at her. The relentless bullying, perpetrated by fellow classmates, was an attempt to make it impossible for Phoebe to go to that school. Nine students faced charges for criminal bodily injury, stalking, harassment, and Civil Rights violations; they were convicted and released to serve probation. The obvious question remains to be answered: Where were the adults?

A growing common phenomenon in schools across the nation and abroad, **bullying,** or **peer abuse**, is defined as a "power differential in which one or more youth repeatedly use aggressive strategies to dominate and cause harm to others of relatively lower status" (Farmer et al., 2010). In other words, bullying isn't about power—it's about the *abuse* of power. *Direct bullying* includes any type of physical abuse or violence; the intent is to physically harm someone (Jungert et al., 2021). *Indirect bullying* involves trying to affect someone negatively, through verbal or emotional abuse and harassment (such as ignoring/excluding someone, laughing/taunting, hurting someone's feelings, showing dislike or disdain). Indirect bullying also takes place when others witness the abuse, but do not report it. When the bullying takes place in an electronic format (such as texting, email, Snapchat, or Facebook), it is referred to as **cyberbullying** (Hinduja & Patchin, 2010).

Because incidences are greatly underreported, we do not know for certain just how many bullying victims there are. In 2019, the National Center for Bullying Prevention research, collected by government and education agencies, found that one of every five students in the United States reports being bullied; 41 percent believe they will be bullied again, despite reporting the actions to school authorities (46 percent) (National Bullying Prevention Center, 2021; National Center for Educational Statistics, 2019). Of those bullied:

- 6 percent of boys are physically harmed compared to 4 percent of girls;
- 18 percent of girls reported being victims of rumors compared to 9 percent of boys;
- Nearly one-fourth of all girls are bullied at school (24 percent) in comparison to 17 percent of boys;

FIGURE 6.5 ■ Percentages Where Peer Abuse Occurs in Public Schools

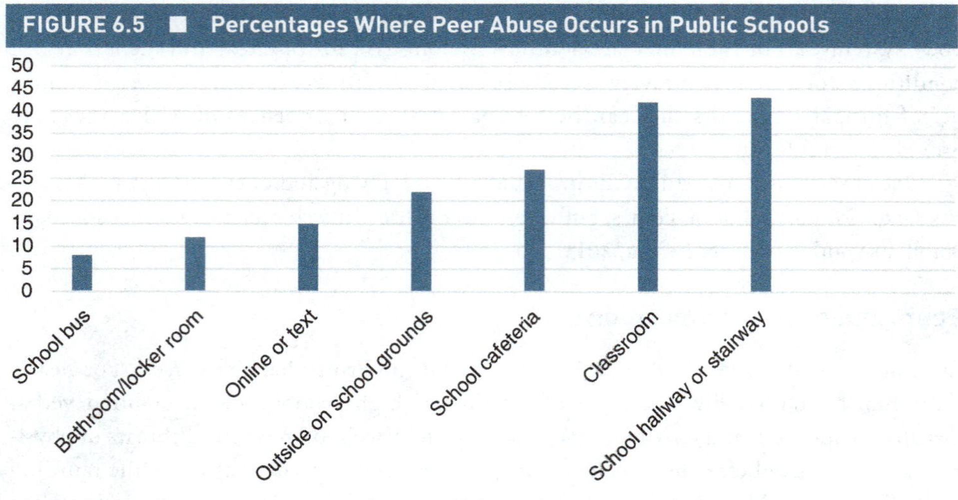

Source: National Center for Education Statistics (2019).

- One-half (49.8 percent) of tweens said they experienced bullying at school, and nearly 15 percent said they have been cyberbullied (Patchin & Hinduja, 2020).

Students report that the most common reasons they are abused by their peers are because of their physical appearance, race, ethnicity, religion, gender, gender identity, disability, and sexual orientation (National Center for Educational Statistics, 2019). Figure 6.5 illustrates the school locations where peer victimization most often occurs.

As with the case of Phoebe Prince, bullying is linked with suicidal ideation: Children, youth, and adolescents who are bullied have significantly increased rates of suicidal thoughts, attempts, and completed suicides (for a full review, see Hinduja & Patchin, 2010). Repeated peer harassment and bullying increase victims' feelings of depression, lower self-esteem and self-worth, and create hopelessness, helplessness, and isolation/loneliness. Because of the increase in the number of cyberbullying-related suicide completions in recent years, researchers have coined the term **cyberbullicide** to describe suicides that are influenced by online harassment and aggression (Hinduja & Patchin, 2010).

The Effects of Social Media on Children's Mental Health

Ella Abi-Jaoude and colleagues evaluated a number of studies related to middle childhood, social media use, and mental health (for a thorough review of the studies, see Abi-Jaoude et al., 2020). Their analysis revealed some troubling findings regarding the impact of technology on children and youth:

- Increase in negative views of self, mental distress, self-injurious behaviors, and suicidality;

- Negative impact on interpersonal relationships due to social comparison;
- Normalization/promotion of eating disorders, self-harm, and suicidality;
- Chronic sleep deprivation, negative impact on cognitive control and self-regulation, and declines in academic performance.

Considering the fact that tech devices are so heavily integrated into society, what is the best way for parents and those who work with youth to appropriately manage technology/social media and to mitigate the potential harms associated with their use? The American Academy of Pediatrics suggests that, because children today do not know a culture without technology and social media, it is vitally important that parents create a home environment in which digital interactions are minimal (American Academy of Pediatrics, 2020). The Academy further suggests that parents and caregivers model healthy technology and social media use.

One of the central responsibilities of parent educators is to be aware of the ways in which changes in society impact the daily lives of children and parents—and today, it is easily seen how the use of and dependence on our devices have influenced parenting and other interpersonal interactions. This cultural change positions helping professionals, teachers, social workers, youth workers, and other adults who work with children, to educate families about the ways in which digital technology can be both a positive and a negative influence on relationships and healthy development (O'Keeffe & Clarke-Pearson, 2011). As helpers, we can educate and advise families, schools, and communities about healthy online use, as well as those things that may have adverse effects on individuals.

The Bullies

Several bodies of research indicate that there are three primary categories of those affected by bullying (Olweus & Limber, 2010; Perren & Alsaker, 2006; Veenstra et al., 2005):

- bullies, but not victim;
- victims, but not bullies;
- those who are both bullies and victims.

Bullies possess common characteristics (for a full review, see Farmer et al., 2010). In kindergarten, bullies tend to be more physically and verbally aggressive than their classmates; they are impulsive and easily frustrated; and they lack empathy. Interestingly, oftentimes they have strong leadership skills and a larger peer group than those who are not involved in bullying. When boys bully, they use physical behaviors; when girls bully, they use words.

These characteristics appear to persist through sixth grade, and about one-half of bullies are well integrated into their classroom and peer structures, and despite their aggressiveness, they are quite popular. Contrary to popular belief, then, not all bullies are socially isolated or rejected. The one consistent characteristic in bullies is that they almost always have aggressive personalities and hot temperaments. When bullies were asked why they pick on one particular person and leave another alone, the most common response is that the victim "provoked" them (Frisén et al., 2007).

While bullying does appear to peak in grades 4 through 7, it doesn't disappear completely. Tragically, bullying is replaced by sexual harassment in later grades. Most acts of bullying occur on school grounds (at recess, in the cafeteria, in the hallways while changing classes, bathrooms, and on the school bus). In almost all of these venues, there is no adult supervision.

The Bullied

In general, bully victims tend to have fewer friends/playmates, are somewhat socially isolated, and have fewer social skills (see Farmer et al., 2010). Other bodies of research indicate that children who are bullied are "different"—in appearance (facial features, weight, height, and hygiene), clothing, behaviors, or speech (Erling & Hwang, 2004). Research confirms these findings. In a study of 119 adolescents, students were asked, "Why do you think children and adolescents are bullied?" (Frisén et al., 2007). The most common reason reported by adolescents was the victim's appearance (40 percent), followed by the victim's behavior (such as being shy or insecure) (36 percent).

Bullying is *not* a normal part of growing up. The effects of bullying are significant and may be long-lasting. Victims of bullies experience (National Academies of Sciences, Engineering & Medicine, 2016)

- anxiety;
- loneliness;
- low self-esteem;
- depression;
- social withdrawal;
- increased absenteeism;
- poor academic performance.

Sadly, oftentimes when children inform an adult that they are the victims of bullying, they are advised by teachers and/or parents to work it out with the offender.

Parents and Teachers

Today, some adults still believe that bullying is a normative experience in childhood and adolescence, and some even maintain that bullying "builds character." The U.S. Department of Health and Human Services (2022) notes that a number of adults and teachers tacitly accept bullying because they themselves experienced it (either as an offender or a victim) when they were younger.

Furthermore, research reveals that adults are barely aware of the bullying that occurs in their schools (Frisen et al., 2007). And, when adolescents were asked what makes bullying stop, only 14 percent of study participants indicated that bullying stops when teachers intervene. Today's students have little confidence in adults' abilities to stop the violence (Frisen et al., 2007). Even in the case of Phoebe Prince, some teachers and school administrators knew that she was repeatedly bullied and harassed—and did nothing to protect her.

Schools can intervene by using such approaches as (U.S. Department of Health & Human Services, 2022):

- Pairing students so they go to and from areas in school using the buddy system.
- Monitoring "bully-prone" areas in the school.
- Displaying written behavioral expectations; expectations contract signed by students, parents, and teachers.
- Applying consistent consequences for those students who do not comply.
- Pairing victim-prone students with older student mentors.

As with any other area of physical and emotional health, parents are a child's first and best educator about the dangers of bullying. Parents and school personnel must always take bullying as the serious threat that it is. If a child reports being bullied, adults should validate (not marginalize) the child's experiences (National Academies of Sciences, Engineering & Medicine, 2016).

They should also immediately speak to the child's teachers, coaches, and other school administrators, and request that those in authority at the school be aware of who the bullies are in the school, and who the bullies' victims are. Parents should also request that their child is not left unsupervised (during lunch, recess, in the restroom, and in the school hallways). Waiting to see if the behaviors change or decrease is not advisable because bullying behaviors persist over time.

Parents can also do their part by making sure their children understand that it is never permissible to taunt, tease, or bully another person, no matter how "harmless" the child or adolescent thinks the behavior is. Adults should also reinforce to youth that watching bullying occur is the same as condoning it, and that bullying *hurts* (National Academies of Sciences, Engineering & Medicine, 2016).

Of course, the ideal time to teach children about bullying is before they experience it. Dinnertime conversations can include such questions as, "Do you ever see anyone putting down your friends or picking on someone?" and, "What do you do when you see that happen?" Although parents cannot protect their children 100 percent of the time, they can buffer their children from bullying by instilling confidence, social skills, and empathy in them.

PROGRAMS FOR SCHOOL-AGE CHILDREN

The older the child, the fewer the programs that exist for parents. Therefore, parent-education programs for those with infants and preschool children far outnumber programs for those with school-age children. As a society, we have assumed that parents with young children need more support and assistance than those with older children. We also have assumed that parent behaviors and attitudes are resistant to change, and we should therefore focus on early parental behavior. Although a variety of agencies—including churches, mental health clinics, and family-counseling agencies—have made sporadic attempts at education for parents of school-age children, the most consistent efforts have been through the public education system.

Parent Involvement in Schools

Efforts to involve parents in school programs are not new. Since the founding of the National Congress of Mothers in 1897, which became the PTA (Parents and Teachers Association) in 1924, attempts to create links between home and school have been evident. A variety of approaches have been used, including parent–teacher conferences, involving parents in fund-raising and open houses, and utilizing parents as volunteers in the classroom and as tutors either at home, online, or in the school. These activities have been most successful with middle-class mothers, with little involvement of fathers or working-class parents. It has been assumed that this kind of involvement contributes to greater adjustment and achievement of children and improved attitudes on the part of parents.

Even so, parent involvement in the schools has left much to be desired, sometimes reaching the point of hostility between parents and school personnel; this has become particularly prevalent in the aftermath of COVID and the COVID vaccination debate between parents, teachers, and school boards of education. It is not unusual for teachers to complain that parents have little interest in their children, leaving the business of childrearing to the schools, and, on the other hand, to resent parents' intrusion into the classroom. Parents, too, may insist that teachers are poorly prepared and assert their perceived parental rights to determine school curricula. Of course, the success with which these issues are resolved varies from teacher to teacher, school to school, and district to district. The rebirth of the "back to basics" movement of the 1980s, however, resulted in state legislation allowing home education and a greater proportion of parents educating their children at home because of dissatisfaction with both the content of public school curricula and the degree of parental input into curriculum decision-making. The issue of parental versus institutional rights in public education is far from resolved, and in fact, it has reached a fever pitch due to the introduction of inclusion and equity education in many American schools.

The importance of parent involvement in the schools has reemerged in recent years as public schools have been increasingly attacked for their failure to educate children properly, and for low standardized test scores. However, since much of the emphasis has been placed on the early childhood period, few successful elementary- and junior high school models have been implemented and tested. Professionals and parents alike are nonetheless renewing their interest in finding ways to work together for the benefit of school-age children.

Afterschool Settings to Promote Healthy Development in Middle Childhood

In the past, not much scientific attention has been paid to the middle childhood developmental period, and perhaps one of the consequences of this lack of empirical understanding of the

Although research consistently demonstrates that afterschool programs significantly contribute in positive ways to children's development, America's youth do not have equal access to these opportunities. For example, children of color and lower SES have less opportunities available to them.

Source: Jim Watson via Getty Images.

school years is the lack of programming that guides and aides children's social-emotional and behavioral health. However, recent post-COVID investments by the United States government provide increasing support for local community efforts that provide afterschool engagement and education to children, and these programs fill the time gaps during which children are out of school and their parents or caregivers return home from work (see Sliwa et al., 2022).

Today, children from higher SES backgrounds attend afterschool programs (66 percent) more than children from lower SES backgrounds (34 percent); involvement of low-income children declined from 4.6 million in 2014 to 2.7 million in 2020 (Afterschool Alliance, 2022). Today, nearly 25 million children are unable to participate in afterschool programs because there are simply not enough opportunities provided for them. Sadly, unmet need is highest among African American and Latinx children: 52 percent of low-income Latinx families and 59 percent of low-income Black families are not able to access afterschool programs (Afterschool Alliance, 2022). There are several facets of afterschool programming (Sparr et al., 2012). These are summarized below and are augmented with information from the Afterschool Alliance (2022).

Effective afterschool programs provide a number of educational and physical activities, and offer significant benefits to youth, families, and communities (youth.gov, 2021). The commonality among all of these programs is that they provide adult-supervised, safe, and supportive environments for children through school–family–community partnerships.

Social and Emotional Learning (SEL)

Children who regularly participate in afterschool programs experience improved social and emotional development in a number of areas. These children typically possess a higher sense of self-concept; have positive attitudes to develop healthy identities; are better able to manage emotions; experience a continuous development of empathy; are more likely to establish healthy relationships; improve decision-making; grow their understanding of equity; experience more positive attitudes about school; and experience an improvement in organizational and concentration skills (Afterschool Alliance, 2017).

Academic Support

Earlier research provides evidence that children who attend afterschool and/or summer programming experience an improvement in their academic performance (Naftzger et al., 2009). Students who regularly attend gain competencies in their math achievement and lower SES students appear to close the achievement gap in math between they and their higher-income peers; similar gains are found in children's reading (Pierce et al., 2013; see Afterschool Alliance, 2017).

School Participation

Children who attend afterschool programs participate more in their school classrooms and experience smoother transitions from grade to grade than children who do not participate. Furthermore, school-aged participants attend school more regularly with fewer absences, experience far less truancy, and have reduced school dropout rates (Westwood Research & Statistical Services, 2017). These findings are especially notable among lower SES students.

There is no question that parental and community involvement in the lives of school-age children tremendously impacts their overall growth and development, and improves the trajectory of their later-in-life development, interpersonal relationships, and experiences. It is, indeed, concerning that the children who are at the most significant risk for poor developmental outcomes and are the most vulnerable have the greatest unequitable, limited access to afterschool opportunities. A call to action to the community of professionals who are committed to improving the lives of children is needed, especially in the aftermath of the COVID-19 pandemic. It is critically important that parent educators work to minimize the disparities and barriers to participating in afterschool programs, such as transportation and neighborhood safety. By implementing a holistic approach to improving the lives of children, these community solutions provide foundational skills that children need as they approach adolescence (Afterschool Alliance, 2017).

PARENTING LIFE EDUCATION: FOSTERING ROOTS AND NURTURING WINGS

When it comes to parenting, there's really not a developmental period when parents can ease off of their responsibilities and commitment. To the contrary! Even though children become far more self-sufficient and independent during the school years, and even though it appears they do not need the intensive, hands-on parenting that is required during the first five years of a child's life, parents and caregivers are still very much needed to ensure their child's healthy development—despite the fact that middle childhood can be a challenging time for parents, particularly as children approach the 'tween years and become even more autonomous (and, perhaps, more opinionated).

Research about the brain growth spurt in the late middle childhood years points to how significant the parent's role is in shaping both the architecture and function of the brain. The parent–child relationship is also immensely important in the establishment of a child's healthy self-concept and the ability to control and regulate emotions, and both of these facets of psychosocial growth impact children's physical, sexual, emotional, and mental health. Further, empirical studies inform us that healthy child growth and development is quite dependent upon a child's secure attachment, brought about by sensitive and responsive interactions between parent and child. It is incumbent upon parents to minimize ACEs and to seek help from mental health professionals if a child should experience harmful environmental circumstances. Positive parenting practices throughout the school years support children's healthy development in all areas. But with the pressures of adulthood and social challenges for children today, it is especially useful for parents to rely on afterschool programming, and other family support programs that guide effective parenting practices and provide links to child development education, and community services and resources if need be.

On the best days, parenting school age children can still be challenging. As children grow and change, it is sometimes difficult to strike a healthy balance between fostering the healthy development of the child's self-concept (the roots that ground them) while encouraging their independence and friendships (the wings that allow them to soar). It's not easy. But today, parent educators and other helping professionals are well equipped to assist parents in the two parenting tasks in middle childhood: Encouraging the healthy development of their child's social and emotional capabilities while simultaneously actively parenting, but from a distance. To be sure, the parent educator's most important task is to provide educational and informational support to parents to help them guide their children through adolescence and into adulthood—from dependency to self-governing adults.

7 THE CHANGING NATURE OF PARENTING: ADOLESCENCE

LEARNING OBJECTIVES

7.1 Summarize the changes in the architecture and functions of the adolescent brain, and how these changes affect executive functions.

7.2 Apply the concepts of the maturity gap to adolescent decision-making and coping skills.

7.3 Describe emotion-related parenting and emotion coaching, and their implications in the parent–teen relationship.

7.4 Explain the process of adolescent individuation and identity development and the ways in which self-governing is important to this process.

7.5 Discuss ways parents can minimize parent–teen conflict.

7.6 Summarize the characteristics of parenting that promote the healthy development of the adolescent's brain development and sense of self.

7.7 Describe teen's friendships and romantic relationships and the role these play in adolescent development.

7.8 Identify adolescent sexual behaviors that pose risks to adolescents.

7.9 Explain anxiety and depression, and their influence on suicidality risk in teenagers.

7.10 Summarize the concept of external and internal assets, and how these impact adolescent development.

Adolescence is the developmental period that spans childhood and adulthood, and it has long been held that this phase of life occurs between the ages of about 12 to 18 or 19 (Sawyer et al., 2018). In contemporary society, however, it is difficult to establish a timeframe for this complex transitional lifestage, and there are multifaceted reasons why trying to do so poses a conundrum (Sawyer et al., 2018).

Aside from early childhood, there is no other time in the lifespan when such tremendous growth and development occurs in an individual. These changes do not just occur in the preadolescent and adolescent's body, they also occur cognitively and socially-emotionally. But, just as with every aspect of human development, the intersectionality of factors impacts the timing of pubertal growth.

Source: iStock.com/MonkeyBusinessImages.

ADOLESCENT DEVELOPMENT

There is substantial physical growth that occurs in the teen's body, from brain growth and maturation, to reproductive growth and maturation, to gains in height, weight, and muscle mass—all of these are significantly impacted by environmental factors, such as the influence of the family (Judd et al., 2020), maltreatment (Natsuaki et al., 2011), the presence or absence of community violence (Butler et al., 2018), the impact of junk foods (Reichelt & Rank, 2017), and adolescent obesity (Ruiz et al., 2020). What is more, these myriad influences also impact the timing of pubertal growth, leading to *earlier* onset of puberty (see Ohlsson et al., 2019, for a full review). And, while puberty appears to begin earlier in nearly all populations than it did five or six decades ago, social changes (including older ages at marriage and parenthood) are simultaneously occurring that *delay* the transition to adulthood (Sawyer et al., 2018). These two factors—earlier onset of pubertal changes and delaying the transition to adulthood—have now extended scientists' beliefs that the adolescent period of development extends from age 10 to age 25 (Jaworska & MacQueen, 2015; Sawyer et al., 2018). Researchers suggest that there are three developmental stages that bridge childhood and adulthood; these stages are presented in Table 7.1. As you saw in the previous chapter, brain development in the preteen and significantly impacts an individual's growth and developmental trajectories, and it is these changes in the brain's structures and functions that trigger all cognitive and social-emotional changes.

TABLE 7.1 ■ Stages of Adolescent Development

Early Adolescence (ages 10–14)	Significant physical growth Increased sexual feelings and interest in romantic partners Limited abstract thought capabilities Development of an internal code of morality
Middle Adolescence (ages 15–17)	Pubertal growth is complete for most Genetic males will continue to grow in height Increased need for autonomy and independence Increasingly egocentric May experience first sexual encounters/relationships Growing capacity for abstract thought Contemplate their existence and meaning of life Metacognition increases Process of individuation intensifies
Late Adolescence/Emerging Adulthood (ages 18–24)	Complete development of the prefrontal cortex Decision-making, coping skills, other executive functions mature to adult levels Increase in emotional and mood stability Individuation complete; a firm sense of identity is in place Psychological, intellectual, academic, financial independence Shift in friendship experiences and romantic relationships

Source: © AMCHP (2021).

The Brain and the Adolescent

At birth, a newborn's brain has nearly 100 billion **neurons**, or nerve cells, and these are the building blocks of the brain and nervous system. During the first five years of life, there is an explosion of the connections between neurons (**synapse formation**) that is fostered by relationships and environmental experiences. The overproduction of connections provides children the means by which they can discover, learn, explore, and excel in a number of different ways (Feinstein, 2009). This first wave of brain growth is referred to as **synaptogenesis**, and between the ages of five and six, a child's brain has reached about 95 percent of its adult size (Grigorenko, 2017).

The changing demands of a child's environment and the demands of development on the child's body require that the brain is able to adapt and refashion its connections (Arain et al., 2013). **Brain plasticity** refers to the brain's ability to modify and reconstruct itself. Once a synapse (connection) is formed, it is either strengthened or weakened by way of heredity and environmental influences (Arain et al., 2013), and over time, the brain removes synapses that are irrelevant, those it no longer needs or uses. **Synaptic pruning** is the process by which the brain eliminates unneeded or extra synapses, and this process is exceptionally advanced in the adolescent brain (Mercurio et al., 2020). This pruning process—the second wave of brain development that begins at about age 11 and continues through about the age of 25—is critically important, as it is the way in which the brain becomes more efficient and more useful to adapt to the complex demands of adulthood (Gill & Caffaso, 2018; Mercurio et al., 2020; Roaten & Roaten, 2012). To be sure, the synaptic pruning process ultimately shapes a more sophisticated brain, and it is the process that "…transforms an unwieldly network of small pathways into a better organized system of superhighways" (Steinberg, 2011, p. 42).

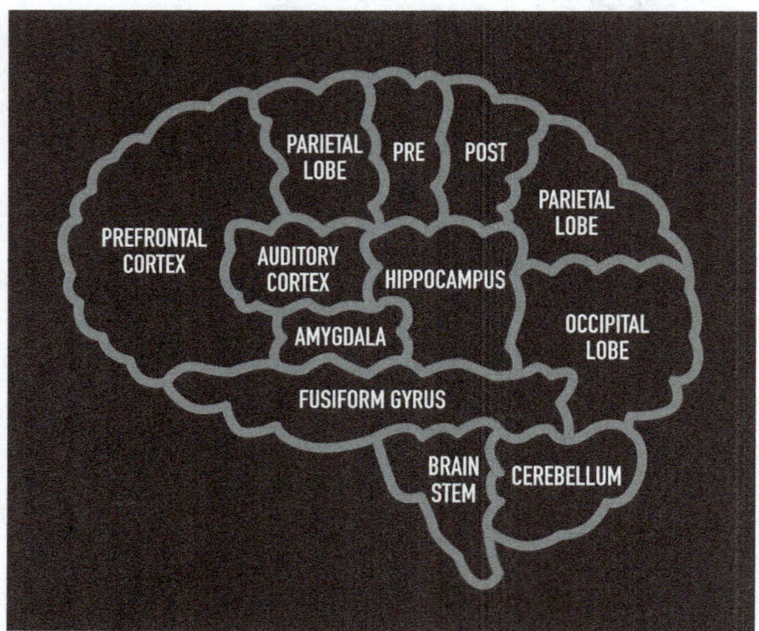

During the adolescent period of development, the brain experiences a growth spurt, particularly in the region of the prefrontal cortex (PFC). Healthy maturation and development of the PFC is critically important because it is this area of the brain that controls a person's executive functions.

Source: iStock.com/jobalou.

The Prefrontal Cortex

The **prefrontal cortex (PFC)** is a part of the brain that is situated at the front of the brain (see the image above), and it is very much under construction during the adolescent period of development. This region of the brain is responsible for an individual's **executive functions** or higher-level cognitive processes (see Arain et al., 2013, for a full review):

- Personality expression
- Focusing attention
- Organizing thoughts
- Problem-solving

- Forming strategies and planning
- Considering the future and weighing possible consequences of behaviors
- Impulse control
- Ability to delay the need for immediate gratification
- Inhibit inappropriate behavior and engage in appropriate behavior
- Decision-making
- Ability to modulate intense emotions
- Self-control

In essence, the prefrontal cortex orchestrates thoughts and actions. However, because the adolescent brain is still immature and its structural changes still incomplete, a teenager's emotions often dictate decision-making and responses. This is important to know because an adolescent's emotions—*not reason*—rule behaviors and decisions (Roaten & Roaten, 2012). Ezequiel Mercurio and colleagues provide a robust review of the empirical literature that describes the ways in which the immaturity of the PFC drives much of a teen's emotional and impulsive decisions, such as having sex on the spur of the moment, engaging in risk-taking behaviors like drug use, and suicide attempts (see especially Eaton et al., 2008; Mercurio et al., 2020); we examine each of these behaviors later in this chapter.

As the PFC becomes more fully developed, teens' abilities to hypothesize, reason, and use logic also expand (Mercurio et al., 2020; Roaten & Roaten, 2012), and these cognitive capabilities prepare the adolescent for the responsibilities of adulthood. And, as our study has shown us up to this point, multiple contexts surround an individual and play a crucial role in shaping a teen's PFC. This is why prefrontal cortex maturation occurs at different rates for different adolescents.

The Maturity Gap

The adolescent brain develops in remarkable ways; however, the brain and emerging cognitive abilities are not in developmental sync. The **maturational imbalance model** explains that during adolescence, the brain regions that seek reward mature more quickly (and are thus more active) than the regions of the brain that promote impulse control (see Mercurio et al., 2020). This developmental imbalance is referred to as the **maturity gap** (Mercurio et al., 2020). For example, one study of 900, 10- to 30-year-olds found that by age 16, adolescents have developed logical reasoning and memory, but social-emotional maturity (specifically, self-control in the presence of peers) does not fully mature until the individual is in their 20s (Steinberg, 2009). A large study of 5,400 of individuals ages 10 to 30 found similar results (Icenogle et al., 2019). This research proposes that, cognitively, 16-year-olds have comparable abilities to adults, yet teens' social-emotional maturity in areas such as impulse control, thinking about the future when making decisions, and peer influence are immature.

Researchers and developmentalists sometimes describe the maturity gap as *cold cognition* and *hot cognition*. **Cold cognition** refers to cognitive processes that do not involve emotions, such as working memory and careful, measured, methodical decision-making and analysis (Icenogle et al., 2019). Conversely, **hot cognition** is significantly influenced by a person's emotions, and commonly leads to impulsive, rapid responses (Lodge & Tabor, 2005). Hot cognition almost always results in biased, poorer decision-making (Huijbregts et al., 2007).

In sum, the adolescent developmental stage is a time of brain maturation that allows teens to think in complex, abstract ways, yet simultaneously make haphazard decisions and choices that are colored by emotion. For parents, caregivers, and parenting professionals, an appreciation of the maturity gap is of the utmost importance because this lag between cognitive abilities and executive functions creates a timespan that is ripe for adolescent risky behaviors and decisions, and faulty reasoning (Mercurio et al., 2020). In a very real way, adolescents' advanced cognitive skills give them a false sense of maturity and security in their psychosocial decisions—putting them at risk for long-term consequences of relatively short-term decisions. A predominant challenge for parents of adolescents, then, is to adapt parenting practices to their teen's developing cognitive capabilities and broadening social orientation while ensuring the healthy development of their child's brain (Kobak et al., 2017).

Positive Parenting, Emotion Socialization, and the Adolescent Brain

The maturity gap in adolescent brain development fundamentally directs parenting tasks and experiences during this lifestage because parents must now balance their role as protector with their role of encouraging and supporting their teen's burgeoning autonomy, self-governing, and decision-making (Kobak et al., 2017).

It is important to remember that the overall effects of past parent–child interactions and childrearing practices carry into adolescence (see Chapters 5 and 6), and parental support, expressed through behaviors such as providing general sustenance, warmth, connectedness, responsiveness, and monitoring, is an important factor that continues to shape the teen's brain. Indeed, one team of researchers observed that the influence of *positive* adolescent environments on PFC development is as important in shaping teens' future life trajectories as negative environments (Whittle et al., 2014). Supportive parenting, from birth through adolescence, has a significant impact on a child's cognitive, social, emotional, and behavioral development and outcomes (Eshel et al., 2006; Landry et al., 2008); positive parenting is also associated with better mental health outcomes for adolescents (Schwartz et al., 2012).

Typically, the greater the degree of parental support, the more favorable the adolescent's personality development and social competence (Shubert et al., 2019). Conversely, a lack of parental and family support is linked to negative outcomes for teenagers, including anxiety, loneliness, low self-esteem, delinquency, drug abuse, and other risky behaviors (Cavanaugh & Buehler, 2015; Hoskins, 2014). One empirical study of 166 adolescents sought to determine the buffering effect of positive parenting among teens in socioeconomically disadvantaged neighborhoods on teen brain development (Whittle et al., 2017). The investigators determined that parents who expressed positivity (i.e., low aggression and irritability, communication, and responsiveness) provide a protective factor against mental health difficulties in their teens and promote healthy adolescent prefrontal cortex development, in spite of the stressors associated with living in an economically disadvantaged neighborhood. In essence, the researchers found that parents' positive, healthy interactions with their teens moderated the negative effects of their living environment.

Just as children are socialized—taught—appropriate behaviors, *emotion coaching* is an effective parenting skill that helps children and adolescents to identify and understand their emotions. Emotion coaching helps teens to cope with feelings in healthy ways.

Source: iStock.com/FGTrade.

Other studies have revealed that parents' emotion regulation can negatively or positively influence the development of the adolescent brain (Ducharme et al., 2013; Jespersen et al., 2021; Schwartz et al., 2012; Shaw et al., 2006). **Emotion-related parenting** practices teach children and adolescents about emotions and emotion-related behavior. Pioneering research by Gottman et al. (1996) suggested that positive parenting includes emotion coaching. **Emotion coaching** is a parenting practice that helps children to self-regulate; it includes labeling and describing emotions that children and adolescents express, helping their children solve problems that caused an emotional response, and comforting them (Spinrad et al., 2020; Valiente et al., 2020). This emotion socialization is essential for optimal adolescent development because as you just learned, adolescents' emotions rule their decisions and behaviors—and they need their parents' assistance and guidance in interpreting and regulating these emotions (Jespersen et al., 2021). Research informs us of the significance of emotion-related parenting in adolescence:

- When parents coach their children and teens about emotions and emotional responses and experiences, youth are better able to successfully regulate their emotions (Jespersen et al., 2021).

- When parents help their children to cope with anger and sadness, children become more skilled at managing their own anger and sadness, and more skilled at identifying what they are feeling (Gottman et al., 1996).
- When parents ignore or do not validate adolescents' feelings, teens have more difficulty with emotion regulation (Eisenberg et al., 1996).
- Only about one-half of parents help adolescents understand and manage their emotions, in both depressed and healthy adolescents (Waller et al., 2014).

There are a number of parenting practices that foster positive parenting, and these are introduced in Table 7.2.

Peers also exert a notable influence on adolescents' emotion socialization (Valiente et al., 2020). We examine the significance of peer relationships a bit later on in this chapter, but here it is important to understand that as adolescents progress through this developmental stage, they place less importance on their parents' emotional guidance and assign more value to their

TABLE 7.2 ■ Parenting Practices That Foster Positive Parenting

Parenting Practice	Parent Behavior	Adolescent Outcomes
Positive engagement	Mutual respect Expressions of affection Mutual emotional support Positive family relationships Available, supportive Family time Predictable routines (including bedtime for teens)	Adaptive emotional regulation Receptive to parents' input Increased self-worth Buffered effects of depression Reduced risk for substance abuse and unprotected sex
Monitoring and supervising teens' behaviors	Balance supervision with support for independence (autonomy granting) Accurately assess teens' behaviors Accurately assess teens' needs and capabilities Adjust supervision based on teen's behaviors	Enhanced self-endorsed values and beliefs Decrease in internalizing and externalizing behaviors Internalizing of parental expectations, boundaries, and rules Increased development of internal locus of control
Open communication	Accurately read teen's communication Respond in flexible ways Attend, listen, empathize, and respond Cooperatively negotiates expectations and goals Consider teens' point of view	Enhanced self-governing and responsible decision-making Increased family relationship satisfaction Advanced conflict-resolution abilities Cooperative negotiations of expectations (e.g., curfew)

Source: Adapted from Kobak et al. (2017).

peers' emotional socialization (Jespersen et al., 2021). More importantly, teens tend to match their emotional expressions to those of their friends (King et al., 2018). Because of this shift to greater reliance on peers, parents must be careful to not abandon their parental roles and responsibilities.

To be sure, this is when balancing adolescents' needs for independence, self-ruling, and autonomous decision-making, yet simultaneously providing safety, becomes challenging for most parents (Kobak et al., 2017). Effective parenting requires that adults are firm, yet flexible; autonomy-granting, yet boundary-enforcing; and trusting, yet knowledgeable about contemporary issues that present obstacles to healthy adolescent development. There is no question that parents play a pivotal role in the healthy development of their adolescent's brain and adolescent identity formation.

It is common for adolescents to "try on" different identities as they begin to individuate from their families of origin. How many identities did you try before you had a firmer idea of "who" you are or want to be? Did any of your identities conflict with your parents' or caregivers' ideals or value systems? Did any of your identities cause your parents or caregivers concern?

Source: iStock.com/FGTrade.

ESTABLISHING IDENTITY AND AUTONOMY

The rapid and extensive physical and social-emotional growth and development that occur during adolescence is second only to the immense changes that occur during the first few years of a child's life. Perhaps the greatest central developmental task for adolescents to successfully navigate is the development of a strong and stable sense of self, or *identity*; this is accomplished through the process of **individuation** (Steinberg, 2008). As our study has shown us, identity development begins to occur well before adolescence, but because of the physical changes in teens' brains, they now have greater capacities to think about "who" they are and how "who" they are affects their lives (Steinberg, 2008). Through the changes associated with individuation, adolescents form an identity that is separate from that of their families of origin. In this section, we explore the characteristics of adolescent individuation and also examine a teenager's need for autonomy and self-governing.

Identity Formation

Erik Erikson was one of the most influential psychologists to shape our current understanding of identity formation in adolescence. According to Erikson and his fifth stage of psychosocial development, the establishment of **identity**, a "subjective sense of an invigorating sameness and continuity," (Erikson, 1968, p. 23), is the central developmental quest for adolescents. Identity is our sense of who we are as a person and who we are as members of society or social groups (Cheon et al., 2020). It forms the foundation for an individual's twofold self-esteem.

- **Self-identity:** How we define ourselves in relation to family, friends, school, and other social environments. Self-identity shapes a teen's perceptions of belonging and inclusion and provides a sense of continuity or self-sameness (Cheon et al., 2020).
- **Social identity:** Constructed by culture through societally assigned traits and characteristics (e.g., society defines a person as "Asian," even though the person doesn't individually define themselves as such) (Koni et al., 2019).

Erikson's theory asserts that there are three interacting factors that converge to shape a person's concept of self and identity:

1. A person's biological traits (including genetics)
2. A person's psychological needs
3. The myriad social and cultural contexts in which the person interacts

Because there is an upsurge of physical, psychological, and social growth during adolescence, searching for an identity is heightened in the teen's awareness, and this growth explosion makes the adolescent period the perfect phase for achievement of self (Adamson & Lyxell, 1996).

As you learned in Chapter 2, *intersectionality* describes the overlap of various social and demographic identities, such as race, ethnicity, gender, sexuality, and class in the experiences of oppression and discrimination (Crenshaw, 1991). An adolescent's subjective perception of the importance of each of these factors also impacts identity development (Cheon et al., 2020; Zell et al., 2018). As one important body of contemporary research accurately suggests, "...the development of identity takes place against the backdrop of the broader society and the value that society places on one's social group membership" (Cheon et al., 2020, p. 1). When a society oppresses, marginalizes, or discriminates against one group (or groups) and gives advantage to another group (or groups), it stands to reason that this oppression and discrimination negatively impact the healthy development of an adolescent's self and social identities.

Intersectionality can be even more complicated for multiracial adolescents because these teens are under constant pressure to identify with one race over another (Weaver & Maselehdan Block, 2020). The opposite of healthy identity development in Erikson's fifth stage is **identity** (or role) **confusion**. This occurs when teens are unsure of who they are and where they fit into society. When an adolescent is forced to identify with one racial or ethnic identity over another, it causes confusion and undermines their sense of self. The consequences of identity or role confusion include difficulties with commitment, a lack of confidence, and difficulties in relating to others and forming/maintaining meaningful relationships (which significantly impacts the next developmental stage in adulthood, *intimacy vs. isolation*) (Cherry & Morin, 2021). For optimal racial and identity development, some researchers have proposed that parents allow their children and teens to explore all aspects of their racial and ethnic makeup, rather than to force a racial identity upon them (Franco & McElroy-Heltzel, 2019). Because identity is dynamic and complex, it changes over time, so how an adolescent identifies at one point in development does not necessarily mean the specific identity will carry over to the next phase of development.

James Marcia (1966, 1993), also studied identity achievement, and his work revealed four identity statuses—*achievement, moratorium, diffusion*, and *foreclosure*. Underlying each of these identity statuses are the processes of commitment and exploration, causing identity formation to be more complex and uncertain:

- **Identity achievement:** Following a period of searching and questioning, an individual commits to a self-defined identity.
- **Identity moratorium:** An individual is currently engaged in the identity questioning and searching process.
- **Identity foreclosed:** The individual unquestioningly accepts parental values without question or the examination of alternatives.
- **Identity diffused:** This individual shows no sign of commitment nor does the person express a need or desire to search for an identity. (Adams & Jones, 1983, p. 249)

In conjunction with identity, teens must also develop autonomy wherein they begin to take responsibility for their actions and decisions that affect themselves, and, in many cases, those around them.

Autonomy and Self-Governing

Scholars have defined autonomy in a number of different ways. **Autonomy** has been described as developing individuation; becoming a self-governing person; directing one's own life with feelings of competency; and the ability to regulate one's own behavior (see Murphy et al., 2008).

Research has also suggested that there are different adolescent behaviors associated with autonomy, including a decreasing dependency on adults; integration of sexuality and gender; and an internal focus on self-esteem (see Murphy et al., 2008). One study found that from ages 9 to 14, children and early adolescents increase their input into decisions regarding such things as appearance, activities, and social life, and this input surges from ages 15 to 20 (Wray-Lake et al., 2010). Through age 20, however, decisions about money and health are still largely influenced by parents and caregivers.

"Because I Said So!": Autonomy-Granting and Control

Although authoritative parenting (see Chapter 5) is characterized by a high degree of support and autonomy-granting in particular areas, it is also characterized by a certain amount of control. *Coercive control* is based on threats, force, or physical punishment and has negative consequences, whereas *inductive control* (i.e., clear limits, rules, and consequences practiced with flexibility) has positive outcomes. Failure to distinguish between these two types of control has resulted in a lot of confusion and inconsistency on the part of parents and adolescents alike (Baumrind et al., 2010; Sorkhabi & Middaugh, 2014).

A large measure of the conflict and stress of parent–adolescent interactions revolves around the issue of control, since teens usually want greater freedom and parents usually seek greater control. Parents have more influence over adolescents when they express a high level of support and exercise inductive control. In fact, by articulating clearly the societal or welfare concerns that complex issues raise, parents are likely to facilitate adolescents' understanding of the limits or boundaries of their personal restrictions. These parents maintain clear boundaries between moral, conventional, and personal issues, while practicing what some researchers refer to as **psychological flexibility** (Brassell et al., 2016).

Conversely, some parents treat both moral and conventional issues as obligatory and subject to parental authority (Smetana, 2011). One body of research found that parental harshness and corporal punishment during adolescence increase the probability of sending approving messages about violence against a spouse or partner in adulthood, sibling aggression, experiencing depression as an adult, and elevated levels of marital conflict (Altschul et al., 2016). These parenting practices in adolescence lead to the increased risk of spousal assault and abuse, regardless of whether the individual witnessed violence between their own parents.

Racial and Ethnic Differences in Autonomy-Granting

While research generally supports that authoritative parenting tends to be the healthiest style of parenting practiced in the United States, this finding represents a Eurocentric perspective, a world view that promotes white, European beliefs, values, and practices as the societal norm. As with every other area of individual development across the lifespan, Eurocentric parenting practices (as described by Baumrind, 1991) are not necessarily validated across ethnicities and cultures (Lerner & Hilliard, 2019). Indeed, developmental contexts such as age and stage of development, geography, nationality, culture, ritual, language, personality, individuality, and identity all influence the bidirectional nature of the parent–child relationship (Lerner & Hilliard, 2019).

Indigenous Americans typically exhibit high levels of warmth and responsiveness to their children. They value autonomy and trust, and therefore tend to engage in lower levels of monitoring their children's behaviors. This parenting style leads to healthy self-regulation in their teens.

Source: iStock.com/theboone.

Some researchers hypothesized that Baumrind's (1991) parenting styles are not adequately representative across all cultures (Rodriguez et al., 2009). In this investigation of Latinx parenting practices, researchers analyzed *warmth* (responsiveness) and *demandingness* (both supportive and nonsupportive); they additionally included another parenting variable, autonomy granting. **Autonomy** granting refers to parents allowing their adolescents the freedom of establishing an identity by encouraging the expression of differences and values, and by allowing mutual participation in decision-making (Kunz & Grych, 2013).

Kunz and Grych's (2013) research revealed that 61 percent of Latinx parents used lower levels of autonomy granting than parents from other racial and cultural backgrounds, and this finding brought to light another style of parenting, *protective parents*. Rodriguez's expanded cultural of view of parenting styles adds four additional types of parenting: protective, cold, affiliative, and a second neglectful style of parenting, neglectful II. This study provides greater distinctions between parenting practices, particularly across ethnic and cultural contexts. Table 7.3 describes the characteristics of parenting styles when autonomy granting is added as a variable.

Other researchers have also found that Native Americans, or Indigenous Americans, are more permissive in their parenting, exhibiting high levels of warmth, low demandingness, and high autonomy granting (Muir et al., 2019). As a result, they tend to value higher levels of

TABLE 7.3 ■ Expanded Understanding of Parenting Styles

Style	Warmth	Demandingness	Autonomy Granting
Authoritative	High	High	High
Authoritarian	Low	High	Low
Permissive	High	Low	High
Neglectful	Low	Low	Low
Protective	High	High	Low
Cold	Low	High	High
Affiliative	High	Low	Low
Neglectful II	Low	Low	High

Source: Rodriguez et al. (2009).

exploration and self-regulation for their children and engage in lower levels of parental monitoring and punishment (Muir et al., 2019).

Asian American parents tend to be more authoritarian in their parenting styles with low warmth, high demandingness, and low autonomy granting. There is so much diversity among these groups, however, that is difficult to qualify one type of parenting style. Asian American parents are generally characterized by the use of logical consequences, high control and exacting obedience, high monitoring of child behavior, and a willingness to use physical punishment when family rules are not followed (Ng & Wang, 2019). Acculturation issues between Asian American parents and teens can be challenging because fathers are less likely to be involved in parenting, emotional restraint is stressed, and sons are given hierarchical and preferential treatment over daughters (Ng & Wang, 2019).

Latinx parents, as noted above, are protective in their parenting styles with high warmth and demandingness and low autonomy granting. They are similar to Asian American parents in that they emphasize high levels of control, demand obedience, and carefully monitor their children's behaviors, but they also emphasize high levels of warmth, connectedness, and bonding. As a collectivist cultural group, Latinx parents also prefer the use of logical consequences, demand loyalty, respect, and the reverencing of their elders, and tend to use a high degree of corporal punishment in their parenting practices (Halgunseth, 2019; Jabagchourian et al., 2014).

White parents are more authoritative in their parenting styles, but this is sometimes mediated by class distinctions in which higher wage-earning parents are positively associated with higher levels of warmth, demandingness, and autonomy granting, and lower wage-earner parents are associated with more control and demandingness, and conformity and obedience (Schneider et al., 2018). In a study of 6,450 parents of young and school-aged children, Schneider and colleagues examined measures of income inequity. They found that parents with lower education levels and who earned lower wages were more likely to use authoritarian parenting practices (i.e., spanking and demanding obedience) than educated, mid- to upper-class parents. Parents who believed their incomes were below average were three times more likely to demand obedience from their children because the parents believed that this obedience is essential for life success. Conversely, parents who believed their income was average were only about twice as likely to adhere to the beliefs that obedience is critical (Schneider et al., 2018). Schneider's (2018) findings also revealed that white parents were more likely to endorse authoritarian childrearing styles and practices than Black parents who were in the same socioeconomic class. Higher levels of psychological punishment rather than physical punishment are also associated with whites of higher social class (Schneider et al., 2018).

African American/Black Caribbean parents are generally more authoritative than authoritarian in their parenting styles, practicing high levels of warmth, demandingness, and autonomy granting. Black parents are generally the most egalitarian across all ethnic and cultural groups in their parenting styles while also valuing independence, creativity, and self-determination in their children (McLoyd et al., 2019).

Parent–Adolescent Conflict

Because of the sweeping changes in adolescence, there is a significant impact on relationships between teenagers and their parents (Branje, 2018). The degree of parent–adolescent conflict varies from culture to culture and from family to family, and its occurrences are very much dependent upon societally accepted adolescent behaviors. Culturally, conflict is greater in periods of rapid social change; familially, conflict is greater when there is a high degree of parental power and authority.

Although some conflict is to be expected with teens' increasing needs for independence, family conflict does affect adolescents' individual and autonomy processes (Steinberg, 2001; see Branje, 2018, for a complete review). Ongoing conflict is associated with teens' externalizing (behavioral) and internalizing (problematic behaviors directed toward self) actions, increased use and abuse of substances, lower levels of self-esteem and well-being, and difficulties in school (Steinberg, 2001). Because of the systemic nature of family relationships, conflict often triggers more conflict.

As you saw earlier, *emotion-related* parenting and *emotion coaching* are two parenting practices that are especially beneficial during adolescence. Some research suggests that this type of parenting allows teens to be negative and argumentative while simultaneously fostering the adolescent's emotion-regulation skills (Granic, 2005). Emotion-related parenting helps the developing adolescent to regulate their negativity in a safe, predictable environment (Granic, 2005). Furthermore, parents who demonstrate flexibility (adjusting and regulating their own emotions) during conflict promote healthier relational development in their teens (Lichtwarck-Aschoff et al., 2009). On the other hand, parents who demonstrate rigidity during conflict do not provide an atmosphere in which teens can discuss opposing views, and this affects them in negative ways in later adult relationships, particularly in being able to renegotiate relationships (Branje et al., 2012). Parents can reduce conflict by being warm, accepting, nurturant, supportive, and autonomy-granting. When conflict does occur between parents and their teens, many parents try to resolve the conflict by exerting more power or control. Usually, this approach is counterproductive, resulting in more conflict.

Teens' Perceptions of Parents

A teenager's perceptions of their parents' attitudes and behaviors are as important as the actual attitudes and behaviors. Naturally, parents tend to view their parenting behaviors more positively than do adolescents (Korelitz & Garber, 2016). Adolescent perceptions of parents are influenced not just by levels of control, monitoring, consistent and harsh discipline, parental warmth and support, inductive reasoning (i.e., explaining how behavior affects others), perceived rejection, and levels of parent–child communication but also by socioeconomic status, neighborhood and community contexts, family structure (e.g., nonresidential fathers, single-parent, step-parent, cohabiting parent, same-sex parents, grandparents as caregivers), and racial and ethnic differences in parenting styles (Cui et al., 2020; Hoskins, 2014; Jager et al., 2016).

Adolescent perceptions of their relationships with their parents are driven in large part by how their parents react to them either positively or negatively, such as with warmth or harshness. In one study (Dimler et al., 2017), researchers found that when adolescents view their parents more negatively than their parents view them, the teenagers are more prone to experience depression and engage in risky externalizing behaviors, such as aggression (Human et al., 2016; Nelemans et al., 2016). For some adolescents, these behaviors are persistent across ages and stages of development (Assink et al., 2015). Adolescent aggressive behavior is known to contribute to lifecourse persistent offending behaviors (Assink et al., 2015), behaviors that are invariably impacted by the bidirectional nature and perceptions of the parent–child relationship.

In general, adolescents tend to perceive lower levels of intimacy and independence, greater differences in personal characteristics, and slightly higher levels of conflict with their parents than parents themselves perceive, but some evidence shows consistency between parents' and adolescents' perceptions. In one study, both mothers and fathers who perceived themselves as competent parents had adolescents who also reported their parents as being competent (e.g., warm, accepting, and helpful) (Hou et al., 2018). Positive affect or warmth shown by adolescents toward their parents is associated with better psychological functioning of adolescents, whereas negative affect is associated with problematic psychological functioning. Another study revealed that older adolescents tend to have more positive and fewer negative feelings about their mothers than about their fathers (Phares & Renk, 1998). In a different study, levels of warm parental involvement were shown to positively influence adolescent's perceptions of their parents, while autonomy granting seemed to influence the teen's views of themselves (Karavasilis et al., 2003).

There is no question that parenting styles are vitally important variables in parent–child interactions and teens' overall development, and the importance of parental roles does not diminish because a teen progresses through adolescence and becomes more independent. Another critical factor in adolescent healthy development is the interaction with peers.

We have seen that as children develop throughout early childhood and the school years, peers become increasingly important, and also to the formation of the capacity for intimacy. Perhaps more than at any other time in lifecourse development, friends are most significant during adolescence and the entrance into adulthood. Through friendships, teens learn to be open and honest, to self-disclose, to validate others, to resolve conflict, to share empathy, and to trust.

ADOLESCENT RELATIONSHIPS

Support by way of friendships and peers is important in the healthy developmental processes of identity formation, autonomy, and resilience (Ioannidis et al., 2020). *Social support* is defined as the extent to which a person is cared for and accepted, and it is experienced as *received/actual* support or *perceived/quality* support (van Harmelen et al., 2021). Between the ages of 13 and 17, teen friendships grow deeper, stronger, and are more equal in their give-and-take and reciprocity in meeting others' needs (Burnett Heyes et al., 2015; see also van Harmelen et al., 2021).

Friendships and Romantic Relationships

The importance of adolescent friendships cannot be stressed enough. Empirical study has shown that positive peer relationships (for a full review, see van Harmelen et al., 2021)

- improve adolescent's mental health and well-being;
- increase self-esteem;
- help to develop healthy coping skills and behaviors;
- lower daily stress;
- promote help-seeking behaviors.

Furthermore, adolescent friendships are highly influenced by parental acceptance and support. For example, researchers in one meta-analytic study looked at teenagers across 31 countries and found associations between parental acceptance and adolescents' reduced socioemotional difficulties, as well as their development of positive worldviews (Khaleque & Ali, 2017). In another study, mothers' support was positively linked with prosocial interactions (intentional behaviors that benefit the well-being of others) among family members while fathers' support was positively linked with prosocial interactions with friends (Padilla-Walker et al., 2016).

Of course, peer influence goes both ways, and an abundance of scholarly work reveals that friends have influence over problematic, health-risk behaviors as well. It is well established, for example, that peers sway alcohol use and truancy (Steers et al., 2019), drug use and abuse (Jorge et al., 2018), sexual decisions and behaviors (Peçi, 2017), bullying others to fit in (Espelage, 2002), tobacco use (Loke & Mak, 2013), and posting sexual images online (Nesi, 2018).

As teens go through individuation, they are especially susceptible to the opinions of their friends—positive or negative—because they are particularly sensitive to being excluded from a group or left out (Henneberger et al., 2020). So, it is not uncommon for adolescents to align their values, beliefs, and behaviors to the norms of a peer group they desire to belong to—for better or worse (Andrews et al., 2020). This is known as *peer socialization* (Henneberger et al., 2020). Due to hot cognition and the inability to think about long-term consequences because of the immature prefrontal cortex, being a part of a desired peer group outweighs any negative health risks or consequences of illegal choice (Blakemore, 2018; Henneberger et al., 2020).

Romantic relationships also become increasingly important in the lives of adolescents, especially because these interactions fulfill a number of significant needs (Furman, 2002; see also Williams & Russell, 2013). For example, while 10th graders rely primarily on close friends for emotional support, by 12th grade, romantic partners become a major source of support (Furman & Buhrmester, 1992). About one-third of 13-year-olds has had a romantic relationship, and 70 percent of 17-year-olds have had at least one (CDC, 2020a). Even though there are high amounts of conflict in adolescent romantic relationships, most experience strong emotional support within the relationships.

Romantic relationships almost always form and exist within the context of the larger peer group, and the peer group's beliefs and attitudes about dating (positive and negative) are important to teens (van Zantvliet et al., 2018). Some bodies of research suggest that the peer-to-peer information that is shared about romantic relationships is important in the development of social learning and relationship skills (see van Zantvliet et al., 2018, for a full review). And, although teenage romantic relationships are rarely initiated online (only about 8 percent), social media plays a big role in teen romance, as Figure 7.1 shows us (Pew Research Center, 2015).

Of course, not all flirting is welcome: One-fourth of all teens have blocked or unfriended someone because the flirtatious behavior was felt to be inappropriate or harassment (Pew Research Center, 2015). Social media also leads to jealousy in adolescent romantic partners.

Just as with peer interactions, romantic relationships also contribute to a person's identity formation, the transition to adulthood, psychological functioning in adulthood, and the development of sexuality (Kansky & Allen, 2018). These relationships, however, do not fulfill the same functions that adult romantic relationships do. Although adults, for instance, turn to one another for caregiving and emotional support, adolescents still often turn to their peers, not the romantic partner, for such support (Furman, 2002). Although caregiving, emotional support,

FIGURE 7.1 ■ Social Media and Teen Romance

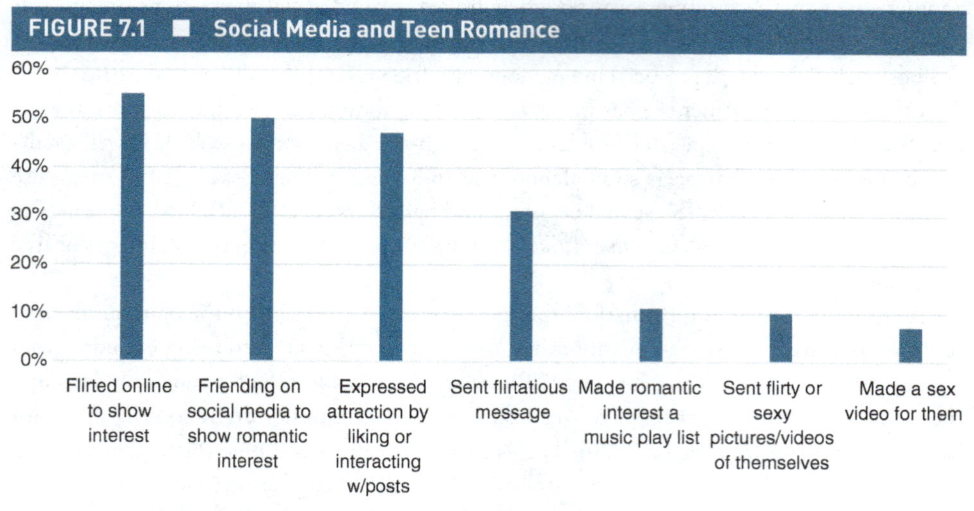

Source: Pew Research Center (2015).

Sexual and gender minority teens experience a wide variety of friendship types. Research shows us that sexual minority females tend to have same-sex friends, while LGBTQ+ males have more female than male friendships.

Source: iStock.com/DisobeyArt.

and other functions develop over time, the need for affiliation with another person as well as sexual needs are often met first in adolescent romantic relationships.

Sexual and Gender Minority Adolescents and Friendships

Sexual and gender minority adolescents (SGMA) can sometimes experience disrupted friendship and romantic relationship development (Feinstein et al., 2018; Montano et al., 2018; Thoma et al., 2021). One investigator's decade review (2010–2020) of SGM family patterns provides important insight into the challenges and difficulties SGM adolescents face (Reczek, 2020). Issues associated with stigmatization, rejection, relationship dissolution, conformity and nonconformity, and disclosure are particularly relevant (Haines et al., 2018). Successfully or unsuccessfully negotiating these issues is positively correlated with family and friendship relationship patterns among SGM adolescents.

Regarding SGM friendships, Diamond and Dubé (2002) reported that same-sex peers are the norm, with some differences. For example, sexual minority females place more emphasis on same-sex friends, while sexual minority males have more female than male friendships. Additionally, when compared to heterosexual males, sexual minority males place more emphasis and importance on their friendships in general and have lower levels of attachment to romantic partners. Sexual minority females, in contrast, place a lot more emphasis on their relationships with romantic females. The authors noted that there was no general pattern of same-sex or cross-sex friendship development. The researchers observe:

> Heterosexual youths were not systematically oriented toward cross-gender friends, and sexual-minority youths were not systematically oriented toward same-gender friends. Thus, although adolescents' developing sexual attractions might render interactions with some peers more stimulating and rewarding than interactions with others, this does not appear to unilaterally influence the number and quality of friendships with cross-gender versus same-gender friends. (p. 162)

According to Korchmaros and colleagues (2015), SGMAs, like sexual and gender majority teenagers, tend to meet their romantic partner at school. However, because approximately 9.5 percent of teenagers today identify as LGBTQ+ (UCLA Williams Institute, 2020), they tend to be more limited in their potential access to romantic partners. As a consequence of this limited access, gay male adolescents are more likely to find a romantic partner and initiate a romantic relationship online than non-LGBTQ+ teenagers (Korchmaros et al., 2015). More specifically, those who experience high levels of social anxiousness and loneliness and low levels of social competence are more likely to use online technologies to initiate and form relationships. However, as noted, initiating romantic relationships online may be more a matter of accessibility for LGBTQ+ adolescents than social competence.

Being oppressed, ridiculed, or bullied tends to increase social anxiety and loneliness. Adolescents who are socially anxious and lonely are less likely to communicate in-person or online and, therefore, they are less likely to initiate and form meaningful friendships and romantic relationships. Of course, the opposite is also valid. Those who are less socially anxious and more outgoing are more likely to communicate in-person or online and, therefore, they are more likely to initiate and form meaningful friendships and romantic relationships.

The skills associated with healthy and unhealthy relationships, generally, are more similar than they are different, regardless of sexual and gender minority status (Harris, 2013). It is important to keep in mind that the development of adolescent relationship skills and related inter- and intrapersonal adjustments are highly associated with the nature of parenting and the parent–child relationship (Mills-Koonce et al., 2018; Reczek, 2020).

With changes in the adolescent's cognition, they now have new ways to think about relationships in their social worlds. And, along with the sexual maturation and functions of the reproductive system, teenagers now have new ways to experience others.

Growing Up, Hooking Up

Hookups are brief, noncommitted, emotionally charged sexual encounters that range from kissing to sexual intercourse. Between partners, there are no expectations of a romantic or committed relationship following the hookup (Garcia et al., 2019). Hookups are generally thought of as recreational sex, and approximately 28 percent of today's teens hook up (CDC, 2020a). Two-thirds of all sexually active teens engage in sexual behaviors with people they are not dating; sexual hooking up experiences peak at around the age of 21 (Garcia et al., 2019; Lyons et al., 2015). The popular slang *body count* refers to the number of people an adolescent has engaged in sexual behaviors with, and today, one in five teens have had two or more sexual encounters within a three-month period (CDC, 2020a). In 2019, slightly more than one-half used condoms in comparison to 63 percent in 2015 (CDC, 2020a). Because most sexual hookups are unplanned, significant and serious consequences are associated with teen sexual hookups (Garcia et al., 2019):

- Each year, nearly 10 million of the 19 million new cases of sexually transmitted infections are diagnosed in adolescents
- Unintended pregnancy
- Sexual assault and victimization
- Experiences often co-occur with alcohol use

Other empirical investigations reveal that there are possibly negative mental health outcomes following hookups (see Garcia et al., 2013). For example, Owen and colleagues (2011) discovered that among 394 later adolescents, students reported an increase in feelings of depression and loneliness. Other researchers have similarly found that regret and depressive symptoms are experienced after uncommitted sex (Grello et al., 2003, 2006; Lewis et al., 2012; Oswalt et al., 2005).

Studies today reveal that teens believe that casual sex—separating sex from emotions—is freeing. However, there are risk factors and consequences associated with hooking up.

Source: iStock.com/Nikada.

While alcohol consumption certainly contributes to adolescent hookups, one social scientist who followed 101 teens in late adolescence asserts that the hookup culture in the United States validates teenager's ideas about casual sex (Wade, 2017). Wade observes, "Hooking up is immanently defensible in hookup culture. Students believe, or believe that their peers believe, that virginity is passé and monogamy prudish; that separating sex from emotions is sexually liberating; and that they're too young for commitment. All of these ideas are widely circulated … validating the choice to engage in casual sex while invalidating both monogamous relationships and the choice to have no sex at all" (Wade, 2017, p. 66). Others purport that a lack of sexual activity may actually thwart older adolescent's social and emotional development and reduce their physical gratification (Julian, 2018). Others assert that casual sexual encounters help adolescents determine if a long-term relationship is desirable (Manning et al., 2006).

Investigations regarding sexual minority hookups are scant. One small study of 17 participants, however, found that LGBTQ+ individuals in late adolescence experience more positive outcomes after hooking up than do heterosexual teens (Watson et al., 2018). The study also found that gay adolescent males used social media to find hookup partners, while lesbian and bisexual teens typically met at social gatherings.

Some bodies of research have pointed to social and contextual variables as determinants and predictors of whether hooking up is likely to occur (Garcia et al., 2019; Lyons et al., 2015). Low self-esteem, depression, and permissive personality types have been identified as some of the risk factors that predicted hooking up (Dickenson & Huebner, 2016; Mendle et al., 2013; Paul et al., 2000). Peers and schoolmates who are hooking up, along with a lack of sexual risk communication from parents, constitute additional risk factors for teens engaging in risky sexual behaviors (Wang et al., 2018).

ADOLESCENT SEXUALITY

Most adolescents become aware of their sexuality and experience their first sexual attraction prior to or at the start of puberty (CDC, 2020a). The United States Youth Risk Behavior Survey found that the majority of the 17,000 teens surveyed identify as heterosexual (see Figure 7.2).

Today, romantic partnerships and sexual contact begin between the ages of 11 and 14 (CDC, 2020a). Because of the same-sex nature of friendships among younger adolescents, it is not uncommon for first sexual experiences and sexual exploration to occur with same-sex friends; frequently, younger adolescent sexual behavior also occurs with ex-partners (Tolman & McClelland, 2011). Hookups are also common, particularly among later-adolescent teens (CDC, 2020a).

As adolescents experience changes in cognition and thought processes, the need for intimacy changes. As they individuate, develop their own identities, and are given more freedom, their capacities to experience intimate and sexual relationships change. These developments can be observed not only in the formation and maintenance of peer relationships but also in the new ways teenagers are intimate with others. As you have seen in this chapter, the area of the teen's brain (the PFC) involved in impulse control and the ability to delay the need for immediate gratification is not fully developed until a person's early- to mid-20s. This area of the brain also

FIGURE 7.2 ■ Adolescent Sexual Orientation, 2020

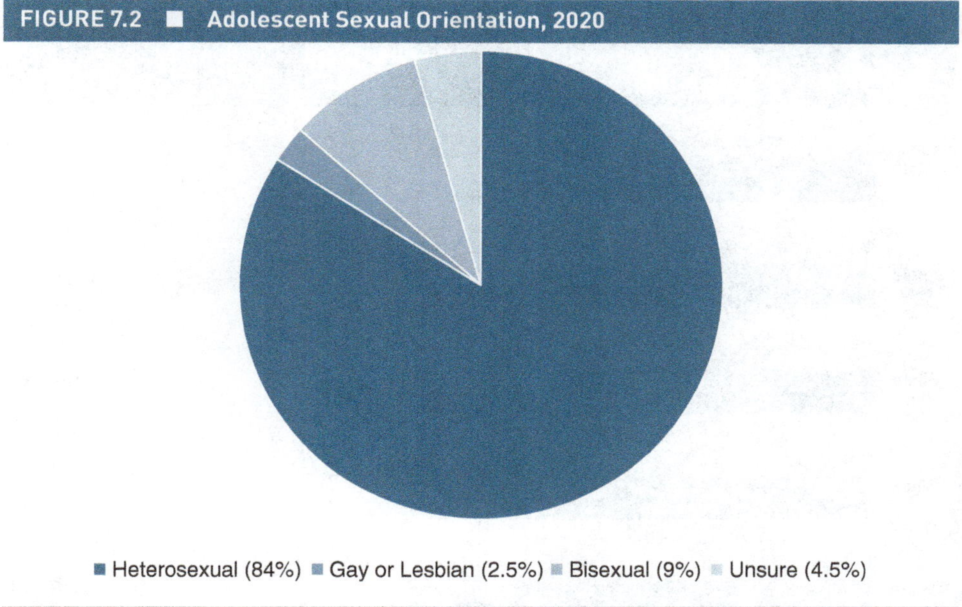

Source: CDC (2020a).

plays an important role in reward-seeking behaviors, such as sex. An in-depth discussion about adolescent sexual behaviors is beyond our scope and purposes, but here it is important to understand contemporary sexual trends among teens, and how risky behaviors may compromise the adolescent's overall healthy development.

Experiencing a Wide Range of Behaviors

Young people are engaging in sexual activity and that their attitudes about sexuality and sexual expression are becoming increasingly open-minded. Adolescent sex and sexuality are of great interest to social science researchers and demographers because teenage behaviors often put them at risk for a number of health concerns, such as unwanted pregnancies, sexually transmitted infections, and violence (Spencer et al., 2020); sexual and gender minority youth are especially at risk for dating violence (Martin-Storey & August, 2016).

Teens in the United States have sex on average at much younger ages than most young people in other countries do (about 16.8 years of age for males and 17.2 for females) (Kinsey Institute, 2020). Nearly 40 percent of high schoolers have had sex; this represents a 6 percent decline in the numbers of teens having sex in 2009 (CDC, 2020a). Figure 7.3 presents the percentage of high school students who are currently sexually active (have had sex within the past 12 months) and the percentage of those who used a condom at last intercourse.

"Having sex" is defined by teenagers as engaging in vaginal, anal, or oral sex (CDC, 2021a). During the teenage years, adolescents engage in a number of sexual practices:

FIGURE 7.3 ■ Percentage of High School Students Who Ever Had Sex, Are Currently Sexually Active, and Have Used a Condom, by Sex and by Race/Ethnicity

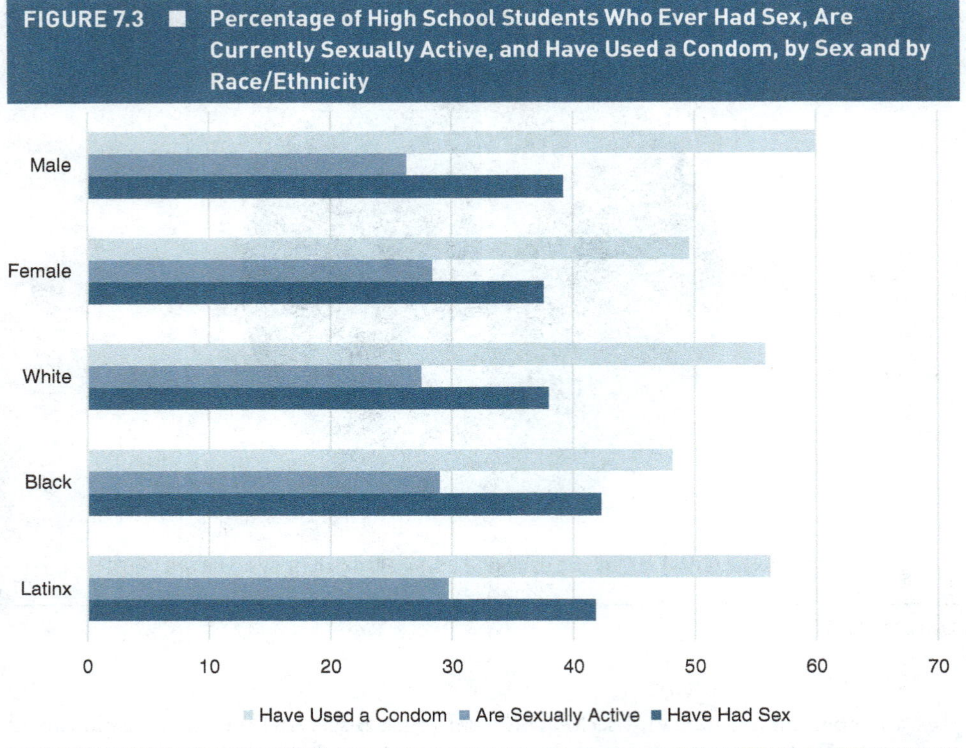

Source: CDC (2020a).

- *Vaginal intercourse/sexual intercourse:* Since 1998, rates of sexual intercourse have declined among both male and female adolescents, with 38 percent reporting they have had sexual intercourse. Bisexual students experience higher percentages of sexual intercourse (46 percent). More than one-half of males (55 percent) and females (55 percent) report having intercourse by age 18. Over 80 percent of lesbian/bisexual identified females report having sex with men at least once (CDC, 2021b).
- *Oral sex:* Those aged 15 to 19 have had oral sex with at least one partner. Many younger teens consider oral sex to be more socially acceptable than intercourse, and white adolescents have more oral sex than Black or Latinx teenagers do (CDC, 2021b; Strome et al., 2022).
- *Anal sex:* Among teens aged 15 to 17, 5 percent of males and 5.5 percent of females have had anal sex; of those aged 15 to 19, 11 percent have had anal sex with a different-sex partner (CDC, 2021b).
- *Same-sex oral or anal sex:* Among adolescent women aged 15 to 19, 11 percent have had oral sex with a female; among gay/bisexual adolescent males aged 15 to 19, 3 percent have had oral or anal sex with a male.

While sexual interests, curiosity, and exploration are all a normative part of adolescent development, certain behaviors do pose risks of acquiring an STI and/or an unwanted pregnancy. Of particular concern are those teens who have first sexual intercourse before age 16, because many times these students are less likely to use contraception; there is also a risk that sexual intercourse is not consensual (CDC, 2020a). Having multiple sex partners also raises the likelihood of poor outcomes. When sex is defined by adolescents as including oral, anal, and vaginal sex, 45 percent of females and 55 percent of males have had at least three sexual partners (CDC, 2020a).

There is also a trend among sexually experienced adolescents to subsequently and purposefully practice sexual avoidance because they do not enjoy sex, find it pleasurable, or they associate sex with negative emotions such as fear, pain, or a bad physical experience. These teens may also report avoiding sex because they do not want to ruin a relationship or friendship, because it is contrary to their value and belief systems, or simply that they have other interests and priorities (Byers et al., 2016).

Consequences of Adolescent Sexual Behaviors

As you have learned in this chapter, risk-taking in the adolescent years is common, and these behaviors occur in large part because of the immature teen brain. Risk-taking is also a way for teenagers to develop autonomy and form an identity separate from that of their parents. Even so, there are a number of consequences of adolescent sexual behaviors, and we briefly discuss them here. It is important to remember that no two adolescents are alike, and therefore teens will experience potential consequences differently.

Sexually Transmitted Infections

STIs include chlamydia, human papillomavirus (HPV), herpes, gonorrhea, syphilis, and human immunodeficiency virus (HIV). In 2019, there were 26 million new STI diagnoses in the United States—and one-half of the new infections occurred in people aged 15 to 24 (CDC, 2021b). Nearly one-fourth (21 percent) of new HIV cases occurred among adolescents aged 13 to 24 (CDC, 2021c). It is important to note, however, that because adolescents are not likely to get tested for STIs, these numbers are vastly underreported. STIs are transmitted via vaginal, oral, and anal sex, but rarely do adolescents use a dental dam (a thin, flexible, square piece of latex that prevents germs from spreading during oral sex) or condoms during anal sex (Planned Parenthood, 2017). Figures 7.4 and 7.5 report the percentages of high schoolers who have been tested for STIs and HIV. As you can see, in comparison to the number of teens who are having sex, the testing rate is quite low.

HPV Cancers

Today, it is estimated that 85 percent of the American population will acquire an HPV infection (CDC, 2020b). HPV infections that do not resolve cause certain types of cancer: cervical; vaginal; vulva; back of the throat (including the base of the tongue and tonsils); penile cancer. With the HPV vaccine, beginning at about age 11 or 12 (for both males and females), there has been an 86 percent decline in these cancers (Planned Parenthood, 2017).

FIGURE 7.4 ■ Percentage of High School Students Who Have Been Tested for STIs and HIV, by Sex and Race/Ethnicity, 2019

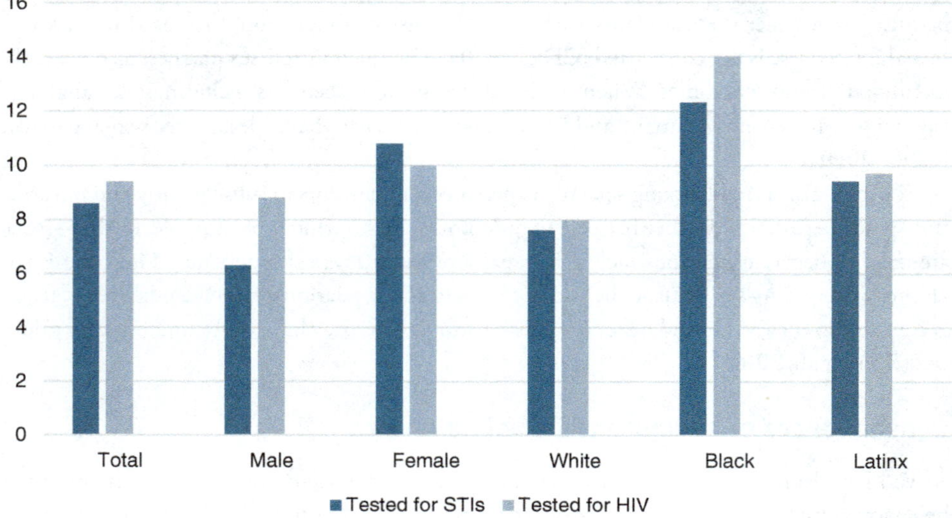

Source: CDC (2020a).

FIGURE 7.5 ■ Percentage of High School Students Who Have Ever Been Tested for STIs/HIV, by Sexual Identity and by Sex of Sexual Contacts

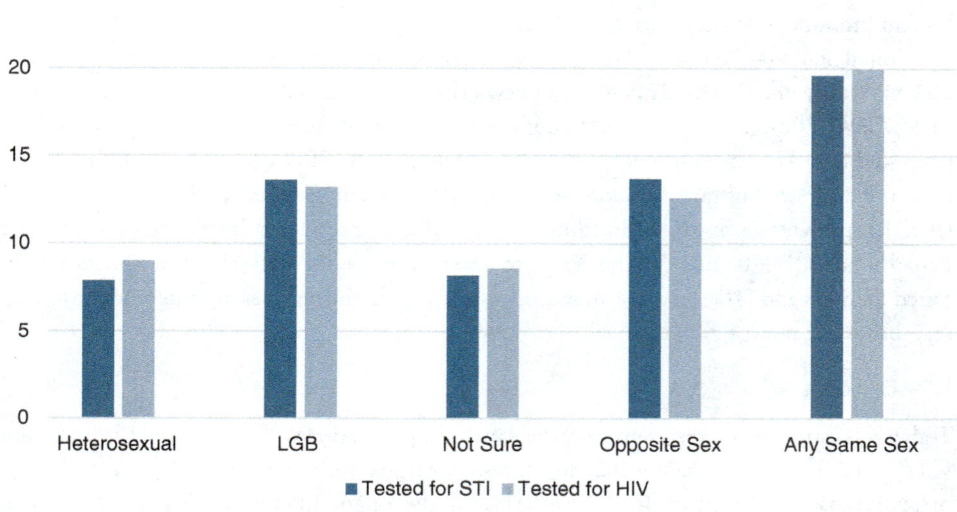

Source: CDC (2020a).

Teen dating violence is on the rise in the United States. It is a type of intimate partner violence that includes (but is not limited to) physical and sexual violence. Dating violence profoundly affects a teen's lifelong health and well-being. *If you see something, say something!*

Source: iStock.com/EgoitzBengoetxea.

Teen Dating Violence

Teen dating violence (TDV) is a type of intimate partner violence that can include *physical violence* (hurting a partner by using physical force, such as hitting, kicking, pushing, slapping, and biting) and *sexual violence* (forcing a partner or an acquaintance to engage in sexual acts or sexual touching without consent, or without the ability to consent; also includes posting sexual images online or sexting) (see Figure 7.6) (CDC, 2021d).

Teenage Pregnancy

Each year, about 750,000 teens become pregnant unintentionally (Office of Population Affairs, 2022). But for the first time since 1940, the teen birth rate in the United States is at a record low, and it is less than half of what it was in 2008; this change in the rates of teens becoming pregnant is lower than any other age group (Pew Research Center, 2019a). This encouraging decline is seen among all racial and ethnic groups, as Figure 7.7 illustrates. The teen abortion rate has similarly declined (Maddow-Zimet & Kost, 2021; Maddow-Zimet et al., 2021). Demographers believe that the 10-year decline is the result of three efforts in the United States: the availability of effective contraception; less numbers of teens having sex; and more pregnancy prevention information and education (Pew Research Center, 2019a).

Births to teen mothers are linked to a host of deleterious outcomes: poverty, overall child/teen mother health and well-being, sexuality and health concerns, education/academic declines

FIGURE 7.6 ■ Percentage of High School Students Who Experienced Physical and or Sexual Dating Violence by Sex and by Race/Ethnicity

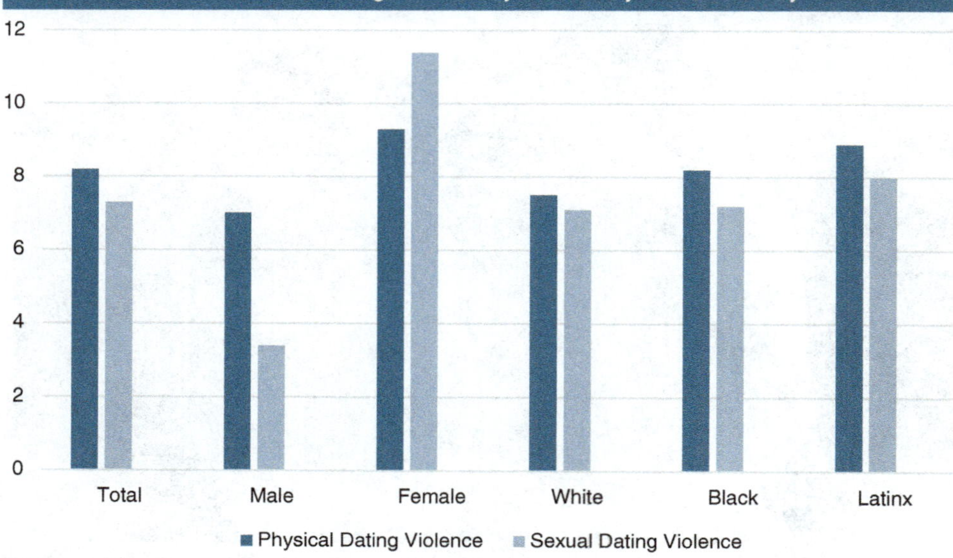

Source: CDC (2020a).

FIGURE 7.7 ■ Teen Birth Rate Across Race and Ethnicity, 2008–2018

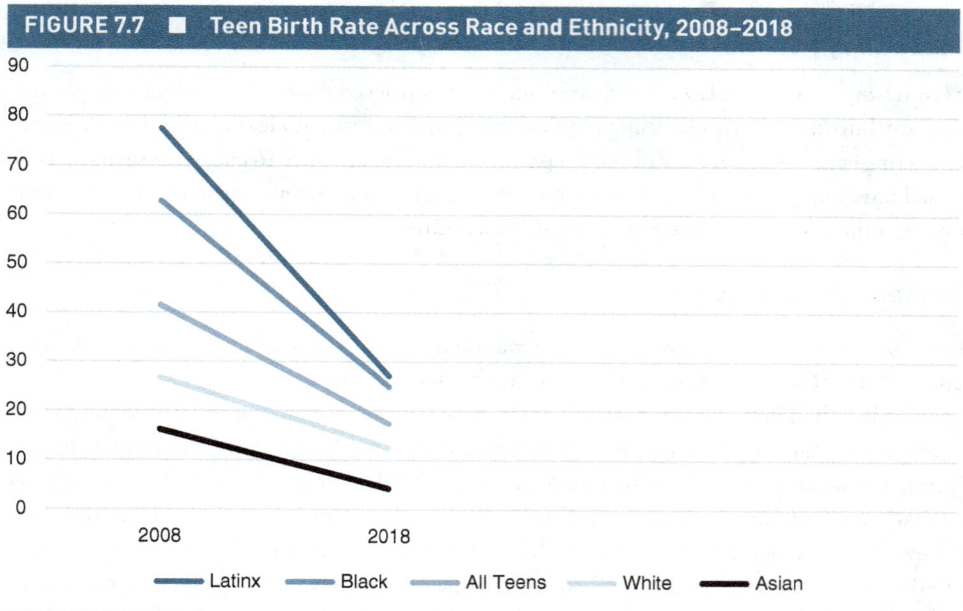

Source: Pew Research Center (2019a).

Note: Births per 1,000 females ages 15–19Note:. Births per 1,000 females ages 15–19.

and dropping out of high school, child abuse and neglect, and other risky behaviors, such as alcohol substance use/abuse (Clark et al., 2018). Without question, teen mothers face a range of developmental risks.

Impacts of Teen Pregnancy on the Mom

Teen parents and their babies start out with many disadvantages. When the head of the family is an adolescent girl, both the teen parent and her child are at increased risk for medical, psychological, developmental, financial, and socioemotional problems.

Medical/psychological: The medical risks for adolescent mothers and their babies are significant, especially for younger adolescent mothers (10- to 14-year-olds). For example, infant mortality rates are much higher for teen mothers (CDC, 2020a, 2021c), and their risk of dying during labor and birth is two to four times higher for women at age 17 than it is for women who have children in their 20s (Alan Guttmacher Institute, 2004). While access to medical and psychological sexual and reproductive health services has increased in recent years, there are still gaps in these services, especially services for sexual and gender minority youth that are inclusive of intersectionality and other diverse experiences (Alan Guttmacher Institute, 2019).

Developmental: Research consistently shows that adolescent mothers struggle when trying to form and maintain stable interpersonal relationships and family life (Larson, 2004; Lehrman, 2001; Quinlivan et al., 2004). Many of these teen parents continue their dependency on family members rather than shift to more independence and autonomy (Hanson, 1992). Daughters of teen mothers are at an elevated risk of becoming teen mothers themselves (Hendrick & Maslowsky, 2019).

Financial: Only about one-half of teen mothers earn a high school diploma by age 22, and because of this, they are much more likely to live in poverty and rely on governmental public assistance (NCSL, 2018). According to the National Conference of State Legislatures, each teen birth, on average, costs approximately $16,000. The decline seen in teen births annually saves $4.4 billion in public spending (NCSL, 2018). Teen parents have high levels of unemployment and lower incomes when they do work (Assini-Meytin & Green, 2015; Harding et al., 2017).

Socioemotional: One-half of teen moms experience depressive symptoms (i.e. feeling lonely, loss of appetite, inability to sleep, thoughts of harming self and/or baby) after giving birth—about 25 percent more than in adult mothers (Hodgkinson et al., 2014). Unfortunately, leaving school due to pregnancy and birth reduces the teen's access to necessary educational and support resources (Martin et al., 2013). Because peers do not share similar experiences, it is difficult for teen mothers to receive social and emotional support from their friends (Reid & Meadows-Oliver, 2007). Teen childbearing is also associated with increased risk of substance abuse (Hodgkinson et al., 2014).

An abundance of research offers encouraging results: When effective social and efficient, practical supports are paired, the majority of adolescents mothers have positive outcomes (Hodgkinson et al., 2014).

Services for Expectant and Parenting Adolescents

A team of researchers conducted a comprehensive literature review in an effort to determine types and effectiveness of pregnant/parenting teen support programs (Harding et al., 2020). This work discovered that there is no one-size-fits-all program, but the most effective programs promote teen parents' self-sufficiency (i.e., contraceptive use, delay in subsequent childbearing, and education). The data from this work are robust, and there is great diversity in the types of programs and settings in which the educational information is provided (for a full review, see Harding et al., 2020). However, there is a profound theme among programs that improved teen parents' self-sufficiency: Frequent adult interactions with the expectant or parenting teen. Successful educational programs include

- individual case workers (social workers, teachers, nurses, youth workers);
- home visitations;
- one-on-one interactions;
- small groups;
- longevity (12 months or longer in duration);
- at least weekly meetings.

One particularly effective program, the Teen-Tot Model, provides comprehensive care for both teen moms and their children. This program uses a three-prong approach to advance childrearing parents' overall health and development: (1) medical case management of mother and child; (2) one-on-one visits with a social worker and other parenting professionals (including home visitations); and (3) mental health services integrated into the medical visits (Hodgkinson et al., 2014). Not surprisingly, research to date has found this to be a highly effective model, as it addresses the holistic growth and development of the adolescent.

Today's teens have a lot of other challenges they face on a daily basis, from drug and alcohol use, bullying, and mental health concerns, including depression, anxiety, and suicidality.

CONTEMPORARY ADOLESCENT DIFFICULTIES

Being a teenager is not easy. Figure 7.8 provides an at-a-glance snapshot of adolescent pressures in their daily lives. In the sections that follow, we explore some of the experiences. While the adolescent developmental period is a time of opportunities, it is also a time of great risk.

FIGURE 7.8 ■ Adolescent Experiences, 2019

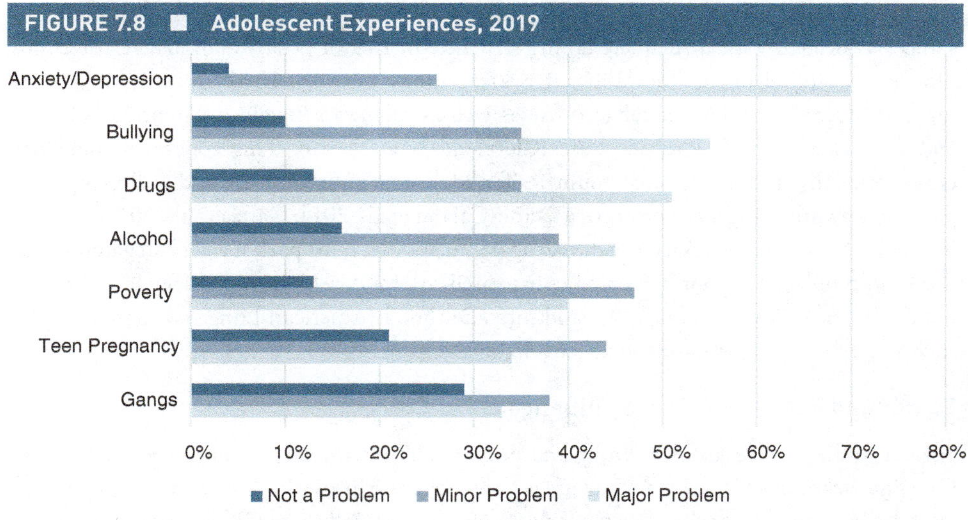

Source: Pew Research Center (2019b).

Adolescent Substance Use and Abuse

Adolescents use tobacco, electronic vaping, alcohol, marijuana, stimulants, and illicit drugs at alarming rates (National Center for Drug Abuse Statistics (NCDAS, 2022). In fact, children are not only introduced to a variety of drugs in middle school but also the availability of drugs has become widespread—one in eight teens abused an illicit substance in 2021, and alcohol is the most commonly abused substance among adolescents (NCDAS, 2022). In the United States:

- Between 2016 and 2020, drug use among eighth graders increased 61 percent.
- One-half of teens have misused a drug at least once.
- By their senior year in high school, 62 percent of adolescents have abused alcohol.
- By the 12th grade, nearly 47 percent of teens have tried illicit drugs.
- In deaths among those aged 15 to 25, 11 percent are due to drug overdose (NCDAS, 2022).

One-fourth of eighth graders have abused alcohol, and 13 million 12- to 20-year-olds report drinking in the last month (NCDAS, 2022). Illegal drug use among early-, mid-, and late adolescence includes marijuana, cocaine, hallucinogens, Molly (Ecstasy), inhalants, methamphetamine, heroin, and fentanyl. Since 1999, opioid overdose deaths have increased 500 percent among 15- to 24-year-olds (NCDAS, 2022). There is no question that drug and alcohol use represent a clear and present danger to today's youth.

The use of substances represents one strategy teenagers use to cope with adverse circumstances associated with inadequate family structure or lack of positive familial relationships. One study, for example, found positive associations between harsh/inconsistent parenting and increased adolescent tobacco use as well as nurturant/involved parenting behaviors and decreased adolescent tobacco use (Cleveland et al., 2010). This appears to hold true cross-nationally in other selected countries for adolescent substance use and well-being, with parental warmth being a key protective factor (Calafat et al., 2014; Garcia et al., 2019). Though tobacco use may not necessarily lead to drug use, it appears to be part of a general gateway syndrome of problem behaviors that predict increased risk for developmental difficulties throughout adolescence (Melby et al., 1993) and into adulthood (American Lung Association, 2022), such as delinquency and dating violence (Collibee et al., 2019).

Family and Peers: Predictive Influencers

Several studies have examined family and peer variables that relate to substance use by teens. One significant risk factor for alcohol use is if someone else in an adolescent's family or peer network has a drinking or other substance use problem, especially a parent (Freisthler & Kepple, 2019), older sibling (Samek et al., 2018), or a peer or best friend. In one study, Black adolescents were more influenced by their siblings with regard to substance use, while white youth were more influence by their peers (Rowan, 2016).

Equally important to the modeling function of parent and sibling behavior is parental/family support. In her decade review of sexual- and gender-minority families, Reczek (2020) found that higher levels of parental involvement, closeness, and support among same-sex attracted youth and were associated with lower levels of teen depression, substance use, and the propensity to run away from home. Transgender youth also benefit from family support with greater positive mental health outcomes and lower rates of substance use when levels of family support and acceptance are high (Ryan et al., 2010). When LGBTQ+ youth feel highly rejected by their parents and family members compared to being accepted by them or only slightly rejected, they are three times more likely to use illicit drugs.

Several studies have examined the effects of family structure on adolescent substance use. One study found that after controlling for race/ethnicity, family structure did not predict regular drinking or deviance (Barnes & Farrell, 1992). On the other hand, another body of research found significantly higher levels of use of cigarettes, alcohol, and marijuana for children in nonintact families (VanderValk et al., 2005). Similarly, a longitudinal study found that adolescents who experienced parents' divorce during adolescence had greater involvement with drugs than children who had experienced parental divorce before adolescence and those who lived in intact families. When mothers remarried, female adolescents increased their drug involvement and male adolescents decreased their use (Needle et al., 1990).

Furthermore, adolescents in father-custody families experienced significantly heightened risk of drug use (Hoffman & Johnson, 1998). Daughters in father-only single families are also much more likely to use drugs (Hemovich & Crano, 2009). These data seem to suggest the relationship between teen substance use and family structure is a complex one—depending on the sex of the child, the sex of the custodial parent, when family disruption occurs, the single or coupled situation of the parent, and whether the custodial parent remarries.

These findings are supported by a global study across 37 countries which showed that multiple micro- and macrofactors help to explain the association between family structure and substance use. Specifically, the researchers found that marijuana use was associated with whether youth lived with both biological parents, while the amount of time spent with peers was most predictive of frequency of alcohol use (Forman-Hoffman et al., 2017). Indeed, as important as family variables are, multiple studies corroborate this international finding: The strongest predictor of drug use for adolescents is the extent to which their friends consume drugs—friends make drugs available to one another, and they model drug and peer group norms which sometimes favor drug use (Walters, 2021). The level of drug use in friendship formation (*selection*) and attributing one's own behavior to the behavior of friends (*projection*) are also important factors that demonstrate the link between peers and substance use.

In summary, research confirms that adolescents who use drugs tend to have close friends who also use drugs (McDonough et al., 2016). Peer orientation, then, is a significant predictor of both drinking and drug behavior, and it also interacts with multiple aspects of parenting.

Parents' Influences on Peer Selection

Researchers have also discovered that parenting practices influence adolescents' orientation toward peers, and that experiences in both the parent and the peer domains influence the likelihood that teens will engage in substance use (Bogenschneider et al., 1998). For example, when parents report higher levels of responsiveness, adolescents report lower orientation to peers, which in turn results in lower rates of substance use. Furthermore, when mothers are less disapproving of adolescent alcohol use in certain circumstances (e.g., as long as drinking and driving do not occur), maternal responsiveness is associated with less substance use. However, when parents disapprove of adolescent alcohol use in every circumstance, maternal responsiveness can be associated with increased substance use (Mahoney & Boyatzis, 2019).

Other research explains that drug-using adolescents are more likely to interact frequently with their friends and be distant from their parents than nonusers are. Some research also indicates that there are *sensitive periods* when changes in peer or parenting relationships can make an adolescent more vulnerable or resilient to drug use (Prins et al., 2020). There is no question that there is a mutual, contingent, and interactive parent–peer linkage for adolescent substance use.

It appears, then, that adolescent personality attributes, parental attitudes and behaviors, and peer orientation all have an impact on drug use. Broadly based programs that combine systemic information with a focus on resisting peer influences and decreasing psychological distress are needed. The success of these programs is due primarily to enhancing an adolescent's ability to resist passive social pressure (e.g., social modeling and overestimation of peer use) rather than to teaching refusal skills to combat active social pressure (i.e., explicit drug offers from friends).

As many as one-third of America's adolescents suffer from some type of mental health disorders. While there are a number of interacting factors that contribute to teen mental health difficulties, many factors can be prevented, such as childhood environments and peer victimization.

Source: iStock.com/VladimirVladimirov.

Anxiety and Depression

In the United States, depression and anxiety disorders are the most common mental health disorders affecting youth and teens (Kalin, 2021). **Depression**, or major depressive disorder, is a serious mood disorder, with symptoms of persistent sadness, hopelessness, helplessness, and loss of interest in activities and peers; some also experience physical symptoms, such as chronic pain or digestive issues (APA, 2013). **Anxiety**, or generalized anxiety disorder, causes excessive worry and apprehension, restlessness, fatigue, irritability, difficulty concentrating, and sleep disturbance; it is most often diagnosed in childhood (APA, 2013). As many as one-third of today's adolescents are diagnosed with generalized anxiety disorder (Healthy Children, 2021), and major depressive disorder affects at least 13 percent of the teen population (SAMHSA, 2017). After they experience puberty, girls are nearly twice as likely as boys to experience anxiety and depression (United Health Foundation, 2021), but it is common for anxiety to begin in childhood, preceding the development of depression, which often develops in adolescence and early adulthood (Kalin, 2021). Two sometimes co-occurring difficulties that overlap teen female depression are *eating disorders* and *self-injury* (cutting) (Steingard, 2021).

Both anxiety and depression are the interacting result of the child/teen's environment and genetics. Kalin's (2021) work points to Levey and colleagues' research that studied 200,000 participants, and found that between 30 and 40 percent of these mental health disorders are due to hereditary factors (Levey et al., 2020). Adverse childhood experiences (ACEs, see Chapter 6) are likely contributors to anxiety and depression (Kalin, 2021), but unfortunately, the utilization of mental healthcare for children is low (Ghandour et al., 2019).

There are a number of sociological factors that are associated with the development of anxiety and/or depression in children and teenagers.

- Poverty (Hodgkinson et al., 2017).
- Alcohol and substance use/abuse in the home by parents or family members (Hellman, 2018).
- An unpredictable childhood environment (Bruhl et al., 2019).
- Child maltreatment (Bruhl et al., 2019).
- Peer victimization (Spiekerman et al., 2021).
- Childhood trauma and ACEs (Yu et al., 2019).
- Prolonged childhood grief (Boelen & Lenferink, 2021).

In children and teens, anxiety and depression may present as social and behavioral problems, both externalizing and internalizing, and when these converge, an infinite feedback loop results: Anxiety/depression → social and behavioral problems → increased anxiety and depression → increased social and behavioral problems, and so on (Pedersen et al., 2019; Piqueras et al., 2019). Ultimately, school functioning is affected, making the feedback loop more problematic: Anxiety/depression → social and behavioral problems → increased anxiety and depression → increased social and behavioral problems → decreased school functioning and academic achievement → increased anxiety/depression, and so on (Pedersen et al., 2019). Sadly, most children and adolescents do not receive the mental and behavioral healthcare they need. In an analysis that included 46.6 million American children and teens, it was learned that one in seven students have at least one treatable mental health disorder, and yet only about one-half of the 7.7 million affected children receive treatment (Whitney & Peterson, 2019).

There is no question that childhood experiences are contributors to later-in-life psychological and mood disorders (Jamnik & DiLalla, 2019)—and there should be no question that early and better access to mental health services are of the utmost importance for the healthy development of children and adolescents.

Adolescent Suicide

Even before the 2020–2021 COVID-19 pandemic caused isolation for most of the world's population, suicide rates among adolescents were already climbing: Between 2007 and 2018, the adolescent suicide rate increased nearly 60 percent (Curtin, 2020). Today, among people aged 10 to 24, suicide is the third leading cause of death (Curtin, 2020). Each day in the United States, there are an average of over 3,700 suicide attempts by youth in grades 9 through 12 (CDC, 2020a). Non-Hispanic white students have higher suicidal ideation rates

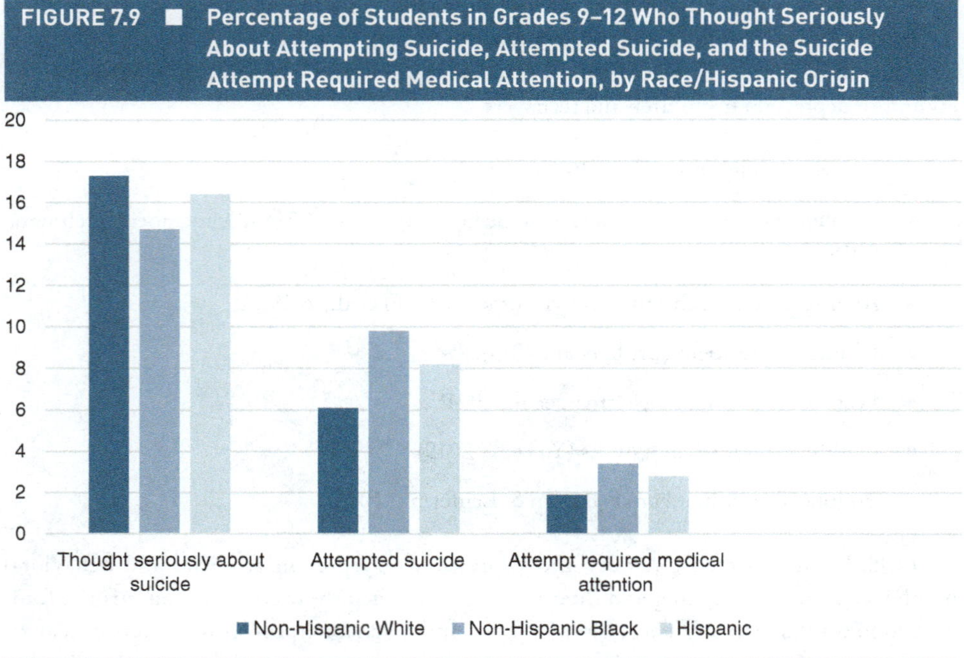

FIGURE 7.9 ■ Percentage of Students in Grades 9–12 Who Thought Seriously About Attempting Suicide, Attempted Suicide, and the Suicide Attempt Required Medical Attention, by Race/Hispanic Origin

Source: Child Trends (2019).

than Black or Latinx students (see Figure 7.9). Females are nearly twice as likely as males to experience suicidal thoughts, attempting suicide, and requiring medical attention; however, males are far more likely to complete suicide (Child Trends Databank, 2019). Emergency department visits for suicide attempts among girls, aged 12 to 17, soared 51 percent in 2021 compared to the same period in 2019; among boys, the suicide attempt rate rose about 4 percent (CDC, 2021e).

Suicidality Risk

Suicidality refers to the risk of suicide and includes suicidal ideation (thoughts) and/or intent. However, today researchers understand that studies regarding child and adolescent suicide are often hindered by this broad definition (Carballo et al., 2020). One body of work suggests that other behaviors should be included in the conceptualization of suicidality, such as suicide attempts, interrupted attempts, aborted attempts, and suicidal acts of preparation (Carballo et al., 2020).

Suicidality also presents differently for youth than it does for adults, particularly in regards to the factor of depression—it is present in some, but not all, suicidal teens, and not all teens with depression experience suicidality (for a thorough review, see Carballo et al., 2020). And, as our study has shown us, human growth and development are very much the result of three interacting forces, biological or physical (including heredity, brain growth and changes, race/

"Go kill yourself" is a popular teen expression. Is cyberbullying avoidable? Should it be punishable by law?

Source: iStock.com/TeroVesalainen.

ethnicity, sex, inborn personality traits); cognitive and psychological (such as hot vs. cold cognition in adolescence, depression, drug/alcohol use and abuse, anxiety, externalizing/internalizing disorders, struggles with sexual orientation and gender identity); and social factors (the home, school, neighborhood, and socioeconomic status). It is important to add, however, that teenagers who have depression are at a fivefold increase for the risk of suicidal thoughts and behaviors (Goldston et al., 2009). Empirical studies have discovered a number of social and emotional risk factors.

Adverse life events: These events, such as family conflict, relationship breakup, bullying, academic stress and pressure, rarely *cause* suicidality, but these are important factors for parents, peers, teachers, and parenting professionals to know because these events interact with other **vulnerability factors** (physical and cognitive/psychological) and increase the risk of suicide (see Carballo et al., 2020, for an analysis of 11 studies that speak to various vulnerability factors).

Family difficulties, conflict, and maltreatment: Difficult and problematic family environments place children and adolescents at greater risk for suicidality. This includes lack of adult supervision and support, such as occurs with *uninvolved parenting* (see Chapter 5); physical, emotional, and sexual harm by a parent; neglect; divorce of parents; socioeconomic status and/or parental job loss; suicidal behavior in either parent or sibling; and family and/or intimate partner violence (see Carballo et al., 2020).

Internal risk factors: An analysis of 66 studies revealed new risk factors for suicidality (for a robust review, see Ati et al., 2020). These now-studied risk factors include: nutritional imbalance (including increased intake of energy drinks), menarche and menstrual problems, poor lifestyle choices, ineffective sleep and rest patterns, maladaptive perfectionism, avoidance coping, emotional focused coping, and external shame.

Smartphone addiction/abuse: Smartphone addiction/abuse is a disorder that involves compulsive overuse of technology and social media, including gaming, and it has recently been linked to suicidality (Ati et al., 2020). Some researchers, however, are hesitant to refer to increased usage of cell phones and other devices as *addiction* and instead prefer to use the term *problematic* (Panova & Carbonell, 2018). Even so, there is no question that its prolonged use for whatever reason (communication, information retrieval, games, etc.) is related to an increase in suicidal behaviors (Ati et al., 2020). Particularly associated with elevated suicide risk is the disruptions in sleep that extended time on cellphones, iPads, and other electronic devises cause.

Trauma experiences: As you learned in Chapter 6, ACEs exert great influence on lifespan growth and development, and they have a tremendous impact on suicidality:

- **Child sexual abuse:** Increases risk of suicidal behaviors by an 11-fold increase in children aged 12 years, and a 6-fold increase between the ages of 13 and 19 years (Bruffaerts et al., 2010; as noted in Carballo et al., 2020).
- **Peer victimization, bullying/cyberbullying:** There are three groups associated with bullying and cyberbullying: victims, perpetrators, and perpetrator/victims (Suicide Prevention Resource Center, 2011). Both victims and perpetrators of bullying are at greater risk for suicidality because both groups are more likely to have depression; those who are cyberbullied have higher risks of depression than victims of face-to-face peer victimization (Wang et al., 2011).
- **Sexual orientation and/or gender identity:** In 2020, one in three LGBTQ+ youth and teens reported they had been physically threatened or harmed because of their LGBTQ+ identity (The Trevor Project, 2020). Of the 40,000 survey respondents, ages 13 to 24, nearly 70 percent indicated that they experience generalized anxiety disorder, and 55 percent experience depression; 40 percent said they asked for mental healthcare, but they did not receive it. There is a 12 percent increase in suicidality when people do not respect transgender and nonbinary youth's preferred pronouns, or youth are not allowed to wear gender-affirming clothing (from 14 percent to 26 percent). Figure 7.10 presents the mental health experiences of 40,000 LGBTQ+, ages 13 to 24.

To be sure, these data are heartbreaking because with proper information, education, and affordable/accessible mental healthcare, children and teens do not need to suffer. Encouragingly, there are protective factors against suicide risk—things that parents, schools, and caring professionals can do to mitigate the risk of suicidality.

FIGURE 7.10 ■ Percentages of LGBTQ+ Youth Experiences, 2020

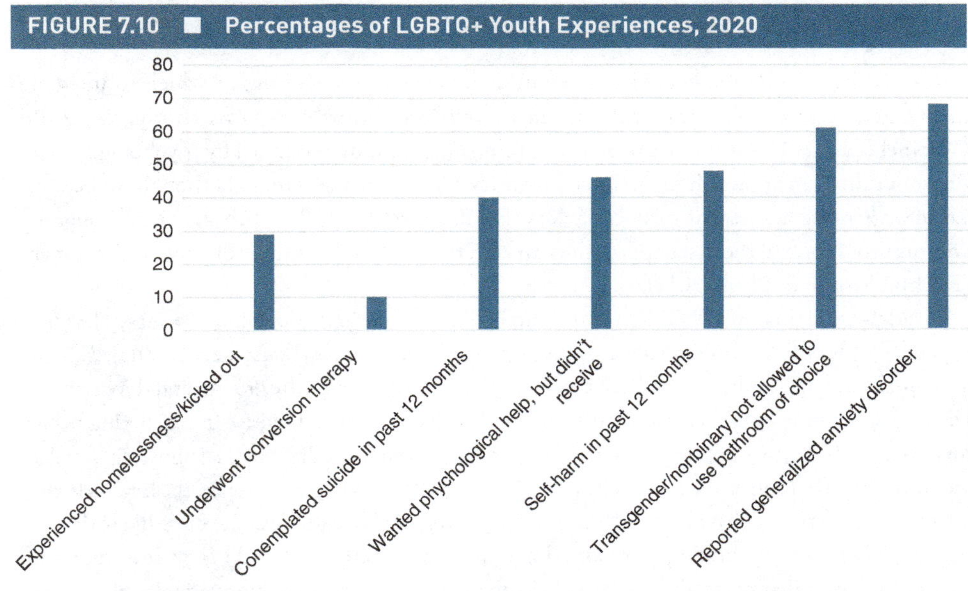

Source: The Trevor Project. (2020). *2020 National Survey on LGBTQ Youth Mental Health.* The Trevor Project.

There Is Hope: Suicidality Protective Factors

Protective factors are influences that can reduce the risk of suicidal behaviors (Nazeer et al., 2020). Parenting matters! Warm, supportive, communicative parenting and caregiving with parental monitoring of youth is the single greatest protective factor against child and adolescent suicidality (Arat & Wong, 2017; Ati et al., 2020; Lensch et al., 2019; Lew et al., 2019). Strong connections to other caring individuals, such as peers, families of peers, teachers, coaches, youth pastors, scout leaders, and mentors significantly reduce youth's intentions to harm themselves or die by suicide (MacKin et al., 2017). Religious practice is also negatively associated with child and adolescent suicide (Cole-Lewis et al., 2016).

Suicide prevention—*and the health, safety, and future of our nation's children, teens, and early adults*—requires a comprehensive, accessible, affordable approach that includes appropriate medical, psychological, and clinical intervention; multifaceted and multiconnected community partnerships; and evidence-based education and programming that addresses each nuance of suicidality. At no other time in our history has such a great task been placed on the shoulders of parents, parenting professionals, and human service providers. As adults, we owe our youth the compassion of all-encompassing, nonjudgmental, unbiased, equitable, socially just care.

POSITIVE ADOLESCENT DEVELOPMENT

Researchers and practitioners alike are continually exploring new ways in which to integrate theory and research into practical preventive and interventive programs (Bornstein, 2019; Ciocanel et al., 2017; Gullotta, 2015). One promising program developed by psychologist Peter Benson utilizes an approach to target and identify adolescent assets that are thought to be critical in preventing adolescent risky behaviors (Fredkova et al., 2019). With strong and ongoing community support, the asset approach is an effective tool for healthy adolescent development (Roehlkepartain & Blyth, 2019).

Initially studying over 250,000 youth from 600 communities nationwide, the survey has now expanded to over three million youth and teens in the United States (Benson et al., 2011). *External* and *internal* assets have been identified as behaviors that promote healthy growth and development, whereas **developmental deficits** are those experiences that lead to an increase in risk-taking behaviors (e.g., alcohol consumption, home isolation, overexposure to media, physical abuse, and violent victimization) (Benson et al., 2011). The more positive assets a teenager possesses, the less likely they are to engage in risky behaviors. Similarly, the more assets adolescents have, the more likely they are to engage in prosocial, thriving behaviors. These assets are briefly described below. It is important to note that regardless of racial and ethnic differences, and other demographic variables, the average American teen only possesses about half of the assets described (Benson et al., 2011).

External Assets

There are four overall categories and associated subcategories of **external assets** (Benson et al., 2011).

1. **Support:** This includes family support; positive family communication; other healthy adult relationships; caring, attentive neighborhoods; caring and safe school climate; and parental involvement in schooling.
2. **Empowerment:** For healthy adolescent development, communities must be safe and value its youth; it must view youth as vital and necessary community resources; adolescents should provide service to others.
3. **Boundaries and expectations:** This asset prioritizes the boundaries of family, school, and neighborhood; the influence of adult role models; positive peer influences; and high behavioral and value expectations in teenagers.
4. **Constructive use of time:** This includes availability and accessibility of creative activities; youth programs; religiosity; and the ability to spend time at home with family.

There are racial and ethnic differences in external assets, and these are illustrated in Figure 7.11; authoritative and authoritarian parenting styles are evident in certain attributes of teens (Benson et al., 2011; Benson & Scales, 2011).

FIGURE 7.11 ■ Percentages of Adolescents' External Assets, by Race/Ethnicity

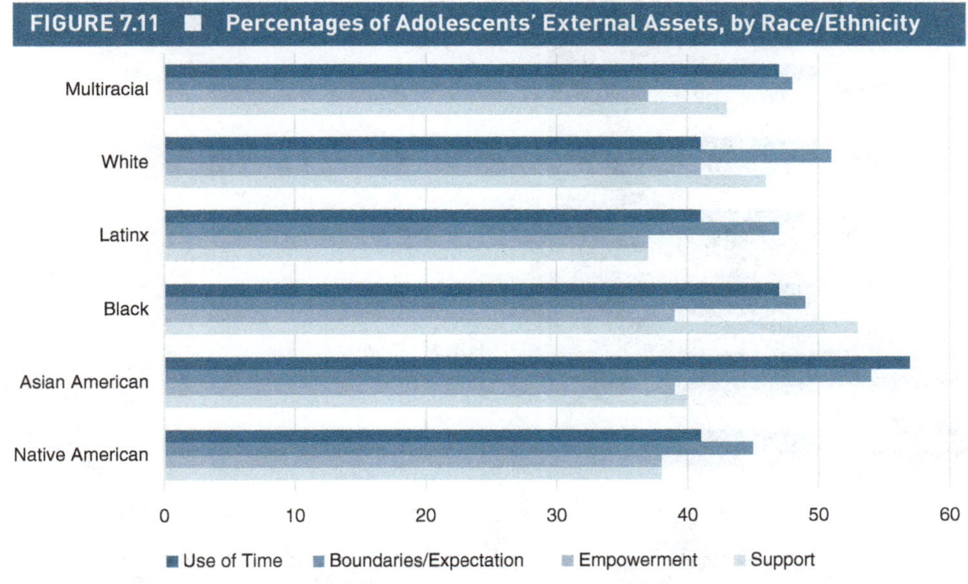

Source: Benson and Scales (2011).

Internal Assets

Just as with external assets, there are four general categories of adolescent internal assets, with corresponding subcategories (Benson et al., 2011).

1. **Commitment to learning:** This includes motivation to achieve; school engagement; attention to homework; bonding to people and the culture of the school; and reading for pleasure.
2. **Positive value system:** This asset prioritizes caring, integrity, honesty, responsibility, and restraint; equality and social justice are valued.
3. **Social competencies:** This encourages planning and decision-making; interpersonal and cultural competence; refusal skills; and the ability to resolve conflicts peacefully.
4. **Positive identity:** This values personal power; self-esteem; a sense of purpose; and a positive view of the future.

Racial and ethnic differences are presented in Figure 7.12.

In short, youth and teens who reported problematic alcohol use, illicit drug use, violent behaviors, academic problems, and suicidality have fewer external and internal assets than those who do not engage in these risky behaviors. Because identity development versus identity (role) confusion is the central developmental task of adolescence (Erikson, 1963, 1968), the asset approach may be key to better understanding adolescent identity formation and development.

FIGURE 7.12 ■ Percentages of Adolescents' Internal Assets, by Race/Ethnicity

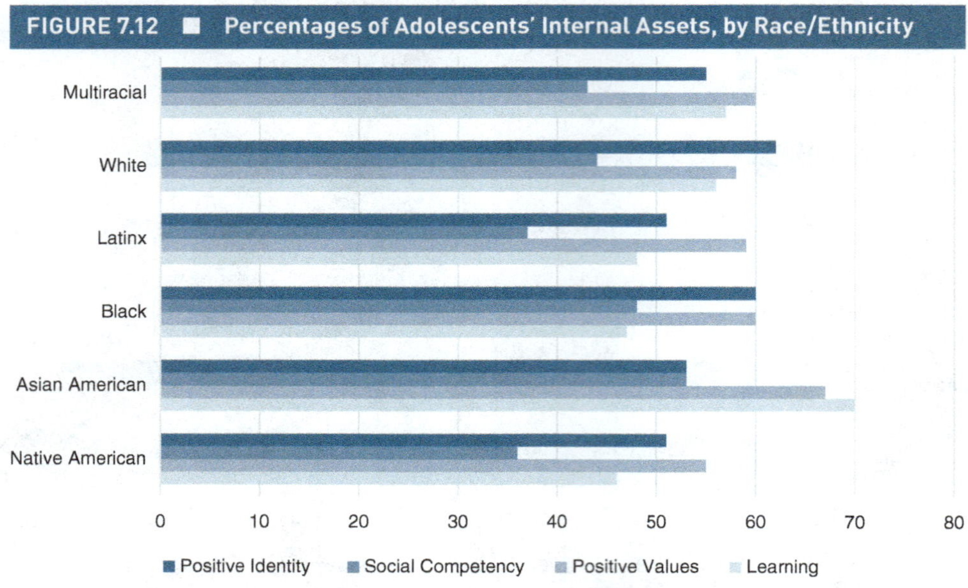

Source: Benson and Scales (2011).

PARENTING LIFE EDUCATION: PROMOTING IDENTITY AND SELF-GOVERNING WHILE PROVIDING A SAFE PLACE TO FALL

One of the underlying tenets of Family Life Education is that the principles of empowering and equipping people through education to "parent" to the best of their capabilities is always relevant—regardless of the family's structure, its demographic makeup, growth and development stage, or life's circumstances (Arcus et al., 1993). As you learned in this chapter, adolescents have fundamental developmental needs that require responsive parenting and caregiving.

First, they have the need for warm, encouraging, supportive, and connecting parents/caregiver relationships that promote the adolescent's physical, sexual, social, and emotional development, and that encourage the teen's need for autonomy and self-governing in their quest for identity. Second, teenagers have the need for family and social relationships that support the healthy development of the adolescent's sense of self (self-worth; self-love; self-esteem) and identity, personality attributes that are vitally important for the successful transition to adulthood, and for future adult relationships. Adolescents also have the need for stable, predictable environments that promote the healthy maturation of their brains.

But our study about parenting teens also showed us that parenting is a complicated, evolving, reciprocal process, and not all adolescents make the transition to adulthood smoothly or without difficulties. To be sure, there are several contemporary societal influences that negatively impact teens' holistic development, including substance use and abuse, peer victimization, social media, and adverse life experiences. To further complicate the developmental process, significant numbers of teenagers today wrestle with their sexual orientations and gender identities, anxiety, and depression, putting them at greater risk for suicidality.

And herein lies the irony: Adolescents strive for independence and autonomy in their search for an identity that is unique and separate from that of their families of origin, yet simultaneously need parents or caregivers (sometimes the very people they're pushing against in an effort to individuate) that create a stable and loving home environment where there exists mutual respect and trust—the safe place for teens that permits age-appropriate independence, teaches them how to assert themselves, and guides them in ways to effectively express their needs and emotions.

The reality is, though, that parents and caregivers cannot do this on their own. To combat against environmental influences and stressors that can hinder—or altogether interrupt—healthy, adaptive adolescent development, communities must work together to create and disseminate educational programming that supports this critical lifestage. As Benson and colleagues keenly conclude, "…[adolescents] need society to pay more attention to their care and nurture" (Benson et al., 2011, p. vii).

8 THE CHANGING NATURE OF PARENTING: FAMILY LIFE AND AGING

LEARNING OBJECTIVES

8.1	Summarize the landscape and trends of aging in contemporary America.
8.2	Explain how experiences of the Family Life Cycle and parenting change throughout aging.
8.3	Discuss the distinguishing characteristics of intergenerational ties in later life.
8.4	Describe the challenges faced by caregivers.
8.5	Relate caregiving experiences to changes in the Family Life Cycle.

The arc of life.

Source: iStock.com/VioletaStoimenova.

It was years ago, very early on a bitterly cold winter morning. My mother had been ill for some time and we were on our way to a cancer specialist, several hours' drive away. I helped her into the car, and after she was situated, I fastened her seatbelt. And then it happened.

Suddenly, for the first time, I noticed that she appeared so weak, and at that moment I knew: *She* needed me. This woman, the very pillar of strength who fought (and beat) cancer twice before, who single-handedly had raised her four children while her husband fought in the Vietnam War, this woman who had supported, encouraged, guided, and taught us, appeared so small and fragile and helpless beneath the blankets. Fighting back tears, I tucked the blanket around her legs, thinking, *"When did this happen? When did I become the parent and she the child?"*

Over the next few weeks, she died by inches. I cared for her every day … bathing her, feeding her, loving her. The stress was indescribable—I left my home every morning at 7:30, as soon as I got my children off to school, cared for her all day, got home in time to get the kids from school, work on homework with them, feed them, bathe them, tuck them into bed.… This was our routine for about six weeks, until she died. Although it was the most difficult thing I had ever done in my life, my relationship with my parents deepened to a level we had never experienced before.… In that situation, you're forced to talk about things you would otherwise never talk about.

My mother held me when I was first born, weak and unable, and I held her at the end, weak and unable. Together, we had traveled the arc of life.

Our nation is moving into an unprecedented time in its history: By the year 2030, one in every five people (roughly 20 percent of the population) will be over the age of 65 living in the United States—more than ever before (Arias et al., 2021). What accounts for this surge in the aging population? Baby Boomers are getting older. *Baby Boomers* are those people who were born between 1946 and 1964. During this time in American history, the birth rates rose sharply because of the economic prosperity following World War II. The first Baby Boomers turned 65 years old in 2011. Is this country prepared for its aging population? And how will this increase in the elderly population affect families and their relationships? How will it affect "parenting"?

This entire generation, accustomed to living in a "youthful culture," is growing old. But do they know how? After the age of 40 or so, is it really downhill until we die? One hundred years ago, few people made it past the age of 70—the average **life expectancy** was 47. Today, the average life expectancy is about 78, depending on a person's race and gender (Arias et al., 2021). White females are expected to live to the age of 80, and Black women have a life expectancy of 75 (Arias et al., 2021). In the United States, between the short span of less than a year, life expectancies among the six Latinx origins decreased, reaching their lowest levels since 2006. Figure 8.1 illustrates life expectancy by race and ethnicity; as you can see, there is a racial gap in life expectancy. How will the aging live out the years that have been added to their lifespan?

FIGURE 8.1 ■ The Racial Gap in Life Expectancy, 2019 and 2020

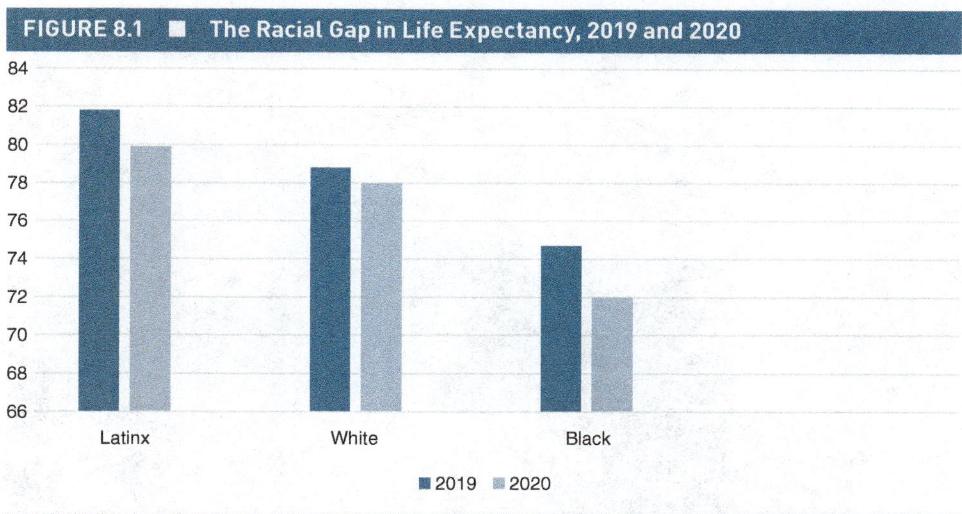

Source: Arias et al. (2021).

In this chapter, we'll examine America's aging population, and the developmental forces involved in aging, such as the biological changes that take place. We will then explore the nature of parent and adult–child relationships as parents age, and look at family relationships and development through aging. We give attention to how intergenerational ties change during the later stages of the lifespan, the experiences of grandparenting, and how these relationships are changing American family experiences. And finally, we'll look at the changes associated with aging lifestyles, such as retirement and caregiving. An understanding of the processes associated with aging are vitally important to understanding parenting because just as the opening vignette illustrates, for most Americans, a decisive shift occurs between parents and their adult children as they age.

AGING AND THE AGED

Understanding the aging is important in our study of parenting because the increasing numbers of this population are challenging American policy makers, healthcare providers, and families (He et al., 2005). How will the nation meet the needs of the increasing numbers of the aging and the aged? How will families care for their aging loved ones?

America is turning gray. One hundred years ago, there were significantly more young people than older Americans. Looking further into the future, from the years 2018 to 2060, the senior population is expected to more than double, from 46 million to nearly 98 million; by 2060, it is expected that one-fourth of the entire United States population will be 65 and older (Mather et al., 2019a).

Today, there are over 50 million older adults (65 and older) living in the United States. Does this photo of "the elderly" align with your image of aging people? Why or why not?

Source: iStock.com/kipgodi.

The Portrait of Age in the United States

In the nearly two decades that spanned 1990–2019, Baby Boomers represented the most expansive generation of any before it.

- **Older population:** In 2021, there were slightly more than 54 million older adults (those aged 65 and older) in the United States, representing 16 percent of its population; in 2000, there were 35 million older adults in America. The median age of the elderly today is 75 years of age (U.S. Department of Health and Human Services, 2021).
- **Diversity:** Within the United States population, there is great diversity among older adults; today, 24 percent of the aging population are members of racial and ethnic minority populations (U.S. Department of Health and Human Services, 2021). Compared with African American/Black Caribbean and white older adults, Latinx are experiencing significantly larger increases. For example, by the year 2050, according to the U.S. Census Bureau (Arias et al., 2021), the percentage of older Latinx will nearly double.
- **Education:** In 2009, about 20 percent of those aged 65 and over had a college degree. Today, 89 percent have graduated from high school, and one-third of the aging population have at least a Bachelor's degree (U.S. Department of Health and Human

Services, 2021). The U.S. Census Bureau (Arias et al., 2021) projects that by the year 2030, as Baby Boomers age, 75 percent will have a college degree.

- **Centenarians:** There were 92,000 centenarians (those aged 100 or more) in 2021 (Statista, 2021). By 2050, it is projected that there will be close to 1 million people in the United States over the age of 100. More than 80 percent of centenarians today are women, and the majority live in metropolitan areas.

To be sure, the face of America is changing! What are the forces that influence their aging? Why do some people age well, and others do not?

Developmental Forces in Aging

Multiple forces influence and affect how people age. **Gerontologists** (scientists who study aging), along with family sociologists, developmentalists, and Family Life Educators, have developed perspectives that help them analyze these influences. The **lifespan perspective** of development emphasizes that from the cradle to the grave, human beings are in a constant, continuous state of growth-motion. This perspective posits that simply because we age does not mean that we completed our intrapersonal and interpersonal developmental tasks and growth. In applying the lifespan perspective, those who study aging are interested in answering the larger question: Why and how do we age the way we do?

One ongoing controversy is the **nature vs. nurture debate**: Are the influences of aging determined by nature (your inborn, hereditary characteristics such as genetic influences) or by nurture (your environmental, experiential, societal, and cultural experiences across your lifespan)? For many years, most social scientists who studied aging focused on the nature side of the argument—that is, they believed that the influences of aging are biologically driven and as such, not much could be done to prevent certain, inevitable outcomes. Today, however, those who study human development and the aging process argue that aging is a process of *both* nature *and* nurture and that the two forces interact to create a unique individual. In particular, there are four interactive forces of development:

1. **Biological forces:** These refer to all genetic and health-related factors. For example, is a person genetically predisposed to getting cancer? Also included in this area of development are lifestyle choices such as diet, exercise, smoking, and alcohol consumption. Race and ethnic differences are also included because some races are more predisposed for certain illnesses such as high blood pressure and diabetes.

2. **Psychological forces:** These refer to all cognitive, emotional, and perceptual factors. Among the aging, things such as cognitive impairment due to certain diseases, and memory loss and retention are considered.

3. **Sociocultural forces:** These include cultural, ethnic, societal, relational, and interpersonal factors. In this area of development, family scientists consider

employment, living arrangements, marital status, parenting and grandparenting, and caregiving.

4. **Lifecycle forces:** All of these forces interact and combine to create a person's unique, individual developmental experiences.

As you have seen, there are certain expected life-course events as well as those that we do not expect or anticipate. Paul Baltes, a psychologist who specializes in aging, and his research associates (Baltes et al., 1998) identify three varying sets of interacting life-course influences: normative age-graded influences, normative history-graded influences, and nonnormative influences.

Normative age-graded influences are developmental changes that are caused by biological, psychological, and sociocultural forces. These age-graded influences are typically highly correlated to a person's chronological age, such as the start of menstruation, puberty growth spurts, menopause, hearing loss, vision loss, or the loss of memory skills. These biological developmental changes are significant because they often signal major transitions in peoples' lives. For example, a teenager who begins menstruating is now capable of bearing children; an individual who begins menopause can no longer bear children. In many cultures, there are rituals or rites of passage that mark progression into different stages of life, and these events correspond to certain ages. Among Israeli women, for instance, menopause is marked with a *croning ceremony.* This rite of passage is celebrated at the age of 50, and during this ceremony, aging women are recognized as the embodiment of wisdom, healing, and teaching. Within this culture, crones are the ones who care for the dying and are the "spiritual midwives," the "knowers of all mysteries" (Alpert, 1991, p. 66).

Every culture establishes norms associated with the timing of the events. This is the culture's *social clock*, and it includes rites of passage, such as graduating from high school or college, getting married, or retiring—all by a socially and culturally accepted age.

Normative history-graded influences are events or conditions that people in a given culture or society experience simultaneously. The history-related events may be *biological* in nature, such as the AIDS epidemic in Africa; *psychological* in nature, such as racism in this country that resulted in the Civil Rights Movement of the 1960s; or *sociocultural*, such as the Great Depression of the 1930s, or the sexual revolution that took place throughout the 1960s and the 1970s. It is these history-graded influences that sometimes give certain generations their nicknames, such as those who grew up during the Great Depression era, the Baby Boomers, or Generation X (those born after 1965). The impact and effect of history-graded influences is great. For example, most people in the United States remember where they were when they learned of the terrorist attacks on September 11, 2001, and many will never forget the experiences of lockdown, masking, and working from home in 2020 and 2021 due to the COVID national health emergency.

Nonnormative influences are things that most people do not experience—these influences are uncommon, rare, or unanticipated events. Some nonnormative influences may be favorable, such as gaining a large, unexpected inheritance from a long-lost uncle, but most often these events are not favorable and cause disruption in individual and family life. Although we expect that we will have to experience the death of our parents, for example, we do not expect that this will occur while we are in college. Similarly, we might expect that we ourselves will experience a serious illness as we enter mid- or later life, but we do not anticipate that we will experience a life-threatening illness in our teens or 20s—or that our children will at any point in their childhood, such as Grit, the newborn cancer warrior introduced to us in Chapter 1.

Our study so far has shown us that *we do not develop in isolation*. Throughout our lifespan, our development is multifaceted, shaped, and reshaped by many interacting influences. Who we are and how we came to be the persons we are is a complex tapestry woven together from biological, psychological, social, and cultural influences. And how we age is no exception.

Many facets of aging are experienced universally and are determined by basic biological processes that are genetically determined. However, there are also environmental and lifestyle influences that significantly impact how we age.

Source: iStock.com/FatCamera.

What Is Aging?

Most of us have heard the cliché, "You're as young as you feel!" But are we? How do we characterize the aging process? Is it a pattern of intricate, genetically timed biological changes? Or is aging a mindset? Aging is not a uniform process for all; certainly, there are universal aging processes, but individual coping and adaptation to lifecourse experiences all affect how we age (Crosnoe & Elder, 2002).

Primary Aging

To better understand the aging process, it is necessary to examine biological, age-related declines. Researchers, gerontologists, and developmentalists alike distinguish between primary aging and secondary aging. **Primary aging** refers to the basic biological processes that are genetically programmed and that take place with the passage of time (Cavanaugh & Blanchard-Fields, 2002). These primary aging processes represent the core aspects of aging (Cavanaugh & Blanchard-Fields, 2002):

- **Biological changes associated with aging:** These changes are genetically programmed and take place over time, and all of the changes are irreversible. Eventually, the biological changes lead to death. Death by primary aging factors is referred to as "death by natural causes."
- **Age-related anatomical and functional changes:** These include changes in the immune system and the ability to fight infection or disease, changes in vision and hearing, changes in the function of joints, and changes in memory retention.
- **Progressive changes:** Starting at about age 30, we begin to lose brain neurons. By the age of 50, our brain size is reduced to 97 percent, and by the age of 70, our brain size is reduced to about 92 percent.
- **Inevitable changes:** This category includes declines in sensory functions. Hearing, vision, taste, and balance become less acute. Reaction times become slower because the speed of nerve impulses slows.
- **Universally experienced changes:** Regardless of society or culture, all primary aging changes are experienced by everyone.

According to biologist Leonard Hayflick (1994), every species in the animal kingdom has a maximum lifespan. For humans, it appears to be about 110 to 120 years. According to Hayflick, each species has a genetically programmed time limit because at a certain point in time, cells lose their ability to replicate. This time limit, known as the **Hayflick limit**, is what accounts for the aging process and life expectancy. Hayflick proposed that there are three cellular factors that cause aging: the diminished capacity to adapt to stressors, a reduction in the speed of performance, and an increased susceptibility to disease (Hayflick, 1994). It appears, then, that there is little a person can do to prevent the inevitability of aging. Are there things we can do, however, to help us slow the aging process?

Secondary Aging

Although the characteristics associated with primary aging cannot be delayed inevitably, to a very large extent we have control over age-related declines that are associated with **secondary aging**—physiological declines that are the result of environmental and behavioral influences that significantly impact how we age. Among other things, secondary aging is influenced by lifestyle choices such as smoking, poor nutrition, lack of exercise, sun exposure, alcohol and/or substance use, and sexual behaviors.

It is often difficult to determine whether the declines associated with aging are due to primary or secondary influences. For example, smoking, which is associated with secondary age-related declines, accelerates the deterioration of the cardiovascular and respiratory systems: Yet it is sometimes difficult to determine whether it is the primary aging influences, such as being more susceptible to disease, or the behavior that causes the greater likelihood that an aged person will develop cancer. The easiest way, then, to determine whether physical deterioration is related to primary or secondary causes is to keep in mind that, as developmental psychologist Barbara Lemme (2011) observed, "primary aging is generally identifiable by its inevitability, universality, and irreversibility, while secondary aging appears only among a part of the population, is related to extrinsic factors such as behavior and socioeconomic status, and may . . . be prevented or perhaps reversed."

Ageism

Ageism refers to the stereotypical attitudes people hold about the aging and the elderly. People who are **ageist** have a fixed and negative mindset about older people, and these ageist beliefs reflect biased understandings about the physical, social, and psychological characteristics of older adults (Weiss & Weiss, 2019; Weiss & Zhang, 2020). As a result of these attitudes, the aging population is often subjected to bias and unfair treatment.

Ageism creates significant consequences for the elderly. For example, studies show that ageism negatively impacts an individual's self-perception and self-worth, as well as their cognitive functions, physical abilities, overall health, and longevity (Barber, 2017; Levy, 2009). Weiss and Zhang (2020) report that while positive perceptions of the aged can somewhat lessen the effects of ageism, the negative attitudes and beliefs are pervasive; one study, in fact, suggests that the negative effects are experienced as nearly three times larger, profoundly impacting the aging experience (Meisner, 2012).

Another problem associated with ageism is that it limits the things people can accomplish, and it denies them the respect and freedom that all people deserve (Lemme, 2011). Ageism may lead to unfair housing, unfair employment, and unfair educational opportunities. For example, a woman with 20 years of administrative office experience may be turned down for a job, or she may be denied a promotion over a younger employee with less experience. Ageism can also interfere with proper medical diagnoses, such as in instances of depression or anxiety in the aging and the elderly; too often these mental diagnoses are misinterpreted or diagnosed as physical conditions and are subsequently either mistreated or left untreated (Lemme, 2011).

There are a number of positive developments, however, among the aging population in the United States (Mather et al., 2019b):

- **Increased education levels:** In 1965, only about 5 percent of people over age 65 had a college degree; in 2018, nearly 30 percent have a bachelor's degree or higher.
- **Narrowing gender gap life expectancy:** In the 1990s, there was a seven-year gap in life expectancies between men and women; in 2017, this gap had narrowed to five years.
- **Lower poverty rates:** Poverty rates vary between men and women, and between age groups. For example, poverty rates for those aged 65 are less than 9 percent, but for women over 80, the poverty rate is about 14 percent (Social Security Administration, 2021).

So what does it mean to age successfully? In a biological sense, it might mean that as a person ages, there is a minimal level of decline in physiological, cognitive, and social and emotional functioning. But for our purposes here, we must consider which life experiences allow some people to age more successfully than others—how do they manage their later years in life? With this in mind, we turn our attention to the effects of aging with regard to family relationships and parenting in middle and old age.

PARENTS AND THEIR ADULT CHILDREN

The traditional concept of the role of parenthood spans the period from the birth or adoption of the first child through the adolescent period of the last child. Parenting, then, has been thought of as a 20- to 30-year commitment. While some parents look forward to launching their children, others do so with much trepidation and doubt, and still others do not successfully manage the shift to an empty nest—the home with no children—well at all. The **empty nest** is a transitional stage in the lives of parenting adults (median age is approximately 50) during which time they guide their adolescents to assume adult roles and responsibilities (Bougea et al., 2019).

While many highlight the earlier years of parenting and the significance of the parent–child relationship during the first two years, preschool years, and school years of a child's life, too often much is left unsaid about the importance of the parent–adult child relationship and its significance to growth and development throughout adulthood.

Renegotiating the Parent–Adult Child Relationship

Prior to and during the empty nest, significant changes take place in parents' roles, as well as in the relationships with the now-grown children. According to Duvall's Family Life Cycle Model, *launching families'* developmental tasks include navigating the evolving adult-to-adult relationships with children, while simultaneously caring for aging family members (Duvall, 1988). As you can see in Table 8.1, the last three stages of the Family Life Cycle encompass the longest timespan.

TABLE 8.1 ■ Family Life Cycle by Length of Time in Each of the Eight Stages

Stage	Length of Time
Married couple without children	2 years
Childbearing families (oldest child is up to 30 months)	2.5 years
Families with preschool children (oldest child is 30 months–6 years)	3.5 years
Families with schoolchildren (oldest child is 6–13 years)	7 years
Families with teenagers (oldest child is 13–20 years)	7 years
Families launch young adults (children leave home)	8 years
Middle-aged parents (empty nest to retirement)	15+ years
Aging family members (retirement to death of both spouses)	10–15+ years

Source: Based on Duvall, Evelyn Millis & Miller, Brent C. Marriages and Family Development 6/E © 1985. Published by Allyn and Bacon Boston, MA.

As you learned in the previous chapter, when a child enters into early adolescence, the overarching goal is for a teen to successfully transition to an established adult identity that is separate from the family of origin. But during this time, an important turning point is also reached in the parent–child relationship: It is during this phase of development that parents and children alike establish intimacy levels that will, to a very large extent, define their subsequent *parent–adult child* relationship.

It is also during these middle years of the Family Life Cycle that parents and children begin to renegotiate their relationship, and parents begin to reflect back on their parenting experiences, and "accept their life choices, relate to their children, and adjust to how [the children] have turned out'" (Lemme, 2011, p. 274). These reflections about their success or failure as parents greatly affect the parents' purpose in life, their self-acceptance, and their well-being, and thus how they interrelate with and support their child.

Little attention has been given to parenting young adult (YA) children. Adult children are considered to be those 18 years of age or older, married or single, living in or out of the parental home. The **age of majority** is the legally defined age "at which a person is considered an adult, with all the attendant rights and responsibilities of adulthood; it is defined by state laws, which vary by state" (U.S. Legal, 2017). Thus, when people say that an adolescent has reached the *age of maturity* or the *age of majority*, they are referring to when an individual is thought to be an adult. The age of majority, or adulthood, in the United States is between 18 and 21 (depending upon the state in which one lives), and it is when an emerging adult gains legal control over their own person, choices, actions, lifestyle, and living arrangements—and when the parents' or guardians' parental rights legally end (U.S. Legal, 2017).

According to Jeffrey Arnett (2000, 2004), **emerging adulthood** is a distinct stage of the developmental lifespan, and typically spans between the ages of 18 and the mid- to late-20s. Arnett (2004) describes five developmental tasks associated with emerging adulthood, and these are summarized in Goldsmith's work (2018): identity exploration; instability; self-focus; feeling "in-between"; and endless possibilities. In essence, then, emerging adulthood is a time of simultaneous rapid, powerful growth and insecurity/uncertainty. Historically, there have been culturally determined milestones or experiences deemed essential to becoming an adult. Table 8.2 describes the cultural, expected age norms at which young adults should reach a milestone, and the percentages of today's YAs who achieve these markers by the desired age. Clearly, the majority of contemporary emerging adults do not meet the social expectations.

Due to the multiple roles required of parents while adolescents develop to and through adulthood, successfully navigating the transition to emerging adulthood requires flexibility on the parts of the YA and the parents or caregivers (Goldsmith, 2018). One researcher observes that it is difficult for parents to know what their soon-to-be-adult child needs because parenting during this life phase demands different roles at different times (Goldsmith, 2018). For example, sometimes a young adult needs the parent to be actively involved in problem-solving and decision-making, yet other times the adult child needs the parents to be hands-off. Sometimes the YA needs a parent to be a confidant and friend, while other times the emerging adult wants firm boundaries and no intrusion. Above all, the adult child needs parents or caregivers who are flexible enough to allow the parent–child relationship to mature into a parent–adult child

TABLE 8.2 ■ Milestones of Adulthood

Milestones	Ideal Age for Completing Milestone	Percent Who Complete Milestones by Ideal Age
Complete formal schooling	22	51.8
Employed full-time	22	36.7
Support family financially	25	42.1
Not living in parents' home	21	47.1
Financially independent	21	28.9
Married	25	23.5
Have a child	25	38.0

Source: Vespa (2017).

relationship, and to lay aside relationship patterns that are no longer effective or controlling (Goldsmith, 2018).

There is scant research that helps us to understand the characteristics of parenting during their child's shift to adulthood. However, there are a number of ways in which parents can assist their child's transition during this period of vulnerability and change. First and foremost, the parent–adult child relationship is built upon the relationship formed throughout the child's life, and, not surprisingly, healthy later-in-life relationships include warm, supporting, caring interactions (Jewsbury Conger et al., 2013). And, similar to the adolescent developmental period, emerging adults require social support from their parents, while at the same time require that their parents relinquish control (Steinberg, 2001). Even though the age of majority is 18 in most of the United States, parents are responsible for providing physical, psychological, social, emotional, and financial support until "...their children are safely and securely launched, whenever that may be" (Jewsbury Conger et al., 2013). This is challenging, indeed, because parents who provide too much support risk interfering with and diminishing the YA's autonomy, self-governing, and self-reliance (Jewsbury Conger et al., 2013).

Dr. Katherine Jewsbury Conger and her colleagues were commissioned by the Institute of Medicine and the National Research Council to study the well-being of young adults (Jewsbury Conger et al., 2013). Their robust review of empirical studies suggests key areas in which parents can successfully support and nurture their young adult children; their work is augmented here with additional research studies.

1. **Communication:** Healthy parent–child relationships are built upon effective communication from childhood, through adolescence, into adulthood. Strong parent–adult child relationships are those in which there is mutual respect, responsiveness (sensitivity), reciprocity, and is nonintrusive (Hamalainen & Arpino, 2020).

2. **Social support:** While one of the milestone developmental tasks in adolescence is the formation of independence, effective parent–adult child relationships require interdependence, a mutual reliance on one another; researchers describe this as the development of autonomy with connectedness (Aquilino, 2006; Settersten & Ray, 2010).

3. **Personal responsibility:** This requires that YAs are taught by their parents the social norms and societal expectations of adulthood; this is also referred to as *relational maturity* and includes attributes such as becoming other rather than self-centered; showing empathy and greater concern for others; accepting responsibility for personal actions and behaviors; and setting and maintaining healthy boundaries (Nelson et al., 2007; Scales et al., 2016; Sharon, 2015).

4. **Physical, psychological, and emotional well-being:** Successful emerging adulthood requires that individuals engage in healthy lifestyle choices (such as quality nutrition and regular exercise) and behaviors. This includes low degrees of risk-taking; minimizing the use of substances, alcohol, and tobacco; engaging in safe sexual behaviors and having fewer sex partners; and leaving violent or abusive relationships (see Scales et al., 2016 for a comprehensive review of each area). Psychological and emotional well-being require that YAs operate from an internal locus of control and have healthy levels of self-efficacy. If they have mental health concerns, they are proactive in and dedicated to maintaining prescribed care. A substantial body of research underscores the importance of parents in helping emerging adults develop physical, psychological, and emotional health (Jewsbury Conger et al., 2013; Scales et al., 2016).

There is no question that the perception of adulthood and the experiences of young adults have changed drastically over the past 20 or 30 years. In the past, when adolescents reached the age of 18, they were considered to be "adults." But as we saw in the previous chapter, both the architecture and functions of the brain are not fully mature until a person's mid-20s. And today, long-established benchmarks of adulthood, such as completing schooling, full-time employment, financial independence, moving out of the family home, and getting married, are achieved at later ages (Fingerman, 2017; Sharon, 2015; Vespa, 2017). Because of the efforts of neuroscientists and researchers, we now have a more nuanced understanding that there is a distinct developmental phase between adolescence and adulthood—emerging adulthood.

This raises an interesting question: Is this shift away from the traditional understanding of adulthood why it is more common for young adults to reside in the family home?

Adult Children Living at Home

In the past, it has been the practice in the United States for young adults to leave the parental home in their late teens or early 20s to establish homes of their own or to attend college. In the 1970s, for example, 8 in 10 people were married by the time they were 30—today, not until the age of 45 are 80 percent married (Vespa, 2017).

There is also empirical evidence that suggests that, traditionally, midlife adults experienced **filial obligation,** the social norm that prescribes they provided care for their older family members (Muresan & Haragus, 2015). Researchers today, however, observe that filial obligation is loosening, "...rendering the parent/child relationship more chosen and voluntary in nature" (Fingerman, 2017). Fingerman posits that because of this societal change, parent and adult child relationships in emerging adulthood today do not necessarily follow "the norms of autonomy," and therefore grant parents and their grown children to experience relationships in ways that benefit them and bring satisfaction.

Based on recent trends reported by the U.S. Census Bureau (see Figure 8.2), it seems that for many families today the parenting career is extended, either because the launching stage is postponed or because it resumes again after a brief empty-nest period. This phenomenon is referred to as the *cluttered nest* or the *elastic nest.* So common and widespread is the trend of adult children returning home after launching, in 2010, President Barack Obama's Healthcare Reform legislation mandated that single, adult children are to be covered under their parents' health insurance plans until the age of 26; before this, adult children were no longer covered under their parents' insurance after the age of 21 or 23. Since then, the share of adults living with their parents has increased sharply, as Figure 8.2 illustrates.

Who Lives at Home?

Recent social challenges, such as the COVID-19 health crisis that swept the United States in 2020 (and the associated economic crisis and job loss in the aftermath), have contributed to an expanded conception of parenthood. These changes have resulted in children remaining in the parental home longer and, for some adult children, returning to live, at least for a brief period (Pew Research Center, 2020).

FIGURE 8.2 ■ Percentage of Adults Living With Their Parents, 2010 and 2017

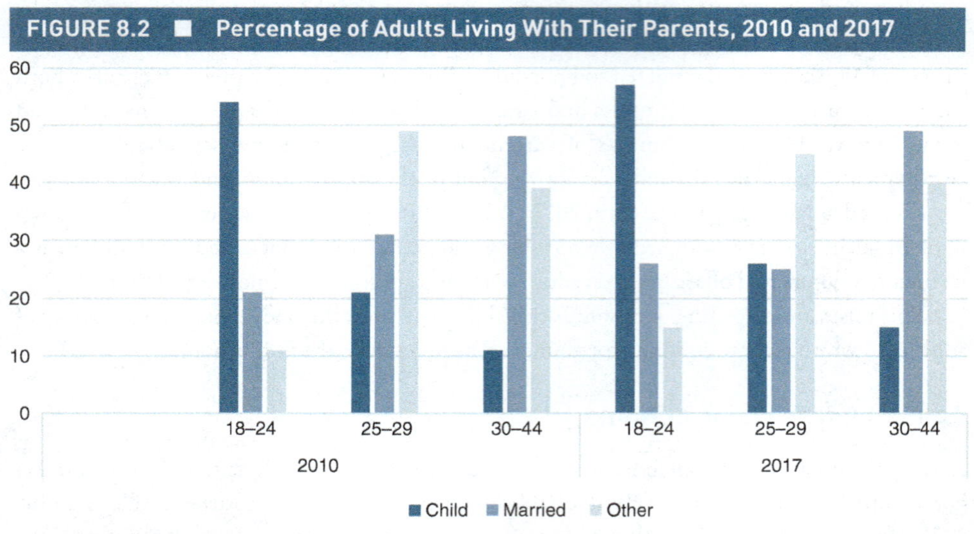

Source: © 2020 PRB.

FIGURE 8.3 ■ Percentages of 18- to 29-Year-Olds Living With At Least One Parent, 2020

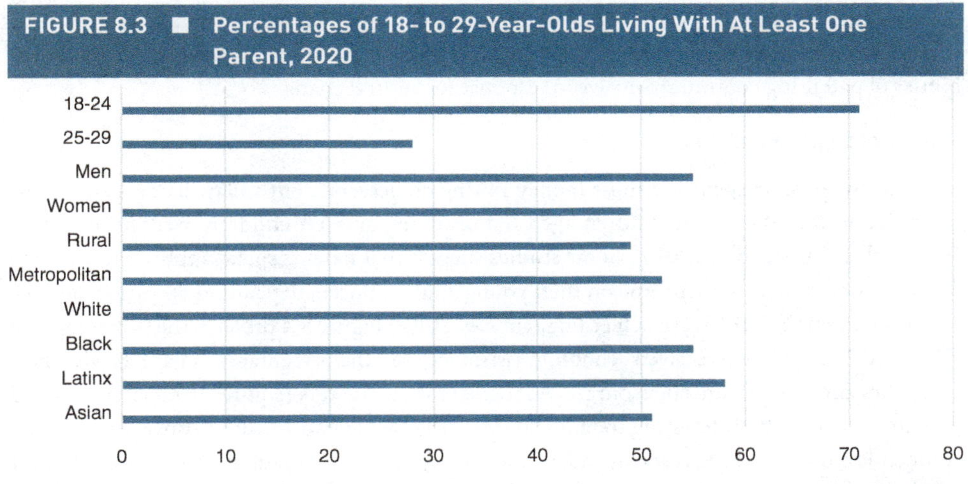

Source: Pew Research Center (2020).

Indeed—for the first time since the Great Depression, over one-half (52 percent) of young adults aged 18 to 29 live with their parents (or one parent) (Pew Research Center, 2020). Historically, whites have been less likely to move back home than other racial and ethnic individuals, but during the COVID-19 restrictions, whites accounted for slightly over 70 percent of the increase in YAs (aged 18 to 24) who resided with their family of origin (Pew Research Center, 2020). Figure 8.3 presents the trends in living arrangements of YAs in the United States during the COVID pandemic.

Emerging adults' co-residency with parents was occurring well before the pandemic, however. One body of research provides an extensive review of the literature and suggests many sociological factors that are delaying emerging adults' independent living and financial responsibility. These include (Copp et al., 2017; Fingerman, 2017):

- Poor employment opportunities
- Increasing cost of housing
- Student loan debt
- Delayed age at first marriage
- The majority of those ages 18 to 25 in the United States do not consider themselves to be adults.

Vespa (2017) and Fry (2016) determined that about one-third of YAs who live with their parents are not employed or attending school. Vespa's work (2017) also highlights the fact that about 10 percent of co-residing young adults have a disability that prevents them from living on their own, and another 2.2 million have addictions or life circumstances that prevent them from leaving the familial home.

Researchers conclude that societal circumstances contribute in substantial ways to the extension of the parenting role (Copp et al., 2017; Fingerman, 2017). To be sure: The responsibilities of parenting continue to evolve in response to cultural changes.

Parental Support of Emerging Adults

Historically, parents spent the most money raising adolescents, but today, parents spend the most financial resources on children aged 6 and under, and YA children over the age of 18 (Kornrich & Furstenberg, 2013). Some studies suggest that parents spend approximately 10 to 33 percent of their annual income on their young adult children, depending on socioeconomic strata (Fingerman, 2017; Kornrich & Furstenberg, 2013). Figure 8.4 presents the percentages of YAs, aged 18 to 29, who received economic assistance, and the percentages of parents who indicated they provided financial resources. As the data show us, YAs require financial help—and parents provide it. It's interesting to note, however, that while two-thirds of Americans say that adult children should be financially independent by age 22, only about one-fourth are, and over one-half of American adults believe that parents do too much for their young adult children (Pew Research Center, 2019). It is clear that today, emerging adults are financially dependent on their parents.

Regardless of SES, parents provide financial assistance to their adult children, but parents from higher SES provide more economic resources (Fingerman et al., 2015, 2016). When

FIGURE 8.4 ■ Percentage of Young Adults (18–29) Who Received Parental Financial Support and Percentage of Parents Who Provided Support, 2019

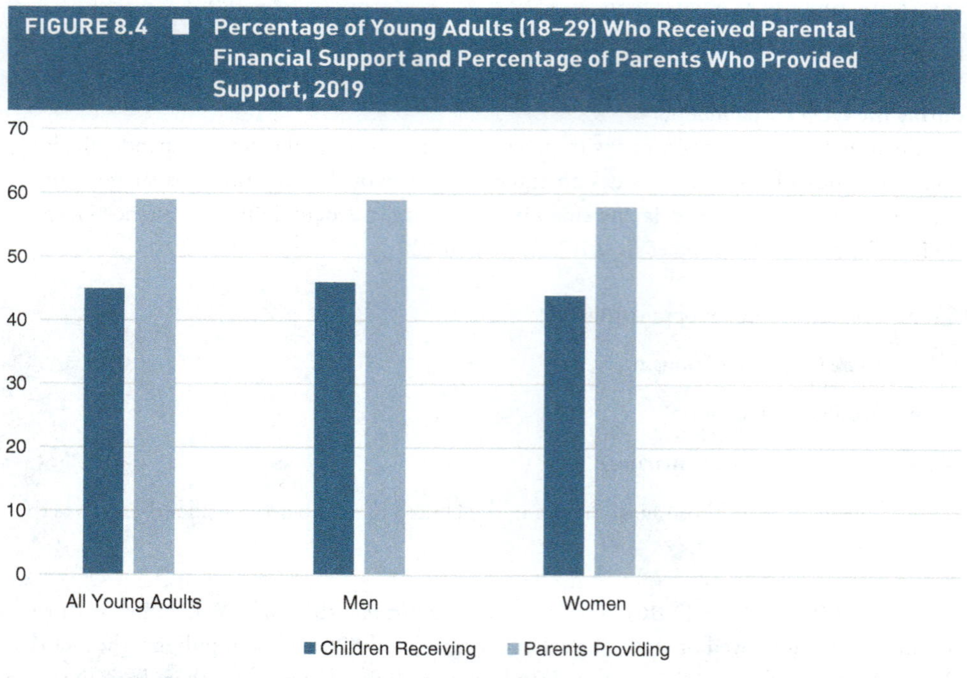

Source: Pew Research Center (2019).

FIGURE 8.5 ■ Percentages of Types of Financial Assistance From Parents to Adult Children

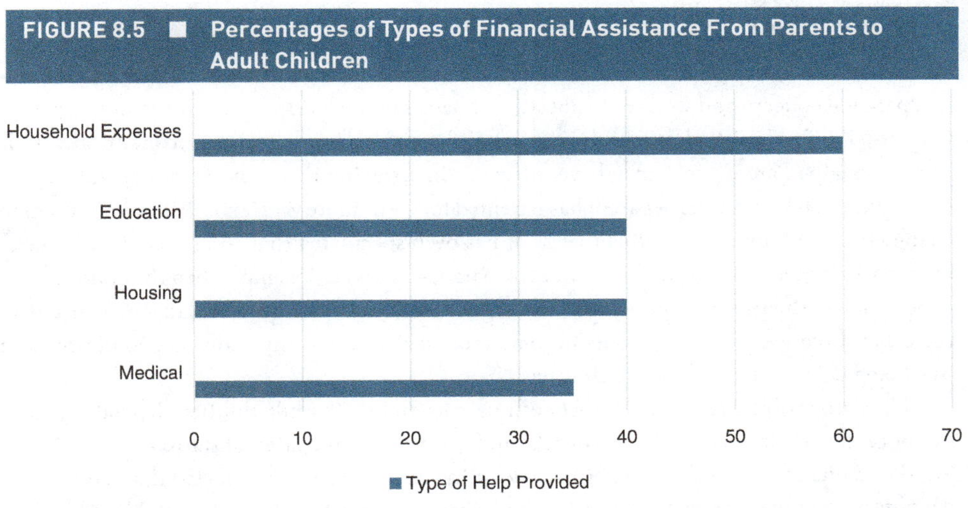

Source: Pew Research Center (2019).

parents provide financial support for their adult children, it is most often to assist them with household expenses, as Figure 8.5 illustrates (Pew Research Center, 2019).

Parents also offer much in the way of nonmaterial/nonfinancial support. Fingerman's (2017) work provides insight into the ways in which parents assist their children in the emerging adulthood years. For example, while most understand the time-intensive nature of parenting young children, today's parents remain highly involved in day-to-day tasks, such as making appointments for adult children, providing emotional and informational support, and child care for grandchildren.

Coming and Going: Need to Know?

One of the biggest developmental losses associated with co-residency is the emerging adult's loss of autonomy, independence, privacy, and setting one's own boundaries (Kreiczer-Levy, 2019). The issue of rules and regulations looms large for many families with adult children at home. To what extent do parents have a right to know where their children are, when they will be home, and whom they are with? Should parents set down rules about socializing, curfews, use of parents' possessions, and the use of alcohol and drugs?

Many parents feel the need to apply rules that make their own lives more comfortable, yet they feel guilty that they are not accepting their child's level of maturity and sense of responsibility. There also exists a social stigma that adult children who live with their parents are immature (Kreiczer-Levy, 2019). Creating an atmosphere of peaceful coexistence while maintaining mutual respect often is difficult, but some evidence suggests that when parents allow their adult child to participate in family decision-making, help with household needs, and assume responsibility in the family's day-to-day functions, the YA better assimilates into the family system (Leopold, 2012).

Adult Children Living Away From Home

When children leave home to establish independence and to begin their own careers and families, parental concern and worries do not stop—there is no such thing as a "postparental" period (Aldous, 1985). Nevertheless, children may still be dependent on parents economically and/or emotionally. Parents, too, may have difficulty in resolving their emotional dependency on their children because when a parent has parented for 20 or more years, it is difficult for them to change roles and not parent. Nonetheless, it has been speculated that emotional dependencies are more balanced in adulthood than in early parent–child relationships when the child is more dependent on the parent (Thompson & Walker, 1984). Still later an imbalance may occur in the other direction as aging parents become more dependent—physically, economically, and psychologically—on their mature children.

The nature of the relationships between parents and their adult children depends to some extent on the marital status of the parent(s) and the marital and parental status of the children, but the results of studies show inconsistencies. One body of research reported that parents and daughters are more involved with each other's lives than parents and sons are (Aldous, 1985). However, parents may show greater concern for their divorced children/grandchildren than for their other adult children who are not divorced. Parents are also more likely to provide child care for these grandchildren, to give comfort to their own divorced children, and to help them with housework.

Other studies have shown that divorced children receive less support from parents and experience more strain in relationships with them than married children (Umberson, 1992). For example, parental divorce and remarriage are associated with significantly less social, instrumental, and financial support to adult children (White, 1992). The reduced financial support to adult children might be accounted for by the lower earnings and assets, and greater obligations of divorced parents, but the reduced support in other areas appears to be the result of lower parent–child solidarity. It seems, then, that structural circumstances influence the quality of relationships and the degree of intergenerational transfers between adult children and their parents (Umberson, 1992).

Transfer of aid or assistance among the generations is never really symmetrical because almost always it is transferred from parent to child. Only by grown children transferring to their own children is there any balancing of material and emotional investment. Transfer of aid was examined in two generations of mother–daughter relationships; most of the youngest generation of daughters (who were university students) were single (Thompson & Walker, 1984). The investigators found that nonreciprocity existed in the transfer of aid: The mothers essentially were the givers, and the daughters were the receivers. Some research reported greater closeness and reciprocity of aid between mothers and their YA daughters when the mothers were widowed as opposed to married. It may be the family member in the nonreciprocating position (receiving but not giving help) who avoids contact with kin.

Our discussion so far has shown us that relationships between mature adults and their adult children, whether the children are living at home or not, are complex and little understood. There is great diversity in the degree and extent of contact and in the transfer of financial resources and services, and the reciprocity of emotional support. Because of this, few generalizations can be made, and few guidelines can be established. Therefore, it appears that an interesting and promising area of research would be the relationship between parents and their adult children.

As adults age through later adulthood, intergenerational ties become increasingly important because these relationships often provide the foundation for intimacy throughout the aging process (Fingerman, 2001). In the section that follows, we'll explore the importance of multigenerational relationships, and how relationships change as we age.

In the following section, we will examine how parenting changes when grandchildren enter the picture.

INTERGENERATIONAL TIES

Intergenerational ties refer to the relationships between family members across multiple generations, and these relationships are indeed important to the aging population. Women over the age of 65, for example, are three times more likely to be widowed than men (U.S. Census Bureau, 2021). Figures 8.6 and 8.7 show us the percentages of widows and widowers from the age of 65. Thus, as adults grow older through later adulthood, their interpersonal relationships across generations become increasingly important because these intergenerational ties provide the foundation for intimacy throughout the aging process (Fingerman, 2001).

In everyday language, the term *generation* describes people who were born during the relatively same time period (such as the "Baby Boomer" generation). When discussing intergenerational relationships, however, the term *generation* is used to describe family members who are "on the same rung of the family ladder," or who are related to one another either biologically or

FIGURE 8.6 ■ Male Marital Status by Age: 2016

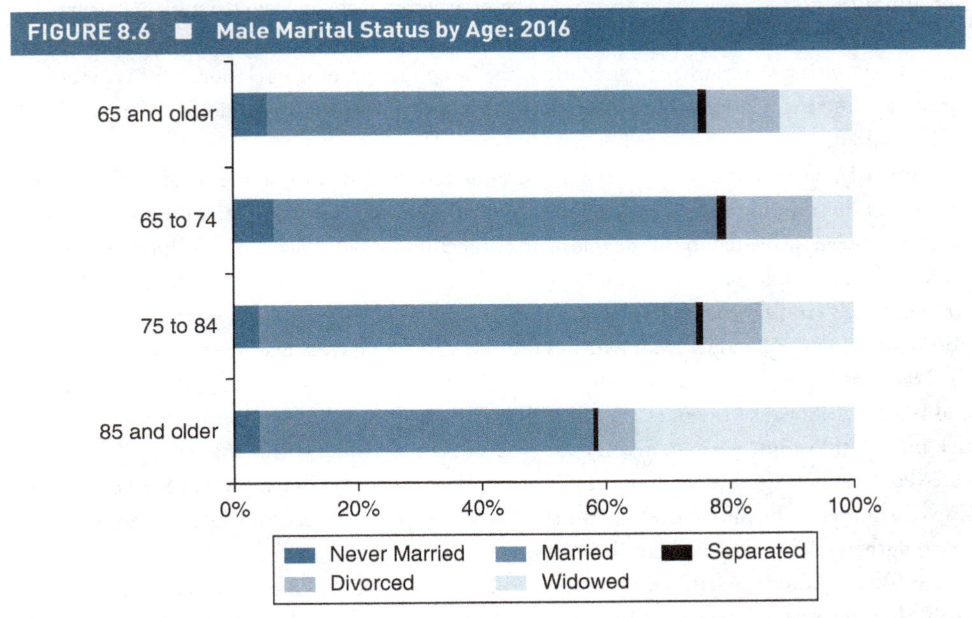

Source: U.S. Census Bureau (2018).

FIGURE 8.7 ■ Female Marital Status by Age: 2016

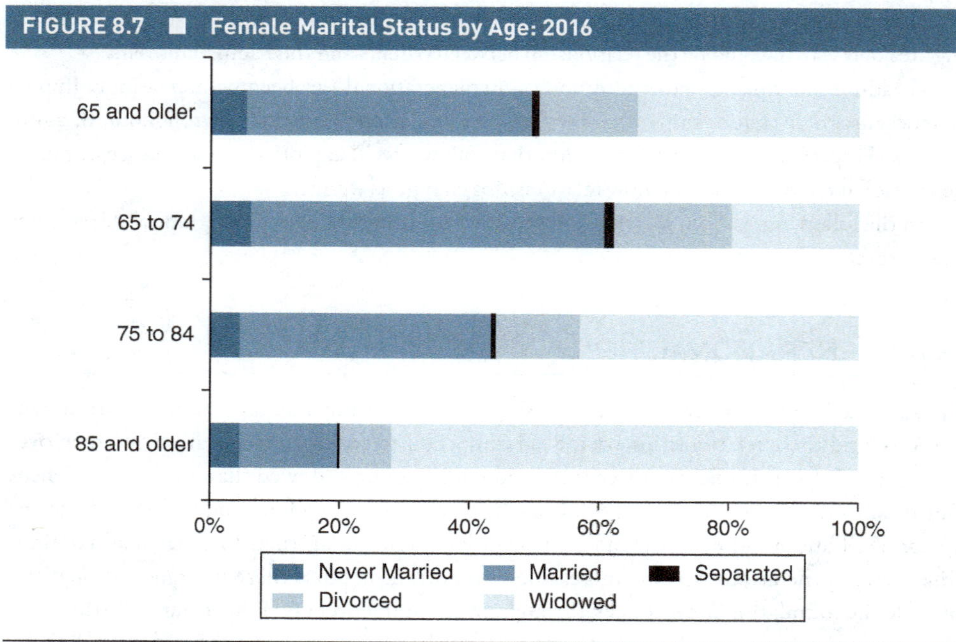

Source: U.S. Census Bureau (2018).

through adoption. Most intergenerational relationships are offshoots of the parent–child relationship, although biological ties are not a necessary prerequisite in order for someone to experience a sense of family, kinship, and intimacy (Fingerman, 2001). For example, sometimes after many years with a stepmother or stepfather, the "step" aspect of the relationship becomes less significant and the relationship becomes as meaningful as those between biological parents and their children.

Similarly, older Black adults frequently do not distinguish "kin" along biological lines; for instance, it is common for nieces, nephews, godchildren, or even younger adults who are not blood or otherwise related to fill the role of an adult child for older Black males (Johnson, 1999). **Fictive kin** are people who are not biologically related to someone, but who fulfill a family role. Among Black families, fictive kin are important sources of emotional support, as well as support in meeting the elderly's needs (MacRae, 1992). A team of investigators examined data from the National Survey of American Life regarding fictive kin networks among Black Americans and Black Caribbeans (Taylor et al., 2022). Their study found that 87 percent experienced fictive kin relationships, with an average kin size of 7.5; nearly one-third (61 percent) routinely received care and support from their fictive network. This study concludes that fictive relationships do not serve the purpose of substituting for losses in family relationships, but rather, serve to strengthen relationship and family bonds.

As Black Americans/Black Caribbeans age, they tend to enjoy warmer relationships with their brothers, sisters, children, and fictive kin than white aging Americans do (MacRae, 1992). Aging Latinx and Asian families also experience extended kin and fictive kin relationships more often than white families do (Institute for Latino Studies, 2010; MacRae, 1992). Importantly, later in the developmental lifecourse, intimacy "may exist between individuals who *define themselves* as parent and offspring" (Fingerman, 2001, p. 23, italics added). Of the many different and varying interpersonal intimate relationships we form throughout our lives, none is as important to some people as the relationship between parent and child.

It is not uncommon for middle-life couples to become emotionally disconnected from one another while they're in the trenches raising their children. When the children leave the nest, oftentimes couples are faced with relationship difficulties they may have ignored or not been aware of.

Source: iStock.com/DrazenZigic.

Parenting: Are We There Yet?

Some parents look forward to launching their children, while others do so with much trepidation and doubt. Still others do not successfully manage the transition to an empty nest—the home with no children—well at all. As parents begin to empty the nest, there are changes that occur in the family system and common struggles that most couples encounter:

- **Change in roles/loss of roles:** When children leave, it's not uncommon for parents to feel a void once their parenting rote is diminished or lost. Some parents try to fill this void with volunteer or other activities. Parents also need to shift to the role of parents of *adult* children.

- **Marital issues:** Raising children requires so much time, energy, and attention that sometimes children are a diversion that keeps parents from working on problems in their marriage. When children leave the nest, the diversion is no longer there. Parents need to reexamine their goals as a couple as they enter the second half of their marriage.
- **Career change:** Frequently, emptying the nest coincides with changes in one or both parents' careers. While men may be thinking of early retirement, women who entered the workforce later because of childrearing responsibilities may be just reaching a peak in their careers.
- **Caregiving shifts:** Typically, as children leave the home, parents find that their own parents need more care and attention. Caregiving responsibilities don't lessen—they simply shift to a different generation.
- **Relationships with children:** For many parents, accepting their children as adults is difficult; other parents accept that their children are adults and require less advice and support. What is more important to midlife parents, however, is *how* children leave the nest: Are the parents and children on good terms?

As you can see, significant changes take place in the family members' roles, as well as in the relationships with the now-grown children. While human growth and development courses emphasize the earlier years of parenting and the significance of the parent–child relationship during the early years, preschool years, and school years of a child's life, too often much is left unsaid about the importance of the parent–adult child relationship.

When a child enters into early adolescence, an important turning point is reached in the parent–child relationship. It is during this phase of development that parents and children alike establish intimacy levels that will, to a very large extent, define their subsequent parent–adult child relationship. This developmental stage of the Family Life Cycle brings important questions to the forefront, such as: How do adolescent children affect the well-being of their parents? Because children come of age during this period of family development and eventually leave the nest (and perhaps return to the nest again and again), what impact does this have on midlife parents?

In many families, children's entry into adolescence coincides with the parents' transition to midlife. As young adolescents strive for increased independence and autonomy, they often begin to challenge their parents' authority. In late adolescence/early adulthood, parents encounter their own developmental tasks associated with midlife, such as caring for their aging parents and preparing for retirement. These normative lifecourse events introduce many challenges into the family system, as parents are forced to play simultaneous roles as caretaker and parent. But typically, marital satisfaction and stability increase as children enter into their early adulthood years (Davis et al., 2016; Lee et al., 2016; Lee & Szinovaca, 2016; see Polenick et al., 2018, for a full review). This increase is likely because conflicts over childrearing and adolescent issues decline.

It is also during a child's adolescent and early adulthood years that parents and children begin to renegotiate their relationship, and parents begin to reflect on their parenting experiences, and "accept their life choices, relate to their children, and adjust to how [the children] have turned out" (Lemme, 2011). These reflections about their success or failure as parents greatly affect the parents' purpose in life, their self-acceptance, and thus their well-being.

Adults' relationships with their parents are affected by their gender, geographic distance, their parents' marital status, and their culture.

Source: iStock.com/grandriver.

The Parent–Adult Child Relationship in Late Adulthood

As parents age and begin to experience physiological and cognitive changes, their roles within the family change, also. The parent–adult child relationship is central to the lives of the elderly: Aside from having their adult children there to provide care when needed, having warm and close relationships with their children provide aging parents a sense of well-being (Fingerman & Birditt, 2011; Thomas et al., 2017). According to aging developmentalist Karen Fingerman (2001), four primary factors influence intimacy between older adults and their adult children: gender, geographic distance, a parent's marital status, and culture.

1. **Gender:** Gender plays a significant role in the intimacy levels of the elderly and their grown children. Women, for example, tend to express greater emotional intensity than do men in their intergenerational ties (Fingerman, 2001; Troll & Fingerman, 1996). Subsequently, elderly mothers and their adult daughters and daughters-in-law experience greater intimacy than do fathers and sons.

2. **Geographic distance:** One national survey indicated that 63 percent of elderly parents see at least one of their children weekly (Crimmins & Ingegneri, 1990). Of the 11,000 senior citizen respondents in the national study, only 20 percent noted that they see their children once per month (or less).

3. **Parent's marital status:** The older parent's marital status also influences the quality of intimacy between elderly parents and their children. Widowed or single older people (particularly women) frequently turn to their grown children or grandchildren for companionship and emotional support.

4. **Culture:** Culture and ethnicity are key determinants in how intergenerational relationships develop and how intimacy is fostered within these relationships. In the United States, for example, involvement in the aging parent's daily life is not supported by American culture, whereas in Japan and other Asian cultures, such involvement is a dominant belief. These cultural differences may explain in part the discrepancies seen in the research as it relates to the impact of adult–child involvement in aging parents' lives, such as in India and among Mexican Americans. But clearly, although the "intimacy parents and offspring share in late life does not involve the close sense of oneness they could derive from a romantic partner" (Fingerman, 2001, p. 31), older adults take pleasure in these intergenerational ties.

Today, some of the most enjoyable, enriching intergenerational relationships the aging experience are with their grandchildren.

If we had known how much fun grandparenting is, we would have skipped parenting all together and jumped right to this phase!

Source: Kelly Welch.

Grandparents as Parents: A Growing Phenomenon

We admit it—we love being grandparents to our collective [9] grandchildren! We confess that we are the type of grandparents who are armed and ready with photos and videos on our phones, ready to spring them on unsuspecting victims, including you, as you can see in the photos. We love being a grandma and grandpa so much, we often quip often that if we had known grandparenting was this much fun, we would have skipped parenting altogether and jumped right into this phase.

Becoming a grandparent is an exciting time for most people (Somary & Stricker, 1998). As adults enter their middle years, they begin to take on several new roles, such as in-law, grandparent, and caregiver to their aging parents. In the United States, some parents become grandparents in their 30s (Szinovacz, 1998), but typically most do so while in their 40s (about one-third), and about one-half of women become grandparents while in their 50s. Today a significant number of grandparents assume the parenting role.

Figure 8.8 provides a snapshot of the percentage of grandparents who are responsible for their grandchildren. In the United States, nearly 4 million children receive their daily care from their grandparents; of these, 2.5 million live in three-generation households (Pebley & Rudkin, 2020; Wiltz, 2016). At any given time in America, about 5 to 6 percent of all grandchildren live in grandparent-grandchild households. These types of families are referred to as **grandfamilies** (Dunn & Wamsley, 2018).

FIGURE 8.8 ■ Grandparents Who Were Caregivers for Their Grandchildren by Age: 2016

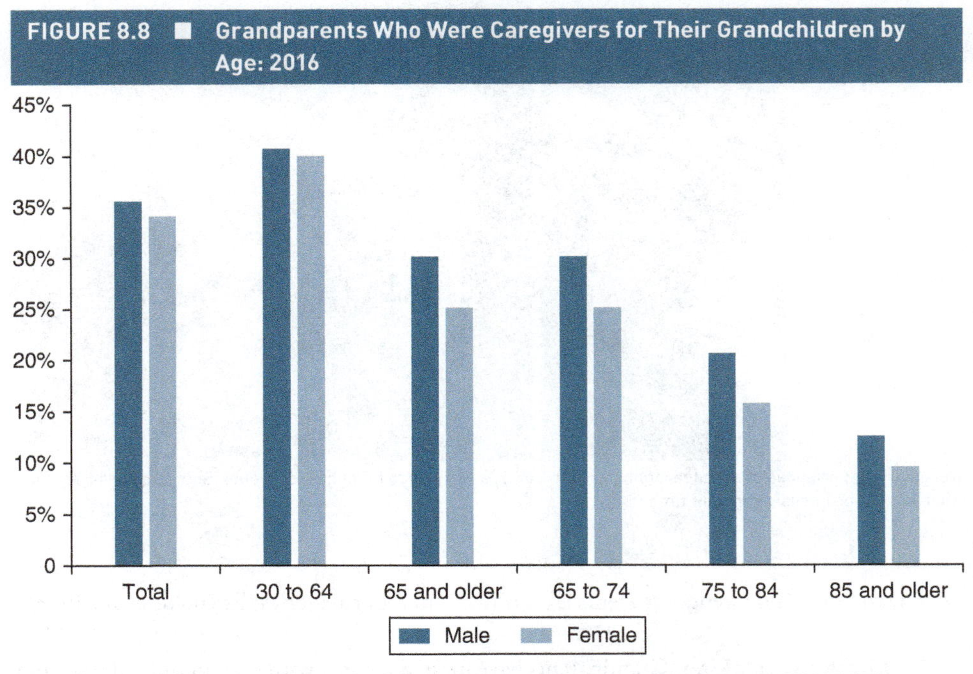

Source: U.S. Census Bureau (2018).

Known as *kinship care*, grandparents provide a living environment for their grandchildren for a number of reasons, but particularly because the parents struggle with substance abuse, mental illness, economic hardship, divorce, domestic violence, and incarceration (Raphel, 2008). Most of these living arrangements are informal, private, and voluntary—the court system and/or the social welfare system are typically not involved in these arrangements. Parents commonly retain legal custody and can make decisions regarding their children, although in some cases, the grandparents share legal custody. Although not common, some grandparents adopt the grandchildren, and the rights of the parents are legally terminated.

Overall, the experiences of grandparenting are incredibly satisfying to most grandparents. Some, however, find the experience to be intrusive on their time.

Source: iStock.com/Sironosov.

The role of grandparents as parents is classified into four categories (Reynolds et al., 2003):

1. **Limited caretaking:** Grandparents have limited contact with their grandchildren, and parents have primary responsibility.

2. **Participatory caretaking:** In these situations, grandparents are engaged and involved in their grandchildren's lives, such as taking an active interest in the children's education and their activities. Care may be provided for grandchildren while the parents are at work, but parents have primary responsibility for them.

3. **Voluntary caretaking:** Grandparents assume the parental role and responsibilities for raising their grandchildren. Although situations vary, typically these types of caregivers assume the role of grandparents as parents to make sure their grandchildren are in a safe, stable environment in the absence of their parents.

4. **Involuntary caretaking:** These grandparents are full-time caregivers of their grandchildren, and most often they have little to no warning; many times, it is not the grandparents' preference—the situation was more or less thrust on them. These types of arrangements are often difficult for children because of the unexpected shift in environments and caregivers.

Many grandparents welcome the opportunity to care for their grandchildren, but others experience financial, social, and emotional intrusions, as well as an increase in health problems. As one body of research suggests, for many grandparents, the role of second parenthood limits their independence and their personal development in mid- to later adulthood (Glass & Hunneycutt, 2002). However, other research suggests that there are rewards, such as getting a chance to raise a child differently, to nurture family relationships, and to receive love and companionship from their grandchildren (Burton et al., 1995).

Grandparents raising their grandchildren is a growing phenomenon in the United States, and much more study needs to be done so family practitioners understand the unique needs of the grandparents and the children they are parenting. With this knowledge, human service providers, such as teachers, social workers, ministers, and mental health workers can begin to successfully implement parenting classes and other resources for caregiving grandparents in order to equip them with the necessary skills to best raise their grandchildren.

Overall, the experience of grandparenting appears to be immensely satisfying; to be sure, 92 percent of survey respondents in one study expressed high levels of satisfaction with their grandparenting role (Kaufman & Elder, 2003; Segatto & Di Filippo, 2003). Studies have shown that grandparents wish to see their grandchildren on a frequent basis, and these relationships have positive outcomes on grandchildren's development (Adkins, 1999). Of course, there are many different ways that people grandparent.

Styles of Grandparenting

Just as there are different parenting styles, there are different styles of grandparenting. In a classic study by a pioneer in the study of aging, Bernice Neugarten and her colleague, K. K. Weinstein (1964) identified five primary styles of grandparenting: formal, fun seeker, remote, involved, and dispenser of wisdom.

In the **formal grandparenting** role, grandparents see their role along common, traditional lines. These grandparents babysit every now and then and indulge their grandchildren on occasion, but when it comes to childrearing and discipline, they play a "hands-off" role; they are content to leave that aspect of parenting to the parents. About one-third of the grandparents in this study practiced this grandparenting style. One study surveyed a representative sample of grandparents and found that more than one-half of their research participants had a **companionate relationship** with their grandchildren (Cherlin & Furstenberg, 1986). Similar to the formal relationship, companionate grandparents enjoy warm, loving, and nurturing relationships with their grandkids, although they are happy to send them home when it is time!

Another common style of grandparenting is the **fun seeker**. These grandparents have a relationship with their grandchildren that is characterized by an informal, spontaneous playfulness. On the other hand, the distant grandparent has little or no contact with grandchildren and is only involved on occasional holidays or birthdays. This grandparenting style is defined as a **remote relationship**.

As you know, many grandparents today assume the role of parent and are *surrogate* parents; this grandparenting style is described as an **involved relationship**. Overall, Black Americans/Black Caribbeans, Asian Americans, Italian Americans, and Latinx are more likely to be actively involved in their grandchildren's lives than are whites because the sense of family is a core value among these cultures (Dunn & Wamsley, 2018). Finally, the **dispenser of wisdom grandparent** offers information and advice to their grandchildren—often whether it is asked for or not.

Indeed, there are many changes that take place in family relationships as people age. Central to the lives of the aging are intergenerational relationships, whether they are with biological kin or with fictive kin. As you learned in Chapter 1, many couples today are forgoing parenting altogether; given the significance of intergenerational relationships in later life, it will be interesting to see the impact of childlessness on couples in the future.

As individuals and couples near the later years in life, there are other substantial changes that must be navigated. In the section that follows, we'll explore other factors associated with aging, including retirement and family caregiving.

FAMILY CHANGES TOWARD THE END OF LIFE

Throughout this text, we have discussed how marital and intimate relationship development and family development involve multiple processes that unfold over the life of the relationship. To fully understand family development, we must take into account the cultural and social contexts in which the family evolves and understands that each transition or milestone has both positive and negative ramifications.

So far in this chapter we've discussed how marriages and other family relationships change as people age and enter the later years of their lifespans. But a discussion about parenting life through the maturing years would not be complete without examining other significant life transitions that also have significant impact on a person's later years. These are the changes that take place within a family's day-to-day living. External factors affect the daily lives of aging adults and their families, including retirement and caregiving.

Sitting on the porch in a rocker and dozing off? Or exploring the Incan ruins of Machu Picchu with teen grandkids? *Successful aging* is a pattern of well-being.

Source: iStock.com/VorDa.

Retirement and Leisure

Contemporary themes of aging research focus on the successful adaptation to the later years by viewing aging as a series of multiple, interrelated processes (Crosnoe & Elder, 2002). Beyond the biological and physiological changes that people experience as they age are external factors that determine how people's later years will progress. If we consider "aging" as a holistic experience that involves changes not just in people's bodies but also in their marital and other interpersonal relationships, as well as in their ability to use their leisure time in productive and meaningful ways, we can reassess our view of the aging process. Let's expand our definition of aging, then, to an even broader view; that is, "successful aging" is a *pattern* of well-being and adaptation to the challenges of middle adulthood and later life (Rowe & Kahn, 1998). With this definition in mind, we consider later-in-life changes that significantly affect the later years in the lifecourse: retirement and family caregiving.

Retirement as a Developmental Process

Retirement is not an isolated event but a developmental process requiring several adjustments and adaptations. It is also considered a life stage because it spans many years of middle and late adulthood. Most of us will spend anywhere from 5 to more than 20 years in the retirement stage of life. Some researchers refer to retirement as *the encore stage* or a *third age* comprised "an on-going engagement with meaningful activities" (Moen & Flood, 2013, p. 206). Although many adults diligently plan for financial security by the time they retire, such as preparing a financial portfolio, all too often they neglect their "psychological" portfolio and do not prepare themselves for the psychological aspects of retirement (American Psychological Association, 2005).

To address the transitional processes associated with permanently exiting the workforce, gerontologist Robert Atchley (2000) identified six phases associated with the processes of retirement as the result of numerous research studies. Atchley's phases provide a general framework of the steps associated with retirement, but keep in mind that retirement is experienced on an individual level that is influenced by a person's culture: Every phase identified by Atchley will not be experienced by everyone. The phases do provide a framework, however, with which to

FIGURE 8.9 ■ The Phases of Retirement

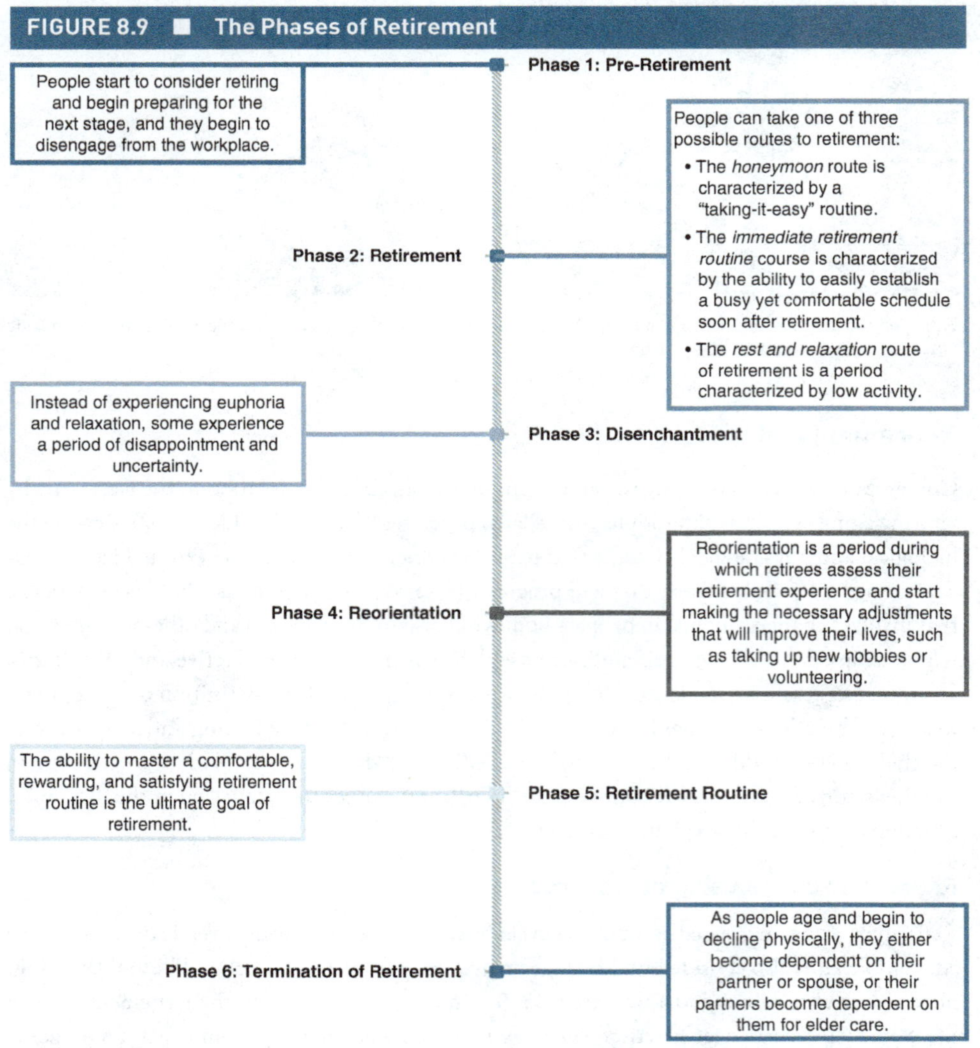

Source: Atchley (2000).

understand the multiple transitions necessary to navigate this normative change in the lifecourse. Figure 8.9 presents the six phases of retirement. As you can see, the retirement process typically unfolds gradually, from someone slowly disengaging from the workplace (sometimes this is referred to as *phased retirement*) to reorienting to establishing a daily routine that does not involve going to work. This stage in the lifespan ends when a person's health begins to decline and she or he can no longer live independently, or when a person's spouse or partner becomes dependent on the other for care. The important thing to keep in mind about retirement is that it is a unique experience for each person. How do relationships fare when someone retires?

Marital Life After Retirement

A substantive body of research concludes that because social relationships and acquaintances that originate in the workplace dissolve after retirement (Bosse et al., 1990), pensioners tend to place greater emphasis on family life and will gain support, love, and friendship from these family relationships (Kulik, 1999). Because retirement is such a significant marker of transition and adaptation for the retiree and their family, one body of research examined the impacts of a number of factors on the lives of male retirees. In a sample of 137 men on the verge of retirement and a sample of 211 men who had already retired, empirical investigation revealed some significant findings among the two groups (Kulik, 1999).

First, both groups of men attached greater importance to their marriages than they did to their own health status, but there were significant differences between the two groups of men in their life orientation. **Life orientation** refers to the emphasis pre-retirees or retirees place on various aspects of life, such as family life and economic security. For instance, pre-retired men focused more on the economic factors, such as career, finances, and material possessions than did retired men. Retired men attached greater significance to their marital and family relationships than did the pre-retired men.

Second, there were also significant differences between the two groups' attitudes regarding gender role behaviors, particularly with respect to household labor. Retired husbands expressed more conservative, traditional values about gender roles than did pre-retired men. In both groups, husbands of working women expressed more liberal views regarding gender role behaviors than did the men whose wives did not work outside the home. Interestingly, gender role behaviors, such as the division of household labor, present in the early years of the marital relationship, are apparently central issues in marital interaction and family living in the later years of life, too.

Third, Kulik's (1999) research also looked at marital intimacy in the later years of life and found three distinct types of intimacy: *reciprocity*, in which both spouses confide in one another and self-disclose; *nonreciprocity*, in which one spouse confides and shares, but the other spouse has a confidant outside of the marriage; and *segregative*, in which neither spouse shares with the other, but instead shares with someone outside the marriage. The research revealed that among the study participants, reciprocity is the most commonly expressed type of intimacy (approximately 70 percent), and nonreciprocity is the least common type (11 percent). A recent review of a vast body of contemporary literature indicates that overall, men have more positive attitudes about retirement than women do (for a complete review, see Hyde et al., 2018).

As you have come to know throughout our study together, there are gendered experiences across the lifespan. Although there is a wealth of empirical studies that examine men's retirement experiences, far less research has explored how gender affects well-being in retirement; because of this lack of research, the role gender plays in women's psychological well-being in retirement is unclear (Kubicek et al., 2011). However, in one study, 778 retired women were asked, "How long did it take you to get used to retirement?" and "How difficult has it been for you to adjust to retirement?" Women reported that they had more difficulties adjusting to retirement than men did; the researchers posited that these postretirement adjustment difficulties were due to the loss of social connections in the workplace (van Solinge & Henkens, 2005). Interestingly, using the same sample of women and asking similar questions, Damman et al. (2013, 2015) found that women's postretirement dissatisfaction and adjustment aren't necessarily about loss of identity and loss of social contacts at work; instead, postworking life adjustment has more to do with the *loss of a previous role*, rather than *adjustment to the current role*.

In summary, certain aspects of marital life are characterized by change as older adults approach and enter their retirement years. It appears that both pre-retired men and retired men alike find their marital lives to be enjoyable and positive, although retired men report higher degrees of marital satisfaction. As people approach retirement and enter retirement, their families and family life become central to their lives (Kulik, 1999).

Family Caregiving

Many people hold the common misconception that elderly people who can no longer "do" for themselves reside in a long-term care facility, such as a retirement home or a nursing home. On the contrary: For every one person who resides in a healthcare facility, there are at least two who live out their remaining years with the help of family caregivers (He et al., 2005). A **caregiver**—sometimes referred to as an **informal caregiver**—is an unpaid individual who is involved in assisting others with daily living (Family Caregiver Alliance, 2018). These family members provide the lion's share of medical and personal health assistance, in addition to emotional, spiritual, and financial support. In the United States, today (AARP, 2020; Family Caregiver Alliance, 2018):

- About 42 million Americans provide unpaid care to an adult aged 50 or older.
- About 26 percent of adult family caregivers care for someone with dementia or Alzheimer's disease; this figure has sharply risen from 22 ercent in 2015.
- Nearly one-fourth of caregivers provide support for a "frail" parent.
- Annually, the value of services provided by informal caregivers is estimated at $470 billion.

Today's longer lifespans present a new challenge to spouses and adult children alike because providing care for aging spouses and parents extends the caregiving career by a number of years. In most cases, caregiving is not isolated to a single period in the Family Life Cycle but instead exists throughout the entire Family Life Cycle. The **caregiving career** consists of the years that caregivers tend to dependent children, aging parents, grandchildren, and eventually, dependent spouses or lifetime partners (Brody, 1985). By the latter part of the human life cycle, it is often the spouse who provides the necessary help or assistance for their aging partner (Zarit et al., 1989). If the spouse cannot provide the necessary care, the burden shifts to the adult children—most typically to the adult daughters (Lemme, 2011).

Characteristics of Caregivers

There is great variability among caregivers and their experiences. Race, ethnicity, SES, education level, marital status, and personality characteristics affect both the caregiver and the person receiving the care. In most cases, family members work together to decide who will help with what in providing various caregiving tasks (Ingersoll-Dayton et al., 2003).

Research has shown that people who have launched all of their children are not working outside of the home and are not married are more likely to provide care for aging parents (Brody & Schoonover, 1986). According to the Family Caregiver Alliance (2018) and AARP's annual caregiving research report (2020), there are other general characteristics of caregivers. For example, the caregiving landscape is dominated by women, making daughters and daughters-in-law the most common caregiver: Three-fourths of all informal caregivers are female and spend at least 50 percent more time providing care than males do. Male caregivers are less likely to provide personal care to their loved ones compared with female caregivers. However, among spousal caregivers over the age of 75, both men and women provide equal amounts of care (Family Caregiver Alliance, 2018). There are racial and ethnic differences among caregivers, as well. These are illustrated in Figure 8.10.

Table 8.3 presents for us the types of caregiving tasks older family members provide for their loved ones, and Figure 8.11 shows us how many hours caregivers dedicate to caregiving.

Developmentalists Denise Boyd and Helen Bee (2009) offer two suggestions. One factor may be that women experience greater emotional closeness to their parents, and consequently

FIGURE 8.10 ■ Caregivers, by Race and Ethnicity, 2020

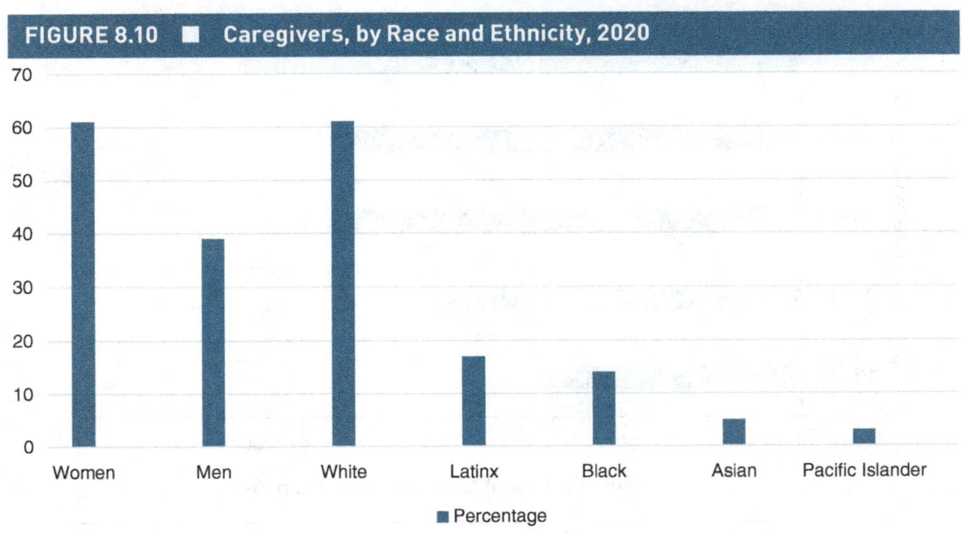

Source: (c) 2020 NAC and AARP.

TABLE 8.3 ■ Caregiving Tasks

On average, caregivers spend:

- *13 days* each month on tasks such as shopping, food preparation, housekeeping, laundry, transportation, and giving medication
- *6 days* per month on feeding, dressing, grooming, bathing, and other assistance
- *13 hours per month* researching care and services

Those who provide complex care:

- *46 percent* of time on nursing tasks (dressing wounds, giving medications)
- *96 percent* help with daily activities (dressing and undressing, toileting, feeding, etc.)
- *75 percent* help with housekeeping tasks

Significant decision-making regarding:

- *66 percent* monitor the care (recipient's care and adjusting care)
- *63 percent* communicate with healthcare professionals on behalf of the care recipient
- *50 percent* act as advocate for the care recipient

Source: Family Caregiver Alliance (2018).

FIGURE 8.11 ■ Number of Hours Dedicated to Caregiving by Age of Family Caregiver

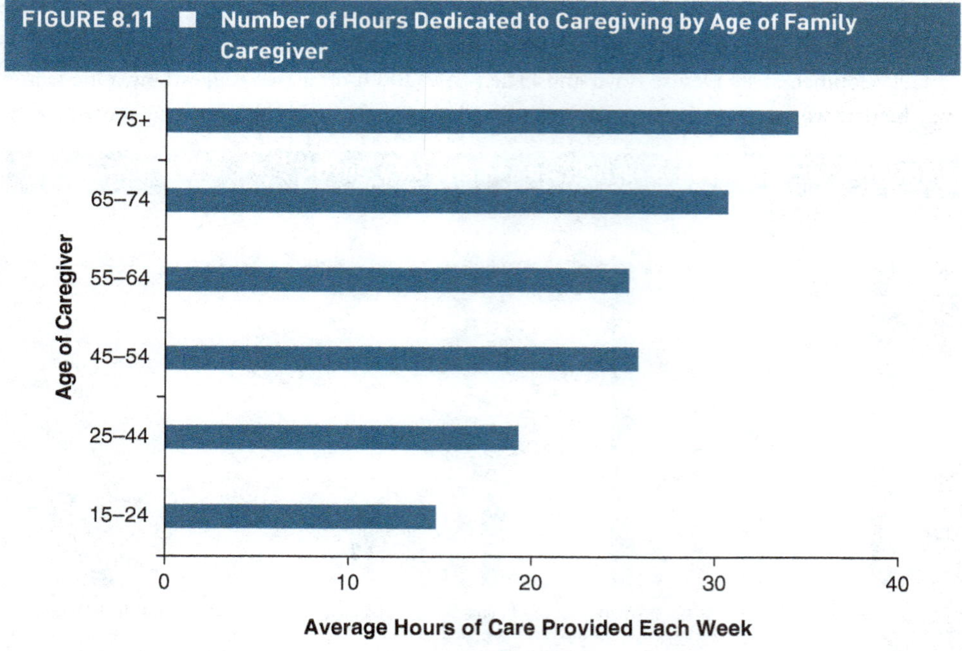

Source: Family Caregiver Alliance (2018).

they feel a greater need to care for them as they age. Another factor may be related to the ways in which women are socialized.

Caregiving responsibilities exert physical and emotional wear and tear on caregivers. This is called **caregiver burden**.

Stressors Associated With Caregiving

Providing care for aging loved ones is a stressful experience, both for the caregiver and for the entire family system. So stressful is caring for an aging loved one that depression rates for caregivers are between 30 and 50 percent (Lemme, 2011). The more stressful aspects of caregiving include the following (NCOA, 2005):

- **Transformation of a cherished relationship:** For many caregivers, it is difficult when an interdependent relationship is transformed to a dependent relationship. When the caregiver is a spouse, the caregiving role becomes the overarching aspect of the marital relationship.
- **Problematic physical behaviors:** Because the caregiver is responsible for helping a loved one with dressing, bathing, toileting, and communicating, many caregivers feel a great deal of stress from these perpetual responsibilities.
- **Cognitive impairments:** When caregivers are taking care of a cognitively impaired spouse or parent, such as those with dementia or Alzheimer's disease, emotional distress is felt greatly by both patient and caregiver.

A number of stressors and rewards are commonly reported by adult child caregivers. Psychologist Mary Ann Parris Stephens and several colleagues undertook numerous studies to determine the types of stressors caregivers experience when caring for a loved one (among many others, Stephens et al., 1997, 2001; Stephens & Franks, 1999).

The stressors include the following:

- Receiving complaints and criticisms from parents
- Uncooperative or demanding parents
- Agitated parents
- Forgetful or unresponsive parents
- Helping with personal care needs
- Managing a parent's financial or legal affairs
- Receiving little help from family or friends

Although caregiving is often difficult and demanding, it also provides many rewards. Stephens's multiple research studies show many rewards:

- Knowing the parent is well cared for
- Spending quality time with a parent
- Enjoying the parent's affection and appreciation
- Seeing a parent derive pleasure from small things
- Seeing a parent calm and content
- Experiencing a closer relationship with a parent

The stressors are not isolated to individual caregivers, however. As we have discussed throughout this text, any life event—anticipated or not—produces ripple effects that reverberate throughout the entire family system. When a parent or family member becomes a caregiver for a spouse or elderly parent, not only does it cause stress and strain on the caregiver but these also radiate throughout the entire family system and, in turn, affect the family's balance. This stress causes increased family tensions, reduced time families have to spend together, role conflict and role strain, changes in individual and family lifestyles, and financial strain (Lemme, 2011). And according to Lemme, the tensions created by family caregiving can exacerbate previously existing strengths or weaknesses in the family system.

Today, a significant number of middle-aged adults are pulled in two directions as they provide care for their children and their elderly parents. While there are a number of stressors associated with being a part of the sandwich generation, can you think of possible benefits or rewards?

Source: Gordon Chibroski/Portland Press Herald via Getty Images.

The Sandwich Generation

Being in the middle of two generations—parenting adolescents or younger children while at the same time caring for aging parents—is known as the **sandwich generation**, and it presents many challenges to middle-aged adults, as the opening story of this chapter illustrates for us.

As Boyd and Bee (2009) observe, being squeezed between two generations is perhaps one of the greatest distinguishing features of families today compared with the family decades ago. Note the authors:

> In middle adulthood ... the family role involves not only giving assistance in both directions in the generational chain but also shouldering the primary responsibility for maintaining affectional bonds. These responsibilities produce what is sometimes called the midlife "squeeze," and those being squeezed form the sandwich generation. (p. 433)

When the tables turn and middle-aged adults begin to parent their parents, they are suddenly taking on conflicting roles. In negotiating these competing roles, many of these adults experience losses associated with providing care to their aging parent. Understanding these losses are key in understanding and coping with the feelings associated with parenting parents (Conway & Conway, 2000).

Parents' losses and needs: As parents age and lose their independence, their children notice other gradual losses along the way. In addition to losing their financial stability, for example, aging parents also lose what was once an important social network, an important source of identity. As their aging friends begin to die, their social identity is further eroded. With the loss of their social network, losses associated with physical decline become that much more pronounced. With their vision, hearing, mobility, memory, strength, and independence in jeopardy, many older adults feel that they will lose their usefulness and their worth. Therefore, it is essential that aging parents are shown that they have continued dignity, and that they are still valued and useful to society. Older parents may also need to have their business needs met, such as helping them pay bills and care for their property. While caring for the parents, adult children also have needs and experience losses, too.

Adult children's losses and needs: The caregiver—the adult child—experiences losses, too. As we have discussed, middle-aged adults lose their time and freedom and take on a number of additional stressors that may affect their own personal health and intimate relationships. As they devote increasing amounts of time to their parents' needs, adult children have less time to spend with their own spouses and children, or to furthering their careers. By and large, parents have been backups throughout life, providing for their children's every need. Thus, when they age, "not only are they weakening physically and shrinking physically in size, [they also] shrink in their capacity to help" (Conway & Conway, 2000). As we observe the gradual deterioration and decline in our parents, we realize (often quite suddenly, as in my experience) that our parents are mortal—and that death is an eventuality.

It is important to understand, then, that when adult children assume the role of caregiver for their aging parents, new needs and family challenges emerge (Conway & Conway, 2000), Being the "squeeze" generation often means that in the process of meeting the needs of two generations, the adult children's personal needs are squeezed out and forgotten. Consequently, it is important for sandwiched caregivers to nurture their marital and other intimate relationships by making time to spend with one another (Conway & Conway, 2000). It's also imperative that adult-children caregivers guard their own mental, emotional, and physical health. This may include learning coping techniques that help buffer the stress associated with caregiving, and doing things that nourish mental health and the physical body. Finally, middle-aged children caring for their parents need to be realistic. A parent may sometimes require "tough love," just as parenting a child does. It is necessary to balance being rational with sensitivity and compassion.

Managing the dual roles of parenting two generations simultaneously brings a variety of conflicting feelings. But if family members understand the legitimate needs of the family members and can make the adaptations and adjustments necessary to meet those needs, then parenting parents while parenting children can be a deeply rich and rewarding life experience.

As adult children grow, their relationships across multiple generations become increasingly important.

Source: iStock.com/EdwinTan.

PARENTING LIFE EDUCATION: REMOVING BARRIERS AND ASSISTING IN TRANSITIONS

Throughout our study, one central parenting theme continues to profoundly resonate: Regardless the age of children or the stage of parenting, *warm, supportive, sensitive, responsive, communicative, connected parenting*—whether we're parenting babies and toddlers, school age children, adolescents, or young adults (and perhaps, our elderly parents)—*is vitally important to the health and well-being of family members.*

As adults grow older through mid- and later adulthood, their interpersonal relationships across generations become even more important because these relationships provide the foundation for intimacy throughout the aging processes. During the middle years of the Family Life Cycle, parents and children begin to renegotiate their relationship, and parents begin to reflect on their success or failure as parents. These reflections greatly affect the parents' purpose in life, self-acceptance, and thus their well-being.

Inevitably, as the opening vignette of this chapter portrays, a profound shift occurs between the parent–adult child relationship, when the child assumes the caregiving role for the aging parents. And, while grandparenting experiences are, by and large, immensely rewarding and enjoyable, this life phase commonly coincides with parenting the last children leaving the nest and simultaneously providing care for aging parents. These multiple demands and roles challenge families today.

Based on the knowledge of the physical, emotional, cognitive, social, and unique differences that people in interpersonal relationships can experience, and on the awareness about the ebbs and flows of transitions in the Family Life Cycle, parenting and Family Life Educators, and other family practitioners, are equipped to help those couples and families in later life, and to remove barriers that prevent them from attaining their relationship, parenting, and family goals. Given the increasing numbers of the aging and elderly in the United States population, it is of the utmost importance that empirical studies are dedicated to better understanding life phase, where a dynamic shift takes place between parents and their children.

9 PARENTING IN SINGLE-PARENT FAMILIES AND STEPFAMILIES

LEARNING OBJECTIVES

9.1 Describe the transitions to postdivorce experienced by men and women.

9.2 Assess the multiple effects of divorce on children and adults.

9.3 Discuss the challenges single parents face following divorce.

9.4 Summarize the transitions to repartnering and stepfamily living experienced by children and adults.

As playing cards scatter on the floor, divorce often creates chaos and "scattered," disorganized lives and relationships. *Source:* iStock.com/HernanCaputo.

I fell for it every time when I was younger. Every time my brothers asked, "Do you wanna play 52-pick-up?", I zealously jumped at the chance to "play cards" with them. I felt grown up and proud that I was included in their card game. It wasn't until I was five or six that I realized the game of 52-pick-up was only a game for them because they had a lot of fun watching me pick up 52 cards that were scattered all over the floor!

When my parents divorced, and then when each of them remarried, a recurring thought I had was, "This is just like 52-pick-up." Our lives were a mess of scattered pieces, flipped upside down. Just like the cards in the game, our lives were disorganized and thrown all over the place. And someone had to pick them up and reorganize them again. It took time, but we all did eventually get all the pieces picked up, and got everything back in order—not in the same order, a different order. But it works for us.

When parents go through a divorce, the entire family system is thrown into turmoil, with each family member feeling the disturbance in different ways. For those who are divorcing, the ramifications weigh heavily as family life undergoes reconstruction. The transitions associated with divorce include (Ahrons, 1994; Duck, 1982):

1. *The decision* to terminate the marriage.
2. *The announcement* to children, family, and friends that the relationship is beyond repair and will be ending.
3. *The separation*, whether orderly or disorderly, ultimately results in a period of time marked by multiple disruptions in the "normal" way of family living.
4. *The formal divorce* is a period of time during which grueling decisions relating to the division of property, spousal support, child support, and child custody must be made.

The events leading up to the family court's decree finalizing the divorce involve changes in all aspects of family life. Not only do spouses lose their marriage, they also are at risk of losing important networks of social support (McPherson et al., 2006) and experience lower psychological and emotional well-being; there are also declines in physical well-being (Sbarra, 2015). Decades of empirical study has shown us that divorce is deeply experienced as profound stress and family crisis, for both parents and children alike.

Beyond the challenges, demands, and stressors associated with divorce, there is a final transition that must be traversed—the *aftermath* of divorce. It is during this transition that families reestablish their identities. Well after the decision to divorce is made public to family and friends, well after the separation takes place, and well after the legal divorce is finalized, the reconstruction continues. Just as there is no universal pathway to uncoupling, there is no universal pathway to rebuilding following divorce. In this chapter, we discuss the transitions and the ways in which families rebuild their new lives. Different families' structures bring them certain challenges, which we explore in the context of binuclear families, single-parent families, and remarriage and stepfamilies.

THE AFTERMATH OF DIVORCE: TRANSITIONS

Just as the opening student comments illustrate, divorce ultimately results in a complex mix-up of existing family relationships. The transition of status from married to divorced often leads to upheaval and disorganization within the family system. To cope with these changes, families must take on the central task associated with the aftermath of divorce—the reorganization of the family. This requires reconstructing the single nuclear family into a *binuclear family*, a process that creates two family systems from one family of origin.

The experiences associated with divorce are so disrupting to families that divorce is ranked as one of the most stressful life events a family can encounter. The aftermath of divorce must be navigated well so that families can successfully rebuild themselves.

Source: iStock.com/PeopleImages.

The Binuclear Family

The term **binuclear family** refers to the separate, distinct households that form after marital separation or divorce. This dramatic change in family life reverberates throughout the entire family system, and this turn of events often brings the entire family to new levels of stress and crisis. The two subsystems that have been formed—the maternal and the paternal—are now the child's family of origin. This restructuring from one central family into two accounts for much of the upheaval and confusion associated with divorce.

Constance Ahrons is a therapist and an internationally recognized lecturer and top professional in the area of divorce. Based on their landmark research, she and her colleague, therapist Roy Rodgers (1987), believe that the major goal of family reorganization centers on establishing healthy patterns of relating within *all* areas of family life. This transformation involves replacing old patterns of interrelating with new patterns and replacing existing family boundaries with new ones. *Over time, these changes help to redefine the family into a binuclear family.* As the former spouses navigate this rocky transition, they must find a way to establish their independence while continuing to fulfill their obligations to their children, their families, their friends, and their careers (Ahrons & Rodgers, 1987). According to anthropologist Paul Bohannan (1971), the co-parental divorce is the most painful, difficult, and complex aspect of the divorce. To better understand co-parenting in the aftermath of divorce, it helps to understand former spouse relationships.

Former Spouse Relationships

Despite the frequency of divorce in today's families, the ongoing relationship between divorced partners is often marked by bitterness, anger, hurt, and hostility. Former spouse relationships are especially important to consider because the relationship between ex-spouses lays the groundwork and sets the emotional climate for the newly defined binuclear family (Ahrons & Rodgers, 1987). Research characterizes five former spouse relationship styles (Ahrons & Rodgers, 1987; Gold, 1992):

- **Perfect Pals:** These are divorced partners who remain friends after they divorce, and they try to accommodate their ex-partner's needs so that they can better focus on parenting. In most cases, these ex-spouses have joint legal custody of their children.
- **Cooperative Colleagues:** Following divorce, a considerable number of ex-spouses are able to cooperate as parents, but they do not feel that they are friends as do Perfect Pals. Even though they may still have disagreements and differences of opinion regarding childrearing and financial issues, they work diligently to keep the conflicts to a minimum so their children will not experience any additional trauma.
- **Angry Associates:** Anger is an integral part of this type of postdivorce relationship. Not only is the divorce experience marked with long, heated battles over property, custody, visitation, and other matters, the fighting continues for many years following the divorce. Effective co-parenting is not a goal of these divorced partners; consequently, children of Angry Associates are all too often caught in the middle of their parents' battles.
- **Fiery Foes:** These divorced couples are incapable of co-parenting. The anger is so intense that they will not allow the other to parent—the other parent represents the enemy. These divorces are marked by significant litigation, with the legal battles continuing for several years following the divorce, and children become pawns in their parents' ongoing battles.
- **Dissolved Duos:** After the divorce, these couples break off all contact with one another. In some instances, one partner (typically the man) literally "disappears," and

thus leaves the mother with the entire burden and responsibility of reorganizing and redefining the family.

By any definition, the dissolution of a marriage is a stressful life event. There is no question that **primary divorce stressors**, such as custody arrangements, visitation, and child support, are demanding and that they exert a number of strains on the entire family. **Secondary divorce stressors** are those things that occur following the divorce. In essence, secondary stressors are the "fallout" associated with divorce. For example, hundreds of studies have revealed that divorced individuals experience more depression, are less happy, and are at greater risks for health problems than married individuals are (for a complete review, see Stephenson & DeLongis, 2018). But are there differences between how women and men experience divorce? Is there such a thing as his-and-her divorces?

Divorced Moms

Divorced women—particularly those who have children—face a number of negative, life-altering experiences following divorce (for a detailed review, see Leopold, 2018):

- Health declines (Shor et al., 2012)
- Taking on bad health and lifestyle habits (Umberson, 1992)
- Increased mortality (Bernsten & Kravdal, 2012; Sbarra et al., 2011)
- Greater decline in satisfaction with family life (Leopold & Kalmijn, 2016)
- Greater feelings of loneliness (Dykstra & Fokkema, 2007)
- Social isolation (Dykstra & Fokkema, 2007)

In addition, they must contend with role overload when they assume the roles of both mother and father to their children. These financial limitations directly influence things such as housing, food, clothing, transportation, medical care, child care, and the opportunities for recreational and/or leisure activities (Lynch & Kaplan, 2000).

Such difficulties not only have immediate negative impacts on women and their children, but they may also have cumulative impacts on the single mother. First, the ongoing stressful conditions associated with divorce exert negative health effects on a person, causing such things as a lowered ability to fight infections and an increased risk to cancer (Wickrama et al., 2006). Second, the stressors and strains associated with divorce also affect emotional health, and oftentimes mothers experience increased levels of depression, anxiety, stress, self-doubt, and pessimism about the future. For example, after a divorce, mothers tend to stay angrier longer and are less likely to forgive than fathers (Bonach et al., 2005; Hetherington & Kelly, 2002). Furthermore, the adverse social conditions associated with divorced single motherhood expose mothers to disadvantaged social positions that include such things as long work weeks and single-handed parenting and child care—that mothers are often solely responsible for their children's well-being is especially difficult for divorced moms (Braver et al., 2006; Wickrama et al., 2006).

In addition to these findings, research reveals another disturbing finding: The demands of single motherhood following divorce are so great that it appears to substantially increase the probability of alcohol abuse in mothers of young children (Williams & Dunne-Bryant, 2006). In a study of nearly 5,000 postdivorce women, the investigators found that among parents of preschool children, women reported greater consumption of alcohol than men did. The researchers attach some caution to these findings because they did not assess the mothers' and fathers' *predivorce* levels of alcohol use. However, they speculate that an increase in mothers' drinking may be the result of social drinking (such as attending more clubs or bars following their divorces) or the result of a decline in social support; feeling alone, the women turn to alcohol. Because of the ramification of these findings for children's well-being, family and social scientists need to explore whether mothers are at greater risk of abusing alcohol following divorce.

Divorced Dads

While mothers' difficulties following divorce are commonly due to financial worries and single-handed parenting, divorced dads' greatest stressors are associated with the decreased contact they have with their children (Braver et al., 2006). A number of studies show that fathers are more depressed, stressed, and disheartened than mothers after divorce because of their inability to be with their children, and because they miss their children so much (Baum, 2006; Bokker et al., 2005; Hallman et al., 2007; Stone, 2007). Often, the father doesn't have control over how often he sees his children because frequent contact with the children may be impeded or altogether prohibited by his former wife who continues to carry hostile, angry, or bitter feelings toward her ex-husband. For example, about one-third of divorced mothers move the kids 400 to 500 miles away from their fathers within the first two years following divorce; this drastically reduces the amount of time fathers can spend with their children (Bailey & Zvonkovic, 2003; Kelly, 2007). Other research also suggests that custodial moms discourage children's contact with their fathers by denying access to the children, by engaging in conflicts or confrontations at the time of picking up the children, and by cutting into the time fathers have with their kids by not having them ready when the father arrives to pick them up (Lehr & MacMillan, 2001; Leite & McKenry, 2002). Many times, fathers will reduce or greatly avoid contact with their children in an effort to keep away from the ongoing conflict with their former wives (Hetherington & Kelly, 2002). In addition, some mothers act as *gatekeepers* of their children, but too frequently, mothers not only guard the gate—they lock it. A number of studies show that many mothers acknowledge that they deny visitation, make it difficult for fathers to see their children, and that they do not intend to share parenting with the father (Cookston et al., 2007; Criddle & Scott, 2005; Henley & Pasley, 2006; Markham et al., 2007).

Children's involvement with their fathers following divorce is important to their development. Studies show that children who experience a warm postdivorce relationship with their fathers have higher self-esteem, fewer behavioral problems, and better social, academic, and cognitive skills (Anderson, 2014; Hetherington, 1991). This appears to be especially true for African American children (McLanahan & Sandefur, 1994). Fathers' involvement in the lives of their children matters because children without fathers are more likely to drop out of high school, become dependent on alcohol or other substances, become delinquent, run away from home, end up in prison, or complete suicide (Anderson, 2014; Finley, 2003; Parke & Brott, 1999).

The greatest stressor divorced fathers face is the lack of contact with their children. This decreased involvement with children often leads to fathers taking on the role of friend, rather than parent, when they are with their children.

Source: iStock.com/AleksandarNakic.

Unfortunately, however, divorce often brings with it significant changes in the ways in which fathers parent, particularly the noncustodial father. For example, postdivorce noncustodial fathers are more likely to be permissive in their parenting and take on a recreational, companion role rather than the role of disciplinarian (Furstenberg & Cherlin, 1991). This phenomenon of fathers taking on the "friend" role following divorce is so common that some have labeled noncustodial fathers as "Disneyland Dads." While these fathers are happy to entertain their children, fathers who do not have custody tend to be less sensitive to their children's emotional needs and are less supportive of them in times of crisis and stress (Stewart, 1999). Other research findings suggest that children have a more difficult time trusting their father following divorce, than they do their mothers (King, 2002), and adolescents rate their fathers as less caring postdivorce (Dunlop et al., 2001).

This inability to effectively parent may, in turn, contribute to the amount of contact a father seeks to have with his children following divorce. For instance, some research suggests that many newly divorced dads feel overwhelmed with their new parenting role because their experiences with their children before divorce were most often limited to day-to-day tasks and responsibilities (Pleck, 1997). Because of this lack of parenting skills, many fathers take on the "friend" role. Others may completely withdraw from their children rather than risk being inadequate.

Each year, over 1 million children experience the divorce of their parents (U.S. Census Bureau, 2019). Understandably, over the past several decades, much attention has been given to the effects of divorce on children, as divorce is one of the most common stressors experienced by today's children (Anderson, 2014; Haimi & Lerner, 2016; Sbarra, 2015; Stephenson & DeLongis, 2018).

The Psychological Impact of Divorce

In an effort to educate physicians about the effects of divorce on men's and women's psychological health, researcher and physician, Basem Abbas Al Ubaidi (2017), put forth a five-stage model that describes the psychological and emotional stages of divorce. In this model, the author distinguishes between the *initiator* (the spouse who initiates the divorce proceedings) and the *receiver* (the spouse on the receiving end of the partner's intent to dissolve the marriage). Unlike other models that describe the processes of divorce, this model is particularly interesting because it describes how the helping professional, such as a parent educator, can help the couple to prepare early on for their postdivorce relationship (Al Ubaidi, 2017):

Stage 1—Blaming the spouse and disillusionment of one party: The couple places blame on one another for past, present, and future relationship problems. The initiator experiences feelings of dissatisfaction, anger, anxiety, depression, guilt, and negative self-image. The receiver experiences helplessness, lack of control, fear of the unknown, and shock. During this time, the *couple and family therapist's* role or the Family/Parent Life Educator's role is to help foster a sense of control in the divorcing couple and to neutralize the couple's fears. The counselor can also help the couple to prepare themselves and their children for the upcoming physical separation.

Stage Two—Mourning the loss and expressing dissatisfaction: In this stage, both partners experience feelings of grief and experience intense preoccupation with the situation. Each partner also has difficulty concentrating; it's not uncommon to see a deterioration of the parenting role. The counselor or Family/Parent Life Educator can assist the couple by helping them through the grieving process and by redirecting the couple's energy to short-term, necessary tasks.

Stage Three—Anger and resentment: The anger and resentment can stem from past and present "wrongs" that occurred in the marriage, and this is typically the stage in which both partners experience roller-coaster emotions. But it's important for the Family Life Educator to help couples to understand that the anger is stemming from the fears and uncertainty about the future. The receiver typically experiences more fear, anger, and resentment than the initiator does. A therapist or Certified Family Life Educator (CFLE) can help to redirect the anger to constructive tasks, such as improving the couple's communication and long-term problem-solving skills to prepare them for co-parenting postdivorce.

Stage Four—Being single and moving ahead with the divorce: The initiator tries out new experiences of independency and singlehood. It is during this time that emotional distance between the spouses is the greatest. The helping professional's role in this stage is to help the divorcing couple focus not on the losses associated with divorce but on the potential that moving forward can bring.

Stage Five—New beginnings: Here, both the initiator and the receiver have accepted the end of the marriage on their own timeframe and begin to settle into the "new normal." The couple negotiates a fair divorce settlement and child custody arrangements. The therapist or CFLE can help couples get to this stage by encouraging them to focus on their own emotional health and that of their children, rather than on the problems of the past.

There is no question that divorce is intensely painful for most people. However, it's important to remember that most people cope well with the stressors associated with divorce, and resiliency is the most common response (Sbarra, 2015). In the section that follows, we'll take a closer look at how divorce affects children and adolescents.

HOW DIVORCE AFFECTS CHILDREN AND ADOLESCENTS

A substantive body of research shows that divorce has detrimental impacts on both short- and long-term adjustment in children and adolescents. As one researcher notes, "Divorce [diminishes] a child's future competence in all areas of life, including family relationships, education, emotional well-being, and future earning power" (Anderson, 2014). Without question, divorce impacts children's mental health and various behaviors (Haimi & Lerner, 2016). In a landmark work in 1991, two researchers examined the results of 92 studies (involving 13,000 children of divorce); the overwhelming results indicated that children of divorce are "less well" than children who had not experienced the divorce of their parents. In general, it was found that children were affected in these ways (for a complete review, see Haimi & Lerner, 2016):

- More difficulties in school
- More behavioral problems
- More negative self-concept
- More social problems with their peers
- More difficulties getting along with their parents

With 67 percent of second marriages ending in divorce, and nearly three-fourths of third marriages ending in divorce (U.S. Census Bureau, 2019), is there a cumulative effect of divorce on children? Table 9.1 shows us the factors that may contribute to children's postdivorce outcomes.

TABLE 9.1 ■ How Are Children Affected?

Loss of parent(s)	Divorce brings the loss of a parent, and with this loss brings emotional, physical, and financial losses.
Economic loss	Single-parent families, particularly mothers, often experience near-poverty or poverty levels of financial constraints.
Emotional security loss	Divorced mothers and fathers are less emotionally available to their children. Children also experience the loss of grandparent relationships.
Lower coping	Parents experience a reduction in their abilities to cope because of the many new demands.
Parent's lack of skills and knowledge	The competence of the parents regarding postdivorce living and parents has a significant impact on children's outcomes.
Parental conflict	The level of conflict to which children are exposed has a tremendous impact on the well-being of children.

Sources: Anderson (2014) and Haimi and Lerner (2016).

Of course, in some instances, divorce is beneficial to children, such as when there is physical, sexual, or emotional violence, but in most instances, divorce has some negative effects on children (Cartwright, 2006; Haimi & Lerner, 2016; Hetherington, 2003; Kelly & Emery, 2003; Wallerstein & Lewis, 2004). Because divorce is a social norm in our culture, how do children respond today to the divorce of their parents?

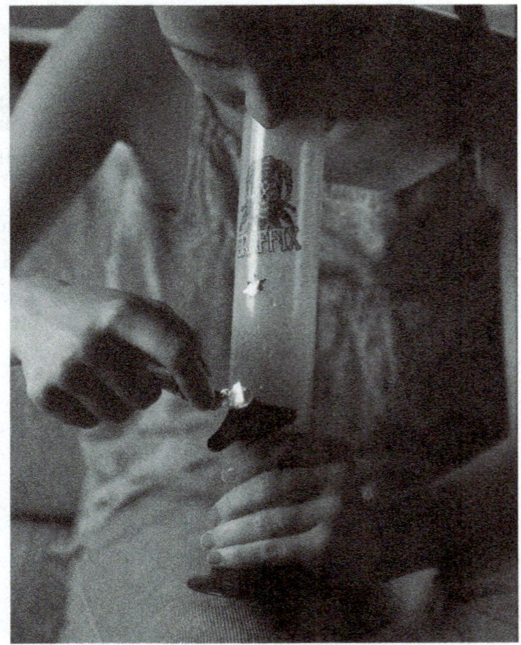

Children who are struggling with the breakup of their parents' marriage may exhibit external behaviors, such as rebellion, smoking or drinking, and skipping school. These behaviors are referred to as *acting out*.

Source: Gary Friedman/Los Angeles Times via Getty Images.

The Negative Effects of Divorce

An abundance of empirical research concludes that children who experience their parents' divorce are at increased risk for certain difficulties. Postdivorce effects on children and adolescents are broken down into three areas: acting out, emotional problems, and problems in school (Shaw & Ingoldsby, 1999). Children **externalize difficulties** through their behavior when they grapple with the inner turmoil, confusion, anger, and hurt they feel in the aftermath of their parents' divorce. Commonly known as **acting out**, children and adolescents externalize their feelings about the divorce, typically through aggressive misbehaviors, noncompliance, disobedience, delinquency, increased absences from school, and increased aggressiveness (Amato, 2010; Fincham, 2002; Hetherington & Kelly, 2002; Stanley & Fincham, 2002). Children of divorce are also more likely to become teenage parents and leave home earlier (Hetherington, 2003). It is not surprising that boys exhibit externalizing behaviors more frequently than girls. This may be due to boys' increased vulnerability to stressor experiences in general. This also explains why boys experience greater postdivorce adjustment difficulties than girls do (Fincham, 2002).

Internalizing difficulties results in emotional problems such as worry, feelings of unhappiness, anxiety, depression, distress, guilt, and poor self-concept. When compared with children whose parents' marriages are intact, children of divorced families have been shown to have a lower concept of self, as well as a lower sense of well-being, and they also have less problem-solving skills (Gohm et al., 1998; Hetherington, 2003; Parish & Wigle, 1985). Additionally, children of divorced parents report lower levels of intimacy with parents and friends and experience interpersonal relationship problems, including difficulty in trusting others (Fincham, 2002; Hetherington, 2003; King, 2002; Stanley & Fincham, 2002). The correlation between divorce and internalizing problems is especially high for girls (Fincham, 2002; Furstenberg & Allison, 1989; Stanley & Fincham, 2002).

In general, children who experience their parents' separation or divorce have more difficulties in the classroom and performing academically than children who have not had similar experiences (Carlson, 1995). In fact, children from established households headed by one parent or children who live in an established stepfamily perform better academically than those children who have recently experienced their parents' divorce.

Why is this so? To a large extent, the reasons children whose parents are divorcing demonstrate poor academic performance are intrinsically tied to the internalization problems encountered by children of divorced families. The emotional aspects of divorce, such as anxiety, depression, guilt, and possibly aggression, affect the children's ability to concentrate in school, negatively affecting their ability to meet scholastic expectations (Dacey & Travers, 2002). This emotional toll may also affect children's ability to interact socially with teachers and peers.

Shaw and Ingoldsby (1999) point to a body of research that speaks to the fact that children of divorced families often experience a subsequently lower socioeconomic status, which has consistently been linked to poor school achievement. This tends to be the case especially among those children who reside in single-parent families that have little interaction with the other parent. Although some children experience great resilience after family dissolution, a significantly large number of children are not as fortunate.

Children's and Adolescents' Adaptation

In terms of those aspects that determine how children and adolescents adjust to family reorganization and redefinition, empirical evidence strongly suggests that it is not the divorce *per se* that ultimately influences postdivorce adaptation; rather, there appear to be mediating family process variables that account for children's responses to divorce. Shaw and Ingoldsby (1999) outline the interrelated family factors that affect children's and adolescents' long-term adjustment to divorce.

Separation From an Attachment Figure

Recall from Chapter 5 that emotional attachment between a child and a caregiver is critical to a child's development. Central to the concept of attachment is the idea that as a result of this initial attachment, children develop a sense of security and trust, allowing for optimal development. When a child experiences the loss of a primary attachment figure, such as in the case of divorce, it may trigger difficulties in interpersonal relationships, including friendships and love relationships (Hannum & Dvorak, 2004; Hinderlie & Kenny, 2002; McIntyre et al., 2003). Research has shown us the common reactions children have to divorce, by age group (Broadwell, 2019):

- **Infants:** Infants may react to their parents' distress by losing their appetites, changing their sleep patterns, or exhibiting changes in other routines, such as being fussy during play time. Parents should try to maintain a daily routine and relate physically and emotionally to the infant.
- **Toddlers:** Toddlers may react to the absence of the parent by crying more and becoming clingy. They may have trouble eating and sleeping, and they may regress to behaviors they had as infants, such as thumb sucking or needing diapers. Parents should reassure their toddler that they will always love her or him. Regular contact with both parents is essential.
- **Preschoolers:** Preschoolers are often called the "forgotten mourners." They know something is wrong and they grieve the loss of the absent parent, but they do not know how to put their feelings into words. They often blame themselves for their parents' breakup. Parents should reassure them that the children did nothing to cause the divorce, and that they will always be loved. Regular contact with both parents is essential.
- **School-aged:** Children at this age understand that their parents don't love each other and that they can't live together. Children may fantasize about ways to reunite their parents. They feel a tremendous sense of loss and rejection, and they worry a lot about the future, about who will care for them and what will happen if their remaining parent dies. They may have physical symptoms such as headaches and stomach aches, and they may have problems sleeping. They may show signs of depression, such as withdrawing from friends and activities. Parents need to be good listeners and reassure

children that the divorce is not the children's fault. They need to have predictable contact with the absent parent.

- **Preteens and Adolescents:** Although children of this age understand the permanence of divorce, they don't like it, and they don't readily accept it. It is not uncommon for children of this age to act out and become rebellious. Parents need to talk about the adolescent's feelings and concerns, not about the problems the parents are having with their ex-spouses. Parents need to make sure the child's responsibilities are age-appropriate and not so demanding that they have to grow up too soon.

Haimi and Lerner (2016) recognize that it is difficult to determine conclusively whether these relationship difficulties are due to the separation from the parent, or whether the problems are due to the multifaceted, multidimensional family processes associated with divorce and the resulting family reorganization.

When a child loses routine contact with a primary attachment figure, it may cause negative impacts on their security and trust with others. Toddlers may react by becoming more and more clingy, and they may regress in toilet training.

Source: iStock.com/SolStock.

Children's and Adolescents' Reactions to Parents Dating

Dating following divorce is common. For example, in a study of 1,700 divorced women in the United States, the study found that 78 percent of the women surveyed indicated that they started thinking about dating before their divorces were finalized, and 65 percent began dating within the first year following divorce (Worthy, 2019). In a study of 1,220 divorced individuals, the researcher discovered that men repartner sooner than do women; within three to five years postdivorce, 40 percent of men are with another partner (Leopold, 2018). According to family scientists, there are certain age-specific reactions that children have to their divorced parents dating (Anderson-Burdine & Armstrong, 2014):

Early Childhood: Common fears include the safety of the mother, whether she will return from the date, that the dating partner will be scary, and that the parents will never get back together.

Middle Childhood: Children see themselves as a part of their parent ("we" and "us"), so they see themselves as dating the partner, as well; they may view the parent's dating partner in a personally beneficial or nonbeneficial way (i.e., "What material things can the partner give to me? What fun things will the partner let me do?").

Adolescents: Teens become easily annoyed at their parents; the parent's dating relationship can reignite the teen's relationship struggles. The parenting role boundaries are often altered due to the new dating activities.

The researchers suggest that when parents begin dating again postdivorce, they should be honest with their children about what their intentions are with the dating partner; parents should also accept that the child will be affected, at least initially, by the dating relationship. The researchers also note that it's important for the parent to introduce the topic of dating again before introducing the dating partner to the children/teens. Most importantly, it is imperative that a parent does not place the emotional burden of dating on the child or put the child in the role of the supporter.

The Passage of Time

Is it true that time heals all wounds? The effects of **temporal influences**, such as the passage of time and the child's age at the time of divorce, may play a role in children's long-term adjustment to their parents' divorce, although there is conflicting evidence. For example, Shaw and Ingoldsby (1999) observe, "As time passes, many of the stressors associated with divorce are lessened in intensity as adults and children adapt to new living situations" (p. 350). Other research offers conflicting findings.

Psychologist Judith Wallerstein devoted more than two decades to studying the effects of divorce on children. In her landmark longitudinal study in the early 1970s of 131 children from dissolved families, she found that one-half to two-thirds of the children in her study carried with them feelings of vulnerability and fear and noted that for children of divorce, growing up was harder every step of the way than it was for children whose parents did not divorce. In *The Unexpected Legacy of Divorce*, Wallerstein, Lewis, and Blakeslee (2000) discuss a research finding that materialized some 30 years after her research had begun—that children carried with them these same feelings of vulnerability and fear well into adulthood. Notes Wallerstein, "When children of divorce become adults, they are badly frightened that their relationships will fail, just like the most important relationship in their parents' lives failed. Their decisions about whether or not to marry are shadowed by the experience of growing up in a home where their parents could not hold it together" (p. 8).

Another body of research appears to confirm Wallerstein's findings. Using data gathered from life story interviews of 40 young adults, ages 19 to 29, the researcher discovered that although a majority of the study participants were positive about their parents' divorces, the majority also considered that they were currently experiencing negative effects related to their parents' separations (Cartwright, 2006). One study participant discussed her hesitancy to enter relationships:

> I've never really had any boyfriend from 14 onwards.... I don't [know] whether that's a reflection of me and not wanting to because of my parents breaking up. I kind of almost think, I've almost got a bad way of thinking. Like, I don't want to start something if I know it's going to be a waste of time, where it's not going to ever go anywhere, cuz then it's wasting my time, I kind of don't ever open up to anyone, so I think [their divorce] affected me. (p. 132)

Is Divorce Hazardous to a Person's Health?

From tobacco to sugar, the federal government has made it standard practice to warn us of impending danger. But what if you were to learn that there was something as hazardous to your health as a pack-a-day Marlboro habit? Would you consider this important information?

We have discussed the emotional impact, financial issues, and more—but what about physical health? What kind of impact does uncoupling have on our bodies? According to research (Dilulio, 1997):

- Becoming single shortens a person's lifespan by seven years.
- Married men and women are half as likely as divorced men to die prematurely from heart disease.
- Divorced or separated adults are 4.5 times more likely to become addicted to alcohol than are those who are married.
- The risk of becoming seriously ill is 12 times greater for divorced and separated adults than it is for married adults.

- People going through a divorce or separation are at double the risk for being involved in an accident.

Interestingly, results such as these cross all racial and ethnic lines. Couples in Europe and Asia share similar statistics. Things like economic stability and emotional support, found commonly in marriages, allow for things such as better diet, safer living environments, fewer hours spent at work, and more hours spent on leisure activities.

People have only so much stress reserve, and indeed, experiencing a divorce is one of the greatest stressors an individual and a family can endure. To help minimize stress, therapists suggest:

- Set realistic goals and priorities—family reorganization takes time.
- Talk about your feelings with someone you trust, and cry when you need to.
- Eliminate blame, criticism, "should have," "could have," and "would have" from your vocabulary—none of these changes the situation.
- Exercise and get plenty of rest.
- Let others help.

Studies have shown that children who experience close relationships with their parents following the divorce are provided a cushion against the negative side effects of divorce.

Source: iStock.com/georgeclerk.

The Relationship Between the Custodial Parent and the Child

Without question, the greatest change to which children and adolescents need to adapt postdivorce is their relationship with their parents. These changes are so significant that researchers have coined the phrase **diminished parenting** to describe this new relationship that takes place during the first few years following divorce. Today, an estimated 13.6 million custodial parents lived with 22.4 million children under the age of 21—more than one-fourth of all children under the age of 21 in the United States—live with a custodial parent, while the other parent lived somewhere else (Grall, 2018). In 2018, 8 of every 10 custodial parents were mothers (80 percent), and nearly 20 percent were fathers (16 percent). The racial and ethnic differences in custodial and noncustodial parenting are presented in Figure 9.1.

Research has revealed changes in the custodial parent's (most typically the mother) behavior, such as less frequent displays of showing affection, particularly to boys, and less nurturing behavior (Amato, 2010). One body of research shows that the conflict between the custodial parent and the children increases, and the ability to communicate with the children declines (Amato & Rezac, 1994). This study is of particular note because the researchers studied over 12,000 children in all types of single-parent homes. During the first year or so following divorce, many children assume more household responsibilities and often exhibit greater independence. Meanwhile, the custodial parent's parenting becomes more negative and less consistent. Some custodial mothers may become permissive in their parenting style and emotionally dependent on their children. But there are any number of family process variables (such as economic difficulties or support, the mother's emotional state, her extended family and social support) that contribute to disturbances in parenting.

The Relationship Between the Noncustodial Parent and the Child

One of the single greatest adjustments required for family reorganization into a binuclear family is that of incorporating a noncustodial parent into the family system. In the United States, it is

FIGURE 9.1 ■ Percent of Children in Custodial Families, by Race: 2018

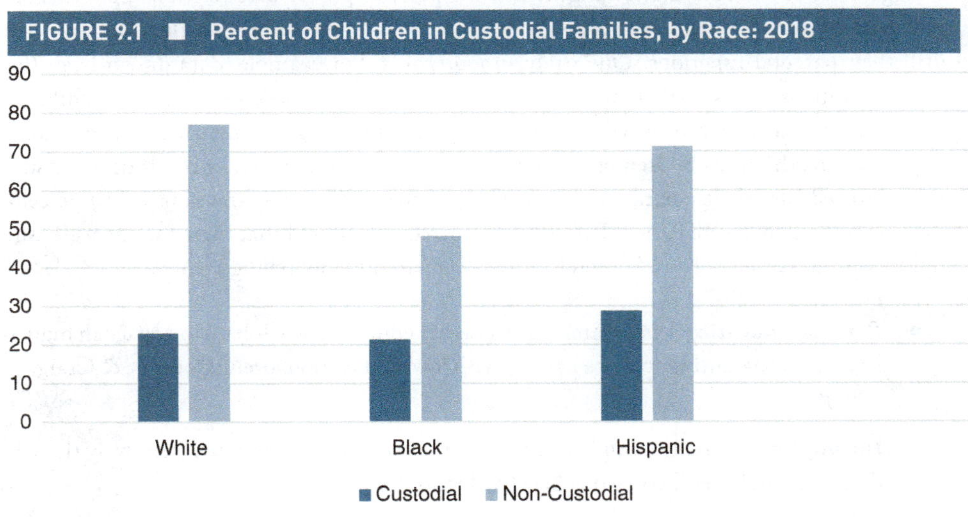

Source: Grall (2018).

more than likely that the nonresident parent is the father (Grall, 2018). The success or failure of this adjustment depends largely on the frequency of visitation the noncustodial parent has with his or her children. One-third of today's children—33 percent—have no contact or visitation with their fathers following divorce, but nearly one-fourth of nonresident fathers see their children at least once a week (U.S. Census Bureau, 2019). For those who do have visitation arrangements, the children spend significantly less time with the nonresidential parent than they did with that parent prior to the divorce. As the length of time increases following the divorce, the amount of time nonresident parents typically spend with their children decreases (Lehr & MacMillan, 2001).

But as with any parent–child relationship, the frequency of contact and the length of visitations are not as important as the quality of the interactions and the relationship between the child and the parent. A strong, intimate relationship with the noncustodial parent, then, bodes well for children's adjustment to a binuclear family, as it appears that good parent–child relationships cushion and shield against the adverse effects of divorce (Davis & Friel, 2001; Institute for Family Studies, 2019; Lehr & MacMillan, 2001; White & Gilbreth, 2001). One study indicated that as children of divorce became adults, 62 percent of those studied noted that their relationships with their fathers improved or stayed the same over the 20 years since their parents' divorce (Ahrons & Tanner, 2003).

Co-parenting in Binuclear Families

It has been said that it is difficult for suffering parents to be effective parents. Divorced parents understandably have many adjustments of their own to make following the dissolution of their marriage, such as adjusting to custody arrangements and binuclear family parenting, financial support, and relocation, but these do not lessen the parents' responsibilities in assuring the needs of their children are met.

Regardless of the custodial arrangements, the parents' postdivorce relationship—such as those detailed in Ahrons and Rodgers's couple relationship types—greatly influences how they fulfill their parental functions. One study supports this. For example, data drawn from the binuclear family study, a study that followed the lives of 98 pairs of spouses and their children for 20 years, revealed that over half of the participants indicated that their parents got along fairly well, now that the children were grown (Ahrons, 2007). Further, one-half of those surveyed reported that their parents were now Cooperative Colleagues, and another 10 percent believed their parents were Perfect Pals. Only 22 percent indicated that their parents were still Angry Associates or Fiery Foes. Several factors affect parenting following divorce:

- **Parents' education level:** Parents with higher education levels lend to engage in higher levels of co-parenting than do parents with lower education levels (Cooksey & Craig, 1998).
- **Income level:** Parents in higher SES brackets tend to co-parent more effectively than do parents in lower income brackets (Arditti, 1999).

- **Duration of the marriage:** Couples who were married longer are more likely to engage in more cooperative postdivorce parenting (Ahrons & Rodgers, 1987).
- **Time elapsed since the divorce:** If other variables, such as higher education levels and higher SES levels are present, divorced couples are more apt to effectively co-parent over time as "wounds begin to heal" (Furstenbcrg & Cherlin, 1991).
- **Remarriage of one or both spouses:** Remarriage often negatively impacts former spouses' ability to co-parent (Ahrons & Rodgers, 1987).
- **Who initiated the divorce:** Most commonly, the spouse who initiates the divorce is the more cooperative co-parent (Duran-Aydingtug, 1995).
- **The legal process of divorce:** If the divorce process involved hostility and conflict or was difficult and protracted, the father tends to be less involved with his children (Madden-Derdich & Arditti, 1999).

While more parents share joint custody of their children following divorce than in past decades, as you saw earlier, significantly more children live with their mothers following divorce than with their fathers (Grall, 2018). This distinction is important because family study researchers have determined that there are considerable differences between mothers and fathers and how they fulfill their parental duties and functions following divorce—for example, the majority of custodial mothers carry out their parenting responsibilities in the same way they parented before they divorced (Baum, 2003). And while some fathers also continue to parent in the same way as before they divorced, other fathers' parental involvement increases, and as we saw earlier, others' involvement decreases.

For the past several decades, social norms dictated that because mothers are the more "nurturing" parent, they should be awarded custody of the children following divorce. Yet because recent scientific studies have revealed that children fare better when both parents are involved in their growing up, legal and social policies have changed to accommodate the needs of the children. Family courts today are more likely than in the past to award joint custody (Emery, 1994).

Living, Loving, and Parenting in Postdivorce Families

Decades of research indicate that, by and large, the picture of divorce for children isn't usually bright or optimistic. Emerging findings, however, show that Americans are finding newer and better ways to "live, love, and parent" in a divorce-saturated society. Hetherington and Kelly (2002) found, after studying 1,400 families, that the multiple processes of divorce can result in healing and ultimate fulfillment. Their research addresses past research findings:

- **Divorce only has two outcomes: Win or lose.** Hetherington and Kelly (2002) maintain that there are a number of different ways that people adjust to divorce. The process of divorce does *not* produce only winners or losers. Each of these patterns of adjusting are not permanent and will change over time.

- **Children always lose out after a divorce.** Divorce is not a rosy experience for children, but *over time* children demonstrate their resiliency to their parents' divorce.
- **The pathways following divorce are fixed and unchanging.** According to the researchers, the effects of divorce are not irrevocable. A negative experience can be offset by later positive experiences.
- **Men are the big winners in divorce.** Although women experience greater economic losses following divorce, overall they do better emotionally following divorce than do men. Even though women frequently fall into poverty following divorce, this trend is changing as women become better educated, and as federal and state agencies become stricter about enforcing child support payments.
- **The absence of a father is the greatest risk to children.** Indeed, fathers matter. But it's not the mere *presence* of a father that makes a difference. The researchers discovered that involved, supportive mothers can counter the adverse effects of a father's absence.

Divorce presents many disruptions in children's and adolescents' lives. Some of these changes require coping and adaptation beyond their years, and clearly put the child at risk for short- and long-term developmental, academic, and interpersonal problems. The interconnected family and environmental variables influencing a youth's adjustment and adaptation to divorce point to the need for effective parenting and co-parenting when establishing a binuclear family. Reorganizing and redefining a family from one nuclear family into a binuclear family is a multifaceted transition that requires tremendous efforts of both parents to assure the best interests of the children are met. Former spouse relationships that promote collaborative, cooperative shared parenting foster positive parent–child relationships that benefit both the parents and the children. The divorce transition still involves many challenges, particularly for single mothers. In the next section, we'll explore the difficulties faced by single mothers.

CHALLENGES FOR SINGLE PARENTS

Households headed by single parents include impoverished, never-married ethnic minority women or teenaged mothers, gay and lesbian parents whose unions are not legally recognized, never-married women who have adopted or borne a child, widows and widowers, and people who find themselves single after a marital breakup (Gottfried & Gottfried, 1994). Additionally, many families instantly became single-parent families when a spouse is called to war, or when a spouse dies in combat.

Regardless of its makeup, each single-parent family has its own unique starting point and its own unique developmental history (Anderson & Sabatelli, 2011). Because mothers with children compose the largest segment of single-parent households, our discussion will center on the issues and challenges faced by single mothers.

As you have learned, family structure is a crucial determinant for the health and well-being of children and adults alike. While the majority of children who are brought up in single-parent homes fare well, there are risks associated with single-parent living. Children from single-parent homes are twice as likely to repeat a grade in school and/or to drop out of high school, and they are at much greater risk of being unemployed (Hetherington, 2003; McLanahan & Sandefur; 1994). And while every family structure is prone to its fair share of problems, single mothers face issues that magnify the stress of raising children. Anderson and Sabatelli (2011) identify the most significant challenges that face single-parent mothers following divorce: changes in financial status, changes in residence, changes in boundaries for children, changes in the emotional environment, and postdivorce dating.

Postdivorce economic hardship is a harsh reality for many women because less than half receive the child support owed them. The *feminization of poverty* is a concept that depicts the increase in poverty in divorced women.

Source: iStock.com/Geber86.

Changes in Household Finances

Another interrelated family factor that affects children's and adolescents' long-term adjustment to divorce is the state of family economics before and after divorce. Economic hardship is a postdivorce reality for many families, particularly for women—less than half (43 percent) receive the full child support they are owed (Grall, 2018). Part of the legal terms of a divorce is determining child support due to the custodial parent. Even if the noncustodial parent (usually the father) faithfully pays child support, however, the amount is rarely sufficient to meet the living expenses of the mother and children. In 2018, for example, 30 percent of single mothers lived below the poverty line, while only 17 percent of solo fathers did; this is in comparison to 8 percent of married couples (Pew Research Center, 2018). The **feminization of poverty** refers to the experience in which women experience poverty rates that are disproportionately high in comparison to men (McLanahan & Kelly, 2006). And, it appears that women suffer more from divorce than men do, especially in disproportionate declines in household income (De Vaus et al., 2015; Leopold, 2018). Further, women are at a greater risk of losing their homes following divorce (Dewilde, 2008).

The economic toll of divorce often translates into still more adjustments for children (Amato, 2010; Grall, 2018). These adjustments may require enduring potentially poorer quality of parenting as the custodial parent must take on more work, and coping with the effects of financial pressures and strains on the family. While some children are more fortunate and are able to remain living in the family home, the financial pressures may mean that they need to make other sacrifices, such as forgoing music lessons and/or sports lessons in order to make ends meet.

When economic hardship afflicts single-parent households, other challenges arise for families already struggling to reorganize and redefine themselves following divorce. Because of the interrelated nature of family living, economic hardship then affects every other aspect of family life, including the challenges newly divorced families face.

Changes in Residence

A common expression in the realm of Family Life Education is that divorce brings with it "new everythings"—a new family structure, a new way of interacting with parents, and perhaps at some point, a new family if one or both parents remarry. In many cases, these transitions include relocating to a new home. Unless the move is within the same neighborhood, a move to a new home introduces other "new everythings," for it also brings new neighborhoods, new peers, new schools, and new teachers.

Divorced single parents often find that because of the radical changes in their finances, they are no longer able to live in their predivorce home (Kelly & Emery, 2003). Quite frequently, in an effort to lessen the strain on the family budget that comes with transitioning to single-parent living, divorced women find that they are forced to sell their homes. Additionally, this transition involves not just an economic rebalancing but also an emotional rebalancing (Anderson & Sabatelli, 2011). When recently divorced single parents then move to a different neighborhood and into a less expensive home, they and their children are faced with the harsh reality of a new beginning that redefines the family system (Kelly & Emery, 2003). Perhaps Trisch, a divorced woman who is selling her home and moving forward, sums it up best:

> Goodbye to the home that I spent endless afternoons and weekends looking for—making sure it met all of the rigid requirements. I'll probably never find another house like that again. It was so much more than a house—it represented an achievement of a goal, a new beginning of the beginning. And now I've lost it all. Goodbye to the home we were making. Goodbye to the tulips planted in the fall but that we never saw together in the spring when it came time for them to bloom. (Fisher & Alberti, 2000, p. 106)

Changes in Boundaries

Central to the challenges of postdivorce parenting is the issue of reworking parenting roles. And as Anderson and Sabatelli (2011) note, even for those parents who are willing, strongly desiring of, and firmly committed to parenting cooperatively, divorce is always accompanied by greater separateness and autonomy, along with a decline in interdependence—and this change in the relationship between parents and children adds to the other everyday, ordinary stresses associated with parenting.

In essence, the reestablishment of parenting roles ensures that what was once shared by both parents is now covered independently by each parent. Some tasks associated with establishing new parental roles following divorce include the following (Graham, 2005):

- Forming new relationships with children that do not include ongoing input, support, and the collaboration from the other parent. Even in the best of circumstances where both parents are actively involved in the children's lives, one parent is still absent from the home.
- Creating a working business relationship with the former spouse that ensures successful completion of childrearing tasks, such as helping children with homework, taking them to after-school activities, or taking them to doctor or dentist appointments.
- Establishing methods of discipline that do not rely on the other parent's input or aid.
- Developing a parenting plan. The parenting plan outlines the rights and responsibilities of each parent and establishes an appropriate working relationship between the parents (for issues regarding the children's health, education, and well-being).
- Communicating clearly and accurately to the other parent those things that are taking place in the child's life. At the forefront of such communication are the child's emotional stability and the protection of the child's best interests. Making these the priority of communication minimizes the children's exposure to ongoing parental conflict and minimizes the temptation to drag the child into the parents' battles.

It is beyond question that the exit of one member from the family system disrupts the balance of the entire system. However, if proper care and attention are given to the reestablishment of parental roles following divorce, over time the family will reestablish itself and find a new, reorganized balance.

Changes in the Emotional Environment

There is no other way to state it: Divorce hurts! Managing the emotional climate of the binuclear family is just as important as managing finances and new parenting roles.

Single mothers' ability to become sole administrator of the home hinges on their ability to manage the emotional climate of their newly defined single-parent homes. In other words, the mother must assume all authority and responsibility, as well as provide love, understanding, and support. While many single mothers rely on their former spouses, day-care providers, or the children's grandparents to assist them, many others decide that if they are the custodial parent, they should have complete authority in whatever decisions are made (Anderson & Sabatelli, 2011; Graham, 2005). This shift in authority allows single mothers to separate from former spouses and gain autonomy. Without this authority, boundaries may not be clear and, all too often, children, former spouses, and/or grandparents may undermine the mother's efforts and render her ineffective—thus ensuring that inconsistent, dysfunctional parenting roles are established.

According to Anderson and Sabatelli (2011), fathers also have difficulties in managing the emotional tasks of the postdivorce family. Divorced fathers tend to struggle with managing the emotional climate of the home because of a frequent inability to maintain a sense of home and family, even if he is the noncustodial parent. Typically, when the father is the nonresident parent, he experiences these feelings of loss and he may feel that he has lost control and influence over his children (Kruk, 2012). Fathers will often experience an even greater sense of loss and powerlessness if there remain high levels of conflict between the father and his former wife, if his ex-spouse limits his visitations to his children (in order to exert control over him or punish him), or if the custodial and visitation agreements are not strictly adhered to (Wallerstein, 1998).

Dating

When women and men experience being single after they divorce, many feel a mix of positive and negative emotions. Some choose to date because they simply do not like being alone. In fact, for some individuals, being single is particularly difficult if they never learned how to live as a single before their marriage, perhaps moving straight from their parents' homes to their marital homes (Fisher & Alberti, 2000). But many may find their newfound status to be liberating—a time to invest in themselves. As one newly divorced man explains:

> I've become aware that living as a single person is an affirmation of strength and self—not an embarrassing admission of failure. I'm more relaxed in the company of others. Postmarital guilt, self-doubts, and questions like "Will I ever love again?" are greatly diminished. I am happy as a single person—something I had not thought possible before. (p. 235)

Most people, however, are not disenchanted with marriage and are not content to remain single following their divorce. Indeed, it is not unusual for many men and women to rush into dating following their marital separation or divorce. For many of these individuals, dating helps them fill the void of their loss with a new, more intense love (Ahrons, 1994). The way men and women handle postmarital romance differs, however. According to Anderson and Sabatelli (2011):

- Postdivorce men initiate dating relationships sooner than do postdivorce women.

- Following divorce, men rely more on their dating partners for intimacy and support than do women.
- Women have stronger, more intimate social support networks than do men and turn to these rather than to a dating partner for intimacy and support.
- Men have greater financial resources to pursue a new partner.
- The demands of single parenting and economic pressures leave women with less energy to pursue a dating relationship.

There are further reasons why newly divorced individuals choose whether or not to date. Some may delay dating to protect themselves from being hurt; others may delay dating in an attempt to gain independence and autonomy; and still others may rush into dating and courtship in an effort to quickly remarry. Beyond not wanting to be "alone," some of these individuals may want to quickly reestablish "normalcy" or find supportive relationships that will help them redefine their identities. While the reasons for dating following divorce are complex and varied, creating new relationships helps restructure an individual's social network in a way that more closely meets the individual's changing needs (Anderson & Sabatelli, 2011).

Not all dating relationships end with another trip down the aisle, but about 64 percent of men and 52 percent of divorced women remarry (Pew Research Center, 2018), and today, nearly four million children in the United States live in a stepparent home (U.S. Census Bureau, 2019). In America, over 40 percent of adults have at least one step relative (U.S. Census Bureau, 2019).

There are a number of transitions associated with repartnering following divorce. Perhaps the greatest difficulty of repartnering is subsequent relationship stability. As one researcher notes, "[Repartnering] can help improve the well-being of adults and children, [but] it appears that the challenges of divorce are rarely overcome completely" (Jensen et al., 2015).

Helping Kids Cope With Divorce

There is no concrete formula or recipe that guarantees that children will come out of divorce unscathed, but there are things that parents can do to help reduce the impact of their decision to end their marriage. Three are a number of ways divorcing parents can ease the impact of divorce on their children; these are described below (Mayo Clinic, 2004).

How to Tell Them

Child psychologists and family therapists recommend that, if possible, spouses should be together when they tell their children about their divorce.

- Parents should reaffirm their love and commitment to their children, and assure them they will always take care of them.
- Parents should assure children that the children are not responsible for the divorce.
- Parents should speak honestly and simply, but they should leave out all of the ugly details.

Keep the Kids Out of the Fight

How ex-spouses act toward each other and toward the children impacts children's adjustment.

- Children should never be forced to side with one parent over the other; they are not pawns or weapons to be used to hurt the other parent.
- Children should never be used as messengers, and parents should never speak badly about the other parent to the children.
- Child support issues should never be talked about in front of children.

Don't Spoil Them

Although it's tempting to spoil children or to lavish them with gifts to help absolve some of the guilt parents feel, child psychologists believe this only makes children feel more insecure.

- Don't relax the household rules or boundaries; these should be similar for both parents.
- Kids and adolescents need stable routines and stable boundaries, even though they will push the limits.

Put the Children First

Angry, hurting, vengeful ex-spouses can make angry, hurting, vengeful parents. Even though it is understandable that ex-spouses want little interaction with each other, parents need to make co-parenting work for the sake of the children. Custody arrangements should center on what the *children* need, not what the parents need or want. Working on parenting goals together, such as meeting monthly to discuss upcoming schedules and plans, enhances children's well-being.

TRANSITIONS TO REPARTNERING

Although remarriages are common today, there remains a stereotypical view that these marriages are not as functional as "traditional" marriages (Ganong & Coleman, 2004). To better understand the transitions associated with forming a new family system following divorce, in the following section, we'll examine the stages of the remarriage experience, remarriage stability, and the many characteristics of stepfamilies today.

Remarriage

Today in the United States, 4 out of 10 new marriages involve remarriage (Pew Research Center, 2018). As you can see in Figure 9.2, 40 percent of all marriages in the United States are remarriages, either for one spouse or for both spouses. The data in Figure 9.3 present for us the percentage of those who remarry, by age group. Overall, whites are more likely to remarry than are other races:

FIGURE 9.2 ■ Percent of New Marriages in the United States, by Type

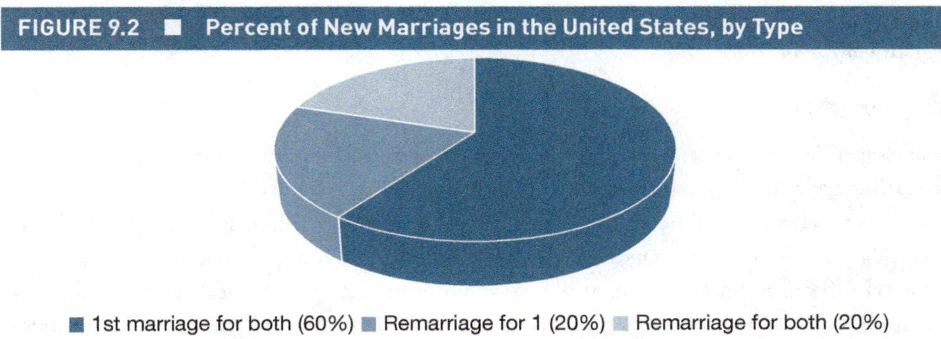

Source: Pew Research Center (2018).

- White: 60 percent
- Hispanic: 51 percent
- Black: 48 percent
- Asian: 46 percent

Transitioning to a new family structure involves a developmental process, just as with any other change encountered throughout the life cycle of the family. As you know, with the dissolution of the nuclear family system because of divorce, two separate family forms emerge, creating a binuclear family. When either one or both of the former spouses choose to remarry, a stepfamily is formed. Like many of the family processes we have discussed throughout this text,

FIGURE 9.3 ■ Percent of Previously Married Individuals Who Remarried, by Age

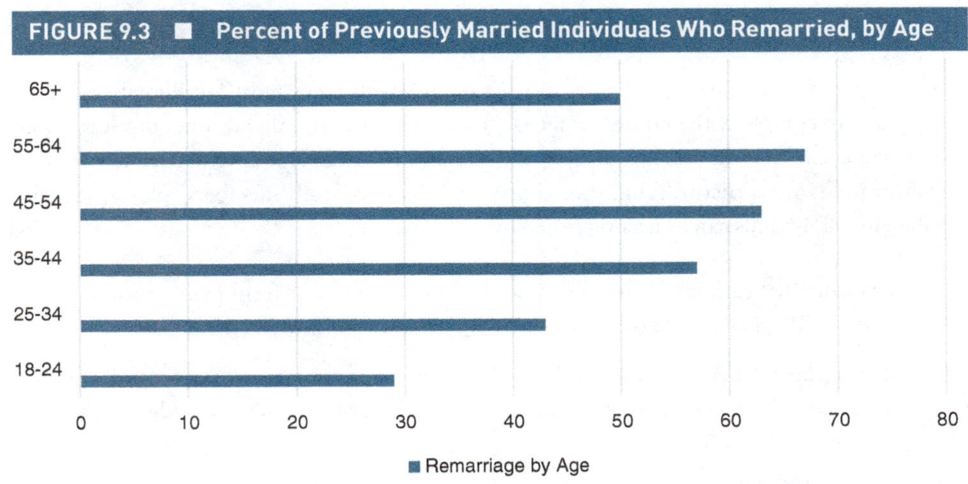

Source: Pew Research Center (2014).

remarriage is also a process of different developmental stages. These stages include *early remarriage* and *late remarriage.*

Early Remarriage

Psychologist Patricia Papernow (1984, 1993) has addressed the patterns commonly seen in the family life cycle development of remarried and stepfamilies. **Remarriage** refers to instances when either one or both of the spouses have been previously married. As its name implies, **early remarriage** refers to the early stages of the new relationship and brings with it not only the developmental difficulties of a traditional marriage, but also carries with it difficulties unique to stepfamilies. When one or both of the married partners bring children from a previous relationship into the new marital relationship, the newly merged family is referred to as a **stepfamily**.

When two families come together, histories, rituals, and family customs must be merged. As noted family scientist and psychologist Hara Marano (2000) explains, "culture clash" is built into any marriage because of the different histories brought to a marriage. This culture clash within a new family occurs because each of us has preferred patterns of interacting along with shared memories and shared histories—*each family of origin has its own shared identity.* When families merge, members from each family of origin may feel that new family members are intruding into their family, and in a very real sense, intruding into their identity. As Papernow points out, however, this is the starting point for every remarried or stepfamily. A lack of shared patterns of interacting and a lack of shared histories are expected and normal at this stage of remarriage. Because newly formed stepfamilies lack shared experiences, the two families interact primarily with their biological parents, siblings, grandparents, and other extended family members during the early remarriage stage (Anderson & Sabatelli, 2011). These interaction patterns may last for up to two to three years after remarriage or the formation of a stepfamily; thus, one of the central developmental tasks of remarriage is to allow time for the newly merged family system to grow and share new experiences together.

Middle Remarriage

During the **middle remarriage** stage of development, which takes most families about three to five years to complete, the family becomes a more cohesive system and functions less along strictly biological lines. In order to successfully transition to this stage of remarried family life, the family needs to restructure family boundaries and identity-family members' roles (Anderson & Sabatelli, 2011). This can be accomplished by

- ensuring that each family member's needs, expectations, and feelings are considered equally. This is achieved through honest communication and shared empathy.
- compromising between "old" and "new" ways of doing things such as homework or celebrating holidays. "Out with the old, in with the new" doesn't apply when it comes to remarried families.
- clarifying family boundaries and expectations with regard to the noncustodial parent, biological relatives, and steprelatives.

If the family makes this successful transition, the family will emerge as not only a more cohesive system with unambiguous boundaries, but also as a family with a shared purpose and a shared family identity (Papernow, 1984).

Late Remarriage

During **late remarriage**—approximately 6 to 10 (or more) years after the remarriage—the family's boundaries and roles are restructured to the point where there is a greater deal of "authenticity" in interactions and shared intimacy within the family system (Anderson & Sabatelli, 2011). If family members are flexible and successful in realigning their boundaries to accommodate the realities of remarried and/or stepfamily living, then closer, warmer, more endearing relationships are likely to form among stepfamily members. This doesn't mean that family living is sunshine and roses all of the time. As with any family, there will be times of conflict, anger, and hurt feelings. There will be times when one family member feels excluded or when another family member feels awkward including a nonbiological family member in decision-making or family rituals. In some remarried families, members may simply agree to accept more distant, less involved relationships with one another (Anderson & Sabatelli, 2011). To be a successful remarried family not only requires a realization from the married partners that "there's a history of something that came before" (Marano, 2000), it also requires the belief that trust and understanding will grow as families share experiences over time.

Remarriage Stability

In the case of remarriage, practice does not make perfect. In comparison to first marriages, remarriages have, for several decades, consistently demonstrated higher rates of divorce (for a complete review of the literature, see Jensen et al., 2015). **Relationship stability** is defined by clinical social worker Todd Jensen (University of North Carolina Chapel Hill) as "the perceptions and behaviors associated with the dissolution of a marriage or committed relationship" (Jensen et al., 2015). In other words, these factors are indicators of a couple's proneness to divorce. And today, one indicator of divorce proneness is remarriage. Indeed, marital instability is more marked among remarried couples than it is in one-marriage couples (Amato, 2010; Sweeney, 2010). Why is the future of remarriage so grim?

There are several reasons. For example, as we just discussed, when couples embark on a second marriage, they often do not have a firm understanding of their identity as a stepfamily, or what it means to merge two families (Gerlach, 2005). Many remarrying partners enter into a second marriage with unrealistic expectations and without a sound understanding of the complexities of stepfamily life. As a result, these couples lack the necessary coping skills to traverse the many transitions as they rebuild their lives together. According to Peter Gerlach (2005), a social worker and board member of the Stepfamily Association of America, remarried families also face greater differences than once-married families in the emotional, legal, social, and financial environments of their families. Gerlach explains that there are as many as 60 significant ways a second marriage differs from a first-marriage environment.

Other research suggests that instability in subsequent marriages is the result of a breakdown in the commitment, cohesion, and communication in first marriages (Ihinger-Tallman

& Pasley, 1987). For example, some couples use divorce to resolve marital conflict, and others experience deep emotional wounds following divorce. These situations often result in partners who have difficulty making another commitment. Other couples have difficulties establishing cohesion, or the emotional ties that bind families together, because of the lack of a shared family history. Finally, unless remarrying couples address communication problems—near the top of the list of reasons why people seek divorce—they run the risk of carrying the same problems into a subsequent marriage.

According to Gerlach (2005), the essence of remarriage is not really different from first marriages: "The relationship objectives are the same—to lovingly help each other fulfill a set of core personal needs over time… while each partner evolves as a unique individual in a changing world. The shared [goals] needed to grow and keep a healthy, satisfying love relationship are the same in both cases." The key to establishing a successful subsequent marriage and family system is a joint commitment from both partners. This will help ensure that all members of the newly formed family system are met. Today, it is important to understand that stepfamilies are not one-size-fits-all in their characteristics.

Today, 40 percent of all marriages in the United States are remarriages. When spouses remarry a new partner, a stepfamily is formed.

Source: iStock.com/vorDa.

Stepfamilies Today

Stepfamilies are very common in today's world, but there used to be negative undertones associated with the term *stepfamily*, such as the "evil" stepmother who is cruel to her stepchildren, so often portrayed in children's storybooks. Due to the increasing incidence of stepfamilies, there have been attempts over the years to soften the terminology and to use other terms that do not carry the negative connotation, such as "integrated family," "complicated family form," "merged family," or "reconstituted" or "combined family." The alternate term with which most of us are familiar is the term **blended families.** The Stepfamily Association of America (SAA, 2009), however, disagrees with the use of this term, pointing out that when two family systems join together, they do not "blend." Notes the SAA, "A stepfamily does not *recreate* a first family (or, blend into something entirely new with all prior connections severed and the former existence obliterated)." Thus, according to the SAA, to "blend" a family would mean that children and spouses in stepfamilies must lose their identity, their individuality, and their active attachment to the absent parent, to the former first family. All other family forms are defined by the relationship that exists between the parent and child, such as foster, adoptive, single-parent, or biological. The SAA holds, then, that it is more accurate and preferred to use the term *stepfamily.* They also assert that implying that two distinct family systems can fold into one sets the new family structure up for unrealistic expectations and "doom" (SAA, 2009).

Stepfamily Types

While the presence of children from a previous marriage defines a stepfamily, the composition of stepfamilies differs. In some instances, members of a stepfamily may or may not live full time within the stepfamily household; in many cases, children are members of *two* stepfamily households. Table 9.2 summarizes the different types of stepfamilies, each defined by the parent–child relationship. Also, in stepfamilies, children are described in different ways. For example, *siblings* share the same two biological parents, while *stepsiblings* are not biologically related, but have parents who are married to one another. A *mutual child* is the child (or children) who is born to the remarried couple. Some researchers refer to this as the "cement" child, as they are thought to cement the relationship.

Stepfamily Characteristics

Many students often mistakenly assume that stepfamilies are no different than first families since there are two parents in the home who share in the everyday tasks of rearing children.

TABLE 9.2 ■ Types of Stepfamilies

Biological mother/stepfather	The household comprises the mother's biological children and her stepchildren (the children of the stepfather).
Biological father/stepmother	The household comprises the father's biological children and his stepchildren (the children of the stepmother).
Complex stepfamily	Both partners have children from previous relationships or marriage, although the children may reside in different households.
Joint biological-stepfamily	The couple has at least one biological child that is the product of both married parents, and at least one biological child of either parent (meaning the other parent would be the stepparent).

Source: Stepfamily Association of America (2009).

While on the surface it may appear that there are not significant differences, the complex combination of roles and relationships makes stepfamily living very different from a nuclear family's, as Table 9.3 shows us. Certain characteristics distinguish stepfamilies from first families (Parziale & Parziale, 2002).

The Stepfamily Is Born of Loss: Every stepfamily has one thing in common: They have all faced loss (Wallerstein & Kelly, 1980). Unlike first marriages, a stepfamily is typically born of loss—of a parent or family through death, through divorce, or through desertion. And because divorce is frequently accompanied by relocation, the members of a stepfamily may also be mourning the loss of other family members (such as a grandmother or grandfather, a favorite aunt or uncle), previous friends, their former home or school, their former neighborhood, or their dreams. The grief is exacerbated during holidays, birthdays, school events, and other special family times. According to the SAA (2009), adults and children each grieve over certain

TABLE 9.3 ■ The Ways That Stepfamilies and Nuclear Families Differ

Structural Factor	Typical Stepfamily	Typical Nuclear Family
Number of co-parenting homes	Usually homes linked by legal documents, emotions, finances, genes and ancestry, shared history, responsibilities, and memories	Usually one home
Grandparents (living and dead)	Usually six or eight or more	Usually four
Physical and legal child custody	Sole, joint, or split; usually subject to legal decree(s) and often legally contested	Shared; no legal suits or decrees
Spouses' parenting values and styles (e.g., child discipline)	Preformed before remarrying and cohabiting; often needs compromising	Evolved together over years; differences are usually less stressful
Caregivers' legal parenting rights and responsibilities regarding minor kids' school/ health/ custody/etc. (varies by state)	Fewer and less clear rights (stepparents and stepgrandparents); responsibilities more confusing; a legal parenting agreement may exist, which excludes any stepparents	More and clearer rights (bioparents and biograndparents); responsibilities far clearer; no legal documents to enforce or litigate
Last names	Rewedded biomom's names may differ from their kids' names: without adoption, stepsibs have different last names	Adults and kids usually all have the same last name, so less chance of identity and loyalty (priority) confusions
Family member loyalty, bonding, and cohesion	Initially, pseudo or little among merging families; may or may not improve with time; much more fragile	Generally much stronger throughout the Family Life Cycle; they usually transcend traumas

Source: Adapted from Gerlach (2005).

specific losses associated with divorce. For example, adults typically grieve over the loss of a partner and the loss of the marital relationship, while children grieve the loss of a parent and stability.

The Family Boundaries and Roles Are Ambiguous: The frequent entrances and exits of family members from the various stepfamily households, such as stepchildren/stepsiblings leaving for visitations or coming for visitations, may lead to indistinct or blurred boundaries. This ambiguity creates confusion and uncertainty as to who is "in" the family and who is not, and causes doubt about family affiliations. Further, the roles in stepfamilies have no clear, traditionally understood labels, no clear definitions, and no clear expectations (Parziale & Parziale, 2002). In a biological family, the role of Mom or Dad is typically well understood by the family, the community, and society. In a stepfamily, however, there is no how-to manual or job description for the roles of "stepparent" or "stepchild," and these roles are not clearly defined by society. Additionally, there are different roles depending on the composition of the stepfamily structure (such as biological mother, biological father, etc.). Further compounding the complexity of stepparenting relationships and heightening the ambiguity is that there is no legal relationship between stepparents and stepchildren: Stepparents cannot authorize emergency medical care, access the child's academic records, or sign legal documents relating to the child.

There Is a Disparity of Individual, Marital, and Family Life Cycles: When two family systems form a stepfamily, an obstacle that all family members face is the fact that they do not share a common history, common traditions, or common life experiences. Compounding these differences is the fact that there will be children with varying developmental needs. It is also quite likely that there will be differences in parenting styles, career aspirations, finances, retirement goals, and lifestyles. As Parziale and his colleague note, when developmental phases among family members are crossed, individual family members' needs may be out of sync with those of other family members, which adds to the stressors associated with role ambiguity.

There Are Several Loyalty Conflicts: Because children have strong emotional ties to their biological parents, their loyalty to the biological parents remains strong. The most common loyalty conflict involves the stepparent whenever children feel that their relationship with their biological parent(s) is threatened as a result of the stepparent joining the family system (Parziale & Parziale, 2002). Another common loyalty conflict exists among siblings. For example, what happens if one sibling *likes* the new stepparent and other siblings *do not?* Is it okay to "love" the new stepparent? Because of these types of loyalty conflicts, the cohesion of the stepfamily is seldom at the same level as the first family's.

Stepfamilies Experience More Stress Than Nuclear Families: Unlike first families, stepfamilies sometimes face years of instability due to the inherent multiple changes. The first two years are often quite turbulent; it may take as long as eight years for the family to reorganize and adjust. All too often, stepparents and children are immediately thrust into conflicting multiple roles. Stepparents walk into a parenting role before emotional or attachment ties with the children have been established. In the meantime, children are expected to instantly love Mom or Dad's new spouse and to get along with their new stepsiblings. All of these changes and expectations are sources of great stress for all involved. Is it any wonder that stepfamily formation and stepfamily life is so challenging?

Stepfamily Challenges

It takes a long time for stepfamily members to get used to the new roles each are being assigned, as well as the new relationships and boundaries intrinsic to new stepfamilies. Because of the inherent "relational overload" that accompanies the numerous and complex steprelationships, stepfamilies face many more challenges than do those in first-time families (Parziale & Parziale, 2002).

Common Challenges for Adults

Even though remarriage is rapidly becoming the most common family form in the United States (Bramlett & Mosher, 2002), it still carries with it a stigma of sorts. In general, first-time marriages receive substantially more emotional and physical support from family and friends, as well as from their place of worship. When adults remarry, they inherit new responsibilities and obligations to their new family. These additional responsibilities may cause added strain and may include:

- **Financial difficulties:** Financial strain is common in stepfamilies as stepfathers and stepmothers alike may be under a court order to pay child and/or spousal support to their former families (Manning et al., 2003; Mason et al., 2001).
- **Adjusting to new parenting roles:** Stepping immediately into the role of stepparent is difficult because it requires learning how to share parenting. Stepparents find that they must change existing parenting techniques, developing new techniques that fit the new family—and developing a new role with the children (Bray, 1999). Because children of divorce experience higher rates of emotional, behavioral, and academic problems than do children of never-divorced families, stepparents have a formidable task as they try to establish a sense of normalcy (Coleman et al., 2000).
- **Establishing discipline:** Exerting authority and discipline are two of the biggest obstacles associated with stepparenting. The SAA (2009) recommends that stepparents initially adopt a "friend" role with their stepchildren, rather than the role of instant parent. Giving children time to get to know a new stepparent affords the stepfamily the opportunity to begin to build a shared history. Reassuring children that the stepparent is not trying to replace the child's biological parent also helps to ease the transition (Coleman et al., 2000).
- **Bonding as a couple:** It is essential that the couple take time to nurture one another and their relationship. This requires finding time to spend time alone together in order to affirm each other and to demonstrate affection (Kheshgi-Genovese & Genovese, 1997).
- **Grieving past losses:** Most divorce adults are wounded in some way and frequently experience guilt, shame, fear, distrust, and a feeling of failure. Even if the individual is the one who initiated the divorce, he or she may experience deep feelings of loss—the

loss of dreams, the loss of goals, the loss of security, or the loss of a fairytale type of love. The sense of loss is one of the most difficult obstacles to overcome.

When two families merge, it is common for each side to feel that the other is intruding into their family. These feelings often compound the interactions of stepfamilies and significantly contribute to why it takes stepfamilies two to three years to adjust to stepfamily living.

Source: iStock.com/skynesher.

Common Challenges for Children

Children enter into a stepfamily with a history of loss that is beyond their control. They tend to respond to this transition with feelings of helplessness and anger. Too often, parents mistakenly assume that because children are young, they are oblivious to the changes that surround them, or they believe that because children are young, they will quickly "bounce back." As we have seen throughout this chapter, a child's ability to bounce back is largely dependent on how they are parented during the turbulent processes of transition—not only by their biological parents but also by their stepparents. To help children thrive as they transition to stepfamily living, adults must understand the common challenges children face as they enter into this new family system:

- **Loss of power and control:** Children lose more than a parent when their nuclear family dissolves; because they have no choice in how the events unfold, they frequently feel a loss of power and control. This sense of powerlessness can be overwhelming for a child. To help children heal, it is imperative that they be given control over some aspect of their new life. For example, when children are allowed to make small decisions, such as how to spend their allowance or devising new stepfamily rules, this contributes to their feelings of control and minimizes their feelings of helplessness (Kalter et al., 1984; Robson et al., 1995).

- **Guilt:** Children often blame themselves for their parents' divorce. They may believe that they were "bad" or "naughty" and that their behavior drove the other parent away; they may believe that they are too "unlovable" or that they are too "expensive" for the parent to care for them; in the case of a deceased parent, they may have "wished" their parent was dead at some point in time. It is crucial that parents engage in honest communication with their children throughout the many processes of divorce and convey to the children that divorce or death is *never* the fault of the child. It is also of the utmost importance that parents assure their children that their parents love them under any circumstances (Warshak, 2000).
- **Loyalty conflicts:** When a parent remarries, children often feel that if they become close to the new stepparent or if they "love" the stepparent, they are unfaithful and disloyal to their biological parent—they feel they have betrayed that parent. If divorced parents continue arguing in front of their children or use the children as pawns in the divorce process, this heightens these loyalty struggles. Thus, the rejection of a new stepparent or a new home may be more a reflection of their fear of abandoning their biological parent rather than dislike for the stepparent. It is vital that both parents and stepparents assure (again and again!) the children that it is possible to love many people at the same time and that having a relationship with a stepparent in no way means that they love their biological parent any less (Kheshgi-Genovese & Genovese, 1997).
- **Anger:** It is normal for children to feel angry toward their parents following divorce and during the formation of a stepfamily. The anger may be due to the sense of powerlessness and lack of control they have in the situation, and it may be directed toward a parent who visits infrequently or fails to follow through on promises. The anger may also be a response to a move from the family home, neighborhood, or school. However the child's anger is expressed, it is essential that parents and stepparents reassure the children that it is normal to feel angry and to feel whatever they have been feeling (Kelly & Emery, 2003; Strohschein, 2005).

Because stepfamilies are structurally and emotionally different from first families, both adults and children have difficulty adjusting and adapting to the changes swept in by divorce (Seymour et al., 1995). For adults, adjustment centers on their ability to maintain a close relationship with their new spouse. Children's ability to adapt is largely dependent on how sensitive parents and stepparents are to children's feelings and behaviors. "A little understanding [is] the right foundation for the beginning of a strong stepfamily relationship" (Seymour et al., 1995).

Successful Stepfamily Living

With all the added stressors and tensions so commonly experienced in stepfamily life, newly formed families may wonder if it is possible for family life to be high in happiness and satisfaction. Marriage and family therapists Emily Visher and John Visher (1993) provide key characteristics of those families who successfully adapt to the multifaceted changes associated with divorce and remarriage.

- **They develop realistic expectations.** All members within the stepfamily understand that it will never be the same as the first family. They also understand that love and care do not develop instantly; these develop slowly, over time, as the family builds its own history, rituals, and traditions through shared experiences.
- **They allow time for mourning.** Adults and children come to understand that they need time to mourn the loss of the family they once had. By allowing open, honest communication, and by sharing feelings of anger, fear, and guilt, the family begins healing.
- **Remarried couples nurture a strong relationship.** Adults take time to nurture their relationship and pay close attention to their needs as a couple. It is difficult to be effective parents and stepparents when couples suffer in their own relationships.
- **They accept that becoming a stepparent takes time.** While biological parents have time to evolve into their parenting roles, stepparents are instantly thrust into their roles. When stepparents do not force togetherness with their stepchildren, their relationships with their stepchildren have a better chance of thriving.
- **Stepparents slowly develop the role of disciplinarian.** Not only does intimacy take time to be earned, so does the role of authoritarian. Discipline works better if the biological parent takes the lead until the relationship between the stepparent and stepchild is stronger (Shoup Olsen, 1997). In successful stepfamilies, stepparents are able to vary their roles, particularly if they have biological children of their own (taking the lead parenting role with their own children but stepping aside to allow the parent and co-parent of stepchildren to discipline their children).
- **They develop a stepfamily history.** For successful stepfamily living, flexibility is key! It is necessary to give each other permission to do things differently than they did in their first family, from establishing a new homework schedule than in the past, to doing household chores, to establishing new (and perhaps different) birthday and holiday rituals and traditions. Over time, as families share experiences, they weave together their own unique family history—and thus strengthen family ties.
- **They work cooperatively with the absent parent.** Stepparents learn to make arrangements far in advance of events and visitations to ensure collaborative shared parenting. Stepfamilies who have flexible family boundaries that allow for multiple exits and entrances into and from the family system tend to experience more cooperative

parenting, such as is common with African American and Hispanic families. Whether or not residual angry, hostile, or bitter feelings exist, communication is essential.

Those who are successful in transitioning their multiple family systems into a cohesive stepfamily system know that, just as with divorce, remarriage involves multiple, simultaneous processes and is accompanied by common struggles faced by both children and adults.

Divorce hurts.

Source: iStock.com/ProfessionalStudioImages.

PARENTING LIFE EDUCATION: PROTECTING CHILDREN'S AND ADULTS' WELL-BEING

Divorce hurts. It hurts the parents. It hurts the children. It hurts the grandparents. It hurts other family and friends. And the transitions that take place in life after divorce are no less emotionally confusing or painful than is the process of divorce. As noted by the student in the opening of this chapter, divorce is a broken experience that requires time for family members to pick up all of the pieces, to reassemble, and to reorganize their lives. Feelings of despair, disappointment, and helplessness are not uncommon, as it takes years for family members to develop a new orientation to postdivorce life.

Given the psychological distress that divorce and relationship end brings to couples and their families, the role helping professionals play postdivorce is crucial to the well-being of children and adults (Beckmeyer et al., 2018). Family processes such as co-parenting cooperation, ex-spouses' communication, and the realignment of boundaries are known to encourage optimal postdivorce psychological health in children (ages 4 to 9) and youth (ages 10 to 18). Understanding and identifying how former spouses' postdivorce ongoing relationship impacts children and youth is a key role of Family Life Educators. According to Family Life practitioner Johnathan Beckmeyer, when working with postdivorce families, Family Life Educators should (2018):

- Create and implement age-appropriate education programs
- Focus on aspects of the former spousal relationship, such as co-parenting and communication
- Help partners transition from spouses to partners in childrearing
- Establish new communication and relationship boundaries
- Establish identities independent and separate from former spouses

The transition to life following divorce involves many processes, which include emotional, economic, parental, and legal ramifications. For children and adolescents whose parents divorce, there are many negative outcomes. There are also many variables associated with postdivorce outcomes, such as being separated from an important attachment figure, the relationship between the parents and their children, the family's economics, and whether one or both parents remarry. The most critical factor in determining outcomes, however, is the parents' ability to effectively co-parent or share parenting.

Although adapting to single-parent life is difficult for mothers, fathers, and children, the most dramatic changes in family life and family structure come about when parents remarry and form stepfamilies. Despite the fact that popular television shows often portray first families and remarried families as similar entities, the differences between the two are vast. Not only does the family structure vary, but so too do their histories, their experiences, and family members' roles. Becoming a stepfamily requires unique tasks for both adults and children—accepting these changes does not happen overnight but requires years to fully integrate as a family system. Realistic expectations—recognizing that the stepfamily will never be the same as the first family and that love and care do not develop instantly—is the foundation on which strong, successful stepfamilies are built and fostered.

Is there family life after divorce? This is a question that we have posed to many of our students taking our courses. We often ask our students to draw a "picture" of divorce. Quite often, students draw a "broken" or "split" home of sorts, with the children residing with the mother while the father lives in another home. In many of these drawings, students draw tears or expressions of sadness on family members' faces. But one drawing in particular captured our attention. It was an illustration of a mature tree that had split, as if it had been struck by lightning or had been destroyed during a storm. In the midst of the split tree trunk was just a hint of new growth—a sprig of bright green, spring-like growth. That drawing captured the essence of divorce and remarriage, the transitions to stepfamily living. When a marriage breaks down and the nuclear family dissolves, the family feels as though it was struck by lightning or twisted apart by a storm. Left wounded, battered, broken, and damaged, many families feel that the family will never recover. Yet, slowly over time, new growth takes place—a new structure grows from the old.

10 FAMILY LIFE AND WORK: A BALANCING ACT

LEARNING OBJECTIVES

10.1 Articulate what led to the dual-earner couple in the United States, and the current landscape of working couples.

10.2 Summarize the effects of working couples on family well-being.

10.3 Identify the challenges that dual-earner couples confront.

10.4 Explain the ways in which differing attitudes toward money affect a couple's relationship and family living today.

"There's nowhere on the [budget] worksheet for the other stuff, [like] daughter needs therapy." Today, the financial demands of raising a family cause enormous stressors for parents. *Source:* iStock.com/Kiwis.

A friend of mine recently confided in me that he was frustrated, angry, and disheartened about the direction his life, marriage, and parenting were taking. As the conversation continued, it was clear that work and money issues were significantly impacting his overall life and marital satisfaction. He shared,

"I know my life stopped being my life a long time ago. When you get married and have kids, that's part of the deal, I know that. But when you're sitting there and you're figuring out, 'Okay, can we afford to have a kid? Can we afford to buy a house? A second car?' you work it out, and it all looks good on paper. On your little worksheet.

But there's nowhere on the worksheet for the other stuff. There's no entry for 'Daughter needs therapy.' Or, 'Mom's really sick, fly home three or four times in one month.' Or. 'Wife goes through cancer scare.' There's *always something* and we never get a chance to breathe. And you look up and, like, twenty years have passed and this is how you've lived. Not hand-to-mouth anymore, like when we were a young couple, but never really a chance to get any momentum going. And it just wears on me. I mean, my wife doesn't know this, but this is the stuff that rocks me out of sleep at two in the morning, you know, a couple of times a week at least, and you just lay there, thinking about everything that has to get done. And so I'm tired all day, and then I act like a jerk because I'm tired and *that* upsets my wife and then something else happens and it's just this big pile of angst that never goes away. And at the bottom of that pile, it's always about money. I mean, dig into any issue, and there it is. Money."

Today, work and family play major roles in the lives of adults. Most Americans come face to face on a daily basis with the demands and challenges of trying to balance work and family life—far too often, there are negative effects when work responsibilities spillover into family life. Married and intimate life brings with it things we can't predict or plan for: Spouses get sick, parents get sick, children need medical care, and money becomes the focus of our every thought. Other things happen that also cause financial worry. For example, the COVID-19 pandemic and the resulting economic fallout caused tremendous financial hardship for millions of Americans, with 10 million families behind on rent and 20 million households reporting having too little to eat (Center on Budget & Policy Priorities, 2022). What does a family do in these situations? And what happens to their relationships when they experience such stressors?

Research indicates that money is a major source of relationship concerns for couples today, and that there are potentially serious implications for couples when money issues crop up (Dew, 2007; Papp et al., 2009). One study found that the larger a couple's debt, the more likely they are to say money is the thing they fight most about (Ramsey Solutions, 2018). For these reasons, in this chapter, we will begin our study of work and family by looking at the landscape of dual-earner couples, including the demands faced by military families when a loved one is deployed, as well as the challenges single parents encounter when they try to balance work and family. We'll then shift our attention to the types of strain and stress families face when they try to juggle work with family life. To best equip you with tools for your own family relationships and parenting responsibilities, we'll conclude by exploring the skills that effective working families use in their daily lives, and how best to manage your money.

WORKING FAMILIES: THE TRANSFORMATION OF AMERICAN HOMES

Economic stability and the ability of families to meet their daily needs is an important measure of family health and well-being (Allegretto, 2005; Hardie & Lucas, 2010; Killewald, 2016; Lewin, 2005). The **socioeconomic status (SES)** of a family is the government's measure of the family's relative economic and social ranking within a community (Krieger, 2001). Measures of

SES typically include the adults' occupation, education level, community/group associations, and income. Other measures may include location of residence and certain home amenities such as a television, computer, telephone, books, and so forth. *Attained SES* refers to the parents' SES, and *SES of origin* is the term used when describing a child's family's SES (Krieger, 2001).

As our nation moved into the second half of the 20th century, a number of sociocultural, economic, and political changes occurred that changed the face of families in the United States. These changes include lowered birth rates and delays in marriage, women's abilities to control their fertility through contraceptives, the legalization of abortion in 1973 and the adoption of no-fault divorce laws, and Civil Rights legislation in 1965 that banned discrimination. All of the factors worked in tandem not only to change how we experience family life but also to change America's workforce as many of these social and cultural factors propelled women into the workplace.

Women Enter the Workforce

The 1960s ushered in many changes that helped to shape our conceptions and experiences of women in the workplace today. A new-wave feminist movement, referred to as **Women's Liberation**, put forth the idea that women suffered oppression in patriarchal, male-dominated cultures such as the United States. Equality in the job place and economic equality were primary goals of feminist organizations (such as the National Organization for Women) throughout the 1960s and 1970s. This was referred to as **gender equality,** and in 1964, a last-minute addition to Civil Rights legislation mandated that discrimination based on a person's gender was illegal.

Signed by President Kennedy in 1963, the Equal Pay Act mandates equal pay for equal work by forbidding employers from paying men and women different wages or benefits for doing jobs that require the same skills and responsibilities. Sixty years later, wages are still not equal.

Source: iStock.com/lankogal.

This is not to say, however, that women have achieved equality. In the ensuing decades since the passage of the Civil Rights Act, women continue to fight against bias, prejudice, discrimination, and sexual harassment as they attempt to break down barriers and stereotypes, and as they enter occupations traditionally held by males. The term **glass ceiling** refers to discrimination against women in the workplace, specifically in situations where advancement in an organization is stopped because of **occupational sexism**, or beliefs that the male gender is more capable of certain work-related tasks and professions than women are. Types of glass ceiling barriers include different pay for comparable work, sexual discrimination in the workplace, and lack of family-friendly work policies (Thomas-Hunt & Phillips, 2004). For example, in 2009, the U.S. Census Bureau estimated that women make 77.6 cents on the dollar compared to men (Institute for Women's Policy Research, 2008). This disparity in earnings is referred to as the **gender wage gap**. It's important to know that the gap isn't closing—in fact, it has remained relatively stable the past 15 years (Pew Research Center, 2019). In 2018, women earned only 85 percent of what men earned. On average, it takes a woman an extra 39 days of work to earn what men do (Pew Research Center, 2019).

While a large portion of the wage gap can be explained by such things as education, occupation, and skills and experience, it is necessary to account for the fact that *wage discrimination* may be at play. **Wage discrimination** is the discrimination shown in the payment of wages, salaries, and earnings to minority groups. More often than not, the targets of wage discrimination are people of color (both men and women) and white women. When wage discrimination takes place, the employee earns less for the same jobs with the same performance levels and responsibilities as white males. In a recent survey, about four-in-ten working women (roughly 42 percent) said they have been the victims of gender wage discrimination; in comparison, only about 5 percent of men have reported the same type of discrimination (Pew Research Center, 2019). Figure 10.1 illustrates for us the various ways in which they experienced gender discrimination at work.

Identifying and challenging wage discrimination in the workplace has been an uphill battle, despite the passage of the Equal Pay Act of 1963. For example, in 2004, the case known

FIGURE 10.1 ■ Discrimination in the Workplace

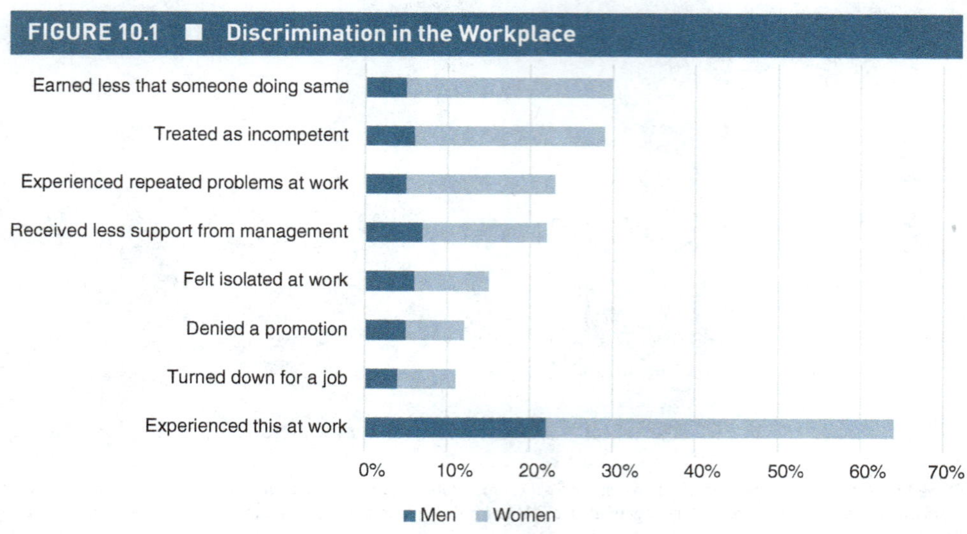

Source: Pew Research Center (2019).

as *Dukes v. Wal-Mart* became the largest class action lawsuit in history—approximately 1.5 million women were parties to the lawsuit and claimed that they received less pay and promotion opportunities than their fellow male coworkers. Additionally, in what is now a historic case, Lilly Ledbetter, a former employee of the Goodyear Tire and Rubber Company, sued the company to receive back pay and damages. After her retirement from the company, she discovered that for years she was paid at significantly lower rates in comparison to her male counterparts. Although she was awarded back pay from a lower court, the U.S. Supreme Court overturned the lower court's decision in 2007. However, in 2009, in his first week in office, President Barack Obama signed into law the *Lilly Ledbetter Fair Pay Act.* Although this law removes the legal obstacles for women seeking equal pay in the workforce, it is also a tool to combat workplace discrimination in all forms. As President Obama observed at the signing of the law:

> Ultimately, equal pay isn't just an economic issue for millions of Americans and their families, it's a question of who we are—and whether we're truly living up to our fundamental ideals; whether we'll do our part, as generations before us, to ensure those words put on paper some 200 years ago really mean something—to breathe new life into them with a more enlightened understanding that is appropriate for our time. That is what Lilly Ledbetter challenged us to do.

When comparing women with other women in the workforce, the earnings gap is widened even further when race and ethnicity are added to the picture. As you have seen, the concept of *intersectionality* looks at the ways in which the interaction of sex, race, ethnicity, and gender form barriers to people in society (U.S. Census Bureau, 2019a)—in this case, the intersection creates barriers to equal pay and wages in the workplace. The data in Table 10.1 show us that women of all racial and ethnic groups earn less than men of the same group; they also earn less than men overall (Institute for Women's Policy Research, 2019). To help you to better understand the significance of the differences, if a man makes $48,000 per year, a white woman in the

TABLE 10.1 ■ Gender Earnings Ratio by Race and Ethnicity

Racial/Ethnic Background	Female Earnings as % of Male Earnings of Same Group	Female Earnings as % of White Male Earnings
All races/ethnicities	81.1%	N/A
White	81.5%	81.5%
Black	89.0%	65.3%
Hispanic	85.7%	61.6%
Asian	75.5%	93.5%

Source: Institute for Women's Policy Research (2019).

same job doing the same tasks with the same skills and abilities would make $39,000; a Black woman would make $31,200; a Latino woman would make slightly over $29,500; and an Asian woman would make $44,880.

Deborah Chalfie, senior counsel of the National Women's Law Center observes, "One of the problems that women and women of color face in the work force is that female-dominated and jobs dominated by women of color are undervalued and underpaid" (Sullivan, 2009, p. 1). That is to say, women tend to be concentrated in certain occupational categories—this is referred to as the **pink-collar phenomenon.** For example, in 2018, 55 percent of the entire workforce was made up of pink-collar workers in "traditionally female" jobs: healthcare, child care, education, customer service, sales, and administrative positions (U.S. Department of Labor, 2019). And, frequently, these jobs are generally rated as deserving less pay than more "masculine" occupations.

This shift from one-earner families to dual-earner families has not only advanced women's opportunities in society but it also dramatically changed the face of American families and how they experience family living today.

A Portrait of Contemporary Dual-Earner Couples

Dual-earner couples are defined as marriages or relationships in which both partners work. Workforce participation varies among dual-earner couples. For example, two-thirds (66 percent) of married couples in the United States today are dual-earners, whereas in about one-fourth of couples, only the male works, and in 5 percent, only the female is employed (Pew Research Center, 2019b). In many such couples, one partner works full time while the other partner works part time; in other families, both partners work full time. Many factors influence labor force participation and earnings among dual-earner couples, such as education level, urban living, unemployment, and discrimination. There are also racial and ethnic differences in dual-earner couples.

White couples are highly involved in the workforce, and only Asian couples are more likely to be involved in the workforce than whites. One reason for white couples' high participation in the workforce is that they tend to have higher levels of education, which are strongly associated with higher levels of employment. As a result, whites generally earn more than Hispanic men and women, even within the same occupation (U.S. Census Bureau, 2019b). The median annual income of white families and these higher earnings are associated with enhanced marital quality among whites (we discuss marital quality later in the chapter) (Amato et al., 2003; Bianchi et al., 2012; Killewald, 2016).

Educational attainment is a key factor in employment and earnings for Black couples. Black/Black Caribbean men are the least likely to be employed among each of the ethnic groups, whereas Black women are the most likely to be employed. In fact, African Black/Black Caribbean men are more than twice as likely to be unemployed than whites. Both African American men and women are typically **blue-collar workers**, which means they are highly represented in the service sector (such as sales, office, production, and transportation); as a result, their earnings are generally lower than those employed in **white-collar professional occupations** (such as attorneys, bankers, and doctors) (U.S. Department of Labor, 2018). Of all racial and ethnic groups in the United States, Black/Black Caribbean families suffer the highest levels of unemployment and poverty and the lowest median family income—about $42,000 annually (Pew Research Center, 2022).

Asian men and women are more likely than any of the other ethnic groups to be employed in professional positions (U.S. Bureau of Labor Statistics, 2020). Low divorce rates, high education levels, a strong work ethic, self-sufficiency, familism, and high participation in the labor force have led to the "model minority" status for many Asian couples (Taylor, 2002). With an annual income of over $80,000 per year, Asian American families have the highest median household income of all racial groups in the United States (U.S. Census Bureau, 2019c). This is perhaps because Asian Americans have the highest educational qualifications of all ethnic groups in the United States—over one-half of all Asian American adults have attained at least a bachelor's degree (U.S. Census Bureau, 2019c).

Influenced by Confucian ideology, Asian households are typically patriarchal with well-defined roles (Choi et al., 2018). Their cultural traditions and roles tend to provide them with order and stability between work life and family life. Additionally, their collectivist perspective has led to a willingness of on the part of many Asian Americans to sacrifice personal needs in order for their families and employees to be successful (Choi et al., 2018; Fong, 2002).

Hispanic couples are similar to Asian couples in that they tend to be patriarchal, familistic, and traditional in their views of men's and women's work roles (Constante et al., 2019). Hispanic men are generally highly employed, while Hispanic women tend to have lower employment rates than each of the other ethnic groups (U.S. Department of Labor, 2019). While Hispanic couples are becoming more educated and, therefore, more represented in professional occupations, they are less likely to have completed high school than each of the other ethnic groups; as a result, they are still highly employed in the service sector, resulting in lower earnings than those employed as professionals (U.S. Department of Labor, 2019).

One of the poorest ethnic groups in America today, Latinx families earn, on average, about $50,000 per year (U.S. Census Bureau, 2019d). It's important to keep in mind that many Hispanic immigrants may have successful businesses in other countries or professional degrees from other countries, but because of the language barrier when they arrive in the United States, they are unable to secure high-paying jobs. Many immigrants today also face discrimination in the workplace; for example, it is not uncommon in California for field workers to earn as little as $10,000 per year for full-time work—about $800 per month (NFWM, 2019). Furthermore, the transnational (families who are divided because they live in different countries) and binational (families whose legal citizenship is mixed) status of many Hispanic families has challenged their ability to manage work and family roles (Baca Zinn & Pok, 2002). In the United States, Hispanic children are at least twice as likely to live in poverty as their non-Hispanic counterparts (Child Trends, 2019).

Arab American couples are typically patriarchal and traditional—men are often the family's providers, and women are homemakers and raise the children (Aboulhassan & Brumley, 2018). Arab American men and women tend to be highly educated and are, therefore, well represented in the professional labor force with higher earnings than the national average. In the United States, Arab Americans' educational attainment levels are similar to the general public, with 31 percent who have graduated from college; 11 percent have a postgraduate degree (Pew Research Center, 2017b). Today, over two-thirds of Arab American adults are in the labor force and are employed in a wide array of occupations (Arab American Institute, 2019). Their median annual income is about $60,000.

Limited education, high unemployment, divorce, single-mother families, and substance abuse rates have contributed to labor force participation among Native Americans that is varied and sporadic (U.S. Census Bureau, 2019e). Although nearly 80 percent of this population have at least a high school diploma, the median household income of single-race American Indian and Alaska Native households is slightly over $39,000. This compares with $58,000 for the nation as a whole.

In recent years, families in the United States have been challenged in new ways as service men and women have been deployed overseas due to military engagements in Iraq and Afghanistan. The challenges are many, and all affect the portrait of wage earners in America.

Military families face the same day-to-day struggles and stressors that all working couples face, but they also face unique situations when they are deployed overseas for months at a time.

Source: Craig F. Walker/The Denver Post via Getty Images.

Service Men and Women

The United States military, which comprises the Army, Navy, Air Force, Coast Guard, and Marines, deployed nearly 200,000 men and women; about 15 percent of American Armed Forces personnel are deployed each year to regions around the world (Pew Research Center, 2017). While military families deal with stressors that are common to all families, such as parenting concerns, child care, juggling work with family, and career decisions, they are also subject to unique stressors because of the separation from family members (van der Wal et al., 2019).

Preparing for Deployment

Until recently, most military personnel had a period of one to two years between deployments. Recently, however, deployments can often occur in quick succession or tours of duty are extended for prolonged periods of time. For example, during the Gulf War in the early 1990s, single parents and dual-career couples were mobilized so quickly that these families had only a few hours to find child care for their children—both immediate child care, extended child care while the parent(s) was deployed overseas in a combat zone (Drummet et al., 2003). Army personnel are deployed more frequently than any other branch; their deployments range from 11 months, followed by a few months at home, to 11 months deployed again (Congressional Research Service, 2021).

Alongside frequent moves, financial worries are of particular concern to deployed military families (Military Family Advisory Network, 2019). What makes the financial picture much worse for so many military families today is that anywhere from 40 percent (Air Force) to 60 percent (Marines) of soldiers are 18 to 24 years of age (Council on Foreign Relations, 2019). Because of this, young couples have not yet learned effective money management skills, and this puts them at significantly higher risk for money troubles during deployment.

Financial Difficulties for Deployed Families

Today, there are increasing incidents of burgeoning financial difficulties among service families because separations due to deployment often catch families financially unprepared. In a survey of over 5,600 service men and women, nearly two-thirds said they didn't have enough savings to cover three months of living expenses (Bushatz, 2018). Furthermore, paying for mental health care was cited as the major barrier to getting help for those suffering with mental health problems, such as post-traumatic stress disorder (PTSD), and nearly 80 percent said that military moves cause high financial burdens and stress. Over one-fourth of all service members have more than $10,000 in credit card debt, and, sadly, food insecurity issues were also uncovered in this study, with about 22,000 active-duty troops using food stamps (Bushatz, 2018).

The bottom line? "Military family described [many] financial burdens: They're going into debt to pay for moving expenses, unable to find child care, unwilling to move forward in their education, forgoing necessary health care, and feelings the mental and physical effects of financial stress" (Bushatz, 2018).

Among those family practitioners who work with military families to improve their financial well-being, current programs are used that focus on financial situations that are unique to the military. Financial programs for military personnel, such as *Money Sense* and *Financial*

Fitness, are preventive educational programs that provide information to service members and their spouses/significant others about ways to manage their financial resources. These types of curricula, especially tailored to the needs of military men and women, teach money management skills and include such things as learning how to budget, keep financial records, develop healthy spending habits, establish realistic savings habits, and manage credit card debt. Research demonstrates that financial education as a part of deployment readiness reduces the frequency of families' money problems (Varcoe et al., 2002).

There are, of course, numerous other issues military families face, and we'll explore those a bit later in this chapter when we look at what it takes for all families to juggle work and family life. Here, it's important to recognize the unique financial situations military families experience, and that Family Life Educators and other family practitioners can provide invaluable resources to these families to assist them during these stressful work-related situations.

Single Parents in the Workforce

As our study has shown us thus far, there is great diversity among single-parent, or *lone parent*, households. For example, households headed by single parents include impoverished, never-married ethnic minority women or teenaged mothers, wealthy never-married women who have adopted or borne a child, widows and widowers, and women and men who find themselves single after a marital breakup (Gottfried & Gottfried, 1994; Richter & Lemola, 2017). Today (U.S. Census Bureau, 2020a):

- About one-half of all single mothers have never married.
- 29 percent are divorced.
- 21 percent are separated from their spouse or are widowed.

Regardless of its makeup, each single parent family has its own unique starting point and its own unique developmental history (Anderson & Sabatelli, 2011). Because mothers with children compose the largest segment of single-parent households—80 percent of single-parent families are headed by single mothers—our discussion begins with looking at work/money issues and challenges faced by single women who are parenting (Single Mother Statistics, 2021; U.S. Census Bureau, 2020a).

Single-Parent Mothers

A large majority of single women with children of all ages work outside the home in the paid labor force. Employment rates among single mothers have significantly increased since the 1990s, where 44 percent of single mothers worked; in 2020, slightly over two-thirds of single moms worked outside the home, more than the share of married mothers who also worked outside the home (U.S. Census Bureau, 2020a). Less than a quarter (22 percent) of single moms receive unemployment benefits. On average, single mothers earn about $48,000 per year (U.S. Census Bureau, 2020a).

As you can see from the information in Figure 10.2, there are a number of factors that affect the economic well-being of women and their children. As Figure 10.3 shows us, single mothers fare worse economically than married couples and single fathers do. Importantly,

FIGURE 10.2 ■ Single-Mother Characteristics

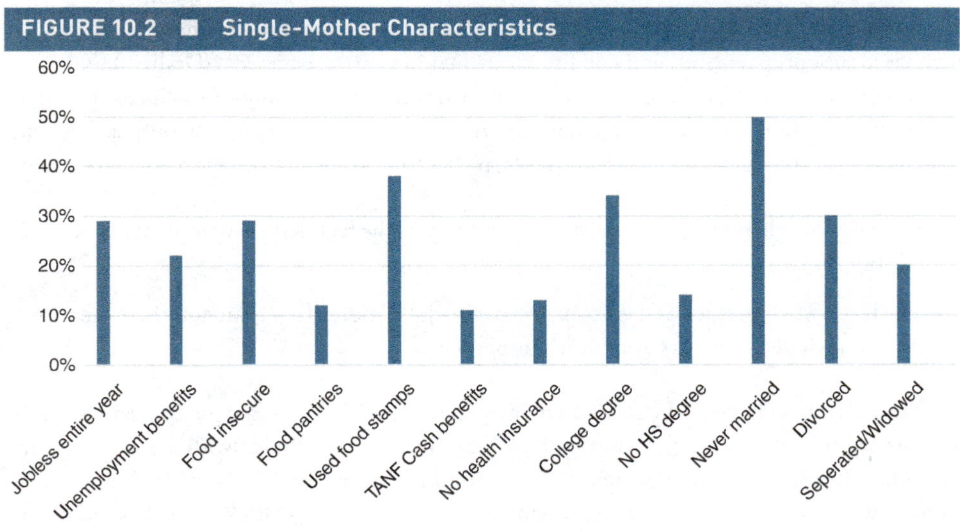

Sources: USDA (2017), HUD (2018), and U.S. Census Bureau (2016).

FIGURE 10.3 ■ Children in Poverty, by Family Type and Race

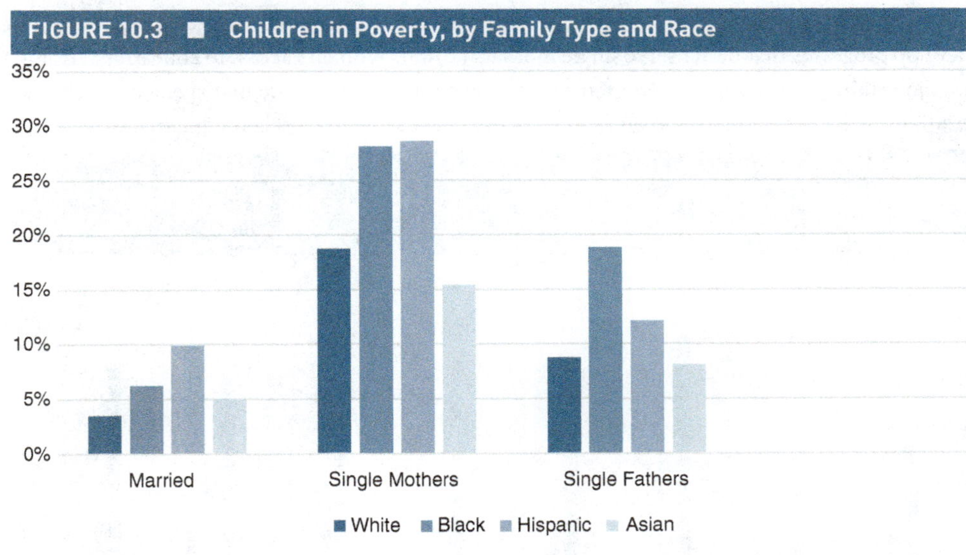

Source: Statista (2019).

any spousal support, child support, or public assistance (welfare) the woman receives typically does not come close to offsetting the differences in income between single-mother parents and married parents. Only one-third of single mothers today receive child support from the child's father, and if a mother does receive support, it is only about $400 a month (U.S. Census Bureau, 2020b). Today, nearly one-third (30.2 percent) of mothers do not receive child support ordered by the court (Grall, 2020), and *$113 billion is owed in back child support to mothers and their* *children* (Office of Child Support Enforcement, 2021). Only 46 percent of parents are current in their child support payments, and one-fourth are making partial payments (Grall, 2020).

A study sponsored by the Congressional Caucus on Women's Issues (2005) revealed that "single mothers find themselves on a downward slide in their struggle to establish secure and solid footing in the workforce" (Corbett, 2005, p. 2). Other key data from the report reveal that:

- Single mothers are "poor" or "near poor," despite the fact that they work, many of them full time.
- Those who are employed work in low-paying jobs; more often than not, these jobs do not include benefits such as health insurance.

Not much has changed since this study was undertaken. In 2017, the poverty rate for children under age 18 was highest among those who lived in households with a parent or parents who did not complete high school; these findings are shown in Figure 10.4 (American Community Survey, 2019). For example, among Blacks, poverty was highest for those children whose parent(s) didn't complete high school (68 percent), and substantially lower among those children who have a parent who completed a college degree (8 percent). Regardless of race or ethnicity, the less education a child's parent has, the more likely the child is to live in poverty.

As the Congressional Caucus notes, local, state, and federal policy makers must begin to develop programs that better serve single mothers (2005). Women's access to educational training, job training, and support programs that provide skills such as life management and work readiness will contribute to women's successes in the workforce—and consequently, parenting.

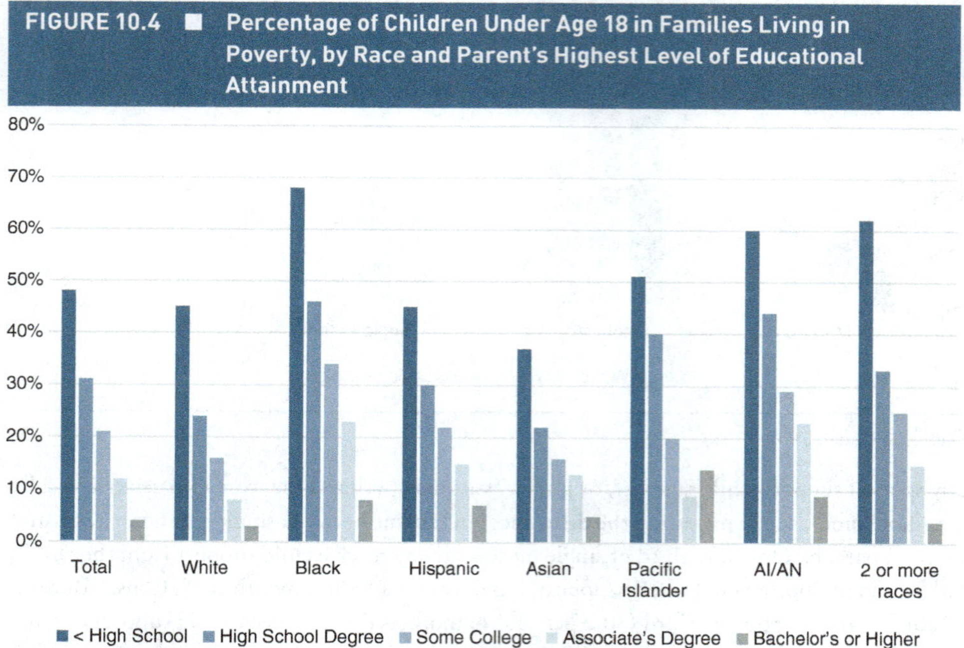

FIGURE 10.4 ■ Percentage of Children Under Age 18 in Families Living in Poverty, by Race and Parent's Highest Level of Educational Attainment

Source: American Community Survey (ACS) (2017).

Single-Parent Fathers

There is an abundance of literature about single mothers, their income levels, their education attainment, and their occupation status, but virtually none exists about single fathers as household heads. That's not to say, however, that there are not increased incidences in single-dad households. Although most single parents are females, the proportion of families headed by single fathers is increasing in the United States, as well as in many other developed countries. Today, about one of every six custodial parents are fathers (16 percent) (U.S. Census Bureau, 2021a).

Family and social scientists attribute the increased numbers of single-father households to a variety of reasons. For instance, more judges are awarding custody to fathers in divorce cases, more women are opting to pursue careers rather than seek custody of their children in divorce cases, and today more fathers are seeking joint custody arrangements (this arrangement reduces their monthly child support payments). Still, single-father households constitute only a small percentage of the overall picture of single-parent homes. Poverty rates are higher among single-father households than they are among married-couple households.

As you have seen consistently throughout our study, family structures and processes affect every aspect of children's development and well-being. As recent COVID-related economic downturns in the United States and the mushrooming student loan debt continue to squeeze parents and families past their emotional and financial coping abilities, countless children will suffer without sufficient economic resources. There is no doubt about it: A family's economic well-being and health are crucial to a child's overall development. Today, a significant number of American families are struggling just to make ends meet.

Although there are a number of challenges associated with dual-career couples, such as increased stress on personal lives and role conflict, many couples experience an increase in equality in the relationship.

Source: iStock.com/kate_sept2004.

COUPLES AND WORK: JUST TRYING TO MAKE ENDS MEET

Economic stability and the ability of families to meet their daily needs is an important measure of family well-being (Allegretto, 2005). **Basic budgets,** or the amount of money families need to manage at the most basic level, must cover costs associated with housing, food, transportation, child care, health care, clothing, personal care items, school materials, and taxes. However, a significant number of Americans today have difficulty meeting their family's economic needs.

- The average U.S. employee works 2,080 each year; this figure represents a 38-hour increase (nearly a full week) since 1990 (U.S. Department of Labor, 2018).
- There are nearly 75 million women in the workforce today, about 47 percent of all American workers (U.S. Department of Labor, 2017).
- 70 percent of mothers with children under the age of 18 are in the workforce, with over three-fourths employed full-time (U.S. Department of Labor, 2017).
- At least one parent is employed in 91 percent of families with children (U.S. Department of Labor, 2019).
- Three-fourths of adults who care for their aging, ill, or disabled parents are also working at a paying job during their caregiving experience (AARP, 2019).

Depending on where you live in the United States, the annual salary you need to support your family can vary significantly. For example, if you and your partner have two children and live in New York or California, you will need at least $88,000 a year to make ends meet (U.S. Department of Labor, 2019). If you live in Kansas or Tennessee, you can get by on about $55,000 or $60,000. When determining a family's financial needs, factors such as food, housing, child care, health care, utilities, and food costs are included. Housing costs typically consume the major portion of the family's income. Table 10.2 provides a quick, at-a-glance look at housing costs around the country. As you can see, it's no surprise that in many parts of the United States, families must be supported by two incomes.

Dual-Earner Couples and Family Well-Being

For both men and women, job status, job complexity, job autonomy, and the number of hours worked are some of the important variables that influence child and family well-being (Perry-Jenkins et al., 2001). **Job status** refers to a type or kind of job that offers some kind of prestige in an organization or community (such as managers or executive officers). **Job complexity** occurs when jobs are at the same time challenging and stimulating, and **job autonomy** happens when employees are allowed a high degree of independence and self-direction. Maureen Perry-Jenkins and her colleagues' (2001) decade review of couples who juggle work with family revealed that when fathers' and mothers' jobs have a high degree of complexity and autonomy, they are more apt to create a positive home environment and show greater warmth in parenting. Job complexity and autonomy are also linked with child outcomes such as enhanced verbal and reading skills and decreases in problem behaviors.

TABLE 10.2 ■ Selected Housing and Food Costs in the United States

State	Income Needed Before Income Taxes	Estimated Housing Costs	Estimated Food Costs
Arkansas	**$59,000**	$5,585	$8,822
California	**$81,056**	$19,875	$10,529
Connecticut	**$74,216**	$15,670	$10,245
Florida	**$66,057**	$13,239	$8,822
Georgia	**$63,209**	$10,932	$8,882
Illinois	**$69,760**	$11,564	$9,011
Kentucky	**$64,017**	$8,872	$8.822
Louisiana	**$61.643**	$10,261	$8,822
Massachusetts	**$75,418**	$17,721	$10,245
Minnesota	**$68,948**	$11,607	$9,011
Missouri	**$62,943**	$9,597	$9,011
Nevada	**$67,137**	$11,581	$10,529
New Jersey	**$75,884**	$17,409	$10,245
Oregon	**$72,311**	$13,166	$10,529
South Carolina	**$59,902**	$10,168	$8,822
Texas	**$61,501**	$11,880	$8,822
Virginia	**$72,223**	$14,900	$8,822
West Virginia	**$72,673**	$16,321	$10,529

Source: U.S. Bureau of Labor Statistics (2019).

Interestingly, most studies about couples and work focus on the well-being of the *couple*, not well-being at the *family* level (Behnke & MacDermid, 2004). But because of the systems nature of family living—when one family member struggles, all others are affected—it is essential that we gain an understanding of how work affects the lives of families. Generally speaking, *family well-being* includes (Behnke & MacDermid, 2004):

- Psychological health, such as low levels of depression and anxiety, and high levels of life satisfaction
- High levels of self-esteem, sense of power, and internal locus of control
- Good physical health

- Low behavior/conduct problems, such as alcohol abuse
- Good social support, such as friendships and contact with extended family
- High marital quality
- High marital stability
- Healthy parent–child relationships

If a family member is struggling at work, or if work conditions are not conducive to a quality family life, then every family member eventually suffers—a family member's occupational well-being is directly related to a good, healthy, comfortable state for the family. Given the importance of family health and functioning in our lives, it is essential to have an awareness and understanding of the interrelated nature of the workplace and the home. Toward the end of this chapter, we'll explore at length those factors necessary for couples to balance work life with family life to promote the family's health and well-being.

Money and Power

Couple and family therapist, Dr. Assaei Romanelli, stresses that money and power are almost always at play if a couple is experiencing relationship difficulties (2019). Romanelli describes the dynamic that occurs when one partner in the relationship earns more money than the other; he refers to this couple type as $$$ and $ (2019). Notes Romanelli, "The dynamic often manifests as follows: The $$$ partner implicitly and semi-consciously expects $ partner to compensate for their diminished income by investing extra time in the relationship, the house, the cooking, and the kids. The $ partner is grateful for the extra income their partner makes, but the financial dependence can generate feelings of guilt, which motivates them to constantly show the $$$ partner how essential they are. Ultimately, both partners act out their frustrations with mutual contempt, criticism, defensiveness, and stonewalling . . . which eventually lead to the relationship ending" (Romanelli, 2019, p. 1). Romanelli offers suggestions for couples who have a discrepancy in their earnings—and thus, a power differential:

- **Know your worth:** The $-partner is valuable, whether it's because they are covering their own expenses through their employment, or because they contribute to the couple's and family's well-being in other, nonquantifiable ways. Romanelli encourages couples to openly discuss their feelings of worth with each other, and to encourage partners who feel guilty for not pulling their financial weight.
- **Say it out loud:** Money and power is a topic that couples rarely discuss, so it is important that couples give each other the time and space to share their experiences. It is equally important for each partner to listen and to validate the other's feelings.
- **Renegotiate the power differential:** Once couples have validated each other's worth, and the importance of each partner to the relationship and to the family, couples can slowly begin to renegotiate financial agreements or boundaries that have already been established. This *takes time* because it challenges the existing balance of the family system.

By making efforts to clarify the financial power dynamic in a relationship, couples can confront head-on any issues this differential poses, rather than ignoring it and allowing it to become a potent, powerful point of resentment in the relationship.

Too Many Hours. Not Enough Hours. Too Much Debt. Nowhere to Turn.

Researchers and family practitioners are interested not only in the total number of work hours that couples put in each week, but they're also interested in how those hours are structured throughout the week (Grosswald, 2004). In many dual-earner families today, one partner works on a schedule that is different from the typical 8:00 to 5:00 schedule. **Shift work** can mean that a partner works nonstandard hours, such as working from 6:00 in the morning until 2:00 in the afternoon, or it could mean working a schedule other than the typical workweek (Monday through Friday in the United States) (Grosswald, 2004). For example, contemporary couples may have a partner that works 11-hours shifts, four times a week, which are common shifts for nurses, emergency personnel, and firefighters.

A number of advantages and disadvantages are associated with shift work schedules. Potential positive effects of these work schedules include such things as working fewer days each week, having more family time, and getting more time to be away from the job (for a complete review, see Loudoun, 2008).

However, there are negative impacts of shift work on families. For example, although shift workers may physically have more time to be with their families than standard-shift workers do, researchers believe the *quality* of these interactions is significantly less (White, 2018). This is because of the fatigue that intensifies throughout the shift week—some research has revealed that after a shift worker comes home from work and sleeps, he or she has less than two hours a day to attend to family duties, do household tasks, and prepare for the next workday. One law firm (Rudgard, 2017) noted that the proportion of divorce cases it has dealt with which involved shift workers increased from 7 percent to 35 percent from 2014 to 2017. So common are marital breakups with shift workers, some now refer to them as *shift work divorces* (Rudgard, 2017). Other studies have demonstrated that shift work significantly impacts family relationships (for a full review, see Davis et al., 2006):

- **Parental involvement:** There is a "mismatch" in parents' shift schedules and time for children. Overall, studies show that shift workers spend less time with their children than standard, daytime workers do.
- **Marital conflict:** Sometimes, high stress and work demands associated with shift work lead to increased levels of marital conflict. As one divorce attorney noted, "[Shift work marriages] effectively mean living under the same roof but leading separate lives" (Rudgard, 2017).

With the evolving global economy and the increase in shift work within different industries, much more needs to be understood about the effects of nonstandard work hours on family life. As some family practitioners note, these types of hours make it difficult for parents to create routines, rituals, and family activities—the very things that help to knit family members together and provide the foundation for family closeness (Davis et al., 2006).

The Demands of Overtime

Organizations typically define **overtime** as the hours a person works beyond their normal 40-hour per week schedule (Baird & Beccia, 1980). Working overtime often leads us to feel overworked, burned out—and just plain cranky. But given the systems nature of family living, it's important to keep in mind that these feelings of "enough is enough!" not only influence working moms and dads, but they also impact their families.

Decades of research have shown that long work hours increase workers' perceptions that their jobs interfere with their emotional states, and these, in turn, increase marital tension between spouses (for a complete review, see Crouter et al., 2001). Other studies have demonstrated that when fathers are pressured or stressed at work, they tend to have more conflict with their adolescent children (Crouter, 1995). Finally, research has revealed that wives' overtime work (46+ hours per week) decreases marital interaction and happiness, and increases the potential of divorce (Amato et al., 2003).

Working overtime can be successfully managed in the short term, but for many couples it is challenging to manage and balance their family relationships over the long haul due to the limited amount of time they can time spend with one another. That's not to say, however, that families can't make it work. As one family practitioner observed, quality time in great quantity is a staple of creating strong family relationships (Defrain, 2000).

Even though the federal government suspended student loan payments during the COVID-19 pandemic, many who carry student loan debt report that they feel they are drowning, sinking, or being crushed by their student loans. Do you own student loan debt? How do you feel when you think about repaying the loans?

Source: Cem Ozdel/Anadolu Agency/Getty Images.

Student Loan Debt: Credit Hostages

Today, few things impact parenting and family life as significantly as student loan debt (Robb et al., 2018). So extensive is the debt in the United States, the topic is becoming central in policy concerns (Robb et al., 2018) and took center stage as a primary concern of American adults in the 2020 Presidential Election. In 2020, 44 million student loan borrowers owed a total of 1.5 trillion dollars (Pew Foundation, 2020). As one borrower said: "I'm a credit hostage" (Proctor, 2020).

Student loan debt is money that is owed on a loan that was taken out by a student to pay for educational expenses, and currently over one *trillion* dollars are owed. In 2019, 15 percent of all adults in the United States carried student loan debt (Pew Foundation, 2020); over one-third of all adults aged 18 to 29 have student loan debt. And this debt is taking its toll on marriages and families. A recent survey of nearly 1400 adults who owe student loan debt found (Proctor, 2020):

- **Interfering with dating:** One in eight survey respondents indicated that dating has been affected by their student loan debt because potential partners to not want to "marry" significant debt.
- **Delaying marriage:** Over one-fourth of borrowers are delaying marriage until they are in a better financial position.
- **Delaying childbearing:** 51 percent indicated that although they desire to start a family, they feel they must delay having children until their student loan debt is paid down or off. One in three have opted to delay having children or forgo having children due to student loan debt.
- **Relationship stress:** Nearly 60 percent of those surveyed said that student loan debt is a significant source of stress and conflict in the relationships.
- **Divorce:** Slightly over 20 percent of student loan borrowers in this study indicated that they would divorce their marriage partner if it would result in a lower student loan payment.

There is also a great deal of psychological and emotional pain that borrowers feel due to the "weight of the debt" (Lockert, 2019). In a study of 829 student loan borrowers, the research revealed that student loan debt is linked to depression and suicidal thoughts (Lockert, 2019):

- **Anxiety:** 90 percent of borrowers experience "life-impeding" anxiety due to student loan debt.
- **Depression:** Over one-half of the borrowers surveyed noted that they experience depression due to their unpaid student loans.

- **Suicidal thoughts:** One in 15 student loan borrowers have considered suicide. When survey respondents were asked if they knew someone who had completed suicide because of student loans, the study participants reported one in 11 deaths.

What makes this type of debt so much different than home mortgages or credit card debt? As one survey respondent said, "If you want to have a good life, you get an education. It *has* to be college. There's an unspoken promise that if you follow this plan, the golden doors will open, everything will be fine" (Lockert, 2019). Another borrow succinctly said, "There is a [prevailing] feeling of hopelessness—you feel like you'll never recover."

While student loan forgiveness programs and lower payment programs exist, annually only about one percent of those who apply are accepted into these programs (Lockert, 2019). As the researcher observes, when an individual or a couple have student loan debt, there is uncertainty about how to pay back the debt, and borrowers also have significantly more pressure to find a high-paying job that accommodates large student loan payments. Finally, the inability to live life as planned creates anxiety and depression among those who are repaying student loan debt. In short, "Student loan debt [causes problems in relationships] because it impacts overall economic stability and flexibility for young Americans at a critical point in the life cycle" (Robb et al., 2018, p. 51). Something needs to give.

Economic hardship decreased somewhat when the U.S. federal government provided COVID-19 economic relief, but the inability to have consistent access to food sources continues to persist today. Millions of Americans face food insecurity, and this hardship is particularly prevalent among people of color.

Source: Chandan Khanna via Getty Images.

Coping With Unemployment: It's Not About the Money

In 2020, the COVID-19 pandemic threw an unprecedented 22.4 million Americans into unemployment (Congressional Research Service, 2021). Still today, countless families are trying to recover from the financial ruin brought about by sudden and prolonged global closures of businesses. The Center on Budget and Policy Priorities provides a snapshot of the economic hardships U.S. families faced during the first 12 months of the pandemic (CBPP, 2022):

- 20 million families reported having too little to eat.
- 10 million households reported they were behind on rent.
- 30 percent of all adults had difficulty covering usual household expenses (i.e. car payment, medical expenses).

Not surprisingly, households of color were likelier to suffer greater and protracted hardship, as Figures 10.5–10.7 illustrate.

Hopelessness. Anger. Hurt. Depression. Apprehension. Powerlessness. Fear. Helplessness. Worry. Anxiety. Worthless. Nervousness. Useless. Losing a job or not being able to find a job is more than losing an income—for many people, being jobless also carries with it severe emotional and psychological distress, as well as a loss in self-esteem, self-confidence, and professional identity (Hiswals et al., 2017). Without question: Job loss and financial hardship rank among the most severe stressors that individuals and families can encounter, and for many, this constitutes living in active trauma (Hiswals et al., 2017).

FIGURE 10.5 ■ Households of Color Lacking Sufficient Food During the Pandemic, 2020

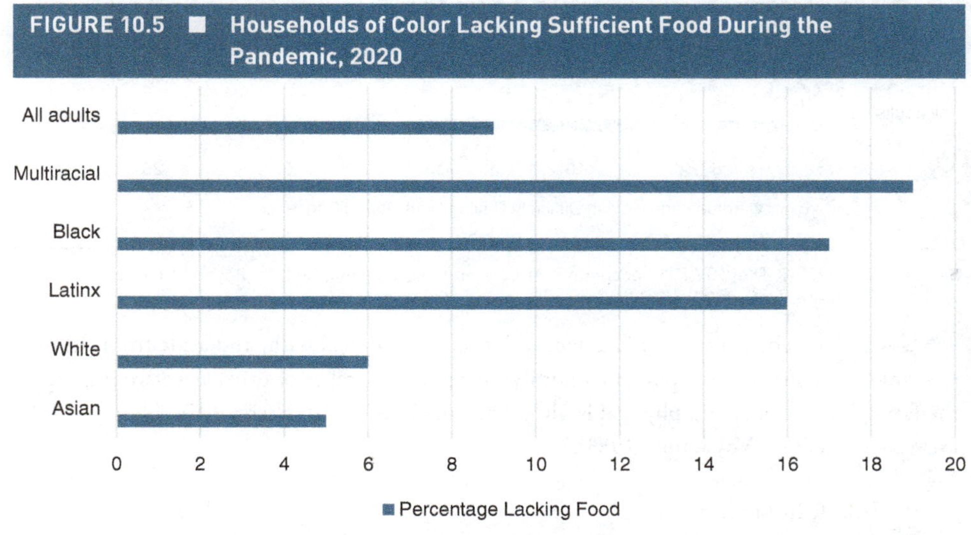

Source: CBPP (2021). The COVID-19 economy's effects on food, housing, and employment hardships. https://www.cbpp.org/sites/default/files/8-13-20pov.pdf

FIGURE 10.6 ■ Difficulty Paying for Household Expenses During Pandemic by Race, 2020

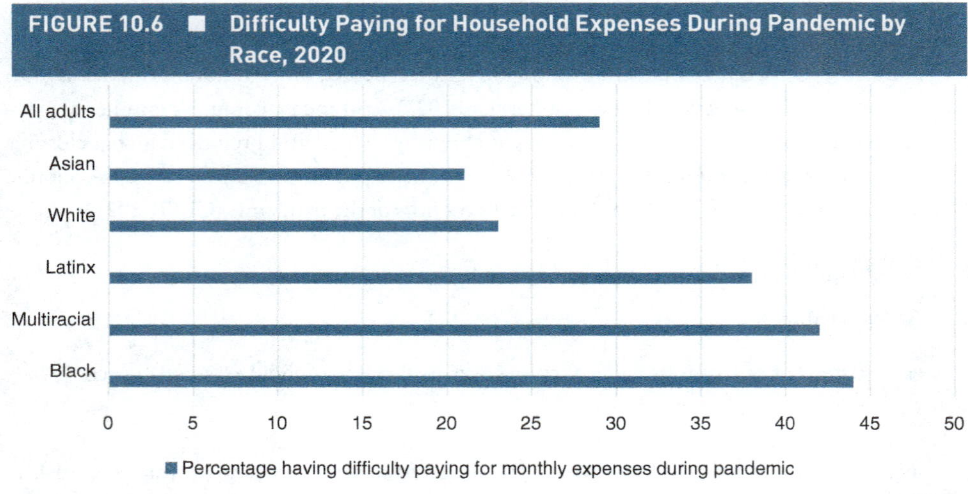

Source: CBPP (2021). The COVID-19 economy's effects on food, housing, and employment hardships. https://www.cbpp.org/sites/default/files/8-13-20pov.pdf

FIGURE 10.7 ■ Households Experiencing Difficulty Paying Rent During Pandemic, 2020

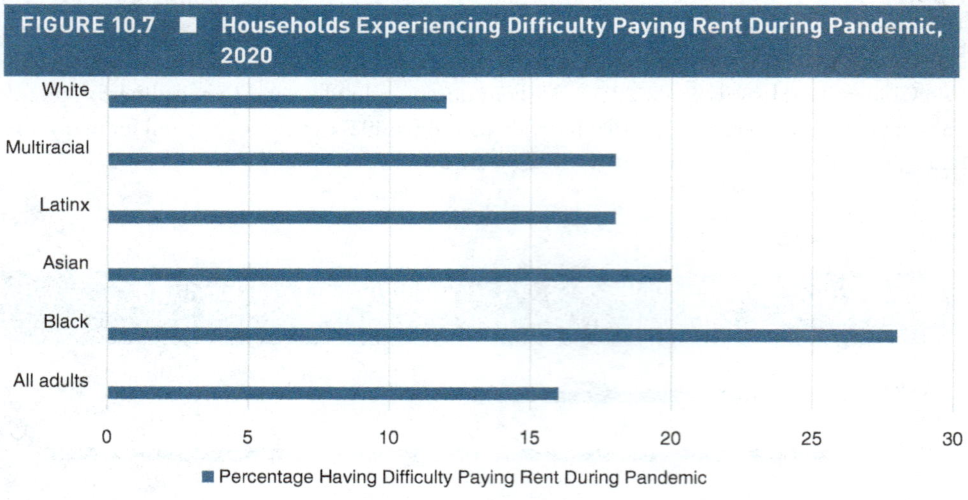

Source: CBPP (2021). The COVID-19 economy's effects on food, housing, and employment hardships. https://www.cbpp.org/sites/default/files/8-13-20pov.pdf

Unemployment is a traumatic situation for families to deal with, and aside from the obvious financial constraints it puts on a family, there are a number of other negative impacts on the family's emotional and physical health. These include (Furstenberg, 1974; Hanisch, 1999; Hiswals et al., 2017; Voydanoff, 1983):

- Family instability
- Decreased family interactions

- Increased levels of family violence
- Increased mental hospital admissions
- Loss of social capital
- Individual and family isolation

In a study that sought to better understand unemployed individuals' experiences and their perceptions of self and family, study participants revealed the pain they were experiencing when they noted (Hiswals et al., 2017, p. 995):

> I belong to nothing. When you have a job, you belong to something. You're included in something. But now I'm not that. Now I'm just something being tossed around somewhere.
>
> Work means security, the feeling that you are safe, that you have a role in life. Now you are not.
>
> You are affected all the time. Your entire life is affected.

As you can see—it's not just about money, or loss of money. It's about *everything else that comes with it*. So, when you look at the figures depicted in this section, we encourage you to look beyond the numbers and the percentages, and see not just the financial impact, but also the emotional and psychological pain. The truth about unemployment and job loss is, it *hurts*. Its effects are long lasting.

Previous research suggests that being married and having children seems to buffer against the negative impacts of unemployment for women but tends to have the reverse effect for men (Artazcoz et al., 2004). This may be because when women are unemployed, frequently they still have their basic economic needs met by their husbands; periods of job loss also lessen women's multiple demands and allow them greater involvement in family life. The risks of poor mental health for men may be higher than it is for women because of the pressures of traditional patriarchal gender roles that dictate that men are to protect and provide for their families. Certainly, job loss may make them feel that they are not living up to their prescribed role of breadwinner. And, because men are traditionally less involved in the care and nurturing of children, the researchers speculated that these activities can't successfully replace their jobs, as they may do with women.

In many ways, the stress associated with unemployment is similar to other transitions some families have to weather, such as divorce, acquiring a disability, or losing a home—and it can be as disrupting to a family's balance and health. But research has shown that people can cope well with unemployment and maintain mental health and well-being if they employ certain strategies. If faced with the loss of a job, healthy families should (Fetsch, 2009):

- Allow themselves to grieve, to feel anger, and be depressed or anxious.
- Adopt the attitude. "We're a strong family. We *can* bounce back from this setback!"

- Maintain consistent daily and weekly routines that provide structure and stability for the family.
- Seek emotional support from friends, relatives, and neighbors.
- Assess personal strengths, skills, and values. Often, new directions emerge after doing so.
- If signs of depression emerge, immediately seek counseling either from a professional source or from a pastor, priest, or rabbi.
- Communicate often and honestly with family members.

Opting Out: Stay-at-Home Moms

Some mothers have decided that staying at home with their children is how they can best experience personal, partner, and family needs with their partner's work responsibilities.

These mothers have opted out of the workforce and choose instead to stay at home and nurture their children; this is referred to as *household work.* Of the millions of mothers in the United States today, prior to the COVID-19 pandemic in 2020, about 7 in 10 mothers (30 percent) stayed home with their children during the day (U.S. Census Bureau, 2021b). At the onset of the pandemic in March, 2020, nearly one-half of all working mothers (45 percent) were no longer working (U.S. Census Bureau, 2021b). To date, nearly one million mothers have still not returned to work.

The fact that household work is still a critical component of a successful home for dual-earner couples has led some economists to try to place a value on household work. The **opportunity cost method** asks the question, *what would a person be paid in wage labor for one hour of household work?* Because what people earn in wage labor varies, this method can tend to skew the real value of household work. An alternative method is the **market alternative cost method**, which estimates the value of household labor by looking at what it would cost in the current market to pay someone to do the household labor the mother performs, such as preparing three meals a day, doing the laundry, caring for the children, and taking care of the home. For example, a group that tracks salaries and wages conducted a survey of stay-at-home moms and found if paid, stay-at-home moms would earn $162,581 annually (Salary.com, 2018). They also discovered that stay-at-home moms work 97 hours per week: spending 13 hours as a daycare provider/teacher to her children; nearly 4 hours as "household CEO"; almost 8 hours as a psychologist; 14 hours as a chef; 15 hours as a housekeeper; almost 7 hours as a laundress; about 9 hours as a computer operator; and nearly 11 hours as a facilities keeper. And they sleep about six hours per night.

Senior Vice President of the company, Bill Coleman, noted that this study "is an eye-opener for many people when they see the real market value of the work moms perform."

Of course, moms aren't the only ones who opt to stay at home and care for the children and the home. Today, an increasing number of fathers are doing the same.

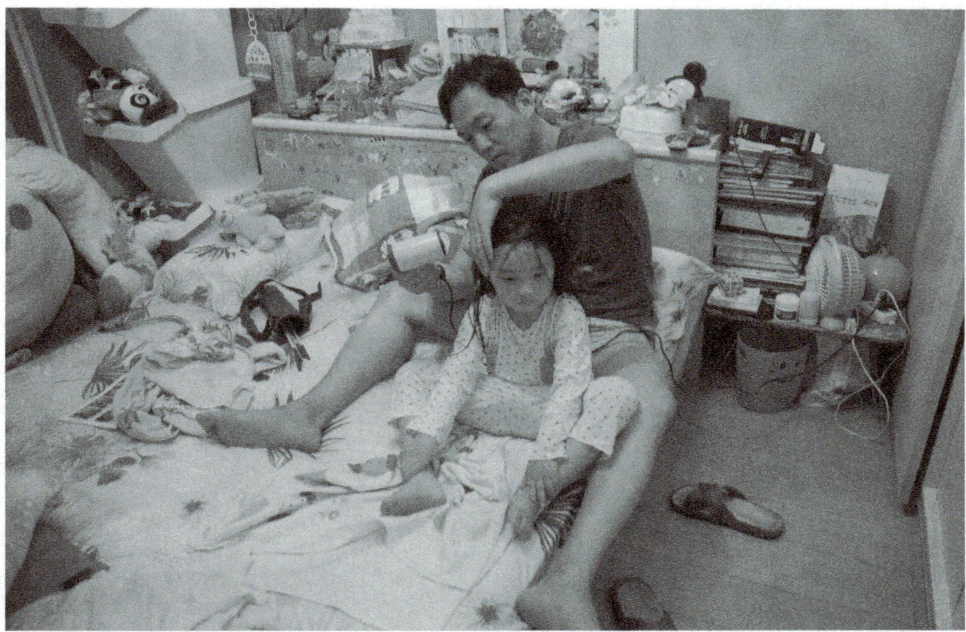

Today, more and more dads are leaving the workforce and are staying home to raise the kids and to care for household tasks.

Source: Shi Yangkun/Visual China Group via Getty Images.

Leaving the Workforce: Stay-at-Home Dads

A growing number of men have decided to stay at home. *Stay-at-home dads* are those who have remained out of the labor force for at least one year primarily so they can care for their children while their wives or partners work outside of the home. In 2020, 20 percent of all stay-at-home parents were fathers (U.S. Department of Labor, 2021). For most of these dads, the wife/partner has the better, higher-paying job and the couple believes that it is in the best interest of the family if the father stays home while the other works. This is a good example of how each individual and every family must make a choice that is good, better, or best for them in order to balance work and family successfully. As you can see in Table 10.3, there are both gender and racial/ethnic differences in parents who do not work outside of the home.

In today's economic environment, there appear to be three social circumstances that are contributing to the increasing numbers of dads who stay home to care for their children. First, among married fathers, the family's economic considerations make it more appealing for him to stay home than they do for her to do so. Second, today's increased divorce rates have resulted in some fathers becoming their children's primary caregiver; because some fathers have economic security, they may opt to stay at home and care for their children, rather than place the children in child care. Finally, a number of stay-at-home dads today are gay men whose husbands or partners work outside of the home, while they care for the

TABLE 10.3 ■ Stay-at-Home Parents

Characteristic	Stay-at-Home Dads Who Aren't Working...		Stay-at-Home Moms Who Aren't Working...	
	In Order to Care for Home/ Family	For Some Other Reason	In Order to Care for Home/ Family	For Some Other Reason
White	49	51	49	48
African American	15	19	7	23
Latinx	21	20	32	20
Asian/Pacific Islander	11	7	32	20
Married w/ working spouse	61	42	77	35
Married w/ nonworking spouse	15	27	5	11
Cohabiting	15	15	7	10
Single	9	16	11	43
At least one child <5	44	29	50	31

Source: Pew Research Center (2018).

children and assume household tasks. The prevalence of dads staying at home and opting out of the paid workforce will likely increase as this movement continues, and as social acceptance becomes more widespread and attitudes change.

THE BALANCING ACT: JUGGLING FAMILY LIFE AND WORK

"Come on, we're late!" "Let's *go!*" "Do you have your [backpack, briefcase, trumpet, book report, science project]?" "Where are my car keys?" Balancing work and family is nothing new. Since the women's movement in the 1960s and the surging flood of women into the workplace the past few decades, working families across the United States engage in similar morning rituals in their dash to get the kids off to school and parents off to work.

After the birth or the adoption of a child, dual-earner families must make numerous adjustments to accommodate the schedules and needs of both relationship partners and the children. Unlike the traditional homemaker/breadwinner family configurations found in the

1950s, once a baby arrives, contemporary couples must not only incorporate sleepless nights into their daily lives but they must also find a way to juggle the responsibilities, stressors, and struggles associated with managing the multiple roles of mother/father, employee, and wife/husband/partner.

Conflicting Demands: Heartstrings Versus Purse Strings

Sometimes our obligations to our jobs come into direct conflict with the needs of our families. When we take on (or have assigned to us) many roles simultaneously—for example, when the family role demands are incompatible with or conflict with the stresses from the work role—**interrole conflict** occurs (Hammer & Thompson, 2003). Such conflict can result in increased work absenteeism, intentions to leave the work force, decreased job satisfaction, decreased family satisfaction, decreased life satisfaction, negative mental and physical health, strain associated with dependent care responsibilities (both child care and elder care), and increased interpersonal conflict or divorce.

Something's Gotta Give: Work–Family Conflict

Work–family conflict falls into three specific areas and is bidirectional—the conflict goes both ways (Greenhaus & Beutell, 1985):

1. **Time-based conflict** takes place when demands from the work domain and the family domain vie for a parent's time and attention. This is the most common type of role conflict found in working families. For instance, a meeting that runs late at work might make one parent late for coaching a son's soccer game. A last-minute business call might make another parent late for a parent–teacher conference.

2. *Strain-based conflict* occurs when the demands in one domain make it difficult to carry out effective role performance in another domain. For example, consider a mother who finds it difficult to concentrate on her job or complete her job tasks on time because she is also caring for her elderly ill father.

   In recognition of the multiple roles with which most American families must now cope, in 1993, the federal government enacted the **Family and Medical Leave Act (FMLA)**. Under the FMLA, federal and state employees and those who work for employers with 50 or more employees are able to take up to 11 weeks of unpaid leave in order to care for an ill child, parent, or spouse, or for one's own serious illness, without fear of losing their job, benefits, or status. Unpaid leave can also be taken for the birth or adoption of a child, or when placing a child for adoption or foster care. Both working men and women are protected by this legislation.

3. *Behavior-based conflict* occurs when incompatibilities exist between the demands of the work role and the demands of the family role. For example, on the job, police officers may need to be aggressive, forceful, emotionally detached, and uncompromising.

"Something's gotta give." Today, parents face demands on their time and their role expectations at both work and at home. It is difficult for most to not bring home the emotional events and tensions from work to home. Would you choose a career that pays less so that you could be home more often with your family? Why or why not?

Source: iStock.com/ EmirMemedovski.

> Airline pilots need to be task oriented, detail oriented, hard driving, and single-minded in their purpose. Although these behavior traits may help these professionals be successful in their careers, bringing home these same behaviors to parenting and family life may not settle well with the spouse and the children.

Family life is a balancing act. Deciding who will work, who will care for the children, when and how to coordinate schedules, and determining who will transport the children to and from events and activities undoubtedly leads to role conflicts. Commonly, the partner with more flexibility in work schedules is called on to "pick up the slack" when it comes to trying to balance work and family. Oftentimes, though, this leads to frustration and a feeling of being "used" and "unappreciated." Consider, for example, a mother who is frequently frustrated with her husband after the birth of their first child. Because they both work full time, she feels that he should shoulder more of the childrearing responsibilities. Sleep deprivation for both partners is a daily reality and, unfortunately, can result in a cycle of escalating conflict: He feels she should appreciate his efforts more and she believes that she shouldn't have to express appreciation because he was just doing his duty as a father. Good communication and a willingness to avoid criticism, contempt, defensiveness, and stonewalling are important keys to negotiating work–family role conflicts effectively (Gottman, 1994), When conflicts do arise, learning to calm down, speak without causing defensiveness, and to validate our partner can help us reduce the possibility that these conflicts will harm the successful balancing of our work and family relationships (see also Gottman, 1999).

Work–Family Spillover/Crossover

Research psychologist Patricia Roehling and her colleague, professor and sociologist Phyllis Moen (2003), conclude that dual-earner couples are vulnerable to work–family conflict, as well as **work–family spillover/crossover**, which occurs when a relationship partner brings the emotional events and tensions of one environment to the other. This spillover/crossover can occur from *family-to-work*; for example, if a parent has an argument with a teenager before leaving for work, it can lead to poor concentration at work. In the case of *work-to-family* conflict, a "bad day at the office" for either parent may end up being a bad day for everyone else at home. Work–family spillover/crossover can also have positive individual and family outcomes. Roehling and Moen (2003) note that good relationships at home energize people, which in turn improves a person's productivity at work; a great day at work can translate to a great day for everyone else at home. The researchers also note that much scientific study shows that couples who combine work, married life, and family report the following:

- Levels of well-being are higher for both men and women.
- Women experience less anxiety and depression.
- Women report better physical health and higher self-esteem.
- Husbands are more involved with the children.
- Children have a stronger network of social support and social relationships.
- Two wages allow the couple to more adequately provide for their children.
- Marital satisfaction is high when the woman's employment is consistent with the husband's and wife's gender role beliefs.

Current economic trends indicate that dual-career relationshps are here to stay, but there are things couples can do to better handle the challenges associated with juggling work and family. In addition to promoting the physical well-being and the health of the children through shared caregiving, and in addition to ensuring the economic survival of the family, parents are also charged with the tremendous responsibility of fostering their children's optimal growth.

Balancing It All

When our lives are in balance, life just seems better, doesn't it? When it comes to work and family, balance can be thought of as the positive psychological state we achieve through regularly meeting our own and others' work-related needs. It is the state of equilibrium we feel when these needs—and their accompanying responsibilities—are fulfilled to improve our own well-being and the well-being of those we love (Harris, 2008).

Perhaps we can think about balance in another way by using the *Triangular Theory of Balancing Work and Family*, presented in Figure 10.8 (Harris, 2008). This theory maintains that the interaction of our personal needs, others' needs, and work responsibilities creates ever-changing situations that cause either balance or imbalance in a family. Individuals can choose and change how their needs and responsibilities interact to create greater balance in their relationships and improve subsequent happiness and well-being. In other words, we have a choice in how we attempt to balance our work and family relationships while, at the same time, try to meet our own personal needs. When we are out of balance in any of the three areas (personal needs, others' needs, and work needs/responsibilities), we intuitively sense that a change needs to occur; how we approach these changes makes all the difference in how happy and satisfied we are in our relationships. Other research redemonstrated that family health and **family cohesion**—the extent to which family members feel emotionally close and bonded to one another—are influenced by how well working couples are able to integrate the demands of work and family life (Stevens et al., 2006). One of the biggest challenges working couples face is who is going to do the tasks necessary to keep the house running and when?

Who Does What and When? Dividing Household Chores

Couples may marry with the intent to share household chores just as they intend to share childrearing. But when children enter into the family system, these intentions often do not become reality. Discrepancies between who does what often becomes a source of recurring conflict. With the majority of mothers today working at least 30 hours a week outside the home, the expectation that they are still responsible for the lion's share of running the household and performing household tasks can become a source of resentment. Sociologist Arlie Hochschild (1989) referred to this burden of taking on the dual responsibilities of wage earner and housekeeper as the **second shift**.

During this second shift, women spend three times as much time performing household tasks as men do, spending 32 hours compared to men's 10 hours (Coltrane, 2000). These tasks include house cleaning, meal preparation, grocery shopping, cleanup after meals, and laundry

FIGURE 10.8 ■ The Triangular Theory of Balancing Work and Family

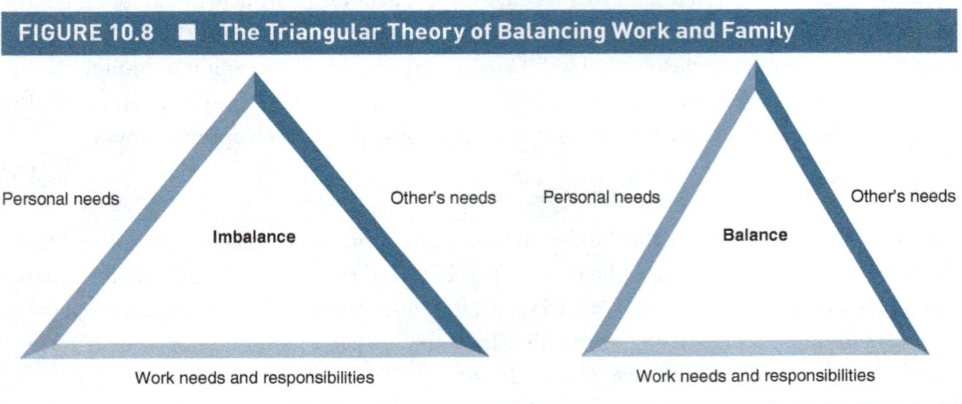

Source: Annotated from ©V.W. Harris (2008).

(Blair & Lichter, 1991). Coltrane (2000) refers to these essential tasks as "routine housework" but maintains that "this family work or social reproductive labor is just as important to the maintenance of society as the productive work that occurs in the formal market economy" (p. 1109), and that these tasks keep the household, the family, and society going. The author cites numerous studies that indicate that, for the most part, neither women nor men enjoy performing routine household chores. They tend to find occasional **residual tasks**, such as bill paying, yard work, and chauffeuring children to be more flexible in nature and more enjoyable to carry out.

Like parenting roles, the division of household duties tends to fall along traditional gender roles once a child is born, even if such tasks were previously handled fairly equally (Baxter, 1993). Coltrane (2000) identifies several factors that contribute to the division of household chores. These factors include *women's employment* (the more hours a woman works outside the home, the more men share in household tasks); *men's employment* (men who work fewer hours outside the home tend to pitch in more around the house and with childrearing); *earnings* (women who earn more hire someone to perform household chores); *education* (men with higher education levels tend to engage in more household labor); and the *presence of children* (when children enter the picture, women assume the majority of housework).

Although gender appears to be an important factor that generally dictates who does what housework and how often, the research does seem to indicate that the division of labor along traditional gender roles is slowly giving way to changing roles of men and women in contemporary

Household chores are still oftentimes divided along "traditional" gender roles, but contemporary families are more likely to share these tasks, or to do whatever is necessary to get the work done.

Source: iStock.com/PollyanaVentura.

society. This is a "ray of hope" for those who struggle with balancing marital and parenting roles, because, as Coltrane (2000) concludes, "We now know that when men perform more of the routine household work, employed women feel that the division of labor is fairer, are less depressed, and enjoy higher levels of marital satisfaction" (p. 1126).

Ten Strategies for Family and Work Balance

Although money doesn't buy happiness, it can definitely provide opportunities for more comfortable daily living and better educational opportunities, health care, family vacations, marriage getaways, and other leisure activities. It can also reduce many of the stressors and strains that those who lack economic advantage inevitably endure (Dyk, 2004). Although the demands of balancing work and family can sometimes be draining on a family, research suggests that most employed couples believe that there are strong benefits to combining work and family, and that the benefits far outweigh the costs (Barnett & Rivers, 1996). Though it takes some effort, it is possible for families to successfully blend and manage these two most important domains in their lives.

In a study that examines the work/family lives of 47 married couples who appear to successfully manage both spheres, the data revealed that these couples structured their lives around 10 major strategies (Haddock et al., 2001). We discuss these in the sections that follow.

Value family: Dual-earner couples who make their relationship and their children a priority experience greater satisfaction and well-being in their family relationships (Eyre & Eyre, 2008). Through words and actions, couples who do well at balancing work and family work hard to keep their family as their number one priority, and all of their decisions reflect this priority. Couples can proactively create opportunities for family time and couple time, and during these times can create family rituals and routines—special family times—that are unique to them. Above all, couples need to remember to nurture their relationship: *Strong couples make stronger parents!* Successful couples also emphasize family happiness and well-being over professional responsibilities.

Strive for partnership: Stressing equality and partnership in the marital relationship is critical to working couples' success. While certainly there are varying degrees of equality among couples, and while there is no doubt that some situations call for greater degrees of partnership than others, partners who possess an overall high degree of equality fare better than those who do not. There appear to be three principle areas where equality is a must: the division of household labor, making decisions together as a couple, and having a "team" mentality. As one partner noted, "If I win and she loses, then we both lose. If she wins and I lose, then we both lose. [This belief] has probably made all the difference... because you just can't live your life trying to always win. The couple will lose, period."

Derive meaning from work: Even if it's not always possible to love their jobs, couples who are successful at balancing work and family note that being able to derive meaning out of what they do is important. For these couples, experiencing enjoyment and purpose from their jobs brings energy, enthusiasm, and excitement to their lives: It also seems to buffer them against work-related fatigue and burnout.

Maintain work boundaries: If couples are able to keep their families as their top priority, it's easier for them to maintain clear—and immovable—boundaries between their home life and their work life. As researchers note, couples who are committed to not allowing work to dictate the pace of their lives are better able to compartmentalize their lives and prevent overlap between their personal and professional lives. As one study participant said, "I think the biggest [strategy] is: When you're at home, you're at home; and when you're at work, you're at work. There's not the crossover. You don't get to think about work unless there's a huge problem."

Be focused and productive at work: Many couples talked about the importance of being productive while at work. They observed that even though they set boundaries, their employers tended to better support their commitment to family if they were efficient while they were on the job.

Prioritize family fun: You gotta have fun! Successful working families make a point to enjoy a lot of fun time together as a family. Not only is family fun a way to relax and de-stress, it's also a way that families build emotional connections and create family rituals, stories, and histories. Family time together doesn't have to be a costly trip to Disneyworld—it can be an every Friday night board game or movie and popcorn night, a spontaneous bike ride on a Saturday, or a quick toss of the Frisbee in the backyard. Of course, a sense of humor goes a long way in buffering the stressors associated with the demands of balancing work and family. Successful families strive to make laughter and humor the general atmosphere in the family.

Families who carve out time to be together and have fun experience healthier relationships, both at home and at work.
Source: iStock.com/jarenwicklund.

Take pride in dual earning: Although the reality of family life for many today means that both partners are in the paid labor force, some women today still feel that there are negative societal messages about them working instead of staying home with the children. Couples who successfully balance work and home life adopt the attitude that dual earning is positive for every member of their family, and they refuse to accept negative comments from family or friends. Overall, these couples do not struggle with feelings of guilt, and they don't fret over not spending every spare minute with their children—if they had to sit down to pay the bills, they did so in lieu of playing with the kids. As one parent noted, "I think it's a big benefit for [my son] to have a working mom.... He's going to grow up understanding that women and men share equally in what's going on, and he's growing up expecting that he's going to share what happens in [his house.]"

Live simply: A number of successful couples have learned to simplify their lives. For example, rather than allowing their children to be involved in as many activities as they wanted to, parents limit each child to one or two activities that they really enjoy doing. Limiting activities in this way helps minimize the chaos of family living. Couples also note the importance of controlling their finances and living within their budgets as a way to simplify their lives. They also find creative time-saving strategies that make family life more efficient and less complicated. For example, one family helps their children line up their clothes for the entire week; this minimizes the "Where's my other Nike?" and "Where'd you put my belt?" last-minute disorder and confusion in the mornings.

Learn to say "no": Keeping a clear sense of priorities helps couples make decisions that are in the best interest of their marriage, children, families, and careers. Successful couples don't allow the pace of their *lives* to dictate their schedules—their schedules dictate the pace. As one husband noted, "I view it as my choice. I have control over what I'm going to do. Rather than, 'This schedule is driving me crazy this week!' I remind myself, 'If it's crazy, then I need to make some other choices—I need to say no.'" Couples who balance family life and work well also note the importance of consistent and frequent communication so they can stay on top of their priorities and always keep the big picture in mind; this keeps them from getting off track by focusing on things that aren't important.

Value time: Couples realize that their time together and time with their families is a valuable commodity and a resource to be spent with great care. They are protective of their family time and seldom allow others or other things to get in the way of the time they've carved out for each other. They carefully determine how their time will be best utilized. Couples also find ways to do things together, such as learning to play golf, so that when their kids are grown, they have shared interests.

All too often, families struggle with work–family balance, and frequently these difficulties can begin to erode the couple's relationship. These adaptive strategies, individualized to each family's needs, can significantly help couples' abilities to become active participants in creating a successful balance of family and work.

RELATIONSHIPS AND MONEY

Most couples undergo some degree of financial culture shock when they begin to merge their finances. According to family financial expert Alena Johnson (2008), spending styles are directly related to financial personality styles, and these personality styles develop through past experiences with money. Answering questions such as, *Was money readily available or pretty tight growing up in your home?* and *What do you like to spend money* on? and *What kinds of things have you saved money for in the past?* are just a few of the questions that help us identify whether we are a spender or a saver, a worrier about or an avoider of money issues, and a risk-inclined or risk-averse financial personality type (see also Mellan, 1994). For example, complete this sentence: "If I had a lot more money, I would ________." Would you pay off your student loans? Or would you go to Vegas? In most cases when our financial personalities are not in sync, conflict occurs.

Interestingly, it is common that one partner possesses a dominant financial personality, and this personality overrides the other partner's. In some cases, the dominant partner is able to persuade the more submissive partner to become more like his or her own financial personality profile (Johnson, 2008). What often happens, though, is that the submissive partner becomes even more entrenched in their own financial personality style. According to Johnson, this "can create an opposite spending style." When this happens, conflict over money is sure to occur,

Johnson also asserts that financial issues are usually more of a catalyst to revealing underlying, hidden, or deeper couple issues than the actual financial problems are themselves. In other words, couples may fight about finances, but often the financial issues are symptomatic of a couple's communication, intimacy, loyalty, or commitment problems. And oftentimes money is an emotional issue.

Money as an Emotional Issue

Whether rich or poor, middle class or low income, money is intricately connected with emotion. Have you ever

- worried yourself sick over a bill you couldn't pay?
- felt fantastic because you loaned your friend in need some money to get by until payday?
- splurged on something and felt excited—until the reality of the cost hit you and then you became upset for spending that much?

There is no question that each of us has felt an array of emotions when it comes to money: The lack of it can cause stress and strain, while the abundance of money can engender feelings of security and opportunity (Dyk, 2004).

People spend money when they are sad, happy, angry, excited, content, or depressed, and often they spend it *because* they are sad, happy, angry, excited, content, or depressed. Indeed, the media are very aware of the close connection between emotion and spending money, and millions of dollars are spent each year to exploit this connection. Their attempts to speak to who we are or who we would like to be, to get us to interact emotionally with their promotional advertisements, and to eventually convince us to purchase their products are their primary goals. For example, think about the latest movie you went to see, the last restaurant you ate at, or the newest technology toy you purchased. Can you pinpoint where you learned about them, what caused you to identify with them, and why you eventually chose to purchase them?

Many of us indulge in spending (or as I refer to it, *retail therapy*) to cope with stress, cure the blues, diffuse feelings of anger or frustration, ease boredom, or soothe ourselves after a bad day. While an occasional little pick-me-up is probably therapeutic to some extent, it's important not to underestimate how these impulsive purchases can create or perpetuate financial problems. Unfortunately, our emotional connection with money can lead to unmanageable debt.

Dealing With Debt

Household debt is at an all-time high. In 2018, *consumer debt* (credit card debt, student loans, and auto loans) reached $14 trillion—almost double the rate from 2004. Collectively, Americans owe over one-fourth of their monthly income to debt, and spend 10 percent of their month income on car loans, credit card debt, and student loans (Statista, 2019).

Debt is a significant topic when discussing families and work; money problems and economic hardship can lead to financial ruin, filing for bankruptcy, the breakup of relationships, and eventual divorce. Today, nearly 45 percent of Americans carry credit card debt, and over two-thirds owe on installment loans (such as auto loans) (Statista, 2019). Two previous studies revealed that couples cited financial and economic problems as the fifth and sixth leading causes of their divorces (Johnson et al., 2000; Schramm et al., 2003). Another study also found that financial matters significantly affect overall marital satisfaction and quality of life (Copur & Eker, 2014).

Among newlyweds' top relationship concerns were debt brought into marriage and financial decision-making (Schramm et al., 2005). Another study of newly married couples found that consumer debt greatly inhibited these couples' attempts to form their new family system (Dew, 2008). Because of their high debt, couples had difficulty finding time together because they worked greater hours in attempts to pay down their debt.

These findings are important to our understanding of parenting and family life, and work. They provide insight for family practitioners who work with premarital couples, such as those who provide premarital education; through educational programs, these practitioners can sensitize couples to debt issues prior to their marriages. If couples learn about debt prior to marriage (Dew, 2008):

- They may decide to postpone their wedding until their debt is paid down or is paid off.
- They may decide to marry, but with the understanding that paying off their debt will yield higher levels of relationship satisfaction.

- They may decide not to acquire credit cards and incur debt because they know that such debt creates declines in marital happiness.
- They are better able to construct effective plans to pay down their debt and to minimize conflict while doing so.

Of course, beyond learning about debt and its consequences, couples should take efforts to learn about financial management strategies, such as learning how to budget so that debt isn't a necessary way of life (Dew, 2008). Understanding money and its significance to married life is perhaps one of the ways in which couples can best prepare for parenting responsibilities.

Saving for the future also takes discipline and planning. There are several principles that people intent on saving might want to consider (Evans, 2004):

1. Is this expenditure really necessary? (Or is it possible to get the same personal affect without using money or using less of it?)
2. Is this expenditure contributing to my wealth or taking from it?
3. Is this an impulse purchase or a planned purchase?
4. Am I being pressured to make an expenditure I'm not certain about?

All couples need to talk about money and its significance to their relationships. The best time to talk about it is all the time! Topics such as acquiring and managing debt, goal setting, distinguishing between wants and needs, and establishing and maintaining a monthly budget are just a few of the issues couples should address on a regular basis. How healthy are your money matters?

PARENTING LIFE EDUCATION: HELPING FAMILIES TO HELP THEMSELVES

A key role of the Family Life Educator or parent educator is to assist and aid families as they make decisions about allocating their resources to meet individual family members' and family goals (NCFR, 2020). All too often, though, when people think of "resources," they think in terms of money, income, or personal assets—and neglect to consider the human side of resources, such as personal, familial, professional, and community resources. *All* of these are important to help individuals, couples, and families to navigate the complexities of making ends meet.

Today, balancing the demands of work and parenting/family life is a challenging—but necessary—task for a significant number of American families. In this chapter, we spent some time looking at the differences in work experiences among various racial and ethnic groups, as well as the differing configurations (such as married or single parents) of working families. While a number of trends were presented, it's important to have an understanding of these trends because they give us a real picture of what's happening in our economic lives today, what a lot of parents are up against, and what their day-to-day struggles are. Given the interrelated nature of family living, it's easy to see how what goes on at work can significantly impact a family's well-being, functioning, and overall health.

Managing complex, multifaceted work/family roles is also a reality for many Americans today. There are a number of ways in which families can ease the stress and strain associated with work, such as keeping their families a priority, managing time more effectively, and carving out time for one another. But today it's just as important to have realistic expectations about trying to balance work and family life. There will be times when things won't get done around the house—the carpet will be in desperate need of vacuuming, children will be able to drive their Hot Wheels cars through the dust on the furniture and become excited about the "road" they created, and sometimes it will just be easier to put dirty dishes in the dishwasher with the clean ones, and wash them all—again. There will be times when couples yell and fight and scream at one another because they're so overworked and overwhelmed, and just plain tired. That's the reality of balancing work and family. Much like a circus act where the performer is trying to keep a number of plates spinning in the air at the same time, sometimes in work and parenting life, we can't keep all the plates going. And certainly today, money constraints due to the economic crisis make matters worse—as the man noted in the opening vignette of this chapter, money seems to be at the base of all of his worries and anxieties.

Can combining work and family really work today? We learned a number of strategies that families who effectively balance the two employ. But above all, it's necessary to keep in mind that we can't possibly control everything. If families keep a sense of humor about the neglected housework, if they're willing to revise plans and schedules as necessary to accommodate everyone's needs, and if they communicate often, they can minimize the stressors associated with work and family. Learning to let go of things that won't really matter in the long run is fairly easy to do. When confronted with work/family stressors, ask yourself: Is this going to make a difference in five years? If not, let it go and focus on the things that *will* make a difference a few years from now.

11 PARENTING IN TIMES OF CRISIS

LEARNING OBJECTIVES

11.1 Distinguish between family crisis and family stress.

11.2 Describe the determinants of the Family Crisis Model.

11.3 Explain the major adaptive tasks families must navigate to successfully adjust to a crisis or stressor.

11.4 Summarize the various ways in which families cope.

11.5 Discuss the various aspects of family resilience.

11.6 Describe the types of family violence.

11.7 Explain the long-term effects of domestic and child violence on the development of children.

11.8 Summarize the ways in which homelessness impacts children's development and on family relationships.

No one can predict what tomorrow or the months and years ahead will bring for any given family. The very nature of parenting and family living involves countless complexities, and along with it, inevitable change. At this point in our study of contemporary parenting, we need to understand there are expected, or *normative*, changes that take place throughout the Family Life Cycle. Some of these changes are considered "vulnerability points," such as getting married; starting a sexual relationship; having a baby; parenting a teenager; juggling dual careers, financial commitments and overcommitments; and caring for aging parents. *Nonnormative* life events, or things we cannot predict or anticipate, or things that are not commonly experienced by most families, also bring much disruption to family living. These would include life events such as a child being diagnosed with cancer, as our story of young Grit in the opening chapter poignantly illustrates; unemployment; the COVID-19 pandemic; mothers fighting in combat; a child or teenager who desires to transition their sexual identity; or a loved one's suicide.

Numerous factors influence the degree of risk that might be involved in parenting for any particular family or any specific group of families. Risk factors may be related to health, medical, psychological, structural, economic, developmental, or social aspects of family life, or to any combination of these. It is probably accurate to say that some risks exist in every family situation, but many families are able to minimize the risk factors by a network of support systems. Sadly, others are unable to do so with any degree of success.

Certain groups of families attempt to function in relatively high-risk situations and are in greater need of support services than other families. In Chapter 7, we discussed what factors put teenaged parents and their children at risk. Here, we examine two more high-risk parenting family types: abusive or neglectful parents and homeless parents. Abusive parents represent a serious risk situation for children and their parents—a risk that is often deadly, at least for the children involved. Homeless parents with children are growing in number, and these families are at risk economically, socially, psychologically, and educationally. These types of families have unique needs and require special kinds of support and intervention services. First, we explore the nuances of family crisis and change.

There is no way for parents to predict the joys and sorrows that parenting brings. Sometimes the crisis is so great, it doesn't feel survivable.

Source: Chandan Khanna via Getty Images.

FAMILY CRISIS

It is a certainty that families grow, change, and experience many transitions, but whether the family experiences these changes and transitions as family *stress* or family *crisis* largely depends on whether the family has the ability to adapt to the changes in the family environment.

In cases of family stress, there is an imbalance between the stressor(s) placed on the family and their ability to meet the demands of the stressor(s). If the family adapts to meet these demands, they will weather this significant, but temporary, period of family stress. If, however, they cannot make the adjustments necessary to cope with these inevitable changes, reorganizations, and disruptions, the stressors may develop into a family crisis. There are four categories of family stress, and each stressor places different demands on the family system. Family stress is said to occur when the demands of the stressor(s) outweigh the family's ability to meet those demands. The four categories of family stress are dismemberment, demoralization, accession, and demoralization plus dismemberment or accession (Duvall & Hill, 1960):

Dismemberment family crisis depicts the separation or isolation of an individual from the rest of his or her family. This includes hospitalization, loss of a child, loss of a spouse, being orphaned, and physical separation (military, work, etc.).

Demoralization family crisis describes crises that tend to bring disgrace or embarrassment to a family system, such as alcoholism, substance use/abuse, crime, and delinquency. This also includes infidelity, nonsupport from a divorced spouse, and ongoing conflict or discord in the family system.

Accession family crisis is when turbulence occurs due to the addition of a family member, such as with the pregnancy or birth of a child, adoption, fostering, relatives moving in, a parent remarries (creating a stepfamily system), and the reunion after a separation.

Demoralization plus dismemberment or accession occurs when a family is thought to be demoralized because of "embarrassing" stressors, such as the imprisonment or the suicide of a family member, or for some families, an out-of-marriage birth.

Like family stress situations, when a family crisis occurs, family members must use their problem-solving and coping skills to navigate the situation until balance is restored. Typically, however, because a crisis is almost always unexpected, families find themselves in unfamiliar territory, and their established repertoire of problem-solving strategies is not effective. This shortage of coping and problem-solving skills increases fear, anger, guilt, and anxiety—and these feelings lead to an increased state of turbulence or family crisis (Moos, 1987). The following foundational theoretical models will shed light on the "how" and "why" some families experience change as stress, while others experience it as crisis.

The ABCs of Family Crisis: The Family Crisis Model

For decades, family researchers and social scientists have been intrigued with why some families who face a given stressor, such as the death of a spouse or child or the serious illness or injury of a close family member, seem to adjust, while others who face the same stressor do not. To examine this difference, family therapist Rueben Hill (1949) conducted research to understand the stressors that families experienced during times of war. From his early work that examined war separation and reunion, Hill advanced the **ABC-X Family Crisis Model**, still considered a major contribution to the area of family stress and family vulnerability research. Hill's model explains why families vary in the way they adapt and adjust to change, transition, and stress.

Hill's ABC-X model views a family crisis situation as a combination of various factors: *A* factors are the initial crisis-causing events; *B* factors are the resources a family has at its disposal to meet the demands of the crisis; *C* factors are the meanings families ascribe to the event; and *X* factors are the outcomes of the event, the results of whether or not a family copes effectively with the crisis event. Figure 11.1 illustrates Hill's (1958) interactive ABC-X Family Crisis Model.

The *A* Factor

The ***A* factor** is the event that initially causes the stress. This stressor can be a normative development in the Family Life Cycle, such as the birth of a child or the marriage of an adult child. It can also be a nonnormative event, such as the early death of a spouse, job loss, or winning the lottery. It is important to note that *A* factors can fall anywhere along the continuum of expected family developmental tasks, to individual developmental tasks, to catastrophic life events. *A* factors are *family-specific:* What one family perceives as a stressor or vulnerability, another family may not. Whatever the stressor, because of the interconnected nature of the family, it provokes change within the *entire* family system—changes in such aspects as family boundaries, family roles, family communication, or family processes (Burr, 1973). When the change is significant, the stressor induces a disturbance in the family's routine way of functioning. According to Hill, then, it isn't just the nature of the stressor event that influences the depth of a person's reaction to the stressor. Whether "stress" becomes a "crisis" depends on the amount of disruption the stressor causes in the family system. The *A* factor then interacts with the *B* factor.

The *B* Factor

The ***B* factor** refers to the family resources that will help the family meet the demands of the stressor or crisis. Some families possess particular strengths within the family system, such as effective communication skills and problem-solving or coping strategies. Other families are weaker in these areas. Some families have access to extended family and community resources. To illustrate, consider a

FIGURE 11.1 ■ Hill's Interactive ABC-X Family Crisis Model

Why do some families adapt and adjust to stress, and other families have difficulty doing so? The ABC-X model helps us understand the variances in family coping.

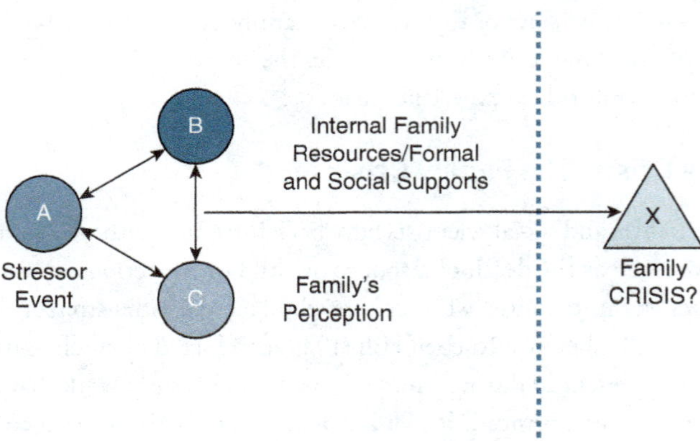

Source: Based on information from Hill (1958).

family in which a parent has a serious illness. Sometimes family and friends may pitch in and prepare meals for the family for a period of weeks or months to get them through the most critical period. This community may also arrange for rides for the children to and from school, take in the children after school, and provide comfort to the individual who is ill as well as the spouse who is taking care of the house, the expenses, and the children. Having friends and family "pitching in" minimizes the disruption—and, in turn, the vulnerability—a family may experience during a parent's illness. Hill theorized that the *A* and *B* factors then interact with the *C* factor.

The *C* Factor

The ***C* factor** refers to the definition the family assigns to the change, transition, stressor, or disruption. *This is why A factors are said to be family-specific;* whether a family experiences a stressor as a crisis depends on their *perception* or *interpretation* of the event. According to Hill, the amount of change (such as changes in family boundaries, family roles, family rules, communication, and routine) that occurs and induces stress influences the severity of the crisis; thus, the family's vulnerability depends on how the family perceives these changes. Factors that come into play include how families answer questions such as, Are the changes serious? Are they minor? Are they short term? Ultimately, the definition the family assigns to the stressor event produces the *X* factor.

The *X* Factor

The ***X* factor** can be thought of as the end product of the initiating event, the family's resources to cope with it, and the meaning they assign to it—the combination of the *A, B,* and *C* factors. The *X* factor could be a momentary bump in the family's life journey, or it could be a life-altering family crisis. Each person processes and perceives stress in unique ways. Families operate with the same uniqueness and subjectivity, and the outcome—the *X* factor—is wholly dependent on the resources the family has to meet life's challenges, in tandem with their perception of the stressor or the definition they assign to the challenge.

At one time or another, we have all reached a point of complete exasperation and uttered the words, "If *one more thing* happens," or "This is the *last straw!*" We all have felt the effects of *pile-up*. Using Hill's ABC-X Model as the foundation, noted family researchers Hamilton McCubbin and Joan Patterson (1982) developed the **Double ABC-X Model** to understand the effects of the accumulation, or pile-up, of stressors and strains and how families adapt to them. Pile-up can result from either a single stressor that coincides with life events/changes, multiple stressors, or multiple stressors that coincide with life events/changes. Regardless of the nature of the pile-up, this model recognizes that the effects of prior stresses and strains are exacerbated and intensified when another stressor is added into the mix. Figure 11.2 illustrates the Double ABC-X Model.

We have now established that the stressors, or the life changes, aren't necessarily the key elements that lead to crisis. More important is the family's ability to make the necessary adaptations and adjustments in the family system to accommodate the change. When the appropriate adjustments are made, not only are families able to add to their repertoire of problem-solving and coping skills, but stressors and life crises can actually propel both individuals and families to develop more intimate, satisfying levels of functioning. Nevertheless, in order to achieve those intimate levels of functioning—in order to survive a family crisis—the family must learn to complete a standard set of adaptive tasks demanded by life's many transitions, changes, and stressors.

FIGURE 11.2 ■ McCubbin's Double ABC-X Model of Family Stress and Crisis: Pile-Up

Why do some families adapt and adjust to stress, and other families have difficulty doing so? The ABC-X model helps us understand the variances in family coping.

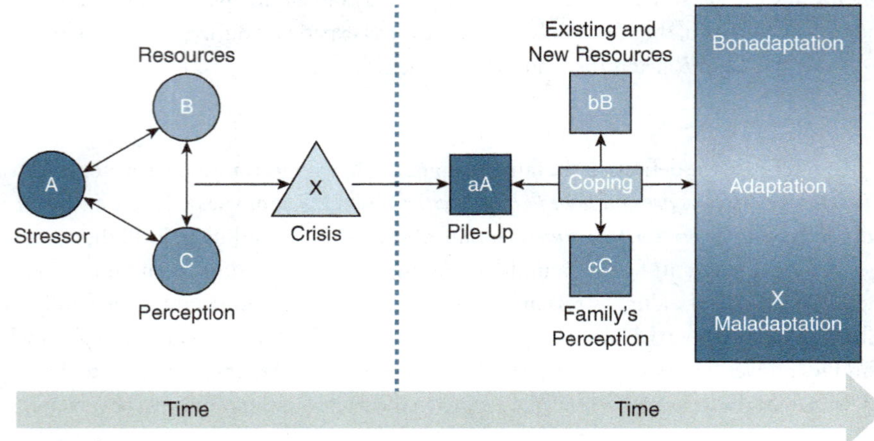

Source: Based on information from McCubbin and Patterson (1982).

Although easier said than done, sustaining and maintaining family ties and other relationships during times of stress and crisis is essential in helping people to weather the storm. Although it's tempting to isolate from others, struggling well often requires the help of others.

Source: iStock.com/FG Trade.

Family Adaptive Tasks

Professor of psychiatry and behavioral sciences Rudolf Moos and research health scientist Jeanne Schaefer (1987) created a framework to help guide students of family life as well as professionals in the field of parent education and Family Science to understand and appreciate those adaptive tasks and adjustments that families need to successfully navigate normative and nonnormative life transitions and changes. Families facing change encounter five major adaptive tasks they must perform in order to successfully adjust:

1. **Establish the meaning and understand the personal significance of the situation.** When a stressor is introduced into the family system, the family as a collective system tries to make sense of what is happening. Charles Darwin once noted that "human beings cannot adapt to their environment alone; they are *interdependent* and must make collective efforts to survive." Sometimes the stressor is of such great magnitude, such as discovering that a spouse is having an extramarital affair or learning that parents are divorcing, that common initial reactions may include numbness, shock, confusion, and disbelief. A family member or members confronting a stressor may also have a keen sense that there is no reality or past experience on which they can draw to handle this stressful event. As disbelief gives way to reality, the life event becomes clearer and the family attempts to "wrap their minds around it," to cognitively grasp what is unfolding. Eventually, the family must acknowledge the reality of the circumstances; at this point, individual family members and the family as a collective system assign significance to the situation. As Moos and Schaefer (1987) explain, it is important to understand that major life events are not "singular" in nature. Finding out that a spouse or an intimate partner has been cheating, for example, potentially involves other stressors, such as the realization that the marriage or the relationship is in trouble, the possibility of divorce, and contemplating the losses associated with a marital dissolution. The potential for this type of "domino" effect exists for many life changes. Consequently, establishing the meaning of transition and change is an ongoing process.
2. **Confront reality and respond to the requirements of the external situation.** Stressor events demand our attention: A loved one who dies must be buried and their personal items sorted through; a family who experiences violence must cope with not only the trauma of the physical violence but also the need to realign family roles and rules. Moos and Schaefer's (1987) point is that sometimes, in the midst of the confusion and shock associated with life change and crisis, families must still cope with the immediate needs of the situation.
3. **Sustain relationships with family members and friends as well as with other individuals who may be helpful in resolving the crisis and aftermath.** This is perhaps not as easy as it may seem. Many times people who experience change and

crisis turn inward, becoming private in their grief as a result of their experiences. Whether a family opens up to other extended family members or friends depends on their cultural and ethnic backgrounds, as some cultures and ethnicities are more open and willing to share than are others. Culture and society are the sculptors that shape what events a particular family perceives as stressful (Pearlin, 1982), and culture also dictates which coping strategies and problem-solving skills are appropriate and acceptable to use (Cordon, 1997). Moos and Schaefer (1987) suggest that these interpersonal relationships often "help individuals obtain information necessary to make wise decisions, find emotional support for them, and secure reassurance about the problems they face" (p. 12).

4. **Preserve a reasonable emotional balance by managing distressful feelings in response to the situation.** Life transitions and change are often accompanied by powerful, sometimes overwhelming, emotions. According to Moos and Schaefer (1987), the feelings of anger, guilt, self-blame, resentment, fear, anxiety, worry, hopelessness, and helplessness may be overpowering. Being able to maintain some level of emotional balance is necessary in order for a family to adapt to the change and maintain a sense of hope, even when that hope is temporarily overshadowed by the circumstances.

5. **Preserve a satisfactory self-image and maintain a sense of competence and mastery.** It is important to maintain a sense of confidence in the family's ability to adapt to, adjust to, and overcome life's challenges; the family must have a sense of an internal locus of control. When families are able to recognize that *all* families face struggles and challenges, with sufficient support networks and time, *all* families can successfully navigate change.

No family is immune from stress, change, and transition. Perhaps now you have a better understanding of why some families weather the storms of crisis and change and come out stronger, and why other families can experience similar situations and circumstances only to become weaker or dissolve altogether. You should now understand how the family's perception of the event and the ability of family members to face it head on, while making the necessary adjustments within the family system, help push the family toward adaptation. When lines of communication remain open among family members and friends, and when these individuals are able to simultaneously accept help and yet do what they can for themselves, they are able to avoid crisis and manage stress. According to family sociologist Ronald L. Pitzer (2004):

> In every life crisis [and change] there is danger and opportunity … a turning point for better or worse. Things will never be quite the same again. They may not necessarily be worse; perhaps they will be better, but they will definitely be different. Though not entirely masters of our fate, neither are we prisoners.

FAMILY COPING AND RESILIENCE

Finding a way to cope with the pile-up of daily stressors and transcending profound life crises is possible. Yet, to overcome the stresses and crises many families experience, family members must have an awareness of those behaviors that promote coping and resiliency to help lessen the influence and impact of a quickly changing, demanding, difficult life circumstance.

Family Coping

A family's ability to cope effectively in the face of adversity and change increases if the family possesses a variety of coping strategies. By using personal, family, and community resources, families are better able to make the necessary adaptations to reduce the impact of stressors. Rudolf Moos and Jeanne Schaefer (1987) provide an overview of the major types of family coping skills that families tend to use in times of change and crisis.

Appraisal-Focused Coping

With **appraisal-focused coping**, families try to understand why the crisis occurred and to find meaning in the circumstances that caused the crisis. Skills needed include the ability to analyze the situation logically and to prepare mentally for certain events to unfold. **Cognitive redefinition** occurs when families attempt to reframe the life event or stressor in ways that are more

In an attempt to cope with the tragic murder of her son, Trayvon Martin's mother, Sybrina Fulton, ran for public office. This type of coping strategy following a tragedy is known as *problem-focused coping*.

Source: Joe Raedle/Getty Images.

favorable. If a spouse loses a job, for example, a family might reframe the situation by saying, "Well, at least she has her health." This type of coping mechanism appears to take the "sting" out of the reality/threat of the situation. **Cognitive avoidance or denial** is an attempt to deny the seriousness of the situation, saying, for example, "He isn't cheating on me—I'm sure there is a reasonable explanation for why they were together."

Problem-Focused Coping

The **problem-focused coping** strategy allows the family to confront the reality of the crisis head on by seeking and obtaining information about the crisis, thereby allowing family members to regain a sense of control over their situation. Families who lose a child to a violent act, for example, might petition lawmakers to create legislation to protect other children from similar acts of violence, as does Mothers Against Drunk Driving (MADD). In cases such as these, families seek the support from the community as well from family members. Problem-solving actions are concrete, tangible ways of meeting the demands of the crisis that provide a sense of competence and that bolster the family's esteem.

Emotion-Focused Coping

Family crises often evoke a wide range of feelings and emotions. In many cases, these feelings and emotions are so new that just experiencing them produces fear and anxiety. To manage their feelings, families might develop **emotion-focused coping** skills or capacities to maintain hope. One coping strategy families develop is **progressive desensitization**, in which family members gradually allow themselves increasing exposure to the varying aspects of the stressor. This was evidenced after the attacks of September 11, 2001, when family members of those who lost their lives in the Twin Towers ventured to "Ground Zero." **Emotional discharge**, another coping skill, is just what the term implies—venting! Emotional discharge entails venting anger, frustration, confusion, disappointment, hatred, and despair in response to tragic or sudden and unexpected news. While some families tend to vent their emotions, other families use humor. All of these strategies have one goal—to reduce the tension produced by the stressor event. **Resigned acceptance** occurs when the family ultimately accepts the situation and recognizes that nothing will change the course their family life has taken.

Couple and Family Therapy

Over several decades, stress and coping in couples and families has received wide attention from family scientists, psychologists, social workers, researchers, couple and family therapists (CFTs), and other family practitioners (Bodenmann, 2010). For good reason—as you have seen so far in our study together, even with everyday stressors such as job and work strain, the challenges associated with parenting, role conflict, and financial constraints can have a negative impact on a couple's relationship quality and satisfaction. Today, couples do not need to struggle alone and in isolation. With the guidance of a qualified mental health professional, such as a marriage and family therapist (MFT), family members can learn to identify the specific behaviors that affect their relationship and other relationships within the family. They can also learn new, healthier ways of relating to each other, how to effectively resolve conflict, and how to communicate in ways that serve to promote the well-being of the couple's relationship as well as the family's (American Association for Marriage and Family Therapists [AAMFT], 2020).

Because of the systems nature of relationships and family life, MFTs and CFTs do not focus on an individual person (even if it is an individual who is seeking treatment); rather, therapy focuses on the interrelated relationships in which the person is embedded, and the treatment plan is focused on the long-term, overall health of the couple and/or their family (AAMFT, 2020). Therapists focus on a wide range of problems, such as anxiety, addictions, child–parent relationships, anxiety, post-traumatic stress disorder (PTSD), depression, and children's conduct disorders. Treatment is brief (about 12 sessions on average), and it is solution-focused. As the term implies, the *solution-focused therapy model* focuses on the default solution patterns individuals, couples, or families are using, not talking about the problem(s) over and over. The aim of therapy, then, is for the clients and the therapist to find alternative problem-solving approaches that work (AAMFT, 2020).

Family Resilience

Family resilience refers to a family's ability to function in a healthy fashion during times of change, stress, adversity, crisis, and transition. Successful adaptation to periods of family stress and crisis involves resilience and a certain "hardiness" that allows the family to "withstand and rebound from disruptive life changes" (Walsh, 2003, p. 1). Often, a crisis serves as a wake-up call to the family—the "heart attack" that gets their attention. Confronted with a crisis, family members often reevaluate their priorities and tend to invest more deeply in meaningful relationships and life pursuits. The crisis may even serve as a time of personal and relational growth, as the newfound personal exploration that accompanies crises can often help family members "discover or develop new insights and abilities ... through weathering a crisis together, relationships [can be] enriched and more loving than they might otherwise have been" (Walsh, 2003, p. 3).

Key Family Resilience Processes

Family resilience is reinforced by numerous family resilience processes that help guide families through the times of change and challenge. These processes also help foster a speedier recovery and help family members create deeper interpersonal relationships following the stressor or crisis event (Cowan et al., 1996). By drawing from these family resiliency resources, the family system can "rally in times of crisis, buffer stress, reduce the risk of dysfunction, and support optimal adaptation—emerge stronger and more resourceful in meeting future challenges" (Walsh, 2003, p. 3). Professor of psychiatry and co-director of the University of Chicago's Center for Family Health, Froma Walsh (2003), refers to a number of empirical family stress/crisis research findings and delineates the key processes in family resilience.

For many people, a spiritual belief system helps them cope in times of crisis. Research indicates that spirituality helps families to be more resilient to the effects of change or crisis.

Source: iStock.com/RyanJLane.

Family Belief System and Spirituality

A family's belief system has a powerful effect on how a stressor, such as the loss of a job, or a tragedy, such as the death of a child, is viewed. The belief system informs the meaning the family assigns to the event. It also determines whether a family has a shared meaning or a shared reality. Walsh (2003) refers to empirical research, which suggests that family belief systems help families organize their family processes and their approaches to family crisis and change; this, in turn, fosters resiliency by promoting problem-solving, healing, and growth.

In addition, medical studies consistently offer evidence that spiritual beliefs and the practice of faith, prayer, and other spiritual rituals not only help families frame their life changes and challenges with shared meaning and purpose but they also give meaning to situations that are "beyond ourselves." For example, we may be able to tap into resources to help empower us to leave an abusive relationship, but some of life's challenges are beyond us. Walsh (2003) further notes that cultural, ethnic, and religious beliefs and traditions help families find strength, comfort, and guidance and ultimately facilitate passage through life's transitions.

Making Meaning of Adversity

As we discussed earlier, the meaning a family attaches to family change and challenge greatly influences how families cope with and adapt to the life event. Families who approach change as a *shared challenge*, as opposed to an individual's problem, have an enhanced ability to overcome adversity.

Walsh (2003) notes that highly functioning and healthy families understand that becoming a family entails continuous growth and motion across the family's life cycle. The family researcher notes:

> A Family Life Cycle orientation helps [family] members see disruptive transitions as *milestones* in their shared life passage. By normalizing and contextualizing distress, family members can enlarge their perspective to see their reactions and difficulties as understandable ... The tendency for blame [and] shame is reduced in viewing their complicated feelings and dilemmas as "normal," common, and *expectable* among families facing similar predicaments.

Highly functioning families also have a positive view of life. Even in the midst of the grimmest circumstances, these families remain optimistic and maintain a positive outlook rather than prematurely giving up and giving in. This "can-do" spirit promotes shared confidence and encouragement, bolsters courage and determination, and fuels shared initiative and perseverance—all hallmarks of family resilience (Walsh, 2003).

Flexibility

Walsh (2003) refers to flexibility in this family process as the ability to "bounce forward" or to change whatever needs to be changed in the family system in order to accommodate new challenges. This reorganization of the family system allows families to reconstruct and recalibrate what is "normal" and allows members to adjust their interactions and behaviors to fit the current conditions into the family's daily life. Flexibility and adaptability are key factors in family resilience.

Communication

In determining those factors that foster family resiliency, Walsh (2003) posits that the family communication processes of bringing clarity to the situation, encouraging open emotional expression by all family members, and promoting collaborative problem-solving are each key elements. For example, *delivering clear messages* removes any ambiguity that might exist; this, in turn, helps to facilitate the meaning the family assigns to the situation and also promotes informed decision-making and problem-solving. Walsh notes that allowing *open emotional expression* promotes a family climate of trust, empathy, and tolerance. Further, when family members cannot or are not allowed to be open with their feelings, self-destructive behaviors may result. *Collaborative problem-solving* helps facilitate "bouncing forward." Families who share in decision-making and conflict resolution promote resiliency by setting clear goals and by taking the necessary steps toward meeting those goals.

Walsh's (2003) work presents for us an empirically based resiliency framework that enables us to see the importance of fostering a strong, healthy family system that helps families navigate the normative and nonnormative twists and turns that naturally accompany family life and parenting relationships. This framework is based on the basic family system premise that takes into account the interconnections that exist between family members and the idea that key family processes influence adaptation and adjustment for each family member. Furthermore, the resiliency framework supports families' efforts to "work well, play well, and love well." According to Walsh, understanding the importance of a shared perception of the situation, shared hope,

In the United States today, nearly 20 people every minute (typically women) suffer at the hands of a batterer.

Source: iStock.com/Geber86.

shared resources, and a shared commitment to struggle together may ultimately result in personal growth and surprisingly deep levels of intimacy. "In bouncing forward … each family must find its own pathways through adversity, fitting their situation, their cultural orientation, and their personal strengths and resources. Families build on small successes and use failures as learning experiences" (p. 15).

THE CRISIS OF FAMILY VIOLENCE

Divorce. Poverty. Suicide. Illness. Sexual violence. Mental illness. Family separation because of war. Bankruptcy. Foreclosure. Job loss. Families today are experiencing a wide variety of changes, transitions, and challenges and are often called on to confront simultaneous challenges. Entire chapters could be written about dealing with each of these family crises, but an increasingly widespread social problem in the United States demands our attention—family violence. Today alone, more than 30,000 American women will find refuge in a domestic violence shelter as the result of having been severely abused by their male intimate partner; between 3 and 10 million children will witness violence taking place in their homes (Bureau of Justice Statistics, 2019).

In this section, we'll take a close look at the number of family members who were battered in the United States over a five-year period. It is important to keep in mind that behind the numbers are countless lives that are, undeniably, forever changed because of the violence committed against them. We begin by considering the following experience of a college student (Welch, 2004).

Melanie is a 20-year-old university sophomore. She carries a pretty full class load, she juggles her academic load with her job responsibilities, and she tries to find time to be with her fiancé, friends, and family. She dreads finals week. But Melanie lives with past childhood experiences that make her day-to-day college life tougher to handle than that of many students. From the age of 10, her stepfather repeatedly sexually assaulted her. She recalls:

> When I was in fourth grade, my stepdad one morning before work and after my mom had already left for work sexually molested me at least 30 or 40 times. [In my 7th-grade year], it was at least once or twice a week during that time period ... It was always after my mom went to bed ... he came into my room and then ....
>
> Flashbacks still haunt me ... where I wake up in the middle of the night, curled up in a ball because I'm scared and I can still, after all these years, feel him on my skin ... it's like, you wake up and you know he's in the room with you .... Even though I'm in college now, there are some nights I can't sleep, and I'm still absolutely terrified of someone who is dead.
>
> I'm engaged and my wedding is less than a month away. [Aside from the normal fears of getting married], I also have to deal with, if Danny holds me a certain way, or touches me a certain way, I remember something that Alan did to me .... It's so unfair that Alan stole that part away from Danny, that there are some things that Danny can't do with me because Alan did them to me. I am absolutely terrified because of what happened to me when I was 10 and then when I was 14. Things like this stay with you.
>
> The effects are long lasting.

Domestic Violence

Violence that takes place in the home is a prevalent, multifaceted social ailment in the United States. Contributing to these assaults are individual factors, such as family of origin patterns, psychopathology, mental illness, and genetic causes; community factors, such as poverty, educational levels, absent or inaccessible family services; and cultural factors, such as media influences.

Domestic violence, or family violence, is violence perpetrated against family members by an offender who is related to the victim either biologically or legally, such as by marriage or through adoption (U.S. Department of Justice, 2018). Although most people think of family violence as something that takes place between intimate partners and children, the people who carry out family violence—the **batterer**—include current or former spouses, parents or adoptive parents, legal guardians or foster parents, biological or adopted children, current or former stepchildren, a sibling, grandchildren, grandparents, in-laws, or other relatives, such as aunts, uncles, nephews, and nieces.

Domestic violence is an umbrella term that encompasses any behavior designed to intentionally inflict emotional, sexual, or physical harm. Acts of domestic or family violence may result in harming children, intimate partners (spouse, cohabiting partner, and gay or lesbian partner), and/or elderly family members. There are three broad categories of domestic violence:

- **Physical violence** includes such acts as hitting, punching, pushing, slapping, biting, or throwing something at the victim.
- **Emotional violence** includes such acts as controlling the amount of contact a family member has with family and friends, name-calling, constant criticism, threats to leave the partner or throw them out, displays of intense jealousy/accusations that one is being unfaithful, controlling the spending and distribution of money, excessive rule-making, and threats of physical or sexual harm.
- **Sexual violence** includes marital rape (unwanted, forcible sex by a person's marital partner), battering rape (rape along with other acts of physical violence), and forced sexual acts (such as forced oral or anal sex).

Demographers measure family violence in two ways: through survey interviews with the victims and through statistics gathered by police. The National Intimate Partner and Sexual Violence Survey (NIPSVS), a division of the U.S. Centers for Disease Control and Prevention (CDC), collects lifetime and past-year information about people's experiences with rape, physical violence, and stalking. Our figures here present some of their 2018 findings.

The Battered

Although no one is immune from abuse, there are specific factors that place some at greater risk for experiencing violence than others. For example, women who have less education (especially women who do not attend college), who come from lower socioeconomic status (SES), or who are single parents or young teenage parents are more likely to be victims of violence. Also, women who have witnessed a parent being battered are at higher risk of being victims themselves. Generally, women who have low self-esteem, feel a sense of inferiority, are passive, or believe that they are responsible for the batterer's actions are more likely to be abused. When violence is perpetrated against a partner, it is referred to as **intimate partner violence (IPV)**.

No gender or racial/ethnic group is immune from family violence, as the data in Figure 11.3 illustrate. Although women (5.4 per 1,000 population) are victimized more frequently than men, about 7 percent of all acts of IPV are perpetrated against men by women (National Center for Victims of Crime, 2018). In addition, intimate partner violence and family violence cross every SES and educational level and every family type, including married, single-parent, gay, straight, and cohabiting families.

Gender-Based Violence Gays, lesbians, bisexuals, and transgender people experience higher rates of violence than heterosexuals, as Figure 11.4 shows us. Violence against LGBTQ+ people includes rape, emotional or psychological violence, physical violence, or stalking by an intimate partner. **Gender-based violence (GBV)** is broadly defined as violence

FIGURE 11.3 ■ Intimate Partner Violence by Race, Ethnicity, and Sex

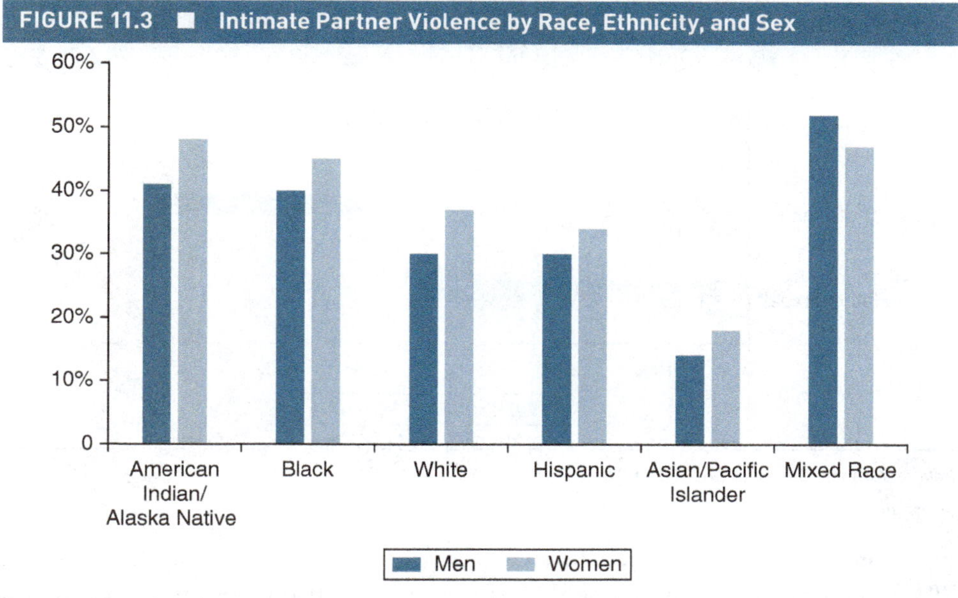

Source: National Center for Victims of Crime (2018).

N = 25,000.

LGBTQ+ people experience higher rates of violence than heterosexuals do. Sadly, there are few safe shelters for gay or trans men who are battered by their partners.

Source: Kentaroo Tryman via Getty Images.

FIGURE 11.4 ■ Rape, Physical Violence, and/or Stalking by an Intimate Partner by Sex and Sexual Orientation

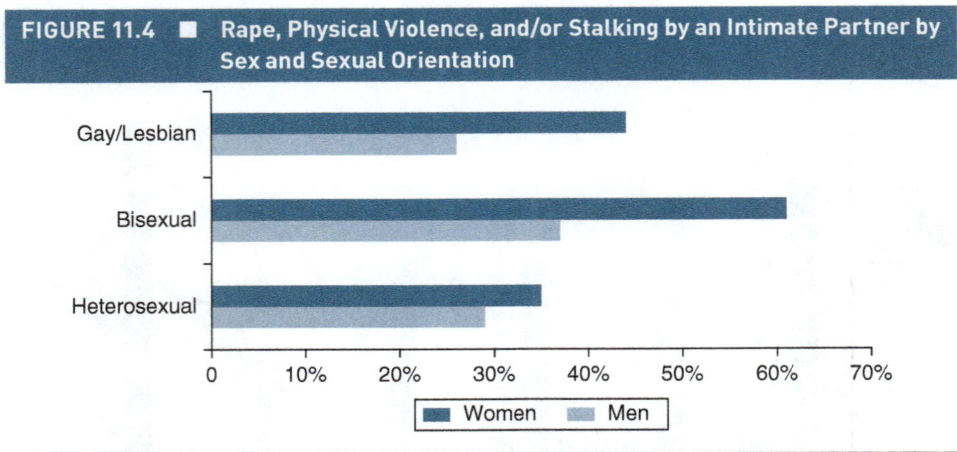

Source: National Center for Victims of Crime (2018).

N = 25,000.

perpetrated against an individual because of their gender/gender identity (Leddy et al., 2019). It's important to understand that GBV is *any* harm that is done to another person against that person's will, and this harm results from power imbalances and inequalities (Wirtz et al., 2020). In a publication that sought to highlight GBV and to determine why GBV is tolerated still today, Elisabeth Duban observes, "GBV is rooted in gender norms regarding masculinity, including the need to assert control or power, enforce roles or prevent, discourage, or punish behavior considered unacceptable because it does not conform to socially constructed norms" (Duban, 2018, p. 8).

Globally, it is estimated that one in three women experience some form of GBV—most often from an intimate partner (Leddy et al., 2019); however, this estimate almost always refers to the experiences of cisgender, heterosexual women (Wirtz et al., 2020). Marginalized women, such as transgender women, experience higher rates of gender-based violence (Leddy et al., 2019), and they are targeted because of their gender nonconformity or gender expression (Wirtz et al., 2020).

In the United States, one in four women and one in nine men suffers physical and/or emotional violence at the hands of an intimate partner—nearly 20 people every minute (U.S. Department of Justice, 2018). The statistics regarding violence perpetrated at the hands of an intimate partner or a family member are staggering and include the following (National Center for Victims of Crime, 2018; U.S. Department of Justice, 2018):

Domestic Violence

- Women aged 18 to 24 are most commonly abused by an intimate partner.
- One in three women and one in four men have experienced slapping, shoving, pushing, and other forms of physical violence by an intimate partner.

- One in ten women have been raped by an intimate partner.
- One in four women and one in seven men have been victims of severe physical violence (beating, burning, and strangling) by an intimate partner
- Each day in the United States, 20,000 calls are placed to national domestic violence hotlines.
- Only one-third injured by intimate partners receive medical care for their injuries.

Dating Violence/Teen Violence

- One in four teen girls in a relationship report being pressured into performing oral sex or having sex against their wishes.
- One in three high school students experience either physical or sexual violence perpetrated by someone they are dating or going out with.
- 9 percent of high school girls and 7 percent of high school boys report being a victim of dating violence.
- Black students report the highest proportion of physical dating violence, as seen in Figure 11.5.

FIGURE 11.5 ■ Percentage of Students in Grades 9–12 Reporting Dating Violence, by Race

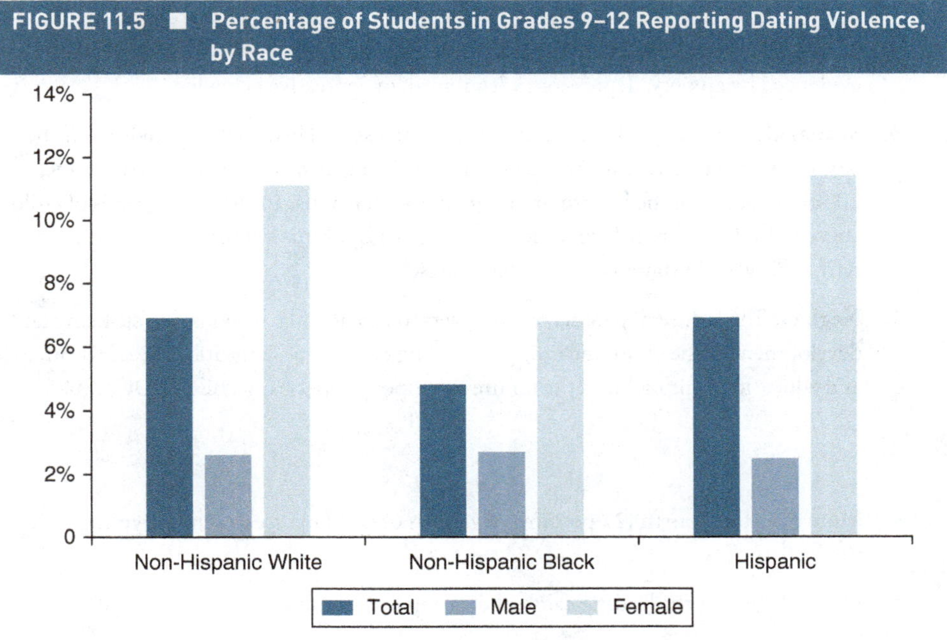

Source: CDC (2018).

Domestic Murders

- Each year, nearly 2,000 women in the United States are killed by their intimate partners.
- IPV is the second leading cause of death among pregnant women in the United States (second only to car accidents).
- Pregnancy is a time of increased risk—most pregnant women who experience violence have been abused before, but pregnancy increases the frequency and severity of attacks by intimate partners.
- Intimate partners are responsible for more than one-half of all female homicides each year and 5 percent of all male homicides.

Violence Against Children **Child maltreatment** is any act, intentional or not, that results in harm to a child, the threat of harm, or the potential for harm (CDC, 2020). There are four types of child maltreatment:

1. **Physical abuse:** Generally defined as "any nonaccidental physical injury to the child" (Child Welfare Information Gateway, 2019). These injuries are usually caused by a parent or person in a position of responsibility, power, or trust (CDC, 2020).
2. **Emotional abuse:** The failure to provide a supportive environment for the child (CDC, 2020) that results in "injury to the psychological capacity or emotional stability of the child" (Child Welfare Information Gateway, 2019). Emotional abuse is typically evidenced by anxiety, depression, withdrawal, or aggressive behavior.
3. **Sexual abuse:** The involvement of a child in any sexual behavior or activity that the child is unable to give informed consent to and is against the laws of society (CDC, 2020). All states in the United States include sexual abuse in their definitions of child abuse (Child Welfare Information Gateway, 2019). Human trafficking is currently only a crime in 15 states in the United States.
4. **Neglect:** The failure of parents or caregivers to provide for the holistic well-being and development of the child, including safe living conditions, education, medical care, and education; this includes the failure to properly supervise a child (CDC, 2020).

Today,

- More than one-fourth (27 percent) of victims of child maltreatment are younger than three years.
- Physical abuse is the leading cause of death in infants under four years of age.
- Each year, four million children experience some type of maltreatment by a parent/caregiver; sadly, these numbers are believed to be vastly underreported.

Figure 11.6 shows us the racial and ethnic differences in children who are abused each year.

Indeed, these trends are alarming, and it's distressing that the United States is not successful in addressing the violence perpetrated against women, children, and sexual minorities. But

FIGURE 11.6 ■ Victims of Child Abuse by Race and Ethnicity (Rate Per 1,000)

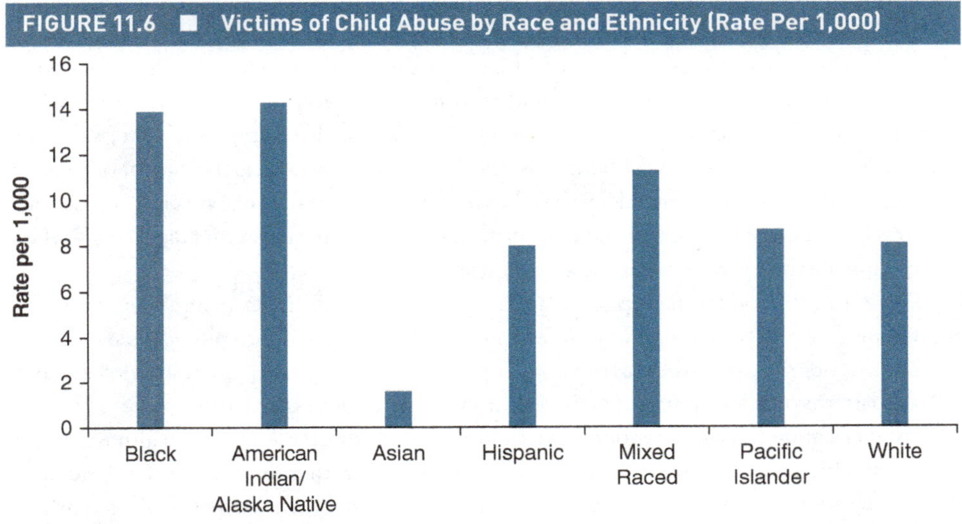

Source: U.S. Department of Health and Human Services (2018).

Perpetrators of domestic violence are driven by the need for power and control. It is almost never a situation of an argument that went too far or got "out of hand."

Source: iStock.com/South_agency.

why do people batter? What are the characteristics of those who abuse their family members or intimate partners? We'll examine these questions in the following section.

The Batterer

As the statistics reveal, men are more likely to abuse a family member more than are women. Those who abuse their partners or their children share some common characteristics; for example, most batterers have low self-esteem and tend to blame everyone else for their behavior. They are also typically extremely jealous and often use sex as their weapon of aggression and ultimate instrument of control. Although violence is the way they express their anger or frustration, they underestimate or even deny that their behaviors are "really that violent" or harmful. Batterers have the need to control and dominate, and they become master manipulators—they can manipulate their partner's weaknesses and strengths.

There is a common misconception that family violence results from an argument that "got out of hand," or that a partner "flew out of control," then escalated into physical blows. Most often, this is not the case—the batterer doesn't just lose control. Rather, domestic violence and IPV are patterns of behavior in which the abuser exerts power over the victim.

Another common misconception is that alcohol use or substance abuse are almost always associated with acts of family violence. Today, it is estimated that in America, England, and Wales, only about one-half (55 percent) of victims believed that their partners had been drinking prior to the physical or sexual assault (World Health Organization, 2018).

Although on the surface, domestic violence appears to be acts of physical, emotional, or sexual aggression against a victim, the central issues in family violence are not the acts of aggression at all. Rather, the central issues of domestic violence are *power, control,* and *domination*—and are commonly perpetuated by the strongest against the weakest (McGoldrick et al., 1999). And batterers use a lot of strategies to control and dominate their partners: verbal abuse, isolation, controlling the finances, reproductive coercion (such as mandating whether birth control can or will be used), or sabotaging birth control so a partner gets pregnant. The important message here is this: *Rarely* is violence a one-time incident. Instead, domestic violence and intimate partner violence are patterns of behaviors that are consistently repeated over time, and over time, they instill great fear in the partner victim. Table 11.1 presents information to help people determine whether they are in an abusive relationship.

The Domestic Abuse Intervention Project (2020) created a tool that helps to describe the many ways in which an abusive partner uses *power* and *control* to manipulate a relationship. Physical battering and sexual assaults (or the threats to commit them) are common abusive behaviors, but other forms of abusive actions often contribute to the overall pattern of abuse:

- intimidation
- emotional abuse
- isolation
- minimizing, denying, and bullying

TABLE 11.1 ■ Signs of an Abusive Partner

Everyone has a right not to be abused in a relationship. *Abuse is not inevitable*, and there are ways to minimize your risk of encountering abuse in your relationships. Following are signs that you may be in an abusive relationship. Pay attention to these signs—they don't go away. They don't get better. If he promises it will never happen again, just remember: *It will.*

- **Overly protective mannerisms:** Your boyfriend berates your friends and tries to keep you from seeing them. He repeatedly asks for detailed descriptions of who you were with, where you went, and why you were with them.
- **Problems with anger:** Trivial and mundane things set him off. He has random and erratic mood swings, putting you at the mercy of his emotional states.
- **Rigidity and belligerence:** Instead of a balanced view of relationship roles, he insists on defining the relationship in his terms, and his terms only. He ignores your needs and forges ahead with his desires.
- **Highly critical:** He is always making comments about your appearance. Healthy relationships are affirming relationships.

Source: National Coalition Against Domestic Violence (2020).

Have you ever ignored signs of abuse in your interpersonal relationships? Have your friends or other loved ones tried to warn you about what they were seeing or hearing? If so, how did you handle their concerns?

Source: iStock.com/AtnoYdur.

- using children against the woman (such as threatening to take the children away)
- male privilege
- economic abuse
- coercion and threats

These behaviors are not commonly identified as "abusive" by some women, but they contribute to the larger system of abuse and are often used to reinforce the physical and/or sexual abusive behaviors by the batterer. These behaviors send the clear message that a physical or sexual assault can be just around the corner.

As you can see, abusive and battering men use a whole host of tactics, ranging from degrading and humiliating comments to physical hits, punches, and kicks; false imprisonment; various forms of sexual abuse; threats and intimidation; economic exploitation; and murder to control and dominate.

Other researchers identify three categories of means that batterers use to control and dominate (Dalton & Schneider, 2001):

- **The ruler and the ruled:** Batterers often set stringent, unreasonable rules at home while also exerting extreme control in every facet of family life. For example, a husband might dictate which route the spouse must use when driving to the grocery store or taking the children to school. Any violation of the rules results in subsequent punishment.
- **Internalizing the rules:** Over time, batterers need to use less and less overt methods of control and can rely on more subtle forms of control due to a *generalized climate of abuse.* This change is a result of the spouse and the children internalizing which behaviors result in abuse. Family members learn to suppress themselves in order to ensure the batterer is not "set off." For example, a mother may put the children to bed early so they are not present when the batterer comes home from work, or a woman may not voice her opinion—even over a trivial issue, such as where she would like to eat dinner—for fear of being hit.
- **Rules enforced by punishment:** According to Dalton and Schneider (2001), batterers "cement" their enforcement of the rules through the use of fear, emotional abuse, and social isolation. Batterers maintain an environment of control and fear through humiliation, criticism, financial abuse, sexual abuse, and emotional abuse. By cutting victims off from family and friends, a batterer's domination is enhanced. Furthermore, victims cannot leave if they do not have access to economic resources. As a wife battered for 17 years recounts, "When he wasn't hitting me, he was reminding me that he could. He was reminding me and getting me ready. Like the cat playing with the bird, letting it live a bit longer before he killed it" (p. 72).

FIGURE 11.7 ■ Lenore Walker's Cycle of Violence

The Cycle of Violence, created by Lenore Walker, illustrates the three phases of violence in abusive relationships: tension-building, acute battering, and the respite phase.

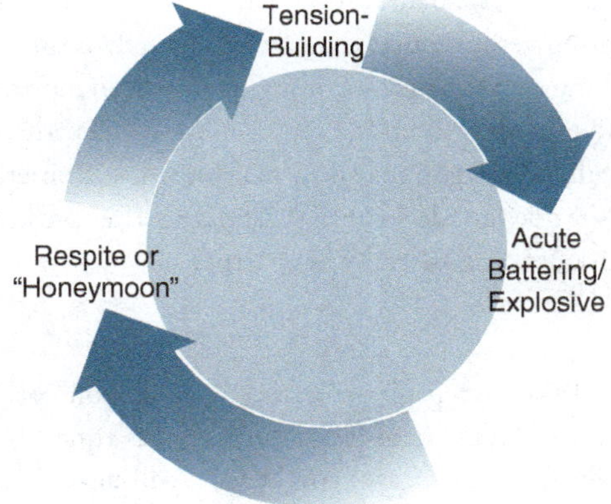

Source: Walker (1979).

The Cycle of Violence

In 1979, a professor of psychological studies and victim advocate for battered women, Lenore Walker, pioneered research that resulted in her **Cycle of Violence model**. In her research, she examined the lives of battered women and found that two-thirds of the 1,600 study respondents recounted similar patterns of intimate partner abuse. Not every abusive relationship experiences every phase of this cycle every time, but Walker's research shows how abusive relationships are cyclical in nature.

The Cycle of Violence, shown in Figure 11.7, illustrates three phases of violence commonly seen in abusive relationships: the *tension-building* phase, the *acute battering* or violent act, and the *respite* (nonviolent) phase.

Tension Building

In this phase, the victim senses that an explosive, violent incident is about to take place. The batterer begins to isolate his partner, threaten her, slap her, pinch her, belittle her, destroy her property, and withdraw affection. As the victim begins to feel tension and fear, her fear builds, and in response, she tries to keep her partner calm and happy by being agreeable, nurturing, and kind. At this point, some women begin to withdraw from or isolate themselves from their family and friends. All of her efforts have one goal: To keep the batterer from becoming violent. According to Walker (1979), the psychological anguish that accompanies this phase is the worst aspect of relationship violence. In fact, the psychological anguish may become so unbearable that many women antagonize or provoke the batterer in order to "just get it over with."

Acute Battering Incident

Unrestrained. Destructive. Out of control. Brutal. This is how Walker (1979) describes the next phase of the Cycle of Violence. During this phase, the violence from the tension-building phase escalates into an acute battering incident during which the violence can become deadly. Along with degrading, humiliating verbal abuse, the batterer severely beats his partner, either by hitting, punching, and kicking or by using a weapon. He may even rape her. The battered woman cannot control when the episode will end. According to Walker, the victim usually does not fight back because she realizes doing so may only make it worse. Sometimes the victim may call the police, but typically she does not do so until several days after the incident. If she attempts to leave, she is at a greater risk of being killed by her partner.

Respite

This phase is often called the loving phase or the "honeymoon" or "flower" phase. Walker (1979) terms this as a time of "illusion of bliss." During this time, the abuser apologizes profusely. He may cry, beg for forgiveness, and vow that he will never harm the victim again. He will often give her gifts to express his regret and lavish her with attention and love. In fact, this may provide an answer to a common question: Why does she stay? Perhaps she stays because she has a sense of renewed hope that things are getting better. Research has identified eight reasons why women typically stay in abusive relationships (Cravens et al., 2015; Whiting, 2016):

1. **Distorted thoughts:** Over time, emotional control and physical pain is traumatizing, and this leads to everything from confusion to self-blame.
2. **Damaged self-worth:** Repeated abuse causes mental, emotional, and physical damage to a person's sense of self.
3. **Fear:** The continued threat of harm—spoken or unspoken, acted upon or not acted upon—is powerful.
4. **Hoping to change him:** "I believed I could love the abuse out of him" (Institute of Family Studies, 2016). Some women's commitments to their marriages or other internal values systems make it difficult for them to leave.
5. **Children:** Women sacrifice their own safety for the children. Some women say they stay because they want their children to have a father; others say they stay so *they* will be the one who is abused, not the children.
6. **Past family experiences:** Many women describe how past experiences of violence in their childhood betrayed their sense of what a healthy relationship is.
7. **Financial constraints:** From having no income, to losing jobs because of their abuser's control, to having a partner accrue thousands of dollars in credit card debt in her name, to having no family, often women have financial limitations that prevent them from leaving.

TABLE 11.2 ■ Resources for Women and Children

The following resources are available for more information about relationships, violence, and safety and leaving abusive relationships
• Office on Women's Health Helpline: 800-994-9662
• National Coalition of Anti-Violence Programs: 212-714-1141
• Domestic Violence Hotline: 800-799-SAFE
• National Sexual Assault Hotline: 800-656-HOPE
• Victim Connect Resource Center: 855-484-2846

Source: Smith et al. (2017).

8. **Isolation:** It is common for abusers to emotionally and physically separate their victim from family, friends, co-workers, and sometimes, society at large.

If a victim has filed charges against her abuser, her renewed sense of hope might cause her to drop the legal charges or to cancel appointments with mental health counselors or victims' advocates because she really believes he will change for good this time. Her renewed sense of hope leads her to believe that the violence won't happen again. *But it will.* Table 11.2 offers resources for battered women and their children. We encourage you to snap photo of this table on your phone so you always have access to it.

Child Sexual Abuse

Some of the content in this section may cause distress to some readers. If you have been affected by child sexual abuse and are distressed, please skip this section.

Every nine minutes in the United States, Child Protective Services confirms a claim of child sexual abuse. **Child sexual abuse (CSA)** is a form of child abuse that involves sexual activity with a minor (a child under the age of 18) (RAINN, 2022). Today, two-thirds of CSA victims are aged 12 to 17 and one-third are under the age of 12 (U.S. Department of Health & Human Services, 2018). Each year in America, 1 in 9 girls and 1 in 53 boys under the age of 18 experience sexual abuse at the hands of an adult (U.S. Department of Health & Human Services, 2018). In our culture today, girls between the ages of 16 and 19 are *four times* more likely than the general population to be victims or rape, attempted rape, or sexual assault (U.S. Department of Health & Human Services, 2018). *A child cannot consent to any form of sexual activity.* Thus, *all* sexual behaviors with a child are crimes.

Characteristics of Child Sexual Abuse

Physical contact between a child and a perpetrator is not necessary for an act to be CSA. Child sexual abuse includes the following:

- Exhibitionism (exposing genitals to a minor child)
- Fondling

TABLE 11.3 ■ The Warning Signs of Child Sexual Abuse

Physical Signs

- Bleeding, bruises, and swelling in the genital area
- Bloody, torn, or stained underpants
- Difficulty walking or sitting
- Frequent urinary or yeast infections
- Pain, itching, and burning in genital area
- Genital discharge

Behavioral Signs

- Develops fears
- Depression
- Difficulties in school (absences, drops in grades)
- Inappropriate sexual knowledge or behaviors
- Nightmares
- Bed-wetting
- Self-harm
- Ducks away from physical contact
- Regressive behaviors, such as thumb-sucking or wetting pants
- Using words that are "too adult" for their age

Source: RAINN (2022).

- Intercourse
- Masturbation in the presence of a minor
- Obscene phone calls, text messages
- Producing, owning, or sharing pornographic images of children
- Sexual harassment (RAINN, 2022)

It's important to understand that CSA is rarely perpetrated by a stranger: 93 percent of victims under the age of 18 know their abuser (RAINN, 2019). It's also important to note that the abuser does not have to be an adult—any person (including siblings, peers, and minor neighbors) who takes advantage of a child's vulnerability is an abuser. As with batterers and perpetrators of domestic violence and IPV, child sexual abusers use their position of power, control, and domination to coerce or intimidate the child. There are several warning signs that a child is being sexually abused. We present these in Table 11.3.

The Lasting Effects of Child Sexual Abuse: "It Never Stops Shaping You"

The effects of child sexual abuse are potentially life long and include later physical, psychological, and behavioral consequences (Okur et al., 2018; Vrolijk-Bosschaart et al., 2018). Because of the differences in our individual development, families of origin, and other lifecourse experiences, outcomes are, understandably, not the same for every victim. However, a very large body of scientific evidence helps us to appreciate the many consequences of CSA. As one survivor stated, "It never stops shaping you."

Physical Health Consequences There are a number of physical health consequences of CSA, including immediate injuries, such as bleeding, tearing, and bruising of young genitalia and rectal tissue, as well as the threat of sexually transmitted infections (ACOG, 2019). Child sexual abuse and trauma also impact the development of the child's brain, which leads to differences in both structure and function; these alterations in the development of the brain have lifelong consequences for the child's mental health and well-being, which we will discuss in just a bit (Edwards, 2018). CSA has also been linked to *future* health problems, including the following:

- Diabetes
- Poor nutrition, malnutrition

Clergy sexual abuse survivor Alexa MacPherson, 42, holds up a photograph of herself as a seven-year-old child during a press conference regarding the death of Cardinal Bernard Law. MacPherson says she was sexually abused by Father Peter Canchong in Dorchester from the time she was three or four years old until she was nine. The press conference was organized by attorney Mitchell Garabedian, who played a key role in battling for victims and unmasking Law's practice of secretly circulating predatory priests around Greater Boston parishes.

Source: Boston Globe via Getty.

- Heart attack
- High blood pressure
- Bowel disease
- Migraine headaches
- Chronic lung disease
- Chronic fatigue syndrome
- Cancer (Afifi et al., 2016; Monnat & Chandler, 2015; Widom et al., 2012)

What is the link between these later-in-life physical difficulties and CSA? Some researchers have found that those who experience CSA are more likely to use and abuse alcohol and other substances; they are also more likely to smoke cigarettes, have a poor diet, and be morbidly obese (De Bellis, 2002; Felitti & others, 1998; Hart & Rubia, 2012; Putnam, 2003). These subsequent lifestyle habits and choices—perhaps used as coping mechanisms and self-medicating techniques due to the violence perpetrated against them as children—lead to down-the-road negative health consequences.

Psychological Consequences Child sexual abuse causes a number of immediate and long-term psychological consequences (for a complete review of the literature, see Edwards, 2018). In the immediate wake of the violence, children experience isolation, fear, and distrust (National Scientific Council on the Developing Child, 2014). Substantive bodies of research show us that when children are victims of sexual abuse, children experience:

- **Diminished cognitive skills:** Due to the disruptions in brain development and the subsequent alterations in the anatomy and function of the brain, CSA victims experience difficulties in working memory, learning, and paying attention (Bick & Nelson, 2016).
- **Attachment difficulties:** As you learned in Chapter 5, in the early years of life, children develop the ability to emotionally attach to others, and these attachment bonds promote the ability to trust others. Victims of CSA are more likely to develop attachment disorders, and these disorders negatively affect a child's ability to form positive peer and social relationships and impact their ability to form intimate and love relationships later in life (Doyle & Cicchetti, 2017).
- **Poorer mental and emotional health:** There is no question that CSA creates risk factors for developing depression, anxiety, and suicidal thoughts, both immediately and later in life (Choi et al., 2017).

Behavioral Consequences All behaviors are a form of communication, and children who are victims of CSA often exhibit behavioral difficulties. For the school-age child, behavioral difficulties can be displayed as outbursts of anger, inability to get along with peers, and difficulties in attention or staying on task (National Scientific Council on the Developing Child, 2014). When the victim either ages into adolescence, or is an adolescent at the time of the assault(s), they commonly experience the following:

- **Risky sexual behaviors:** Risky sexual behaviors include early onset of sexual behaviors, greater number of sexual partners, infrequent use of contraception, and transactional sex (sex exchanged for money, gifts, drugs, etc.).
- **Alcohol and drug use:** Adolescent and adult survivors of CSA are at a significantly greater risk to use and abuse alcohol and other substances than people who are not victims.
- **Juvenile delinquency and/or adult criminality:** Victims of CSA and other types of child abuse are more likely to develop antisocial behaviors than those who are not victims (Child Welfare Information Gateway, 2019; Choi et al., 2017).

Keeping Our Kids Safe

There is no question that CSA is devastating, both in the immediate aftermath and in its long-lasting consequences. Despite its prevalence in our society, there are things we can do, together as a community of human service providers who care, to prevent CSA and minimize its effects. First, there are a number of online resources that provide a wealth of information, such as the Child Welfare Information Gateway's Preventing Child Abuse & Neglect and Responding to Child Abuse & Neglect (2019). We can also stem the effects of abuse by utilizing the many known *protective factors* we have (Child Welfare Information Gateway, 2019), most of which we have discussed in our study together throughout this textbook:

- Parenting knowledge, competencies, and education
- Child nurturing and the importance of the healthy development of attachment
- Knowledge of child development
- Knowledge of the development of intimacy across the lifespan and healthy relational skills
- Knowledge of the social and emotional development of children
- Knowledge of the development of relationships
- Understanding of the importance of peers and healthy peer relationships
- Parent or caregiver well-being
- Strong communication skills
- Stable family environments and living situations

- Positive community involvement
- Strong local, state, and federal policies that support the family's well-being

Equipped with this knowledge, we *can* work together to build a stronger, safer society for our children and our children's children. We now turn our attention to one of the most visible and persistent social problems in the United States—homelessness. With the economic downturn that began in the United States in 2020 due to the COVID-19 pandemic, the number of homeless people continues to grow.

HOMELESS FAMILIES

Debate has occurred over how to define homelessness. Typically, **homelessness** refers to persons living in areas not designated as human habitats (U.S. Department of Housing and Urban Development, 2021). The United States Department of Housing and Urban Development (HUD) considers persons to be homeless if their nighttime residence is in public or private emergency shelters; in the streets, parks, subways, bus terminals, railroad stations, airports; under bridges or aqueducts; in abandoned buildings without utilities; in cars or trucks; or in any other public or private space that is not designated a shelter (U.S. Department of Housing and

Homelessness is caused by a number of factors, most of which are not within the control of the family who is homeless. But homelessness looks different for different families: Some live in temporary shelters, such as an RV, while others live in hotel rooms.

Source: Jeff Pachoud via Getty Images.

FIGURE 11.8 ■ Racial and Ethnic Experiences of Homelessness in the United States, 2020

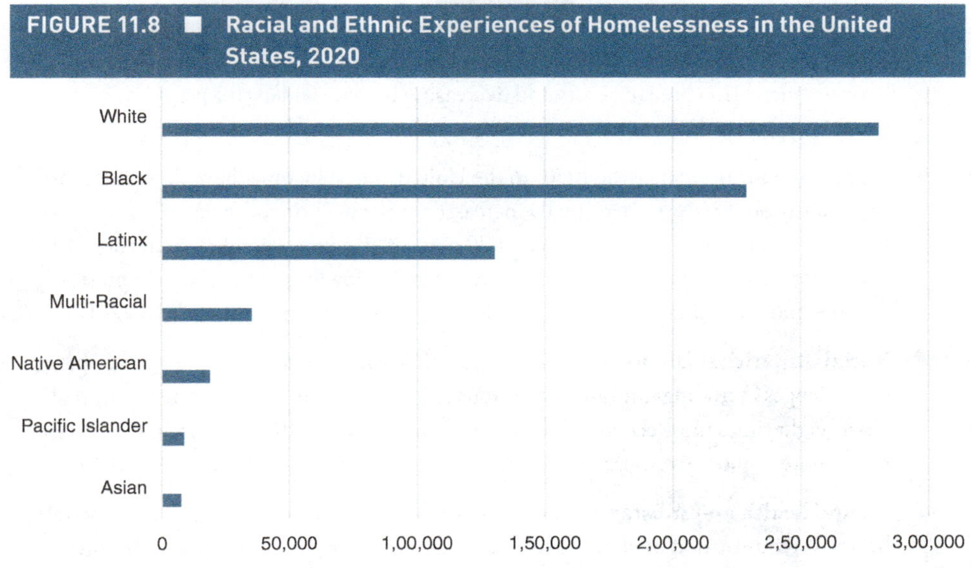

Source: National Alliance to End Homelessness (2021).

Urban Development, 2021). Sometimes those who are living temporarily in hotel rooms, as well as those residing in social and health service facilities without a permanent address, are defined as homeless. Although circumstances that lead to homelessness vary, it occurs when people are unable to acquire and/or maintain affordable housing.

Who Are the Homeless? What the Numbers Say

On any given night in the United States, nearly 600,000—about 18 per 10,000—people are homeless (National Alliance to End Homelessness, 2021). Of these, one-third are families with children, and two-thirds are single individuals. There are differing racial and ethnic experiences with homelessness, as you can see in Figure 11.8. Risk of homelessness is also significantly linked to gender: Males (58 percent) are far more likely than females (37 percent) to be without a home. Transgender and nonbinary individuals are also impacted. In 2021, it was estimated that LGBTQ+ young people were 120 percent more likely to experience homelessness than their cisgendered counterparts; in 4 out of 10 cases, the person's sexual orientation and/or identity contributed to their homeless status (Stasha, 2021).

The causes of homelessness are multifaceted, and oftentimes they intersect and are interconnected. Although each family or person's experiences are unique, there are a number of common societal factors that contribute to homelessness in this country (National League of Cities, 2021):

- **Housing affordability:** In communities where people spend 30 percent or more of their income on rent, there are higher rates of homelessness (Casey, 2018).

Cost-burdened families are those who pay 30 percent of their total household income on housing; **severely cost-burdened** families pay 50 percent or more. As the gap between increasing housing costs and decreasing income widens for poor Americans, the homeless population continues to rise.

- **Income inequality:** Since the 1970s in the United States, incomes have skyrocketed for the wealthy but have only marginally increased for the majority of wage earners (U.S. Census Bureau, 2020). Today, the upper 20 percent of wage earners brings in about 14 times more than the lower 20 percent. Because of the slow/stagnant growth in most families' incomes, children have a difficult time moving upward (Chetty et al., 2017).
- **Racial disparities:** Due to historical, structural racism, people of color face a number of challenges in finding safe, affordable housing. In 2019, the average white family had nearly eight times more economic resources than the average Black family and about five times more economic resources than the average Latinx family (Bhutta et al., 2020).
- **Mental health and substance use:** About one-fourth of unsheltered homeless people have severe, untreated mental illnesses, and about one-firth have chronic substance use (U.S. Department of Housing and Urban Development, 2021).
- **Domestic violence:** Violence against women, children, and youth accounts for one-fourth to nearly 60 percent of homeless women in the United States (Institute for Children, Poverty, & Homelessness, 2019).

Homeless mothers have been found to experience high prevalence of disruptive family events, including divorce, illness, and physical and/or sexual abuse. The vast majority are homeless for economic reasons—they were poor before becoming homeless, frequently struggling to pay bills. Many lived in neighborhoods characterized by violence, persistent unemployment, poor schools, and limited access to medical and social services. Although eviction or relationship problems sometimes cause homelessness for many single-parent households, the reality is that neither federal assistance nor minimum-wage earnings of these low-skilled women are sufficient to pay the rent, cover child care, and meet healthcare and other living expenses. Such economic problems may increase feelings of hopelessness, dependency, and depression and contribute to family dysfunction (for a full review, see Haskett & Armstrong, 2019; Letiecq et al., 1998).

Homelessness and Shelters

In general, emergency shelters provide from one night to several months of shelter. In the United States today, there are eight different types of homeless shelters; each offers its own distinct elements that meet the diverse needs of the homeless (Backpacks, USA, 2021).

1. **Emergency shelters:** Some shelters offer night-only services, requiring that temporary residents leave during the day; others operate as day shelters, meaning that residents can stay both during the day and through the night. Day sheltering is important because oftentimes emergency shelters are located in unsafe neighborhoods.

2. **Domestic violence/women's shelters:** These shelters serve victims of IPV and their children. Often, these shelters provide other services, such as counseling and social policy resources to help families find safe and secure housing. It is important to note that there are few such shelters for LGBTQ+ battered men and their children.

3. **Faith-based shelters:** These shelters are offered by churches, temples, and mosques, and provide warm, secure sleeping facilities and meals.

4. **Youth shelters:** LGBTQ+ youth are 120 percent more likely to experience homelessness than their straight peers (National Coalition for the Homeless, 2021). Youth shelters serve a limited age range and offer counseling, job training, and educational opportunities. The goal of these facilities is to promote self-sufficiency and healthy foundations for success.

5. **Family shelters:** These shelters do not keep men away; rather, these shelters strive to keep families together.

6. **Wet shelters:** A relatively new concept, wet shelters open their doors to people who are drunk and/or actively using substances. Residents are not required to be sober before using these services.

7. **Transitional housing:** Similar to youth and family shelters, transitional housing gives residents time to recover from the initial trauma that forced them out of their homes. These shelters provide mental health and financial counseling, job training, access to social policy resources, and assistance in finding permanent housing.

8. **Permanent housing:** Today, a substantial number of wage earners work full-time, yet there is not affordable housing available. A number of federal programs exist to help individuals and families transition to safe, affordable living quarters, such as the Low-Income Housing tax credit; project-based rental assistant programs; public housing; and the National Housing Trust fund.

Homelessness is a pervasive problem in the United States, and its causes are diverse. And, while by the numbers the white population is the largest group affected by homelessness, historically disregarded racial groups are more likely to experience chronic homelessness (National Alliance to End Homelessness, 2021). Segregation, discrimination in employment and workplace advancement opportunities, higher unemployment rates, lower rates of education and the ability to obtain quality education, and higher incarceration rates are all deeply embedded structural social factors that lead to increased vulnerability to homelessness in people of color. There is no question that homeless experiences have a lasting impact on children's development.

Homelessness and Child Development

Each year in the United States, a staggering 2.5 million children go to bed without the access to stable housing (Yamashiro & McLaughlin, 2020). The majority of children in homeless shelters are below the age of 12, as Figure 11.9 presents (Child Trends, 2019). Sadly, homeless experiences for children are not without negative consequences.

FIGURE 11.9 ■ Percentage of Children in Homeless Shelters, by Age

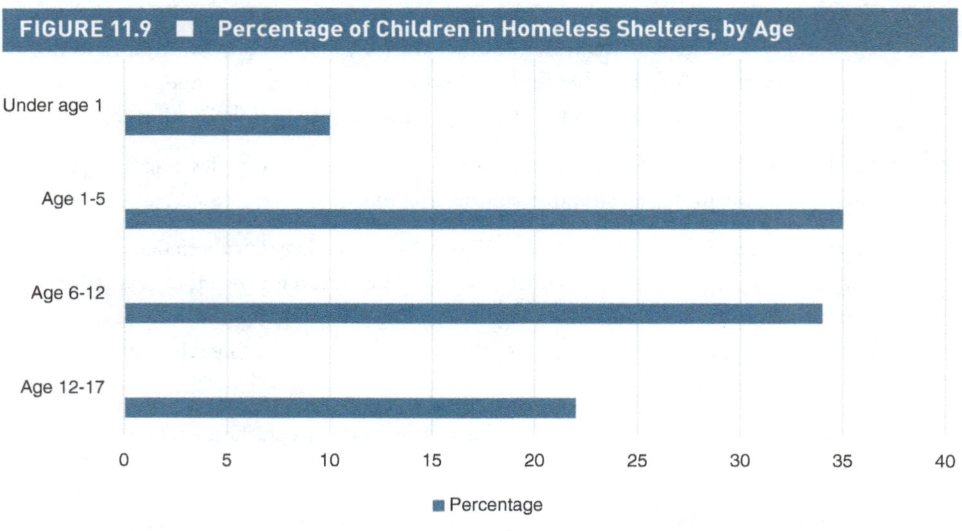

Source: Child Trends (2019).

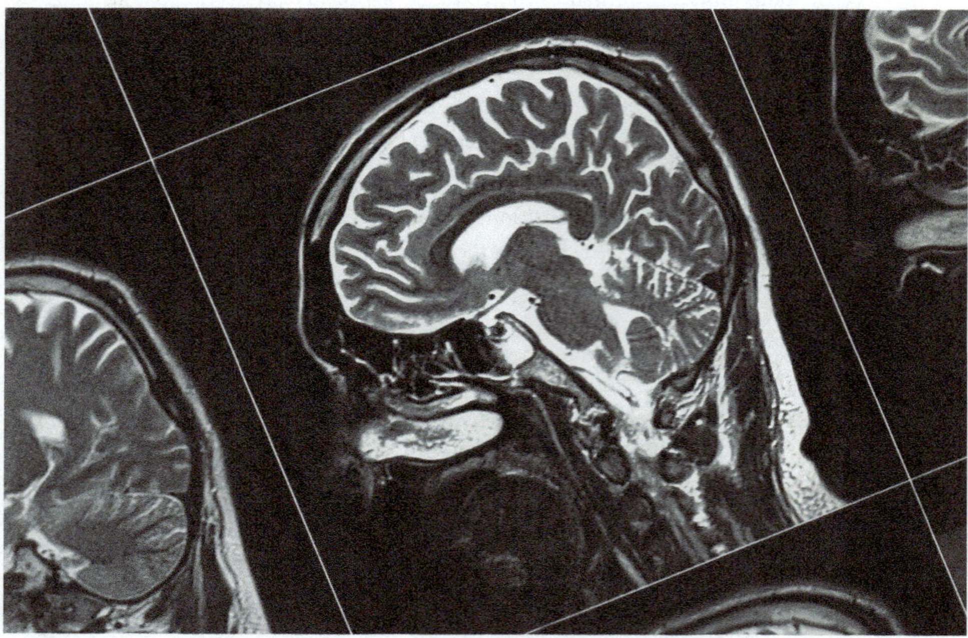

Strong and ongoing stress, such as in the case of homelessness, is referred to as toxic stress. This prolonged exposure to stress creates a toxic coating of sorts on the child's brain, causing long-last negative impacts on the child's development.

Source: iStock.com/sudok1.

As you have seen in our study, early childhood experiences profoundly shape the architecture and functions of the brain, laying the groundwork for the child's future physical and emotional growth and health, future learning, and behavior. Homeless experiences in early childhood are known to significantly impact children's academic accomplishments and success (such as math and ELA proficiencies), as well as their school-day interactions with teachers and peers (Perlman & Fantuzzo, 2010, 2013). Overall, children who experience homelessness are four times more likely to have slowed development and twice the rate of learning disabilities as those children in poverty who have stable housing (National Child Traumatic Stress Network, 2022).

Among those children enrolled in preschool, 54 percent of homeless children experience significant developmental delays; by the age of 17, one-half of the children who have been homeless at any point in their childhood have repeated one grade and school, and nearly one-fourth have repeated at least two grades (Annie E. Casey Foundation, 2022). Among homeless children under the age of five, more than three-fourths experience speech delays, and one-third have motor-visual delays.

In a study of 328 children living in homeless shelters, the researchers found that overall, functions in physical, cognitive, and socioemotional development were significantly lower than children who did not reside in homeless shelters; furthermore, 25 percent were found to need mental health services (Haskett et al., 2016). Another study examined the social and academic outcomes of 4,594 first graders to determine the effects of childhood homelessness (Brumley et al., 2015). This body of evidence revealed that poor academic outcomes (i.e., reading achievement, academic engagement, and engagement with peers) are not due to homelessness alone; rather, these children typically experience multiple, co-occurring poverty risks, such as being born to teen parents or to parents who have low education attainment, or who are abused or neglected by their parent(s).

Children who are homeless also face greater risks to their physical health. For example, homeless children experience illnesses four times more than housed children; they have five times more stomach and bowel infections, twice as many ear infections, have high rates of asthma, and are more likely to be overweight/obese (Gewirtz et al., 2008; Grant et al., 2007).

There is no question that teachers play a critical role in the lives of homeless children. First and foremost, educators need to be aware of classroom indicators of homelessness, although it is not always apparent. For example, prior to teaching at universities, we had high school teaching experiences. To our dismay, we did not discover until the end of the first semester that one of our high school students was living in a single hotel room with his five siblings and his parents. The hotel room had one bed, one chair and desk, and no kitchen appliances, such as a microwave. Had we been more observant, we could have perhaps connected this student and his family to community resources much sooner. Seattle University's *Project on Family Homelessness* provides a snapshot of classroom indicators of child homelessness. These are presented in Table 11.4.

The significance of the school's role in positive academic and developmental outcomes in homeless children cannot be overstated. As one cohort of researchers observes, "The child's classroom may be the only place where the child can experience quiet, interact with children [their] age, and experience success ... School is the most normal activity that homeless children experience. For homeless children, [school] is much more than a learning environment—it is a

TABLE 11.4 ■ Classroom Indicators of Homelessness

Lack of continuity	• Sporadic attendance at a number of schools • "Misplacement" of student records • Gaps in test scores
Transportation/attendance problems	• Irregular attendance • Tardiness • Truancy • Excessive absences
Poor health/hygiene	• No immunizations/records • Medical and dental neglect • Food insecurity (food hoarding; chronic hunger; stuffing food) • Falling asleep in class • Wearing unclean clothes for many days in a row • Inconsistent bathing and grooming
Inconsistent/lack of school readiness	• Consistent incomplete or missing assignments • Lack of school supplies at home • Overprotective of belongings at school
Social and behavioral concerns	• Inability to concentrate or pay attention • Unable/unwilling to form friendships • Self-isolation in the classroom/recess • Outbursts of anger • Anxiety/panic attacks • Uncontrollable crying/inability to self-regulate • Difficulty in comforting/consoling the child
Student/parent statements	• Doesn't "remember" address or phone number • "I don't remember the name of my previous school." • "We move a lot." • "My dad gets moved a lot because of his job." • "I left my backpack on the bus."

Source: Seattle University's Project on Family Homelessness Information from The National Center for Homelessness Education (2014) at http://center.serve.org/nche/nche/warning.html

place of safety, personal space, friendships, and support" (Driver & Spady, 2013; Reed-Victor & Stronge, 2003, p. 2).

Barbara Driver and Pam Spady (2013), Virginia Department of Education, describe the ways in which homelessness affects young learners, and the ways in which educators can meet these unique needs. For example, because homeless children oftentimes experience a lack of positive peer relationships, teachers can provide cooperative learning experiences where students "buddy up" to complete assignments (Driver & Spady, 2013). Because of the lack of financial resources, homeless students do not have basic school supplies for use in the classroom and at home. Teachers can meet these needs by supplying textbooks and supplies to local homeless shelters, and privately providing school supplies to the student. Providing quiet time for learners, having a safe place for students' belongings, and allowing children to do homework at school also promote the educational and socioemotional well-being of homeless children (Driver & Spady, 2013).

Without shelter, homeless families have no place in which to conduct the daily activities necessary to function. Without an address, the homeless find it difficult to secure a job or obtain welfare benefits. They lack privacy and a place to keep possessions. Further, the lack of shelter contributes over time to other problems, such as poor nutrition, poor physical and/or mental health, victimization, apathy, loneliness, and dejection. Families with minor children are in jeopardy of losing custody. Many families are alone, without knowledge of how and where to find a support system.

How does homelessness affect family relationships?

Housing Instability and Family Relationships

Not surprisingly, housing instability and homelessness place enormous stress on parents and their children. As you saw earlier in this chapter, there are a number of interacting factors that contribute to how well a family copes with a stressor event. Central to a family's adaptation in any crisis is the family's ability to maintain their healthy interactions and family routines (Linver et al., 2002; Weisner et al., 2005). The nature of homelessness presents significant challenges to parenting.

- Commonly, shelter living is noisy and crowded, and housing rules usurp parental authority (Mayberry et al., 2014).
- Homelessness often separates family members. In a study of 2,307 families in family shelters, 230 were separated from their partners, and 576 parents were separated from one or more of their children (Shinn et al., 2015).
- Family routines (such as meal- and bedtime routines and schedules) are disrupted when families are in shelter living or temporary housing. These predictable schedules are essential to healthy parenting and family relationships (for a thorough review, see Perlman et al., 2014).

Today there exist many resources for families experiencing homelessness, from agencies that provide emergency financial assistance, to school supplies and winter coats for children, to mental and financial health counseling for parents. Overcoming poverty and homelessness requires a commitment from society to better the lives of those less fortunate.

Source: iStock.com/ sergeyryzhov.

- There is a disruption in parenting styles and parental disciplinary patterns. This is sometimes referred to as "parenting in public," and it is not uncommon for shelter staff or residents to criticize what they believe to be "inappropriate" parenting (Friedman, 2000). This disruption erodes actively engaged parenting and parental authority.
- As our study has shown us, some racial and ethnic families embrace extended family relationships and fictive kin. Because most shelters or temporary housing do not permit visitors, families experience social isolation due to the lack of intergenerational support and comfort (Gaurino et al., 2009).
- Homeless fathers face other challenges, due to the fact that most temporary housing supports female-headed families (Perlman et al., 2014). This is problematic because as we saw in Chapter 1, a number of contemporary families are headed by single fathers; today gay parenting men who are victims of IPV have few options when in need of emergency shelter (SAMHSA, 2016). As one body of research concludes, "These separations result in fathers being rendered invisible in the lives of their children" (Perlman et al., 2014, p. 13).

There is no question that the family is critical to the healthy growth and development of children, and perhaps it is even more important during the crisis of housing instability and homelessness. When the very nature of parenting—"loving, protecting, nurturing, guiding, and teaching"—is stripped from struggling mothers and fathers, children and their parent(s) suffer from feelings of depression, anxiety, guilt, and shame (Paquette & Bassuk, 2009, p. 292). It is incumbent upon human service providers, social workers, counselors, schools, religious organizations, child welfare authorities, and law- and policymakers to minimize family separations and buffer against the impact of the destabilizing effects of homelessness.

Support for Homeless Families

In 1987, lawmakers signed the first major piece of federal legislation to deal with the needs of the homeless in a comprehensive manner—the *Stewart B. McKinney Homeless Assistance Act*. In the 1990s, Congress passed legislation that increased funds for shelters and housing, job training, health and counseling services, and education for homeless children and adults. Still today, however, a large percentage of the homeless work full- or part-time, but low wages cannot provide for rent and other living expenses. In 2021, the *Emergency Homelessness Assistance Act* was enacted by the U.S. Congress. This legislation provides funding for rental assistance, the development of affordable/sustainable housing, and supportive community services. Individuals do not have to become homeless in order to qualify for this federal assistance: Those who are at risk of homelessness (such as veterans and single mothers) or who are attempting to leave a violent home situation are also eligible.

Invisible People (2021) is a nonprofit organization in the United States that educates and advocates for the homeless. They rightly maintain that there is no one, single federal, state, or community agency that can turn the tide of homelessness in this country. While rental assistance is important, solutions to homelessness must be comprehensive and also include livable wages, access to affordable healthcare and mental health services, reliable transportation to work and school, and quality/affordable child care. To be sure, families most at risk should be identified early and intervention efforts begun as soon as possible. Table 11.5 offers ways in which the helping profession can further promote the health and wellness of homeless families.

Finally, because homeless families differ on many dimensions (including family structure, family size, racial/cultural background, housing history, and pathways to homelessness), homeless policies must address the diversity of homeless family life. Other family factors that need to be considered are extent of parental education, intergenerational interaction, family cohesion, family conflict, life stress, and amount of social support. Above all, policy must empower families to become self-sufficient, encourage involvement in parenting, recognize interdependency of family members, build social-support networks, and strengthen neighborhoods and communities.

TABLE 11.5 ■ Support Homeless Families Through Practice and Policy

Practice	Policy
Actively involve parents in decision-making and parenting children of all decisions	Allow families with children to stay together
Provide parenting skills education that support the growth and development of children	Extend all education, training, and other support services for several months after leaving shelters
Connect residents to workforce training and employment programs	Provide long-term follow-up services
Provide families the time and space for independent living and maintain family routines and traditions	Make family reunification a primary goal
Actively engage extended family, fictive kin, and other social-support networks	Assist parents in regaining custody of their children who may have been placed in foster care
Employ culturally sensitive practices	Provide services, interventions, and best practices that strengthen families
Connect residents to substance use treatment services	
Coordinate services with early childhood programs	
Foster education connections	
Adopt proactive practices that help to identify those at highest risk	

Sources: Adapted in part from Gaurino et al. (2009), United States Interagency Council on Homelessness (2021), Reed-Victor and Popp (2013), SchoolHouse Connection (2019).

PARENTING LIFE EDUCATION: #TEAMGRIT

Stress and crisis are inevitable experiences in parenting life. It's not a question of *if* parents and families experience difficulties—it's a question of *when.* Family Life Educators, therapists, social workers, family practitioners and scientists, and child life specialists, with their knowledge of family strengths and weaknesses, best parenting practices, and how family members relate to each other, are valuable resources to today's families: They have the knowledge necessary to help individuals and families acquire the necessary skills to traverse these inevitabilities or other crises for which no one can be prepared, such as childhood abuse and homelessness.

Nolan and Laura brought their three-month-old son, Grit, to the emergency room, with symptoms of dehydration and the flu. Within 48 hours, the lives of this young family were forever changed: Grit was diagnosed with a rare form of childhood prostate cancer.

The baby was only the second three-month-old in history to be diagnosed with this cancer, and in a matter of days, the parents headed to St. Jude's Children's Research Hospital several states away to begin the uphill battle to save their baby's life. They left their daughter in the care of family members. They left their jobs as high school teachers and coaches. They left their home. They left their community. They left all that they knew was certainty in their young marriage. Grit spent the majority of his early childhood years at St. Jude's. Before his third birthday, he had received countless chemotherapy treatments, 40 radiation treatments, and had parts of his pelvis, prostate, bladder, and lung removed to thwart the cancer's spread.

Fast forward to 2022. With a head full of blonde hair, mischievous blue eyes that sparkle with rambunctious energy, and an infectious laugh, Grit is in remission! Although he still has routine monthly chemotherapy treatments and scans every 90 days, Nolan and Laura are slowly beginning to rebuild the lives they put on hold while they waged the war against the vicious cancer that tried to take their baby's life. It will take time to rebuild their marriage and their family relationships. It will take time to reestablish family routines. It will take time to recover from the financial onslaught and fallout from having to step away from work. But as Nolan says, "You just fight another day. That's how he did it. That's how we're doing it."

Grit means courage, resolve, strength of character, perseverance, determination, and tenacity. These are the characteristics that so well describe this child's personality. And, without question, these are the characteristics that propel determined parents and families to do whatever it takes in the face of family stress, crisis, and change to "fight another day."

12 PARENTING DISABLED CHILDREN

LEARNING OBJECTIVES

12.1 Compare the similarities and differences between the Medicalization and Social Models of disability.

12.2 Identify the common emotions that parents, caregivers, and families experience upon receiving a diagnosis of a child's disability(ies).

12.3 Discuss the availability, as well as the challenges, of quality healthcare for disabled children.

12.4 Describe the Individuals with Disabilities Act (IDEA) and the categories of disabilities it addresses.

12.5 Differentiate between parent–child relationships among the various disabilities that affect children.

12.6 Demonstrate the ways in which helping professionals can best advocate for disabled children and their families.

In 2015, the National Council on Disability (United States) launched a campaign, #SayTheWord, to encourage people to use the word *disabled* rather than popular euphemisms such as special needs, differently abled, handicapable, exceptional children, person with a disability, and physically/mentally/emotionally challenged. Lawrence Carter-Long, activist and public affairs specialist for the National Council on Disability, notes, "If you 'see the person and not the disability,' you're only getting half of the picture. Broaden your perspective...[It's the same as saying] they 'see the person and not the gender,' or they 'see the person and not the race.' By suggesting disability is simply a 'difference' and has no impact on a person's life is a very privileged position to take. [It] minimizes the very real discrimination disabled people face" (King, 2016, p. 1). Long-Carter concludes that today's euphemisms disenfranchise the disabled and marginalize the fact that they are a "diverse and vibrant community with a history, and a legacy all our own" (King, 2016, p. 1).

In the United States, several federal organizations define disability, including the American Association on Intellectual and Developmental Disabilities and the U.S. Centers for Disease Control and Prevention. They state:

> Intellectual and developmental disabilities are disorders that are usually present at birth and that negatively affect the trajectory of the individual's physical, intellectual, and/or emotional development. Many of these conditions affect multiple body parts or systems. Intellectual disability starts any time before a child turns 18 and is characterized by problems with both intellectual functioning or intelligence, which include the ability to learn, reason, problem solve, and others skills, such as adaptive behavior, which includes everyday social and life skills. The term "developmental disabilities" is a broader category of often lifelong disability that can be intellectual, physical, or both.
> *(National Academies of Sciences, Engineering, and Medicine, 2016, p. 232)*

The U.S. Department of Education has also conceptualized and defined disabilities. All of these definitions are important because these are the guidelines by which children and families qualify for intervention and education services. We discuss these later in this chapter.

In an effort to encourage people to use the word disabled rather than popular substitutes, such as exceptional children, activists begin the #SayTheWord campaign.

Source: iStock.com/tzahiV.

To use identity-affirming language, throughout our discussion, we employ the term *disabled* to affirm the experiences and expertise of disabled children and adults. A group of researchers further proposed that it is necessary to understand disability in terms of its relationship between health, functioning, and the environment. They note that disability is "an environmentally contextualized, health-related limitation in a child's existing or emergent capacity to perform developmentally appropriate activities and participate, as desired, in society" (Halfon et al., 2012, p. 13).

In this chapter, we first explore the history of meeting the needs of disabled children as we discuss the dominant historical narratives of medicalizing disabilities and the paradigm shift to the social model. We'll then examine Critical Disability Theory, and the Individuals with Disabilities Education Act and other legislation that provides for special education. We will conclude with looking at the lived experiences of parents of disabled children.

HISTORICAL NARRATIVES ABOUT DISABILITIES

It is important to understand the historical perspectives and narratives about disabilities and children because helping professionals are positioned to help change unconstructive, adverse, harmful, and negative opinions and perceptions about the experiences of disabled people (Garden, 2010). We first explore the medical model of disability.

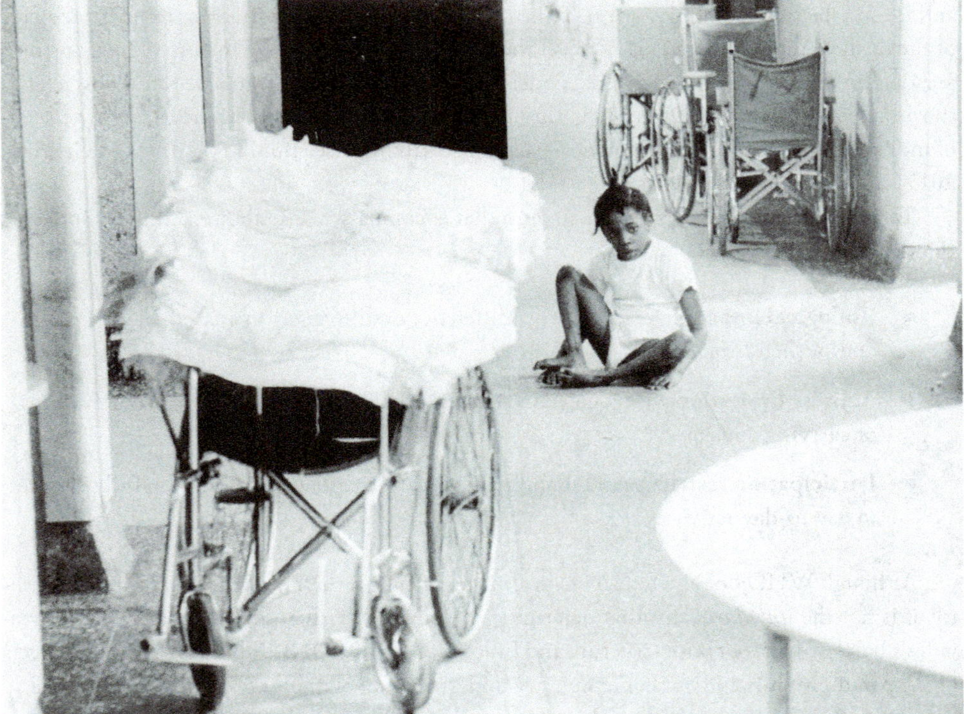

When societies adopt the *medical model* of disability, which was popular in the United States through the early 2000s, disabled people are expected to adapt to society's expectations of ableness.

Source: New York Daily News Archive via Getty Images.

The Medicalization and Social Models of Disability

For most of the 20th century, disability was thought to be a condition within an individual that caused limitations and/or disadvantages to the person (Dodd et al., 2010). Historically, the **medical model** or **medicalization** held that the person's biological, cognitive, or intellectual deficit required some sort of medical, clinical, or therapeutic intervention (Conrad, 2004; Lalvani & Polvere, 2013). This model also supported the idea that disabilities render people dependent on others and are "pitiable," and viewed them as unhealthy or ill (Bunbury, 2019; Giallo & Gavidia-Payne, 2006, p. 937). A perhaps unintentional outcome of the medical model was the prevailing view that disabled people had limited autonomy—and thus, a restricted ability to participate in society (Bunbury, 2019). As Bunbury rightly concludes, this hindered participation "leads to social exclusion" (Bunbury, 2019, p. 27). Some authors contend that the medicalization of disability has been largely responsible for the stereotyping and discrimination of disabled people and has led to defining people by their disability(ties) (Dodd et al., 2010).

In 2001, the World Health Organization (WHO) redefined disability by adopting the *social model* of disability. The **social model** separates disabled persons from *impairment*, or the notion that disabled people are diminished in their capacities to participate in life; thus, the more a society makes accommodations to support disabled people, the less disability(ties) impact daily lives and life satisfaction (Bunbury, 2019). This model of disability was borne out of the inadequacy of the medical model to explain and meet the needs of disabled people: Instead of focusing on a person's limitations or "deficits," this model focuses on society and its barriers and obstacles to the disabled (Bunbury, 2019). As such, this model asserts that society's failure to meet the needs of individuals affected by impairments results in "disability" (see Bunbury, 2019; and Goering, 2015 for comprehensive reviews).

Today, the term disability is a broad term that encompasses several interacting components (Dodd et al., 2010):

- **Biological impairments:** There is a difference or differences in anatomical structures and/or their functions.
- **Activity limitations:** Biological impairments may cause difficulties in accomplishing or carrying out a task.
- **Participation restrictions:** Disability may make it difficult for people to fully engage in day-to-day activities.

Although WHO does include biological impairments in their conceptualization of disability, it is not the *singular* factor that determines "disability"; rather, the current definition provides a balanced view of both structure and function (WHO, 2011). Table 12.1 presents aspects of the paradigm shift and our contemporary understanding of disability and disabled people.

Another dominant narrative is that parents and families of children with disabilities experience a lower quality of life and "suffer" chronic and persistent helplessness, sorrow, and caregiver weariness (for a complete review, see Lalvani & Polvere, 2013).

TABLE 12.1 ■ The Paradigm Shift in the Concepts of Disability

Defining Disability	
Traditional Concept	**Paradigm Shift**
• A medical or clinical diagnosis • A medical "defect" or emergency that needs to be treated, repaired, or cured • A person is limited and/or defined by the impairment, and/or the "damaged" structure or function	• A social, environmental, or contextual issue that requires accessibility, accommodations, and equity • Individuals can and should lead productive, independent lives, and may require accommodations to do so
Strategies to Address Disability	
Traditional Concept	**Paradigm Shift**
• Institutionalize, "hide," or segregate the individual • Correct the deficit • Exclusion due to harmful stereotypes and biased assumptions • Provide a wide range of *rehabilitation services*, such as medical, mental health, vocational (i.e., physical and/or occupational therapy)	• Remove all physical, intellectual, cultural, and educational barriers so that disabled persons can actively and inclusively participate in society • Create and maintain access through accommodations, universal design, and equitable/inclusive learning environments • Address disabled people's needs not just through a restorative lens but also through accepting, accommodating, adaptive practices
Role of the Disabled Person	
Traditional Concept	**Paradigm Shift**
• The patient • The client • The object of intervention • A research subject • Passive and dependent	• An independent community member • An active participant in culture • An advocate for self • A person with equal access and opportunity

Sources: Adapted for use in part from Art Beyond Sight Disability Awareness Training (2014); Dodd et al. (2010); WHO (2011).

Parents' and Families' Emotions About Disabled Children

Although we all long for a healthy baby, not all of us will have the "perfect" baby. Birth defects and anomalies can range from barely noticeable to life-threatening to fatal. No matter how severe the defect, parents of infants with birth defects and physically challenged babies mourn the loss of the healthy child they imagined they'd deliver. The birth of a child with disabilities into a family requires considerable adjustment on the part of family members.

As you learned in Chapter 4, a *congenital birth defect* is a physical anomaly that is present at birth; it may be inherited, or it may be the result of environmental influences during pregnancy and/or birth (March of Dimes, 2022). Major birth defects can have serious effects on a child's health and development and may impact the functional ability of the child (CDC, 2020). Today, one in every 33 babies—about 3 percent of all babies—born in the United States have a birth defect (CDC, 2020). These defects account for 20 percent of infant deaths and are the leading cause of deaths in infants. Birth defects include (CDC, 2020):

- Brain/spine: 2,649 per year
- Eye: 751 per year
- Heart: 17,380 per year
- Mouth/face: 6,253 per year
- Stomach/intestine: 2,706 per year
- Muscle/bone: 17,723 per year
- Chromosome (genetic): 7,286 per year

Each of these birth anomalies will impact a child's development and life experiences, in small to significant ways.

Much of the literature from the 1950s through the 1970s described only the negative experiences and outcomes for disabled people and their families (Munyi, 2012). Despite the significant number of changes in the treatment of and care for disabled individuals over the past four decades, and the addition of early intervention resources and education services, the beliefs persist that families who have a disabled child are long-suffering (Lalvani & Polvere, 2013). And, without question, there are sometimes seemingly insurmountable obstacles parents and families face. To ignore these experiences would be grossly marginalizing and dismissive of the realities of caregiving.

Most parents suffer a period of shock, grief, and anger when they learn of their child's impairment(s), and research continues to report these common experiences (Durand et al., 2013; Kandel & Merrick, 2003; Woodman, 2014). Frequent reactions and emotions are shown in Table 12.2. Many of these emotions are similar to the reactions parents and family members experience when they learn about the death of a loved one (Kandel & Merrick, 2003).

Some experts believe that grieving is the process by which individuals can separate from a significant lost dream, and it begins spontaneously (Moses, 1983). According to Moses, there are several states of grieving, which have no time limits.

- **Denial:** The existence of, the permanence of, or the impact of the disability may be denied. Denial buys time for parents to gain the internal strength and the external supports necessary to cope. This requires (and uses up) enormous physical, emotional, and spiritual energy.

TABLE 12.2 ■ How Parents Express Emotions When Their Child Is Diagnosed With a Disability

Emotion	How It Is Expressed
Denial	Parent ignores the initial diagnosis or may seek alternative explanations or other opinions about the child's impairment.
Anxiety	Parents' attitudes, beliefs, values, routines, and goals may change; parents experience a sense of impending doom.
Fear	Parents become protective of their child and are afraid to let their child do certain things, lest the child becomes injured; parents express uncertainty or fear about their child's future.
Depression	Parents experience overwhelming and uncontrollable tears, sadness, regret, remorse, sadness, and feelings of hopelessness.
Guilt	Parents feel that they are somehow to blame for the situation or the impairment(s).

Sources: Adapted in part from Bunjnowska et al. (2019), Lee (2013), Padden and James (2017), Gallagher et al. (2015).

- **Anxiety:** A feeling of internal imbalance occurs. Anxiety facilitates the restructuring of attitudes concerning responsibility and serves as a mobilizer of energy.
- **Guilt:** This is the most disconcerting of all grief states. Commonly, it is expressed in three ways: (1) the parent feels that they have caused the disability; (2) the parent feels that having a child with a disability is a just or fair punishment for some specific or awful action committed in the past; or (3) the parent feels generalized or unspecified guilt because the disability exists.
- **Depression:** Self-anger, or anger turned inward, causes depression. If parents have the support needed to deal with the depression, it can help them to rework a definition of competence for their child.
- **Anger:** People have an internal sense of justice. The anger they feel when their child is born with a disability can be frightening and can result in aggression, overprotection, or overpunitiveness toward the child.

It must be noted, however, that the prevailing research is often carried out within the medical model, which inherently views disabled children as patients, and their life-long caregivers as burdened with impossible obstacles (Emerson & Hatton, 2008).

Several bodies of research support this characterization that parents and families of children with various disabilities view the child's impairment(s) as a *negative stressor*; as such, parents are thought to experience low levels of psychological wellness and general health (Beighton & Wills, 2017; Emerson & Hatton, 2014; Miodrag & Hodapp, 2010; Woodman & Hauser-Cram, 2013). Indeed, about 75 percent of parents caring for a child with disabilities care for their children for 20 years or more (Emerson & Brigham, 2014). Some researchers further suggest that the longer parents and families care for a disabled child, the more distress their caregiving role causes them (see Beighton & Wills, 2017). However, with early intervention, the increase in resources and services, and the availability of these resources and services, contemporary parents of children with disabilities also report positive aspects of their experiences.

Contrary to popular belief, not all parents express or experience distress and dismay over their child's disabilities. It is important for the parenting practitioner to validate parents' feelings, whatever they may be.

Source: iStock.com/ DTatiana8.

Beighton and Wills (2017) provide a robust literature review about the ways in which parents view some aspects of caring for a child with impairments and found that parents describe their gains as: positive impacts (among several, Blacher & Baker, 2007; Blacher et al., 2013); positive perceptions (Vilaseca et al., 2013); finding benefits in the circumstances (Rapanaro et al., 2008); positive rewards, experiences, and contributions (Kimura & Yamazaki, 2013); and positive growth through stress (King & Patterson, 2000). Another group of researchers culled the results of five studies and found a number of positive experiences identified by parents (Hastings & Taunt, 2002, p. 118):

- A pleasurable and satisfying experience in caring for the child
- The child brings joy and happiness to the family

- A sense of accomplishment in caring for and rearing a child with impairments
- The love between the child and the family members
- Fortified family and marriage bonds
- A renewed sense of purpose in life
- A clarity of what is important in life
- Increased spirituality
- An increase in personal strength
- Increased social and community relationships

The coping strategies of family members, the degree of marital/relationship stability, and the availability and use of support systems also affect how parents grieve and respond to/cope with their children's disabilities.

Emerging thought helps us to further progress in our understanding and conceptualization of "disability." In the section that follows, we explore *critical disability theory* at in introductory level.

CRITICAL DISABILITY THEORY

As we've seen so far, historical interpretations of disability carry with them assumptions (i.e., that individuals with disabilities are "less than" societal norms) that consequently oppress disabled people and interfere with their basic human rights (Gillies, 2014). **Critical disability theory (CDT)** seeks to understand disability as a construct that is multifaceted, an experience that, in addition to its biophysical aspects, is also a cultural, social, and political one (Hall, 2019). As Devlin and Pothier observe, "...disability is not fundamentally a question of medicine or health, nor is it just an issue of sensitivity and compassion; rather, it is a question of politics and power(lessness)" (Pothier & Devlin, 2016, p. 2). As Gillies concludes, CDT challenges able-bodied supremacy and its inherent oppression due to well-established social barriers (Gillies, 2014).

The Elements of Critical Disability Theory

While an in-depth discussion of CDT is beyond our purposes here, it is necessary for helping professionals to understand the current and progressing conceptualizations of what it means to be disabled in the United States: It is both a lived and political experience (Hall, 2019; Hosking, 2008).

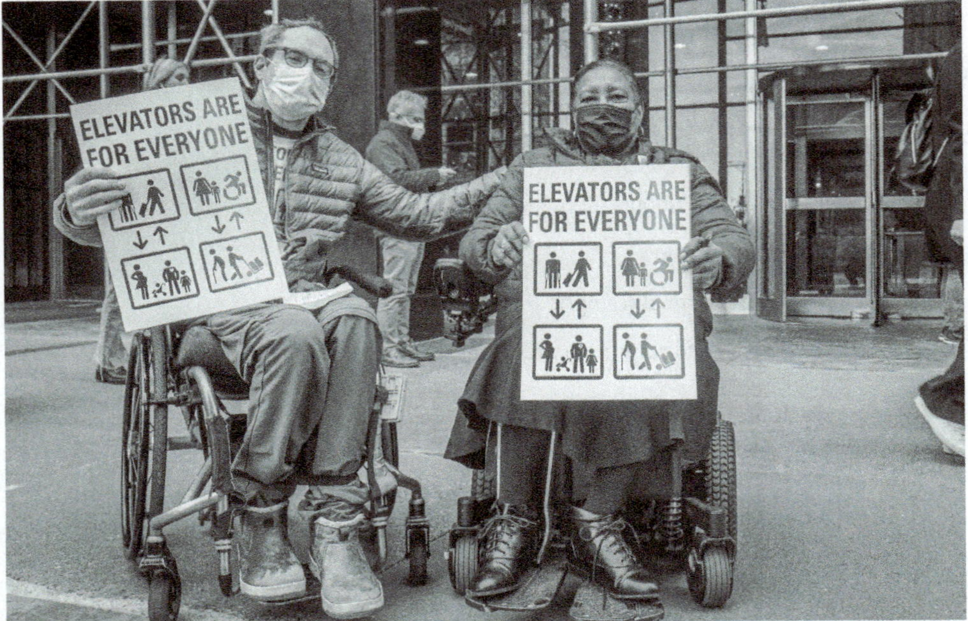

Critical Disability Theory stresses the importance of valuing the voices, experiences, and rights of disabled people.

Source: Erik McGregor via Getty Images.

CDT comprises foundational beliefs: multidimensionality; valuing diversity; rights; voices of disability; and language (Hall, 2019; Hosking, 2008).

- **Multidimensionality:** Similar to Crenshaw's (1989) work *of intersectionality*—when one area of societal oppression intersects with another—disabled individuals also experience intersectionality with gender, race, indigeneity, age, sexual orientation and identity, varying degrees of ableism, language, education, and immigration/refugee status (Holley et al., 2016).
- **Valuing diversity:** People with disabilities are culturally diverse, and each person experiences their disability in unique ways. It is important that individual differences are accepted and respected (Disabled World, 2022).
- **Rights:** CDT supports disabled individuals' rights to autonomy and their full, unincumbered right to participate in society (Hosking, 2008).
- **Voice:** "Able bodied people think about disability from their abled perspective" (Hosking, 2008, p. 13). Historically, disabled persons have not had a voice. The #SayTheWord campaign seeks to remove the stigma that disability experiences are those of impairment, lack, pity, and inability (King, 2016).

- **Language:** Any time that language is used to convey that disability is a family or personal tragedy, it renders individuals "powerless, vulnerable, and dependent" (Hosking, 2008, p. 14)—even when euphemisms are used, as we discussed in the opening of this chapter.

Critical disability theory's primary focus is to support the transformation and evolution of society's perspectives of disabled people and their experiences, and to rid the systemic biases against this diverse group.

Merging the Medical Model and Critical Disability Theory

CDT begins with the precept that disability is a historical social construct based on an individual's physical, intellectual, or behavioral impairments (the medical model). As you saw in Chapter 4, the prevention of disabilities through healthy prenatal care and healthy labor and birth experiences, treatment, intervention, and the provision of supportive services are all the result of the medical model.

But there are also unintended consequences of the medical model: The goal of treatment and intervention (and even with some support services) is to "approximate normal functioning" (Goering, 2015, p. 135). The problem with the medical model, then, is that a person's impairments are viewed as the *cause* of societal barriers and disadvantages—and the only way to remove those barriers is to "fix" or "cure" the impairment (Crow, 1996; Silvers, 1998). For example, when a person in a wheelchair is confronted with stairs, the medical model asserts that *the person* must be treated so the stairs are manageable. The social model, on the other hand, contends that the structure provided by society is problematic and must be accommodated to meet the needs of the disabled.

In a call to rethink disability, Goering's article speaks to the fact that the primary disadvantages experienced by disabled people isn't because of their limitations, but instead from social attitudes and structures that exclude them (Goering, 2015)—much like the experiences of oppression and exclusion in the "race/class/gender triad" (Davis, 2001, p. 535). Haskell notes that "in order for disability and disability attitudes to be viewed as a [societal] issue, [the disabled] must become as visible" as races and genders seeking identity affirmation (Haskell, 2010, p. 20).

It is important to pause at this point and synthesize the ideas that, while the medical model advanced the health and well-being of disabled people, it has also contributed to the undesired effect of reducing individuals to one trait—their specific limitation(s). This is a critical point for helping professionals to understand because governmental policies and funding are shaped by and reflected in societal attitudes (Haskell, 2010).

A significant number of disabled children require special education and related services. In the next section, we will explore the history of the United States government's role in developing and implementing programs and services for disabled children so they are able to reach their full potential of development in safe, supportive, and nurturing environments.

SUPPORTING DISABLED CHILDREN AND THEIR FAMILIES

For more than 100 years, the United States has invested in improving the well-being and health of children with disabilities, by the creation, implementation, and delivery of evidence-based interventions and services for families (National Academies of Sciences, Engineering, & Medicine, 2016). This rich history has had—and continues to have—one singular goal: To promote positive living, educational, and occupational outcomes, and to minimize negative circumstances.

Child- and family-centered policies, interventions, and programs are **publicly funded**, money that is most often generated through taxes; the government then distributes this funding to federal, state, and local agencies. For children without disabilities, state public education institutions receive from $4,000 to $10,000 per nondisabled student and $10,000 to $20,000 per disabled student (U.S. Department of Education, 2021a). Throughout the COVID-19 epidemic of 2020/2021, the federal government released more than $3 billion to service nearly eight million infants, toddlers, and students. In the sections that follow, we will explore two principle needs of disabled children—healthcare and education.

Disabled Children's Healthcare Needs: Coverage and Affordability

The physical, emotional, relational, and psychological burdens of caring for a disabled child can be substantial for parents and families (Anderson et al., 2007). Childhood disabilities also result in both short- and long-term financial costs, both direct costs and out-of-pocket costs, ranging anywhere from $1,000 per year to nearly $70,000 (Shahat & Greco, 2021). Consider the following:

- Among children with autism spectrum disorder (ASD), experts estimate that on average, children and adolescents have 4.1 to 6.2 times greater medical expenditures than children who do not have ASD (Autism Speaks, 2021). On average, medical costs for autistic children without intellectual disability is approximately $60,000; costs increase when a child has an intellectual disability. Because mothers serve in the roles of their child's advocate and their case manager, they work 56 percent fewer hours per week than mother of children who are not disabled; they work 35 percent fewer hours per week than mothers of children with other disabilities (Autism Speaks, 2021).
- The lifetime cost of cerebral palsy to a family is estimated to be $921,000 (Cerebral Palsy Group, 2021).
- For children with severe to profound hearing loss, it is estimated that the lifetime cost of disability-related healthcare is $297,000 (Hearing Loss Association of America, 2021).

Furthermore, in 2020, 4.3 million children in the United States did not have health insurance (Towner, 2020). In 2019, of those families with disabled children who do have health insurance, 38 percent paid $1,000 or more in out-of-pocket expenses in the past 12 months, and one-fourth reported they had problems paying their child's medical bills (Williams & Musumeci, 2021).

Medicaid, public health insurance that is jointly funded by the federal government and individual states, provides coverage of healthcare expenses for low-income families; it is the largest source of funding of healthcare costs for low-income families and individuals. The **Children's Health Insurance Program (CHIP)** also provides healthcare coverage for low-income children. Almost one-half of all American children with special healthcare needs are covered by Medicaid/CHIP, and in 2019, nearly 14 million children with special needs were covered (Williams & Musumeci, 2021). Figure 12.1 illustrates the health insurance status of children with special needs. It is noteworthy that two-thirds of Medicaid/CHIP-only children live at or below the poverty line, and, sadly, people in poverty are less able to receive early diagnosis, treatment, intervention, resources, and support; the delay in diagnosis means that the child's impairment(s) are untreated longer and thus potentially become more severe (Goodman et al., 2019). As shown in Figure 12.2, the majority of healthcare costs of disabled children are met through private insurance. The majority of children with special healthcare needs who have Medicaid/CHIP-only are from a racial or ethnic minority group (Williams & Musumeci, 2021). The intersectionality of poverty, race, and disability is evident.

The Individuals With Disabilities Education Act

As early as 1893, disabled students were excluded from public education and kept at the margins of society (Esteves & Rao, 2008), but in 1954, the United States Supreme Court case of Brown v. Board of Education (1954) determined that segregation of a child based on race violated the child's access to equal education opportunities. This landmark decision not only paved the way for all people, regardless of race, to have access to educational opportunity but also

FIGURE 12.1 ■ Health Insurance Status of Children With Special Healthcare Needs, 2019

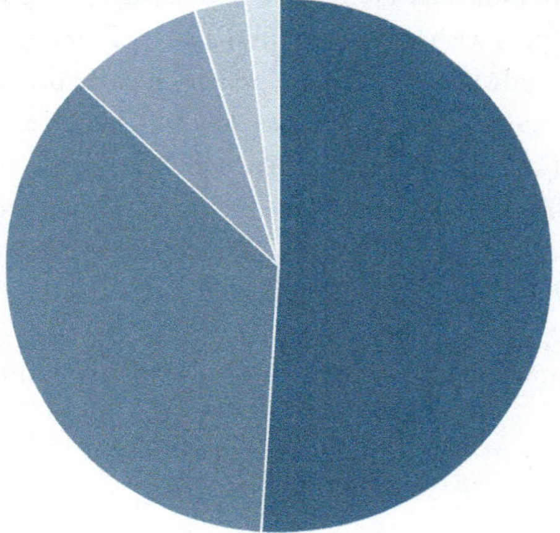

Source: National Survey of Children's Health (2019).

FIGURE 12.2 ■ Healthcare Coverage by Race/Ethnicity, 2019

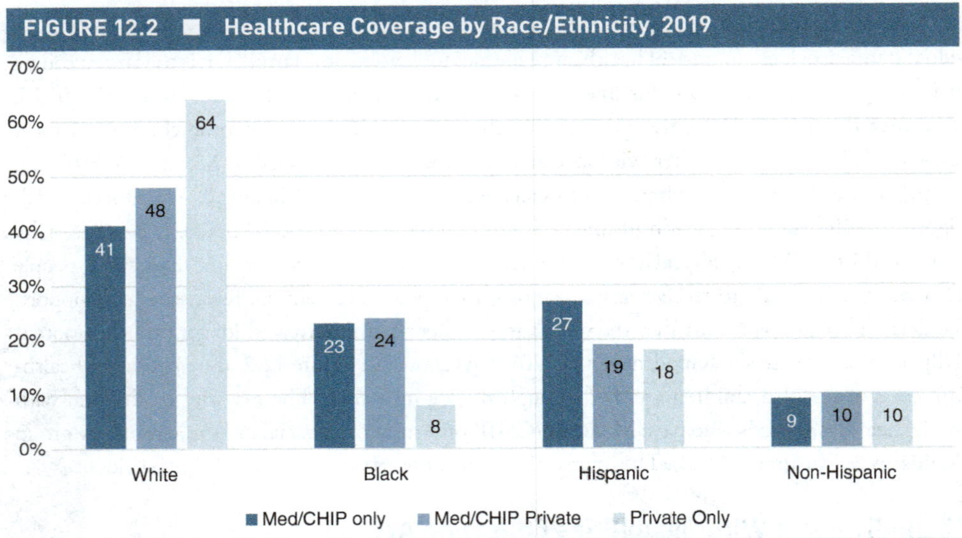

Source: National Survey of Children's Health (2019).

eventually opened the door to free and public education for all people, regardless of race, gender, or disability.

The Evolution of Free and Appropriate Education (FAPE)

In 1965, the federal *Elementary and Secondary Education Act* made it possible for public schools to receive federal monies, and in 1966, this act made it possible to fund education for disabled students (Esteves & Rao, 2008). The 1973 *Rehabilitation Act*, Section 504, provides that, "No otherwise qualified individual with a disability in the United States...shall, solely by reason of her or his disability, be excluded from the participation in, be denied the benefits of, or be subjected to discrimination under any program or activity that received federal financial assistance" (Americans with Disabilities Act, 2021). Today, Section 504 requires every school district in the United States to provide **free and appropriate education (FAPE)** regardless of the type or severity of a person's disability. For PreK, elementary, and secondary education programs, disability is defined as any person who (Rehabilitation Act, 1973):

- Has a physical or mental impairment which substantially limits one or more major life activities.
- Has a record of the impairment(s).
- Is regarded as having the impairment.

Thus, any school-aged disabled or impaired child is entitled to FAPE. In 1990, the **Individuals with Disabilities Education Act (IDEA)** required public schools to meet the educational needs of Prek-12 students, and in 2020, more than 7.1 million students in the United

United States federal law mandates that all children have equal access to free and public education, regardless of their disabilities.

Source: iStock.com/FatCamera.

States received services—about 14 percent of all public school students (National Center for Education Statistics, 2021a). This is in stark contrast from prior to 1975, when 1.8 million disabled children were *excluded* from public schools because of their impairments (U.S. Department of Education, IDEA, 2021a). Today, over two-thirds of children with disabilities are in public school classrooms and spend at least 80 percent of their days in school.

Those Served by IDEA

Under IDEA, *early intervention services* are provided to infants and toddlers under the age of three and their families, and those aged 3 to 21 receive *special education and related services*. **Special education** refers to a wide range of educational and social services for people with disabilities (Gargiulo & Bouck, 2018). The education differs from traditional public schooling in that it provides disabled children with education that addresses their unique, individual differences.

Infants, toddlers, children, and adolescents: Those who are experiencing developmental delays in their cognitive, physical, communication, socioemotional, or adaptive development. **Developmental delays** describe children from three to five years of age who exhibit significant delays in one or more domains of physical, cognitive, communicative, social and emotional, and adaptive development; as a result of their delays, they need special education and services. It is a useful category for ensuring early services. The label itself is an acceptable and nonjudgmental term that allows children access to services they need. The term also minimizes the possibility of inaccurate diagnosis in young children because of the wide variability in development.

Ages 3–21: There are 13 different disability categories (described in the next section) that qualify individuals for services and special education.

To qualify for services, all of the child's developmental delays must be appropriately measured by verified diagnostic instruments and procedures. Figure 12.3 describes the distribution of students (ages 3 to 21) by their disability type who were served under IDEA during the 2019–2020 school year. As you can see, one-third of students were diagnosed with a **specific learning disability**, which is one or more impairments, characterized by an inability to "listen, think, speak, read, write, spell, or do mathematical calculations" (National Center for Education Statistics, 2021b). Racial and ethnic groups served under IDEA are shown in Figure 12.4.

IDEA's Disability Categories

Each of the 13 disability categories in IDEA cover a wide range of impairments and difficulties. To be covered by IDEA, a child's school performance must be "adversely affected" (U.S. Department of Education, IDEA, 2021b). Unless otherwise noted, the disability categories are described by the National Dissemination Center for Children with Disabilities (2021). It is important to note that the terminology adopted by IDEA may not reflect contemporary cultural sensitivity and identity-affirming language for disabled people.

FIGURE 12.3 ■ Percentage of Students Aged 3–21 Served Under IDEA, 2019–2020, by Disability

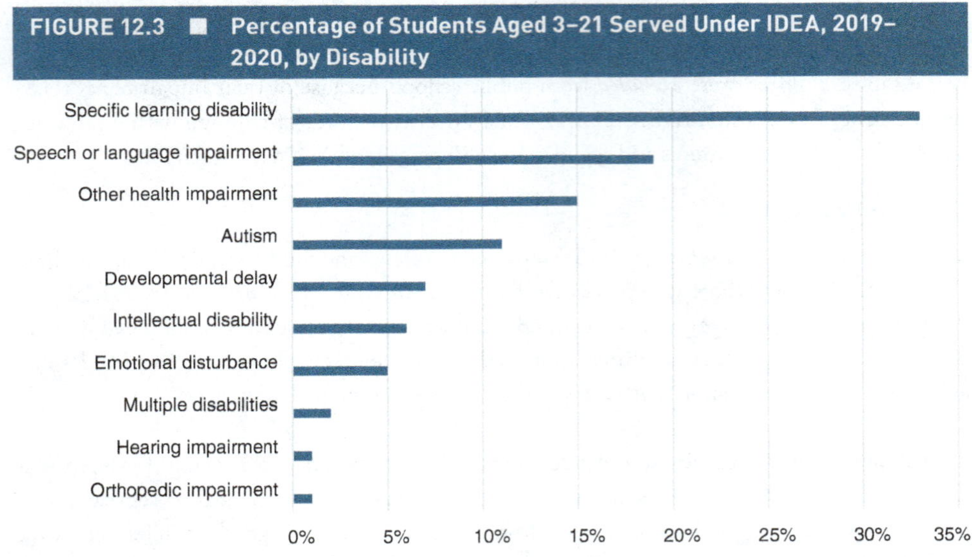

NOTE: Visual impairment, traumatic brin injury, and deaf-blindness are not shown because they each account for less than 0.5 percent of students served under IDEA; detail does not sum to 100 percent

Source: U.S. Department of Education, Office of Special Education Programs, IDEA (2021b).

FIGURE 12.4 ■ Percentage of Students Aged 3–21 Served Under IDEA, 2019–2020, by Race/Ethnicity

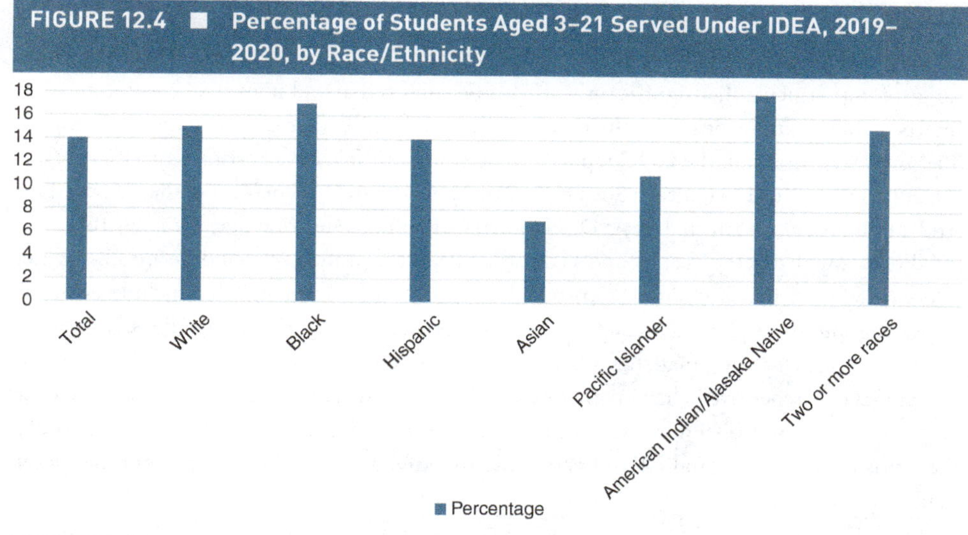

Source: U.S. Department of Education, Office of Special Education Programs, IDEA (2021b).

In America, 1 in 54 individuals have autism, a condition that results due to anomalies in the structure or function of the brain and causes a wide array of neurodevelopmental disorders. Lyte, for example, is nonverbal—he has difficulty orally communicating with others.

Source: Photo courtesy of Annie Crank.

Autism

Autism, or **autism spectrum disorder (ASD)**, is a developmental disability comprised of a broad range of impairments that significantly affect a person's verbal and nonverbal communication, interpersonal relationships, and their social interaction skills (Autism Society, 2021; Autism Speaks, 2021). In 2020, the CDC reported that 1 in 54 people have autism—twice as great as the 2004 rate of 1 in 125 (Autism Society, 2021). Approximately 1.5 percent of the United States student population is affected by ASD (National Center for Education Statistics, 2021b).

These impairments affect a child's educational abilities and may include **stimming**, which refers to ways in which children self-stimulate. Some stimming behaviors include **echolalia** (repeating sounds or phrases); repetitive movements such as hand flapping and rocking; *visual stimming* in which a child may stare blankly, blink repeatedly, or line up toys; **tactile stimming**, which includes repetitive behaviors that help a child to connect to their sense of touch (such as tapping fingers); and **vestibular stimming**, such as twirling or spinning (Barloso, 2021). Today, the terms **neuroatypical** and **neurodiverse** refer to individuals who have autism or other developmental differences.

Deaf-Blindness

Deaf-blindness refers to people who simultaneously experience hearing and vision impairments, and these impairments cause severe communication, developmental, and educational needs that cannot be served in programs for children who have only deafness or blindness (National Center on Deaf-Blindness, 2021). In 2019, there were 658 infants and toddlers (birth to 2), and 9,867 children and adolescents (aged 3 to 21) affected. White children experience deaf-blindness more frequently than other races/ethnicities (53 percent); 20 percent are Latinx; and 14 percent of deaf-blind children are Black (National Center on Deaf-Blindness, 2021). Children are declared *legally blind* if their visual acuity is 20/200 or less in the better eye, even with the use of glasses, or if their field of peripheral vision is extremely narrow.

Deafness

Deafness is disability that is so severe, a child has difficulty processing through hearing, even with amplification (hearing aids), and this difficult adversely affects a child's educational performance. Deafness also is categorized as *prelingual* (occurring at birth) or *postlingual* (occurring at some point after the development of speech and language). Hearing loss affects about 17 in every 1,000 children in the United States; more than 90 percent of deaf children have hearing parents (National Deaf Children's Society, 2021).

Deaf children have great difficulty in the comprehension and production of spoken language. It is more difficult for children who are prelingually deaf to speak than it is for children postlingually deaf because they have never had a spoken-language model—they are unable to receive feedback on the sounds they attempt to produce. Therefore, it is important for deaf children to be taught an effective communication system. Most educators use a *total communication approach*, which is a combination of oral production and manual production (sign language).

Deaf children are not necessarily intellectually deficient, but oftentimes their academic achievement suffers because so much of academic work—especially reading—depends on mastering the spoken language. Social interaction, too, is difficult for deaf children who have no way of communicating with their hearing peers unless the peers learn American Sign Language. This need for social interaction may be one reason why deaf individuals, both children and adults, seek to associate with other deaf individuals with whom they can communicate (Andrews et al., 2011).

Emotional Disturbance

The National Dissemination Center for Children with Disabilities (2021) describes **emotional disturbance** as "...a condition exhibiting one or more of the following characteristics over a long period of time and to a marked degree that adversely affects a child's education performance:

- An inability to learn that cannot be explained by intellectual, sensory, or health factors.
- An inability to build or maintain satisfactory interpersonal relationships with peers and teachers.
- Inappropriate types of behavior or feelings under normal circumstances.
- A general pervasive mood of unhappiness or depression.
- A tendency to develop physical symptoms or fears associated with personal or school problems.
- A tendency to develop physical symptoms or fears associated with personal or school problems. This term does not apply to children who are socially maladjusted" (p. 3).

Less than 1 percent of the student population in this country is affected by emotional disturbance (National Center for Education Statistics, 2021b).

It's particularly difficult to arrive at a definition for children who have extreme social-interpersonal or intrapersonal problems. In the past, these children have been described as abusive, defiant, irritable, destructive, withdrawn, irresponsible, jealous, hostile, aggressive, and unpredictable. For a number of years, children have had labels attached to them—emotionally impaired, behaviorally impaired, socially/emotionally impaired, emotionally disturbed, socially maladjusted, and so on. Currently, the term *emotional or behavioral disorders (EBD)* is accepted. Despite definition difficulties, however, most experts agree that children who fit this category demonstrate extreme behavior that is not productive within the social and cultural context, and the problem is chronic rather than situational. Often the phrase "[the behavior] adversely affects educational performance" is added as a qualifier (Hallahan & Kauffman, 2000; Smith & Luckasson, 1992).

There are two types of disordered behavior: externalizing and internalizing (Achenbach et al., 1991; Walker & Severson, 1990).**Externalizing behaviors** consist of aggressive behaviors expressed outwardly toward others, such as aggression, acting out, or disruption. The most common behaviors of children being served by special education are externalizing; boys with these behaviors outnumber girls 5 to 1. **Internalizing behaviors** are expressed in a more socially withdrawn fashion and include anxiety and depression.

Several researchers have described other specific behaviors that represent the following dimensions: conduct disorder, socialized aggression, attention problems/immaturity, anxiety/withdrawal, psychotic behavior, and motor excess. Children may demonstrate several behaviors that represent more than one dimension. For example, a child might exhibit behaviors considered to be in the conduct disorder dimension, such as disruption, temper tantrums, and fighting, and at the same time show motor excess behaviors, such as an inability to sit still and excessive talkativeness (from Hallahan & Kauffman, 2000).

Dysfunctional family relationships, especially negative parent–child interactions, often are associated with behavioral disorders. The same is true for school experiences, which can influence a child's behavior in either negative or positive ways. Contextual factors, such as poverty, exposure to violence and drugs, and standards and expectations for behavior, are potential influencers. Children with emotional/behavioral disorders have a severely limited ability to effectively interact with adults and peers (Hallahan & Kauffman, 2000).

Hearing Impairment

Distinct from deafness, **hearing impairment** refers to a child who has difficulty hearing. A child has a hearing impairment if, with a hearing aid, they have enough residual hearing to successfully process language information through auditory means. This hearing impairment is not enough to warrant a diagnosis of "deaf," but it does adversely affect a child's educational performance.

Intellectual Disability

Intellectual disability (ID) is diagnosed when there is significantly subaverage intellectual functioning; this may be present from birth or early infancy (although most children do not develop noticeable symptoms until they are two to three years old); the diagnosis is made after formal testing. Today, both intellectual functioning and adaptive skills are taken into consideration for diagnosis, and the lower-limit IQ score to be considered "normal" has been reduced to 70. The American Association of Intellectual or Developmental Disabilities (AAIDD) classifies children by the degree of support they need to function as competently as they can (AAIDD, 2021).

IDs cause mild to substantial limitations in a person's day-to-day living, such as in a person's ability to (Sulkes, 2022):

- communicate
- live independently
- take care of oneself (such as daily hygiene and nutrition)
- make decisions
- cope with multiple tasks at the same time
- care for their personal health, safety, and well-being

Most individuals have mild limitations and are capable of functioning adequately in society with little or no assistance (Hallahan & Kauffman, 2000).

There are varying degrees of ID: mild, moderate, severe, and profound. For example, those with mild levels are able to develop social and communication skills and can learn up to about a sixth grade level; as an adult, they are usually self-supportive (Sulkes, 2022). Conversely, those with profound ID experience extreme cognitive limitations, have poor motor skills, and may achieve only limited self-care. Today, about 1 percent of the American student population is thought to be affected by some degree intellectual disability (National Center for Education Statistics, 2021b).

ID is usually not detectable at birth unless there is an obvious birth defect, such as an unusually large head (hydrocephaly), an unusually small head (microcephaly), Fetal Alcohol Spectrum Disorder (see Chapter 4), or the physical characteristics of Down syndrome.

Multiple Disabilities

About 3 in 10 disabled children have **multiple disabilities**, which are co-occurring impairments, such as ID-blindness (National Center for Education Statistics, 2021b). The simultaneous disabilities cause severe education needs.

Orthopedic Impairments

Bone-, joint-, or muscle-related disabilities that negatively affect a child's educational performance are known as **orthopedic impairments**. The causes can be due to genetic disorders (such as genetic limb difference); congenital anomalies (such as spina bifida); disease (such as muscular dystrophy); birth injury (including cerebral palsy); and injury (such as fractures, burns, and amputations).

Other Health Impairment

Sometimes, children's chronic or acute health problems, such as asthma, diabetes, epilepsy, and sickle cell anemia, affect a child's strength and energy, and this results in the child's inability to engage well in a learning environment. About 2 percent of disabled children under IDEA suffer from other health impairments (National Center for Education Statistics, 2021b).

Specific Learning Disability

Affecting nearly 5 percent of IDEA-supported disabled children, **specific learning disability** refers to a disorder in which one or more learning processes (i.e., language, listening, thinking, speaking writing, etc.) is adversely impacted. **Dyslexia**, a disorder that makes it difficult for affected children to learn to read or write letters, words, and other symbols, is a form of specific learning disability. More than two million children—about 3.5 percent of students—receive IDEA services for their disordered reading.

Speech and language pathologists (SLPs) help students with a wide range of speech- and language-related problems.
Source: iStock.com/FatCamera.

Speech or Language Impairment

Speech is the vocal production of language, and *language* is the method of communication. Communication is either impaired or unsuccessful if the sender or the receiver cannot use the signals or symbols adequately. **Communication disorders** affect either/both a child's ability to send/receive messages. These disorders have the potential to influence most aspects of a child's life, including social interaction, and affect approximately 3 percent of today's students (National Center for Education Statistics, 2021b).

It is useful to distinguish between speech disorders and language disorders. A **speech disorder** is an impairment of voice, articulation of speech sounds, and/or fluency (Hallahan & Kauffman, 2000):

- *Voice disorders* occur when there is an absence or an abnormal production of voice quality, pitch, loudness, resonance, and/or duration.
- *Articulation disorders* are the abnormal production of speech sounds.
- *Fluency disorders*, the abnormal flow of verbal expression, are characterized by impaired rate and rhythm that may be accompanied by struggle behavior.

Language disorder is the impairment or deviant development of comprehension and/or use of a spoken, written, and/or other symbol system; it may involve the form, the content, and/or the function of language.

Traumatic Brain Injury

Traumatic brain injury (TBI) occurs when a child's brain has experienced an injury because of some type of force; TBI does not apply to congenital or birth trauma brain injuries. TBIs can cause multiple co-occurring disabilities and can profoundly affect cognition, language, memory, attention, judgment, problem-solving, and motor abilities.

Visual Impairment

Like hearing impairments, **visual impairments** fall into two categories: the blind and the partially sighted. As with hearing impairments, there is more than one definition of the categories. *Partially sighted* children have visual acuity between 20/70 and 20/200 in the better eye with glasses. Some definitions indicate that blind children must learn to read Braille or use aural methods (such as screen reading software, auditory books, and recording devices), whereas partially sighted children are able to read using glasses and/or magnification.

Visual impairment/blindness is one of the least prevalent disabilities in American children. The most common visual problems, such as nearsightedness, farsightedness, and astigmatism, may be serious enough to cause significant impairment, but most can be corrected with glasses or contact lenses. Most of the visual impairments that affect children are due to prenatal causes, many of which are hereditary. Other causes include maternal prenatal infectious diseases such as syphilis and rubella—both of which are preventable (German measles) (Hallahan & Kauffman, 2000).

Children who are visually impaired are usually not significantly disabled in their ability to understand and use language, but their early language development may be restricted by the lack of visual experiences, making their language more self-centered. There is no evidence to suggest that sight impairment results in lower intelligence, but children who are visually impaired may rely more heavily on the senses of hearing and touch to perceive and learn about their world.

Attention Deficit Hyperactivity Disorder (ADHD)

Attention deficit hyperactivity disorder (ADHD) is a behavioral disorder that makes it difficult for children to stay focused and presents them with difficulties in controlling their behaviors; some children are also affected by hyperactivity (Learning Disabilities Association of America, LDA, 2021). It is characterized by chronic, impairing levels of attention, hyperactivity, or their combination.

ADHD describes a set of symptoms in children reflecting excessive inattention or overactivity and impulsive responding, within the context of developmentally appropriate behavior for the child's age and gender group. Unable to sustain responses long enough to accomplish assigned tasks, these children show considerably less persistence than their peers.

Today, about six million children—about 10 percent of American students—have been diagnosed with ADHD (LDA, 2021). In a typical classroom of 24 to 30 students, it is likely that at least one student will have ADHD (LDA, 2021). Under IDEA, ADHD is not considered to be a learning disability. However, about 30 percent of children with ADHD have a specific learning disability which qualifies them for IDEA services. Educators, psychologists, and other professionals support the use of behavior modification and/or social skills training to improve a child's behavior.

Giftedness

Giftedness is the only exceptionality not included in the category of disabilities. There is little agreement about the definition of **giftedness**, except that *gifted children* excel in some way(s) when compared with their peers; federal laws do not require special services for gifted students as they do for students with disabilities. Most states mandate programs for gifted students, and each state has its own definition of gifted. The most common features of these state definitions are general intellectual ability, specific academic aptitude, creative-thinking ability, advanced ability in the fine arts and performing arts, and leadership ability (Hallahan & Kauffman, 2000). A variety of educational models exist for gifted children, but research on the effectiveness of these models is sparse.

It is understandable that parents are perhaps fearful when they have a child who is diagnosed with disabilities because as we have seen, such a reality dashes the dreams for the hoped-for child. It is important to remember, however, that despite a child's differences and variations from an abled child, impaired children—with supportive, loving, encouraging environments—can (and do!) achieve their full developmental potentials.

THE LIVED EXPERIENCES OF FAMILIES

Parenting disabled children can, at times, be overwhelming, and parents experience significantly more adverse physical, emotional, and psychological outcomes than parents of children without disabilities (Gallagher & Whitely, 2012; Hsiao et al., 2018; Scherer et al., 2019). In fact, there is considerable literature related to stress and coping in these families, and most of it reports increased tension, anxiety, and strain between couples, siblings, and other kin (Anderson et al., 2007; Dervishaliaj, 2013). Benson (2012, 2014, 2016) described the ways in which both short- and long-term caregiving causes stress in every area of a parent's life (i.e., marriage, other family relationships, peer relationships, and career/work) and found that many experienced fractured relationships and overall relationship satisfaction.

But because every disabled child faces unique challenges of their own, there is substantial variation in the nature and extent to which individual families experience and report stress.

Family Caregiver Stressors and the Power of Resilience

Research has identified several potential causes for increased stress in families with disabled children. These include increased caregiving demands, the need to feel a sense of "normalcy," lack of information about their children's condition, uncertainty about their children's future, severity/type of disability, increased financial burden, lack of available and appropriate child care, single parenthood, and lack of support systems (see Masefield et al., 2020). Specifically, caregiver stress is the result of a number of concurrent factors,

- Time commitments and role strain (Goudie et al., 2014; Ritzema & Sladeczek, 2011).
- Managing and coping with the child's seemingly endless medical appointments and treatments (Baker et al., 2003; Hsiao, 2017; Ritzema & Sladeczek, 2011).
- Dealing with a child's behavioral challenges (Woodman et al., 2015).
- Financial burdens (Anderson et al., 2007; Goudie et al., 2014; Stabile & Allin, 2012).
- Relationship strain (Bagby et al., 2012; Kirby et al., 2015; Osborne & Reed, 2009).
- Low self-efficacy and poor physical health due to demands (Hung et al., 2010; Micsinszki et al., 2018; Murphy et al., 2007; Smith & Grzywaca, 2014).
- Insufficient support systems (Butcher et al., 2008).

Despite these stress-inducing circumstances, families with disabled children appear to adapt remarkably well, and a wealth of research substantiates this.

Resilience: Bouncing Back Well

As we've seen throughout our study of contemporary parenting, *resilience* refers to the ability to maintain flexibility and adapt to life's events. Specific to parenting disabled children, one body of research conceptualizes resilience as an adaptation process, a process that is fluid and changes over time (Suzuki et al., 2013, 2018). Elements of this adaptive process are numerous and include a strong parental internal locus of control and self-efficacy, positive perceptions of the situation, various communication and other relational skills, coping strategies, and social support (Widyawati et al., 2020; Whiting et al., 2019); another study speaks to the importance of parents acquiring personal mastery (i.e., personal growth through a sense of purpose) (Keniş-Coşkun at al., 2020). Ultimately, if parents successfully navigate this adaptive process, there are more positive outcomes for the child (Cappe et al., 2011; Fereidouni et al., 2021; Widyawati et al., 2020). Resilience—the ability to "bounce back well"—is perhaps one of the strongest psychological interventions that can enhance the lives of parents, the disabled child, and other family members (Buckner et al., 2003, 2009; Fereidouni et al., 2021). **Resilience-based interventions** are resources and programs that help parents and caregivers adapt well to psychological stress and are known to positively enhance parents' and families' emotions, mental health, overall well-being, and quality of life (for a full review, see Helmreich et al., 2017). Helmreich et al. (2017) reviewed a number of resiliency studies, and Table 12.3 presents their findings, as well as the findings of other bodies of research, of scientifically validated resilience factors among parents; the table also shows various parent education training methods that would benefit parents of children with complex needs.

The Impact of Support From Helping Professionals

The research is unequivocal about the positive impact of support on families of children with disabilities: The greater the level of social support, especially informal support, the lower the level of stress. And, when parents are supported, children are supported.

Understandably, raising a disabled child places significant stressors on parents, caregivers, and siblings. Support from helping professionals helps these families to "struggle well."

Source: iStock.com/olesiabilkei.

TABLE 12.3 ■ Factors That Enhance Parental and Family Resilience

Resilience Factor	Parent Education Training
Meaning/purpose in life	• Help parents set priorities • Assist parents in identifying aspects of their lives that bring them meaning and contentment • Guide parents in defining their values
Sense of coherence (a mix of optimism combined with a sense of control)	• Comprehensibility—help parents see the situation in an orderly, coherent, clear way • Manageability—provide parents assistance in identifying their available resources • Meaningfulness—motivate parents to explore meaning in the circumstances
Positive emotions	• Identifying emotions and feelings • Mindfulness techniques • Spirituality and religiosity • Activities that bring pleasure and down-time

Resilience Factor	Parent Education Training
Active coping	• Problem-solving techniques • Intentional focusing • Using internal resources • Reframing
Self-esteem/self-efficacy	• Help to identify personal and relational strengths • Help to identify past successful management of stressors • Help to challenge self-criticism • Help to evaluate and modify expectations

Sources: Drageset and Haugan (2015), Helmreich et al. (2017), Idan and Margalit (2014), Eriksson and Mittelmark (2017).

Georgetown University Child Development Center and the Center for Child Health (2021) provides a comprehensive educational program, Serving Children with Disabilities, to improve the support skills of helping professionals who work with disabled children and their families. The guiding principle of the program is that children should be understood within the context of their family—including their rich cultural and ethnic histories and experiences—and that each family brings unique expertise and perspectives to helping professionals as they seek support (Georgetown University, 2021).

In addition to educational support received from IDEA, families often need guidance and assistance to meet not only the demands of parenting their disabled child but also with the everyday demands of raising a family. Helping professionals and educators cannot only direct parents and families to resources, but they can also:

- **Promote family interaction:** Because of the unique stressors and the multiple demands and needs associated with a disabled child, it is not uncommon for families to experience a disconnection in family relationships and to interact as a family system on an infrequent basis. Helping professionals can help families find ways to be inclusive of siblings and extended family and to "work and play" as a family.
- **Increasing support from the family network:** Every family has strengths, and oftentimes it is necessary for the helping professional to help families identify their strengths and tap into their resiliencies. It is also beneficial for families to identify people in their social support network and to evaluate what strengths they may bring to ease the burden of caregiving. It is also valuable for families to identify those who can provide respite care.
- **Accessing help from the community:** To some extent, every community has supports and services, be it formal educational programs or smaller-scale support that

is provided by churches or community religious organizations. Services such as food pantries, transportation, volunteer in-home respite care or child care, and financial support from religious or neighborhood benevolence funds or crowd source funding, all help to alleviate the caregiving stressors.

- **Helping families to help themselves:** Helping families to establish an internal locus of control is essential to them becoming empowered. The Serving Children with Disabilities program encourages professionals to assist families in gathering and organizing school, medical, and other records about their child and information about the child's disability. It is also beneficial for service providers to offer education that promotes parents' and caregivers' communication skills, so they are better able to convey their needs and to confidently discuss their child with service providers.

Being an effective advocate for a disabled child is a learned skill. But, due to the nature of the unique stressors parents and families face, it is not uncommon for families to need additional advocacy, because, "… disabilities and [their] impact on families are not always easily recognized, or well understood by either family members or professionals" (Georgetown University, 2021, p. 22).

Parent–Child Relationships

Throughout this book, we have discussed parent–child interactions in a variety of types of families. There are many elements or characteristics common to all families that facilitate positive outcomes. On the other hand, each family type has its particular challenges, and each family within those types has its unique characteristics. Families with disabled children share similar challenges, regardless of the type of disability. However, each type of disability brings with it additional unique, special challenges, which are described briefly below.

Physical Disabilities

The burden of care for a child with physical disabilities depends on the type and severity of the particular disability (Feizi et al., 2014; Shyam et al., 2014). When a child has severe neurological problems that prevent independent locomotion, she remains dependent on her parents long after the infancy stage. Lifting and transporting become more difficult as the child matures, and toilet learning and self-feeding may occur much later than usual. Parents may become socially isolated if they are reluctant or unable to take their disabled children to public places. This reluctance may be especially strong when the child's disability is extremely visible. Increased demands by children and fewer rewards to parents may cause angry feelings toward the child and subsequent guilt.

Many physical disabilities require the use of special equipment or prosthetic devices, which may create logistical problems. If the child has difficulty getting around, parents may be tempted to be overprotective and/or intrusive, doing things for the child that he may be able to do for himself if given time and patience and thereby encouraging unnecessary dependence. This dependence may be exacerbated if the child is unable to enter into extracurricular activities with his peers because of his physical limitations. Parents should be encouraged to nurture the child's self-concept and body image, focusing on his strengths.

Intellectual Disability

The initial diagnosis of an ID may be especially difficult for parents because they must accept that the child will be forever limited in intellectual development. During the early days and months of the child's life, parents are almost always able to get off to a good start with the child without the trauma associated with a diagnosed disability. These early positive patterns may make it easier for parents to cope with their grief at a later time. On the other hand, delayed diagnosis may be confusing and frustrating to parents if the cause of the disability is not known and if they perceive their roles in the child's optimal development as ambiguous or hopeless.

As the Loss and Grief Cycle illustrated for us in Chapter 4, parents of children with ID experience recurring crises arising from the lack of their child's lack of normative developmental progression. The slowed rate of development and the discrepancy from the expected trajectory become a source for heightened stress and grief (Feizi et al., 2014; Jess et al., 2018; Shyam et al., 2014). These crises are likely to occur at the age when children who are typically developing ordinarily would begin to walk and talk, begin kindergarten, experience the onset of puberty, and celebrate their 21st birthdays. Further, parents may experience a crisis when a younger sibling's development surpasses that of the intellectually disabled child.

Setting reasonable expectation levels for the disabled child's behavior and performance can be extremely difficult for parents. Parental warmth, nurturance, and acceptance, focusing on the child's total development, are important.

Learning Disabilities

There is no "prototype" of a learning-disabled child—these children are characterized as much by their differences as by their similarities. Because of the diversity of characteristics, the lack of a visible disability, problems with definitions, and the difficulty in early identification, parents may experience unique stressors (Panicker & Chelliah, 2016).

Unfortunately, many children with learning disabilities develop emotional/behavioral disorders, partly because their learning problems have led to repeated experiences of failure, and perhaps coupled with rejection by parents, teachers, and peers. These children have been found to have lower self-concepts, more anxiety, and lower peer acceptance than typically achieving children (Heiman & Olenik-Shemesh, 2020).

Children with learning disabilities need an abundance of affection, praise, and approval from parents and peers. Parents need to be supported in their efforts to provide as many successful experiences for these children as possible—even a series of small accomplishments. A partnership between parents and teachers to provide appropriate intervention while setting reasonable expectations can help these children lead more rewarding lives.

Communication Disorders

Communication-disordered children are faced with major obstacles to social communication. An inability to convey their thoughts and feelings leads to frustration and, often, aggression.

Most parents of children with communication disorders, including parents of children with autism and ASD, have periods of increased emotional instability, prolonged grief, ambivalence, and mood swings; they are "intensely affected by the ways their child is accepted or rejected by society" (Naniwadekar, 2018, p. 142). Parents of children with communication disorders experience more marital dissatisfaction and conflict than parents of children with other disabilities, and mothers tend to socially isolate themselves.

For mildly impaired preschool children, language development can be facilitated by parents listening attentively and empathically, providing appropriate language models, encouraging children to use their communication skills appropriately, asking open-ended questions, and offering many opportunities for language learning. However, early intervention for children with communicative disorders is critical, and parental efforts may need to be augmented by the intervention of a speech therapist. Nonverbal children will require a specialist in language training to help them acquire functional language. Some children will require a system of augmentative or alternative communication, such as manual signing or utilization of communication boards or electronic devices.

Hearing Impairments/Deafness

Deafness usually is unexpected and may be difficult to detect in infants, especially by hearing parents. The average age for the detection of congenital hearing loss has been reported to be 20 months of age (Canale et al., 2006). However, the increased practice of screening newborns who are at biological risk before they leave the hospital can result in much earlier diagnosis for many children.

Some researchers suggest that the full impact of deafness is not felt by parents until the preschool years, when the communication gap between deaf and hearing children becomes more evident (Meadow-Orlans, 1994). Experts report that frequent interaction with and positive feedback from family members can account for much of the impact of the hearing impaired/deaf child's development of positive self-identity, especially in light of their risk for negative peer interactions; furthermore, in families with hearing impaired/deaf infants, the early parent–child bonding relationship may also be negatively impacted (for a complete review, see Blank et al., 2020; Brown et al., 2013).

Undoubtedly, the biggest challenge facing the parents of hearing impaired/deaf children is establishing an effective communication system because the child's hearing loss affects the communication dynamic between parents and their child; this negatively impacted relationship, in turn, may contribute to other suboptimal developmental outcomes in the child (Cruz et al., 2013).

Hearing parents face a significant challenge in trying to unlearn habitual communication patterns and replace them with patterns more appropriate to the visual mode. Many experts advocate the use of deaf adults as models of effective sequential communicators (Bodner-Johnson, 1991).

Visual Impairments/Blindness

One of the most significant problems of parents with infants who are visually impaired or blind is the inability to establish eye contact. The infant's gaze is an important cue in sustaining reciprocal interactions with a caregiver, and it promotes positive social and emotional behaviors (Senju et al., 2013). Also, babies who are blind do not display the clearly differentiated facial expressions of sighted babies. They smile less often and often fail to smile even at the sound of the mother's voice, and the signals they give to their caregivers are more subdued. As a result, the inability of parents and other caregivers to interpret their babies' signals may lead to disruption in the bonding and attachment process. Research has shown that blind children, during the second year, do not have a mental representation of the mother that can sustain them in the mother's absence (see van den Broek et al., 2017).

Programs directed at supporting parents of children who are blind teach parents to provide many experiences that stimulate their young children's senses—hearing, touch, taste, smell, and movement. To develop communicative competence, parents learn to respond to all of the child's attempts to communicate, by using alternative signals such as verbal response, soft touch, the imitation of vocalizations, and expanding on child utterances.

Emotional/Behavioral Disorders

This disability may be the most challenging of all for parents because the child's behavior eventually impacts every area of family life, where simply "waking up the child for school and getting them dressed becomes an emotionally exhausting event" (Lukowiak, 2010, p. 26). Some families also experience social isolation because family and friends are less likely to visit if a child has continuing or escalating behavioral difficulties.

When young children do not respond well to usual disciplinary techniques, parents are likely to become angry, frustrated, and ineffective (Ricci et al., 2017). Other parental behaviors associated with behavioral disordered children include:

- unreasonable or punitive discipline
- emotional deprivation or rejection
- severe marital conflict
- requiring perfectionism
- overindulgence
- detachment
- authoritarianism

When severely withdrawn children do not react or respond to parents' attempts to communicate and interact with them, parents may feel helpless, hurt, and guilty. Understandably, the negative feedback from the child affects the parent and causes they/him/her to respond in a negative manner, so that a vicious cycle of unhealthy behaviors—from child and parents alike—occurs (Vaughan et al., 2013). It is no wonder that many parents search avidly for a diagnosis to explain the child's behavior.

There are almost as many ways to deal with emotional/behavioral disorders as there are types of behaviors. Treatment often depends on the provided explanation of the behavior. For example, if a biological/medical model is accepted, parents are likely to use medication to regulate the child's behavior; if the behavior is explained through a psychoanalytic model, parents are likely to seek therapy to uncover the underlying causes of the behavior. If it is viewed through the behavioral lens, behavior modification techniques are likely to be used. Sometimes a combination of techniques is used. In any event, parents of children who are emotionally or behaviorally disordered need ample support to deal effectively with their children's behavior.

High Ability Learners

Gifted children, or *high ability learners*, do not present the same types of challenges to parents presented by children with disabilities. However, some parents of gifted children may demonstrate behaviors that are on the opposite end of a continuum: They may fail to nurture the child's giftedness, not understanding the child's precocity, or they may exploit the exceptional traits and push the child beyond reasonable limits. Oftentimes it is difficult for parents to find the right balance of nurturance and stimulation of giftedness and realistic expectations. Furthermore, parents of gifted children sometimes struggle to find adequate resources, support, and assistance (Renati et al., 2017).

Parents of gifted children can learn to encourage original thinking, questioning, and experimentation without being overly demanding. Avoiding interference with the child's work and resisting the temptation to dominate or control the child's activities all are ways in which parents can nurture giftedness and encourage initiative and independence. To avoid conflict between gifted and nongifted siblings, the gifted characteristics of one sibling should not be overemphasized.

BEST PRACTICES FOR PARENTS OF DISABLED CHILDREN

Today, many more children with exceptionalities are being served at younger ages. Federal legislation promotes the idea of **family-centered support services**, a notion that embraces the idea that services should center on and be responsive to the needs of all family members as they relate to the child's development. An *Individualized Family Service Plan (IFSP)* is required, targeting the whole family, not just the child, for intervention. Principles for a family-centered philosophy include the recognition that the family is the constant in the child's life, and as such, recognize family strengths; a family-centered strategy also respects a family's choices regarding their desired outcomes for their child (Bruder & Staff, 1998).

Similar to family-centered services, **empowerment principles** allow families to control the direction and outcomes of support services (Hsiao et al., 2018; Turnbull et al., 2015). They, too, promote family strengths and decision-making. Below, we'll discuss several contemporary family support and empowerment strategies that promote children's and families' health and well-being. Unless otherwise noted, these strategies are adapted from the work of Barbara

Van Haren, Director of Special Education for the Cooperative Extension Agency, Brookfield, Wisconsin, and Craig Fiedler, professor of special education at the University of Wisconsin (2008).

Be Empathic and Foster Hope

As with any other type of family service, those of us who work with families and their children should be empathic and demonstrate understanding and compassion. When we display empathy for families, it allows us to approach families in judgment-free ways. When we are able to lay our judgments and personal opinions aside, we can then best put ourselves in the place of the families we are serving, and better understand the day-to-day challenges and frustrations they face. By showing empathy and understanding, we can then oftentimes be the voice of hope for parents and families. Careful not to be unrealistic of a disabled child's future, we can be optimistic and hopeful for a child's continual progress.

When working with parents, it is critically important for the parenting professional to honor the parents and other family members as experts.

Source: iStock.com/AsISeeIt.

Recognize Families as Experts and Enhance Their Self-Efficacy

As professionals who work with individuals and families, we oftentimes forget that we are not the experts—the parents and family members who interact with their disabled child are the ones who best know the child. While we as service providers, educators, and family scientists might be able to help families identify their strengths and competencies, from time to time we must step out of our expert roles and allow families to see that they, indeed, "have what it takes" to help their child reach his/her/their developmental potentials. When we take a step back, families feel better supported and their strengths emerge—they feel empowered and motivated.

Enhance Family Access and Offer Family Networking

As our study has shown us, family support can come from a number of sources. Families who have accessible means of support, such as being able to place their disabled child in the neighborhood school, are better able to build networks—both with other families who may share common ground and with families of children who do not have a disabled child. These family connections may assist parents in accessing new information, such as with parent-to-parent programs where matches are made between a "veteran" parent of a disabled child and a more experienced parent. Family connection networking may also help them to become more comfortable with the setting they have chosen to educate their child(ren). Schools can also serve as conduits between families and federal/state programming.

Encourage Effective Problem-Solving and Coping Skills

There are a number of processes involved in effective problem-solving. First, families must be able to define the problem. As you saw in the previous chapter, this can be difficult because each of us assign different meanings to different situations. Next, families need to generate possible solutions; depending on the child's severity of disabilities, solutions will vary. Families then need to choose a solution or solutions, and they then need to implement the solution. Of course, these are difficult—if not impossible—steps without trained professionals guiding the way. Finally, parents must evaluate the effectiveness of their chosen solution(s).

You can see why support and empowerment from service providers and educators are necessary to help parents and children alike. As a colleague of a disabled child recently shared with us, "When we learned that our son was hearing impaired and cognitively delayed, we were devastated. I have my graduate degree in Special Education, and even still, when we first got the news, I felt like I was being smothered. I looked at my husband and said, 'If we feel this helpless, imagine how families with fewer resources and access to those resources feel'. Our child's diagnosis made me that much more committed to my chosen profession."

PARENTING LIFE EDUCATION: AFFIRMING IDENTITIES, ADVOCATING FOR RIGHTS AND SERVICES, AND PROMOTING DEVELOPMENTAL OUTCOMES

Prior to the 1850s, people with disabilities (of all ages) were institutionalized, hidden away from society. The medical model that emerged in the mid-19th century shed new light on both the experiences and the treatment of those with impairments, and it conceptualized disability as an illness or physical condition that is a part of the person's body. It was believed that the impairment(s) negatively impacted an individual's quality of life, and that the person lived at a disadvantage. In essence, the medical model is centered on *what a person cannot do and what they cannot be or become.*

In the 1960s, American citizens fought for the civil rights of Black, Indigenous, and people of color (BIPOC) individuals and other races and ethnicities, and for the prohibition of exclusion based on sex, national origin, and religion. At this same time, disability rights activists and people with disabilities began their battle to be removed from the fringes of society and be recognized as a minority group who has experienced discrimination, marginalization, and disenfranchisement that the medical model of *limitations* imposed upon them. From the 1970s through the 1990s, the social model of disability became the prevailing theory of advocating for individuals with impairments. This model conceptualizes "disability" as impairments due to the barriers imposed upon them from their environments—physical, attitudinal, and other social barriers. This foundational premise is what led the way to federal legislation that provides FAPE for children of all abilities.

Today, many in this country are calling for the *human rights model* of disability. This paradigm recognizes that having a disability is a part of the whole fabric of human diversity, and that all individuals deserve equitable treatment and respect. A first step that we can take, as helping professionals and educators of young children, is to use identity-affirming language, where the *person* comes before the disability. For example, a social worker or parent educator might use the phrase, "the child with autism," rather than "the autistic child." This model calls for the end of using euphemisms to describe disability, and this intentional language suggests that we recognize the child as a person first—not by a label that stigmatizes what they may and may not be able to do (Liebowitz, 2015).

Parents of children with disabilities face many challenges. The initial diagnosis of a disability in a child shatters a dream, and most parents experience a period of grieving for the loss of a healthy child. Overwhelming evidence suggests that parenting a child with a disability is stressful. The intensity and duration of stress vary, depending on a variety of child, family, professional, and cultural factors, and increased stress may surface at various times throughout the life cycle. However, most research suggests that with appropriate support, these families are little different from other families in healthily functioning family environments.

Furthermore, families of children with disabilities share many characteristics, but each disability brings its special challenges and rewards to parents. Many families demonstrate resilience—a remarkable capacity to adapt to stress and adversity and to achieve much higher levels of self-mastery and self-esteem than would be expected. Specific parental behaviors seem to contribute to a child's resiliency.

Early intervention services for young disabled children and their families are federally and locally mandated to implement a family-centered philosophy, whereby parents are full partners in the decision-making and in the assessment of and delivery of services to their children. Today, there are many family-centered support and empowerment strategies that professionals can use in their efforts to enhance the lives of disabled children and their families.

As teachers, social workers, therapists, Family Life Educators, healthcare professionals, and parenting educators, it is incumbent upon us to recognize the impact of the various social and cultural trends on parenting (National Council on Family Relations, 2021). Working with parents and families in contemporary society requires that we affirm the identities of disabled children and recognize their strengths and contributions, rather than their "limitations." We must advocate for they and their parents/caregivers to promote the healthiest developmental outcomes, both for children and their families.

APPENDICES

CHAPTER 2 APPENDIX

The Varied Experiences of Parenting

Contemporary Families

- It is incumbent upon parent and family practitioners to know and understand the cultural differences in and approaches to parenting among American contemporary parents. Only then can biases and micro-aggressions be set aside.
- *African Heritage theory* helps us to understand the ways in which **African American/ Black Caribbean** cultures distinctly differ from white, European American cultures, such as Black cultures' rich heritages of valuing extended families and kinship, and the value of shared emotional and instrumental support in family life and rearing children. Thus, when using the term "parents," African American/Black Caribbeans are not only referring to the child's parents but also to the extended family and fictive kin who participate in childrearing. Furthermore, while Euro-Americans may view parent–child interactions in the Black families as harsh and controlling, yet Black children report that their parents' behaviors are acts of love, care, and protection.
- **Latinx** embrace their cultural heritage of community, and place high value on immediate, extended, and fictive kin (i.e., close friendships) family relationships. *Familismo* or *familism* describes the mutual support shared between family members, and this ideology places the well-being of a family member and family over the needs of an individual. Parenting practitioners need to be knowledgeable of and sensitive to the ways in which intergenerational relationships influence parenting and family decisions.
- Among **Asian Americans**, *filial piety* governs intergenerational family experiences. Asian parents are warm, affectionate, and lenient with their infants and young children, but as children grow into school-age and adolescence, discipline becomes strict. Parental goals—not the goals of the individual child—take precedence, and children are expected to be self-governing; firm expectations and obedience/ obligation to parents characterize Asian American parent–child relationships. Parent professionals need to be cautious about interpreting these parenting behaviors as parental control/child submission because the ultimate goal of Asian parenting is to rear children who internalize the value of individual responsibility.
- **Native American/Alaska Native (NA/AN)** family systems are vastly different from other extended families in the United States. Unlike Euro-American families where

children attach or bond to close family, Indigenous families expose their children to an array of persons to whom they can become attached. Thus, the extended family plays as large a role in childrearing as parents do—parenting is very much a communal effort. From pregnancy, Native parents instill in their children they are gifts and are the very center of Indigenous life. Those who work with Native children and families must understand that families and children very much feel stranded between two vastly different cultures. It is therefore of great importance that family practitioners make biculturalism a priority.

- The most common living arrangement among **Arab American** families is a multigenerational household in which rich cultural beliefs and traditions are upheld. Similar to Asian American parents who believe that their children are a reflection of them, honor to parents is stressed. Because parents value conformity, Arab American parents are viewed as strict, demanding, rigid, and undemocratic. It's important to stress, however, that because Arab Americans come from a vast number of countries, parenting styles vary greatly in this people group. For example, those from Lebanon use the authoritative Western approach to parenting, families from Egypt, Algeria, and Palestine equally use permissive parenting and authoritarian parenting styles. Love shown by Arab parents may be expressed in symbolic ways (i.e., providing protection, housing, food, and education), not in explicit ways (such as saying "I love you" repeatedly to a child). Indeed, country of origin significantly influences parenting styles and practices. When working with Arab families, practitioners must first ascertain the family's country of origin to best understand the cultural lens through which the children are being raised.

How Do Children Learn About Their Racial/Ethnic Identity?

- Racial/ethnic socialization practices have been linked to a number of positive outcomes in minority children and adolescents: *well-developed racial identity; heightened self-esteem; higher academic functioning*; and *decreased levels of depression and anger.*
- The practice of cultural socialization is protective against racial discrimination because children and adolescents develop coping and problem-solving strategies to help buffer racism and deal with prejudice.
- It is critically important that parent professionals examine their values and beliefs, and diligently work to eliminate biases and micro-aggressions held toward people of racial/ethnic backgrounds differing from their own. In today's diverse American society, a one-size-fits-all approach to parenting education and to imparting skills is irresponsible.
- To avoid prejudice and discrimination, we must:
    - Model the values, attitudes, and behaviors we want our children to develop. This requires being aware of our own conscious and unconscious stereotypes and behaviors.

- Expose children to people and experiences from other cultures and belief systems.
- Encourage children to see that relationships with people who are different from themselves can be rich and rewarding experiences.
- Talk with children about the similarities and differences between themselves. Help them to see that being "different" from someone does not mean the person is "worse" than someone else.
- Integrate diversity information and communication into conversations and activities.
- Teach children to be sensitive, critical thinkers, so that through examining and questioning they can better understand any issue.
- Adopt a "zero tolerance" policy about racism, prejudice, bias, and discrimination.
- Teach them that words *do hurt*.

CHAPTER 5 APPENDIX

The Changing Nature of Parenting

Infancy and Toddlerhood

Parenting Infants and Toddlers

- Parenting infants and toddlers involves an interplay between the traits and characteristics of the parents and their children. Just as infant characteristics affect how a parent responds to the baby or the toddler, a parent's traits or mood affects how a baby responds. Across time, these interactions significantly affect a child's overall development and social and emotional well-being.

- When parents understand how contextual situations, life events, individual parent and child characteristics, and couple interaction patterns mutually shape the parent–child relationship (Ecological Model), they are more able to focus on beliefs and practices that positively influence child development outcomes.

- Research has provided us with an understanding of three basic types of infant temperament: easy, difficult, and slow to warm up. When parents have knowledge of their baby's innate personality, they can more easily adjust or align their interactions to their child's. This is known as *goodness of fit*, and it is the center of healthy parent/infant relationships.

- There is no question that *difficult babies* and *slow-to-warm-up babies* are more demanding and more challenging, and that they cause more strain on family relationships. It's important to remember, however, that the concept of *differential susceptibility* goes both ways—even though it may seem like nothing the parent does will calm or soothe the infant, the baby or toddler is actually highly susceptible to high-quality parenting. It just takes time and patience for parents to learn their child's temperaments and ways of interacting.

From Partners to Parents: Making the Transition

- Dispelling the cultural myths and unrealistic beliefs about idyllic parenting can help parents confront the challenges and realities of the new roles, stress, and conflict that occur with the transition to parenting. By intentionally nurturing individual psychological well-being and the quality of the couple relationship while leveraging family support and other resources, new parents can successfully adjust to their new roles and the often, unanticipated realities of limited time, energy, and resources that adding a newborn to their family system brings.
- Parents who practice supportive coparenting by assisting each other when needed and directly or indirectly agreeing to send coordinated and consistent messaging to their child can help provide predictability and stability in establishing and reinforcing family rules, practices, and discipline. Positive coparenting is linked to child emotional well-being, academic success, social competence, and self-regulation.

Trust, Attachment, and Reciprocity

- Because social and emotional development is a lifelong process, parents who are committed to their child's development work to help their child meet important milestones at each stage of development. According to Erik Erikson, a child's social and emotional development occurs in at least eight stages. The first stage of development from about 0 to 24 months is *Trust versus Mistrust*. During this stage, parents provide a secure, consistent, and nurturing environment for their child by meeting her physical and emotional needs when they arise, quickly removing her discomforts, cuddling, fondling, playing with, and talking to her so she can develop a sense of her world as a safe place to be and of people as helpful, dependable, and trustworthy.
- Parents who practice limit-setting parenting balance responding to child signals (infant cues) and gradually introducing routines and delayed response times. With limit-setting parenting of infants, parents *do* respond to the needs of the child, but over time parents reduce their interactions, and infants begin to self-regulate.
- Equally important as prompt, consistent attention to the infant's needs is the maintenance of an orderly and predictable environment. Consistent routines, patterns of responses from caregivers, such as tones of voice, scents, and the way their body feels when held closely, help a child learn she is competent, that she can depend on others, and to develop effortful control, or the ability to inhibit certain behaviors in order to regulate emotions.
- Parents who understand the importance of attachment as an emotional or affectional bond that ties or binds the child to the parent build secure parent–child attachment bonds through being sensitive and responsive to a child's signals. By perceiving an infant's cues accurately and responding to them promptly, appropriately, affectionately, tenderly, and positively, the child learns to trust his caregiver.

- Developing *synchrony* and *mutuality* in parent–child social and emotional interactions occur when the parent–child exchanges are reciprocal, positive, and mutually rewarding. Engaging in activities such as paying attention to the same things, mutual gazing at each other, and recognizing cues, signals, and patterns of behaviors, such as when a baby seeks stimulation, is drowsy, or averts her gaze because the stimulation is too overwhelming, are some ways parents can positively interact with their child.

Brain Development and Infant Stimulation

- Parents who provide repeated positive sensory experiences and stimulating environments, such as interesting things to look at, loving and responsive care, talking and singing to help their infants' brains to thrive. Visual stimulation should consist of bright colors, light-and-dark contrasts (stripes, bull's-eye patterns, and geometric shapes), objects that move, and contoured surfaces. Auditory stimulation can include vocalizing (such as imitating coos and babbles, talking, singing), exposure to music, daily sounds in and out of the house, and regular reading. Touching should include holding, cuddling, stroking, rocking, and movement.
- It is important to balance the infant's day with self-initiated, independent activities and interactive exchanges. An effort should be made to keep these interactions spontaneous, fun, and consistent with the needs of both parent and child, while striving for high mutuality. Remembering always that quality of stimulation is more important than quantity, infant stimulation should be varied, appropriately timed, linked to the infant's actions, and presented in a context of basic trust.

Parents as Protectors

- As a child becomes mobile, the role of parents gradually takes on the new dimension of protector. As protectors, parents must provide the safest environment possible for toddlers in order to allow them to exercise their growing independence and increased capacity for learning. Parents can encourage compliance and reduce hearing "No's" from a child by phrasing statements in the form of expectations, when offering choices is not warranted, such as "When your toys are picked up, we would be happy to have you join us in the living room to play a game." On other occasions, when appropriate, parents can offer the child potential choices such as, "Would you rather pick up your toys now or after we play a game?"
- During the second stage (*Autonomy versus Shame and Doubt*) of Erikson's theory of psychosocial development, parents recognize the young child's need to do what he is capable of doing at his own pace and in his own time. As they do, the toddler develops a sense that he can control his own muscles, impulses, himself and, not insignificantly, his environment. Letting him dress himself in the morning, pour his own milk, or put away his toys when appropriate helps protect him from parental overprotection and other critical, harsh, or unthinking practices.

- Setting firm limits and enforcing them consistently in a loving manner while avoiding extremes during this stage is critical to healthy child development. The most important limits have to do with the child's own safety and well-being. Expressing expectations and offering choices is important when setting limits.
- One important purpose of parental control through setting limits is to make it possible for the child to know how and when to control herself. Forcing a contest of wills or giving in to her desires during a temper tantrum are inappropriate techniques for helping her learn how to control herself. Contests of wills can be avoided by making expectations simple, clear, and consistent. Taking her by the hand and leading her in the desired direction, modeling the expected behavior for her, and offering realistic choices so that she can exercise her independence are potential appropriate techniques.
- Autonomy supportive parenting, a parenting style (authoritative) in which parents promote age-appropriate child involvement in decision-making, helps to diminish externalizing behaviors and increases his sense of responsibility, competence, self-confidence, and self-respect. Giving the child the opportunity to make as many developmentally appropriate choices as possible throughout the day, listening to his perspective, validating his feelings, and asking open-ended questions are healthy strategies for encouraging problem-solving and decision-making skills.
- Parents play a unique role in facilitating the acquisition of social skills, language, curiosity, and the formation of the roots of intelligence critical to their child's social and intellectual development. Social skills can be encouraged through providing exposure to interactions with children her own age. Labeling familiar objects and events, reinforcing language attempts, modeling good quality and quantity of language spoken in the home, asking/answering questions, and reading to her help facilitate strong language development. Providing learning experiences that involve touch, taste, smell, vision, and hearing will help to expand her curiosity and intelligence as she explores basic concepts related to color, shape, size, weight, distance, and causality.

Parents as Nurturers

- Nurturing, warm, responsive parenting is critical to healthy child development, particularly during the preschool period. Discovering the optimal amount of supervision without interference, assistance without indulgence, and warmth and love without suffocation are important strategies. Frequent expressions of love, consistency in making and enforcing rules, and administering discipline are critical to help a child develop his sense of competence. Partners who agree on the goals they have for him and who show love and respect for each other and for him create a positive emotional climate in the home.
- A positive emotional climate and positive child outcomes are much more likely to be created in the home when both parents choose to parent using an authoritative

parenting style. Authoritative parents set clear boundaries for their child's behavior, but they are flexible and will change these boundaries if the situation warrants. They are warm and responsive and encourage open parent–child communication. She is expected to follow the rules of the house but is still allowed to be autonomous. With this style, parents use a balance of power and reason.

- There are many racial, ethnic, cultural, income, and living environment differences in parenting that influence parenting styles and child well-being. Parenting goals such as fostering independence, compliance, autonomy, maintenance of cultural identities, increased educational, economic, and social success influence specific choices of parenting style and subsequent child outcomes. For example, African (and Asian) American parents typically utilize more authoritarian parenting styles (involving more physical discipline and higher control) than other parenting styles. One reason African American parents practice the increased use of strictness and discipline is as a protective factor for the child's safety, to show affection, demand compliance, and teach respect for authority. The manner in which parents interact with and guide him influences his development in more ways than are immediately visible (such as behavior and school performance). Children learn how to love and be loved when they feel secure and accepted and form strong attachment bonds with parents.
- Parents who use inductive discipline emphasize process goals, stressing the "how" rather than the "what" of behavior. This is in contrast to a parent telling a child that some of her behaviors are good and others are bad, which is more likely to produce unnecessary feelings of guilt and shame. It is important to show her why her present behavior pattern is inappropriate, how to act instead, and demonstrate the expectation that she will change her behavior in the desired positive direction.
- Parents who use *natural consequences* allow the child to learn naturally from his behavior (a child who refuses to eat goes hungry). Parents who use *logical consequences* pair a specific positive or negative consequence to a specific behavior (a child who disturbs the rest of the family at mealtime is given the choice to settle down or to leave the table). When using this type of discipline, the parent's actions must be based on respect for the child as a person separate from his deeds. The parent should also be firm in following through with the consequences, yet kind and encouraging in the tone of voice used when disciplining him.

Building Self-Concept, Initiative, and Learning

- Parents who help a child feel like he belongs and feels worthwhile are instrumental in helping him develop his self-concept. Paying particular attention to helping him successfully interact with his environment is critical to his success and well-being.
- *Initiative versus Guilt* is the third stage of Erikson's psychosocial development model. During this stage, parents encourage a sense of initiative in their child—a sense that

she can learn and accomplish anything—by promoting and reinforcing security, freedom, moral responsibility, opportunity, controlling her behavior, encouraging her to initiate play, such as fantasy play, and to ask questions.

CHAPTER 6 APPENDIX

The Changing Nature of Parenthood

Middle Childhood

Child Brain Maturation and the Environment

- Optimal brain development requires direction from experiences in the environment. The parent–child relationship/family relationships are central to the architecture and function of the child's developing brain. Providing a child with multiple opportunities to get involved in *stimulating environments, experiences, and interactions*, such as clubs, sports, music lessons, after-school activities, and summer programs, are great ways to *support and promote their individual capacities and capabilities.*
- Because parenting, childhood experiences, and childhood environments influence structural brain changes during preadolescence and adolescence, it is important that parents protect their child from adverse childhood experiences as much as possible. Monitoring friends, social media, and other influences are some good strategies. In addition, practicing warm, responsive, and supportive parenting is crucial because it is linked to positive cognitive, behavioral, and psychological growth and development throughout the individual's life. Warm parenting includes using soft tones, being empathetic, and available for a child. Responsive parenting includes being encouraging, conversational, and staying connected. Supportive parenting includes not only monitoring what is going on with a child but also setting boundaries and being consistent.

Child Sexual Development

- Because most children don't know the proper names for their sexual anatomy or understand the maturational and sexual changes that are occurring during puberty, parents need to communicate early and regularly with their child about the changes that occur during this important stage of development. Communicating in warm and sensitive ways about his sexual health, discussing sexual values, beliefs, and expectations, and being open and honest when answering questions are key strategies. It is critical that parents make sure he is well informed with correct information about sexual matters throughout the developmental process and that they don't rely on schools or peers to inform him about responsible sexual health.

- Talking to children about specific healthy sexual behaviors should occur developmentally with a different focus during middle childhood (5 to 8 yrs.) than late middle childhood (9 to 12 yrs.). Discussions about healthy sexual behaviors during middle childhood could include how children experience their gender identity, sexual orientation, the basics of human reproduction, personal body rights and responsibility. During late middle childhood, parents can communicate about accurate sexual health education, reproduction, pregnancy, STIs, respect for privacy, family values about dating and sex, appropriate and safe boundaries, expectations about social media use, and rights and responsibilities within friendships and relationships as they try to normalize her feelings and uncertainties. The key is to keep the conversation going.
- Parental support of a sexual or gender minority child is critical to his growth, development, physical and psychological well-being. Affirming his sexual orientation and expressions of gender, openly talking about his LGBTQ+ identity, defending and protecting him when he experiences bullying, and welcoming his LGBTQ+ peers into their lives and families are some common ways parents of a sexual or gender minority child can show their support.

Middle Childhood: Fostering Social and Emotional Growth

- Due to a child's limited experiences in dealing with her social world during middle childhood, she needs important assurances from her parents that they are a secure base and are available for support. Fostering mutuality of contact (i.e., quantity and quality of time spent together), open communication, and a collaborative relationship help cement the parent–child attachment bond.
- Helping a child develop self-control and regulate his emotions during middle childhood is a primary task for parents. A healthy attachment bond evolves to a mechanism that helps children learn to self-govern and regulate their emotions. Warm, responsive, connected parents guide and assist their child when he experiences negative emotions or struggles to manage his negative feelings. Staying keenly attuned to his feelings allows authoritative parents to more accurately and insightfully assess and evaluate his feelings and to support him in identifying, understanding, accepting, and managing them.
- The middle childhood period of development provides a critical window for prevention, early detection, and intervention of mental health disorders. Parents are integral to helping their child access the needed mental health resources and healthcare supports, particularly when they experience low SES. Becoming informed and reaching out to professionals, practitioners, and organizations who provide mental health resources and healthcare supports is critical in order to maintain both parent and child well-being.

- Parents need to be aware of and sensitive to youths' intersecting identities and the inequalities, inequities, and disparities that can negatively impact child development. Documentation status, sexual orientation, gender identity, physical ability, and race represent some of the intersecting identities that are influenced by multiple forces in society which interact and work together to shape a child's physical, cognitive, and social-emotional development. Open, affirming communication about these identities and powerful forces reinforces that she is secure and supported by her parents as she navigates the complexities of her social world.

Middle Childhood: Developing Industry

- When the child's use of his expanding skills and competencies meets with success, when he receives support and approval form parents, peers, and teachers, then he develops a sense of industry, the fourth stage of Erikson's psychosocial development. Parents who provide their child with multiple developmentally appropriate work-oriented tasks and competency experiences, such as home chore duties and support for doing well in school, assist him to believe in himself and his capabilities. Erikson believed that many of the attitudes toward work and work habits that are exhibited later in life are formed during this developmental period. It is therefore important that both parents and teachers provide many and ongoing opportunities for him to succeed at a variety of work experiences.
- Parenting style and the quality of interactions between parents and children are significantly related to a child's development of a healthy self-concept, which includes her sense of belonging, worth, and competence. How her parents talk to her and reinforce that they accept and support her strongly influences how she begins to see herself. Because she tends to behave in ways consistent with how she sees herself, achievement orientation and academic success are good indicators of the strength of her self-concept.
- Providing in-home and out-of-home learning experiences are critical to a child's growing sense of industry as he works to expand both his body skills and his perceptual skills. Sports, music or dance, clubs, and church activities, among others, allow him to associate with peers and other adults, make friendships, learn about others' cultural backgrounds, spend time with those who share similar interests, and learn how to play by the rules and be a good sport. Parents need to be aware of the "more is better" trap when planning for his out-of-home activities so there is time to pursue meaningful interaction or other interests and activities, such as planned and unplanned in-home activities.
- Parental proactive teaching, calm discussion in disciplinary encounters, warmth, and interest and involvement in the child's peer activities are parenting practices that are important for her behavioral, social, and academic adjustment. Supportive and aware parenting, characterized by affection, approval, attentiveness, responsiveness,

guidance, and receptivity to emotions, is associated with higher positive self-concept, higher academic achievement, greater popularity with peers, and decreased psychological and behavior problems. Supportive and aware parenting is particularly salient for boys, in that it appears to be associated with decreased externalizing behavior, whereas for girls, it appears to serve as a buffer against a decline in self-esteem.

Middle Childhood: Exit Parents, Enter Friends

- Perhaps the most difficult adjustment that parents must make when their child is a preadolescent is that of understanding and accepting his rejection of some of the adult standards and his loyalty to peers. Parents can soften these adjustments and potential conflicts by understanding the stages of friendship development, including the developmental changes in peer group structures and the significance of friendships, while making sure to foster empathy.
- Supportive parents support positive friendships—and the intimacy they provide—knowing that they positively impact their child's development because of the social and emotional benefits they offer. Supporting LGBTQ+ friendships is particularly important because they serve to buffer gender and sexual minorities from social isolation or rejection associated with homophobia and transphobia. Emotional support in processing their orientation and identity minority statuses, opportunities to share experiences with coming out and transitioning, and receiving needed counseling from like-minded peers, help to fill in the gaps of support in society—vitally necessary in a society where LGBTQ+ identities are at odds with established social norms.
- Because of the historical disparaging and marginalizing views of people of color, and because of historical racial barriers in equal opportunities, racial and ethnic minority parents are faced with the challenges of insulating their children from the negative consequences of racism. They can deal with these challenges by teaching their children how to "navigate and negotiate" the racism terrain through a process referred to as racial/ethnic socialization. By teaching a child the values and norms associated with his race/ethnicity, parents help shape his attitudes and help him to cope with race-related barriers. Helping him develop a strong sense of his racial/ethnic identity, heightened self-esteem, high academic functioning, and decreased levels of depression and anger are critical to navigating and negotiating the barriers, stereotypes, prejudices, biases, bigotry, and discrimination associated with racism that he will inevitably face.
- When children have unwavering networks of predictable, warm, communicative relationships with parents and caregivers, they are better able to cope with threatening racial trauma. Stable, orderly, and safe neighborhoods, and emotionally supportive and responsive schools with positive teacher–student relationships serve as protective factor against racial trauma by promoting children's autonomy and self-concept.

Tweens: Contemporary Challenges for Preadolescents

- Parents and parenting professionals must work at all three levels—the individual, the family, and the community—to provide effective buffers against the effects of ACEs and toxic stress. Providing nurturing, safe, consistent, predictable, stable support and care, engaging in parental monitoring, supervision, and consistent enforcement of expectations and boundaries, practicing a warm, responsive, communicative parenting style, resolving conflicts in healthy ways, and providing concrete support in times of need are some strategies parents can use at the family level.
- Parents can help quell the tide of peer abuse and victimization by getting involved with and supporting schools who intervene using approaches such as: (1) Pairing students so they go to and from areas in school using the buddy system; (2) Monitoring "bully-prone" areas in the school; (3) Displaying written behavioral expectations; (4) Having an expectations contract signed by students, parents, and teachers; (5) Applying consistent consequences for those students who do not comply; and (6) Pairing victim-prone students with older student mentors.
- Parents of bullied children should request that their child is not left unsupervised (during lunch, recess, in the restroom, in the school hallways). Waiting to see if the behaviors change or decrease is not advisable because bullying behaviors persist over time. Parents can also do their part by making sure their children understand that it is never permissible to taunt, tease, or bully another person, no matter how "harmless" the child or adolescent thinks the behavior is. Adults should also reinforce to youth that watching bullying occur is the same as condoning it, and that bullying *hurts*.
- Because children today do not know a culture without technology and social media, it is vitally important that parents create a home environment in which digital interactions are minimal. Parents and caregivers should model healthy technology and social media use and educate their child about the ways in which digital technology can be both a positive and a negative influence on relationships.

CHAPTER 7 APPENDIX

The Changing Nature of Parenting

Adolescence

Adolescent Development

- It has long been understood that teens experience substantial skeletal, muscular, and reproductive growth from about the ages of 12 through 18, during which time their bodies gain in height, weight, and muscle mass; sexual organs also mature to adult size and functions.

- Because of the changing pressures of a child's environment and the demands of growth and development on the child's body, the brain must adapt and reconstruct its connections so that it can become more efficient and more useful in adulthood. An individual's *second wave of brain growth* begins at about age 11, and continues through about the age of 25. During this time, the adolescent brain undergoes *synaptic pruning*, during which time, cognitive skills rapidly expand, and executive functions (i.e., problem-solving, weighing possible consequences of behaviors, impulse control, ability to modulate intense emotions) begin to emerge. In short, an adolescent's logical memory and reasoning develop before social-emotional maturity develops.
- Parental support (warmth, connectedness, responsiveness, and monitoring) is as important to the adolescent's healthy development as it is to the infant, toddler, and the child. Low aggression and irritability, and high communication and responsiveness promote healthy adolescent brain development.
- Parental emotional regulation modeling teaches adolescents how to successfully understand and control their own emotions by helping teens to describe and express emotions in healthy ways, solve problems, and comfort them. This is known as *emotion socialization*, and it is essential to healthy adolescent development. Emotional regulation skills that parents can model include accurately reading each other's communication; responding in flexible ways; attending, listening, empathizing, and responding; and considering each other's points of view.

Establishing Identity and Autonomy

- The central developmental task for adolescents is to successfully navigate the development of a strong and stable sense of self, or *identity*; this is accomplished through the process of *individuation*. Through the changes associated with individuation, adolescents form an identity that is separate from that of their families of origin.
- Intersectionality is especially important to understand when considering an adolescent's identity development because of the importance the teen may place on various social identities such as race, ethnicity, gender, sexuality, and class. Evidence strongly suggests that parents allow teens to explore all aspects of their racial and ethnic identities, rather than force an identity upon them, for optimal identity outcomes.
- As adolescents strive for autonomy, skillful parents know how to accurately assess their teen's behaviors, needs, and capabilities, and adjust their parental supervision based on their child's behaviors and needs. In other words, parenting isn't a one-size-no-matte r-the-situation-fits-all job. Parenting teens requires flexibility and a willingness to negotiate. It requires balancing control with trust. It requires balancing freedom with restrictions. But none of this is possible unless there is an environment of mutual

respect and an environment where emotionally supportive parents are consistently available.

- Healthy adolescent identify formation is significantly linked to parents who encourage the promotion of their teen's independence and autonomy. Parents who understand that part of the adolescent's "job" is to distance from parents and to begin to try on new roles and responsibilities are more likely to attempt to understand their child's emerging points of view and differences of opinions. By way of contrast, parents who do not foster their teen's autonomy often demand conformity, and this lack of autonomy promotion sends teens the message that they need to rely on their parents—not themselves—to make choices, decisions, or plans. These teens ultimately develop lower decision-making and coping skills.

Adolescent Peer and Parent Relationships

- The goal of parenting is to help teenagers form positive internal working models of self-love, self-acceptance, self-worth, and self-esteem.
- There are a number of ways in which parents can positively engage with their teens to promote adolescent autonomy, increase their self-worth, and improve emotional self-regulation: create a home environment of mutuality and reciprocity; establish stable, predictive routines; establish and maintain boundaries that respect the teen's growing need for independence; and encourage family time.
- In teens, support by way of friendships and peers is important in the healthy developmental processes of identity formation, autonomy, and resilience, and these relationships are highly influenced by parental acceptance and support.
- Ideally, the adolescent–parent relationship is such that the teen feels secure, heard, and accepted, so when they begin to seek individuality and autonomy by way of peer and romantic relationships, they have both a safe space in which to share ideas or vent, and a safe place to land.
- Through frequent, open, nonjudgmental dialogue that includes encouragement and guidance along with expectations and accountability, parents can model the healthy language, attitudes, and behaviors that help their teens to choose healthy friendships and romantic relationships.
- It's especially important for parents to share their own personal beliefs, values, and opinions about sex and sexuality with their teens. Several decades of research has provided evidence that parents who engage in frequent, informal conversations with their kids about sex have teens who tend to wait to have sex until they are older, and who will practice safer sex when they do have it. These conversations typically go well beyond the how-not-to-get-pregnant-and-not-to-get-an-STI talk; however, communicative parents also talk to their teens about sexual consent, sexting, dating violence, bullying, drug and alcohol use, and staying safe online.

Contemporary Adolescent Difficulties and Positive Adolescent Development

- *Connectedness* refers to a teen's sense of being cared for and belonging, whether it's feeling connected to family or to school. This feeling of connectedness by adolescents is a belief that adults and peers care about them on an individual level (i.e., about their feelings, their goals, their moods, their experiences, etc.).
- Overall, adult connectedness has positive effects on teens' academic achievement, school attendance, sexual health and risk, school violence, substance use, and mental health.
- Parents, teachers, and other adults in the community can be powerful buffers against contemporary adolescent difficulties, and positively contribute *support* in significant ways.
- There are three evidence-based parenting practices that are known to reduce teen's risk for substance abuse, unprotected sex, and decreased internalizing/externalizing behaviors, and to increase adolescent's internalizing parents' expectations and boundaries: *Positive engagement* (consistent, meaningful interactions and communication); *Consistent monitoring and supervision of teen's peers, behaviors, school attendance/performance, and technology use* (in warm, supportive, responsive ways—not harsh, punitive, and unsupportive ways); and *Open communication* (active listening; validating the teen's thoughts, feelings, and beliefs; and showing trust).
- Adolescents need to know that their parents are interested in their everyday lives, and that they care. It's important that parents give unconditional love, without judgment or criticism. When the teen "messes up," it's important that parents convey the message that they are disappointed in the adolescent's *behavior*—not the teen.
- The stronger the relationship a parent has with their teen, the more influence the parent has on the adolescent's developmental outcomes. It is crucially important for parents, then, to begin to build parent–child relationship in infancy, and carry the relationship strengths into and through adolescence.

CHAPTER 12 APPENDIX

Parenting Disabled Children

The Lived Experiences of Families

- Parenting children with disabilities can, at times, be overwhelming, and parents experience significantly more adverse physical, emotional, and psychological outcomes than parents of children without disabilities. Parent support by way of parenting education is of the utmost importance:

- Promote family interaction: Helping professionals can help families find ways to be inclusive of siblings and extended family, and to "work and play" as a family.
- Increasing support from the family network: Oftentimes it is necessary for the helping professional to help families identify their strengths and tap into their resiliencies. It is also beneficial for the parent educator to help families identify people in their social support network, and to evaluate what strengths they may bring to ease the burden of caregiving. It is also valuable for families to identify those who can provide respite care.
- Accessing help from the community: To some extent, every community has supports and services, be it formal educational programs or smaller-scale support that is provided by churches or community religious organizations. Services such as food pantries, transportation, volunteer in-home respite care or child care, and financial support from religious or neighborhood benevolence funds or crowd source funding, all help to alleviate the caregiving stressors.
- Helping families to help themselves: Helping families to establish an internal locus of control is essential to them becoming empowered. The Serving Children with Disabilities program encourages professionals to assist families in gathering and organizing school, medical, and other records about their child, and information about the child's disability. It is also beneficial for service providers to offer education that promotes parents' and caregivers' communication skills, so they are better able to convey their needs and to confidently discuss their child with service providers.

Bouncing Back Well: Resilience-Based Parent Education

- **Resilience-based interventions** are resources and programs that help parents and caregivers adapt well to psychological stress, and are known to positively enhance parents' and families' emotions, mental health, overall well-being, and quality of life. Parent education training:
  - Helps parents set priorities.
  - Assists parents in identifying aspect of their lives that bring them meaning and contentment.
  - Guides parents in defining their values.
  - Helps parents see the situation in an orderly, coherent, clear way.
  - Provides parents assistance in identifying and obtaining available resources.
  - Motivates parents to explore meaning in the circumstances.
  - Educates parents about active coping strategies: problem-solving techniques, intentional focusing, using internalized resources, and reframing.
  - Helps parents identify personal and relational strengths and challenge self-criticism.

Best Practices for Parents of Disabled Children

- *Family-centered support services* embraces the idea that services should center on and be responsive to the needs of all family members as they relate to the child's development. To this end, parenting professionals and practitioners are poised to:
  - Show empathy and foster hope.
  - Recognize parents and families as experts and enhance their self-efficacy.
  - Enhance family access to services and offer family and social networking.
  - Encourage effective problem-solving and coping skills.

REFERENCES

CHAPTER 1

Abma, J. C., & Martinez, G. (2006). Childlessness among older women in the United States: Trends and profiles. *Journal of Marriage and Family, 68*(4), 1045–1056.

Adamec, C. (2004). *The complete idiot's guide to adoption*. Penguin.

Agrillo, C., & Nelini, C. (2008). Childfree by choice: A review. *Journal of Cultural Geography, 25*(3), 347–363.

Al-Fadhli, H. M., & Smith, J. C. (1996). Assessing the impact of violence on motivation for parenthood among Blacks and Whites. *Journal of Negro Education, 65*(4), 424–433.

American Psychological Association. (2004). *Sexual orientation, parents, and children*. https://www.apa.org/about/policy/parenting

Anderssen, N., Amlie, C., & Ytteroy, E. A. (2002). Outcomes for children with lesbian or gay parents: A review of studies from 1978 to 2000. *Scandinavian Journal of Psychology, 43*, 335–351.

Arcus, M. (1993). *Handbook of family life education*. SAGE.

Arcus, M. E., Schvaneveldt, J. D., & Moss, J. J. (1993). The nature of family life education. In M. E. Arcus, J. D. Schvaneveldt, & J. J. Moss (Eds.), *Handbook of family life education: Foundations of family life education* (Vol. 1). SAGE.

Arendell, T. (2000). Conceiving and investigating motherhood: The decade's scholarship. *Journal of Marriage and the Family, 62*, 1192–1207.

Arnold, L. B. (2005). Don't you know what causes that? Advice, celebration, and justification in a large family's bulletin board. *Communication Studies, 56*(4), 331–351.

Bahtiyar-Saygan, B., & Sakalli-Ugurlu, N. (2019). Development of attitudes toward voluntary childlessness scale and its associations with ambivalent sexism in Turkey. *Journal of Family Issues, 40*(17), 2499–2527.

Barbeta, M., & Cano, T. (2017). Toward a new model of fatherhood? Discourses on paternal involvement in urban Spain. *Revista Española de Investigaciones Sociológicas, 159*, 13–30.

Berkowitz, D., & Marsiglio, W. (2007). Gay men: Negotiating procreative, father, and family identities. *Journal of Marriage and Family, 69*(2), 366–381.

Blake, J. (1981). Family size and the quality of children. *Demography, 18*, 421–442.

Blake, L., Carone, N., Raffanello, E., Slutsky, J., Ehrhardt, A. A., & Golombok, S. (2017). Gay fathers' motivations for and feelings about surrogacy as a path to parenthood. *Human Reproduction, 32*(4), 860–867.

Bonkowski, S. (2003). Gay and lesbian parenting. *Family Law Advisor*. www.divorcenet.com/il/ilart-15a.html

Bornstein, M. H. (2002). Parenting infants. In M. H. Bornstein (Ed.), *Handbook of parenting: Vol 1. Children and parenting* (2nd ed., pp. 3–43). Erlbaum.

Bos, H. M. W., Knox, J. R., van Rijn-van Gelderern, L., & Gartrell, N. K. (2016). Same-sex and different-sex parent households and child health outcomes: Findings from the National Survey of Children's Health. *Journal of Developmental and Behavioral Pediatrics, 37*(3), 179–187.

Bos, H. M. W., Kuyper, L., & Gartrell, N. K. (2018). A population-based comparison of female and male same-sex and different-sex parent households. *Family Process, 57*(1), 148–164.

Bos, H. M. W., van Balen, F., & van den Boom, D. C. (2004). Experience of parenthood, couple relationship, social support, and child-rearing goals in planned lesbian mother families. *Journal of Child Psychology and Psychiatry, 45*, 755–764.

Bowen, M. (1966). The use of family theory in clinical

practice. *Comprehensive Psychology, 7*, 345–374.

Brewster, K. L., & Rindfuss, R. R. (2000). Fertility and women's employment in industrialized nations. *Annual Review of Sociology, 26*, 271–296.

Brooks-Gunn, J., & Markman, L. B. (2005). The contribution of parenting to ethnic and racial gaps in school readiness. *Future of Children, 15*(1), 139–168.

Business Insider. (2019). *More than a third of millennials share Rep. Alexandria Ocasio-Cortez's worry about having kids while the threat of climate change looms*. https://www.vox.com/2019/3/11/18256166/climate-change-having-kids

Campbell, N. (2003). *Be fruitful and multiply*. Vision Forum.

Cano, T., Perales, F., & Baxter, J. (2018). A matter of time: Father involvement and child cognitive outcomes. *Journal of Marriage and Family, 81*(1), 1–22.

Cao, H. I., Mills-Koonce, W. R., Wood, C., & Fine, M. A. (2016). Identity transformation during the transition to parenthood among same-sex couples: An ecological, stress-strategy-adaptation perspective. *Journal of Family and Theory Review, 8*(1), 30–59.

Carter, B., & McGoldrick, M. (1999). *The expanded family life cycle: Individual, family, and social perspectives* (3rd ed.). Allyn & Bacon.

Cartwright, R. (1999, Autumn). Childless or childfree? *Journal of Fertility Counseling*.

Centers for Disease Control and Prevention (CDC). (2018). Births in the United States: 2017. *NCHS Data Brief*, 318. https://www.cdc.gov/nchs/products/databriefs/db318.htm

Centers for Disease Control and Prevention (CDC). (2019a). *Births: Final data for 2018. National Vital Statistics Report, 68*(13). https://www.cdc.gov/nchs/data/nvsr/nvsr68/nvsr68_13-508.pdf]

Centers for Disease Control and Prevention (CDC). (2019b). *Reproductive health: Teen pregnancy*. https://www.cdc.gov/teenpregnancy/about/index.htm

Centers for Disease Control and Prevention (CDC). (2019c). National population-based estimates for major birth defects, 2010–2014. *Birth Defects Research, 111*(18), 1420–1435.

Centers for Disease Control and Prevention (CDC). Division of Vital Statistics. (2005). Births: Preliminary data for 2004. *National Vital Statistics Report, 54*(8). www.cdc.gov/nchs/data/nvsr/nvsr54/nvsr54_08.pdf

Ciano-Boyce, C., & Shelley-Sireci, L. (2002). Who is Mommy tonight? Lesbian parenting issues. *Journal of Homosexuality, 43*, 1–13.

Congress.gov. (2008). *S.1790: Communities of color teen pregnancy prevention act of 2007*. 110th Congress 2007–2008. https://www.congress.gov/bill/110th-congress/senate-bill/1790

Costa, P. A., & Tasker, F. (2018). We wanted a forever family: Altruistic, individualistic, and motivated reasoning motivations for adoption among LGBTQ individuals. *Journal of Family Issues, 39*(18), 4156–4178.

Craig, L. (2006). Do fathers care mean father's share? *Gender & Society, 20*, 259–291.

Crockenberg, S. C., & Leerkes, E. M. (2003). Parental acceptance, postpartum depression, and maternal sensitivity: Mediating and moderating processes. *Journal of Family Psychology, 17*, 80–93.

Czaplewski, S. R., & Jorgensen, J. R. (1993). *Handbook of family life education*. SAGE.

Darling, C. A. (1987). Family life education. In M. B. Sussman & S. K. Steinmetz (Eds.), *Handbook of marriage and the family* (pp. 815–833). Plenum.

Davenport, D. (2018). *Adoption is the United States: 2018*. https://creatingafamily.org/adoption-category/adoption-blog/adoption-cost-length-time/

Downs, M. (2019, May 19). Defining motherhood. *The Washington Post*. https://www.washingtonpost.com/news/style/wp/2019/05/09/feature/the-protector-the-multitasker-the-holder-of-rocks-10-moms-define-motherhood/

Duvall, E. M. (1977). *Marriage and family development* (5th ed.).

Fitzpatrick, K. E., Tuffnell, D., Kurinczuk, J. J., & Knight, M. (2017). Pregnancy at very advanced maternal age: A UK population-based cohort study. *British Journal of Gynecology, 124*(7), 1097–1106.

Gallup. (2018). *Americans, in theory, think larger families are ideal*. https://news.gallup.com/poll/236696/americans-th

eory-think-larger-families-ideal.aspx

Gartrell, N., Bos, H., & Koh, A. (2018, July 19). *Mental health of young adults with lesbian parents*. The Williams Institute School of Law. https://williamsinstitute.law.ucla.edu/research/mental-health-kids-lesbian-parents/

Gates, G. J. (2013). *LGBT parenting in the United States*. The Williams Institute.

Gato, J., Santos, S., & Fontaine, A. M. (2016). To have or not to have children? That is the question. Factors influence parental decisions among lesbians and gay men. *Sexuality Research and Social Policy, 14*(3), 310–323.

Gauthier, A. H., Smeeding, T. M., & Furstenberg, F. F. (2004). Are parents investing less time in children? Trends in selected industrialized countries. *Population and Development Review, 30*(4), 647–671.

Gerson, M. J. (1980). The lure of motherhood. *Psychology of Women Quarterly, 5*(2), 207–218.

Gerson, M. J. (1985). *Hard choices: How women decide about work, career, and motherhood.* University of California Press.

Gerson, M. J. (1986). The prospect of parenthood for women and men. *Psychology of Women Quarterly, 10*, 49–62.

Gerson, M-J., Posner, J-A., & Morris, A. M. (1991). The wish for a child in couples eager, disinterested, and conflicted about having children. *American Journal of Family Therapy, 19*(4), 334–343.

Goldberg, S. K., & Conron, K. J. (2018). *How many same-sex couples in the U.S. are raising children?* The Williams Institute. https://williamsinstitute.law.ucla.edu/research/parenting/how-many-same-sex-parents-us/

Goldberg, A. E., Downing, J. B., & Moyer, A. M. (2012). Why parenthood, and why now? Gay men's motivations for pursuing parenthood. *Family Relations, 61*, 157–174.

Goldberg, A. E., Downing, J. B., & Richardson, H. B. (2009). The transition from infertility to adoption: Perceptions of lesbian and heterosexual couples. *Journal of Social and Personal Relationships, 29*, 938–963.

Goldberg, A. E., Gartrell, N., & Gates, G. J. (2014, July). *Research report on LGB-parent families*. https://williamsinstitute.law.ucla.edu/publications/report-lgb-parent-families/

Goldberg, A. E., & Smith, J. Z. (2014). Preschool selection considerations and experiences of school mistreatment among lesbian, gay, and heterosexual adoptive parents. *Early Childhood Research Quarterly, 29*, 64–75.

Gunnarsson, V., Orazem, P., & Sanches, M. (2006). Child labor and school achievement in Latin America. *World Bank Economic Review, 20*, 31–54.

Hagestad, G. O., & Call, V. R. A. (2007). Pathways to childlessness: A life course perspective. *Journal of Family Issues, 28*(10), 1338–1361.

Hartill, L. (2001). Life with a supersized family. *Christian Science Monitor, 93*, 15.

Hatloy, I. (2013). Understanding postnatal depression. *Mind*.

Hayford, S. R., & Morgan, S. P. (2008). Religiosity and fertility in the United States: The role of fertility intentions. *Social Forces, 86*(3), 1163–1189.

Hays, S. (1996). *The cultural contradictions of motherhood*. Yale University Press.

Hoffman, L. W., & Hoffman, M. L. (1973). The value of children to parents. In J. T. Fawcett (Ed.), *Psychological perspectives on population* (pp. 19–76). Basic Books.

Humphries, J. (2010). *Childhood and child labour in the British industrial revolution*. Cambridge University Press.

Irfan, U. (2019). We need to talk about the ethics of having children in a warming world. *Vox.com*. https://www.vox.com/2019/3/11/18256166/climate-change-having-kids

Jeffries, W. L., Marsiglio, W., Tunalilar, O., & Berkowitz, D. (2019). Fatherhood desires and being bothered by future childlessness among U.S. Gay, bisexual, and heterosexual men—United States, 2002–2015. *Journal of GLBT Family Studies*, 1–16.

Johnson, S. M., & O'Connor, E. (2002). *The gay baby boom: The psychology of gay parenthood.* New York University Press.

Karoly, L. A., Kilburn, M. R., & Cannon, J. S. (2005). *Early childhood interventions: Proven results, future promise*. RAND.

Kerckhoff, R. K. (1964). Family life education in America. In H. T. Christensen (Ed.), *Handbook of marriage and the family* (pp. 881–911). Rand McNally.

Knitzer, J., & Lefkowitz, J. (2006). *Helping the most vulnerable infants, toddlers, and their families: Executive summary.* https://files.eric.ed.gov/fulltext/ED522729.pdf

Koropeckyj-Cox, T., & Pendell, G. (2007). The gender gap in attitudes about childlessness in the United States. *Journal of Marriage and Family, 69*(4), 899–915.

Kretchmar, M. D., & Jacobvitz, D. B. (2002). Observing mother-child relationships across generations: Boundary patterns, attachment, and the transmission of caregiving. *Family Process, 41*, 351–374.

Lamb, M. E. (1987). The father's role: Cross-cultural perspectives. *Erlbaum.*

Lawson, K. (2004). Development and psychometric properties of the perceptions of parenting inventory. *The Journal of Psychology, 138*(5), 433–455.

Leal, D., Gato, J., & Tasker, F. (2019). Prospective parenting: Sexual identity and intercultural trajectories. *Culture, Health, and Sexuality, 21*, 757–773.

Lerner, R. M., Castellino, D. R., Terry, P. A., Villarruel, F. A., & McKinney, M. H. (1995). A developmental contextual perspective on parenting. In M. H. Bornstein (Ed.), *Handbook of parenting: Biology and ecology of parenting* (Vol. 2, pp. 285–309). Erlbaum.

Lerner, R. M., Noh, E. R., & Wilson, C. (2004). *The parenting of adolescents and adolescents as parents: A developmental contextual perspective.* https://parenthood.library.wisc.edu/Lerner/Lerner.html

Lesthaeghe, R. (2014). The fertility transition in Sub-Saharan Africa into the 21st century. PSC Research Report, No. 14–823.

Longman, P. (2004). *The empty cradle. How falling birthrates threaten world prosperity [and what to do about it].* Basic Books.

Martin, S. P. (2002). *Delayed marriage and childbearing: Implications and measurement of diverging trends in family timing.* University of Maryland Department of Sociology and Maryland Population Research Center.

McGoldrick, M., & Carter, E. A. (1982). The family life cycle. In F. Walsh (Ed.), *Normal family processes* (pp. 167–195). The Guilford Press.

McMorris, J., & Glass, J. (2018). Contemporary approaches to gender and religion. In B. Risman, C. Froyum, & W. Scarborough (Eds.), *Handbook of the sociology of gender. Handbooks of sociology and social research.* Springer.

McQuillan, K. (2004). When does religion influence fertility? *Population and Development Review, 30*(1), 25–56.

Medina, S., & Magnuson, S. (2009). Motherhood in the 21st century: Implications for counselors (practice & theory). *Journal of Counseling and Development, 87*(1), 90–98.

Mercer, R. T. (1986). *First-time motherhood: Experiences from teens to forties.* Springer.

Mercer, R. T. (2004). Becoming a mother versus maternal role attainment. *Journal of Nursing Scholarship, 36*(3), 226–232.

Mills, M., Rindfuss, R., McDonald, P., & te Velde, E. (2011). Why do people postpone parenthood? Reasons and social policy incentives. *Human Reproduction Update, 17*(6), 848–860.

Molina-Garcia, L., Hidalgo-Ruiz, M., Cocera-Ruiz, E. M., Conde-Puertas, E., Delgado-Rodriguez, M., & Martinez-Galiano, J. M. (2019, December 30). *The delay of motherhood: Reasons, determinants, time used to achieve pregnancy, and maternal anxiety level. PLOS.* https://journals.plos.org/plosone/article?id=10.1371/journal.pone.0227063

Morison, T. (2013). Heterosexual men and parenthood decision making in South Africa: Attending to the invisible norm. *Journal of Family Issues, 34*(8), 1125–1144.

National Organization on Adolescent Pregnancy, Parenting, and Prevention. (2008). www.healthyteennetwork.org

National Vital Statistics Reports. (2017). Pregnancy and childbirth demographics. *National Vital Statistics Reports, 67*(8), 1–49.

National Vital Statistics Reports. (2018). Births: Final data for 2016. *National Vital Statistics Report, 67*(1).

National Vital Statistics Report. (2019). Births: Final data for 2018. *National Vital Statistics Report, 68*(13), 1–47. https://www.cdc.gov/nchs/d

ata/nvsr/nvsr68/nvsr68_13-508.pdf

National Vital Statistics Reports. (2021). Births: Final data for 2019. *National Vital Statistics Report*, *70*(2). https://www.cdc.gov/nchs/data/nvsr/nvsr70/nvsr70-02-508.pdf

Park, K. (2005). Choosing childlessness; Weber's typology of action and motives of the voluntarily childless. *Sociological Inquiry*, *75*(3), 372–402.

Patterson, C. (2000). Family relationships of lesbians and gay men. *Journal of Marriage and Family*, *62*, 1052–1069.

Perrin, E. C. (2002). *Sexual orientation in child and adolescent health care*. Kluwer Academic/Plenum.

Perrin, E. C., Hurley, S. M., Mattern, K., Flavin, L., & Pinderhughes, E. E. (2019). Barriers and stigma experienced by gay fathers and their children. *Pediatrics*, *143*(2), 1–9.

Peterson, H., & Engwall, K. (2013). Silent bodies: Childfree women's gendered and embodied experiences. *European Journal of Women's Studies*, *20*(4), 376–389.

Pew Research Center. (2015). *Parenting approaches and concerns*. https://www.pewsocialtrends.org/2015/12/17/3-parenting-approaches-and-concerns/

Pew Research Center. (2017). *The changing global religious landscape*. https://www.pewforum.org/2017/04/05/the-changing-global-religious-landscape/pf_17-04-05_projectionsupdate_birthsdeaths640px/

Pew Research Center. (2018a). *Most parents and non-parents don't expect to have kids in the future*. https://www.pewresearch.org/fact-tank/2018/12/12/most-parents-and-many-non-parents-dont-expect-to-have-kids-in-the-future/

Pew Research Center. (2018b). *More than a million Millennials are becoming moms each year*. https://www.pewresearch.org/fact-tank/2018/05/04/more-than-a-million-millennials-are-becoming-moms-each-year/

Pleck, E. H., & Pleck, J. H. (1997). Fatherhood ideals in the United States: Historical dimensions. In M. Lamb (Ed.), *The roles of the father in child development*. Wiley.

Powell, D. (2005). Divorce-on-demand: Forget about gay marriage—What about the state of regular marriage? In E. Schroeder (Ed.), *Taking sides: Clashing views on controversial issues in family and personal relationships* (pp. 243–246). McGraw-Hill.

Power to Decide: The Campaign to Prevent Unplanned Pregnancy. (2019). Unplanned pregnancy: National data. https://powertodecide.org/what-we-do/information/national-state-data/national

Priel, B., & Besser, A. (2001). Bridging the gap between attachment and object relations theories: A study of the transition to motherhood. *British Journal of Medical Psychology*, *74*, 85–100.

Rankin, S. H. (2000). Life-span development: Refreshing a theoretical and practice perspective. *Scholarly Inquiry for Nursing Practice*, *14*(4), 379–388.

Rathus, S. A., & Nevid, J. S. (1992). *Adjustment and growth: The challenges of life* (5th ed.). Harcourt Brace Jovanovich.

Riskind, R. G., & Tornello, S. L. (2017). Sexual orientation and future parenthood in a 2011–2013 nationally representative United States sample. *Journal of Family Psychology*, *31*(6), 792–798.

Riswick, T., & Engelen, T. (2018). Siblings and life transitions: Investigating the resource dilution hypothesis across historical contexts and outcomes. *The History of the Family*, *23*(4), 521–532.

Rodgers, R. H., & White, J. M. (1993). Family development theory. In K. E. Fitzpatrick, D. Tuffnell, J. J. Kurinczuk, & M. Knight (Eds.), Pregnancy at very advanced maternal age: A UK population-based cohort study. *BJOG*. 2017, *124*(7), 1097–1106. PMID:27581343

Rogers, S. J., & White, L. K. (1998). Satisfaction with parenting: The role of marital happiness, family structure, and parents' gender. *Journal of Marriage and the Family*, *60*(2), 293–308.

Rotundo, E. A. (1993). *American motherhood*. Basic Books.

Rubin, R. (1967). Attainment of the maternal role. *Part I. Nursing Research*, *16*, 237–245.

Russell, C. S. (1993). Family development theory as revised by Rodgers and White. Implications for practice. In G. Pauline, P. G. Boss, W. J. Doherty, R. LaRossa, W. R. Schumm, & S. K. Steinmetz (Eds.), *Sourcebook of family theories and methods: A contextual approach* (pp. 255–257). Kluwer/Plenum Press.

Satir, V. (1972). *People making*. Science & Behavior.

Scandurra, C., Bacchini, D., Esposito, C., Bochicchio, V., Valerio, P., & Amodeo, A. L. (2019). The influence of minority stress. gender, and legalization of civil unions on parenting desire and intention in lesbian women and gay men: Implications for social policy and clinical practice. *Journal of GLBT Family Studies, 15*, 76–100.

Seccombe, K. (1991). Assessing the costs and benefits of children: Gender comparisons among childfree husbands and wives. *Journal of Marriage and the Family, 53*, 191–202.

Shenkman, G. (2012). The gap between fatherhood and couplehood desires among Israeli gay men and estimations of their likelihood. *Journal of Family Psychology, 26*(5), 828–832.

Shenkman, G., Bos, H., & Kogan, S. (2019). Attachment avoidance and parenthood desires in gay men and lesbians and their heterosexual counterparts. *Journal of Reproductive and Infant Psychology, 37*, 344–357.

Smith, W. M., Jr. (1968). Family life education—Who needs it? *The Family Coordinator, 17*, 55–61.

Solomon-Fears, C. (2008). *Nonmarital childbearing: Trends, reasons, and public policy interventions*. CRS Report for Congress, Order Code RL.34756. https://sgp.fas.org/crs/misc/RL34756.pdf

Strohschein, L., Gauthier, A. H., Campbell, R., & Kleparchuk, C. (2008). Parenting as a dynamic process: A test of the resource dilution hypothesis theory. *Journal of Marriage and Family, 70*, 670–683.

Tanturri, M. L., & Mencarini, L. (2008). Childless or childfree? Paths to voluntary childlessness in Italy. *Population and Development Review, 34*(1), 51–77.

Tate, D. P., & Patterson, C. J. (2019). Desire for parenthood in context of other life aspirations among lesbian, gay, and heterosexual young adults. *Frontiers in Psychology, 10*, 2679. https://doi.org/10.3389/fpsyg.2019.02679

Tate, D. P., Patterson, C. J., & Levy, A. J. (2019). Predictors of parenthood intentions among childless lesbian, gay, and heterosexual adults. *Journal of Family Psychology, 33*, 194–202.

The Alan Guttmacher Institute. (2018). *U.S. pregnancy and births*. https://www.guttmacher.org/news-release/2017/us-rates-pregnancy-birth-and-abortion-among-adolescents-and-young-adults-continue

Theisen, C. (2004). *The parent coach plan: Eight parenting responsibilities*. www.parentcoachplan.com

van Doorne-Huiskes, A., & Doorten, I. (2011). The complexity of parenthood in modern societies. In G. Beets, J. Schippers, & E. Velde (Eds.), *The future of motherhood in western societies. Springer.* https://doi.org/10.1007/978-90-481-8969-4_8

Veevers, J. E. (1980). *Childless by choice*. Butterworth.

Walker, K. (2017). What issues do lesbian co-mothers face in their transition to parenthood? *Perspective, 34*, 1–7.

Watkins, E. S. (2008). Conceiving the future: Pronatalism, reproduction, and the family in the United States, 1890–1938. *Journal of Interdisciplinary History, 39*(1), 144–145.

Weiss, H. B. (1990). Beyond parens patriae: Building policies and programs to care for our own and others' children. *Children and Youth Services Review, 12*, 269–284.

Yamaguchi, K., & Fergusson, L. R. (1995). The stopping and spacing of childbirths and their birth history predictors: Rational choice theory and event history analysis. *American Sociological Review, 60*, 272–289.

Yogman, M., & Garfield, C. F. (2016). Fathers' roles in the care and development of their children: The role of pediatricians. *Pediatrics, 138*(1). https://doi.org/10.1542/peds.2016-1128

Zizzo, G. (2009). Lesbian families and the negotiation of maternal identity through the unconventional use of breast milk. *Journal of Gay Lesbian Issues, 5*(2), 96–109.

CHAPTER 2

Abudabbeh, N. (2005). Arab families. In M. McGoldrick, J. Giordano, & N. Garcia-Preto (Eds.), *Ethnicity and family therapy* (pp. 423–436). Guilford Press.

Al-Darmaki, F., & Sayed, M. A. (2009). Counseling challenges within the cultural context of the United Arab Emirates. In L. H. Gerstein, P. P. Heppner, S. Ægisdóttir, S.-M. A. Leung & K. L. Norsworthy (Eds.), *International handbook of cross-cultural counseling: Cultural assumptions and practices worldwide* (pp. 465–474). SAGE.

Alberts, M. (2002). *The ecological model of human development: The foundation for a family policy perspective*. The University of Minnesota Children, Youth, and Family Consortium. http://www.cyfc.umn.edu/publications/connettion/pubs/05summer/0l-foundationfamilypolicy.html

Allen, M., Svetaz, M. V., Hardeman, R., & Resnick, M. D. (2008). *What research tells us about Latino parenting practices and their relationship to youth sexual behavior.* The National Campaign to Prevent Teen Pregnancy. https://www.rhyclearinghouse.acf.hhs.gov/sites/default/files/docs/17153_What_research_tells_us_about_latino_parenting_practices_and_their_relationship_to_youth_sexual_behavior.pdf

Amos, P. M. (2013). Parenting and culture: Evidence from some African communities. In M. L. Seidl-de-Moura (Ed.), *Parenting in South American and African contexts*. https://www.intechopen.com/books/parenting-in-south-american-and-african-contexts/parenting-and-culture-evidence-from-some-african-communities

Andersen, C. H. (2020). *11 surprising reasons French children are so well-behaved*. https://www.rd.com/list/french-parenting/

Arab American Institute. (2019). *Who are Arab Americans?* www.aaiusa.org

Atkinson, D. R., Morten, G., & Sue, D. W. (1998). *Counseling American minorities*. McGraw-Hill.

Austin, B. (2019). *1619: Virginia's first Africans*. Hampton History Museum. https://hampton.gov/DocumentCenter/View/24075/1619-Virginias-First-Africans?bidId=

Bain, H. (2006). Parenting in Latino families. In R. L. Smith & R. E. Montilla (Eds.), *Counseling and family therapy with Latino populations* (pp. 161–175). Routledge.

Banerjee, M. (2019). *More than one-third of American kids have lived in extended family households*. www.phys.org/news/2018-01-one-third-american-kids-family-households.html

Banks, J. A., & McGee-Banks, C. A. (2019). *Multicultural education: Issues and perspectives*. Wiley.

Barbour, C., Barbour, N., & Scully, P. A. (2005). *Families, schools and communities: Building partnerships for educating children*. Pearson/Prentice Hall.

Baumrind, D. (1972). An exploratory study of socialization effects on black children: Some black-white comparisons. *Child Development*, *43*(1), 261–267.

Berlin, L. J., Brooks-Gunn, J., Spiker, D., & Zaslow, M. J. (1995). Examining observational measures of emotional support and cognitive stimulation in Black and White mothers of preschoolers. *Journal of Family Issues*, *16*(5), 664–686.

Bernstein, R. (2016). *Parenting around the world: Child-rearing practices in different cultures*. https://www.tuw.edu/health/child-rearing-practices-different-cultures/

BigFoot, D. S., & Funderburk, B. W. (2006). *Honoring children, making relatives: The cultural translation of parent-child interaction therapy for American Indian and Alaska Native families*. University of Oklahoma Health Sciences Center. http://www.icctc.org/Honoring percent20Children percent-20Making percent20Relatives percent2006-21-2011Final percent20Submission.pdf

BigFoot, D. S., & Braden, J. (2007). Adapting evidence-based treatments for use with American Indian and Native Alaskan children and youth. *Focal Point*, *21*(1), 19–22.

Binghalib, Y. (2007). *Family dynamics between Arab Muslim parents, Western parents, and their bi-ethnic children*. California State University. https://s3.amazonaws.com/na-st01.ext.exlibrisgroup.com/01CALS_USL/storage/alma/2B/69/1D/1E/46/3D/AE/C7/4B/A0/85/C1/DE/50/12/E8/FAMILY%20DYNAMICS%20BETWEEN%20ARAB%20MUSLIM%20PARENTS.pdf?response-content-type=application%2Fpdf&X-Amz-Algorithm=AWS4-HMAC-SHA256&X-Amz-Date=20221106T154503Z&X-Amz-SignedHeaders=host&X-Amz-Expires=119&X-Amz-Credential=AKIAJN6NPMNGJALPPWAQ%2F20221106%2Fus-east-1%2Fs3%2Faws4_request&X-Amz-Signature=c

02dcd8847796fe71d0ed56db1983ad2790095b1b531a060b1a64ed90f90289f

Binghalib, Y. (2011). *A product of two worlds: Family dynamics between Arab Muslim parents, Western parents, and their bi-ethnic children*. LAP LAMBERT Academic.

Boellstorff, T. (2005). Between religion and desire: Being Muslim and gay in Indonesia. *American Anthropologist*, *107*(4), 575–585.

Bornstein, M. H. (2012). Cultural approaches to parenting. *Parenting: Science & Practice*, *12*(2–3), 212–221.

Brayboy, B. M. J., Fann, A. J., Castagno, A. E., & Solyom, J. A. (2012). Postsecondary education for American Indian and Alaskan Natives: Higher education for nation building and self. *Journal of Student Affairs Research & Practice*, *51*(2), 227–229.

Bronfenbrenner, U. (1979). *The ecology of human development: Experiments by nature and design*. Harvard University Press.

Bronfenbrenner, U., & Morris, P. A. (1998). The ecology of developmental processes. In W. Damon & R. M. Lerner (Eds.), *Handbook of child psychology: Vol. 1. Theoretical models of human development* (5th ed., pp. 993–1023). Wiley.

Brown, M. C., Dancy, T. E., & Davis, J. E. (2013). *Educating African American males: Contexts for consideration, possibilities for practice*. Peter Lang.

Brown, J., & Johnson, S. (2008). Childrearing and child participation in Jamaican families. *International Journal of Early Years Education*, *16*(1), 31–40.

Brown, T. N., Tanner-Smith, E. E., Lesane-Brown, C. L., & Ezell, M. E. (2007). Child, parent, and situational correlates of familial ethnic/race socialization. *Journal of Marriage and Family*, *69*(1), 14–26.

Calderon-Tena, C. O., Knight, G. P., & Carlo, G. (2011). The socialization of prosocial behavioral tendencies among Mexican American Adolescents: The role of familism values. *Cultural Diversity & Ethnic Minority Psychology*, *17*(1), 98–106.

Calzada, E. J., Huang, K. Y., Linares-Torres, H., Singh, S. D., & Brotman, L. (2014). Maternal familismo and Dominican immigrant families. *Journal of Latinx Psychology*, *2*(3), 156–171.

Cardona, B., & Softas-Nall, L. (2010). Family therapy with Latino families: An interview with Patricia Arrendondo. *The Family Journal: Counseling and Therapy for Couples and Families*, 1–5. https://doi.org/10.1177/1066480709356543

Carlson, J., & Dermer, S. B. (2017). *The SAGE encyclopedia of marriage, family, and couples counseling*. SAGE.

Carmichael, S., & Hamilton, C. V. (1967). *Black power: Politics of liberation*. Vintage.

Carranza, M. A., Gouveia, L., Cogua, J., & Ondracek-Sayers, K. (2002). *The integration of Hispanic/Latino immigrant workforce*. University of Nebraska. https://www.unomaha.edu/college-of-arts-and-sciences/ollas/_files/pdfs/publications-presentations/report-integration-latino-workforce-2002-gouveia-carranza.pdf

Carson, D., Dail, P., Greeley, S., & Kenote, T. (1990). Stresses and strengths of Native American reservation families in poverty. *Family Perspective*, *24*(4), 383–400.

Carteret, M. (2011). *Cultural values of Latino parents and families*. *Dimensions of cultures*. https://www.dimensionsofculture.com/2011/03/cultural-values-of-latino-patients-and-families/

Cengage. (2020). *African-American families*. https://www.encyclopedia.com/reference/encyclopedias-almanacs-transcripts-and-maps/african-american-families

Chao, R. K. (1994). Beyond parental control and authoritarian parenting style: Understanding Chinese parenting through the cultural notion of training. *Child Development*, *65*(4), 1111–1119.

Chen, X., & French, D. C. (2008). Children's social competence in cultural context. *Annual Review of Psychology*, *59*, 591–616.

Child Trends. (2018a). *Immigrant children*. www.childtrends.org/indicators/immigrant-children

Child Trends. (2018b). *Births to unmarried women*. www.childtrends.org/indicators/births-to-unmarried-women

Choi, Y., Harachi, T. W., Gillmore, M. R., & Catalano, R. F. (2005). Applicability of the social development model to urban ethnic minority youth: Examining the relationship between external constraints, family socialization, and problem behaviors. *Journal of Research on Adolescence, 15*(4), 505–534.

Cilluffo, A., & Cohn, D. (2019). *Six demographic trends shaping the U.S. and the world in 2019.* www.pewresearch.org/fact-tank/2019/04/11/6-demographic-trends-shaping-the-u-s-and-the-world-in-2019/

Clair, M., & Denis, J. S. (2015). Sociology of racism. In James D. Wright (Ed.), *The International Encyclopedia of the Social and Behavioral Sciences* (Vol. 19, pp. 857–863).

Coard, S. I., Foy-Watson, S., Zimmer, C., & Wallace, A. (2007). Considering culturally relevant parenting practices in intervention development and adaptation: A randomized controlled trial of the Black Parenting Strengths and Strategies (BPSSP) Program. *The Counseling Psychologist, 35*(6), 797–820.

Coleman, P. A. (2015). *Why Norwegian parents let their kids nap in below-freezing temperatures.* Fatherly. https://www.fatherly.com/health-science/why-norwegian-babies-sleep-outside/#:~:text=In%20Norway%20and%20most%20other,for%20up%20to%203%20ho urs

Constante, K., Marchand, A. D., Cross, F. L., & Rivas-Drake, D. (2019). Understanding the promotive role of familism in the link between ethnic-racial identity and Latino youth school engagement. *Journal of Latinx Psychology, 7*(3), 230–244.

Coontz, S. (1992). *The way we never were: American families and the nostalgia trap.* Basic Books.

Coontz, S. (1999). *American families: A multicultural reader.* Routledge.

Cross, C. J. (2020). Racial/ethnic differences in the association between family structure and children's education. *Journal of Marriage and Family, 82*(2), 691–712.

Crensahw, K. (1991). Mapping the margins: Intersectionality, identity politics, and violence against women of color. *Stanford Law Review, 43*(6), 1241–1299.

Delgado-Gaitan, C. (1994). Socializing young children in Mexican-American families: An intergenerational perspective. In P. M. Greenfield & R. R. Cocking (Eds.), *Cross-cultural roots of minority child development* (pp. 55–86). Lawrence Erlbaum.

Dixon, F. (2020). *How parents can raise resilient children.* Best Parenting Books.

Dixon, S. V., Graber, J. A., & Brooks-Gunn, J. (2008). The roles of respect for parental authority and parenting practices in parent-child conflict among African American, Latino, and European American families. *Journal of Family Psychology, 22*(1), 1–10.

Doi, S., Fujiwara, T., Isumi, A., Ochi, M., & Kato, T. (2018, May 25). *Relationship between leaving children home alone and their mental health: Results from the A-CHILD Study in Japan. Frontiers in Psychiatry.* https://www.frontiersin.org/articles/10.3389/fpsyt.2018.00192/full

Domenech, R. M. M., Donovick, M. R., & Crowley, S. L. (2009). Parenting styles in a cultural context: Observations of protective parenting in first-generation Latinos. *Family Process, 48*(2), 195–210.

Druckerman, P. (2020, April 19). *The decade of the parenting manual. The New York Times.*

Dutton, M. A. (1998, March/April). Cultural issues in trauma treatment. *Centering Newsletter, 3*(2), 1–2.

Dwalry, M., Achoui, M., & Farah, A. (2006). Parenting styles in Arab societies: A first cross-regional research study. *Journal of Cross-Cultural Psychology, 37*(3), 230–247.

Dykeman, C., & Nelson, J. (1995). Building strong working alliances with American Indian families. *Social Work in Education, 17*(3), 148–159.

Elliott, S., & Aseltine, E. (2013). Raising teenagers in hostile environments: How race, class, and gender matter for mothers' protective carework. *Journal of Family Issues, 34*(6), 719–744.

Fleming, W. C. (2007). Getting past our myths and stereotypes about Native Americans. *The Educational Digest, 72*(7), 51–58.

Folicov, C. J. (2007). Working with transnational immigrants: Expanding meanings of family, community, and culture. *Family Process, 46*(2), 157–171.

Fong, T. P. (2002). *The contemporary Asian American experience: Beyond the model minority* (2nd ed.). Prentice Hall.

Forehand, R., & Kotchick, B. A. (1996). Cultural diversity: A wake-up call for parent training. *Behavior Therapy, 27*(2), 187–206.

Franklin, J. H., & Moss, A. A. (1988). *From slavery to freedom: A history of Negro Americans* (6th ed.). Alfred A. Knopf.

Gaille, B. (2017). *21 noteworthy statistics of blended families.* https://brandongaille.com/20-noteworthy-statistics-of-blended-families/

Gallardo, A. M. (2019). Cognitions and parental practices in the context of migration. *Summa Psicológica, 16.* https://doi.org/10.18774/0719-448x.2019.16.412

Goldberg, A. E., Smith, J. Z., & Perry-Jenkins, M. (2012). The division of labor in lesbian, gay, and heterosexual new adoptive parents. *Journal of Marriage and Family, 74*(4), 812–828.

Gonzales, N. A., Cauce, A. M., Friedman, R. J., & Mason, C. A. (1996). Family, peer, and neighborhood influences on academic achievement among African American adolescents: One-year prospective effects. *American Journal of Community Psychology, 24*, 365.

Gorman, J. (1998). Parenting attitudes and practices of immigrant Chinese mothers and adolescents. *Family Relations, 47*, 73–80.

Greene, B. (1995). African American families: A legacy of vulnerability and resilience. *National Forum, 75*(3), 20.

Guilamo-Ramos, V., Dittus, P., Jaccard, J., Johanson, M., Bouris, A., & Acosta, N. (2007). Parenting practices among Dominican and Puerto Rican Mothers. *Social Work, 52*, 17–30.

Gutman, H. G. (1977). *The Black family in slavery and freedom: 1750-1925.* Vintage.

Haboush, K. L. (2007). Working with Arab American families: Culturally competent practice for school psychologists. *Psychology in the Schools, 44*(2), 183–198.

Hale-Benson, J. (1988). African Heritage theory and Afro-American cognitive styles. *Educational Considerations, 15*(1). https://doi.org/10.4148/0146-9282.1609

Hallam, J. (2004). *The slave experience: Family.* https://www.thirteen.org/wnet/slavery/experience/family/history2.html

Hamilton, J. C., & Roy, D. R. (2020). When they see us: An unshaken history of racism in America. *Journal of Family Theory & Review*, 100–107. https://doi.org/10.1111/jftr.12360

Haneef, M. A. M. (1997). Islam, the Islamic worldview and Islamic economics. *Journal of Economics and Management, 5*(1), 39–66.

Hellerstedt, W. L., Peterson-Hickey, M., Rhodes, K. L., & Garwick, A. (2006). Environmental, social, and personal correlates of having ever had sexual intercourse among American Indian youths. *American Journal of Public Health, 96*(12), 2228–2234.

Henry, H. M., Stiles, W. B., Biran, M. W., & Hinkle, S. (2008). Perceived parental acculturation behaviors and control as predictors of subjective well-being in Arab American college students. *The Family Journal, 16*, 28–34.

Hill, S. A. (2001). Class, race, and gender dimensions of child rearing in African American families. *Journal of Black Studies, 31*(4), 494–508. https://www.history.com/this-day-in-history/first-african-slave-ship-arrives-jamestown-colony

Hill, N. E., Bush, K. R., & Roosa, M. W. (2003). Parenting and family socialization strategies and children's mental health: Low-income Mexican-American and Euro-American mothers and children. *Child Development, 74*, 189–204.

Huffman, T. (2008). *American Indian higher educational experiences: Cultural visions and personal journeys*. Peter Lang.

Hughes, D., Smith, E. P., Steven, H. C., Rodriquez, J., Johnson, D. J., & Spice, P. (2006). Parents' ethnic-racial socialization practices: A review of research and directions for future study. *Developmental Psychology, 42*, 747–770.

Huitt, W. (2003). *A systems model of human behavior.* Educational Psychology Interactive. Valdosta State University.

Hull, K. (2018). Conventional and cutting-edge: Definitions of family in LGBT communities. *Sexuality Research and Social Policy, 1*(16), 1–13.

Huynh, V. W., & Fuligni, A. J. (2008). Ethnic socialization and the academic adjustment of adolescents from Mexican, Chinese, and European backgrounds. *Developmental Psychology, 44*(4), 1202–1208.

Institute of Family Studies. (2019). *Cohabitation is pervasive.*

www.ifstudies.org/blog/cohabitation-is-pervasive

Johnson, T., Kulesa, P., Cho, Y., & Shavitt, S. (2005). The relation between culture and response styles: Evidence from 19 countries. *Journal of Cross-Cultural Psychology, 36*, 264–277.

Kelley, M. L., & Tseng, H. M. (1992). Cultural differences in child rearing: A comparison of immigrant Chinese and Caucasian American mothers. *Journal of Cross-Cultural Psychology, 23*(4), 444–455.

Kennedy, T. M., & Ceballo, R. (2013). Latino adolescents' community violence exposure: After-school activities and familismo as risk and protective factors. *Social Development, 22*(4), 663–682.

Kids Count Data Center. (2019a). *Children in single-parent families by race in the United States*. https://datacenter.kidscount.org/data/tables/107-children-in-single-parent-families-byrace#detailed/1/any/false/871,870,573,869,36,868,867,133,38,35/10,11,9,12,1,185,13/432,431

Kids Count Data Center. (2019b). *Children who live in two-parent families, by race ethnicity in the United States*. https://datacenter.kidscount.org/data/tables/8053-children-who-live-in-two-parent-families-by-race-ethnicity#detailed/1/any/false/1491,1049/4217,4218,4215,3301,4216,2664/15474,15473

Kim, S. Y., Wang, Y., Orozco-Lapray, D., Shen, Y., & Murtuza, M. (2013). Does "Tiger Parenting" exist? Parenting profiles of Chinese Americans and adolescent developmental outcomes. *Asian American Journal of Psychology, 1*(4), 7–18.

Kobeisy, A. N. (2004). *Counseling American Muslims: Understanding the faith and helping the people*. Praeger/Greenwood.

Kupperbusch, C., Matstumoto, D., Kooken, K., Loewinger, S., Uchida, H., Wilson-Cohn, C., & Yrizarry, N. (1999). Cultural influences on nonverbal expressions of emotion. In P. Philippot, R. S. Feldman, & E. J. Coats (Eds.), *The social context of nonverbal behavior* (2nd ed., Vol. 1, pp. 17–44). Cambridge University Press.

LaFromboise, T., & Low, K. (1989). American Indian children and adolescents. In J. Gibbs et al. (Eds.), *Children of color* (pp. 114–147). Jossey-Bass.

LeCuyer, E. A., Christensen, J. J., Kearney, M. H., & Kitzman, H. J. (2011). African American mothers' self-described discipline strategies with young children. *Issues in Comprehensive Pediatric Nursing, 34*(3), 144–162.

Leung, P. W. L., & Kwon, K. S. F. (1998). Parenting styles, motivational orientations, and self-perceived academic competence: A mediational model. *Merrill-Palmer Quarterly, 44*(1), 1–19.

Li, N., & Hein, S. (2019). Parenting, autonomy in learning and development during adolescence in China. *New Directions for Child and Adolescent Development, 163*, 67–80.

Lin, C., & Liu, W. (1993). Intergenerational relationships among Chinese immigrant families from Taiwan. In H. McAddo (Ed.), *Family ethnicity: Strength in diversity* (pp. 271–286). SAGE.

Little Soldier, L. (1992). Working with Native American children. *Young Children, 47*(6), 15–21.

Liu, S. S., Morris, M. W., Talheim, T., & Yang, Q. (2019). Ingroup vigilance in collectivist cultures. *Proceedings of the National Academy of Sciences, 116*(29), 20181758.

Mack, L. (2019). *Filial piety: An important Chinese cultural value*. https://www.thoughtco.com/filial-piety-in-chinese-688386

Makes Marks, L. F. (2007). Great mysteries: Native North American religions and participatory visions. *ReVision, 29*(3), 29–37.

Markus, H. R., & Moya, P. M. L. (2010). *Doing race: 21 essays for the 21st century*. W.W. Norton.

McKay, M. M., Atkins, M. S., Hawkins, T., Brown, C., & Lynn, C. J. (2003). Inner-city African American Parental involvement in children's schooling: Racial socialization and social support from the parent community. *American Journal of Community Psychology, 32*(1–2), 107–114.

McLoyd, V. C., & Smith, J. (2002). Physical discipline and behavior problems in African American, European American, and Hispanic children: Emotional support as a moderator. *Journal of Marriage and Family, 64*(1), 40–53.

McWilliams, P. (1998). *Ain't nobody's business if you do: The absurdity of consensual crimes in a free country.* Prelude Press.

Mench-Tum, R. (2001). *The UN works to fight racism.* United Nations Department of Public Information, DPI, 2193.

Mitchell, V. (2008). Choosing family: Meaning and membership in the lesbian family of choice. *Journal of Lesbian Studies, 12*(2–3), 301–313.

Montgomery, L. M., & Colwell, C. (2019). *Objects of surveillance: A material history of the American Indian school experience.* University Press of Colorado.

Mourad, M. R., & Carolan, M. T. A. (2010). An ecological approach to culturally sensitive intervention for Arab American women and their families. *The Family Journal, 18*(2), 178–183.

Myers, D. G. (2008). *Social psychology* (9th ed.). McGraw-Hill.

Neto, F. (2007). Forgiveness, personality and gratitude. *Personality and Individual Differences, 43,* 2313–2323.

Nord, W. A., & Haynes, C. C. (1998). *Taking religion seriously across the curriculum.* Association for Supervision & Curriculum Development.

Okere, E. I. (2017). *Bicultural socialization experiences of Black immigrant students in selective predominantly white institutions in America.* Seton Hall University Dissertations and Theses (ETDs). 2301. https://scholarship.shu.edu/dissertations/2301

Oxford Learner's Dictionary. (2019). *People in society: Gender identity.* https://www.oxfordlearnersdictionaries.com/us/definition/english/non-binary

Paniagua, F. A. (2005). *Assessing and treating culturally diverse clients: A practical guide.* SAGE.

Parra-Cardona, J. R., Córdova, D., Holtrop, K., Villarruel, F. A., & Wieling, E. (2008). Shared ancestry, evolving stories: Similar and contrasting life experiences described by foreign born and U.S. born Latino parents. *Family Process, 47*(2), 157–172.

Pew Research Center. (2015). *Parenting approaches and concerns.* https://www.pewsocialtrends.org/2015/12/17/3-parenting-approaches-and-concerns/

Pew Research Center. (2017a). *Number of Muslims in the U.S. continues to grow.* https://www.pewforum.org/2017/07/26/demographic-portrait-of-muslim-americans/pf_2017-06-26_muslimamericans-01new-12/

Pew Research Center. (2017b). *Religion and public life.* https://www.pewforum.org/2017/07/26/demographic-portrait-of-muslim-americans/pf_2017-06-26_muslimamericans-01new-02/

Pew Research Center. (2018a). *About one-third of US children are living with an unmarried parent.* www.pewresearch.org/fact-tank/2018/04/27/about-one-third-of-u-s-children-are-living-with-an-unmarried-parent

Pew Research Center. (2018b). *They're waiting longer, but U.S. women today more likely to have children than a decade ago.* www.pewsocialtrends.org/2018/01/18/theyre-waiting-longer-but-u-s-women-today-more-likely-to-have-children-than-a-decade-age

Pew Research Center. (2018c). *A record 64 million Americans live in multigenerational households.* https://www.pewresearch.org/fact-tank/2018/04/05/a-record-64-million-americans-live-in-multigenerational-households/

Pew Research Center. (2019). *Race in America: 2019.* https://www.pewresearch.org/social-trends/2019/04/09/race-in-america-2019/

Piñ-Watson, B., Gonzalez, I. M., & Manzo, G. (2019). Mexican-descent adolescent resilience through *familismo* in the context of intergeneration acculturation conflict on depressive symptoms. *Translational Issues in Psychological Science, 5*(4), 326–334.

Pittman, C. T. (2012a). Racial microaggressions: The narratives of African American faculty at a predominately white university. *The Journal of Negro Education, 81*(1), 82–92.

Pittman, L. (2012b). African American families: Still a band of slaves? In S. Akhtar (Ed.), *The African American experience: Psychoanalytic perspectives* (pp. 229–270). Rowman & Littlefield.

Popenoe, D., & Whitehead, B. D. (2005). *The state of our unions.* National Marriage Project.

Prioste, A., Narciso, I., Goncalves, M. M., & Pereira, C. R. (2015). Family relationships and parenting practices: A pathway to adolescents' collectivist and individualist values? *Journal of Child and Family*

Studies. https://doi.org/10.1007/s10826-015-0129-3

Ramirez, O. (1989). Mexican American children and adolescents. In J. T. Gibbs & L. N. Huang (Eds.), *Children of color: Psychological intervention with minority youth*. Jossey-Bass.

Read, J. G. (2003). The sources of gender role attitudes among Christian and Muslim Arab-American women. *Sociology of Religion*, *64*, 207–222.

Reese, L. (2002). Parental strategies in contrasting cultural settings: Families in Mexico and "el norte.". *Anthropology & Education Quarterly*, *33*, 30–59.

Richards, P. (2018). *Teaching 'race" in our schools is more important than ever*. https://drpaulrichards.wordpress.com/2018/02/

Ritchie, J., & Ritchie, J. (1983). Polynesian child rearing: An alternative model. *Alternative Lifestyles*, *5*, 126–141.

Rothstein, R. (2017). *The color of law: A forgotten history of how our government segregated America*. Liveright.

Rudy, D., & Grusec, J. E. (2001). Correlates of authoritarian parenting in individualist and collectivist cultures and implications for understanding the transmission of values. *Journal of Cross-Cultural Psychology*, *32*(2), 202–212.

Sabogal, F., Marín, G., Otero-Sabogal, R., Marín, B. V., & Perez-Stable, E. J. (1987). Hispanic familism and acculturation: What changes and what doesn't? *Hispanic Journal of Behavioral Sciences*, *9*(4), 397–412.

Santiago-Rivera, A. L., Arredondo, P., & Gallardo-Cooper, M. (2002). *Counseling Latinos and la familia: A practical guide*. SAGE.

Sarkisian, N., & Gerstel, N. (2004). Kin support among blacks and whites: Race and family organization. *American Sociological Review*, *69*(6), 812–837.

Schwartz, S. J., & Unger, J. B. (2010). Biculturalism and context: What is biculturalism, and when is it adaptive? *Human Development*, *53*(1), 26–32.

Shumow, L., Vandell, D. L., & Posner, J. K. (1998). Harsh, firm, and permissive parenting in low-income families: Relations to children's academic achievement and behavioral adjustment. *Journal of Family Issues*, *19*(5), 483–507.

Sikorski, M. F., Niemiec, R. P., & Walberg, H. J. (1999). Designing school volunteer programs. *NASSP Bulletin*, *83*(103), 114–116.

Skenazy, L. (2010). *Free-range kids: Giving our children the freedom we had without going nuts with worry*. Jossey-Bass.

Smith, P. D., Easterbrook, M. J., Koc, Y., Lun, V. M. C., Papastylianou, D., Grigoryan, L., Torres, C., Efremova, M., Hassan, B., Abbas, A., Ahmad, A. H., al-Bayati, A., Selim, H. A., Anderson, J., Cross, S. E., Delfino, G. I., Gamsakhurdia, V., Gavreliuc, A., Gavreliuc, D., ... Chobthamkit, P. (2021). Is an emphasis on dignity, honor, and face more an attribute of individuals or of cultural groups? *Cross-Cultural Research*, *55*(2–3), 95–126.

Smith, R. L., & Montilla, R. E. (2006). Working with Latino population: Background and historical perspectives. In R. L. Smith & R. E. Montilla (Eds.), *Counseling and family therapy with Latino population* (pp. 27–40). Routledge.

Solot, D., & Miller, M. (2004). *Affirmation of family diversity*. Alternatives to Marriage Project. www.unmarried.org/family.html

Stamkou, E., van Kleef, G. A., Homan, A. C., Gelfand, M. J., Fons, J. R., van Egmond, M. C., Boer, D., Phiri, N., Ayub, N., Kinias, Z., Cantarero, K., Efrat Treister, D., Figueiredo, A., Hashimoto, H., Hofmann, E. B., Lima, R. P., & Lee, I. C. (2019). Cultural collectivism and tightness moderate responses to norm violators: Effects on power perception, moral emotions and leader support. *Personality and Social Psychology Bulletin*, *45*(6), 947–964.

Stein, G. L., Cavanaugh, A. M., Castro-Schilo, L., Mejia, Y., & Plunkett, S. W. (2019). Making my family proud: The unique contribution of familism pride to the psychological adjustment of Latinx emerging adults. *Cultural Diversity and Ethnic Minority Psychology*, *25*(2), 188–198.

Stein, G. L., Coard, S. I., Kiang, L., Smith, R. K., & Mejia, Y. C. (2018). Socialization and adolescence: A closer examination at stage-salient issues. *Journal of Research on Adolescence*, *28*(3), 609–621.

Stein, G. L., Gonzalez, L. M., Cupito, A. M., & Kiang, L. (2013). The protective role of familism in the lives of Latino adolescents. *Journal of Family Issues*, *36*(10), 1255–1273.

St. Vil, N. M., McDonald, K. B., & Cross-Barnet, C. (2018). A qualitative study of Black married couples' relationships with their extended family networks. *Families in Society: The Journal of Contemporary Social Services*, *99*(1), 56–66.

Sudarkasa, N. (2007). Interpreting the African heritage in African American family organization. In H. P. McAdoo (Ed.), *Black families* (pp. 29–48). SAGE.

Taylor, R. L. (2000). Diversity within African American families. In D. H. Demo, K. R. Allen, & M. A. Fine (Eds.), *Handbook of family diversity* (pp. 232–251). Oxford University Press.

Taylor, T. S. (2005, January 19). *When a marriage can't make room for daddy*. Chicago Tribune. http://www.turnonyourinnerlight.com/ChicagoTribune01192005.htm

Transatlantic Slave Trade Database. (2020). *Intra-American slave trade database: Slave voyages*. https://www.slavevoyages.org/american/database

Trask-Tate, A. J., Cunningham, M., & Francois, S. (2014). The role of racial socialization in promoting the academic expectations of African American adolescents: Realities in a post-Brown era. *Journal of Negro Education*, *83*(3), 281–299.

Triandis, H. C., & Suh, E. M. (2002). Cultural influences on personality. *Annual Review of Psychology*, *53*(1), 133–160.

UCLA, Equity, Diversity, & Inclusion. (2020). *Native American and indigenous peoples FAQS*. https://equity.ucla.edu/know/resources-on-native-american-and-indigenous-affairs/native-american-and-indigenous-peoples-faqs/

United States Census Bureau. (2018a). *Black (African American) history month*. www.census.gov/search-results.html?q=African+American&page=1&stateGeo=none&searchtype=web&cssp=SERP&_charset_=UTF-8

United States Census Bureau. (2018b). *Household income by race and Hispanic origin: 1957 to 2017*. www.census.gov/content/dam/Census/library/visualizations/2018/demo/p60-263/figure1.pdf

United States Census Bureau. (2019a). *Current Population Survey (CPS): Subject definitions*. www.census.gov/programs-surveys/cps/technical-documentation/subject-definitions.html#household

United States Census Bureau. (2019b). *America's family and living arrangements*. Current population survey (CPS). www.census.gov/data/tables/2017/demo/families/cps-2017.htm

United States Census Bureau. (2019c). *Characteristics of same-sex couple households: 2005 to present*. www.census.gov/data/tables/time-series/demo/same-sex-couples/ssc-house-characteristics.html

United States Census Bureau. (2019d). *Selected population profile in the United States: 2018 American Community Survey 1-year estimates*. www.factdinder.census/gov/faces/tableservices/jsf/pages/producview.xhtmlZsrec=bkmk

United States Census Bureau. (2019e). *Census Information Centers (CIC): Asian American data links*. www.census.gov/about/partners/cic/resources/data-links/asian.html

United States Census Bureau. (2019f). *American Indian and Alaska Native heritage month*. www.census.gov/newsroom/facts-for-features/2017/aian-month.html

Urban Institute. (2020). *Structural racism in America*. https://www.urban.org/features/structural-racism-america

Van Kleef, G. A., Wanders, F., Stamkou, E., & Homan, A. C. (2015). The social dynamics of breaking the rules: Antecedents and consequences of norm-violating behavior. *Current Opinion in Psychology*, *6*, 25–31.

Vazquez, C. I. (2004). *Parenting with pride Latino style*. Harper-Collins.

Wan, Y. (2017). The significance of the variation theory in cross-cultural communication. *Comparative Literature and Culture*, *19*(5). https://doi.org/10.7771/1481-4374.3113

Waterman, S. J. (2019). New research perspectives on Native American students in higher education. *Journal Committed to Social Change on Race and Ethnicity*, *5*(1). Spring, 2019. https://journals.shareok.org/jcscore/article/view/76

Watson, H. L. (1990). *Liberty and power: The politics of Jacksonian American*. The Noonday Press.

White-Johnson, R. L., Ford, K. R., & Sellers, R. M. (2010). Parental racial socialization profiles: Association with demographic factors, racial discrimination, childhood socialization, and racial identity. *Cultural Diversity and Ethnic Minority Psychology, 16*(2), 237–247.

Yaman, A., Mesman, J., van IJzendoorn, M. H., & Bakermans-Kranenburg, M. J. (2010). Parenting and toddler aggression in second-generation immigrant families: The moderating role of child temperament. *Journal of Family Psychology, 24*(2), 208–211.

Zahedi, A. (2007). Contested meanings of the veil and political ideologies of Iranian regimes. *Journal of Middle East Women's Studies, 3*(3), 75–99.

Zhao, Y. (2007). China and the whole child. *Educational Leadership, 64*(8), 70–73.

Zhao, Y., & Qiu, W. (2009). How good are the Asians? Refuting four myths about Asian-American academic achievement. *Phi Delta Kappan, 90*(5), 338–344.

Zong, J., Batalova, J., & Burrows, M. (2019). *Frequently requested statistics on immigrants and immigration in the United States*. www.migrationpolicy.org/article/frequently-requested-statistics-immigrants-and-immigration-united-states?gclid=EAIaIQobChMIj5Pc4KG84gIV0LfACh3w5g-VEAAYASAAEgL0-fD_BwE

CHAPTER 3

Adetunji, R. R., & Sze, K. (2012). *Understanding nonverbal communication across cultures: A symbolic interactionism approach.* International Conference on Communication and Media, 2012, Penang, Malaysia, Vol. 103, November 2012. https://papers.ssrn.com/sol3/papers.cfm?abstract_id=2178486

Akechi, H., Senju, A., Uibo, H., Kikuchi, Y., Hasegawa, T., & Hietanen, J. K. (2013). Attention to eye contact in the West and East: Autonomic responses and evaluative ratings. *PLoS One, 8*(3), e59312. https://doi.org/10.1371/hournal.pone.0059312

American Academy of Pediatrics, Committee on Psychosocial Aspects of Child and Family Health. (2002). Coparent or second parent adoption by same-sex parents. *Pediatrics, 109*, 339–240.

Anderson, S. A., & Sabatelli, R. M. (2011). *Family interaction: A multigenerational developmental perspective* (5th ed.). Pearson.

Annie E. Casey Foundation. (2020). *2020 kids count profile: National trends.* https://www.aecf.org/m/databook/2020KC_profile_US.pdf

Bagarozzi, D. A., & Anderson, S. A. (1989). *Personal, marital, and family myths: Theoretical formulations and clinical strategies*. Norton.

Baiocco, R., Carone, N., Ioverno, S., & Lingiardi, V. (2019). Same-sex and different-sex parent families in Italy. *Journal of Developmental & Behavioral Pediatrics, 39*(7), 555–563.

Baiocco, R., Santamaria, F., Ioverno, S., Fontanesi, L., Baumgartner, E., Laghi, F., & Lingiardi, V. (2015). Lesbian mother families and gay father families in Italy: Family functioning, dyadic satisfaction, and child well-being. *Sexuality Research and Social Policy, A Journal of the NSRC, 12*(3), 202–212.

Barlow, J., & Coren, E. (2018). The effectiveness of parenting programs: A review of Campbell reviews. *Research on Social Work Practice, 28*(1), 99–102.

Bernardes, J. (2000). *Family studies: An introduction*. Routledge.

Blumer, H. (1969). *Symbolic interaction*. Prentice Hall.

Bos, H. M., Know, J. R., van Rijn-van Gelderen, L., & Gartrell, N. K. (2016). Same-sex and different-sex parent households and child health outcomes: Findings from the National Survey of Children's Health. *Journal of Developmental and Behavioral Pediatrics, 37*(3), 179–187.

Boss, P. G., Doherty, W. J., LaRossa, R., Schumm, W. R., & Steinmetz, S. K. (1993). *Sourcebook of family theories and methods: A contextual approach*. Plenum.

Carter, B., & McGoldrick, M. (2005). *The expanded family life cycle: Individual, family, and social perspectives* (4th ed.). Allyn & Bacon.

Child Welfare Information Gateway. (2019). *Long-term consequences of child abuse and neglect*. U.S. Department of Health and Human Services, Administration for Children and Children's Bureau.

Child Welfare Information Gateway. (2020a). *Prevention*

and parent education programs. https://www.childwelfare.gov/topics/preventing/prevention-programs/

Child Welfare Information Gateway. (2020b). *Children's Bureau timeline*. https://www.childwelfare.gov/more-tools-resources/resources-from-childrens-bureau/timeline1/

Cowan, C. P., & Cowan, P. A. (2018). Enhancing parenting effectiveness, fathers' involvement, couple relationship quality, and children's development: Breaking down silos in family policy making and service delivery. *Journal of Family Theory & Review, 11*(1), 92–111.

Dunn, C. G., Kenney, E., Fleischhacker, S. E., & Bleich, S. N. (2020). Feeding low-income children during the Covid-19 pandemic. *New England Journal of Medicine, 382*, e40. https://doi.org/1056/NEJMp2005638

Farr, R. H. (2017). Does parental sexual orientation matter? A longitudinal follow-up of adoptive families with school-age children. *Developmental Psychology, 53*(2), 252–264.

Fox, R. C., Lidz, V., & Bershady, H. L. (2005). *After Parsons: A theory of social action for the twenty-first century*. Russell Sage Foundation.

Galvin, K. M., Braithwaite, D. O., Schrodt, P., & Bylund, C. L. (2019). *Family communication: Cohesion and change*. Routledge.

Golombok, S. (1983). Children in lesbian and single-parent households: Psychosexual and psychiatric appraisal. *Journal of Child Psychology, 24*(4), 551–572.

Golombok, S. (1999). Lesbian and gay families. In A. Bainham, S. Day Sclater, & M. Richards (Eds.), *What is a parent?* Hart.

Gottman, J. M. (1994a). *What predicts divorce? The relationship between marital process and marital outcomes*. Erlbaum.

Gottman, J. M. (1994b). *Why marriages succeed or fail*. Simon & Schuster.

Gottman, J. M. (1999). *The marriage clinic: A scientifically based marital therapy*. Norton.

Gottman, J. M., Markham, J. J., & Notarius, C. I. (1977). The topography of marital conflict: A sequential analysis of verbal and nonverbal behavior. *Journal of Marriage and the Family, 39*, 461–477.

Gottman, J. M., & Porterfield, A. (1981). Communicative competence in the nonverbal behavior of married couples. *Journal of Marriage and the Family, 43*, 817–824.

Gottman, J. M., Ryan, K. D., Carrere, S., & Erlye, A. M. (2002). Toward a scientifically based marital therapy. In H. A. Liddle, D. A. Santisteban, R. F. Levant, & J. H. Bray (Eds.), *Family psychology: Science-based interventions* (pp. 147–174). American Psychological Association.

Ictech, B. (2018). Smartphones and face-to-face interaction: Digital cross-talk during encounters in everyday life. *Symbolic Interaction, 42*(1), 27–45.

Kapetanovic, S., Boele, S., & Skoog, T. (2019). Parent-adolescent communication and adolescent delinquency: Unraveling within-family processes from between-family differences. *Journal of Youth & Adolescence, 48*(9), 1707–1723.

Kellogg, T. (1990). *Broken toys, broken dreams: Understanding and healing boundaries, codependence, compulsion, and family relationships*. BRAT.

Mead, G. H. (1934). *Mind, self, and society* (C. Morris, Introduction and Ed.). University of Chicago Press.

Moen, P., & Coltrane, S. (2005). Families, theories, and social policy. In V. L. Bengston, A. C. Acock, K. R. Allen, P. Dilworth-Anderson, & D. M. Klein (Eds.), *Sourcebook of family theory and research*. SAGE.

Natenshon, H. (1999). *A day center for adolescents with eating disorders within Southern Health*. Paper presented to the Butterfly-Southern Health Rating Disorder Conference.

National Academies of Sciences, Engineering, and Medicine. (2016). *Federal policies and investments supporting parents and children in the United States*. Parenting matters: Supporting parents of children ages 0–8. The National Academies Press.

National Council on Family Relations. (2020). *Understanding families: Research and practice*. https://www.ncfr.org/membership

Neighbour, R. H. (1985). The family life cycle. *Journal of the Royal Society of Medicine, 78*(Suppl. 8), 11–15.

Nichols, M. P., & Schwartz, R. C. (2009). *The essentials of family therapy* (4th ed.). Allyn & Bacon.

O'Keeffe, G. S., & Clarke-Pearson, K. (2011). The impact of social media on children, adolescents, and families. *Pediatrics, 127*(4), 800–804.

Olson, D. H., Sprenkel, D. H., & Russell, C. S. (1979). Circumplex model of marital and family systems: Cohesion and adaptability dimensions, family types, and clinical applications. *Family Process, 18*, 3–28.

Parsons, T. (1951). *The social system*. Free Press.

Pew Research Center. (2016). *Americans increasingly use smartphones for more than voice calls, texting*. https://www.pewresearch.org/internet/ft_01-27-16_smartphoneactivities_640/

Pew Research Center. (2018). *Teens, social media, and technology*. https://www.pewresearch.org/internet/2018/05/31/teens-social-media-technology-2018/

Pew Research Center. (2020). *Unemployment rose higher in three months of COVID-29 than it did in two years of the Great Recession*. https://www.pewresearch.org/fact-tank/2020/06/11/unemployment-rose-higher-in-three-months-of-covid-19-than-it-did-in-two-years-of-the-great-recession/

Phoon, A. (2017). Social media and its start influences on society. *Journal of First-Year Writing, 1*(1). https://scholarworks.bgsu.edu/cgi/viewcontent.cgi?article=1004&context=writ

Pitts, J. R. (1964). The structural functional approach. In E. T. Christensen (Ed.), *Handbook of marriage and the family*. Rand McNally.

Povenmire-Kirk, T. C., Bethune, L. K., Alverson, C. Y., & Guttman Kahn, L. (2015). A journey, not a destination: Developing cultural competence in secondary transition. *Teaching Exceptional Children, 47*, 319–328.

Procentese, F., Gatti, F., & Di Napoli, I. (2019). Families and social media use: The role of parents' perceptions about social media impact on family systems in the relationship between family collective efficacy and open communication. *International Journal of Environmental Research and Public Health*, 16(24), 5006, 1–38.

Richardson, B. (2012). *Cultural awareness to help while serving Native veterans*. Office of Rural Health. https://www.ruralhealth.va.gov/docs/webinars/richardson-cultural-sensitivity-062712.pdf

Rosenblatt, P. C. (1994). *Metaphors of family systems theory: Toward new constructions*. Guilford.

Sabatelli, R. M. (1988). Exploring relationship satisfaction: A social exchange perspective on the interdependence between theory, research, and practice. *Family Relations, 37*, 217–222.

Sandstrom, H., Adams, G., & Pyati, A. (2019). *Wellness check: Material hardship and psychological distress among families with infants and toddlers*. Urban Institute.

Smith, M. (1993). Changing sociological perspectives on change. *Sociology, 27*(3), 513–531.

Smith, S. (1995). Family theory and multicultural family studies. In B. B. Ingoldsby & S. Smith (Eds.), *Families in multicultural perspective* (pp. 5–35). Guilford.

Sorokowska, A., Sorokowsi, P., Hilpert, P., Cantarero, K., Frackowiak, T., Ahmadi, K., Alghraibeh, A. M., Aryeetey, R., Bertoni, A., Bettache, K., Blumen, S., Bł;ażejewska, M., Bortolini, T., Butovskaya, M., Castro, F. N., Cetinkaya, H., Cunha, D., David, D., David, O. A., ... Pierce Jr., J. D., *Jr.* (2017). Preferred interpersonal distances: A global comparison. *Journal of Cross-Cultural Psychology, 48*(4), 577–592.

Stanley, S. (2017). *Reasons people give for divorce*. Institute for Family Studies. https://ifstudies.org/blog/reasons-people-give-for-divorce

Torres, M. N. (1993, July). Cultural sensitivity. *Advance for Nurse Practitioners*, 16–18.

Turner, L. H., & West, R. (2006). *Perspectives on family communication* (3rd ed.). McGraw-Hill.

Turner, L. H., & West, R. (2018). *Perspectives on family communication* (5th ed.). McGraw-Hill.

Urban Institute. (2018). *State and local financial initiative*. https://www.urban.org/policy-centers/cross-center-initiatives/state-and-local-finance-initiative/state-and-local-backgrounders/state-and-local-expenditures

Urban Institute. (2019). *Kids' share: Report on federal expenditures on children through 2018 and future projections*. https://www.urban.org/sites/default/files/publication/101020/kids_share_2019_report_on_federal_expenditures_on_children_through_2018_and_future_projections.pdf

Waxman, E., Joo, N., & Pyati, A. (2019). *The social safety net in 2019: Four trends to watch in SNAP*. Urban Wire. https://www.urban.org/urban-wire/social-safety-net-2019-four-trends-watch-snap

White, J. M., Klein, D. M., & Martin, T. F. (2014). *Family theories: An introduction* (4th ed.). SAGE.

CHAPTER 4

Ahlborg, T., Dahlof, L. G., & Hallberg, L. R. (2005). Quality of intimate and sexual relationship in first-time parents six months after delivery. *Journal of Sex Research*, *42*(2), 167–174.

Ahlborg, T., Dahlof, L. G., & Strandmark, M. (2000). First-time parents' sexual relationships. *Scandinavian Journal of Sexology*, *3*, 127–139.

American College of Obstetricians and Gynecologists. (2019). *Pelvic inflammatory disease*. https://www.acog.org/Patients/FAQs/Pelvic-Inflammatory-Disease-PID?IsMobileSet=false

American Society for Reproductive Medicine. (2015, September). Disparities in access to effective treatment for infertility in the United States: An ethics committee opinion. *Fertility and Sterility*, *104*(5), 1104–1110.

American Society for Reproductive Medicine. (2019). *Female infertility*. https://www.asrm.org/topics/topics-index/female-infertility/

Barrett, G., Pendry, E., Peacock, J., Victor, C., Thakar, R., & Manyonda, I. (2000). Women's sexual health after childbirth. *British Journal of Obstetrics and Gynecology*, *107*, 186–195.

Becher, E. H., Kim, H., Cronin, S. E., Deenanath, V., McGuire, J. K., McCann, E. M., & Powell, S. (2019). Positive parenting and parental conflict: Contributions to resilient coparenting during divorce. *Family Relations*, *68*(1), 150–164.

Belsky, J. (1990). Children and marriage. In F. Fincham & T. Bradbury (Eds.), *The psychology of marriage: Basic issues and applications*, (pp. 172–200).

Berger, A. P., Potter, E. M., Shutters, C. M., & Imborek, K. L. (2015). Pregnant transmen and barriers to high quality healthcare. *Proceedings in Obstetrics and Gynecology*, *5*(2), 1–12.

Berkowitz, D. (2013). Gay men and surrogacy. In A. Goldberg & K. R. Allen (Eds.), *LGBT-parent families: Innovations in research and implications for practice* (pp. 71–85). Springer.

Blake, L., Carone, N., Raffanello, E., Slutsky, J., Ehrhardt, A. A., & Golombok, S. (2017). Gay fathers' motivations for and feelings about surrogacy as a path to parenthood. *Human Reproduction*, *32*(4), 860–867.

Brummen, H. J., Bruinse, H. W., van de Pol, G., Heintz, A. P. M., & van der Vaart, C. H. (2006). Which factors determine the sexual function 1 year after childbirth? *British Journal of Gynecology*, *113*, 914–918.

Buehlman, K. T., Gottman, J. M., & Katz, L. F. (1992). How a couple views their past predicts their future: Predicting divorce from an oral history interview. *Journal of Family Psychology*, *5*, 295–318.

Campbell, S. B., Cohn, J. F., Flanagan, C., Popper, S., & Meyers, T. (1992). Course and correlates of postpartum depression during the transition to parenthood. *Development and Psychopathology*, *4*, 29–47.

Ceballo, R., Lansford, J. E., Abbey, A., & Stewart, A. J. (2004). Gaining a child: Comparing the experiences of biological, adoptive, and stepparents. *Family Relations*, *53*, 38–48.

Centers for Disease Control and Prevention (CDC). (2019). National population-based estimates for major birth defects, 2010–2014. *Birth Defects Research*, *111*(18), 1420–1435.

Centers for Disease Control and Prevention (CDC). (2020a). *Basics about FASDs*. https://www.cdc.gov/ncbddd/fasd/facts.html

Centers for Disease Control and Prevention (CDC). (2020b). *Fetal alcohol spectrum disorders: Data and statistics*. https://www.cdc.gov/ncbddd/fasd/data.html

Centers for Disease Control and Prevention (CDC). (2020c). *Infant mortality*. https://www.cdc.gov/reproductivehealth/MaternalInfantHealth/InfantMortality.htm

Connolly, A., Thorp, J., & Pahel, L. (2005). Effects of pregnancy and childbirth on postpartum sexual function: A longitudinal prospective study. *International Urogynecological Journal of Pelvic Floor Dysfunction, 16*, 263–267. www.ncibi.nlm.nih.gov/entrez/query.fcgi?cmd=retrieve&db=pubmed&dopt=Abstract&list_uids=15838587&query_hl=53 [March 22, 2006].

Cowan, C. P., & Cowan, P. A. (2000). *When partners become parents: The big life change for couples*. Erlbaum.

Cowan, P. A., & Pape Cowan, C. (2019). The role of parental relationships in children's well-being: A modest set of proposals for improving the lives of children. *Human Development, 62*, 171–174.

Deave, T., Johnson, D., & Ingram, J. (2008). Transition to parenthood: The needs of parents in pregnancy and early parenthood. *BMC Pregnancy Childbirth, 30*(8), 1–11.

Farmer, L. B., & Byrd, R. (2015). Genderism and the LBGTQQIA community: An interpretative phenomenological analysis. *Journal of LGBT Issues in Counseling, 9*(4), 288–310.

Figueiredo, B., Field, T., Diego, M., Hernandez, R.M., Deeds, O., & Ascenio, A. (2008). Partner relationships during the transition to parenthood. *Journal of Reproductive and Infant Psychology, 26*(2), 99–107.

Florsheim, P., Emi, S., McCann, C., Matthew, W., Ritsuko, F., Trina, S., & Moore, D. (2003). The transition to parenthood among young African American and Latino couples: Relational predictors of risk for parental dysfunction. *Journal of Family Psychology, 17*, 65–79.

Gable, S., Crnic, K., & Belsky, J. (1994). Coparenting within the family system: Influences on children's development. *Family Relations, 43*, 380–386.

Gato, J., Santos, S., & Fontaine, A. M. (2016). To have or not to have children? That is the question. Factors influence parental decisions among lesbians and gay men. *Sexuality Research and Social Policy, 14*(3), 310–323.

Gibler, R. C., Kalomiris, A. E., & Kiel, E. J. (2018). Paternal anxiety in relation to toddler anxiety: The mediating role of maternal behavior. *Child Psychiatry & Human Development, 49*(4), 512–522.

Gilliam, J. E., & Coleman, M. C. (1981). Who influences IEP committee decisions? *Exceptional Children, 47*, 642–644.

Goldberg, A. E., & Scheib, J. E. (2015). Why donor insemination and not adoption? Narratives of female-partnered and single mothers. *Family Relations, 64*(5), 726–742.

Golombok, S., Blake, L., Slutsky, J., Raffanello, E., Roman, G. D., & Ehrhardt, A. (2018). Parenting and the adjustment of children born to gay fathers through surrogacy. *Child Development, 89*(4), 1223–1233.

Hahn, M., Sheran, N., Weber, S., Cohan, D., & Obedin-Maliver, J. (2019). Providing patient-centered perinatal care for transgender men and gender-diverse individuals: A collaborative multidisciplinary team approach. *Obstetrics & Gynecology, 134*(5), 959–963.

Hansen, T. (2012). Parenthood and happiness: A review of folk theories versus empirical evidence. *Social Indicators Research, 108*(1), 1–36.

Harwood, K., McLean, N., & Durkin, K. (2007). First-time mothers' expectations of parenthood: What happens when optimistic expectations are not matched by later experiences? *Developmental Psychology, 43*(1), 1–12.

Hill, D. B., & Willoughby, B. L. B. (2005). The development and validation of the genderism and transphobia scale. *Sex Roles, 53*, 531–544.

Hudak, N. C. (2019). *Communicating heterosexism in queer pregnancies: A multiadic interview study.* A dissertation presented to the faculty of the Scripps College of Communication of Ohio University. https://etd.ohiolink.edu/apexprod/rws_etd/send_file/send?accession=ohiou1565777259154463&disposition=inline

Kluwer, E. S., & Johnson, M. D. (2007). Conflict frequency and relationship quality across the transition to parenthood. *Journal of Marriage and Family, 69*, 1089–1106.

Latham, R. M., Mark, K. M., & Oliver, B. R. (2018). Coparenting and children's disruptive behavior: Interacting processes for parenting sense of competence. *Journal of Family Psychology, 32*(1), 151–156.

Lawrence, R., Rothman, A. D., Cobb, R. J., Rothman, M. T., & Bradbury, T. N. (2008). Marital satisfaction across the transition to parenthood. *Journal of Family Psychology, 22*(1), 41–50.

Lazarus, K., & Rossouw, P. J. (2015). Mother's expectations of parenthood: The impact of prenatal expectations on self-esteem, depression, anxiety, and stress post birth. *International Journal of Neuropsychotherapy, 3*(2), 102–123.

Light, A., Wang, L. F., Zeymo, A., & Gomez-Lobo, V. (2018). Family planning and contraception use in transgender men. *Contraception, 98*(4), 266–269.

Lunkenheimer, E., Kemp, C. J., Lucas-Thompson, R. G., Cole, P. M., & Albrecht, E. C. (2017). Assessing biobehavioural self-regulation and coregulation in early childhood: The parent-child challenge task. *Infant and Child Development, 26*(1), e1965.

MacDorman, M., & Declercq, E. (2019). Trends and state variations in out-of-hospital births in the United States, 2004–2017. *Birth, 46*(2), 279–288.

March of Dimes. (2020). *Neural tube defects*. https://www.marchofdimes.org/complications/neural-tube-defects.aspx#:~:text=Neural%20tube%20defects%20(NTDs)%20are,not%20trying%20to%20get%20pregnant

March of Dimes. (2022). *Miscarriage*. https://www.marchofdimes.org/find-support/topics/miscarriage-loss-grief/miscarriage

Marieb, E. N., & Hoehn, K. N. (2019). *Human anatomy & physiology* (11th ed.). Pearson Education.

Massar, K., & Buunk, A. P. (2019). Expecting and competing? Jealous responses among pregnant and nonpregnant women. *Evolutionary Psychology, 17*(1). https://doi.org/10.1177/1474704919833344

Mayo Clinic. (2019). *Sperm donation*. https://www.mayoclinic.org/tests-procedures/sperm-donation/about/pac-20395032

Mayo Clinic. (2020a). *Pregnancy week by week*. https://www.mayoclinic.org/healthy-lifestyle/pregnancy-week-by-week/in-depth/pregnancy/art-20047208

Mayo Clinic. (2020b). *Fetal alcohol syndrome*. https://www.mayoclinic.org/diseases-conditions/fetal-alcohol-syndrome/symptoms-causes/syc-20352901

McHale, J., Rao, N., & Krasnow, A. (2000). Constructing family climates: Chinese mothers' reports of their coparenting behavior and preschoolers' adaptation. *International Journal of Behavioral Development, 24*, 111–118.

Meeussen, L., & Van Laar, C. (2018). Feeling pressure to be a perfect mother relates to parental burnout and career ambitions. *Frontiers in Psychology, 9*, Article 2113.

Merck Manual. (2020). *Spontaneous abortion*. https://www.merckmanuals.com/professional/gynecology-and-obstetrics/abnormalities-of-pregnancy/spontaneous-abortion

Moore, K., Persaud, T. V. N., & Torchini, M. (2019). *The developing human: Clinically oriented embryology* (11th ed.). Elsevier.

Musick, K., Meier, A., & Flood, S. (2016). How parents fare: Mothers' and fathers' subjective well-being in time with children. *American Sociological Review, 81*(5), 1069–1095.

Nelson, C. A., Zeanah, C. H., & Fox, N. A. (2019). How early experience shapes human development: The case of psychosocial deprivation. *Neural Plasticity*, January 14, 2020. https://doi.org/10.1155/2019/1676285

Nomaguchi, K., & Milkie, M. A. (2017). Sociological perspectives on parenting stress: How social structure and culture shape parental strain and the well-being of parents and children. In K. Keater-Deckard, & R. Panneton (Eds.), *Parental stress and early child development*, (pp. 47–73). Springer.

Nomaguchi, K., & Milkie, M. A. (2020). Parenthood and well-being: A decade in review. *Journal of Marriage and Family, 82*(1), 198–223.

Notarius, C. I., Benson, P. R., Sloane, D., Vanzetti, N. A., & Hornyak, L. M. (1989). Exploring the interface between perception and behavior: An analysis of marital interaction in distressed and nondistressed couples. *Behavioral Assessment, 11*, 39–64.

Obedin-Maliver, J., & Makadon, H. J. (2016). Transgender men and pregnancy. *Obstetric Medicine, 9*(1), 4–8.

Ogata, K., & Miyashita, K. (2000). Exploring links between father's participation in family chores, child's empathy, family function, and father's identity development. *Japanese Journal of Family Psychology, 14*, 15–27.

Parfitt, Y., & Ayers, S. (2014). Transition to parenthood and mental health in first-time parents. *Infant Mental Health Journal, 35*(3), 263–273.

Parkes, A., Green, M., & Mitchell, K. (2019). Coparenting and parenting pathways from the couple relationship to children's behavior problems. *Journal of Family Psychology, 33*(2), 215–225.

Penn Medicine. (2019). *IVF by the numbers*. https://www.pennmedicine.org/updates/blogs/fertility-blog/2018/march/ivf-by-the-numbers

Perkins, K. M., Boulet, S. L., Jamieson, D. J., & Kissin, D. M. (2016). National assisted reproductive technology surveillance system (NASS) group. Trends and outcomes of gestational surrogacy in the United States. *Fertility and Sterility, 106*(2), 435–442.

Reis, E. (2020). Midwives and pregnant men: Labouring toward ethical care in the United States. *Canadian Medical Association Journal, 192*(7), E169–E170.

Richardson, P. (1981). Women's perceptions of their important dyadic relationships during pregnancy. *Journal of Maternal and Child Nursing, 10*(3), 159–174.

Roskam, I., Raes, M. E., & Mikolajczak, M. (2017). Exhausted parents: Development and preliminary validation of the parental burnout inventory. *Frontiers in Psychology, 9*. https://doi.org/10.3389/fpsyg.2017.00163

Salmela-Aro, K., Aunola, K., Saisto, T., Halmesmaki, E., & Nurmi, J. E. (2006). Couples share similar changes in depressive symptoms and marital satisfaction anticipating the birth of a child. *Journal of Social and Personal Relationships, 23*(5), 781–803.

Shanely, L. K. (2016). *Unassisted childbirth* (3rd ed.). CreateSpace Independent.

Society of Obstetricians and Gynaecologists of Canada. (2007). No. 372: Statement on planned homebirth. *Journal of Obstetrics and Gynaecology, 41*(2), 223–227.

Society for the Study of Addiction. (2019, April 30). Fetal alcohol spectrum disorder prevalence is very high in susceptible groups Worldwide. *Science Daily*. www.sciencedaily.com/releases/2019/04/190430091840.htm

Staneva, A., & Wittkowski, A. (2013). Exploring beliefs and expectations about motherhood in Bulgarian mothers: A qualitative study. *Midwifery, 29*, 260–267.

Tierney, A. L., & Nelson, C. A. (2009). Brain development and the role of experience in the early years. *Zero Three, 30*(2), 9–13.

United States Department of Health and Human Services. (2019). *Male infertility*. https://www.hhs.gov/opa/reproductive-health/fact-sheets/male-infertility/index.html

U.S. Department of Agriculture. (2019). *The cost of raising a child*. Center for Nutrition Policy and Promotion. https://www.usda.gov/media/blog/2017/01/13/cost-raising-child

U.S. Department of Health and Human Services. (2003, June 17). *Researchers identify a possible cause of infertility in some women with endometriosis*. National Institute of Child Health and Human Development. http://www.nichd.nih.gov/news/releascs/infertility.cfm [August 1, 2009].

von Sydow, K. (1999). Sexuality during pregnancy and after childbirth: A metacontent analysis of 59 studies. *Journal of Psychosomatic Research, 47*, 27–49.

Welch, K. J. (2004). *Development: Journey through childhood and adolescence*. Allyn & Bacon.

Welch, K. J. (2011). *THINK human sexuality* (1st ed.). Allyn & Bacon.

Wells, J. (2019). Deaths triple for births at home as opposed to hospital, study finds. *American Council on Science and Health*. https://www.acsh.org/news/2019/03/19/deaths-triple-births-home-opposed-hospital-study-finds-13895

Williams, J. F., & Smith, V. C. (2015). Fetal alcohol spectrum disorders. *Pediatrics, 136*(5), 31395–e1406.

CHAPTER 5

Aarestrup, A. K., Skovgaard Væver, M., Petersen, J., Røhder, K., & Schiøtz, M. (2020). An early intervention to promote maternal sensitivity in the perinatal period for women with psychosocial vulnerabilities: Study protocol of a randomized controlled trial. *BMC Psychology*, *8*(41). https://doi.org/10.1186/s40359-020-00407-3

Ainsworth, M. D. S. (1979). Infant-mother attachment. *The American Psychologist*, *34*(10), 932–937.

Ainsworth, M. D. S., Blehar, M. C., Waters, E., & Wall, S. (1978). *Patterns of attachment: A psychological study of the strange situation*. Erlbaum.

Allen, L. R., & Kelly, B. B. (2015). *Transforming the workforce for children birth through age 8: A unifying foundation*. National Academies Press.

Altenburger, L. E., & Schoppe-Sullivan, S. J. (2020). New fathers' parenting quality: Personal, contextual, and child precursors. *Journal of Family Psychology*. Advance online publication. https://doi.org/10.1037/fam0000753

Amato, R. P., & Fowler, F. (2002). Parenting practices, child adjustment, and family diversity. *Journal of Marriage and Family*, *64*(3), 703–716.

Barnett, L. (2005). Keep in touch: The importance of touch in infant development. *Infant Observation*, *8*(2), 115–123.

Barrable, A. (2019). Shaping space and practice to support autonomy: Lessons from natural settings in Scotland. *Learning Environments Research*. https://doi.org/10.1007/s10984-019-09305-x

Barr, R. G., Trent, R. B., & Cross, J. (2006). Age-related incidence curve of hospitalized Shaken Baby Syndrome cases: Convergent evidence for crying as a trigger to shaking. *Child Abuse & Neglect*, *30*, 7–16.

Baumrind, D. (1991). The influence of parenting style on adolescent competence and substance use. *Journal of Early Adolescence*, *11*(1), 56–95.

Baumrind, D. (1996). The discipline controversy revisited. *Family Relations*, *45*, 405–414.

Bell, S. M., & Ainsworth, M. D. (1979). Infant crying and maternal responsiveness. *Child Development*, *43*, 1171–1190.

Belsky, J., Crnic, K., & Woodworth, S. (1995). Personality and parenting: Exploring the mediating role of transient mood and daily hassles. *Journal of Personality*, *63*, 905–929.

Belsky, J., Grossman, K., Grossman, K., & Scheuerer-Englisch, H. (1996). Continuity in parent-child relationships from infancy to middle childhood and relations with friendship competence. *Child Development*, *67*, 1437–1454.

Belsky, J., Woodworth, S., & Crnic, K. (1996). Trouble in the second year: Three questions about family interaction. *Child Development*, *67*(2), 556–578.

Bert, S. C., Guner, B. M., & Lanzi, R. G. (2009). The influence of maternal history of abuse on parenting knowledge and behavior. *Family Relations*, *58*, 176–187.

Bilgin, A., & Wolkel, D. (2020). Parental use of "cry it out" in infants: No adverse effects on attachment and behavioural development at 18 months. *Journal of Child Psychology and Psychiatry*, 1–10. https://doi.org/10.1111/jcpp.13223

Black, M. M., Walker, S. P., Fernald, L. C. H., Andersen, C. T., DiGirolamo, A. M., Lu, C., McCoy, D. C., Fink, G., Shawar, Y. R., Shiffman, J., Devercelli, A. E., Wodon, Q. T., Vargas-Barón, E., Grantham-McGregor, S., & Lancet Early Childhood Development Series Steering Committee[Corporate Author]. (2017). Early childhood development coming of age: Science through the life course. *Lancet*, *389*, 77–90.

Blair, C., & Raver, C. C. (2016). Poverty, stress, and brain development: New directions for prevention and intervention. *Academy of Pediatrics*, *16*(3 suppl), S30–S36.

Blair, C., & Razza, R. A. (2007). Relating effortful control, executive function, and false belief understanding to emerging math and literacy ability in kindergarten. *Child Development*, *78*(2), 647–663.

Blunt Bugental, D., Martorell, G. A., & Barraza, V. (2003). The hormonal costs of subtle forms of infant maltreatment. *Hormones and Behavior*, *43*(1), 237–244.

Bornstein, M. H., Suwalsky, J. T. D., & Breakstone, D. A. (2012). Emotional relationships between mothers and infants: Knowns, unknowns, and unknown unknowns. *Developmental Psychopathology*, *24*(1), 113–123.

Bowlby, J. (1958). The nature of the child's tie to his mother. *International Journal of Psychoanalysis*, *39*, 350–373.

Bowlby, J. (1969). *Attachment and loss* (Vol. 1). Basic Books.

Bowlby, J. (1980). *Attachment and Loss*. Separation, anxiety and anger (Vol. II). Basic Books.

Bowlby, J. (1988). *A secure base*. Routledge.

Bowlby, J. (2005). *A secure base: Clinical applications of attachment theory*. Taylor & Francis.

Boyd, D., & Bee, H. (2009). *Lifespan development* (5th ed.). Allyn & Bacon.

Brauner-Otto, S. R., Axinn, W. G., & Ghimire, D. J. (2020). Parents' marital quality and children's transition to adulthood. *Demography*. https://doi.org/10.1007/s13524-019-00851-w

Brazelton, T. B., Koslowski, B., & Main, M. (1974). The origins of reciprocity: The early mother-infant interaction. In M. Lewis & L. Rosenblum (Eds.), *The effect of the infant on its caregiver* (pp. 49–76). Wiley.

Bremner, J. D., & Narayan, M. (1998). The effects of stress on memory and the hippocampus throughout the life cycle: Implications for childhood development and aging. *Developmental Psychopathology*, *10*(4), 871–885.

Brock, R. L., & Kochanska, G. (2016). Interparental conflict, children's security with parents, and long-term risk of internalizing problems: A longitudinal study from ages 2 to 10. *Developmental Psychopathology*, *28*(1), 45–54.

Broman, C. L., Reckase, M. D., & Freedman-Doan, C. R. (2006). The role of parenting in drug use among Black, Latino, and White adolescents. *Journal of Ethnicity in Substance Use*, *5*(1), 39–50.

Brooks-Gunn, J., & Markman, L. B. (2005). The contribution of parenting to ethnic and racial gaps in school readiness. *Future of Children*, *15*(1), 139–168.

Brown, R., & Ward, H. (2013). *Decision-making within a child's timeframe. An overview of current research evidence for family justice professionals concerning child development and the impact of maltreatment*. Childhood Wellbeing Research Centre, Institute of Education.

Cassidy, C. M., & Conroy, D. E. (2006). Children's self-esteem related to school- and sport-specific perceptions of self and others. *Journal of Sport Behavior*, *29*(1), 3–26.

Cebalo, R., Chao, R. K., Hill, N. E., Le, H., Murry, V. M., & Pinderhughes, E. E. (2008). Excavating culture: Summary of results. *Applied Developmental Science*, *12*(4), 220–226.

Cheah, C. S. L., & Rubin, K. H. (2004). Comparison of European American and mainland Chinese mothers' responses to aggression and social withdrawal in preschoolers. *International Journal of Behavioral Development*, *28*, 83–94.

Chen, Z., & Kaplan, H. B. (2001). Intergenerational transmission of constructive parenting. *Journal of Marriage and Family*, *63*(1), 17–31.

Cherry, K. (2018, June 9). *Uninvolved parenting*. https://www.verywellmind.com/what-is-uninvolved-parenting-2794958

Chess, S., & Thomas, A. (1999). *Goodness of fit: Clinical applications for infancy through adult life*. Bruner/Mazel.

Clark, T. T., Yang, C., McClernon, F. J., & Fuemmeler, B. F. (2015). Racial differences inparenting style typologies and heavy episodic drinking trajectories. *Health Psychology*, *34*, 697–708.

Connell, C. M., & Prinz, R. J. (2002). The impact of childcare and parent-child interactions on school readiness and social skill development for low-income African American children. *Journal of School Psychology*, *40*(2), 177–193.

Cox, M. J., & Paley, B. (2003). Understanding families as systems. *Current Directions in Psychological Science*, *12*, 193–196.

Darling, N., & Steinberg, L. (1993). Parenting style as context: An integrative model. *Psychological Bulletin*, *113*(3), 487–496.

Dawson, G., Ashman, S., & Carver, L. (2000). The role of early experience in shaping behavioral and brain development and its implications for social policy. *Development and Psychology*, *12*. https://doi.org/695-712.10.1017/S0954579400004089

Day, R., Peteron, G., & McCracken, C. (1998). Predicting spanking of younger and older children by mothers and fathers. *Journal of Marriage and the Family*, *60*, 79–94.

De Wolff, M., & van IJzendoorn, M. H. (1997). Sensitivity and attachment: A meta-analysis on parental antecedents of infant attachment. *Child Development*, *68*(4), 571–591.

Dinkmeyer, D., McKay, G., & Dinkmeyer, D. (1997). *The parents' handbook (A part of the complete STEP Program)*. American Guidance Service.

Doherty, W. J., Kouneski, E. F., & Erickson, M. F. (1998). Responsible fathering: An overview and conceptual framework. *Journal of Marriage and the Family*, *60*(2), 277–292.

Dreikurs, R., & Grey, I. (1968). *A new approach to discipline: Logical consequences*. Hawthorne.

Durbin, M., DiClemente, R., Siegel, D., Krasnovsky, F., Lazarus, N., & Camacho, T. (1993). Factors associated with multiple sex partners among junior high school students. *Journal of Adolescent Health Care*, *14*, 202–207.

Eamon, M. K., & Mulder, C. (2005). Predicting antisocial behavior among Latino young adolescents: An ecological systems analysis. *American Journal of Orthopsychiatry*, *75*, 117–127.

Eiden, R. D., Teti, D. M., & Corns, K. M. (1995). Maternal working models of attachment, marital adjustment, and the parent-child relationship. *Child Development*, *66*(5), 1504–1518.

Erikson, E. H. (1958). The syndrome of identity diffusion in adolescents and young adults. In J. M. Tanner & B. Inhelder (Eds.), *Proceedings of the third meeting of the child study group, world health organization: Discussions on child development* (Vol. 3, pp. 133–167). International Universities Press.

Erikson, E. H. (1963). *Childhood and society* (2nd ed.). W.W. Norton.

Eshel, N., Daelmans, B., Cabral De Mello, M., & Martines, J. (2006). Responsive parenting: Interventions and outcomes. *Bulletin World Health Organization*, *84*(12), 992–998.

Feldman, R., Granat, A., Pariente, C., Kanety, H., Kuint, J., & Gilboa-Schechtman, E. (2009). Maternal depression and anxiety across the postpartum year and infant social engagement, fear regulation, and stress reactivity. *Journal of the American Academy of Child & Adolescent Psychiatry*, *48*(9), 919–927.

Field, T. (2010). Postpartum depression effects on early interactions, parenting, and safety practices: A review. *Infant Behavior & Development*, *33*(1), 1–6.

Finkelhor, D., Turner, H., Wormuth, B. K., Vandermiden, J., & Hamby, S. (2019). Corporal punishment: Current rates from a national survey. *Journal of Child and Family Studies*. https://doi.org/10.1007/s10826-019-01426-4

Fitzgerald, M. (2020). *Criticism of attachment theory*. https://www.academia.edu/42642393/Amended_Criticism_of_Attachment_Theory_2020_Second_draft?auto=download

Fosco, G. M., & Lydon-Stale, D. M. (2019). A within-family examination of interparental conflict, cognitive appraisals, and adolescent mood and bell-being. *Child Development*, *90*(4), e421–e436.

Fox, N. A. (1995). Of the way we were: Adult memories about attachment experiences and their role in determining infant-parent relationships: A commentary on van IJzendoorn (1995). *Psychological Bulletin*, *117*(3), 404–410.

Giles-Sims, J., Straus, M., & Sugarman, D. (1995). Child, maternal, and family characteristics associated with spanking. *Family Relations*, *44*, 170–176.

Goldberg, J. S., & Carlson, M. J. (2014). Parents' relationship quality and children's behavior in stable married and cohabiting families. *Journal of Marriage and Family*, *76*(4), 762–777.

Gomby, D., Larson, C., Lewit, E., & Behrman, R. (1993). Home visiting: Analysis and recommendations. *The Future of Children: Home Visiting*, *3*(3), 6–22.

Gradisar, M., Jackson, K., Spurrier, N., Gibson, J., Whitham, J., Williams, A. S., Dolby, R., & Kennaway, D. J. (2016). Behavioral interventions for infant sleep problems: A randomized controlled trial. *Pediatrics*, *147*(6), e20151486.

Grogan-Kaylor, A. (2005). Corporal punishment and the growth trajectory of children's antisocial behavior. *Child Maltreatment*, *10*, 283–292.

Gurol, A., & Palot, S. (2012). The effects of baby massage on attachment between mothers and their infants. *Asian Nursing Research*, *6*(1), 35–41.

Halford, W. K., & Pepping, C. A. (2017). An ecological model of mediators of change in Couple Relationship Education. *Current Opinion in Psychology, 13*, 39–43.

Hanappi, D., & Lipps, O. (2019). Job insecurity and parental well-being: The role of parenthood and family factors. *Demographic Research, 40*(31), 897–932.

Harvard Family Research Project. (2006). *Family involvement makes a difference in school success*. http://www.hfrp.org

Heim, C., & Binder, E. B. (2012). Current research trends in early life stress and depression: Review of human studies on sensitive periods, gene-environment interactions, and epigenetics. *Experimental Neurology, 233*, 102–111.

Heim, C., Newport, D. J., Mletzko, T., Miller, A. H., & Nemeroff, C. B. (2008). The link between childhood trauma and depression: Insights from HPA axis studies in humans. *Psychoneuroendocrinology, 33*, 693–710.

Høifødt, R. S., Strøm, C., Kolstrup, N., Eisemann, M., & Waterloo, K. (2011). Effectiveness of cognitive behavioural therapy in primary health care: A review. *Family Practice, 28*(5), 489–504.

Hosokawa, R., & Katsura, T. (2019). Exposure to marital conflict: Gender differences in internalizing and externalizing problems among children. *PLoS One, 14*(9). Article e0222021.

Hyvarinen, L., Walthes, R., Jacob, N., Nottingham Chaplin, K., & Leonhardt, M. (2014). Current understanding of what infants see. *Current Ophthalmology Reports, 2*(4), 142–149.

Isabella, R., & Belsky, J. (1991). Interactional synchrony and the origins of infant-mother attachment: A replication study. *Child Development, 62*(2), 373–384.

Jackson, C., Henriksen, L., & Foshee, V. A. (1998). The authoritative parenting index: Predicting health risk behaviors among children and adolescents. *Health Education Behavior, 25*(3), 319–337.

Kang, Y., & Moore, J. (2011). Parenting style and adolescents' school performance in mainland China. *US-China Education Review, 1*, 133–138.

Kerr, K. L., Cosgrove, K. T., Ratliff, E. L., Burrows, K., Misaki, M., Moore, A. J., DeVille, D. C., Silk, J. S., Tapert, S. F., Bodurka, J., Simmons, W. K., & Morris, A. S. (2020). TEAMwork: Testing emotional attunement and mutuality during parent-adolescent MRI. *Frontiers in Human Neuroscience, 14*, 24. https://doi.org/10.3389/fnhum.2020.00024

Kershaw, T., Murphy, A., Lewis, J., Divney, A., Albritton, T., Magriples, U., & Gordon, D. (2014). Family and relationship influences on parenting behaviors of young parents. *Journal of Adolescent Health, 54*(2), 197–203.

Khaleque, A., & Ali, S. (2017). A systematic review of meta-analyses of research on interpersonal acceptance-rejection theory: Constructs and measures. *Journal of Family Theory & Review, 9*(4), 441–458.

Kiff, C. J., Lengua, L. J., & Zalewski, M. (2011). Nature and nurturing: Parenting in the context of child temperament. *Clinical Child and Family Psychology Review, 14*(3), 251–301.

Kim Halford, W., Rhoades, G., & Morris, M. (2018). Effects of the parents' relationship on children. In M. R. Sanders & A. Morawska (Eds.), *Handbook of parenting and child development across the lifespan* (pp. 97–120). Spring International.

Kim, J. E., Hetherington, E. M., & Reiss, D. (1999). Associations among family relationships, antisocial peers, and adolescents' externalizing behaviors: Gender and family type differences. *Child Development, 70*, 1209–1230.

Kingston, D., Tough, S., & Whitfield, H. (2012). Prenatal and postpartum maternal psychological distress and infant development: A systematic review. *Child Psychiatry & Human Development, 43*(5), 683–714.

Klaus, M. H., Kennell, J. H., & Klaus, P. H. (1995). *Bonding: Building the foundations of secure attachment and independence*. Addison-Wesley.

Kuppens, S., & Ceulemans, E. (2019). Parenting styles: A closer look at a well-known concept. *Journal of Child & Family Studies, 28*, 168–181.

Kurth, E., Kennedy, H. P., Spichiger, E., Hösli, I., & Zemp Stutz, E. (2011). Crying babies, tired mothers: What do we know? A systematic review. *Midwifery, 27*, 187–194.

La Leche League. (2022). *Breastfeeding information, A to Z*. https://www.llli.org/breastfeeding-info/

Lamb-Parker, F., Boak, A. Y., Griffin, K. W., Ripple, C., & Peay, L. (1999). Parent-child relationship, home learning environment, and school readiness. *School Psychology Review, 28*, 413–425.

Landry, S. H., Smith, K. E., Swank, P. R., Zucker, T., Crawford, A. D., & Solari, E. F. (2012). The effects of a responsive parenting intervention on parent–child interactions during shared book reading. *Developmental Psychology, 48*(4), 969–986.

Lansford, J. E., Deater-Deckard, K., Dodge, K. A., Bates, J. E., & Pettit, G. S. (2004). Ethnic differences in the link between physical discipline and later adolescent externalizing behaviors. *Journal of Child Psychology and Psychiatry, 45*(4), 801–812.

Leclère, C., Viaux, S., Avril, M., Achard, C., Chetouani, M., Missonnier, S., & Cohen, D. (2014). Why synchrony matters during mother-child interactions: A systematic review. *PloS One, 9*, E113571. https://doi.org/10.1371/journal.pone.0113571

Liew, J., McTigue, E., Barrois, L., & Hughes, J. (2008). Adaptive and effortful control and academic self-efficacy believes on achievement: A longitudinal study of 1st through 3rd graders. *Early Childhood Research Quarterly, 23*, 515–526.

Lucassen, P. L. B. J. (2001). Systematic review of the occurrence of infantile colic in the community. *Archives of Disease in Childhood, 84*, 398–403.

Lutz, K. F., Anderson, L. S., Riesch, S. K., Pridham, K. A., & Becker, P. T. (2009). Furthering the understanding of parent–child relationships: A nursing scholarship review series. Part 2: Grasping the early parenting experience—The insider view. *Journal for Specialists in Pediatric Nursing, 14*(4), 262–283.

Malik, F., & Marwaha, R. (2020, May 23). Developmental stages of social emotional development in children. *StatPearls*. www.ncbi.nl.nih.gov/books/NBK534819

McAdams, D. P. (1989). *Intimacy: The need to be close*. Doubleday & Co.

McClelland, M., & Cameron, C. E. (2012). Self-regulation in early childhood: Improving conceptual clarity and developing ecologically valid measures. *Child Development Perspectives, 6*(2), 136–142.

McClelland, M. M., Ponitz, C. C., Messersmith, E. E., & Tominey, S. (2010). Self-regulation: Integration of cognition and emotion. In W. F. Overton & R. M. Lerner (Eds.), *The handbook of lifespan development*. Cognition, biology, and methods (Vol. 1, pp. 509–553). John Wiley & Sons.

McClowry, S. G., Rodriguez, E. T., & Koslowitz, R. (2008). Temperament-based intervention: Re-examining goodness of fit. *European Journal of Developmental Science, 2*(1–2), 120–135.

McClun, L. A., & Merrell, K. W. (1998). Relationship of perceived parenting styles, locus of control orientation, and self-concept among junior high age students. *Psychology in the Schools, 35*(4), 381–390.

McFarland, D. H., Fortin, A. J., & Polka, L. (2019). Physiological measures of mother-infant interactional synchrony. *Developmental Psychobiology, 62*(4), 50–61.

McKenna, J. J. (2020). *Safe infant sleep: Expert answers to your breastfeeding questions*. Platypus Media.

McLeod, S. (2018). *Erik Erikson's stages of psychosocial development*. https://www.simplypsychology.org/Erik-Erikson.html

McLeod, J. D., & Nonnemaker, J. M. (2000). Poverty and child emotional and behavioral problems: Racial/ethnic differences in processes and effects. *Journal of Health and Social Behavior, 41*, 137–161.

Micalizzi, L., Wang, M., & Saudino, K. J. (2017). Difficult temperament and negative parenting in early childhood: A genetically informed cross-lagged analysis. *Developmental Science, 20*(2). https://pubmed.ncbi.nlm.nih.gov/26490166/

Mihalec-Adkins, B. P., & Cooley, M. E. (2020). Examining individual-level academic risk and protective factors for foster youth: School engagement, behaviors, self-esteem, and social skills. *Child & Family Social Work, 25*(2), 256–266.

Miller, J. P. (2010). *Whole child education* (1st ed.). University of Toronto Press, Scholarly Publishing Division.

Miller, J. J., Cooley, M. E., & Mihalec-Adkins, B. P. (2022).

Examining the impact of COVID-19 on parental stress: A study of foster parents. *Child and Adolescent Social Work Journal, 39*, 47–156.

Moller, E. L., de Vente, W., & Rodenburg, R. (2019). Infant crying and the calming response: Parental versus mechanical soothing using swaddling, sound, and movement. *PLoS One, 14*(4), E0214548. https://doi.org/10.1371/journal.pone.0214548

Murphey, D., Cook, E., Beckwith, S., & Belford, J. (2018). Parenting knowledge among first-time parents of young children. *Child Trends Publications*. https://www.childtrends.org/publications/parenting-knowledge-among-first-time-parents-of-young-children-a-research-to-practice-brief

Murphy, S. E., Boyd-Soisson, E., Jacobvitz, D. B., & Hazen, N. L. (2017). Dyadic and triadic family interactions as simultaneous predictors of children's externalizing behaviors. *Family Relations: An Interdisciplinary Journal of Applied Family Studies, 66*(2), 346–359.

Nash, J. B., & Schaefer, C. E. (2011). Play therapy: Basic concepts and practices. In C. E. Schaefer (Ed.), *Foundations of play therapy* (pp. 3–13). John Wiley & Sons Inc.

National Association for the Education of Young Children. (2020). *Principles of child development and learning and implications that inform practice*. https://www.naeyc.org/resources/position-statements/dap/principles

National Head Start Association. (2022). *Head start's model: Nationwide, comprehensive, multi-generational*. https://nhsa.org/resource/2022-state-fact-sheets/

National Institute on Deafness and Other Communication Disorders (NIDCD). (2017). *Your baby's hearing and communication development*. https://www.nidcd.nih.gov/health/your-babys-hearing-and-communicative-development-checklist

National Research Council. (2015). *Transforming the workforce for children birth through age 8: A unifying foundation*. The National Academies Press.

Nomaguchi, K., & Milkie, A. (2020). Parenthood and well-being: A decade in review. *Journal of Marriage and Family, 82*(1), 198–223.

Odame-Mensah, S., & Gyimah, E. K. (2018). The role of permissive and neglectful parenting style in determining the academic performance of adolescents in the senior high schools in the Birim Municipality. *Journal of Education and Practice, 9*(4), 73.

Ossa, X., Bustos, L., & Fernandes, L. (2012). Prenatal attachment and associated factors during the third trimester of pregnancy in Tumeco, Chile. *Midwifery, 28*(5), 689–696.

Parfitt, Y., Pike, A., & Ayers, S. (2013). The impact of parents' mental health on parent-baby interaction: A prospective study. *Infant Behavior and Development, 36*(4), 599–608.

Pederson, D. R., & Moran, G. (1996). Expressions of the attachment relationship outside of the strange situation. *Child Development, 67*(3), 915–927.

Penn State Hershey. (2020). *Excessive crying in infants*. https://www.health.pa.gov/topics/programs/Pages/Shaken-Baby-Syndrome.aspx

Piaget, J. (1952). *The origins of intelligence in children* (M. Cook, Trans.). International Universities Press.

Pierrehumbert, B., Torrisi, R., Ansermet, F., Borghini, A., & Halfon, O. (2012). Adult attachment representations predict cortisol and oxytocin responses to stress. *Attach and Human Development, 14*, 453–476.

Pietromonaco, P. R., & Collins, N. L. (2017). Interpersonal mechanisms linking close relationships to health. *American Psychology, 72*, 531–542.

Pietromonaco, P. R., Uchino, B., & Dunkel Schetter, C. (2013). Close relationship processes and health: Implications of attachment theory for health and disease. *Health Psychology, 32*, 499–513.

Pittman, L. D., & Chase-Lansdale, P. L. (2001). African American adolescent girls in impoverished communities: Parenting style and adolescent outcomes. *Journal of Research on Adolescence, 11*, 199–224.

Planalp, E. M., Braungart-Rieker, J. M., Lickenbrock, D. M., & Zentall, S. R. (2013). Trajectories of parenting during infancy: The role of infant temperament and marital adjustment for mothers and fathers. *Infancy, 18*(Suppl 1), E15–E45.

Planalp, E. M., Van Hulle, C., Lemery-Chalfant, L., & Goldsmith, H. H. (2017). Genetic and environmental contributions to the development of positive affect in infancy. *Emotion, 17*(3), 412–420.

Pluess, M., & Belsky, J. (2010). Differential susceptibility to parenting and quality child care. *Developmental Psychology, 46*(2), 379–390.

Pluess, M., Belsky, J., Way, B. M., & Taylor, S. E. (2010). 5-HTTLPR Moderates Effects of life events on neuroticism: Differential susceptibility to environmental influences. *Progress in Neuropsychopharmacology & Biological Psychiatry, 34*, 1070–1074.

Ponnet, K. (2014). Financial stress, parent functioning and adolescent problem behavior: An actor-partner interdependence approach to family stress processes in low-, middle-, and high-income families. *Journal of Youth & Adolescence, 43*(1), 1752–1769.

Radziszewska, B., van der Gaag, E., & Munow, M. (1996). Parenting style and adolescent depressive symptoms, smoking, and academic achievement: Ethnic, gender, and SES differences. *Journal of Behavioral Medicine, 19*, 289–305.

Rees, C. (2007). Childhood attachment. *British Journal of General Practice, 57*(544), 920–922.

Roche, K. M., Ensminger, M. E., & Cherlin, A. J. (2007). Variations in parenting and adolescent outcomes among African American and Latino families living in low-income, urban areas. *Journal of Family Issues, 28*(7), 882–909.

Rosanbalm, K. D., & Murray, D. W. (2017). *Promoting self-regulation in early childhood: A practice brief. OPRE brief #2017-79.* Office of Planning, Research, and Evaluation, Administration for Children and Families, US. Department of Health and Human Services.

Ryan, R. M., & Deci, E. L. (2017). *Self-determination theory: Basic psychological needs in motivation, development, and wellness*. Guilford Press.

Sadeghi, M., & Mazaheri, A. (2007). Comparement of attachment styles in mothers with and without history of fetus abortion (intentional and spontaneous). *Fertility and Infertility Journal, 8*(1), 60–69.

Salehi, K., & Kohan, S. (2017). Maternal-fetal attachment: What we know and what we need to know. *International Journal of Pregnancy and Childbirth, 2*(5), 146–148.

Salehi, K., Taleghani, F., & Kohan, S. (2019). Effect of attachment-based interventions on prenatal attachment: A protocol for systematic review. *Reproductive Health, 16*, 15.

Samaniego, R. Y., & Gonzales, N. A. (1999). Multiple mediators of the effects of acculturation status on delinquency for Mexican American adolescents. *American Journal of Community Psychology, 27*, 189–210.

Sanders, M. (2008). Triple P-Positive Parenting Program as a public health approach to strengthening parenting. *Journal of Family Psychology, 22*, 506–517.

Sanson, A. V., Letcher, P. L. C., & Havighurst, S. S. (2018). Child characteristics and their reciprocal effects on parenting. In M. R. Sanders & A. Morawska (Eds.), *Handbook of parenting and child development across the lifespan* (pp. 337–370). Springer.

Sedgmen, B., Mcmahon, G., Carins, D., Benzie, R. J., & Woodfield, R. L. (2006). The impact of two-dimensional versus three-dimensional ultrasound exposure on maternal-fetal attachment and maternal health behavior in pregnancy. *Ultrasound in Obstetrics & Gynecology, 27*(3), 245–251.

Shemmings, D. (2011). *Attachment in children and young people. (Frontline briefing)*. Research in Practice.

Shucksmith, J., Leo, B., Hendry, L. B., & Glendinning, A. (1995). Models of parenting: Implications for adolescent well-being within different types of family contexts. *Journal of Adolescence, 18*, 253–270.

Simpson, J. A., & Steven Rholes, W. (2017). Adult attachment, stress, and romantic relationships. *Current Opinion in Psychology, 13*, 19–24.

Smetana, J. G. (1995). Parenting styles and conceptions of parental authority during adolescence. *Child Development, 66*(2), 299–316.

Srvanti, L. (2017). Goodness of fit. *Indian Journal of Psychiatry, 59*(4), 515.

Steele, H., Steele, M., & Fonagy, P. (1996). Associations among classifications of mothers, fathers, and their infants. *Child Development, 67*, 541–555.

Steinberg, L., Lamborn, S. D., Darling, N., & Mounts, N. S. (1994). Over-time changes in adjustment and competence among adolescents from authoritative, authoritarian, indulgent, and neglectful families. *Child Development, 65*, 754–770.

Steinberg, L., & Morris, A. S. (2001). Adolescent development. *Annual Review of Psychology, 52*, 83–110.

Steinberg, L., Mounts, N., Lamborn, S., & Dornbusch, S. (1991). Authoritative parenting and adolescent adjustment across various ecological niches. *Journal of Research on Adolescence, 1*, 19–36.

Stephens, K. (2007). Strategies for parenting children with difficult temperaments. *Child Care Exchange*. https://www.easternflorida.edu/community-resources/child-development-centers/parent-resource-library/documents/parenting-the-difficult-temperament.pdf

Takeuchi, H., Taki, Y., Hashizume, H., Asano, K., Asano, M., Sassa, Y., Yokota, S., Kotozaki, Y., Nouchi, R., & Kawashima, R. (2015). The impact of parent-child interaction on brain structures: Cross-sectional and longitudinal analyses. *Journal of Neuroscience, 35*(5), 2233–2245.

Thomas, A., & Chess, S. (1977). *Temperament and development*. Brunner/Mazel.

Tierney, A. L., & Nelson, C. A. (2009). Brain development and the role of experience in the early years. *Zero Three, 30*(2), 9–13.

Tronick, E., & Reck, C. (2009). Infants of depressed mothers. *Harvard Review of Psychiatry, 17*(2), 147–156.

Vaish, A., Hepach, R., & Tomasello, M. (2018). The specificity of reciprocity: Young children reciprocate more generously to those who intentionally benefit them. *Journal of Experimental Child Psychology, 167*, 336–353.

Valiente, C., Lemery-Chalfant, K., Swanson, J., & Reiser, M. (2008). Prediction of children's academic competence from their effortful control, relationships, and classroom participation. *Journal of Educational Psychology, 100*(1), 67–77.

van Ijzendoorn, M. H., & Bakermans-Kranenburg, J. J. (2003). Attachment disorders and disorganized attachment: Similar and different. *Attachment & Human Development, 5*(3), 313–320.

Wake, M. (2006). Prevalence, stability, and outcomes of cry-fuss and sleep problems in the first 2 years of life: Prospective community-based study. *Pediatrics, 117*, 836–842.

Welch, K. J. (2010). *THINK human sexuality* (1st ed.). Pearson Education.

Wells, A. I. (2018). Attachment style and romantic satisfaction as predictors of relationship visibility on facebook. *Senior Independent Study Theses. Paper 7887.*

Wittmer, D. (2011). *Attachment. What works?* Center on the Social and Emotional Foundations for Early Learning, Vanderbilt University.

CHAPTER 6

Abi-Jaoude, E., Naylor, K. T., & Pignatiello, A. (2020). Smartphones, social media use, and youth mental health. *Canadian Medical Association Journal, 192*(6), E136–E141.

Abramson, A. (2021). Children's mental health is in crisis: 2022 trends report. *American Psychological Association, 53*(1), 69.

Abtahi, M. M., & Kerns, K. A. (2017). Attachment and emotion regulation in middle childhood: Changes in affect and vagal tone during a social stress task. *Attachment & Human Development, 19*(3), 221–242.

Advocates for Youth. (2004). *Youth of color—at disproportionate risk of negative sexual health outcomes*. https://www.advocatesforyouth.org/wp-content/uploads/storage/advfy/documents/fsyouthcolor.pdf

Afterschool Alliance. (2017). *What does the research say about afterschool?* http://afterschoolalliance.org/documents/what_does_the_research_say_about_afterschool.pdf

Afterschool Alliance. (2022). *America after 3PM: Core findings*. http://www.afterschoolalliance.org/AA3PM/

Ainsworth, M. S. (1989). Attachments beyond infancy. *American Psychologist, 44*(4), 709–716.

Alegria, M., Green, J. G., McLaughlin, K. A., & Loder, S. (2015). *Disparities in child and adolescent mental health and mental health services in the U.S.* http://www.mamh.org/Portals/0/Uploads/Documents/

Public/Disparities%20in%20Child%20and%20Adolescent%20Mental%20Health.pdf

American Academy of Pediatrics. (2015). *Parenting school-aged children*. https://www.healthychildren.org/English/family-life/family-dynamics/Pages/Parenting-School-Age-Children.aspx

American Academy of Pediatrics. (2020). *What do we really know about kids and screens?* https://www.apa.org/monitor/2020/04/cover-kids-screens

American Psychological Association, Working Group for Addressing Racial and Ethnic Disparities in Youth Mental Health. (2017). *Addressing the mental health needs of racial and ethnic minority youth: A guide for practitioners*. www.apa.org/pi/families/resources/mental-healthneeds.pdf

Atwater, E. (1992). Peers. *Adolescence, 3*, 151–153.

Austin, A., & Wagner, E. F. (2010). Treatment attrition among racial and ethnic minority youth. *Journal of Social Work Practice in the Addictions, 10*, 63–80.

Backes, E. P., & Bonnie, R. J. (2019). *The promise of adolescence: Realizing opportunity for all youth*. National Academies Press.

Bick, J., & Nelson, C. A. (2016). Early adverse experiences and the developing brain. *Neuropsychopharmacology, 41*, 117–196.

Biro, F. M., & Wien, M. (2010). Childhood obesity and adult morbidities. *American Journal of Clinical Nutrition, 91*(5), 1499S–1505S.

Boldt, L. J., Kochanska, G., Grekin, R., & Brock, R. L. (2016). Attachment in middle childhood: Predictors, correlates, and implications for adaptation. *Attachment & Human Development, 16*, 115–140.

Boldt, L. J., Kochanska, G., Yoon, J. E., & Nordling, J. K. (2014). Children's attachment to both parents from toddler age to middle childhood: Links to adaptive and maladaptive outcomes. *Attachment & Human Development, 16*, 211–229.

Bondolo, E., Brady, N., Pencille, M., Beatty, D., & Contrada, R. (2009). Coping with racism: A selective review of the literature and a theoretical and methodological critique. *Journal of Behavioral Medicine, 32*(1), 64–88.

Bowlby, J. (1969). *Attachment and loss* (2nd ed., Vol. 1). Basic Books.

Bronstein, P., Duncan, P., D'Ari, A., Pieniadz, J., Fitzgerald, M., Abrams, C. L., Frankowski, B., Franco, O., Hunt, C., Oh, C., & Susan, Y. (1996). Family and parenting behaviors predicting middle school adjustment: A longitudinal study. *Family Relations, 45*(4), 415–426.

Brooks, R. (2002). Transitional friends? Young people's strategies to manage and maintain their friendships during a period of repositioning. *Journal of Youth Studies, 5*, 449–467.

Brown, G. L., Mangelsdorf, S. C., Neff, C., Schoppe-Sullivan, S. J., & Frosch, C. A. (2009). Young children's self-concepts: Associations with child temperament, mothers' and fathers' parenting, and triadic family interaction. *Merrill Palmer Q, 55*(2), 184–216.

Brumariu, L. E. (2015). Parent-child attachment and emotion regulation. *New Directions for Child and Adolescent Development, 148*, 31–45.

Carter, R. T. (2007). Racism and psychological and emotional injury: Recognizing and assessing race-based traumatic stress. *The Counseling Psychologist, 35*(1), 13–105.

Cassidy, J. (1994). Emotion regulation: Influences of attachment relationships. *Monographs of the Society for Research in Child Development, 59*, 228–249.

Center on the Developing Child. (2021). *Toxic stress*. https://developingchild.harvard.edu/science/key-concepts/toxic-stress/

Centers for Disease Control and Prevention (CDC). (2019). *Violence prevention: Adverse childhood experiences*. https://www.cdc.gov/violenceprevention/aces/index.html

Centers for Disease Control and Prevention (CDC). (2021). *Violence prevention*. https://www.cdc.gov/violenceprevention/aces/riskprotectivefactors.html

Chaarani, B., Hahn, S., Allgaier, N., Adise, S., Owens, M. M., Juliano, A. C., Yuan, D. K., Loso, H., Ivanciu, A., Albaugh, M. D., Dumas, J., Mackey, S., Laurent, J., Ivanova, M., Hagler, D. J., Cornejo, M. D., Hatton, S., Agrawal, A., Aguinaldo, L., ... ABCD Consortium. (2021). Baseline brain function in the preadolescents of the ABCD Study. *Nature Neuroscience, 24*(8), 1176–1186. https:

//doi.org/10.1038/s41593-021-00867-9

Chapman, J. W., Lambourne, R., & Silva, P. A. (1990). Some antecedents of academic self-concept: A longitudinal study. *British Journal of Educational Psychology, 60*(2), 142–152.

Child Mind Institute. (2021). *2020 children's mental health report: Telehealth in an increasingly virtual world*. https://childmind.org/our-impact/childrens-mental-health-report/2020-childrens-mental-health-report/

Child Trends. (2018). *The prevalence of adverse childhood experiences, nationally, by state, and race or ethnicity*. https://www.childtrends.org/publications/prevalence-adverse-childhood-experiences-nationally-state-race-ethnicity

Child Trends. (2021). *New agenda to support and improve children's mental health*. https://www.childtrends.org/news-release/new-agenda-to-support-improve-childrens-mental-health

Collins, W. A., & Madsen, S. D. (2019). Parenting during middle childhood. In *Handbook of parenting*. https://www.routledgehandbooks.com/doi/10.4324/9780429440847

Colombo, J., Gustafson, K. M., & Carlson, S. E. (2019). Critical and sensitive periods in development and nutrition. *Annals of Nutrition & Metabolism, 75*(Suppl. 1), 34–42.

Commendador, K. A. (2010). Parental influences on adolescent decision making and contraceptive use. *Pediatric Nursing, 36*, 147–156.

Common Sense Media. (2019). *The Common Sense census: Media use by tweens and teens*. https://www.commonsensemedia.org/sites/default/files/uploads/research/2019-census-8-to-18-full-report-updated.pdf

Cornell University. (2017). *What does the scholarly research say about the link between family acceptance and LGBT youth well-being?* https://whatweknow.inequality.cornell.edu/wp-content/uploads/2018/04/PDF-Family-acceptance-1.pdf

Curriculum Associates. (2021). *What we've learned about unfinished learning: Insights from midyear diagnostic assessments*. https://www.curriculumassociates.com/-/media/mainsite/files/iready/iready-understanding-student-needs-paper-winter-results-2021.pdf

DelGiudice, M. (2014). An evolutionary life history framework for psychopathology. *Psychological Inquiry, 25*(3–4), 261–300.

DelGiudice, M. (2018). Middle childhood: An evolutionary-developmental synthesis. In N. Halfon, C. Forrest, R. Lerner, & E. Faustman (Eds.), *Handbook of life course health development*. Springer.

Dorn, E., Hancock, J., Sarakatsannis, J., & Viruleg, E. (2020). *COVID-19 and student learning in the United States: The hurt could last a lifetime*. https://www.mckinsey.com/industries/public-and-social-sector/our-insights/covid-19-and-student-learning-in-the-united-states-the-hurt-could-last-a-lifetime

Downing, J., & Bellis, M. A. (2009). Early pubertal onset and its relationship with sexual risk taking, substance use, and anti-social behavior: A preliminary cross-sectional study. *BMC Public Health, 9*, 446.

Dunphy, D. C. (1963). The social structure of urban adolescent peer groups. *Sociometry, 26*, 230–246.

Ember, C., & Cunnar, C. (2015). Children's play and work: The relevance of cross-cultural ethnographic research for archaeologists. *Childhood in the Past, 8*(2), 87–103.

Erikson, E. H. (1963). *Childhood and society* (2nd ed.). Norton.

Erling, A., & Hwang, P. (2004). Swedish 10-year-old children's perceptions and experiences of bullying. *Journal of School Violence, 3*, 33–43.

Eshel, N., Daelmans, B., de Mello, M. C., & Martines, J. (2006). Responsive parenting: Interventions and outcomes. *World Health Organization, 84*, 991–998.

Farmer, T. W., Petrin, R. A., Robertson, D. L., Fraser, M. W., Hall, C. M., Day, S. H., & Dadisman, K. (2010). Peer relations of bullies, bully–victims, and victims: The two social worlds of bullying in second-grade classrooms. *Elementary School Journal, 110*, 364–392.

Fazel, M., Hoagwood, K., Stephan, S., & Ford, T. (2014). Mental health interventions in schools: Mental health interventions in schools in high-income countries. *Lancet Psychiatry, 1*(5), 377–387.

Felitti, V. J., Anda, R. F., Nordenberg, D., Williamson, D. F.,

Spitz, A. M., Edwards, V., Koss, M. P., & Marks, J. S. (1998). Relationship of childhood abuse and household dysfunction to many of the leading causes of death in adults: The Adverse Childhood Experiences (ACE) study. *American Journal of Preventive Medicine*, *14*(4), 245–258.

Flores, D., & Barroso, J. (2017). 21st century parent-child sex communication in the U.S.: A process review. *Journal of Sex Research*, *54*(4–5), 532–548.

Florida State University. (2021). *What is toxic stress?* https://med.fsu.edu/childStress/whatis

Franco, N., & Levitt, M. J. (1998). The social ecology of middle childhood: Family support, friendship quality, and self-esteem. *Family Relations: An Interdisciplinary Journal of Applied Family Studies*, *47*(4), 315–321.

Frisén, A., Jonsson, A. K., & Persson, C. (2007). Adolescents' perception of bullying. Who is the victim, who is the bullying? What can be done to stop bullying? *Adolescence*, *42*(1), 749–761.

Galupo, M. P. (2007). Women's close friendships across sexual orientation: An analysis of lesbian-heterosexual and bisexual-heterosexual women's friendships. *Sex Roles*, *56*, 473–482.

Galupo, M. P. (2009). Cross-category friendship patterns: Comparison of heterosexual and sexual minority adults. *Journal of Social and Personal Relationships*, *26*, 811–831.

Galupo, M. P., Bauerband, L. A., Gonzalez, K. A., Hagen, D. B., Hether, S. D., & Krum, T. E. (2014). Transgender friendship experiences: Benefits and barriers of friendships across gender identity and sexual orientation. *Feminism & Psychology*, *24*(2), 193–215.

Ge, X., & Natsuaki, M. N. (2009). In search of explanations for early pubertal timing effects on developmental psychology. *Current Directions in Psychological Science*, *18*(6), 327–331.

Gilmore, J. H., Knickmeyer Santelli, R., & Gao, W. (2018). Imaging structural and functional brain development in early childhood. *Nature Reviews Neuroscience*, *19*(3), 123–137.

Grossman, J. M., Jenkins, L. J., & Richer, A. M. (2018). Parents' perspectives on family sexuality communication from middle school to high school. *International Journal of Research and Public Health*, *15*(1), 107.

Hafford-Letchfield, T., Cocker, C., Manning, R., & McCormack, K. (2020). Trans and nonbinary parenting. In S. K. Kattari, M. K. Kinney, L. Kattari, & N. E. Walls (Eds.), *Social work and health care practice with transgender and nonbinary individuals and communities: Voices for equity, inclusion, and resilience* (p. 384). Routledge.

Hafford-Letchfield, T., Cocker, C., Rutter, D., Tinarwo, M., McCormack, K., & Manning, R. (2019). What do we know about transgender parenting?: Findings from a systematic review. *Health & Social Care in the Community*, *27*(5), 1111–1125.

Hart, H., & Rubia, K. (2012). Neuroimaging of child abuse: A critical review. *Frontiers in Human Neuroscience*, *6*, 52.

Hicks, M. S., McRee, A. L., & Eisenberg, M. E. (2013). Teens talking with their partners about sex: The role of parent communication. *American Journal of Sex Education*, *8*, 1–1.

Hinduja, S., & Patchin, J. W. (2010). Bullying, cyberbullying, and suicide. *Archives of Suicide Research*, *14*(3), 206–221.

Hines, S. (2007). *TransForming gender: Transgender practices of identity, intimacy, and care*. Policy Press.

Hisle, N. (2022). *The intersectionality of race and trauma in children and teens who are Black, indigenous, and people of color. Strategies and methods for implementing trauma-informed pedagogy.* https://www.igi-global.com/chapter/the-intersectionality-of-race-and-trauma-in-children-and-teens-who-are-black-indigenous-and-people-of-color-bipoc/287203

Human Rights Campaign. (2021). *Understanding the transgender community.* https://www.hrc.org/resources/transgender

Ictech, B. (2018). Smartphones and face-to-face interaction: Digital cross-talk during encounters in everyday life. *Symbolic Interaction*, *42*(1), 27–45.

Johns, M. M., Lowry, R., Andrzejewski, J., Barrios, L. C., Demissie, Z., Mcmanus, T., Rasberry, C. N., Robin, L.,

& Underwood, J. M. (2019). Transgender identity and experiences of violence victimization, substance use, suicide risk, and sexual risk behaviors among high school students—19 states and large urban school districts, 2017. *Morbidity and Mortality Weekly Report*, *68*, 67–71.

Johnson, S. B., Blum, R. W., & Giedd, J. N. (2009). Adolescent maturity and the brain: The promise and pitfalls of neuroscience research in adolescent health policy. *Journal of Adolescent Health*, *45*(3), 26–221.

Jonson-Reid, M., & Wideman, E. (2017). Trauma and very young children. *Child & Adolescent Psychiatry*, *26*(3), 477–490.

Jungert, T., Karatas, P., Iotti, N. O., & Perrin, S. (2021, January 21). Direct bullying and cyberbullying: Experimental study of bystanders' motivation to defend victims and the role of anxiety and identification with the bully. *Frontiers in Psychology*. https://www.frontiersin.org/articles/10.3389/fpsyg.2020.616572/fu

Kamza, A. (2019). Attachment to mothers and fathers during middle childhood: An evidence from Polish sample. *BMC Psychology*, *7*(79). https://doi.org/10.1186/s40359-019-0361-5

Keenan, K., Culbert, K., Grimm, K., Hipwell, A., & Stepp, S. (2014). Timing and tempo: Exploring the complex association between pubertal development and depression in African American and European American girls. *Journal of Abnormal Psychology*, *123*(4), 725–736.

Department of Psychiatry, University of Pittsburgh.

Kerns, K. A., Abraham, M. M., Schlegelmilch, A., & Morgan, T. A. (2007). Mother-child attachment in later middle childhood: Assessment approaches and associations with mood and emotion regulation. *Attachment & Human Development*, *9*, 33–53.

Kerns, K. A., & Brumariu, L. E. (2016). Attachment in middle childhood. In J. Cassidy & P. Shaver (Eds.), *Handbook of attachment* (Vol. 3, pp. 349–365). .

Kessler, R. C., Berglund, P., Demler, O., Jin, R., Merikangas, K. R., & Walters, E. E. (2005). Lifetime prevalence and age-of-onset distributions of DSM-IV disorders in the National Comorbidity Survey Replication. *Archives of General Psychiatry*, *62*(6), 593–602.

Ketsetzis, M., Ryan, B. A., & Adams, G. R. (1998). Family processes, parent-child interactions, and child characteristics influencing school-based social adjustment. *Journal of Marriage and the Family*, *60*, 374–387.

Knudsen, E. I. (2004). Sensitive periods in the development of the brain and behavior. *Journal of Cognitive Neuroscience*, *16*(8), 1412–1425.

Kuhar, R., Monro, S., & Takács, J. (2018). Trans* citizenship in post-socialist societies. *Critical Social Policy*, *38*(1), 99–120.

Lancy, D. F. (2010). Learning 'from nobody': The limited role of teaching in folk models of children's development. *Childhood in the Past*, *3*, 79–106.

Lancy, D. F. (2015). *The anthropology of childhood: Cherubs, chattel, changelings* (2nd ed.). Cambridge University Press.

Lancy, D. F. (2017). *Raising children: Surprising insights from other cultures*. Cambridge University Press.

Landry, S. H., Smith, K. E., Swank, P. R., & Guttentag, C. (2008). A responsive parenting intervention: The optimal timing across early childhood for impacting maternal behaviors and child outcomes. *Developmental Psychology*, *44*, 1335–1353.

L'ng, A. (2010). Attachment and emotion regulation-clinical implications of a non-clinical sample study. *Social and Behavioral Sciences*, *5*, 674–678.

Lantos, H., Manlove, J., Wildsmith, E., Faccio, B., Guzman, L., & Moore, K. A. (2019). Parent-teen communication about sexual and reproductive health: Cohort differences by race/ethnicity and nativity. *International Journal Environmental Research and Public Health*, *16*(5), 833. https://www.ncbi.nlm.nih.gov/pmc/articles/PMC6427285/

Letkiewicz, A. M., Weldon, A. L., Tengshe, C., Niznikiewicz, M. A., & Heller, W. (2021). Cumulative childhood maltreatment and executive functioning in adulthood. *Journal of Aggression, Maltreatment, & Trauma*, *30*(4), 547–563.

Macedo, D. M., Smithers, L. G., Roberts, R. M., Paradies, Y., & Jamieson, L. M. (2019). Effects of racism on the socio-emotional wellbeing of Aboriginal Australian children.

International Journal for Equity in Health, *18*, 132.

Mah, V. K., & Ford-Jones, E. L. (2012). Spotlight on middle childhood: Rejuvenating the "forgotten years." *Paediatrics & Child Health*, *17*(2), 81–83.

Markus, H. R., & Moya, P. M. L. (2010). *Doing race: 21 essays for the 21st century*. .

Mendelson, M. J., & Kay, A. C. (2003). Positive feelings in friendship: Does imbalance in the relationship matter? *Journal of Social and Personal Relationships*, *20*, 101–116.

Morsy, L., & Rothstein, R. (2019). *Toxic stress and outcomes: African American children growing up poor are at greater risk of disrupted physiological functioning and depressed academic achievement*. https://www.epi.org/publication/toxic-stress-and-childrens-outcomes-african-american-children-growing-up-poor-are-at-greater-risk-of-disrupted-physiological-functioning-and-depressed-academic-achievement/

Naftzger, N., Vinson, M., Bonney, C., Murphy, J., & Kaufman, S. (2009). *21st Century Community Learning Centers (21st CCLC) analytic support for evaluation and program monitoring: An overview of the 21st CCLC performance data: 2006–07* (Fourth Report). U.S. Department of Education.

National Academies of Sciences, Engineering, and Medicine. (2016). *Preventing bullying through science, policy, and practice*. The National Academies Press.

National Bullying Prevention Center. (2021). *Bullying statistics: By the numbers*. https://www.pacer.org/bullying/info/stats.asp

National Center for Educational Statistics. (2019). *Student reports of bullying: Results from the 2017 School Crime Supplement to the National Victimization Survey*. US Department of Education. http://nces.ed.gov/pubsearch/pubsinfo.asp?pubid=2015056

National Institutes of Health. (2020). *Puberty and precocious puberty. Eunice Kennedy Shriver National Institute of Child Health and Human Development*. https://www.nichd.nih.gov/health/topics/factsheets/puberty#:~:text=The%20time%20in%20one's%20life,between%20ages%209%20and%2014

National Sexual Violence Center. (2013). *An overview of healthy childhood sexual development*. https://www.nationalcac.org/wp-content/uploads/2016/08/HealthySexualDevelopmentOverview.pdf

NCSL. (2021). *Adverse childhood experiences*. https://www.ncsl.org/research/health/adverse-childhood-experiences-aces.aspx

Nelson, C. A., Bhutta, Z. A., Burke Harris, N., Danese, A., & Samara, M. (2020). Adversity in childhood is linked to mental and physical health throughout life. *BMJ*, *371*, m3048. https://doi.org/10.1136/bmj.m3048

Okami, P., & Shackelford, T. K. (2001). Human sex differences in sexual psychology and behavior. *Annual Review of Sex Research*, *12*, 186–241.

O'Keeffe, G. S., & Clarke-Pearson, K. (2011). The impact of social media on children, adolescents, and families. *Pediatrics*, *127*(4), 800–804.

Olweus, D., & Limber, S. P. (2010). Bullying in school: Evaluation and dissemination of the Olweus Bullying Prevention Program. *American Journal of Orthopsychiatry*, *80*(1), 124–134.

Oswald, D. L., & Clark, E. M. (2003). Best friends forever? High school best friendships and the transition to college. *Journal of Social and Personal Relationships*, *10*, 187–196.

Paris, J. (2019). *Child growth and development: ECE 101*. College of the Canyons.

Parrigon, K. S., Kerns, K. A., Abtahi, M. M., & Koehn, A. (2015). Attachment and emotion in middle childhood and adolescence. *Psychological Topics*, *24*, 27–50.

Patchin, J. W., & Hinduja, S. (2020). Tween cyberbullying in 2020. *Cyberbullying Research Center and Cartoon Network*. https://i.cartoonnetwork.com/stopbullying/pdfs/CN_Stop_Bullying_Cyber_Bullying_Report_9.30.20.pdf

Paul, E. L., & White, K. M. (1990, Summer). The development of intimate relationships during late adolescence. *Adolescence*, *25*(98), 375–400.

Pechtel, P., & Pizzagalli, D. A. (2011). Effects of early life stress on cognitive and affective function: An integrated review of human literature. *Psychopharmacology*, *214*, 55–70.

Perren, S., & Alsaker, F. D. (2006). Social behavior and

peer relationships of victims, bully-victims, and bullies in kindergarten. *Journal of Child Psychology and Psychiatry, 47*(1), 45–57.

Perry, N. E. (2019). Recognizing early childhood as a critical time for developing and supporting self-regulation. *Metacognition and Learning, 14*(3), 327–334.

Pettit, G. S., Bates, J. E., & Dodge, K. A. (1997). Supportive parenting, ecological context, and children's adjustment: A seven-year longitudinal study. *Child Development, 68*(5), 908–923.

Pew Research Center. (2016). *Americans increasingly use smartphones for more than voice calls, texting.* https://www.pewresearch.org/internet/ft_01-27-16_smartphoneactivities_640/

Pew Research Center. (2018). *Teens, social media, and technology.* https://www.pewresearch.org/internet/2018/05/31/teens-social-media-technology-2018/

Phoon, A. (2017). Social media and its stark influences on society. *Journal of First-Year Writing, 1*(1). https://scholarworks.bgsu.edu

Pierce, K. M., Auger, A., & Vandell, D. L. (2013). *Associations between structured activity participation and academic outcomes in middle childhood: Narrowing the achievement gap? Paper presented at the 2013 Biennial Meeting of the Society for Research in Child Development held in Seattle, WA.*

Pierce, K. M., Bolt, D. M., & Vandell, D. L. (2010). Specific features of after-school program quality: Associations with children's functioning in middle childhood. *American Journal of Community Psychology, 45*(3/4), 381–393.

Polanco-Roman, L., Danies, A., & Anglin, D. M. (2016). Racial discrimination as race-based trauma, coping strategies, and dissociative symptoms among emerging adults. *Psychological Trauma, 8*(5), 609–617.

Pollak, S. D., Nelson, C. A., Schlaak, M. F., Roeber, B. J., Wewerka, S. S., Wiik, K. L., Frenn, K. A., Loman, M. M., & Gunnar, M. R. (2010). Neurodevelopmental effects of early deprivation in postinstitutionalized children. *Child Development, 81*(1), 224–236.

Priest, N., Paradies, Y., Trenerry, B., Truong, M., Karlsen, S., & Kelly, Y. (2013). A systematic review of studies examining the relationship between reported racism and health and wellbeing for children and young people. *Social Science Medicine, 95*, 115–127.

Procentese, F., Gatti, F., & Di Napoli, I. (2019). Families and social media use: The role of parents' perceptions about social media impact on family systems in the relationship between family collective efficacy and open communication. *International Journal of Environmental Research and Public Health*, 16(24), 5006, 1–38.

Reiss, F. (2013). Socioeconomic inequalities and mental health problems in children and adolescents: A systematic review. *Social Science Medicine, 90*, 24–31.

Reiss, F., Meyrose, A. K., Otto, C., Lampert, T., Klasen, F., & Ravens-Sieberer, U. (2019). Socioeconomic status, stressful life situations and mental health problems in children and adolescents: Results of the German BELLA cohort-study. *PLoS One, 14*(3), e0213700. https://doi.org/10.1371/journal/pone.0213700

Rodgers, K. B., & McGuire, J. K. (2012). Adolescent sexual risk and multiple contexts: Interpersonal violence, parenting, and poverty. *Journal of Interpersonal Violence, 27*(11), 2091–2107.

Rodrigues, C., de Figueiredo, S., & Dias, F. D. (2012). Families: Influences in children's development and behavior, from parents and teachers' point of view. *Psychology Research, 2*(12), 693–705.

Rybak, A., & McAndrew, F. T. (2006). How do we decide whom our friends are? Defining levels of friendship in Poland and the United States. *The Journal of Social Psychology, 146*(2), 147–163.

Saewyc, E. M., Taylor, D., Homma, Y., & Ogilvie, G. (2008). Trends in sexual health and risk behaviours among adolescent students in British Columbia. *Canadian Journal of Human Sexuality, 17*(1–2), 1–13.

Senn, T. E., Walsh, J. L., & Carey, M. P. (2014). The mediating roles of perceived stress and health behaviors in the relation between objective, subjective, and neighborhood socioeconomic status and perceived health. *Annals of Behavioral Medicine, 48*(2), 215–224.

Singh, S., Roy, D., Sinha, K., Parveen, S., Sharma, G., & Joshi, G. (2020). Impact of

COVID-19 and lockdown on mental health of children and adolescents: A narrative review with recommendations. *Psychiatry Research, 93*, 113429. https://doi.org/10.1016/j.psychres.2020.113429

Skinner, E. A., & Zimmer-Gembeck, M. J. (2007). The development of coping. *Annual Review of Clinical Psychology, 58*, 119–144.

Sliwa, S. A., Lee, S. M., Gover, L. E., & Morris, D. D. (2022). Out of school time providers innovate to support school-aged children during the COVID-19 pandemic. *Preventing Chronic Disease, 19*, 210347.

Smith, W. (2010). *The impact of racial trauma on African Americans*. The Heinz Endowments. http://www.heinz.org/userfiles/impactofracialtraumaonafricanamericans.pdf

Sparr, M., Morrison, C., Miller, K., Bartko, W. T., Strachan, E., & Staples, B. (2012). Masturbation. *Pediatrics in Review, 33*(4), 190–191.

Strachan, E., & Staples, B. (2012). Masturbation. *Pediatric Review, 33*(4), 190–191.

Thompson, R. A. (2008). Early attachment and later development: Familiar questions, new answers. In J. Cassidy & P. R. Shaver (Eds.), *Handbook of attachment: Theory, research, and clinical applications* (pp. 348–365). Guilford Press.

Tice, D. M., Bratslavsky, E., & Baumeister, R. F. (2001). Emotional distress regulation takes precedence over impulse control: If you feel bad, do it! *Journal of Personality and Social Psychology, 80*(1), 53–67.

United States Department of Education. (2021). *Supporting child and student social, emotional, behavioral, and mental health needs.*, https://www2.ed.gov/documents/students/supporting-child-student-social-emotional-behavioral-mental-health.pdf

United States Department of Health & Human Services. (2022). *Prevention: Learn how to identify bullying and stand up to it safely.* https://www.stopbullying.gov/

Veenstra, R., Lindenberg, S., Oldehinkel, A. J., de Winter, A. F., Verhulst, F. C., & Ormel, J. (2005). Bullying and victimization in elementary schools: A comparison of bullies, victims, bully/victims, and uninvolved preadolescents. *Developmental Psychology, 41*(4), 672–682.

Vohs, K. D., & Baumeister, R. F. (2011). *Handbook of self-regulation: Research, theory and applications* (2nd ed.). Guilford Press.

Waters, S. F., Virmani, E. A., Thompson, R. A., Meyer, S. A., Raikes, H. A., & Jochem, R. (2010). Emotion regulation and attachment: Unpacking two constructs and their association. *Journal of Psychopathology and Behavioral Assessment, 32*(1), 37–47.

Waters, T. E. A., Bosmans, G., Vandevivere, E., Dujardin, A., & Waters, H. S. (2015). Secure base representations in middle childhood across two Western cultures: Associations with parental attachment representations and maternal reports of behavior problems. *Developmental Psychology, 51*(8), 1013–1025.

Welch, K. J. (2010). *THINK human sexuality* (1st ed.). Pearson Education.

Westwood Research & Statistical Services. (2017). *2015-16 school year statewide evaluation.*

Whittle, S., Simmons, J. G., Dennison, M., Vijayakumar, N., Schwartz, O., Yap, M., Sheeber, L., & Allen, B. (2014). Positive parenting predicts the development of adolescent brain structure: A longitudinal study. *Developmental Cognitive Neuroscience, 8*, 7–17.

Widman, L., Choukas-Bradley, S., Noar, S. M., Nesi, J., & Garrett, K. (2016). Parent-adolescent sexual communication and adolescent safer sex behavior: A meta-analysis. *JAMA Pediatrics, 170*(1), 52–61.

Wiederman, M. W. (2005). The gendered nature of sexual scripts. *The Family Journal, 13*(4), 496–502.

Wikkeling-Scott, L. F. (2011). *An examination of the influence of mother-child communication and maternal monitoring on sexual behavior in African American high school students.* Dr. P.H. Thesis. Morgan State University.

Wolke, D., & Lereya, S. T. (2015). Long-term effects of bullying. *Archives of Disease in Childhood, 100*(9), 879–885.

Wurtele, S. K., & Kenny, M. C. (2012). Preventing childhood sexual abuse: An ecological approach. In P. Goodyear-Brown (Ed.), *Handbook of child sexual abuse: Identification, assessment and treatment* (pp. 531–565). Wiley Press.

Youth.gov. (2021). *Benefits for youth, families, & Communities.*

https://youth.gov/youth-topics/afterschool-programs/benefits-youth-families-and-communities

Zimmer-Gembeck, M. J., Webb, H. J., Pepping, C. A., Swan, K., Merlo, O., Skinner, E. A., Avdagic, E., & Dunbar, M. (2015). Review: Is parent-child attachment a correlate of children's emotion regulation and coping? *International Journal of Behavioral Development*, *41*(1), 74–93.

Ziv, Y., Benita, M., & Sofri, I. (2017). Self-regulation in childhood: A developmental perspective. In J. L. Matson (Ed.), *Handbook of social behavior and skills in children* (pp. 149–173). Springer International.

CHAPTER 7

Adams, G. R., & Jones, R. M. (1983). Female adolescents' identity development: Age comparisons and perceived child-rearing experience. *Developmental Psychology*, *19*, 249–256.

Adamson, L., & Lyxell, B. (1996). Self-concept and questions of life: Identity development during late adolescence. *Journal of Adolescence*, *19*(6), 569–582.

Alan Guttmacher Institute. (2004). *U.S. teenage pregnancy statistics: Overall trends, trends by race and ethnicity, and state-by-state information*. Alan Guttmacher Institute.

Alan Guttmacher Institute. (2019). *Unintended pregnancy in the United States*. https://www.guttmacher.org/fact-sheet/unintended-pregnancy-united-states

Altschul, I., Lee, S. J., & Gershoff, E. T. (2016). Hugs, not wits: Warmth and spanking as predictors of child social competence. *Journal of Marriage and Family*, *78*(3), 695–714.

American Lung Association. (2022). *State of tobacco control: 2022*. https://www.lung.org/research/sotc

American Psychiatric Association (APA). (2013). *Diagnostic and statistical manual of mental disorders (DSM V)*.(5th ed.). https://doi-org.ezproxy.frederick.edu/10.1176/appi.books.9780890425596

Andrews, J. L., Foulkes, L., & Blakemore, S. J. (2020). Peer influence in adolescence: Public-health implications for COVID-10. *Trends in Cognitive Science*, *24*(8), 585–587.

Arain, M., Haque, M., Johal, L., Mathur, P., Nel, W., Rais, A., Sandhu, R., & Sharma, S. (2013). Maturation of the adolescent brain. *Neuropsychiatric Disease and Treatment*, *9*, 449–461.

Arat, G., & Wong, P. W. C. (2017). The relationship between physical activity and mental health among adolescents in six middle-income countries: A cross-sectional study. *Child & Youth Services*, *38*(3), 180–195.

Arcus, M. E., Schvaneveldt, J. D., & Moss, J. J. (Eds.). (1993). *Handbook of family life education. Vol. 1. Foundations of family life education; Vol. 2. The practice of family life education*. SAGE.

Assini-Meytin, L. C., & Green, K. M. (2015). Long-term consequences of adolescent parenthood among African American urban youth: A propensity matching approach. *Journal of Adolescent Health*, *56*(5), 529–535.

Assink, M., van der Put, C. E., Hoeve, M., De Vries, S. L. A., Stams, G. J. J. M., & Oort, F. J. (2015). Risk factors for persistent delinquent behaviors among juveniles: A meta-analytic analysis. *Clinical Psychology Review*, *42*, 47–61.

Association of Maternal & Child Health Programs. (2021). *Adolescent development: An overview*. http://www.amchp.org/programsandtopics/AdolescentHealth/projects/Pages/AdolescentDevelopment.aspx

Ati, N. A., Praswati, M. D., & Windarwati, H. D. (2020). What are the risk factors and protective factors of suicidal behavior in adolescents? A systematic review. *Journal of Child & Adolescent Psychiatric Nursing*, *34*, 7–18.

Barnes, G., & Farrell, M. (1992). Parental support and control as predictors of adolescent drinking, delinquency, and related problem behaviors. *Journal of Marriage and the Family*, *54*(4), 763–776.

Baumrind, D. (1991). The influence of parenting style on adolescent competence and substance use. *The Journal of Early Adolescence*, *11*(1), 56–95.

Baumrind, D., Larzelere, R. E., & Owens, E. B. (2010). Effects of preschool parents' power assertive patterns and practices on adolescent development. *Parenting*, *10*(3), 157–201.

Benson, P. L., & Scales, P. C. (2011). Developmental assets. In R. J. R. Levesque (Ed.), *Encyclopedia of adolescence*. Springer.

Benson, P. L., Scales, P. C., Leffert, N., & Roehlkepartain, E. C. (2011). *A fragile foundation: The state of adolescent assets among American youth* (2nd ed.). Search Institute.

Blakemore, S. J. (2018). Avoiding social risk in adolescence. *Current Directions in Psychological Science*, *27*, 116–122.

Boelen, P. A., & Lenferink, L. I. M. (2021). Prolonged grief disorder in DSM-5-TR: Early predictors and longitudinal measurement invariance. *Australian & New Zealand Journal of Psychiatry*. https://doi.org/10.1177/00048674211025728

Bogenschneider, K., Wu, M., Raffaelli, M., & Tsay, J. (1998). Parent influences on adolescent peer orientation and substance use: The interface of parenting practices and values. *Journal of Marriage and the Family*, *69*(6), 1672–1688.

Bornstein, M. (Ed.). (2019). *Handbook of parenting: Social conditions and applied parenting* (3rd ed., Vol. 4). Routledge.

Branje, S. (2018). Development of parent-adolescent relationships: Conflict interactions as a mechanism of change. *Child Development Perspective*, *12*(3), 171–176.

Branje, S. J. T., Laursen, B., & Collins, W. A. (2012). The Routledge handbook of family communication. In A. L. Vangelisti (Ed.), *The Routledge handbook of family communication* (2nd ed., pp. 271–286). Routledge.

Brassell, A. A., Rosenberg, E., Parent, J., & Rough, J. N. (2016). Parent's psychological flexibility: Associations with parenting and child psychosocial well-being. *Journal of Contextual Behavioral Science*, *5*, 111–120.

Bruffaerts, R., Demyttenaere, K., Borges, G., Haro, J. M., Chiu, W. T., Hwang, I., Karam, E. G., Kessler, R. C., Sampson, N., Alonso, J., Andrade, L. H., Angermeyer, M., Benjet, C., Bromet, E., de Girolamo, G., de Graaf, R., Florescu, S., Gureje, O., Horiguchi, I., ... Nock, M. K. (2010). Childhood adversities as risk factors for onset and persistence of suicidal behaviour. *British Journal of Psychiatry*, *197*(1), 20–27.

Bruhl, A., Kley, H., Grocholewski, A., Neuner, F., & Heinrichs, N. (2019). Child maltreatment, peer victimization, and social anxiety in adulthood: A cross-sectional study in a treatment-seeking sample. *BMC Psychiatry*, *19*, 418.

Burnett Heyes, S., Jih, Y. R., Block, P., Hiu, C. F., Holmes, E. A., & Lau, J. Y. (2015). Relationship reciprocation modulates resource allocation in adolescent social networks: Developmental effects. *Child Development*, *86*(5), 1489–1506.

Butler, O., Yang, X. F., Laube, C., Kühn, S., & Immordino-Yang, M. H. (2018). Community violence exposure correlates with smaller gray matter volume and lower IQ in urban adolescents. *Human Brain Mapping*, *39*(5), 2088–2097.

Byers, E. S., O'sullivan, L. F., & Brotto, L. A. (2016). Time out from sex or romance: Sexually experienced adolescents' decisions to purposefully avoid sexual activity or romantic relationships. *Journal of Youth and Adolescence*, *45*, 831–845.

Calafat, A., Garcia, F., Juan, M., Becona, E., & Fernandez-Hermida, J. R. (2014). Which parenting style is more protective against adolescent substance use? Evidence within the European context. *Drug and Alcohol Dependence*, *138*, 185–192.

Carballo, J. J., Llorente, C., Kehrmann, L., Flamarique, I., Zuddas, A., Purper-Ouakil, D., Hoekstra, P. J., Coghill, D., Schulze, U. M. E., Dittmann, R. W., Buitelaar, J. K., Castro-Fornieles, J., Lievesley, K., Santosh, P., Arango, C., & STOP Consortium. (2020). Psychosocial risk factors for suicidality in children and adolescents. *European Child & Adolescent Psychiatry*, *29*, 759–776.

Cavanaugh, A. M., & Buehler, C. (2015). Adolescent loneliness and social anxiety: The role of multiple sources of support. *Journal of Social and Personal Relationships*, *33*(2), 149–170.

Centers for Disease Control and Prevention (CDC). (2020a). Youth risk behavior surveillance: United States, 2019. *MMWR*, *69*(1), 1–88.

Centers for Disease Control and Prevention (CDC). (2020b). *Reasons to get vaccinated: Human Papillomavirus (HPV)*. https://www.cdc.gov/hpv/parents/vaccine/six-reasons.html

Centers for Disease Control and Prevention (CDC). (2021a). *STD risk and oral sex: Fact sheet*. https://www.cdc.gov/st

d/healthcomm/stdfact-stdriskandoralsex.htm

Centers for Disease Control and Prevention (CDC). (2021b). *Sexually transmitted diseases: Adolescents and young adults*. https://www.cdc.gov/std/life-stages-populations/adolescents-youngadults.htm

Centers for Disease Control and Prevention (CDC). (2021c). *Adolescent and school health: Sexual risk behaviors can lead to HIV, STDs, and teen pregnancy*. https://www.cdc.gov/healthyyouth/sexualbehaviors/index.htm

Centers for Disease Control and Prevention (CDC). (2021d). *Preventing teen dating violence*. https://www.cdc.gov/violenceprevention/intimatepartnerviolence/teendatingviolence/fastfact.html1

Centers for Disease Control and Prevention (CDC). (2021e). Emergency department visits for suspected suicide attempts among persons aged 12-25 years before and during the COVID-19 pandemic: United States, January 2019-May 2021. *MMWR, 70*(24), 888–894.

Cheon, Y. M., Ip, P. S., Haskin, M., & Hip, T. (2020, May). Profiles of adolescent identity at the intersection of ethnic/racial identity, American identity, and subjective social status. *Frontiers in Psychology, 15*. https://doi.org/10.3389/fpsyg.2020.00959

Cherry, K., & Morin, A. (2021). *Identity vs role confusion in psychosocial development*. https://www.verywellmind.com/identity-versus-confusion-2795735

Child Trends Databank. (2019). *Suicidal teens*. https://www.childtrends.org/?indicators=suicidal-teens, https://www.thetrevorproject.org/wp-content/uploads/2020/07/The-Trevor-Project-National-Survey-Results-2020.pdf

Ciocanel, O., Power, K., Eriksen, A., & Gillings, K. (2017). Effectiveness of positive youth development interventions: A meta-analysis of randomized controlled trials. *J Youth Adolescence, 46*, 483–504. https://doi.org/10.1007/s10964-016-0555-6

Clark, M., Buchanan, R., Kovensky, R., & Leve, L. D. (2018). Partner influences on young women's risky drug and sexual behavior. *Reproductive Health, 15*, 156.

Cleveland, M. J., Feinberg, M. E., & Greenberg, M. T. (2010). Protective families in high- and low-risk environments: Implications for adolescent substance use. *Journal of Youth and Adolescence, 39*, 114–126.

Cole-Lewis, Y. C., Gipson, P. Y., Opperman, K. J., Arango, A., & King, C. A. (2016). Protective role of religious involvement against depression and suicidal ideation among youth with interpersonal problems. *Journal of Religion and Health, 55*(4), 1172–1188.

Collibee, C., Furman, W., & Shoop, J. (2019). Risky interactions: Relational and developmental moderators of substance use and dating aggression. *Journal of Youth and Adolescence, 48*, 102–113.

Crenshaw, K. (1991). Mapping the margins: Intersectionality, identity politics, and violence against women of color. *Stanford Law Review, 43*, 1241–1299.

Cui, Z., Oshri, A., Liu, S., Smith, E. P., & Kogan, S. M. (2020). Child maltreatment and resilience: The promotive and protective role of future orientation. *Journal of Youth and Adolescence, 49*, 2075–2089.

Curtin, S. C. (2020). State suicide rates among adolescents and young adults aged 10–24: United States, 2000–2018. *National Vital Statistics Reports, 69*(11). National Center for Health Statistics.

Diamond, L. M., & Dubé, E. M. (2002). Friendship and attachment among heterosexual and sexual-minority youths: Does the gender of your friend matter? *Journal of Youth and Adolescence, 31*(2), 155–166.

Dickenson, J. A., & Huebner, D. M. (2016). The relationship between sexual activity and depressive symptoms in lesbian, gay, and bisexual youth: Effects of gender and family support. *Archives of Sexual Behavior, 45*, 671–681.

Dimler, L. M., Natsuaki, M. N., Hastings, P. D., Zahn-Waxler, C., & Klimes-Dougan, B. (2017). Parenting effects are in the eye of the beholder: Parent-adolescent differences in perceptions affects adolescent problem behaviors. *Journal of Youth and Adolescence, 46*, 1076–1088.

Ducharme, F., Kergoat, M. J., Antoine, P., Pasquier, F., & Coulombe, R. (2013). The uniqueexperience of spouses in early-onset dementia. *American Journal of Alzheimer's Disease and Other Dementias, 28*(6), 634–641.

Eaton, L. K., Kann, L., Kinchen, S., Shanklin, S., Ross, J., Hawkins, J., Harris, W. A.,

Lowry, R., McManus, T., Chyen, D., Lim, C., Brener, N. D., Wechsler, H., & Centers for Disease Control and Prevention (CDC). (2008). Youth risk behavior surveillance: United States, 2007, surveillance summaries. *Morbidity and Mortality Weekly Report, 57*(SS04), 1–131.

Eisenberg, N., Fabes, R. A., & Murphy, B. C. (1996). Parents' reactions to children's negative emotions: Relations to children's social competence and comforting behavior. *Child Development, 67*, 2227–2247.

Erikson, E. H. (1963). *Childhood and society* (2nd ed.). Norton.

Erikson, E. (1968). *Identity: Youth and crisis*. Norton.

Eshel, N., Daelmans, B., de Mello, M. C., & Martines, J. (2006). Responsive parenting: Interventions and outcomes. *Bulletins of the World Health Organization, 84*, 991–998.

Espelage, D. L. (2002). Bullying in early adolescence: The role of the peer group. *ERIC digest. ERIC clearinghouse on elementary and early childhood education*. (ERIC Document Reproduction Service No. ED471912).

Feinstein, S. G. (2009). *Secretes of the teenage brain: Research-based strategies for reaching and teaching today's adolescents* (2nd ed.). Corwin Press.

Feinstein, B. A., McConnell, E., Dyar, C., Mustanski, B., & Newcomb, M. E. (2018). Minority stress and relationship functioning among young male same-sex couples: An examination of actor–partner interdependence models. *Journal of Consulting and Clinical Psychology, 86*(5), 416–426.

Forman-Hoffman, V. L., Glasheen, C., & Batts, K. R. (2017). Marijuana use, recent marijuana initiation, and progression to marijuana use disorder among young male and female adolescents aged 12-14 living in U.S. households. *Substance Abuse: Research and Treatment, 11*, epub.

Franco, M., & McElroy-Heltzel, S. (2019). Let me choose: Primary caregiver cultural humility, racial identity, and mental health for multiracial people. *Journal of Counseling Psychology, 66*(3), 269–279.

Fredkova, W. M., Gower, A. L., & Sieving, R. E. (2019). Association among internal assets, bullying, and emotional distress among eight grade students. *Journal of School Health, 89*(11), 883–889.

Freisthler, B., & Kepple, J. J. (2019). Types of substance use and punitive parenting: A preliminary exploration. *Journal of Social Work Practice in the Addictions, 19*(3), 262–283.

Furman, W. (2002). The emerging field of adolescent romantic relationships. *Current Directions in Psychological Science, 11*(5), 177–180.

Furman, W., & Buhrmester, D. (1992). Age and sex differences in perceptions of networks of personal relationships. *Child Development, 63*, 103–115.

Garcia, T. A., Litt, D. M., Cue Davis, K., Norris, J., Kaysen, D., & Lewis, M. A. (2019). Growing up, hooking up, and drinking: A review of uncommitted sexual behavior and its association with alcohol use and related consequences among adolescents and young adults in the United States. *Frontiers in Psychology, 10*, 1872. https://doi.org/10.3389/fpsyg.2019.01872

Garcia, R., Reiber, C., Massey, S. G., & Merriwether, A. M. (2013). Sexual hookup culture. *Review of General Psychology, 16*(2), 161–176.

Ghandour, R. M., Sherman, L. J., Vladutiu, C. J., Ali, M. M., Lynch, S. E., Bitsko, R. H., & Blumberg, S. J. (2019). Prevalence and treatment of depression, anxiety, and conduct problems in U.S. children. *Journal of Pediatrics, 206*, 256–267, E3.

Gill, K., & Caffaso, J. (2018). *What is synaptic pruning?* https://www.healthline.com/health/synaptic-pruning

Goldston, D. B., Sergent Daniel, S., Erkanli, A., Reboussin, B. A., Mayfield, A., Frazier, P. H., & Treadway, S. L. (2009). Psychiatric diagnoses as contemporaneous risk factors for suicide attempts among adolescents and young adults: Developmental changes. *Journal of Consulting & Clinical Psychiatry, 77*(2), 281–290.

Gottman, J. M., Katz, L. F., & Hooven, C. (1996). Parental meta-emotion philosophy and the emotional life of families: Theoretical models and preliminary data. *Journal of Family Psychology, 10*, 243–268.

Granic, I. (2005). Timing is everything—developmental psychopathology from a dynamic systems perspective. *Developmental Review, 25*, 386–407.

Grello, C. M., Welsh, D. P., & Harper, M. S. (2006). No strings attached: The nature of casual sex in college students. *Journal of Sex Research, 43*(3), 255–267.

Grello, C. M., Welsh, D. P., Harper, M. S., & Dickson, J. W. (2003). Dating and sexual relationship trajectories and adolescent functioning. *Adolescent & Family Health, 3*(3), 103–112.

Grigorenko, E. L. (2017). Brain development: The effect of interventions on children and adolescents. In D. A. P. Bundy, N. D. Silva, S. Horton, & et al. (Eds.), *Child and adolescent health and development* (3rd ed.). The International Bank for Reconstruction and Development/The World Bank.

Gullotta, T. P. (2015). After-school programming and SEL. In J. A. Durlak, C. E. Domitrovich, R. P. Weissberg, & T. P. Gullotta (Eds.), *Handbook of social and emotional learning: Research and practice* (pp. 260–281). The Guilford Press.

Haines, K. M., Reyn Boyer, C., Giovanazzi, C., & Paz Galupo, M. (2018). "Not a real family": Microaggressions directed toward LGBTQ Families. *Journal of Homosexuality, 65*(9), 1138–1151.

Halgunseth, L. C. (2019). Latino and Latin American parenting. In M. H. Bornstein (Ed.), *Handbook of parenting: Volume 4: Social conditions and applied parenting* (3rd ed., pp. 24–56). Routledge.

Hanson, S. L. (1992). Involving families in programs for pregnant teens: Consequences for teens and their families. *Family Relations, 41*, 303–311.

Harding, J. F., Knab, J., Zief, S., Kelly, K., & McCallum, D. (2020). A systematic review of programs to promote aspects of teen parents' self-sufficiency: Supporting educational outcomes and health birth spacing. *Maternal and Child Health, 24*(Suppl. 2), 84–104.

Harding, J. F., Morris, P. A., & Hill, J. (2017). Understanding associations between low-income mothers' participation in education and parenting. *Journal of Research on Educational Effectiveness, 10*(4), 704–731.

van Harmelen, A. L., Blakemore, S. J., Goodyer, I. M., & Kievit, R. A. (2021). The interplay between adolescent friendship quality and resilient functioning following childhood and adolescent adversity. *Adversity and Resilience Science, 2*, 37–50.

Harris, M. B. (2013). *School experiences of gay and lesbian youth: The invisible minority.* Routledge.

Healthy Children. (2021). *Anxiety in teens is rising: What's going on?* https://www.healthychildren.org/English/health-issues/conditions/emotional-problems/Pages/Anxiety-Disorders.aspx

Hellman, M. (2018). Social causes of depression, anxiety, and stress. *Nordic Studies on Alcohol and Drugs, 33*(3), 149–151.

Hemovich, V., & Crano, W. D. (2009). Family structure and adolescent drug use: An exploration of single-parent families. *Substance Use & Misuse, 44*(14), 2099–2113.

Hendrick, C. E., & Maslowsky, J. (2019). Teen mothers educational attainment and their children's risk for teenage childbearing. *American Psychological Association, 55*(6), 1259–1273.

Henneberger, A. K., Mushonga, D. R., & Preston, A. M. (2020). *Peer influence and adolescent substance use: A systematic review of dynamic social network research. Adolescent Research Review.* file:///Users/11786/Downloads/Peer_influence_in_adolescent_drinking_behavior_A_m.pdf

Hodgkinson, S., Beers, L., Southammakosane, C., & Lewin, A. (2014). Addressing the mental health needs of pregnant and parenting adolescents. *Pediatrics, 133*(1), 114–122.

Hodgkinson, S., Godoy, L., Savio Beers, L., & Lewin, A. (2017). Improving mental health access for low-income children and families in the primary care setting. *Pediatrics, 139*(1), e20151175. https://doi.org/10.1542/peds.2015-1175

Hoffman, J., & Johnson, R. (1998). A national portrait of family structure and adolescent drug use. *Journal of Marriage and the Family, 60*, 633–645.

Hoskins, D. H. (2014). Consequences of parenting on adolescent outcomes. *Societies, 4*(3), 506–531.

Hou, Y., Kim, S. Y., & Benner, A. D. (2018). Parent–Adolescent discrepancies in reports of parenting and adolescent outcomes in Mexican immigrant families. *Journal of Youth and Adolescence, 47*, 430–444.

Huijbregts, S. C. J., Warren, A. J., Sonneville, L. M. J., & Swaab-Barneveld, H. (2007). Hot and cool forms of inhibitory control and externalizing behavior in children of mothers who smoked during pregnancy: An exploratory study. *Journal of Abnormal Psychology, 36*(3), 323–333.

Human, L. J., Dirks, M. A., DeLongis, A., & Chen, E. (2016). Congruence and incongruence in adolescents' and parents' perceptions of the family: Using response surface analysis to examine links with adolescents' psychological adjustment. *Journal of Youth and Adolescence, 45*(10), 2022–2035.

Icenogle, G., Steinberg, L., Duell, N., Chein, J., Chang, L., Chaudhary, N., Di Giunta, L., Dodge, K. A., Fanti, K. A., Lansford, J. E., Oburu, P., Pastorelli, C., Skinner, A. T., Sorbring, E., Tapanya, S., Uribe Tirado, L. M., Alampay, L. P., Al-Hassan, S. M., Takash, H. M. S., ... Bacchini, D. (2019). Adolescents' cognitive capacity reaches adult levels prior to their psychosocial maturity: Evidence for a "maturity gap" in a multinational, cross-sectional sample. *Law and Human Behavior, 43*(1), 69–85.

Ioannidis, K., Askelund, A. D., Kievit, R. A., & van Harmelen, A-L. (2020). The complex neurobiology of resilient functioning after childhood maltreatment. *BMC Medicine, 18*, 32.

Jabagchourian, J. J., Sorkhabi, N., Quach, W., & Strage, A. (2014). Parenting styles and practices of Latino parents and Latino fifth graders' academic, cognitive, social, and behavioral outcomes. *Hispanic Journal of Behavioral Sciences, 36*(2), 175–194.

Jager, J., Mahler, A., An, D., Putnick, D. L., Bornstein, M. H., Lansford, J. E., Dodge, K. A., Skinner, A. T., & Deater-Deckard, K. (2016). Early adolescents' unique perspectives of maternal and paternal rejection: Examining their across-dyad generalizability and relations with adjustment 1 year later. *Journal of Youth and Adolescence, 45*(10), 2108–2124.

Jamnik, M. R., & DiLalla, L. F. (2019). Health outcomes associated with internalizing problems in early childhood and adolescence. *Frontiers in Psychology, 10*(25). https://doi.org/10.3389/fpsyg.2019.00060

Jaworska, N., & MacQueen, G. (2015). Adolescence as a unique developmental period. *Journal of Psychiatry and Neuroscience, 40*(5), 291–293.

Jespersen, J. E., Hardy, N. R., & Sheffield Morris, A. (2021). Parent and peer emotion responsivity styles: An extension of Gottman's emotion socialization parenting typologies. *Children, 8*(319), 1–15.

Jorge, K. O., Ferreira, R. C., Ferreira, E. F. E., Kawachi, I., Zarzar, P. M., & Pordeus, I. A. (2018). Peer group influence and illicit drug use among adolescent students in Brazil: A cross-sectional study. *Cad Saúde Pública, 34*(3), e00144316.

Judd, N., Sauce, B., Wiedenhoeft, J., Tromp, J., Chaarani, B., Schliep, A., van Noort, B., Penttilä, J., Grimmer, Y., Insensee, C., Becker, A., Banaschewski, T., Bokde, A. L. W., Quinlan, E. B., Desrivières, S., Flor, H., Grigis, A., Gowland, P., Heinz, A., ... Klingberg, T. (2020). *Cognitive and brain development is independently influenced by socioeconomic status and polygenic scores for educational attainment. Proceedings of the National Academy of Sciences, 202001228*. https://doi.org/10.1073/pnas/2001228117

Julian, K. (2018). The sex recession. *The Atlantic, 322*(5), 78–94.

Kalin, N. H. (2021). Anxiety, depression, and suicide in youth. *American Journal of Psychiatry, 178*(4), 275–279.

Kansky, J., & Allen, J. P. (2018). Making sense and moving on: The potential for individual and interpersonal growth following emerging adult breakups. *Emerging Adulthood, 6*(3), 172–190.

Karavasilis, L., Doyle, A. B., & Markiewicz, D. (2003). Associations between parenting style and attachment to mother in middle childhood and adolescence. *International Journal of Behavioral Development, 27*(2), 153–164.

Khaleque, A., & Ali, S. (2017). A systematic review of meta-analyses of research on interpersonal acceptance–rejection theory: Constructs and measures. *Journal of Family Theory & Review, 9*(4), 441–458.

King, D., Delfabbro, P. H., Doh, Y. Y., & Wu, A. M. S. (2018). Policy and prevention approaches for disordered and hazardous gaming and Internet use: An international perspective. *Prevention Science, 34*, 233–249.

Kinsey Institute. (2020). *FAQs and sex information.* https://kinseyinstitute.org/research/faq.php

Kobak, R., Abbott, C., Zisk, A., & Bounoua, N. (2017). Adapting to the changing needs of adolescents: Parenting practices and challenges to sensitive attunement. *Current Opinion in Psychology, 15,* 137–142.

Koni, E., Moradi, S., Arahanga-Doyle, H., Neha, T., Hayhurst, J. G., Boyes, M., Cruwys, T., Hunter, J. A., & Scarf, D. (2019). Promoting resilience in adolescents: A new social identity benefits those who need it most. *PLoS One, 14*(1), e0210521. https://doi.org/10.1371/journal.pone.0210521

Korchmaros, J. D., Ybarro, N. L., & Mitchell, K. J. (2015). Adolescent online romantic relationship initiation: Differences by sexual and gender identification. *Journal of Adolescence, 40,* 54–64.

Korelitz, K. E., & Garber, J. (2016). Congruence of parents' and children's perceptions of parenting: A meta-analysis. *Journal of Youth and Adolescence, 45*(10), 1973–1995.

Kunz, J. H., & Grych, J. H. (2013). Parental psychological control and autonomy granting: Distinctions and associations with child and family functioning. *Parenting: Science and Practice, 13*(2), 77–94.

Landry, S. H., Smith, K. E., Swank, P. R., & Guttentag, C. (2008). A responsive parenting intervention: The optimal timing across early childhood for impacting maternal behaviors and child outcomes. *Developmental Psychology, 44,* 1335–1353.

Larson, N. C. (2004). Parenting stress among adolescent mothers in the transition to adulthood. *Child and Adolescent Social Work Journal, 21*(5), 457–476.

Lehrman, G. (2001). *The history of private life: Courtship in early America.* The Gilder Lehrman Institute of American History. http://yalepress.yale.edu

Lensch, T., Clements-Nolle, K., Oman, R. F., Lu, M., & Dominguez, A. (2019). Prospective impact of individual, family, and community youth assets on adolescent suicide ideation. *Journal of Epidemiology & Community Health, 73*(3), 219–224.

Lerner, R. M., & Hilliard, L. J. (2019). A relational developmental systems perspective on parenting. In R. M. Lerner & L. J. Hilliard (Eds.), *Handbook of parenting* (3rd ed., pp. 3–23). Routledge.

Levey, D. F., Gelernter, J., Polimanti, R., Zhou, H., Cheng, Z., Aslan, M., Quaden, R., Concato, J., Radhakrishnan, K., Bryois, J., Sullivan, P. F., & Million Veteran Program, & Stein, M. B. (2020). Reproducible genetic risk loci for anxiety: Results from 200,000 participants in the Million Veteran Program. *American Journal of Psychiatry, 177,* 223–232.

Lew, B., Huen, J., Yu, P., Yuan, L., Wang, D. F., Ping, F., Abu Talib, M., Lester, D., & Jia, C. X. (2019). Associations between depression, anxiety, stress, hopelessness, subjective well-being, coping styles, and suicide in Chinese university students. *PLoS One, 14*(7), e0217372.

Lewis, M. A., Granato, H., Blayney, J. A., Lostutter, T. W., & Kilmer, J. R. (2012). Predictors of hooking up sexual behaviors and emotional reactions among US college students. *Archives of Sexual Behavior, 41*(5), 1219–1229.

Lichtwarck-Aschoff, A., Kunnen, S. E., & Van Geert, P. L. (2009). Here we go again: A dynamic systems perspective on emotional rigidity across parent-adolescent conflicts. *Developmental Psychology, 45,* 1364–1375.

Lodge, M., & Taber, C. S. (2005). The automaticity of affect for political leaders, groups, and issues: An experimental test of the hot cognition hypothesis. *Political Psychology, 26*(3), 455–482.

Loke, A. Y., & Mak, Y. (2013). Family process and peer influences on substance use by adolescents. *International Journal of Environmental Research & Public Health, 10*(9), 3868–3885.

Lyons, H. A., Manning, W. D., Longmore, M. A., & Giordano, P. C. (2015). Gender and casual sexual activity from adolescence to emerging adulthood: Social and life course correlates. *The Journal of Sex Research, 52*(5), 543–557.

MacKin, D. M., Perlman, G., Davila, J., Kotov, R., & Klein, D. N. (2017). Social support buffers the effect of interpersonal life stress on suicidal ideation and self-injury during adolescence. *Psychological Medicine, 47*(6), 1149–1161.

Maddow-Zimet, I., & Kost, K. (2021). *Pregnancies, births and abortions in the United States, 1973–2017: National and state trends by age.* Guttmacher Institute. https://www.guttmacher.org/report/pregnancies-birth

s-abortions-in-united-states-1973-2017

Maddow-Zimet, I., Kost, K., & Finn, S. (2021). *Pregnancies, births, and abortions in the United States, 1973-2017: National and state trends by age*. *Guttmacher Institute*. https://www.guttmacher.org/report/pregnancies-births-abortions-in-united-states-1973-2017

Mahoney, A., & Boyatzis, C. J. (2019). *Handbook of parenting: Parenting, religion, and spirituality* (3rd ed., Vol. 5). Routledge.

Manning, W. D., Giordano, P. C., & Longmore, M. A. (2006). Hooking up: The relationship contexts of 'nonrelationship' sex. *Journal of Adolescent Research*, *21*(5), 459–483.

Marcia, J. E. (1966). Development and validation of ego-identity status. *Journal of Personality and Social Psychology*, *3*, 551–558.

Marcia, J. E. (1993). The relational roots of identity. In J. Kroger (Ed.), *Discussions on ego identity* (pp. 101–120). Erlbaum.

Martin-Storey, A., & August, E. G. (2016). Harassment due to gender nonconformity mediates the association between sexual minority identity and depressive symptoms. *Journal of Sex Research*, *53*(1), 85–97.

Martin, A., Brazil, A., & Brooks-Gun, J. (2013). The socioemotional outcomes of young children of teenage mothers by paternal coresidence. *Journal of Family Issues*, *34*, 1217–1237.

McDonough, M. H., Jose, P. E., & Stuart, J. (2016). Bi-directional effects of peer relationships and adolescent substance use: A longitudinal study. *Journal of Youth and Adolescence*, *45*, 1652–1663.

McLoyd, V. C., Hardaway, C. R., & Jocosn, R. M. (2019). African American parenting. In M. H. Bornstein (Ed.), *Handbook of parenting: Volume 4: Social conditions and applied parenting* (3rd ed., pp. 57–107). Routledge.

Melby, J., Conger, R., Conger, K., & Lorenz, F. (1993). Effects of parental behavior on tobacco use by young male adolescents. *Journal of Marriage and the Family*, *55*(2), 439–454.

Mendle, J., Ferrero, J., Moore, S. R., & Harden, K. P. (2013). Depression and adolescent sexual activity in romantic and nonromantic relational contexts: A genetically-informative sibling comparison. *Journal of Abnormal Psychology*, *122*(1), 51–63.

Mercurio, E., Carcia-Lopez, E., Morales-Quintero, L. A., Llamas, N. E., Marinaro, J. Á., & Muñoz, J. M. (2020). Adolescent brain development and progressive legal responsibility in the Latin American context. *Frontiers in Psychology*, *11*, 627. https://doi.org/10.3389/fpsyg.2020.00627

Mills-Koonce, R., Rehder, P. D., & McCurdy, A. L. (2018). The significance of parenting and parent-child relationships for sexual and gender minority adolescents. *The Journal of Research on Adolescence*, *28*(3), 637–649.

Montano, G. T., Thoma, B. C., Paglisotti, T., Weiss, P. M., Shultz, M. K., McCauley, H. L., Miller, E., & Marshal, M. P. (2018). Disparities in parental support and parental attachment between heterosexual and sexual minority youth: A meta-analysis. *Journal of Adolescent Health*, *62*(2), S32–S33.

Muir, N. M., Bohr, Y., Shepherd, M. J., Healey, G. K., & Warne, D. K. (2019). Indigenous parenting. In M. H. Bornstein (Ed.), *Handbook of parenting (vol. 4): Social conditions and applied parenting* (3rd ed., pp. 170–197). Routledge.

Murphy, D. A., Greenwell, L., Resell, J., Breacht, M. L., & Schuster, M. A. (2008). Early and middle adolescents' autonomy development: Impact of maternal HIV/AIDS. *Clinical Child Psychology & Psychiatry*, *13*(2), 253–276.

National Center for Drug Abuse Statistics (NCDAS). (2022). *Drug use among youth: Facts and statistics*. https://drugabusestatistics.org/teen-drug-use/

National Conference of State Legislatures (NCSL). (2018). *Teen pregnancy prevention*. https://www.ncsl.org/research/health/teen-pregnancy-prevention.aspx#:~:text=to%20older%20parents.-,Economic%20Wellbeing%20and%20the%20Cycle%20of%20Poverty,year%20of%20a%20child's%20birth

Natsuaki, M. N., Leve, L. D., & Mendle, J. (2011). Going through the rites of passage: Timing and transition of menarche, childhood sexual abuse, and anxiety symptoms in girls. *Journal of Youth and Adolescence*, *40*(1), 1357–1370.

Nazeer, A., Latif, F., Mondal, A., Zeem, M. W., & Greydanus, D. E. (2020). Obsessive-compulsive disorder in children and adolescents: Epidemiology, diagnosis, and management. *Translational Pediatrics, 9*(Suppl. 1), S76–S93.

Needle, R., Su, S., & Doherty, W. (1990). Divorce, remarriage, and adolescent substance use: A prospective longitudinal study. *Journal of Marriage and the Family, 52*(1), 157–169.

Nelemans, S. A., Branje, S. J. T., Hale, W. W., Goosens, L., Koot, E. M., Oldehinkel, A. J., & Meeus, W. H. J. (2016). Discrepancies between perceptions of the parent–adolescent relationship and early adolescent depressive symptoms: An illustration of polynomial regression analysis. *Journal of Youth and Adolescence, 45*, 2049–2063.

Nesi, J. (2018). Transformation of adolescent peer relations in the social media context: Part 2 – application to peer group processes and future directions for research. *Clinical Child and Family Psychology Review, 21*, 295–319.

Ng, F.-Y., & Wang, Q. (2019). Asian and Asian American parenting. In M. H. Bornstein (Ed.), *Handbook of parenting: Volume 4: Social conditions and applied parenting* (3rd ed., pp. 108–169). Routledge.

Office of Population Affairs. (2022). *Trends in teen pregnancy and childbearing. U.S. Department of Health and Human Services*. https://actionnetwork.org/forms/sex-ed-for-all-month/

Ohlsson, C., Bygdell, M., Celind, J., Sondén, A., Tidblad, A., Sävendahl, L., & Kindblom, J. M. (2019). Secular trends in pubertal growth acceleration in Swedish boys born from 1947-1996. *JAMA Pediatrics, 173*(9), 860–865.

Oswalt, S. B., Cameron, K. A., & Koob, J. J. (2005). Sexual regret in college students. *Archives of Sexual Behavior, 34*(6), 663–669.

Owen, J., Finchan, F. D., & Moore, J. (2011). Short-term prospective study of hooking up among college students. *Archives of Sexual Behavior, 40*(2), 331–341.

Padilla-Walker, L. M., Nielson, M. G., & Day, R. D. (2016). The role of parental warmth and hostility on adolescents' prosocial behavior toward multiple targets. *Journal of Family Psychology, 30*(3), 331–340.

Panova, T., & Carbonell, X. (2018). Is smartphone addiction really an addiction? *Journal of Behavioral Addiction, 7*(2), 252–259.

Paul, E. L., McManus, B., & Hayes, A. (2000). Hookups: Characteristics and correlates of college students' spontaneous and anonymous sexual experiences. *Journal of Sex Research, 37*, 76–88.

Peçi, B. (2017). Peer influence and adolescent sexual behavior trajectories: Links to sexual initiation. *European Journal of Multidisciplinary Studies, 2*(3), 96–105.

Pedersen, M. L., Holen, S., Lydersen, S., Martinsen, K., Neumer, S-P., Adolfsen, F., & Sund, A. M. (2019). School functioning and internalizing problems in young school children. *BMC Psychology, 7*(88). https://doi.org/10.1186/s40359019-0365-1

Pew Research Center. (2015). *Teens, social media, & technology*. https://www.pewresearch.org/internet/2015/04/09/teens-social-media-technology-2015/

Pew Research Center. (2019a). *Why is the teen birth rate falling?* https://www.pewresearch.org/fact-tank/2019/08/02/why-is-the-teen-birth-rate-falli

Pew Research Center. (2019b). *Most U.S. teens see anxiety and depression as a major problem among their peers*. https://www.pewresearch.org/social-trends/2019/02/20/most-u-s-teens-see-anxiety-and-depression-as-a-major-problem-among-their-peers/

Phares, V., & Renk, K. (1998). Perceptions of parents: A measure of adolescents' feelings about their parents. *Journal of Marriage and Family, 60*, 646–659.

Piqueras, J. A., Soto-Sanz, V., Rodriguez-Marin, J., & Garcia-Oliva, J. (2019). What is the role of internalizing and externalizing symptoms in adolescent suicide behaviors? *International Journal of Environmental Research and Public Health, 16*(2511), 1–13.

Planned Parenthood. (2017). *What's a dental dam?* https://www.plannedparenthood.org/learn/teens/ask-experts/whats-a-dental-dam

Prins, S. J., Kajeepeta, S., Pearce, R., Beardslee, J., Pardini, D., & Cerdá, M. (2020). Identifying sensitive periods when changes in parenting and peer factors are associated with changes in adolescent alcohol and marijuana use. *Social Psychiatry and*

Psychiatric Epidemiology, 56, 605–617.

Quinlivan, J. A., Tan, L. H., Steele, A., & Black, K. (2004). Impact of demographic factors, early family relationships, and depressive symptomatology in teenage pregnancy. *Australian and New Zealand Journal of Psychiatry, 38*(4), 197–208.

Reczek, C. (2020). Sexual- and gender-minority families: A 2010 to 2020 decade in review. *Journal of Marriage and Family, 82*(1), 300–325.

Reichelt, A. C., & Rank, M. M. (2017). The impact of junk foods on the adolescent brain. *Birth Defects Research, 109*(20), 1649–1658.

Reid, V., & Meadows-Oliver, M. (2007). Postpartum depression in adolescent Mothers: An integrative review of the Literature. *Journal of Pediatric Health Care, 21*, 289–298.

Roaten, G. K., & Roaten, D. J. (2012). Adolescent brain development: Current research and the impact of secondary school counseling programs. *Journal of School Counseling, 10*(18). http://www.jsc.montana.edu/articles/v10n18.pdf

Rodriguez, M. M. D., Donovick, M. R., & Crowley, S. L. (2009). Parenting styles in cultural context: Observations of "protective parenting" in first-generation Latinos. *Family Process, 48*(2), 195–210.

Roehlkepartain, E. C., & Blyth, D. A. (2019). Developmental assets. In D. T. L. Shek & J. Leung (Eds.), *The encyclopedia of child and adolescent development: Volume 7: History, theory, & culture in adolescence*. Wiley.

Rowan, Z. R. (2016). Social risk factors of Black and white adolescents' substance use: The differential role of siblings and best friends. *Journal of Youth and Adolescence, 45*(7), 1482–1496.

Ruiz, L. D., Zuelch, M. L., Dimitratos, S. M., & Scherr, R. E. (2020). Adolescent obesity: Diet quality, psychosocial health, and cardiometabolic risk factors. *Nutrients, 12*(1), 43. https://doi.org/10.3390/nu12010043

Ryan, C., Russell, S. T., Huebner, D., Diaz, R., & Sanchez, J. (2010). Family acceptance in adolescence and the health of LGBT young adults. *Journal of Child and Adolescent Psychiatric Nursing, 23*(4), 205–213.

Samek, D. R., Goodman, R. J., Riley, L., McGue, M., & Iacono, W. G. (2018). The developmental unfolding of sibling influences on alcohol use over time. *Journal of Youth and Adolescence, 47*(2), 349–368.

SAMHSA. (2017). *Comparison of physical health conditions among adolescents Aged 12 to 17 with and without major depressive episode*. https://www.samhsa.gov/data/sites/default/files/CBHSQ-DR-MH9-HealthCond-2017/CBHSQ%20Physical%20Health%20Conditions%20among%20Adolescents%20Aged%2012%20to%2017%20%E2%80%93%20MH9.pdf

Sawyer, S. M., Azzopardi, P. S., Wickremaranthne, D., & Patton, G. C. (2018). The age of adolescence. *The Lancet Child & Adolescent Health, 2*(3), 223–228.

Schneider, D., Hastings, O. P., & LaBriola, J. (2018). Income inequality and class divides in parental investments. *American Sociological Review, 83*(3), 475–507.

Schwartz, O. S., Dudgeon, P., Sheeber, L. B., Yap, M. B. H., Simmons, J. G., & Allen, N. B. (2012). Parental behaviors during family interactions predict changes in depression and anxiety symptoms during adolescence. *Journal of Abnormal Child Psychology, 40*, 59–71.

Shaw, P., Greenstein, D., Lerch, J., Lenroot, R., Gogtay, N., Evans, A., Rapoport, J., & Giedd, J. (2006). Intellectual ability and cortical development in children and adolescents. *Nature, 440*, 676–679.

Shubert, J., Wray-Lake, L., Syvertsen, A. K., & Metzger, A. (2019). The role of family civic context in character development across childhood and adolescence. *Applied Developmental Science, 26*(1), 15–30.

Smetana, J. G. (2011). Adolescents' social reasoning and relationships with parents: Conflicts and co-ordinations within and across domains. In E. Amsel & J. G. Smetana (Eds.), *Adolescent vulnerabilities and opportunities: Developmental and constructivist perspectives* (pp. 139–158). Cambridge University Press.

Sorkhabi, N., & Middaugh, E. (2014). How variations in parents' use of confrontive and coercive control relate to variations in parent–adolescent conflict, adolescent disclosure, and parental knowledge: Adolescents' perspective. *Journal of Child and Family Studies, 23*(7), 1227–1241.

Spencer, C., Stith, S., Durtschi, J., & Toews, M. (2020). Factors related to college students' decisions to report sexual assault. *Journal of Interpersonal Violence*, *35*(21–22), 4666–4685.

Spiekerman, A. M., Witkow, M. R., & Nishina, A. (2021). Peer victimization and depressive symptoms during adolescence: Examining the roles of social support and internalizing coping. *The Journal of Early Adolescence*, *41*(4), 505–526.

Spinrad, T. L., Morris, A. S., & Luthar, S. S. (2020). Introduction to the special issue: Socialization of emotion and self-regulation: Understanding processes and application. *Developmental Psychology*, *56*, 385–389.

Steers, M. N., Neighbors, C., & Wickham, R. E. (2019). My friends, I'm #SOTALLYTOBER: A longitudinal examination of college students' drinking, friends' approval of drinking, and Facebook alcohol-related posts. *Digital Health*, *6*(5). https://doi.org/10.1177/2055207619845449

Steinberg, L. (2001). We know some things: Adolescent-parent relationships in retrospect and prospect. *Journal of Research on Adolescence*, *11*, 1–19.

Steinberg, L. (2008). *Adolescence*. McGraw-Hill.

Steinberg, L. (2009). Adolescent development and juvenile justice. *Annual Review of Clinical Psychology*, *5*, 459–485.

Steinberg, L. (2011). Demystifying the adolescent brain. *Educational Leadership*, *68*(7), 42–46.

Steingard, R. J. (2021). *Mood disorders and teenage girls*. *Child Mind Institute*. https://childmind.org/article/mood-disorders-and-teenage-girls/

Strome, A., Moore-Petinak, N., Waselewski, M., & Chang, T. (2022). Youth's knowledge and perceptions of health risks associated with unprotected oral sex. *Annals of Family Medicine*, *20*(1), 72–76.

Suicide Prevention Resource Center. (2011). *Suicide and bullying: Issue brief*. https://sprc.org/sites/default/files/migrate/library/Suicide_Bullying_Issue_Brief.pdf

The Trevor Project. (2020). *The national survey on LGBTyouth*. https://www.thetrevorproject.org/wp-content/uploads/2020/07/The-Trevor-Project-National-Survey-Results-2020.pdf

Thoma, B. C., Eckstrand, K. L., Montano, G. T., Rezeppa, T. L., & Marshal, M. P. (2021). Gender nonconformity and minority stress among lesbian, gay, and bisexual individuals: A meta-analytic review. *Perspectives on Psychological Science*, *16*(6), 1165–1183.

Tolman, D. L., & McClelland, S. I. (2011). Normative sexuality development in adolescence: A decade in review, 2000-2009. *Journal of Research on Adolescence*, *21*(1), 242–255.

UCLA Williams Institute. (2020). *LGBT youth population in the United States*. https://williamsinstitute.law.ucla.edu/publications/lgbt-youth-pop-us/

United Health Foundation. (2021). *Anxiety and depression*. https://www.americashealthrankings.org/explore/health-of-women-and-children/measure/depression_children/state/ALL

Valiente, C., Swanson, J., DeLay, D., Fraser, A. M., & Parker, J. H. (2020). Emotion-related socialization in the classroom: Considering the roles of teachers, peers, and the classroom context. *Developmental Psychology*, *56*, 578–594.

VanderValk, I., Spruijt, E., de Goede, M., Maas, C., & Meeus, W. (2005). Family structure and problem behavior of adolescents and young adults: A growth-curve study. *Journal of Youth and Adolescence*, *34*(6), 533–546.

Wade, L. (2017). What's so cultural about hookup culture? *Contexts*, *16*(1), 66–68.

Waller, J. M., Silk, J. S., Stone, L. B., & Dahl, R. E. (2014). Corumination and co-problem-solving in the daily lives of adolescents with major depressive disorder. *Journal of the American Academy of Child and Adolescent Psychiatry*, *53*, 869–878.

Walters, G. D. (2021). Explaining the drug-crime connection with peers, proactive criminal thinking, and victimization: Systemic, cognitive social learning, and person proximity mechanisms. *Psychology of Addictive Behaviors*, *35*(3), 366–376.

Wang, M.-T., Kiuru, N., Degol, J., & Salmela-Aro, K. (2018). Friends, academic achievement, and school engagement during adolescence: A social network approach to peer influence and selection effects. *Learning and Instruction*, *58*, 148–160.

Wang, J., Nansel, T. R., & Iannotti, R. J. (2011). Cyber bullying and traditional bullying:

Differential association with depression. *Journal of Adolescent Health, 48*(4), 415–417.

Watson, R., Shahin, Y. M., & Arbeit, M. R. (2018). Hookup initiation and emotional outcomes differ across young LGB men and women. *Sexualities, 22*(5–6), 932–950.

Weaver, J., & Masalehdan Block, A. (2020). Identity development in biracial children: Contextual factors from social work. *Keystone Journal of Undergraduate Research, 7*(1), 13–22.

Whitney, D. G., & Peterson, M. D. (2019). US national and state-level prevalence of mental health disorder and disparities of mental health care use in children. *JAMA Pediatrics, 14*(4), 389–391.

Whittle, S., Simmons, J. G., Dennison, M., Vijaykumar, N., Schwartz, O., Yap, M. B., Sheeber, L., & Allen, N. B. (2014). Positive parenting predicts the development of adolescent brain structure: A longitudinal study. *Developmental Cognitive Neuroscience, 8*, 7–17.

Whittle, S., Vijayakumar, N., & Simmons, J. G. (2017). Role of positive parenting in the association between neighborhood social disadvantage and brain development across adolescence. *JAMA Psychiatry, 74*(8), 824–832.

Williams, L. R., & Russell, S. T. (2013). Shared social and emotional activities within adolescent romantic and nonromantic sexual relationships. *Archives of Sexual Behavior, 42*, 649–658.

Wray-Lake, L., Crouter, A. C., & McHale, S. M. (2010). Developmental patterns in decision-making autonomy across middle childhood and adolescence: European American parents' perspectives. *Child Development, 81*(2), 636–651.

Yu, M., Linn, K. A., Shinohara, R. T., Oathes, D. J., Cook, P. A., Duprat, R., Moore, T. M., Oquendo, M. A., Phillips, M. L., McInnis, M., Fava, M., Trivedi, M., McGrath, P., Parsey, R., Weissman, M. M., & Sheline, Y. I. (2019). Childhood trauma history is linked to abnormal brain connectivity in major depression. *PNAS, 116*(17), 8582–8590.

van Zantvliet, P. I., Ivanova, K., & Verbakel, E. (2018). Adolescents' involvement in romantic relationships and problem behavior: The moderating effect of peer norms. *Youth & Society, 52*(4), 574–591.

Zell, E., Strickhouser, J. E., & Krizan, Z. (2018). Subjective social status and health: A meta-analysis of community and society ladders. *Health Psychology, 37*, 979–987.

CHAPTER 8

AARP. (2020). *1 in 5 Americans now provide unpaid care.* https://www.aarp.org/caregiving/basics/info-2020/unpaid-family-caregivers-report.html

Adkins, V. (1999). Grandparents as a national asset: A brief note. *Activities, Adaptation, and Aging, 24*, 13–18.

Aldous, J. (1985). New views of grandparents in intergenerational context. *Journal of Family Issues, 16*(1), 104–122.

Alpert, R. T. (1991). Our lives are the text: Exploring Jewish women's rituals. *Bridges, 2*(1), 66–80.

American Psychological Association. (2005). *Controlling anger before it controls you.* www.apa.org/pubinfo/anger.html

Aquilino, W. S. (2006). Family relationships and support systems in emerging adulthood. In J. J. Arnett & J. L. Tanner (Eds.), *Emerging adults in America: Coming of age in the 21st century* (pp. 193–217). American Psychological Association.

Arias, E., Tejada-Vera, B., & Ahmad, F. (2021, February). *Provisional life expectancy estimates for January through June, 2020.* Vital statistics rapid release; no 10. National Center for Health Statistics. http://doi.org/10.15620/cdc:100392

Arnett, J. J. (2000). Emerging adulthood: A theory of development from the late teens through the twenties. *American Psychologist, 55*(5), 469.

Arnett, J. J. (2004). *Emerging adulthood: The winding road from the late teens through the early twenties.* Oxford University Press.

Atchley, R. C. (2000). *Social forces and aging* (9th ed.). Wadsworth.

Baltes, P. B., Lindenberger, U., & Staudinger, U. M. (1998). Life-span theory in developmental psychology. In W. Damon & R. M. Lerner (Eds.), *Handbook of child psychology: Theoretical models of human development* (pp. 1029–1143). John Wiley & Sons Inc.

Barber, S. J. (2017). An examination of age-based stereotype threat about cognitive decline: Implications for stereotype-threat research and theory development. *Perspectives on Psychological Science, 12*, 62–90.

Birditt, K. S., Tighe, L. A., Fingerman, K. L., & Zarit, S. H. (2012). Intergenerational relationship quality across three generations. *The Journals of Gerontology, Series B: Psychological Sciences and Social Sciences, 67*, 627–638.

Bosse, R., Aldwin, C. M., Levinson, M. R., Workman-Daniels, K., & Ekerdt, D. J. (1990). Differences in social support among retirees and workers: Findings from the normative aging study. *Psychology of Aging, 5*, 41–47.

Bougea, A., Despoti, A., & Vasilopoulos, E. (2019). Empty-nest-related psychosocial stress: Conceptual issues, future directions in economic crisis. *Psychiatriki, 30*(4), 329–338.

Boyd, D., & Bee, H. (2009). *Lifespan development* (5th ed.). Allyn & Bacon.

Brody, E. M. (1985). Parent care as a normative family stress. *The Gerontologist, 25*, 19–29.

Brody, E. M., & Schoonover, C. (1986). Patterns of parent care when adult daughters work and when they do not. *The Gerontologist, 26*, 371–281.

Burton, L., Dilworth-Anderson, P., & Merriwether-de-Vries, C. (1995). Context of surrogate parenting among contemporary grandparents. *Marriage and Family Review, 20*, 349–366.

Cavanaugh, J. C., & Blanchard-Fields, F. (2002). *Adult development and aging* (4th ed.). Wadsworth.

Cherlin, A. J., & Furstenberg, F. F. (1986). *The new American grandparent*. Basic Books.

Conway, J., & Conway, S. (2000). *Parenting your parents*. www.midlife.com

Copp, J. E., Giordano, P. C., Longmore, M. A., & Manning, W. D. (2017). Living with parents and emerging adults' depressive symptoms. *Journal of Family Issues, 38*(16), 2254–2276.

Crimmins, E. M., & Ingegneri, D. G. (1990). Interaction and living arrangements of older parents and their children. *Research on Aging, 12*, 3–35.

Crosnoe, R., & Elder, G. H. (2002). Successful adaptation in the later years: A life course approach to aging. *Social Psychology Quarterly, 65*(4), 309–328.

Damman, M., Henkens, K., & Kalmijn, M. (2013). Late-career work disengagement: The roles of retirement and career experiences. *The Journals of Gerontology, 68*(3), 445–463.

Damman, M., Henkens, K., & Kalmijn, M. (2015). Missing work after retirement: The role of life histories in the retirement adjustment process. *The Gerontologist, 55*(5), 802–813.

Davis, E. M., Kim, K., & Fingerman, K. L. (2016). Is an empty nest best? Coresidence with adult children and parental marital quality before and after the Great Recession. *The Journal of Gerontology, Series B: Psychological Sciences and Social Sciences, 73*(3), 372–381. http://doi.org/10.1093/geronb/gbw022

Dunn, B., & Wamsley, B. (2018). Grandfamilies: Characteristics and needs of grandparents raising grandchildren. *The Journal of Extension, 56*(5), 7. https://joe.org/joe/2018september/rb2.php

Duvall, E. M. (1988). Family development's first forty years. *Family Relations, 37*(1), 127–134.

Family Caregiver Alliance. (2018). *Caregiver statistics: Demographics*. https://www.caregiver.org/caregiver-statistics-demographics

Fingerman, K. L. (2001). A distant closeness: Intimacy between parents and their children in later life. *Generations, 25*(2), 26–33.

Fingerman, K. L. (2017, November). Millennials and their parents: Implications of the new young adulthood for midlife adults. *Innovation in Aging, 1*(3), igx026. http://doi.org/10.1093/geroni/igx026

Fingerman, K. L., & Birditt, K. S. (2011). Relationships between adults and their aging parents. In K. W. Schaie & S. L. Willis (Eds.), *Handbook of the psychology of aging* (pp. 219–232). Elsevier Academic Press.

Fingerman, K. L., Kim, K., Birditt, K. S., & Zarit, S. H. (2016). The ties that bind: Midlife parents' daily experience with grown children. *Journal of Marriage and Family, 78*, 431–450.

Fingerman, K. L., Kim, K., Davis, E. M., Furstenberg, F.

F., Birditt, K. S., & Zarit, S. H. (2015). I'll give you the world: Parental socioeconomic background and assistance to young adult children. *Journal of Marriage and Family, 77*, 844–865.

Fry, R. (2016, May). *For first time in modern era, living with parents edges out other living arrangements for 18- to 34-year-olds*. Pew Research Center. https://www.pewresearch.org/social-trends/2016/05/24/for-first-time-in-modern-era-living-with-parents-edges-out-other-living-arrangements-for-18-to-34-year-olds/

Glass, J. C., & Hunneycutt, T. L. (2002). Grandparents parenting grandchildren: Extent of situation issues involved and educational implications. *Educational Gerontology, 28*(2), 139–161.

Goldsmith, J. (2018, August). Emerging adults' relationships with their parents. *Clinical Science Insights*, 1–6. https://www.family-institute.org/sites/default/files/pdfs/csi-emerging-adults-relationships-with-parents.pdf

Hamalainen, H., & Arpino, B. (2020, July). *Is support between parents and adult children reciprocal? Families and Households*. https://www.niussp.org/family-and-households/is-support-between-parents-and-adult-children-reciprocal-le-soutien-entre-parents-et-enfants-adultes-est-il-reciproque/

Hayflick, H. (1994). *How and why we age*. Ballantine.

He, W., Sangupta, M., Velkoff, V. A., & DeBarros, K. S. (2005). *65+ in the United States: 2005*. United States Census Bureau Current Population Reports, 23–209. www.census.gov/prod/2006pubs/p23-209.pdf

Hyde, M., Cheshire-Allen, M., Damman, M., Henkens, K., Platts, L., Pritchard, K., & Reed, C. (2018). *The experience of the transition to retirement: Rapid evidence review*. Centre for Aging Better. https://ageing-better.org.uk/resources/transition-to-retirement-rapid-evidence-review

Ingersoll-Dayton, B., Neal, M., Ha, J., & Hammer, L. (2003). Redressing inequity in parent care among siblings. *Journal of Marriage and Family, 65*, 201–212.

Institute for Latino Studies. (2010). Fictive kinship and acquaintance networks as sources of support and social capital for Mexican transmigrants in South Bend. *Institute for Latino Studies, 1*(1). https://latinostudies.nd.edu/assets/95249/original/3.7_fictive_kinship_and_acquaintance_networks.pdf

Jewsbury Conger, K., Conger, R. D., Russell, S. T., & Hollis, N. (2013). *Background paper: Parenting during the transitions to adulthood. Improving the health, safety, and well-being of young adults: Workshop summary*. Board on Children, Youth, and Families; Institute of Medicine, National Research Council. National Academies Press.

Johnson, C. L. (1999). Fictive kin among oldest old African Americans in the San Francisco Bay area. *Journals of Gerontology: Series B, Psychological Science and Social Science, 54*(6), S368–S375.

Kaufman, G., & Elder, G. H., Jr. (2003). Grandparenting and age identity. *Journal of Aging Studies, 17*(3), 269–282.

Kornrich, S., & Furstenberg, F. (2013). Investing in children: Changes in parental spending on children, 1972-2007. *Demography, 50*, 1–23.

Kreiczer-Levy, S. (2019). Parents and adult children: The elusive boundaries of the legal family. *Law & Social Inquiry, 44*(2), 519–525.

Kubicek, B., Korunka, C., Raymo, J. M., & Hoonakker, P. (2011). Psychological well-being in retirement: The effects of personal and gendered contextual resources. *Journal of Occupational Health Psychology, 16*(2), 230–246.

Kulik, L. (1999). Continuity and discontinuity in marital life after retirement: Life orientations, gender role ideology, intimacy, and satisfaction. *The Journal of Contemporary Human Services, 8*(3), 286–294.

Lee, H. J., & Szinovaca, M. E. (2016). Positive, negative, and ambivalent interactions with family and friends: Associations with well-being. *Journal of Marriage and Family, 78*, 660–679.

Lee, J. E., Zarit, S. H., Rovine, M. J., Birditt, K. S., & Fingerman, K. L. (2016). The interdependence of relationships with adult children and spouses. *Family Relations, 65*, 342–353.

Lemme, B. H. (2011). *Development in adulthood* (4th ed.). Pearson Education.

Leopold, T. (2012). The legacy of leaving home: Long-term effects of co-residence on parent-child relationships.

Journal of Marriage & Family, 74(3), 399–412.

Levy, B. R. (2009). Stereotype embodiment: A psychosocial approach to aging. *Current Directions in Psychological Science, 18*, 332–336.

MacRae, H. (1992). Fictive kin as a component of the social networks of older people. *Research on Aging, 14*, 226–247.

Mather, M., Jacobsen, L., Kilduff, L., Lee, A., Pollard, K. M., Scommegna, P., & Vonorman, A. (2019a). America's changing population: What to expect in the 2020 Census. *Population Bulletin, 74*(1), 1–21.

Mather, M., Scommenga, P., & Kilduff, L. (2019b). Fact sheet: Aging in the United States. *Population Bulletin, 70*(2), 1–20. https://www.prb.org/wp-content/uploads/2019/07/population-bulletin-2015-70-2-aging-us.pdf

Meisner, B. A. (2012). A meta-analysis of positive and negative age stereotype priming effects on behavior among older adults. *The Journals of Gerontology Series B: Psychological Sciences and Social Sciences, 67*, 13–17.

Moen, P., & Flood, S. (2013). Limited engagements? Women's and men's work/volunteer time in the encore life course stage. *Social Problems, 60*(2), 206–233.

Muresan, C., & Haragus, P. (2015). Norms of filial obligation and actual support to parents in central and Eastern Europe. *Journal of Population Studies, 9*(2), 49–82.

National Council on Aging. (2005). *Caregiver research: The latest news*. www.ncoa.org/

Nelson, L. J., Padilla-Walker, L. M., Carroll, J. S., Madsen, S. D., Barry, C. M., & Badger, S. (2007). If you want me to treat you like an adult, start acting like one! Comparing the criteria that emerging adults and their parents have for adulthood. *Journal of Family Psychology, 21*, 665–674.

Neugarten, B. L., & Weinstein, K. K. (1964). The changing American grandparent. *Journal of Marriage and the Family, 26*, 299–304.

Pebley, A. R., & Rudkin, L. L. (2020). *Grandparents caring for grandchildren*. RAND Corporation. https://www.rand.org/pubs/research_briefs/RB5030.html

Pew Research Center. (2019). *Majority of Americans say parents are doing too much for their young adult children*. https://www.pewresearch.org/social-trends/2019/10/23/majority-of-americans-say-parents-are-doing-too-much-for-their-young-adult-children/

Pew Research Center. (2020). *A majority of young adults in the U.S. live with their parents for the first time since the Great Depression*. https://www.pewresearch.org/fact-tank/2020/09/04/a-majority-of-young-adults-in-the-u-s-live-with-their-parents-for-the-first-time-since-the-great-depression/

Polenick, C. A., Birditt, K. S., & Zarit, S. H. (2018). Parental support of adult children and middle-aged couples' marital satisfaction. *The Gerontologist, 58*(4), 663–673.

Raphel, S. (2008). Kinship care and the situation for grandparents. *Journal of Childhood and Adolescent Psychiatric Nursing, 21*(2), 118–120.

Reynolds, G. P., Wright, J. V., & Beale, B. (2003). The roles of grandparents in educating today's children. *Journal of Instructional Psychology, 30*(4), 316–325.

Rowe, J., & Kahn, R. (1998). *Successful aging*. Random House.

Scales, P. C., Benson, P. L., Oesterle, S., Hill, K. G., Hawkins, J. D., & Pashak, T. J. (2016). The dimensions of successful young adult development: A conceptual and measurement framework. *Applied Developmental Science, 20*(3), 150–174.

Segatto, B., & Di Filippo, L. (2003). Relationship and emotions in couples in the retirement and/or empty nest phase. *Eta Evolutiva, 74*(1), 5–20.

Settersten, R. A., & Ray, B. E. (2010). *Not quite adults: Why 20-somethings are choosing a slower path to adulthood, and why it's good for everyone*. Bantam Books.

Sharon, T. (2015). Constructing adulthood: Markers of adulthood and well-being among emerging adults. *Journal of Emerging Adulthood, 4*(3), 161–167.

Social Security Administration. (2021). *Monthly statistical snapshot*. September 2019 – February 2020; September 2020 – February 2021.

Somary, K., & Stricker, G. (1998). Becoming a grandparent: A longitudinal study of expectations and early experiences as a function of sex and lineage. *The Gerontologist, 38*, 53–61.

Statista. (2021). *Number of people aged 100 and over (centenarians) in the United States from 2016 to 2060*. https://www.statista.com/statistics/996619/number-centenarians-us/

Steinberg, L. (2001). We know some things: Parent–adolescent relationships in retrospect and prospect. *Journal of Research on Adolescence, 11*, 1–19.

Stephens, M. A. P., Franks, M. M., & Atienza, A. A. (1997). Where two roles intersect: Spillover between parent care and employment. *Psychology and Aging, 12*, 30–37.

Stephens, M. A. P., & Franks, M. M. (1999). Intergenerational relationships in later-life families: Adult daughters and sons as caregivers to aging parents. In J. C. Cavanaugh & S. K. Whitbourne (Eds.), *Gerontology: An interdisciplinary perspective* (pp. 329–354). Oxford University Press.

Stephens, M. A. P., Townsend, A. L., Martire, L. M., & Druley, J. A. (2001). Balancing parent care with other roles: Interrole conflict of adu1t daughter caregivers. *Journal of Gerontology: Psychological Sciences, 56B*, P24–P34.

Szinovacz, M. E. (1998). Grandparents today: A demographic profile. *The Gerontologist, 38*, 37–52.

Taylor, R., Chatters, L., Cross, C. J., & Mouzon, D. (2022). Fictive kin networks among African Americans, Black Caribbeans, and Non-Latino Whites. *Journal of Family Issues, 43*(1). https://journals.sagepub.com/doi/abs/10.1177/0192513X21993188

Thomas, P. A., Liu, H., & Umberson, D. (2017). Family relationships and well-being. *Innovation in Aging, 1*(3). https://www.ncbi.nlm.nih.gov/pmc/articles/PMC5954612/

Thompson, L., & Walker, A. J. (1984). Mothers and daughters: Aid patterns and attachment. *Journal of Marriage and the Family, 46*, 313–322.

Troll, L., & Fingerman, K. L. (1996). Parent/child bonds in adulthood. In C. Malestesta-Magai & S. McFadden (Eds.), *Handbook of emotion, adult development and aging*. Academic Press.

Umberson, D. (1992). Gender, marital status, and the social control of health behavior. *Social Science & Medicine, 34*, 907–917.

U.S. Census Bureau. (2018). *The population 65 years and older in the United States: 2016*. American Community Survey Reports. https://www.census.gov/content/dam/Census/library/publications/2018/acs/ACS-38.pdf

United States Census Bureau. (2021). *Love and loss among older adults: Marriage, divorce, widowhood remain prevalent among older populations*. https://www.census.gov/library/stories/2021/04/love-and-loss-among-older-adults.html

U.S. Department of Health and Human Services. (2021). *2020 profile of older Americans*. The Administration for Community Living. https://acl.gov/sites/default/files/Aging%20and%20Disability%20in%20America/2020ProfileOlderAmericans.Final_pdf

U.S. Legal.com. (2017). *Age of majority law and legal definition*. https://definitions.uslegal.com/a/age-of-majority/

van Solinge, H., & Henkens, K. (2005). Couples' adjustment to retirement: A multi-actor panel study. *Journal of Gerontology: Social Sciences, 60B*, S11–S20.

Vespa, J. (2017). *The changing economics and demographics of young adulthood: 1975-2016*. U.S. Census Bureau: Current Population Reports. https://www.census.gov/content/dam/Census/library/publications/2017/demo/p20-579.pdf

Weiss, D., & Weiss, M. (2019). Why people feel younger: Motivational and social-cognitive mechanisms of the subjective age bias and its implications for work and organizations. *Work, Aging & Retirement, 5*, 273–280.

Weiss, D., & Zhang, X. (2020). Multiple sources of aging attitudes: Perceptions of age groups and generations from adolescence to old age across China, Germany, and the United States. *Journal of Cross-Cultural Psychology, 51*(6), 407–423.

White, L. (1992). The effect of parental divorce and remarriage on parental support for adult children. *Journal of Family Issues, 13*(2), 234–250.

Wiltz, T. (2016, November 2). *Why more grandparents are raising children*. http://www.pewtrusts.org/en/research-and-analysis/blogs/stateline/2016/11/02/why-more-grandparents-are-raising-children

Zarit, S. H., Birkel, R. C., & Malonebeach, E. (1989).

Spouses as caregivers: Stresses and interventions. In M. Z. Goldstein (Ed.), *Family involvement in the treatment of the frail elderly*. American Psychiatric Association.

CHAPTER 9

Ahrons, C. (1994). *The good divorce: Keeping your family together when your marriage comes apart*. HarperCollins.

Ahrons, C. (2007). *We're still family: What grown children have to say about their parents' divorce*. HarperCollins.

Ahrons, C., & Rodgers, R. H. (1987). *Divorced families: Meeting the challenge of divorce and remarriage*. Norton.

Ahrons, C., & Tanner, J. L. (2003). Adult children and their fathers: Relationship changes 20 years after parental divorce. *Family Relations, 52*, 340–351.

Al Ubaidi, B. A. (2017). The psychological and emotional stages of divorce. *Journal of Family Medicine and Disease Prevention, 3*(3), 1–4.

Amato, P. R. (2010). Research on divorce: Continuing trends and new developments. *Journal of Marriage and Family, 72*, 650–666.

Amato, P. R., & Rezac, S. (1994). Contact with nonresident parents, interparental conflict, and children's behavior. *Journal of Family Issues, 15*, 191–207.

Anderson, J. (2014). The impact of family structure on the health of children: Effects of divorce. *Linacre Quarterly, 81*(4), 378–387.

Anderson-Burdine, A., & Armstrong, J. (2014). *An in depth look at heterosexual single parent dating and effects on children.* Texas Women's University.

Anderson, S. A., & Sabatelli, R. M. (2011). *Family interaction: A multigenerational developmental perspective* (5th ed.). Pearson Education.

Arditti, J. (1999). Rethinking relationships between divorced mothers and their children: Capitalizing on family strengths. *Family Relations, 48*(2), 109–119.

Bailey, S., & Zvonkovic, A. (2003). Parenting after divorce. *Journal of Divorce and Remarriage, 39*(3/4), 59–80.

Baum, N. (2003). Divorce process variables and the co-parental relationship and parental role fulfillment of divorced parents: Family and couple research. *Family Process, 42*, 117–131.

Baum, N. (2006). Post-divorce paternal disengagement. *Journal of Marriage and Family Therapy, 32*, 245–254.

Beckmeyer, J. J., *Krejnik, S., *McCray, J., Markham, M. S., & Troilo, J. (November, 2018). Former spousal relationships and children's post-divorce well-being. In Paper presented at the National Council on Family Relations Annual Conference.

Bernsten, K. N., & Kravdal, O. (2012). The relationship between mortality and time since divorce, widowhood or remarriage in Norway. *Social Science & Medicine, 75*, 2267–2274.

Bohannan, P. (1971). *The curse of culture*. Holt, Rinehart, & Winston.

Bokker, P., Farley, R., & Denny, G. (2005). Emotional well-being among recently divorced fathers. *Journal of Divorce and Remarriage, 41*, 157–172.

Bonach, K., Sales, E., & Koeske, G. (2005). Gender differences in co-parenting quality. *Journal of Divorce and Remarriage, 42*, 1–28.

Bramlett, M. D., & Mosher, W. D. (2002). First marriage dissolution, divorce, and remarriage: United States. *Vital and Health Statistics, 323*. National Center for Health Statistics.

Braver, S., Shapiro, J. R., & Goodman, M. R. (2006). Consequences of divorce for parents. In M. A. Fine & J. H. Harvey (Eds.), *Handbook of divorce and relationship dissolution* (pp. 313–337). Erlbaum.

Bray, J. H. (1999). From marriage to remarriage and beyond. In E. M. Hetherington (Ed.), *Coping with divorce, single parenting, and remarriage* (pp. 253–271). Erlbaum.

Broadwell, L. (2019). *Age-by-age guide on the effects of divorce on children*. https://www.parents.com/parenting/divorce/coping/age-by-age-guide-to-what-children-understand-about-divorce/

Carlson, C. (1995). Working with single-parent and stepfamily systems. In A. Thomas & J. Grimes (Eds.), *Best practices in school psychology* (3rd ed., pp. 1097–1110). National Association of School Psychologists.

Cartwright, C. (2006). You want to know how it affected me? Young adults' perceptions of the impact of parental divorce. *Journal of Divorce and Remarriage, 44*(3/4), 125–143.

Coleman, M., Ganong, L. H., & Fine, M. (2000). Reinvestigating remarriage: Another decade of progress. *Journal of Marriage and the Family, 62*, 1288–1307.

Cooksey, E., & Craig, P. (1998). Parenting from a distance: The effects of parental characteristics on contact between nonresidential fathers and their children. *Demography, 35*(2), 187–200.

Cookston, J. T., Braver, S. L., Griffin, W., deLuse, S. R., & Miles, J. C. (2007). Effects of the dads for life intervention on interparental conflict and co-parenting in the two years after divorce. *Family Process, 46*(1), 123–137.

Criddle, M., & Scott, M. (2005). Mandatory divorce education and post-divorce parental conflict. *Journal of Divorce and Remarriage, 62*, 99–111.

Dacey, J., & Travers, J. (2002). *Human development across the lifespan* (5th ed.). McGraw-Hill.

Davis, E. C., & Friel, L. V. (2001). Adolescent sexuality: Disentangling the effects of family structure and family contexts. *Journal of Marriage and Family, 63*(3), 669–681.

De Vaus, D., Gray, M., Qu, L., & Stanton, D. (2015). *The economic consequences of divorce in six OECD countries* (Research Report No. 31). Australian Institute of Family Studies.

Dewilde, C. (2008). Divorce and the housing movements of owner-occupiers: A European comparison. *Housing Studies, 23*, 809–832.

DiIulio, J. J. (April 7, 1997). *Deadly divorce: Divorce can be hazardous to your health. National Review.* www.findarticles.com

Duck, S. W. (1982). A topography of relationship disengagement and dissolution. In S. W. Duck (Ed.), *Personal relationships, 4: Dissolving personal relationships* (pp. 1–30). Academic Press.

Dunlop, R., Bermingham, S., & Burns, A. (2001). Parent-child relations and adolescent self-image following divorce: A 10-year study. *Journal of Youth and Adolescence, 30*(2), 117–134.

Duran-Aydingtug, C. (1995). Former spouse interaction: Normative guidelines and actual behavior. *Journal of Divorce and Remarriage, 22*, 147–161.

Dykstra, P. A., & Fokkema, T. (2007). Social and emotional loneliness among divorced and married men and women: Comparing the deficit and cognitive perspectives. *Basic and Applied Social Psychology, 29*, 1–12.

Emery, R. E. (1994). *Renegotiating family relationships: Divorce, child custody, and mediation.* Guilford Press.

Fincham, F. D. (2002). Divorce. In N. J. Salkind (Ed.), *Child development: Macmillan psychology reference series.* Macmillan.

Finley, G. E. (2003). Father-child relationships following divorce. In J. R. Miller, R. M. Lerner, L. B. Schiamberg, & P. M. Anderson (Eds.), *Encyclopedia of human ecology* (Vol. 1, pp. 291–293). ABC-CLIO.

Fisher, B., & Alberti, R. (2000). *Rebuilding: When your relationship ends* (3rd ed.). Impact.

Furstenberg, F. F., & Allison, P. D. (1989). How marital dissolution affects children: Variations by age and sex. *Developmental Psychology, 25*, 540–549.

Furstenberg, F. F., & Cherlin, A. J. (1991). *Divided families: What happens to children when parents part.* Harvard University Press.

Ganong, L., & Coleman, M. (2004). *Stepfamily relationships: Development, dynamics, and interventions.* Kluwer Academic/Plenum.

Gerlach, P. (2005). *Forge a healthy remarriage.* http://sfhelp.org/01/bonding.htm

Gohm, C. L., Oishi, S., Darlington, J., & Diener, E. (1998). Culture, parental conflict, parental marital status, and the subjective well-being of young adults. *Journal of Marriage and the Family, 60*, 314–319.

Gold, L. (1992). *Between love and hate: A guide to civilized divorce.* Springer.

Gottfried, A. E., & Gottfried, A. W. (1994). *Redefining families: Implications for children's development.* Plenum.

Graham, L. (2005). *Resource guide for parenting after divorce.* Riley County District Court, State of Kansas.

Grall, T. (2018). *Custodial mothers and fathers and their child support: 2015.* Current

Population Reports, P60-262. U.S. Census Bureau.

Haimi, M., & Lerner, A. (2016). The impact of parental separation and divorce on the health status of children, and the ways to improve it. *Journal of Clinical and Medical Genomics*, *4*, 137.

Hallman, J., Dienhart, A., & Beaton, J. (2007). A qualitative analysis of fathers' experiences of parental time after separation and divorce. *Fathering: A Journal of Theory, Research, and Practice About Men as Fathers*, *5*, 4–24.

Hannum, J. W., & Dvorak, D. M. (2004). Effects of family conflict, divorce, and attachment patterns on the psychological distress and social adjustment of college freshmen. *Journal of College Student Development*, *45*(1), 27–42.

Henley, K., & Pasley, K. (2006). Coparenting following divorce. In M. Fine & J. Harvey (Eds.), *Handbook of divorce* (pp. 24–262). Erlbaum.

Hetherington, E. M. (1991). The role of individual differences and family relationships in children's coping with divorce and remarriage. In P. A. Cowan & E. M. Hetherington (Eds.), *Family transitions* (pp. 165–194). Erlbaum.

Hetherington, E. M. (2003). Intimate pathways: Changing patterns in close personal relationships across time. *Family Relations*, *52*, 318–331.

Hetherington, E. M., & Kelly, J. (2002). *For better or worse: Divorce reconsidered.* Norton.

Hinderlie, H. H., & Kenny, M. (2002). Attachment, social support, and college adjustment among Black students at predominantly white universities. *Journal of College Student Development*, *43*, 327–340.

Ihinger-Tallman, M., & Pasley, K. (1987). *Remarriage*. SAGE.

Institute for Family Studies. (2019). *The adult children of divorce find their voice*. https://ifstudies.org/blog/the-adult-children-of-divorce-find-their-voice

Jensen, T. M., Shafer, K., Guo, S., & Larson, J. H. (2015). Differences in relationship stability between individuals in first and second marriages: A propensity score analysis. *Journal of Family Issues*, *38*(3), 1–27.

Kalter, N., Alpern, D., Spence, R., & Plunkett, J. W. (1984). Locus of control in children of divorce. *Journal of Personality Assessment*, *48*(4), 410–414.

Kelly, J. B. (2007). Children's living arrangements following divorce. *Family Process*, *46*, 35–52.

Kelly, J. B., & Emery, R. E. (2003). Children's adjustment following divorce: Risk and resiliency perspectives. *Family Relations*, *52*(4), 352–362.

Kheshgi-Genovese, Z., & Genovese, T. A. (1997). Developing the spousal relationship within stepfamilies. *Families in Society*, *78*(3), 255–264.

King, V. (2002). Parental divorce and interpersonal trust in adult offspring. *Journal of Marriage and Family*, *64*(3), 642–656.

Kruk, E. (2012). *The vital importance of parental presence in children's lives*. http://www.psychologytoday.com/blog/co-parenting-after-divorce/201205/father-absence-father-deficit-father-hunger

Lehr, R., & MacMillan, P. (2001). The psychological and emotional impact of divorce: The noncustodial fathers' perspective. *Families in Society*, *82*(4), 373–382.

Leite, R. W., & McKenry, P. C. (2002). Aspects of father status and post-divorce father involvement with children. *Journal of Family Issues*, *23*, 601–623.

Leopold, T. (2018). Gender differences in the consequences of divorce: A study of multiple outcomes. *Demography*, *55*(3), 769–797.

Leopold, T., & Kalmijn, M. (2016). Is divorce more painful when couples have children? Evidence from long-term panel data on multiple domains of well-being. *Demography*, *53*, 1717–1742.

Lynch, J., & Kaplan, G. (2000). Socioeconomic position. In L. F. Berkman & I. Kawachi (Eds.), *Social epidemiology* (pp. 13–35). Oxford University Press.

Madden-Derdich, D., & Arditti, J. (1999). The ties that bind: Attachment between former spouses. *Family Relations*, *48*(3), 243–249.

Manning, W. D., Steward, S. D., & Smock, P. J. (2003). The complexity of fathers' parenting responsibilities and involvement with nonresident children. *Journal of Family Issues*, *24*(5), 645–667.

Marano, H. (March/April, 2000). Divorced? Don't even think of remarrying until you read this. *Psychology Today, 33*(2), 57–62.

Markham, M., Ganong, L., & Coleman, M. (2007). Mothers' cooperation in coparental relationships. *Family Relations, 56*, 369–377.

Mason, M. A., Fine, M. A., & Carnochan, S. (2001). Family law in the new millennium: For whose families? *Journal of Family Issues, 22*(7), 859–881.

Mayo Clinic. (2004). *Divorce: Helping your child cope with the breakup*. Children's Health. www.mayoclinic.com/health/divorce/HO00055

McIntyre, A., Heron, R. L., McIntyre, M. D., Burton, S. J., & Engler, J. N. (2003). College students from families of divorce: Keys to their resilience. *Journal of Applied Developmental Psychology, 24*, 17–31.

McLanahan, S. S., & Kelly, E. L. (2006). The feminization of poverty. In *Handbook of the sociology of gender* (pp. 127–145). Springer.

McLanahan, S. S., & Sandefur, G. (1994). *Growing up with a single parent: What hurts, what helps*. Harvard University Press.

McPherson, M., Brashears, M. E., & Smith-Lovin, L. (2006). Social isolation in America: Changes in core discussion networks over two decades. *American Sociological Review, 71*(3), 353–375.

Papernow, P. L. (1984). The stepfamily cycle: An experiential model for stepfamily development. *Family Relations, 33*, 355–363.

Papernow, P. L. (1993). *Becoming a stepfamily: Patterns of development in remarried families*. Jossey-Bass.

Parish, T. S., & Wigle, S. E. (1985). A longitudinal study of the impact of parental divorce on adolescents' evaluations of self and parents. *Adolescence, 20*(77), 239–244.

Parke, R. D., & Brott, A. A. (1999). *Throwaway dads: They myths and barriers that keep men from being the fathers they want to be*. Houghton Mifflin.

Parziale, J., & Parziale, J. B. (2002). *The journey: A traveling guide to Christian stepfamilies*. InStep Ministries.

Pew Research Center. (2014). *The demographics of remarriage*. https://www.pewsocialtrends.org/2014/11/14/chapter-2-the-demographics-of-remarriage/

Pew Research Center. (2018). *The changing profile of unmarried parents*. https://www.pewsocialtrends.org/2018/04/25/the-changing-profile-of-unmarried-parents/

Pleck, J. H. (1997). Paternal involvement: Levels, sources, and consequences. In M. E. Lamb (Ed.), *The role of the father in child development* (pp. 66–103). Wiley.

Robson, M., Cook, P., & Gilliland, J. (1995). Helping children manage stress. *British Education Research Journal, 21*(2), 165–174.

Sbarra, D. A. (2015). Divorce and health: Current trends and future directions. *Psychosomatic Medicine, 77*(3), 227–236.

Sbarra, D. A., Law, R. W., & Portley, R. M. (2011). Divorce and death: A meta-analysis and research agenda for clinical, social, and health psychology. *Perspectives on Psychological Science, 6*, 454–474.

Seymour, T., Francis, C., & Steffens, P. (1995). *Supporting stepfamilies: What do the children feel*? NF 95-223. University of Nebraska Cooperative Extension.

Shaw, D. S., & Ingoldsby, E. M. (1999). Children of divorce. In R. T. Ammerman, C. G. Last, & M. Hersen (Eds.), *Handbook of prescriptive treatments for children and adolescents* (2nd ed., pp. 346–363). Allyn & Bacon.

Shor, E., Roelfs, D. J., Bugyi, P., & Schwartz, J. E. (2012). Meta-analysis of marital dissolution and mortality: Reevaluating the intersection of gender and age. *Social Science & Medicine, 75*, 46–59.

Shoup Olsen, C. (1997). *Stepping stones for stepfamilies*. MF 2238. Kansas State University Cooperative Extension.

Stanley, S. M., & Fincham, F. D. (2002). The effects of divorce on children. *Couples Research and Therapy Newsletter, 8*(1), 7–10.

Stepfamily Association of America. (2009). *What is a stepfamily*? www.saafamilies.org/faqs/fats.htm

Stephenson, E., & Delongis, A. (2018). A 20-year prospective study of marital separation and divorce in stepfamilies: Appraisals of family stress as predictors. *Journal of Social and Personal Relationships, 36*(6), 1600–1618.

Stewart, S. D. (1999). Disneyland dads, Disneyland moms? How nonresident parents spend time with their children.

Journal of Family Issues, *20*, 539–556.

Stone, G. (2007). Father post-divorce well-being. *Journal of Divorce and Remarriage*, *41*, 139–150.

Strohschein, L. (2005). Parental divorce and child mental health trajectories. *Journal of Marriage and Family*, *67*(5), 1286–1300.

Sweeney, M. (2010). Remarriage and stepfamilies: Strategic sites for family scholarship in the 21st century. *Journal of Marriage and Family*, *72*, 667–684.

Umberson, D. (1992). Gender, marital status, and the social control of health behavior. *Social Science & Medicine*, *34*, 907–917.

United States Census Bureau. (2019). *National Stepfamily Day: September 16, 2018*. https://www.census.gov/newsroom/stories/2018/stepfamily.html

Visher, E. B., & Visher, J. S. (1993). *Stepfamilies: Myths and realities*. Citadel Press.

Wallerstein, J., & Kelly, J. (1980). *Surviving the break-up: How children actually cope with divorce*. Basic Books.

Wallerstein, J. S., & Lewis, M. (2004). The unexpected legacy of divorce: Report of a 25-year study. *Psychoanalytic Psychology*, *21*, 353–370.

Wallerstein, J. S., Lewis, J. M., & Blakeslee, S. (2000). *The unexpected legacy of divorce: A 25-year landmark study*. Hyperion.

Warshak, R. (2000). Remarriage as a trigger of parental alienation syndrome. *American Journal of Family Therapy*, *28*(3), 229–241.

White, L., & Gilbreth, J. G. (2001). When children have two fathers: Effects of relationships with stepfathers and noncustodial fathers on adolescent outcomes. *Journal of Marriage and Family*, *63*, 155–167.

Wickrama, K. A. S., Lorenze, F. O., Conger, R. D., & Elder, G. H. (2006). Changes in family financial circumstances and the physical health of married and recently divorced mothers. *Social Science and Medicine*, *63*, 123–136.

Williams, K., & Dunne-Bryant, A. (2006). Divorce and adult psychological well-being: Clarifying the role of gender and child age. *Journal of Marriage and Family*, *64*, 254–268.

Worthy. (2019). *Jumping in: Dating after divorce in 2019*. https://www.worthy.com/blog/knowledge-center/insights/study-on-dating-after-divorce-in-2019/

CHAPTER 10

AARP. (2019). *Understanding the impact of family caregiving on work*. https://www.aarp.org/content/dam/aarp/research/public_policy_institute/ltc/2012/understanding-impact-family-caregiving-work-AARP-ppi-ltc.pdf

Aboulhassan, S., & Brumley, K. M. (2018). Carrying the burden of a culture: Bargaining with patriarchy and the gendered reputation of Arab American women. *Journal of Family Issues*, *40*(5), 637–661.

Allegretto, S. (2005, September 1). *Basic family budgets: Working families' incomes often fail to meet living expenses around the U.S. Economic Policy Institute Briefing Paper #165*. www.epi.org/coinent.cfm/bpl65 (October 5, 2005).

Amato, P. R., Johnson, D. R., Booth, A., & Rogers, S. J. (2003). Continuity and change in marital quality between 1980 and 2000. *Journal of Marriage and the Family*, *65*(1), 1–22.

American Community Survey. (2017). *2017 ACS: 1-year estimates*. https://www.census.gov/programs-surveys/acs/technical-documentation/table-and-geography-changes/2017/1-year.html

American Community Survey. (2019). *Father's day: 2018*. https://www.census.gov/newsroom/stories/2018/fathers-day.html?#

Anderson, S. A., & Sabatelli, R. M. (2011). *Family interaction: A multigenerational developmental perspective* (5th ed.). Pearson.

Arab American Institute. (2019). *Who are Arab Americans?* http://www.aaiusa.org

Artazcoz, L., Benach, J., Borrell, C., & Cortes, I. (2004). Unemployment and mental health: Understanding the interactions among gender, family roles, and social class. *American Journal of Public Health*, *94*(1), 82–88.

Baca Zinn, M., & Pok, A. Y. (2002). Tradition and transition in Mexican-origin families. In R. L. Taylor (Ed.), *Minority families in the United States: A multicultural perspective* (3rd ed., pp. 79–100). Prentice Hall.

Baird, L. S., & Beccia, P. J. (1980). The potential misuse of overtime. *Personnel Psychology, 33*, 557–565.

Barnett, R. C., & Rivers, C. (1996). *She works, he works: How two-income families are happy, healthy, and thriving*. Harvard University Press.

Baxter, J. (1993). *Work at home: The domestic division of labour.* University of Queensland Press.

Behnke, A. O., & MacDermid, S. M. (2004). *Family well-being. A Sloan work and family encyclopedia entry.* http://wfnetwork.bc.edu/encyclopedia_entry.php?id=235

Bianchi, S. M., Sayer, L. C., Milkie, M. A., & Robinson, J. P. (2012). Housework: Who did, does or will do it, and how much does it matter? *Social Forces, 91*(1), 55–63.

Blair, S. L., & Lichter, D. (1991). Measuring the division of household labor: Gender segregation of housework among American couples. *Journal of Family Issues, 12*, 91–113.

Bushatz, A. (2018). *Report shows finances as a top concern for troops, families*. https://www.military.com/daily-news/2018/03/01/report-shows-finances-top-concern-troops-families.html

Center on Budget and Policy Priorities (CBPP). (2022). *COVID-19: Responding to the health and economic crisis*. https://www.cbpp.org/research/resource-lists/covid-19-responding-to-the-health-and-economic-crisis

Child Trends. (2019). *Children in poverty.* https://www.childtrends.org/indicators/children-in-poverty

Choi, Y., Yeun Kim, T., Noh, S., Lee, J., & Takeuchi, D. (2018). Culture and family process: Measures of familism for Filipino and Korean American parents. *Family Processes, 57*(4), 1029–1048.

Coltrane, S. (2000). Research on household labor: Modeling and measuring the social embeddedness of routine family work. *Journal of Marriage and the Family, 62*, 1208–1233.

Congressional Caucus on Women's Issues. (2005). *Chutes & Ladders: The search for solid ground for women in the workforce*. http://www.womenwork.org/policy/chutes.htm [August 11, 2009].

Congressional Research Service. (2021). *Global economic effects of COVID-19: Overview*. https://crsreports.congress.gov/product/details?prodcode=R46270

Constante, K., Marchand, A. D., Cross, F. L., & Rivas-Drake, D. (2019). Understanding the promotive role of familism in the link between ethnic-racial identity and Latino youth social engagement. *Journal of Latinx Psychology, 7*(3), 230–244.

Copur, Z., & Eker, I. (2014). The relationship between financial issues and martial relationship. *International Journal of Arts & Sciences, 7*, 683–698.

Corbett, M. (2005). *U.S. households led by single mothers and displaced homemakers on the rise*. *Women's Work*. www.womenwork.org

Council on Foreign Relations. (2019). *Demographics of the U.S. military.* www.cfr.org/article/demographics-us-military

Crouter, A. C. (1995). Processes linking families and work: Implications for behavior and developing in both settings. In R. D. Parke & S. Kellam (Eds.), *Exploring family relationships with other social contexts* (pp. 55–79). Erlbaum.

Crouter, A. C., Bumpus, M. F., Head, M. R., & McHale, S. M. (2001). Implications of overwork and overload for the quality of men's family relationships. *Journal of Marriage and Family, 63*(2), 404–416.

Davis, K. K., Crouter, A. C., & McHale, S. M. (2006). Implications of shift work for parent-adolescent relationships in dual-earner families. *Family Relations, 55*, 450–460.

Defrain, J. (2000). *Creating a strong family: Qualities of strong families*. University of Nebraska Cooperative Extension, Institute of Agriculture and Natural Resources.

Dew, J. (2007). Two sides of the same coin? The differing roles of assets and consumer debt in marriage. *Journal of Family and Economic Issues, 28*, 89–104.

Dew, J. (2008). Debt change and marital satisfaction change in recently married couples. *Family Relations, 57*, 60–71.

Drummet, A. R., Coleman, M., & Cable, S. (2003). Military families under stress: Implications for family life education. *Family Relations, 52*, 279–287.

Dyk, P. H. (2004). Complexity of family life among the

low-income and working poor: Introduction to the special issue. *Family Relations, 53*(2), 122–126.

Evans, R. P. (2004). *The five lessons a millionaire taught me*. Aurcadia Press.

Eyre, R., & Eyre, L. (February, 29, 2008). *Balancing work and family*. Utah State University.

Fetsch, R. (2009). *Suggestion for maintaining mental health during employment transitions*. Colorado State University, Human Development & Family Studies. www.ext.colostate.edu [February 8, 2009].

Fong, T. P. (2002). *The contemporary Asian American experience: Beyond the model minority* (2nd ed.). Prentice Hall.

Furstenberg, F. F. (1974). Work experience and family life. In J. O'Toole (Ed.), *Work and the quality of life*. MIT Press.

Gottfried, A. E., & Gottfried, A. W. (1994). *Redefining families: Implications for children's development*. Plenum.

Gottman, J. M. (1994). *Why marriages succeed or fail*. Simon & Schuster.

Gottman, J. M. (1999). *The marriage clinic: A scientifically based marital therapy*. Norton.

Grall, T. (2020). *Custodial mothers and fathers and their child support: 2017*. Current population reports. P60-269. https://www.census.gov/content/dam/Census/library/publications/2020/demo/p60-269.pdf

Greenhaus, J. H., & Beutell, N. J. (1985). Sources of conflict between work and family roles. *Academy of Management Review, 10*, 76–88.

Grosswald, B. (2004). The effects of shift work on family satisfaction. *Families in Society, 85*(3), 413–423.

Haddock, S. A., Zimmerman, T. S., Ziemba, S. J., & Current, L. R. (2001). Ten adaptive strategies for family and work balance: Advice from successful families. *Journal of Marital and Family Therapy, 27*(4), 445–458.

Hammer, L., & Thompson, C. (2003). *Work-family role conflict*. Sloan work and family encyclopedia. www.bc.edu/bc_org/avp/wfnetwork/rft/wfpedia/wfpWFRCent.html [August 10, 2004].

Hanisch, K. A. (1999). Job loss and unemployment research from 1994 to 1998: A review of and recommendations for research and intervention. *Journal of Vocational Behavior, 55*, 188–220.

Hardie, J. H., & Lucas, A. (2010). Economic factors and relationship quality among young couples: Comparing cohabitation and marriage. *Journal of Marriage and Family, 72*(5), 1141–1154.

Harris, V. W. (2008). *The triangular theory of balancing work and family*. Unpublished manuscript.

Hiswals, A. S., Marttila, A., Malstam, E., & Marcassa, G. (2017). Experiences of unemployment and well-being after job loss during economic recession: Results of a qualitative study in east central Sweden. *Journal of Public Health Research, 6*(3), 995. http://doi.org/10.4081/jphr.2017.995

Hochschild, A. (1989). *The second shift*. Avon.

HUD. (2018). *Strong families initiative*. https://www.hud.gov/strongfamilies

Institute for Women's Policy Research. (2008). *The gender wage gap: 2007*. Publication IWPR No. C350. https://iwpr.org/wp-content/uploads/2020/08/C464_Gender-Wage-Gap-2.pdf [January 31, 2009].

Institute for Women's Policy Research. (2019). *Median weekly earnings and gender earnings ratio for full-time workers*. https://iwpr.org/publications/gender-wage-gap-2018/

Johnson, A. (2008, October). *Financial first aid. Paper presented at the family consumer science agent in-service*. St. George, UT.

Johnson, N. J., Backlund, E., Sorlie, P. D., & Loveless, C. A. (2000). Marital status and mortality: The national longitudinal mortality study. *Annual of Epidemiology, 10*, 224–238.

Killewald, A. (2016). Money, work, and marital stability: Assessing change in the gendered determinants of divorce. *American Sociological Review, 81*(4), 696–719.

Krieger, N. (2001). *Critical perspectives on racial and ethnic differences in health and later life*. The National Academic Press, Committee on Population. www.darwin.nap.edu/books/0309092116.html

Lewin, A. C. (2005). The effect of economic stability on family stability among welfare recipients. *Evaluation Review, 29*(30), 223–240.

Lockert, M. (2019, September). *Mental health survey: 1 in 14 high student debt borrowers considered suicide. Student Loan Planner*. https://www.studentloanplanner.com/mental-health-awareness-survey/

Loudoun, R. (2008). Balancing shiftwork and life outside work: Do 12-hour shifts make a difference? *Applied Ergonomics, 39*, 572–579.

Mellan, O. (1994). *Money harmony*. Walker and Company.

Military Family Advisory Network. (2019). *2019 military family survey*. https://militaryfamilyadvisorynetwork.org/survey/

National Council on Family Relations (NCFR). (2020). *Understanding families: Research and practice*. https://www.ncfr.org/membership

NFWM. (2019). *Immigration reform*. http://nfwm.org/current-campaigns/immigration-reform-2/

Office of Child Support Enforcement. (2021). *Certified child support arrears shows sharp decline*. https://www.acf.hhs.gov/css/ocsedatablog/2021/05/certified-child-support-arrears-shows-sharp-decline#:~:text=The%20amount%20of%20child%20support,child%20support%20that%20remains%20unpaid

Papp, L. M., Cummings, E. M., & Goeke-Morey, M. C. (2009). For richer, for poorer: Money as a topic of marital conflict in the home. *Family Relations, 58*, 91–103.

Perry-Jenkins, M., Repetti, R. L., & Crouter, A. C. (2001). Work and family in the 1990s. In R. Milardo (Ed.), *Understanding families into the new millennium: A decade in review* (pp. 200–217). NCFR and Alliance Communications Group.

Pew Foundation. (2020). *Law will ease access to affordable student loan repayment if implemented effectively*. https://www.pewtrusts.org/en/research-and-analysis/articles/2020/03/02/law-will-ease-access-to-affordable-student-loan-repayment-if-implemented-effectively

Pew Research Center. (2017a). *U.S. active-duty military presence overseas is at its smallest in decades*. https://www.pewresearch.org/fact-tank/2017/08/22/u-s-active-duty-military-presence-overseas-is-at-its-smallest-in-decades/

Pew Research Center. (2017b). *U.S. Muslims concerned about their place in society*. https://www.pewforum.org/2017/07/26/findings-from-pew-research-centers-2017-survey-of-us-muslims/

Pew Research Center. (2018). *Stay at home moms and dads account for about one in five U.S. Parents*. https://www.pewresearch.org/fact-tank/2018/09/24/stay-at-home-moms-and-dads-account-for-about-one-in-five-u-s-parents/

Pew Research Center. (2019a). *The narrowing, but persistent, gender gap in pay*. https://www.pewresearch.org/fact-tank/2019/03/22/gender-pay-gap-facts/

Pew Research Center. (2019b). *Student loan system presents repayment challenges*. pewtrusts.org/en/research_and_analysis/reports/2019/11/student-loan-system-presents-repayment-challenges/

Pew Research Center. (2022). *Household income, poverty status, and home ownership among Black immigrants*. https://www.pewresearch.org/race-ethnicity/2022/01/20/household-income-poverty-status-and-home-ownership-among-black-immigrants/#:~:text=In%202019%2C%20the%20median%20household,income%20in%202000%20(%2454%2C700)

Proctor, C. (2020). *Refinancing your students loans with SoFi could save you money—and even help you get a better mortgage rate*. https://www.businessinsider.com/personal-finance/sofi-student-loan-refinancing-review-and-how-it-works

Ramsey Solutions. (2018). *Money ruining marriages in America: A Ramsey Solutions study*. https://www.daveramsey.com/pr/money-ruining-marriages-in-america

Richter, D., & Lemola, S. (2017). Growing up with a single mother and life satisfaction in adulthood: A test of mediating and moderating factors. *PLoS One, 12*(6), e0179639. http://doi.org/10.1371/journal.pone.0179639

Robb, C. A., Chatterjee, S., Porto, N., & Cude, B. J. (2018). The influence of student loan debt on financial satisfaction. *Journal of Family and Economic Issues, 40*, 51–73.

Roehling, P. V., & Moen, P. (2003). *Dual-earner couples. Sloan work and family encyclopedia*. www.bc.edu/bc_org/avp/wfnetwork/rft/wfpedia/wfpDECent.html [August 10, 2004].

Romanelli, A. (2019, August). Let's talk about money in our intimate relationships: 3 steps to clarify the financial power dynamic in your relationship. *Psychology Today*. psychology today.com/us/blog/the-other-side-relationships

Rudgard, O. (2017). *Shift work*. https://www.telegraph.co.uk/news/2017/09/02/shift-work-infidelity-ending-marriages/

Salary.com. (2018). *Moms: We know you're worth it*. https://www.salary.com/articles/stay-at-home-mom/

Schramm, D. G., Marshall, J. P., Harris, V. W., & George, A. (2003). *Marriage in Utah: 2003 baseline statewide survey on marriage and divorce*. Utah Department of Workforce Services.

Schramm, D. G., Marshall, J. P., Harris, V. W., & Lee, T. R. (2005). After "I do": The newlywed transition. *Marriage and Family Review, 38*, 45–67.

Single Mother Statistics. (2021). *Single mother statistics*. https://singlemotherguide.com/single-mother-statistics/#:~:text=According%20to%202021%20U.S.%20Census,were%20headed%20by%20single%20mothers.&text=Of%20all%20single%2Dparent%20families,were%20born%20to%20unwed%20mothers

Statista. (2019). *Families with debt in the United States*. https://www.statista.com/statistics/247874/amount-of-family-debt-distributed-by-type-of-debt/

Stevens, D. P., Kiger, G., & Riley, P. J. (2006). His, hers, our ours? Work-to-family spillover, crossover, and family cohesion. *The Social Science Journal, 43*, 425–436.

Sullivan, M. (2009, February 5). *Wage gap is wider for women of color. Women's Policy Research*. www.iwpr.org

Taylor, K. (2002). *Minority families in the United States: A multicultural perspective*. Prentice Hall.

Thomas-Hunt, M., & Phillips, K. W. (2004). When what you know is not enough: Expertise and gender dynamics in task groups. *Personality and Social Psychology Bulletin, 30*(12), 1585–1598.

U.S. Bureau of Labor Statistics. (2019). *Consumer expenditures report: 2019*. https://www.bls.gov/opub/reports/consumer-expenditures/2019/home.htm

U.S. Bureau of Labor Statistics. (2020). *Labor force characteristics by race and ethnicity, 2020*. https://www.bls.gov/opub/reports/race-and-ethnicity/2020/home.htm

U.S. Census Bureau. (2016). *Mother's Day: May 8, 2016. America's family and living arrangements*. https://www.census.gov/newsroom/facts-for-features/2016/cb16-ff09.html

United States Census Bureau. (2019a). *The intersectionality of sex, race, and Hispanic origin in the STEM workplace*. https://www.census.gov/library/working-papers/2019/demo/SEHSD-WP2018-27.html

United States Census Bureau. (2019b). *Households by labor force status of members*. https://www.census.gov/programs-surveys/sipp/publications/tables/hsehld-char.html

United States Census Bureau. (2019c). *Asian-American and Pacific Islander heritage month: May 2019*. https://www.census.gov/newsroom/facts-for-features/2019/asian-american-pacific-islander.html

United States Census Bureau. (2019d). *Hispanic heritage month 2019*. https://www.census.gov/newsroom/facts-for-features/2019/hispanic-heritage-month.html

United States Census Bureau. (2019e). *American Indian and Alaska Native heritage month: November 2019*. https://www.census.gov/newsroom/facts-for-features/2019/aian-month.html

United States Census Bureau. (2020a). *American's families and living arrangements*. https://www.census.gov/data/tables/2020/demo/families/cps-2020.html

United States Census Bureau. (2020b). *Custodial mothers and fathers and their child support*. https://www.census.gov/newsroom/press-releases/2020/custodial-parents.html

United States Census Bureau. (2021a). *Census Bureau releases new estimate on America's families and living arrangements. Release number CB21-TPS, 138*. https://www.census.gov/newsroom/press-releases/2021/families-and-living-arrangements.html

United States Census Bureau. (2021b). *Tracking job losses for mothers of school-aged children during a health crisis*. https://www.census.gov/library/stories/2021/03/moms-work-and-the-pandemic.html

U.S. Department of Agriculture. (2017). *Household food security in the United States, 2017*. https://www.ers.usda.gov/webdocs/publications/90029/ap-079.pdf

U.S. Department of Labor. (2017). *12 stats about working*

women. www.blog.dol.gov/2017/03/01/12-stats-about-working-women

U.S. Department of Labor. (2018). *Unemployment rates 2018*. https://www.bls.gov/opub/ted/2018/unemployment-rate-2-point-7-percent-for-people-ages-45-to-54-8-point-3-percent-for-ages-16-to-24-in-october-2018.htm

U.S. Department of Labor. (2019). *Employment characteristics of families summary*. www.bls.gov/news/release/famee.nr0.htm

U.S. Department of Labor. (2021). *Employment characteristics of families: 2020*. https://www.bls.gov/news.release/pdf/famee.pdf

Varcoe, K. P., Empter, N., & Lee, N. (2002). Working with military audiences to improve financial well-being. *JFCS, 94*(1), 33–34.

Voydanoff, P. (1983). Unemployment: Family, strategies for adaptation. In C. R. Figley & H. I. McCubbin (Eds.), *Stress and the family, II—coping with catastrophe* (pp. 90–102). New York City.

van der Wal, S. J., Gorter, R., Reinjnen, A. l., Geuze, E., & Vermetten, E. (2019). Cohort profile: The prospective research in stress-related military operations (PRISMO) study in the Dutch armed forces. *British Medical Journal, 9*(3), e026670.

White, D. M. (2018). *Shift work and relationships*. www.psychcentral.com/lib/shift-work-and-relationships/

CHAPTER 11

ACOG. (2019). *Sexual assault. Committee on Health Care for Underserved Women*. https://www.acog.org/Clinical-Guidance-and-Publications/Committee-Opinions/Committee-on-Health-Care-for-Underserved-Women/Sexual-Assault

Afifi, T. O., MacMillan, H. L., Boylem, M., Cheung, K., Taillieu, T., Turner, S., & Sareen, J. (2016). Child abuse and physical health in adulthood. *Health Reports, 27*(3), 10–18.

American Association for Marriage and Family Therapists. (2020). *Policy on social and family policies*. https://www.aamft.org/About_AAMFT/Position_On_Couples.aspx

Annie E. Casey Foundation. (2022). *What children and young people need to thrive*. https://www.aecf.org/

Backpacks USA. (2021). *How to make a care package for homeless shelters*. https://www.backpacksusa.com/blogs/blog/how-to-make-a-care-package-for-homeless-shelters

Bhutta, N., Chang, A. C., Dettling, L. J., & Hsu, J. W. (2020). *Disparities in wealth by race and ethnicity in the 2019 survey of consumer finances. Federal Reserve*. https://www.federalreserve.gov/econres/notes/feds-notes/disparities-in-wealth-by-race-and-ethnicity-in-the-2019-survey-of-consumer-finances-20200928.htm

Bick, J., & Nelson, C. A. (2016). Early adverse experiences and the developing brain. *Neuropsychopharmacology, 41*, 177–196.

Bodenmann, G. (2010). New themes in couple therapy: The role of stress, coping, and social support. In K. Hahlweg, M. Grawe-Gerber, & D. H. Baucom (Eds.), *Enhancing couples: The shape of couple therapy to come* (pp. 142–156). Hogrefe.

Brumley, B., Fantuzzo, J., & Perlman, S. (2015). The unique relations between early homelessness and educational well-being: An empirical test of the continuum of risk hypothesis. *Children and Youth Services Review, 48*, 31–37.

Burr, W. R. (1973). *Theory construction and the sociology of the family*. Wiley.

Casey, C. G. A. (2018). *Research demonstrates connection between housing affordability, homelessness. Continuum of Care*. https://dupagehomeless.org/research-demonstrates-connection-between-housing-affordability-homelessness/

Centers for Disease Control and Prevention. (2018). *Youth risk behavior survey, United States 2017. Table 38: Percentage of high school students who experienced sexual dating violence,* by sex, race/ethnicity, grade, sexual references n 647 identity, and sex of sexual contacts*. https://www.cdc.gov/healthyyouth/data/yrbs/2017_tables/contribute_to_violence.htm#t38_down

Centers for Disease Control and Prevention. (2019). *Adverse childhood experiences (ACES)*. https://www.cdc.gov/violenceprevention/childabuseandneglect/acestudy/index.html

Centers for Disease Control and Prevention. (2020). *Preventing child abuse and neglect:*

What are child abuse and neglect? https://www.cdc.gov/violenceprevention/childabuseandneglect/fastfact.html

Chetty, R., Grusky, D., Hell, M., Hendron, N., Manduca, R., & Nargang, J. (2017). The fading American dream: Trends in absolute income mobility since 1940. *Science, 356*(6336), 398.

Child Trends. (2019). *Children and youth experiencing homelessness*. https://www.childtrends.org/indicators/homeless-children-and-youth

Child Welfare Information Gateway. (2019). *Long-term consequences of child abuse and neglect*. U.S. Department of Health and Human Services, Administration for Children and Families, Children's Bureau.

Choi, N. G., DiNitto, D. M., Marti, C. N., & Choi, B. Y. (2017). Association of adverse childhood experiences with lifetime mental and substance use disorders among men and women aged 50+ years. *International Psychogeriatrics, 29*, 359–372. http://doi.org/10.1017/S1041610216001800

Cordon, I. M. (1997). *Stress*. www.csun.edu/~vcpsy00h/students/stress.htm

Cowan, P., Cowan, C. P., & Schulz, M. (1996). Thinking about risk and resilience in families. In E. M. Hetherington & E. Blechman (Eds.), *Stress, coping, and resiliency in children and families* (pp. 1–38). Erlbaum.

Cravens, J. D., Whiting, J. B., & Aamar, R. O. (2015). Why I stayed/left: An analysis of voices of intimate partner violence on social media. *Contemporary Family Therapy: An International Journal, 37*(4), 372–385.

Dalton, C., & Schneider, E. M. (2001). *Battered women and the law*. Foundation Press.

De Bellis, M. D. (2002). Developmental traumatology: A contributory mechanism for alcohol and substance use disorders. *Psychoneuroendocrinology, 27*, 155–170.

Domestic Abuse Intervention Project. (2020). *What is the Duluth model?* https://www.theduluthmodel.org/

Doyle, C., & Cicchetti, D. (2017). From the cradle to the grave: The effect of adverse caregiving environments on attachment and relationships throughout the lifespan. *Clinical Psychology: Science and Practice, 24*(2), 203–217.

Driver, B. L., & Spady, P. M. (2013). *What educators can do: Homeless children and youth*. Virginia Department of Education, Info Brief No. 2. https://education.wm.edu/centers/hope/publications/infobriefs/documents/whateducatorscando2013.pdf

Duban, E. (2018). *Preventing and addressing sexual and gender-based violence in places of deprivation of liberty*. https://www.osce.org/odihr/427448

Duvall, E. M., & Hill, R. (1960). *Being married*. Association Press.

Edwards, D. (2018). Childhood sexual abuse and brain development: A discussion of associated structural changes and negative psychological outcomes. *Child Abuse Review, 27*(3), 198–208.

Felitti, V. J., Anda, R. F., Nordenberg, D., Williamson, D. F., Spitz, A. M., Edwards, V., Koss, M. P., & Marks, J. S. (1998). Relationship of childhood abuse and household dysfunction to many of the leading causes of death in adults. The adverse childhood experiences (ACE) study. *American Journal of Preventive Medicine, 14*, 245–258.

Friedman, D. (2000). *Parenting in public: Family shelter and public assistance*. Columbia University Press.

Gewirtz, A., Har-Shegos, E., & Medhanie, A. (2008). Psychological status of homeless children and youth in family supportive housing. *American Behavioral Scientist, 51*(6), 810–823.

Grant, R., Shapiro, A., Joseph, S., Goldsmith, S., Rigual-Lynch, L., & Redlener, I. (2007). The health of homeless children revisited. *Advances in Pediatrics, 54*, 173–187.

Guarino, K., Soares, P., Konnath, K., Clervil, R., & Bassuk, E. (2009). *Trauma-informed organizational toolkit. Center for Mental Health Services, Substance Abuse and Mental Health Services Administration, and the Daniels Fund, the National Child Traumatic Stress Network, and the W.K. Kellogg Foundation*. www.homeless.samhsa.gov and www.familyhomelessness.org

Hart, H., & Rubia, K. (2012). Neuroimaging of child abuse: A critical review. *Frontiers in Human Neuroscience, 6*, 52.

Haskett, M. E., & Armstrong, J. M. (2019). The experience of family homelessness. In B. H. Fiese, M. Celano, K.

Deater-Deckard, E. N. Jouriles, & M. A. Whisman (Eds.), *APA handbook of contemporary family psychology: Applications and broad impact of family psychology* (pp. 523–538). American Psychological Association.

Haskett, M. E., Armstrong, J. M., & Tisdale, J. (2016). Developmental status and social-emotional functioning of young children experiencing homelessness. *Early Childhood Education Journal, 44*, 119–125.

Hill, R. (1949). *Families under stress*. Harper.

Hill, R. (1958). Generic features of families under stress. *Social Casework, 49*, 139–150.

Institute for Children, Poverty & Homelessness. (2019). *The dynamics of family homelessness in New York City*. https://www.icphusa.org/wp-content/uploads/2019/07/Family-Dynamics-Final.pdf

Institute of Family Studies. (2016). *Eight reasons why women stay in abusive relationships*. https://ifstudies.org/blog/eight-reasons-women-stay-in-abusive-relationships

Invisible People. (2021). *How to help homeless families*. https://invisiblepeople.tv/how-to-help-homeless-families/

Leddy, A. M., Weiss, E., Yam, E., & Pulerwitz, J. (2019). Gender-based violence and engagement in biomedical HIV preventions, care and treatment: A scoping review. *BMC Public Health, 19*, 897.

Letiecq, B., Anderson, E., & Koblinsky, S. (1998). Social support of the homeless and houses mothers: A comparison of temporary and permanent housing arrangements. *Family Relations, 47*(4), 415–421.

Linver, M. R., Brooks-Gunn, J., & Kohen, D. E. (2002). Family processes as pathways from income to young children's development. *Developmental Psychology, 38*(5), 719–734.

Mayberry, L. S., Shinn, M., Biggons-Benton, J., & Wise, J. (2014). Families experiencing housing instability: The effects of housing programs on family routines and rituals. *American Journal of Orthopsychiatry, 84*(1), 95–109.

McCubbin, H. I., & Patterson, J. M. (1982). Family adaptation to crisis. In H. I. McCubbin, M. B. Sussman, & J. M. Patterson (Eds.), *Family stress, coping, and social support*. Thomas.

McGoldrick, M., Broken Nose, M. A., & Potenza, M. (1999). Violence and the family life cycle. In B. Carter & M. McGoldrick (Eds.), *The expanded family life cycle: Individual, family, and social perspectives* (pp. 470–491). Allyn & Bacon.

Monnat, S. M., & Chandler, R. F. (2015). Long-term physical health consequences of adverse childhood experiences. *The Sociological Quarterly, 56*, 723–752.

Moos, R. H. (1987). *Life transitions and crises: A conceptual overview*. Plenum Press.

Moos, R. H., & Schaefer, J. A. (1987). Life transitions and crises: A conceptual overview. In R. H. Moos (Ed.), *Coping with life crises: An integrated approach* (pp. 3–28). Plenum Press.

National Alliance to End Homelessness. (2021). *State of homelessness: 2021 edition*. https://endhomelessness.org/homelessness-in-america/homelessness-statistics/state-of-homelessness-2021/

National Center for Victims of Crime. (2018). *Intimate partner violence*. https://ovc.ncjrs.gov/ncvrw2018/info_flyers/fact_sheets/2018NCVRW_IPV_508_QC.pdf

National Child Traumatic Stress Network. (2022). *Complex trauma: Effects*. https://www.nctsn.org/what-is-child-trauma/trauma-types/complex-trauma/effects

National Coalition Against Domestic Violence. (2020). *What is domestic violence?* https://ncadv.org/learn-more

National Coalition for the Homeless. (2021). *LGBT homelessness*. https://nationalhomeless.org/issues/lgbt/

National League of Cities. (2021). *Unlocking homelessness, Part 1: Who experiences homelessness and why*. https://www.nlc.org/wp-content/uploads/2021/02/UnlockingHomelessnessReportPart1.pdf

National Scientific Council on the Developing Child. (2014). *Excessive stress disrupts the architecture of the developing brain* (Working paper 3). https://developingchild.harvard.edu/resources/wp3/

Okur, P., Pereda, N., Van Der Knaap, L. M., & Bogaerts, S. (2018). Attributions of blame among victims of child sexual abuse: Findings from a community sample. *Journal of Child Sexual Abuse, 28*(3), 301–317. h ttp://doi.org/10.1080/1053871 2.2018.1546249

Paquette, K., & Bassuk, E. L. (2009). Parenting and homelessness: Overview and introduction to the special section. *American Journal of Orthopsychiatry, 79*, 292–298.

Pearlin, L. I. (1982). The social contexts of stress. In L. Goldberger & S. Brenitz (Eds.), *Handbook of stress: Theoretical and clinical aspects*. Free Press.

Perlman, S. M., & Fantuzzo, J. W. (2010). Timing and impact of homelessness and maltreatment on school readiness. *Children and Youth Services Review, 32*, 874–883.

Perlman, S., & Fantuzzo, J. (2013). Predicting risk of placement: A population-based study of out-of-home placement, child maltreatment, and emergency housing. *Journal of the Society for Social Work and Research, 4*, 99–113.

Perlman, S., Sheller, S., Hudson, K. M., & Wilson, C. L. (2014). Parenting in the face of homelessness. In M. Haskett, S. Perlman, & B. A. Cowan (Eds.), *Promoting positive parenting in the context of homelessness* (pp. 57–78). Springer.

Pitzer, R. L. (2004). *Change, crisis, and loss in our lives*. www.extension.mn.edu/distribution/familydevelopmenl/DE2455.html

Putnam, F. W. (2003). Ten-year research update review: Child sexual abuse. *Journal of the American Academy of Child and Adolescent Psychiatry, 42*, 269–278.

RAINN. (2019). *Child sexual abuse: Children and statistics*. https://www.rainn.org/statistics/children-and-teens

RAINN. (2022). *Warning signs for young children*. https://www.rainn.org/articles/warning-signs-young-children#:~:text=Regressive%20behaviors%20or%20resuming%20behaviors,unusual%20amount%20of%20time%20alone

Reed-Victor, E., & Popp, P. (2013). *Using the best that we know: Supporting young children experiencing homelessness*. The College of William and Mary. Virginia Department of Education Information Brief, No. 9.

Reed-Victor, E., & Stronge, J. H. (2003). Homeless students and resilience: Staff perspectives on individual and environmental factors. *Journal of Children & Poverty, 8*(2), 159–183.

SAMHSA. (2016). *L.A. family housing supports single fathers with housing*. https://www.samhsa.gov/homlessness-programspresources/hpr-resources/single-fathers-children-shelters

SchoolHouse Connection. (2019). *Tips for teachers and staff: How to support students experiencing homelessness*. https://schoolhouseconnection.org/tips-for-teachers-staff-how-to-support-students-experiencing-homelessness/

Seattle University. (2014). *Project on homelessness: Building a movement to end homelessness*. https://nationalhomeless.org/issues/lgbt/

Shinn, M., Gibbons-Benton, J., & Brown, S. R. (2015). Poverty, homelessness, and family break-up. *Child Welfare, 94*(1), 105–122.

Smith, S. G., Chen, J., Basile, K. C., Gilbert, L. K., Merrick, M. T., Patel, N., Walling, M., & Jain, A. (2017). *The national intimate partner and sexual violence survey (NISVS): 2010–2012 state report*. National Center for Injury Prevention and Control.

Stasha, S. (2021). *The state of homelessness in the U.S.: 2021*. https://policyadvice.net/insurance/insights/homelessness-statistics/

U.S. Bureau of Justice Statistics. (2019). *Criminal victimization: 2018*. https://www.bjs.gov/index.cfm

U.S. Census Bureau. (2020). *2019 American Community Survey statistics for income, poverty, and health insurance available for states and local areas*. https://www.census.gov/newroom/press-releases/2020/acs-1year.html#:~text=The%202019%20U.S.%20median%20household,the%202018%20and%202019%20ACS

U.S. Department of Health and Human Services. (2018). *Child maltreatment*. https://www.acf.hhs.gov/sites/default/files/cb/cm2017.pdf

U.S. Department of Housing and Urban Development. (2021). *HUD released 2021 annual homeless assessment report: Part 1. HUD No. 22-022, HUD Public Affairs*, https://www.hud.gov/press/press_releases_media_advisories/hud_no_22_022

U.S. Department of Justice. (2018). *Domestic violence*. https://www.justice.gov/ovw/domestic-violence

U.S. Interagency Council on Homelessness. (2021). *The federal strategic plan to prevent and end homelessness*. https://www.usich.gov/fsp

Vrolijk-Bosschaart, T. F., Brillesliper-Kater, S. N., Benninga, M. A., Lindauer, R. J. L., & Teeuw, A. H. (2018). Clinical practice: Recognizing child sexual abuse—what makes it so difficult? *European Journal of Pediatrics*, *177*(9), 1343–1350.

Walker, L. E. (1979). *The battered woman*. Harper & Row.

Walsh, F. (2003). Family resilience: A framework for clinical practice. *Family Process*, *42*, 1–18.

Weisner, T. S., Matheson, C., Coots, J., & Bernheimer, L. P. (2005). Sustainability of daily routines as a family outcome. In A. Maynard & M. Martini (Eds.), *Learning in cultural context: Family, peers, and school* (pp. 47–74). Kluwer Academic/Plenum.

Welch, K. J. (2004). *Development: Journey of a lifetime*. Allyn & Bacon.

Whiting, J. (2016). *Eight reasons women stay in abusive relationships*. https://ifstudies.org/blog/eight-reasons-women-stay-in-abusive-relationships

Widom, C. S., Czaia, S. J., Bentley, T., & Johnson, M. S. (2012). A prospective investigation of physical health outcomes in abused and neglected children: New findings from a 30-year follow-up. *American Journal of Public Health*, *102*(6), 1135–1144.

Wirtz, A. L., Poteat, T. C., Mannat, M., & Glass, N. (2020). Gender-based violence against transgender people in the United States: A call for research and programming. *Trauma, Violence, and Abuse*, *21*(2), 227–241.

World Health Organization. (2018). *Intimate partner violence and alcohol*. https://www.who.int/violence_injury_prevention/violence/world_report/factsheets/fs_intimate.pdfa

Yamashiro, A., & McLaughlin, J. (2020). *Early childhood homelessness: State profiles. U.S. Department of Education*. https://www2.ed.gov/rschstat/eval/disadv/homeless/early-childhood-homelessness-state-profiles-2020.pdf

CHAPTER 12

AAIDD. (2021). *Frequently asked questions on intellectual disability and the AAIDD definition*. https://www.aaidd.org/docs/default-source/sis-docs/aaiddfaqonid_template.pdf?sfvrsn=9a63a874_2#:~:text=What%20is%20the%20official%20AAIDD,before%20the%20age%20of%2018

Achenbach, T. M., Howell, C. T., Quay, H. C., & Conners, C. K. (1991). National survey of problems and competencies among four- to sixteen-year-olds: Parents' reports for normative and clinical samples. *Monographs of the Society for Research in Child Development*, *56*(3), 1–131.

Americans with Disabilities Act. (2021). *A guide to disability rights laws*. https://www.ada.gov/cguide.htm

Anderson, D., Dumont, S., Jacobs, P., & Azzaria, L. (2007). The personal costs of caring for a child with a disability: A review of the literature. *Public Health Reports*, *122*(1), 3–16.

Andrews, J. F., Shaw, P. C., & Lomas, G. (2011). Deaf and hard of hearing students. In J. M. Kauffman & D. P. Hallahan (Eds.), *Handbook of special education*. Routledge.

Art Beyond Sight Disability Awareness Training. (2014). *Disability and inclusion*. http://www.artbeyondsight.org/dic/definition-of-disability-paradigm-change-and-ongoing-conversation/

Autism Society. (2021). *What is autism?* https://www.autism-society.org/what-is/

Autism Speaks. (2021). *Autism statistics and facts*. https://www.autismspeaks.org/autism-statistics-asd

Bagby, M. S., Dickie, V. A., & Baranek, G. T. (2012). How sensory experiences of children with and without autism affect family occupations. *The American Journal of Occupational Therapy*, *66*(1), 78–86.

Baker, B. L., McIntyre, L. L., Blacher, J., Crnic, K., Edelbrock, C., & Low, C. (2003). Pre-school children with and without developmental delay: Behaviour problems and parenting stress over time. *Journal of Intellectual Disability Research*, *47*, 217–230.

Barloso, K. (2021). *Autism stimming and hand flapping: What are the key causes and behaviors?* https://ibcces.org/blog/2021/10/12/autism-stimming-and-hand-flapping-wh

at-are-the-key-causes-and-behaviors/

Beighton, C., & Wills, J. (2017). Are parents identifying positive aspects to parenting their child with an intellectual disability or are they just coping? A qualitative exploration. *Journal of Intellectual Disabilities, 21*(4), 325–345.

Benson, P. R. (2012). Network characteristics, perceived social support, and psychological adjustment in mothers of children with autism spectrum disorder. *Journal of Autism and Developmental Disorders, 42*, 2597–2610.

Benson, P. R. (2014). Coping and psychological adjustment among mothers of children with ASD: An accelerated longitudinal study. *Journal of Autism and Developmental Disorders, 44*, 1793–1807.

Benson, P. R. (2016). The longitudinal effects of network characteristics on the mental health of mothers of children with ASD: The mediating role of parent cognitions. *Journal of Autism and Developmental Disorders, 46*, 1699–1715.

Blacher, J., & Baker, B. (2007). Positive impact of intellectual disability on families. *Journal on Mental Retardation, 112*, 330–338.

Blacher, J., Begum, G. F., & Marcoulides, G. A. (2013). Longitudinal perspectives of child positive impact on families: Relationship to disability and culture. *American Journal on Intellectual and Developmental Disabilities, 118*(2), 141–155.

Blank, A., Frush Holt, R., Pisoni, D. B., & Kronenberger, W. W. (2020). Associations between parenting stress, language comprehension, and inhibitory control in children with hearing loss. *Journal of Speech, Language, and Hearing Research, 63*(1), 321–333.

Bodner-Johnson, B. (1991). Family conversation style: Its effect on the deaf child's participation. *Exceptional Children, 57*(6), 502–509.

Brown, E. D., Ackerman, B. P., & Moore, C. A. (2013). Family adversity and inhibitory control for economically disadvantaged children: Preschool relations and associations with school readiness. *Journal of Family Psychology, 27*, 443–452.

Bruder, M. B., & Staff, I. (1998). A comparison of the effects of type of classroom and service characteristics on toddlers with disabilities. *Topics in Early Childhood Special Education, 18*, 26–37.

Buckner, J. C., Mezzacappa, E., & Beardslee, W. R. (2003). Characteristics of resilient youths living in poverty: The role of self-regulatory processes. *Developmental Psychopathology, 15*, 139–162.

Buckner, J. C., Mezzacappa, E., & Beardslee, W. R. (2009). Self-regulation and its relations to adaptive functioning in low-income youths. *American Journal of Orthopsychiatry, 79*, 19–30.

Bujnowska, A., Rodríguez, C., Garcia, T., Areces, D., & Marsh, N. (2019). Parenting and future anxiety: The impact of having a child with developmental disabilities. *International Journal of Environmental Research and Public Health, 16*(668), 1–16.

Bunbury, C. (2019). Unconscious bias and the medical model: How the social model may hold the key to transformative thinking about disability discrimination. *International Journal of Discrimination and the Law, 19*(1), 26–47.

Butcher, P. R., Wind, T., & Bouma, A. (2008). Parenting stress in mothers and fathers of a child with a hemiparesis: Sources of stress, intervening factors, and long-term expressions of stress. *Child: Health, Care, & Development, 34*(4), 530–541.

Canale, A., Favero, E., Lacilla, M., Recchia, E., & Schindler, A. (2006). Age at diagnosis of deaf babies: A retrospective analysis highlighting the advantage of newborn hearing screening. *International Journal of Pediatric Otorhinolaryngology, 70*(7), 1283–1289.

Cappe, E., Wolff, M., Bobet, R., & Adrien, J.-L. (2011). Quality of life: A key variable to consider in the evaluation of adjustment in parents of children with autism spectrum disorders and in the development of relevant support and assistance programmes. *Quality of Life Research, 20*(8), 1279–1294.

Centers for Disease Control and Prevention. (2020). *U.S.: Data and statistics on birth defects.* https://www.cdc.gov/ncbddd/birthdefects/data.html

Cerebral Palsy Group. (2021). *Treatment costs overview.* https://cerebralpalsygroup.com/treatment/costs/

Conrad, P. (2004). The discovery of hyperkinesis: Notes on the medicalization of deviant behavior. In S. Danforth & S. D. Taff (Eds.), *Crucial readings in special education* (pp. 18–24). Pearson-Merrill, Prentice-Hall.

Crenshaw, K. (1989). Demarginalizing the intersection or race and sex: A Black feminist critique of antidiscrimination doctrine, feminist theory, and antiracist politics. *University of Chicago Legal Forum*, *1*(8), 138–167.

Crow, C. (1996). Including all of our lives. In Morris (Ed.), *Encounters with strangers*. The Women's Press Ltd.

Cruz, I., Quittner, A. L., DesJardin, J., Marker, C., & CDaCI Investigative Team. (2013). Identification of effective strategies to promote language in deaf children with cochlear implants. *Child Development*, *84*, 543–559.

Davis, L. (2001). Identity politics, disability, and culture. In G. L. Albrecht, K. D. Seelman, & M. Bury. (Eds.), *Handbook of disability studies* (pp. 535–545). SAGE.

Dervishaliaj, E. (2013). Parental stress in families of children with disabilities: A literature review. *Journal of Educational and Social Research*, *3*(7), 579–584.

Disabled World. (2022). *Disability benefits, facts, statistics, resources*. https://www.disabled-world.com/disability/

Dodd, J., Jones, C., Joly, D., & Sandell, R. (2010). Disability reframed: Challenging visitor perceptions in the museum. In R. Sandell, J. Dodd, & R. Garland-Thomson (Eds.), *Representing disability: Activism and agency in the Museum* (pp. 92–111). Routledge.

Drageset, J., & Haugan, G. (2015). Psychometric properties of the orientation to life questionnaire in nursing home residents. *Scandinavian Journal of Caring Sciences*, *30*(3), 623–630. https://doi.org/10.111/scs.12271

Durand, V. M., Hieneman, M., Clarke, S., Wang, M., & Rinaldi, M. (2013). Positive family intervention for severe challenging behavior I: A multi-site randomized clinical trial. *Journal of Positive Behavior Interventions*, *15*(3), 133–143.

Emerson, E., & Brigham, P. (2014). The developmental health of children of parents with intellectual disabilities: Cross sectional study. *Research in Developmental Disability*, *35*(4), 917–921.

Emerson, E., & Hatton, C. (2008). *Estimating future need for adult social care services for people with learning disabilities in England*. Centre for Disability Research.

Emerson, E., & Hatton, C. (2014). *Health inequalities and people with intellectual disabilities*. Cambridge University Press.

Eriksson, M., & Mittlemark, M. B. (2017). The sense of coherence and its measurement. In M. B. Mittlemark, S. Sagy, M. Erisksson, G. F. Bauer, J. M. Pelikan, B. Lindström, & G. A. Espnes (Eds.), *The handbook of salutogenesis*. Springer. https://pubmed.ncbi.nlm.nih.gov/28590637/

Esteves, K. J., & Rao, S. (2008). *The evolution of special education: Retracing legal milestones in American history. Principal, November/December, 2008*. https://www.naesp.org/sites/default/files/resources/1/Principal/2008/N-Oweb2.pdf

Feizi, A., Najmi, B., Salesi, A., Chorami, M., & Hoveidafar, R. (2014). Parenting stress among mothers of children with different physical, mental, and psychological problems. *Journal of Research in Medical Sciences*, *19*(2), 145–152.

Fereidouni, K., Kamyab, A. H., Dehghan, A., Khiyali, Z., Ziopour, A., Mehedi, N., & Toghroli, R. (2021). A comparative study on the quality of life and resilience of mothers with disabled and neurotypically developing children in Iran. *Heliyon*, *7*(6), e07285. https://doi.org/10.1016/j.heliyon2021.e07285

Gallagher, S., Phillips, A. C., Lee, H., & Carroll, D. (2015). The association between spirituality and depression in parents caring for children with developmental disabilities: Social support and/or last resort. *Journal of Religion and Health*, *54*, 358–370.

Gallagher, S., & Whitely, J. (2012). Social support is associated with blood pressure responses in patients caring for children with developmental disabilities. *Research in Developmental Disabilities*, *33*, 2099–2105.

Garden, R. (2010). Disability and narrative: New directions for medicine and the medical humanities. *Journal of Medical Ethics; Medical Humanities*, *36*, 70–74.

Gargiulo, R. M., & Bouck, E. C. (2018). *Special education in contemporary society: An introduction to exceptionality* (6th ed.). SAGE.

Georgetown University Child Development Center. (2021). *Serving children with disabilities: Supporting families with children with disabilities*. https://gucchd.georgetown.edu/products/SCWD_2FCD.pdf

Giallo, R., & Gavidia-Payne, S. (2006). Child, parent and family factors as predictors of adjustment for siblings of children with a disability. *Journal of Intellectual Disability Research*, *50*, 937–948.

Gillies, R. M. (2014). The role of assessment in informing interventions for students with special education needs. *International Journal of Disability, Development, and Education*, *61*(1), 1–5.

Goering, S. (2015). Rethinking disability: The social model of disability and chronic disease. *Current Reviews in Musculoskeletal Medicine*, *8*(2), 134–138.

Goodman, N., Morris, M., & Boston, K. (2019). *Financial inequality: Disability, race, and poverty in America*. National Disability Institute. https://www.nationaldisabilityinstitute.org/wp-content/uploads/2019/02/disability-race-poverty-in-america.pdf

Goudie, A., Narcisse, M. R., Hall, D. E., & Kuo, D. Z. (2014). Financial and psychological stressors associated with caring for children with disability. *Families, Systems & Health: The Journal of Collaborative Family Healthcare*, *32*(3), 280–290.

Halfon, N., Houtrow, A., Larson, K., & Newacheck, P. W. (2012). The changing landscape of disability in childhood. *Future of Children*, *22*(1), 13–42.

Hall, M. C. (2019). Critical disability theory. In E. N. Zalta (Ed.), *The stanford encyclopedia of philosophy*. https://plato.stanford.edu/archives/win2019/entries/disability-critical

Hallahan, D. P., & Kauffman, J. M. (2000). *Exceptional learners: Introduction to special education*. Allyn & Bacon.

Haskell, R. (2010). *Evaluating social work students' attitudes toward physical disability. Scholar Commons Graduate Theses and Dissertations*. https://scholarcommons.usf.edu/etd/1655

Hastings, R. P., & Taunt, H. (2002). Positive perceptions in families of children with developmental disabilities. *American Journal on Mental Retardation*, *107*(2), 116–127.

Hearing Loss Association of America. (2021). *Children with hearing loss*. https://www.hearingloss.org/hearing-help/financial-assistance/

Heiman, T., & Olenik-Shemesh, D. (2020). Social-emotional profile of children with and without learning disabilities: The relationships with perceived loneliness, self-efficacy, and well-being. *International Journal of Environmental Research & Public Health*, *17*(2), 7358. https://doi.org/10.3390/ijerph17207358

Helmreich, I., Kunzler, A., Chmitorz, A., Konig, J., Binder, H., Wessa, M., & Lieb, K. (2017, February 2). Psychological interventions for resilience enhancement in adults. *Cochrane Database Systems Review*. https://doi.org/10.1002/14651858.CD012527

Holley, L. C., Tavassoli, K. Y., & Stromwall, L. K. (2016). Mental illness discrimination in mental health treatment programs: Intersections of race, ethnicity, and sexual orientation. *Community Mental Health Journal*, *52*, 311–322.

Hosking, D. L. (2008). *Critical disability theory*. A paper presented at the 4th Biennial Critical Disability Theory A paper presented at the 4th Biennial Disability Studies Conference, Lancaster University, UK, September 2–4, 2008.

Hsiao, Y. J. (2017). Parental stress in families of children with disabilities. *Intervention in School & Clinic*, *53*(4), 201–205.

Hsiao, Y. J., Higgins, K., & Diamond, L. (2018). Parent empowerment: Respecting their voices. *Teaching Exceptional Children*, *51*(1), 43–53.

Hung, J. W., Wu, Y. H., Chiang, Y. C., Wu, W. C., & Yeh, C. H. (2010). Mental health of parents having children with physical disabilities. *Chang Gung Medical Journal*, *33*(1), 82–91.

Idan, O., & Margalit, M. (2014). Socioemotional self-perceptions, family climate, and hopeful thinking among students with learning disabilities and typically achieving students from the same classes. *Journal of Learning Disabilities*, *47*(2), 136–152.

Jess, M., Totsika, V., & Hastings, R. P. (2018). Maternal stress and the functions of positivity in mothers of children with intellectual disability. *Journal of Child & Family Studies*, *27*(11), 3753–3763.

Kandel, I., & Merrick, J. (2003). The birth of a child with disability: Coping by parents and siblings. *The Scientific World Journal*, *3*, 741–750.

Keniș-Coșkun, Ö., Atabay, C. E., Șekeroğlu, A., Akdeniz, E., Kasil, B., Bozkurt, G., & Karadağ-Saygı, E. (2020). The relationship between caregiver burden and resilience and quality of life in a Turkish pediatric rehabilitation facility. *Journal of Pediatric Nursing*, *52*, e108–e113.

Kimura, M., & Yamazaki, Y. (2013). The lived experiences of mothers of multiple children with intellectual disabilities. *Qualitative Health Research*, *23*(10), 1307–1319.

King, B. J. (2016). *'Disabled': Just #SayTheWord*. https://www.npr.org/sections/13.7/2016/02/25/468073722/disabled-just-saytheword

King, L. A., & Patterson, C. (2000). Reconstructing life goals after the birth of a child with Down's syndrome: Finding happiness and growing. *International Journal of Rehabilitation and Health*, *5*(1), 17–30.

Kirby, A. V., White, T. J., & Baranek, G. G. (2015). Caregiver strain and sensory features in children with autism spectrum disorder and other developmental disabilities. *American Journal of Developmental Disabilities*, *120*(1), 32–45.

Lalvani, P. l., & Polvere, L. (2013). Historical perspective on studying families of children with disabilities: A case for critical research. *Disability Studies Quarterly*, *33*(3). https://dsq-sds.org/article/view/3209/3291

Learning Disabilities Association of America. (2021). *ADHD: Affects focus, attention, and behavior and can make learning challenging*. https://ldaamerica.org/disabilities/adhd/

Lee, J. (2013). Maternal stress, well-being, and impaired sleep in mothers of children with developmental disabilities: A literature review. *Research on Developmental Disabilities*, *34*, 4255–4273.

Liebowitz, C. (2015). *I am disabled. On identity-first language*. https://thebodyisnotanapology.com/magazine/i-am-disabled-on-identity-first-versus-people-first-language/

Lukowiak, T. (2010, Winter). Training and support for parents of children with emotional and behavioral disorders. *JAASEP*, 25–35.

March of Dimes. (2022). *Birth defects and other health conditions*. https://www.marchofdimes.org/complications/birth-defects-other-health-conditions.aspx

Masefield, S. C., Prady, S. L., Sheldon, T. A., Small, N., Jarvis, S., & Pickett, K. E. (2020). The caregiver health effects of caring for young children with developmental disabilities: A meta-analysis. *Maternal & Child Health Journal*, *24*, 561–574.

Meadow-Orlans, K. P. (1994). Stress, support, and deafness: Perceptions of infants' mothers and fathers. *Journal of Early Intervention*, *18*(1), 91–102.

Micsinszki, S. K., Ballantyne, M., Cleverley, K., Green, P., & Stremler, R. (2018). Sleep outcomes for parents of children with neurodevelopmental disabilities: A systematic review. *Journal of Family Nursing*, *24*, 217–249.

Miodrag, N., & Hodapp, R. M. (2010). Chronic stress and health among parents of children with intellectual and developmental disabilities. *Current Opinion in Psychiatry*, *23*(5), 407–411.

Moses, K. (1983). The impact of initial diagnosis: Mobilizing family resources. In J. Mulick & S. Pueschel (Eds.), *Parent-professional partnerships in developmental disabilities services* (pp. 11–34). Academic Guild.

Munyi, C. W. (2012). Past and present perceptions towards disability: A historical perspective. *Disabilities Studies Quarterly*, *32*(2). https://dsq-sds.org/article/view/3197/3068&sa=U&ved=0ahUKEwjlpcnlLubKAhULaz4KHX_YDy0QFgg0MAc&usg=AFQjCNEWDZ_0jsTk0B8Q2JDebeZ2Ngp2QQ

Murphy, N. A., Christian, B., Caplin, D. A., & Young, P. C. (2007). The health of caregivers for children with disabilities: Caregiver perspectives. *Child: Care, Health, & Development*, *33*(2), 180–187.

Naniwadekar, K. (2018). Stress and anxiety among parents of children with communication disorders. In S. K. Gupta & S. Venkatesan (Eds.), *Handbook of research on psychosocial perspectives of human communication disorders* (pp. 141–156). IGI Global. https://doi.org/10.4018/978-1-5225-4955-0

National Academies of Sciences, Engineering, and Medicine. (2016). *Parenting matters: Supporting parents of children ages 0–8*. The National Academies Press. https://doi.org/10.17226/21868

National Center on Deaf-Blindness. (2021). *Improving services, results, and quality of life for children and youth who are deaf-blind*. https://www.nationaldb.org/

National Center for Education Statistics. (2021a). *Students with disabilities: Fast facts*. https://nces.ed.gov/fastfacts/display.asp?id=64

National Center for Education Statistics. (2021b). *Students with disabilities*. https://nces.ed.gov/programs/coe/indicator/cgg

National Council on Family Relations. (2021). *Family life education content areas: Content and practice guidelines*. https://www.ncfr.org/sites/default/files/2023/FLE%20Content%20and%20Practice%20Guidelines%202020.pdf

National Deaf Children's Society. (2021). *Staying connected: Impact report, 2020/2021*. https://www.ndcs.org.uk/media/7420/staying-connected_national-deaf-childrens-society-impact-report_2020-to-2021.pdf

National Dissemination Center for Children with Disabilities. (2021). *Categories of disability under IDEA*. https://www.parentcenterhub.org/wp-content/uploads/repo_items/gr3.pdf

National Survey of Children's Health. (2019). *National survey of children with special health-care needs*. https://www.childhealthdata.org/learn-about-the-nsch/archive-prior-year-data-documents-and-resources

Osborne, L. A., & Reed, P. (2009). The relationship between parenting stress and behavior problems of children with autistic spectrum disorders. *Exceptional Children, 76*, 54–73.

Padden, C., & James, J. E. (2017). Stress among parents of children with and without autism spectrum disorder: A comparison involving physiological indicators and parent self-reports. *Journal of Developmental and Physical Disabilities, 29*, 567–586.

Panicker, A. S., & Chelliah, A. (2016). Resilience and stress in children and adolescents with specific learning disability. *Journal of the Canadian Academy of Child & Adolescent Psychiatry, 25*(1), 17–23.

Pothier, D., & Devlin, R. (2016). *Critical disability theory: Essays in philosophy, politics, and law*. UBC Press.

Rapanaro, C., Bartu, A., & Lee, A. H. (2008). Perceived benefits and negative impact of challenges encountered in caring for young adults with intellectual disabilities in the transition to adulthood. *Journal of Applied Research in Intellectual Disabilities, 21*, 4–47.

Rehabilitation Act. (1973). *Rehabilitation act of 1973 (Rehab act)*. https://askearn.org/page/the-rehabilitation-act-of-1973-rehab-act#:~:text=The%20Rehabilitation%20Act%20of%201973%2C%20as%20Amended%20(Rehab%20Act),employment%20practices%20of%20federal%20contractors

Renati, R., Bonfiglio, N. S., & Pfeiffer, S. (2017). Challenges raising a gifted child: Stress and resilience factors within the family. *Gifted Education International, 33*(2), 145–162.

Ricci, F., Levi, C., Nardecchia, E., Antonella, A., & Salvatore, A. G. (2017). Psychological aspects in parents of children with disability and behavior problems. *European Psychiatry, 41*, S792.

Ritzema, A. M., & Sladeczek, I. E. (2011). Stress in parents of children with developmental disabilities over time. *The Journal of Developmental Disabilities, 17*(2), 21–34.

Scherer, N., Verhy, I., & Kuper, H. (2019). Depression and anxiety in parents of children with intellectual and developmental disabilities: A systematic review and meta-analysis. *PLoS ONE, 14*(7), e0219888.

Senju, A., Tucker, L., Pasco, G., Hudry, K., Hudry, K., Elsabbagh, M., Charman, T., & Johnson, M. H. (2013). *The importance of the eyes: Communication skills in infants of blind parents*. https://doi.org/10.1098/rspb.2013.0436

Shahat, S., & Greco, G. (2021). The economic costs of childhood disability: A literature review. *International Journal of Environmental Research and Public Health, 18*, 1–25.

Shyam, R., Govil, D., & Govil, K. (2014). Stress and family burden in mothers of children with disabilities. *International Journal of Interdisciplinary & Multidisciplinary Studies, 1*(4), 152–159.

Silvers, A. A. (1998). A fatal attraction to normalizing. In E.

Parens (Ed.), *Enhancing human traits* (pp. 95–123). Georgetown University Press.

Smith, A. M., & Grzywaca, J. G. (2014). Health and well-being in midlife parents of children with special health needs. *Family, Systems, & Health, 32*(3), 303–312.

Smith, D. D., & Luckasson, R. (1992). *Introduction to special education: Teaching in an age of challenge*. Allyn & Bacon.

Stabile, M., & Allin, S. (2012). The economic costs of childhood disability. *Future Child, 22*(1), 65–96.

Sulkes, S. B. (2022). *Intellectual disability. Merck Manual*. https://www.msdmanuals.com/home/children-s-health-issues/learning-and-developmental-disorders/intellectual-disability

Suzuki, K., Hiratani, M., Mizukoshi, N., Hayashi, T., & Inagaki, M. (2018). Family resilience elements alleviate the relationship between maternal psychological distress and the severity of children's developmental disorders. *Research in Developmental Disabilities, 83*, 91–98.

Suzuki, K., Kobayasi, T., Moriyama, K., Kaga, M., & Inagaki, M. (2013). A framework for resilience research in parents of children with developmental disorders. *Asian Journal of Human Services, 5*, 104–111.

Towner, C. (2020). *What the next administration will spend on children*. Children's Budget Coalition. https://www.childrensbudget.org/news

Turnbull, A., Turnbull, R., Erwin, E. J., Soodak, L. C., & Shogren, K. A. (2015). *Families, professionals, and exceptionality* (7th ed.). Pearson.

U.S. Department of Education. (2021a). *U.S. Department of Education releases more than $3 billion in American Rescue Plan Funds to support children*. https://www.ed.gov/news/press-releases/us-department-education-releases-more-3-billion-american-rescue-plan-funds-support-children-disabilities

U.S. Department of Education. (2021b). *Office of special education programs, individuals with disabilities act (IDEA) database*. https://www.e.ed.gov/programs/osepidea/618-data/state-level-data-files/index.html#bccDigestof Education Statistics, 2020, table 204.30

Van Haren, B., & Fiedler, C. R. (2008). Support and empower families of children with disabilities. *Intervention in School and Clinic, 43*(4), 231–235.

Van den Broek, E. G. C., van Eijden, A., Overbeek, M. M., Kef, S., Sterkenburg, P. S., & Schuengel, C. (2017). A systematic review of the literature on parenting of young children with visual impairments and the adaptions for Video-Feedback Intervention to Promote Positive Parenting (VIPP). *Journal of Developmental & Physical Disabilities, 29*(3), 503–545.

Vaughan, E. L., Feinn, R., Bernard, S., Brereton, M., & Kaufman, J. S. (2013). Relationships between child emotional and behavioral symptoms and caregiver strain and parenting stress. *Journal of Family Issues, 34*(4), 534–556.

Vilaseca, R., Ferrer, F., & Guardia Olmos, J. (2013). Gender differences in positive perceptions, anxiety, and depression among mothers and fathers of children with intellectual disabilities: A logistic regression analysis. *Quality & Quantity, 48*(4), 2241–2253.

Walker, H. M., & Severson, H. H. (1990). *Systematic screening for behavior disorders user's guide and administration manual*. Sopris West.

Whiting, M., Nash, A. S., Kendall, S., & Roberts, S. A. (2019). Enhancing resilience and self-efficacy in the parents of children with disabilities and complex health needs. *Primary Health Care Research and Development, 20*(e33). https://doi.org/10.1017/S1463423619000112

Widyawati, Y., Otten, R., Kleemans, T., & Scholte, R. H. J. (2020). Parental resilience and the quality of life of children with developmental disabilities in Indonesia. *International Journal of Disability, Development, and Education*. https://doi.org/10.1080/1034912X.2020.1834078

Williams, E., & Musumeci, M. (2021). *Children with special healthcare needs: Coverage, affordability, and HCBS access*. https://www.kff.org/medicaid/issue-brief/children-with-special-health-care-needs-coverage-affordability-and-hcbs-access/

Woodman, A. C. (2014). Trajectories of stress among parents of children with disabilities: A dyadic analysis. *Family Relations, 63*(1), 39–54.

Woodman, A., & Hauser-Cram, P. (2013). The role of coping strategies in predicting change in parenting efficacy and depressive symptoms among mothers of adolescents with developmental disabilities. *Journal of Intellectual Disability Research*, *57*(6), 513–530.

Woodman, A. C., Mawdsley, H. P., & Hauser-Cram, P. (2015). Parenting stress and child behavior problems within families of children with developmental disabilities: Transactional relations across 15 years. *Research in Developmental Disabilities*, *36*, 264–276.

World Health Organization (WHO). (2011). *World report on disability.* https://www.who.int/disabilities/world_report/2011/report.pdf

GLOSSARY

A factor: The life event that causes a family stress.

ABC-X family crisis model: A theoretical model that helps to explain how families cope with and adapt to crisis or stress.

Acculturation: The transfer of societal values and customs from one group to another—it is a cultural shift where individuals or people groups adopt the predominant behaviors and traits of a different culture.

ADHD: A behavioral disorder that makes it difficult for children to stay focused, and presents them with difficulties in controlling their behaviors; some children are also affected by hyperactivity.

Adolescence: The developmental period that spans childhood and adulthood, ages 10 to 25.

Adverse Childhood Experiences (ACEs): Specific environmental kinds of adversity children may face.

African Heritage theory: Views African American/Black Caribbean cultures as distinctly different from white, European American cultures; takes into consideration the unique characteristics and elements of West African culture (from where most slaves were captured) that were preserved while they were enslaved in America and the Caribbean.

Age of majority: The legal age (18 in most states) at which a person is considered an adult.

Age-related norms: Socially approved and shaped timelines to when a person should get married, have children, retire, etc.

Ageism: The stereotypical attitudes people hold about the aging and the elderly.

Ageist: A fixed, negative biased mindset about older people.

Alcohol-Related Birth Defects (ARBD): Defects of the internal organs due to the gestational parent's consumption of alcohol during pregnancy.

Alcohol-Related Neurodevelopmental Disorder (ARND): Affects a person's cognitive abilities.

Anencephaly: A baby is born with missing parts of the brain and/or skull.

Angry associates: Anger and resentment characterize these postbreakup relationships; coparenting is not a goal.

Antinatalist: An ideology that discourages childbearing.

Anxiety: Generalized anxiety disorder causes excessive worry and apprehension.

Appraisal-focused coping: Families try to make meaning of the stressor.

Artificial insemination: Donor sperm is inserted into the gestational parent's vagina via medical procedures.

Assisted Reproductive Technology (ART): Treatments that involve fertilization through the hands-on manipulation of ova and sperm.

Attachment theory: Studies the attachment types of infants and adults.

Attachment: The special emotional, enduring bond an infant forms with significant adults.

Authoritarian parenting: Obedience- and status-orientated.

Authoritative parenting: Warm, responsive parenting with clear boundaries and high communication.

Autism (ASD): A developmental disability comprised of a broad range of impairments that significantly affect a person's verbal and nonverbal communication, interpersonal relationships, and their social interaction skills.

Autonomy versus Shame and Doubt: Erikson's second stage of psychosocial development.

Autonomy: Developing individuation and becoming a self-governing individual.

Azoospermia: No sperm cells are produced.

B factor: The resources families have available to them to help them meet the demands of a stressor.

Balance/homeostasis: A family's state of "normal."

Basic budgets: The amount of money families need to manage at the most basic level (housing, food, transportation, child care, health care, etc.).

Basic virtues: Personality strengths.

Batterer: The person who carries out the violence.

Bicultural socialization/biculturalism: Both the aspects of African and/or Caribbean heritages and Western culture are integrated.

Binuclear family: The distinct households that form after marital separation or divorce.

BIPOC: Black, Indigenous People of Color.

Blastocyst: A ball of cells that differentiates into an embryo.

Blended family: Another term for stepfamily; however, the Stepfamily Association of America disagrees with the use of this term because families do not blend because that would imply a loss of identity.

Blue-collar workers: Highly represented in the service sector (plumber, electrician, etc.).

Boundary: A system that serves the purpose of affecting the exchange of information within a family system.

Brain plasticity: The brain's ability to modify and reconstruct itself.

Braxton Hicks contractions: Prelabor or practice contractions that result when the uterus contracts and relaxes.

Bullying/peer abuse: A "power differential in which one or more youth repeatedly use aggressive strategies to dominate and cause harm to others of relatively lower status."

***C* factor:** The family's perception of the stressor event.

Calming response (CR): The ways in which an infant soothes when upset or crying.

Caregiver burden: The physical and emotional wear and tear on caregivers.

Caregiver/informal caregiver: An unpaid individual who is involved in assisting others with daily living.

Caregiver: The person/persons responsible for the primary care of the infant or young child.

Caregiving career: The years that caregivers tend to dependent children, aging parents, and eventually, dependent husbands or wives.

Child maltreatment: Any act, intentional or not, that results in harm to a child, the threat of harm, or the potential for harm.

Child sexual abuse (CSA): A form of child abuse that involves sexual activity with a minor.

Childfree by choice: Remaining childfree as a conscious choice.

Childfree: A conscience choice to not have children.

Childless: If a couple is unable to conceive or bear children of their own or adopt children.

Children's Health Insurance Program (CHIP): Provides healthcare coverage for low-income children.

Chosen family: Nonbiological kinship bonds that often replace blood families and become the bedrock of trust, support, and love for LGBTQ+ individuals and their families.

Chronosystem: Reflects changes in society that happen over time.

Circumplex model of marital and family systems: A theoretical model that addresses family cohesion (emotional closeness), adaptability, and communication.

Cognitive avoidance/denial: Families deny the seriousness of the situation.

Cognitive redefinition: Families reframe the life event to make it more favorable.

Cohabiting couples: Unmarried partners who live together in a single household.

Cold cognition: Cognitive processes that do not involve emotion.

Collectivist cultures: Individuals define their identity in terms of the relationships they hold with others.

Communication disorders: Affect either/both a child's ability to send/receive messages.

Communication rules: Govern what family members can and cannot discuss or share and how they are to interact with their own family members.

Communication: The process of making and sharing meanings.

Companionate relationship: A relationship in which

grandparents and grandchildren are companions.

Conception: Occurs when the product of fertilization embeds in the uterine lining.

Conceptus: The fertilized ovum.

Congenital birth defects: Physical and structural anomalies present at birth.

Constructive conflict: Serves to build relationships and foster loyalty, commitment, and intimacy.

Contexts/ecosystem: Areas of individual and family development that play a role in the relationship between people and their environments; these multiple contexts make up a person's "culture."

Cooperative colleagues: Ex-partners cooperate as parents, but do not consider themselves to be friends.

Cost-burdened: Families who pay 30% of their total income on housing.

Critical disability theory: A person's disability is as much a cultural, social, and political issue as it is a biophysical or biocognitve one.

Critical period of development: Weeks 3 to 8, when all of the baby's organs and physical structures develop.

Crude birth rate: The number of childbirths per 1,000 women, per year.

Cry it out/sleep training: Parents let their infants cry themselves to sleep, rather than comforting or rocking them.

Cultural competence: Accepting and respecting cultural differences, being aware of the dynamics of these differences, and continually expanding cultural knowledge.

Cultural variation approach: The range of social practices (i.e., gender roles, economic systems, and social hierarchy) observed in different cultures around the world, and the maintenance of these ways of life.

Cyberbullicide: Describes suicides that are influenced by online harassment and aggression.

Cyberbullying: Bullying that takes place in an electronic format (such as texting, email, or Facebook).

Cycle of violence model: A model that describes the common patterns of intimate partner abuse.

Deaf-blindness: People who simultaneously experience hearing and vision impairments.

Deafness: A child has difficulty processing through hearing, even with amplification (hearing aids).

Dealing-with-problems focus: An early educational approach that emphasized the problems in culture and the ways in which to cope with the problems.

Depression: Major depressive disorder, a serious mood disorder.

Destructive conflict: Unhelpful and hurtful.

Developing-family-potentials focus: A contemporary educational approach that builds on positive aspects of family life and bring about human capabilities that improve and enhance personal life and family living.

Developmental deficits: Experiences and behaviors that lead to risk-taking in adolescents.

Developmental delays: Children who exhibit significant delays in one or more domains of physical, cognitive, communicative, social and emotional, and adaptive development.

Developmental tasks: Individuals achieve certain biological, physical, cognitive/intellectual, social, emotional, and spiritual tasks across the lifecourse.

Dilate: The cervix opens to 10 centimeters.

Diminished parenting: Initially following a divorce, parents become less involved and less communicative and nurturing with their children.

Discipline: Instruction from another; positive system of guidance.

Disorganized: Infants who do not fit to any of the other 3 attachment types, but who have attachment difficulties.

Dispenser of wisdom grandparenting: Grandparent offers information and advice to their grandchildren—often whether it is asked for or not.

Dissolved duos: After the dissolution of the relationship, the partners have little to zero contact with each other.

Diversity/diverse: The broad spectrum of demographic and philosophical differences among people groups both within and outside of a culture; specifically, differences in age, gender, race, ethnicity, culture, sexual orientation, religion, and socioeconomic status.

Domestic violence: Violence perpetrated against family members by someone who is related either biologically or legally.

Double ABC-X model: A theoretical model that helps to explain the cumulative effects of multiple stressors.

Doula: A professional labor support person.

Dual-earner couples: Marriages or relationships in which both partners work.

Dyslexia: A disorder that makes it difficult for affected children to learn to read or write letters, words, and other symbols.

Early remarriage: The early stages of a new marital relationship.

Echolalia: Repeating sounds or phrases.

Efface: The cervix becomes thin.

Embryonic period: Weeks 3 through 8 of pregnancy.

Emerging adulthood: A developmental phase spanning the ages of 18 to the mid- to late-twenties.

Emotion coaching: A parenting practice that helps children to self-regulate.

Emotion regulation (ER): A person's ability to chance the intensity of emotional experiences.

Emotion-focused coping: Families try to maintain hope.

Emotion-related parenting: Parenting practices that teach children and adolescents about emotions and emotion-related behavior.

Emotional discharge: Commonly referred to as "venting."

Emotional disturbance: Characterized by inappropriate behaviors, or feelings; an inability to learn; difficulty building or maintaining relationships.

Empathy: The capacity to understand another's circumstances or situation, and the ability to feel or express emotional concern for another person.

Empowerment principles: Allow families to control the direction and outcomes of support services.

Empty nest: The family home with no children.

Excessive infant crying: When an infant cries for 3 hours per day, 3 days per week, for at least 3 weeks.

Executive functions: Higher-level cognitive processes.

Exosystem: Elements of society in which policies are made and influenced that ultimately have an impact on the elements of the microsystem and the individual.

Expressive roles: Assigned to the people-oriented mate.

Extended family: A family system where two or more generations of close family relatives live together in one household.

Externalizing behaviors: Aggressive behavior expressed outwardly against others.

Externalizing difficulties/acting out: Feelings about the divorce or stresses associated with parents' breaking up are typically shown in aggressive misbehaviors, disobedience, and increased school absences.

Familismo/familism: The term used by Latinx to describe their loyalty to their collective family, and it refers to the mutual support and obligation shared between family members.

Family and Medical Leave Act (FMLA): Federal and state employees and those who work for employers with 50 or more employees are able to take up to 11 weeks of unpaid leave in order to care for an ill child, parent, or spouse, or for one's own serious illness, without fear of losing their job, benefits, or status. Unpaid leave can also be taken for the birth or adoption of a child, or when placing a child for adoption or foster care. Both working men and women are protected by this legislation.

Family cohesion: Extent to which family members feel emotionally close and bonded to one another.

Family Life Cycle: Comprises multiple entrances and exits from the family of origin.

Family Life Education: Provides organized, programmatic education to help strengthen families.

Family of origin: The family into which we are born or brought into by adoption or circumstance (such as being raised by a grandparent).

Family projection process: The decision to have/not have children based on one's past childhood experiences.

Family resilience: A family's ability to interact in healthy ways during times of change, stress, or crisis.

Family science: The scientific study of children, families, and parenting to gain a comprehensive understanding of the diversity of parenting life.

Family system: A family entity who reside in a household that consists of various individuals and their interconnected, intergenerational patterns of interactions.

Family systems theory (FST): A theoretical paradigm that views families as a whole entity made up of interconnected parts that seek to maintain balance.

Family-centered support services: Embraces the idea that services should center on and be responsive to the needs of all family members as they relate to the child's development.

Family: A group of two people or more related by birth, marriage, or adoption and residing together.

Father involvement: The time a father and their/his child(ren) spend together.

Feminization of poverty: Following divorce or within single-parenting, women experience poverty rates that are higher in comparison to men.

Fertilization: The fusion of the ovum and the sperm.

Fetal alcohol spectrum disorders (FASDs): An umbrella term that includes a group of anatomical and intellectual conditions that affect a developing baby in the womb.

Fetal Alcohol Syndrome (FAS): The most serious FASD condition.

Fetal period: Weeks 9 through 40 of pregnancy.

Fictive kin: People who are not biologically related to someone, but who fulfill a family role.

Fiery foes: The relationship of these exes is intensely anger-filled, and are marked by many trips to attorneys and the court.

Filial obligation: A waning social norm that prescribes that adult children provide care for their aging parents.

Filial piety: A deeply engrained moral foundation in Asian societies that involves a series of obligations of child to parent.

First trimester: The first 12 weeks of pregnancy.

Formal grandparenting: Traditional grandparenting roles.

Framework: A systematic structure for classifying families, their behaviors, or their experiences.

Free and Appropriate Education (FAPE): Every public school district must provide free education appropriate to the child's abilities.

Free-range parenting: A parenting style that promotes the idea of raising children to function as independently as possible, as young as possible.

Freebirth/unassisted birth: Intentionally giving birth without the guidance of a health-care professional.

Full term: A baby born between 37 and 40 weeks.

Fun seeker grandparenting: A relationship characterized by informal, spontaneous playfulness.

Gamete intrafallopian transfer (GIFT): Unfertilized eggs are placed directly into the gestational parent's fallopian tubes.

Gender binary: There are two opposite, distinct genders.

Gender equality: Discrimination based on a person's gender is illegal.

Gender expression: How a person chooses to present their gender to their social world through appearance and behaviors.

Gender identity: A person's concept of male, female, both, or neither.

Gender minority: A person's gender identity is not in alignment with their genetically assigned sex.

Gender nonbinary: Individuals who do not define themselves as male or female.

Gender nonconforming: A person's physical appearance and behaviors do not align with societal norms and mores of "male" or "female."

Gender wage gap: Disparity in earnings between men and women.

Gender-Based Violence (GBV): Violence perpetrated against an individual because of their gender/gender identity.

General Systems theory (GST): A theoretical model that purports that objects do not exist in isolation, but instead are interconnected to parts of a larger whole.

Germinal period: Weeks 0 through 2 of pregnancy.

Gerontologists: Scientists who study the aging processes.

Gestation: The process of carrying human life in the womb.

Gestational parent: The individual who carries human life in the womb.

Giftedness: Children who excel in some way in comparison to their peers.

Glass ceiling: Discrimination against women in the workplace that prevents women from advancing.

Gonadarche: The time during which initial sex hormones are produced in genetic males and genetic females.

Grandfamilies: Families in which grandparents are the primary caregivers for their grandchildren.

Group reliance: The belief instilled into children that anyone in a community can help them.

Gunnysacking: When a person unloads all of the pent-up feelings in the midst of an argument.

Hayflick Limit: The theory that each species has a genetically programmed time limit because at a certain point in time, cells lose their ability to replicate.

Hearing impairment: A child who has difficulty hearing.

Heteronormative: A perspective that asserts that heterosexuality is the norm.

Homelessness: Persons living in areas not designated as human habitats.

Hookup: Brief, noncommitted, emotionally charged sexual encounters.

Hot cognition: Cognitive processes that do involve emotion.

Household: All the people who occupy a housing unit.

Hydrocephalus: A buildup of fluid on the unborn baby's brain.

Identity confusion: Confusion in the establishment of identity and pursuit of self.

Identity: A subjective sense of self.

Immigrant families with children: Children with at least one parent who was born outside of the United States.

Immigrants: People who reside in the United States who were not U.S. citizens at birth.

In Vitro Fertilization (IVF): Eggs are surgically removed from the ovary and mixed with sperm in a laboratory culture dish; they are placed inside of the gestational parent's uterus.

Indian removal act/Trail of tears: Policies that allowed the U.S. Government to remove Native children from their families and relocate them with the sole purpose of forced cultural assimilation.

Individualistic cultures: Where individual goals are promoted over group goals.

Individuals with disabilities education act (IDEA): Requires all public schools in the United States to meet the education needs of every student, regardless of ability.

Individuation: The adolescent process of establishing a strong sense of self, or identity.

Inductive discipline: Encourages children to accept responsibility for their behaviors.

Industry versus Inferiority: Erik Erikson's fourth stage of psychosocial development.

Industry: A sense of achievement, competence, ability.

Inferiority: A persistent sense of inadequacy.

Infertility: The inability to conceive a baby.

Inhibitory control (IC): Withholding responses that may not be appropriate.

Initiative versus Guilt: Erikson's third stage of psychosocial development.

Initiative: A child believes he/she/they can accomplish anything.

Insecure-avoidant: Independent of the parents.

Insecure-resistant: Infants have underinvolved parents.

Instrumental roles: Assigned to the task-oriented mate.

Intellectual disability: Significantly subaverage intellectual functioning.

Intensive mothering ideology: The Western cultural belief that a mother should give of herself unconditionally and focus all of her time, energy, money, love, support, and every other resource she has on raising her children.

Intergenerational ties: The relationships between family members across multiple generations.

Internal/external assets: Psychological and societal factors that promote healthy adolescent development.

Internalizing behaviors: Expressed in a more socially withdrawn fashion and include anxiety and depression.

Internalizing difficulties: Feelings and stress are expressed as emotional problems, such as worry and anxiety.

Interrole conflict: When the demands of one role conflict with the demands of another.

Intersectionality: The interconnected nature of social categorizations—such as race, social economic class, and gender—regarded as creating overlapping and interdependent systems of discrimination or disadvantage.

Intimate partner violence: Violence against an intimate partner.

Involved grandparenting: Grandparents assume the role of parent.

Job autonomy: Employees are allowed a high degree of independence and self-direction.

Job complexity: Are both challenging and stimulating.

Job status: A type of job that offers prestige.

Labor: The rhythmic uterine contractions that help to expel the baby.

Language disorder: An impairment or deviant development of comprehension and/or use of a spoken, written, and/or other symbol system.

Lanugo: A soft downy hair that covers the baby in the womb.

Late remarriage: 6 to 10 years after the remarriage; by this time, family boundaries and roles are restructured.

Latinx: People of Latin American origin or descent; the gender-neutral alternative to Latino or Latina.

Lesbian comothering (LCM): The shared mothering role in lesbian couple relationships.

Life expectancy: The average period a person is expected to live.

Life orientation: The emphasis pre-retirees or retirees place on various aspects of life, such as family life and economic security.

Lifespan perspective: Humans are in a continuous state of growth and development, from birth until death.

Logical consequences: Assigned by the parent to express status quo or order.

Macrosystem: The overarching cultural values and beliefs that affect individual development by establishing either implicit or explicit rules about what is or is not acceptable behavior.

Market alternative cost method: Estimates the value of household labor by looking at what it would cost in the current market to pay someone to do the household labor a parent performs.

Maternal role attainment (MRA): The fluid, continual, fluctuating processes associated with becoming a mother.

Maturation imbalance model: The brain regions that seek reward mature more quickly than the regions of the brain that promote impulse control.

Maturity gap: Developmental imbalance between the maturation rates of various regions in the brain.

Medicaid: Public health insurance that is funded by the federal government and local states.

Medical model/medicalization: Disability is seen as an illness or ailment (biological, cognitive, or intellectual deficit), and must therefore be treated by clinical or therapeutic means.

Mesosystem: The interaction *between* the various elements rather than on the individual.

Microsystem: The developmental context nearest the individual and represents those interactions in which people are directly involved.

Middle childhood: A distinct developmental stage in the lifespan, encompassing ages 6 to 12.

Middle remarriage: About 3 to 5 years after the formation of the new marriage; the family becomes more cohesive.

Mothering: A process whereby someone performs the relational and logistical work of caring for others.

Multiple disabilities: Co-occurring impairments.

Multiple mothering: A common parenting practice that involves aunts, cousins, close friends, and fictive kin who provide Black mothers with a range of modeling and tangible support.

Native American/Alaska Native (NA/AN): Aboriginal peoples of the United States and their descendants, and who maintain tribal affiliation or community attachment.

Natural consequences: Those that occur naturally from a behavior.

Nature versus Nurture debate: The decades-long debate regarding whether aging forces are hereditary or the result of environmental influences.

Neural Tube Defects (NTDs): Defects in the baby's spinal cord and/or brain.

Neuroatypical/neurodiverse: Autistic individuals; may have other developmental differences.

Neurobehavioral Disorder Associated with Prenatal Alcohol Exposure (ND-PAE): A diagnosis involving thinking and memory problems, behavior problems, and problems with day-to-day life skills, caused by the gestational parent's consumption of alcohol during pregnancy.

Neurons: Nerve cells that are the building blocks of the brain and nervous system.

Nonfamily household: Comprised of a householder living alone, such as a widow, or where the householder shares the home with people to whom they are not related.

Nonheteronormative: A perspective that does not adhere to the heteronormative gender binary expectation.

Nonnormative influences: Influences that are uncommon, rare, or unanticipated events.

Nonnormative: Life events that we do not anticipate, and that we cannot predict, but that do have an impact on our developmental lifecourse.

Nonregulated couples: Partners whose interactions tend to be far more negative than positive.

Normative age-graded influences: Developmental changes that are caused by biological, psychological, and sociocultural forces.

Normative history-graded influences: Events or conditions that people in a given culture or society experience simultaneously.

Normative/on-time events: They come at relatively predictable points in our lives and are generally expected. Additionally, sometimes events occur at atypical points in the lifespan, such as when a young adolescent gives birth.

Nuclear family: Consists of a biological father, a biological mother, and their biological or adopted children.

Nurturance: Affectionate care and attention.

Occupational sexism: Beliefs that the male gender is more capable of certain work-related tasks and professions than women are.

Off-time events: Sometimes events occur at atypical points in the lifespan, such as when a young adolescent gives birth.

Oligospermia: Too few sperm cells are produced.

Opportunity cost method: Asks the question, *What would a person be paid in wage labor for one hour of household work?*

Orthopedic impairments: Bone-, joint-, or muscle-related disabilities.

Overtime: Hours a person works beyond her or his normal 40-hour per week schedule.

Parent education: Assist persons who are already parents to be more effective in their roles, as well as to educate individuals who desire to work as a helping professional with parents and their families.

Parenthood aspirations: The desire, hope, or want to become a parent.

Parent–child relationship: Emotional and physical connections between a parent and a child.

Patriarchal family structure: The ideology that the father figure is the authority over his entire household.

Pelvic Inflammatory Disease (PID): A scarring of the fallopian tubes, most often due to infection or an untreated sexually transmitted infection.

Perfect pals: Parents who remain friends after divorce.

Permissive parenting: High levels of warmth, affection, and responsiveness, high levels of parent–child communication; do not attempt to control children's behaviors.

Personalismo: The warmth and familiarity expressed in family and extended kin relationships; it is central to Latinx interpersonal relationships.

Pink-collar phenomenon: "Traditionally female" jobs.

Positive stress response: A stress response that is mild and temporary.

Postpartum depression: Depressive symptoms in the gestational parent following the birth of the baby.

Prefrontal cortex (PFC): A region of the brain is responsible for an individual's executive functions, or higher-level cognitive processes.

Prepubescence: The middle childhood years that lead to puberty in adolescence.

Preterm: A baby born before the 37th week of pregnancy.

Preventing-the-problem focus: An early educational approach that emphasized pointing out the "correct" way to raise children.

Primary aging: Biological processes that are genetically programmed and that take place with the passage of time.

Primary divorce stressors: Immediate concerns such as custody arrangements and child support.

Problem-focused coping: Families focus on solutions to the stressor.

Progressive desensitization: Over a period of time, families allow themselves increased exposure to different aspects of the stressor.

Pronatalism/natalism: An ideology that embraces childbearing.

Prostaglandins: Chemicals that aid in softening the cervix to prepare it for birth.

Protective factors: Individual, family, peer, societal, and other contextual factors that protect against suicidality.

Psychological flexibility: The ways in which parents maintain boundaries between moral, conventional, and personal issues.

Psychosocial development: The social and emotional development of an individual.

Puberty: A time of muscular, skeletal, and reproductive growth.

Publicly funded: Money that is most often generated through taxes; the government then distributes this funding to federal, state, and local agencies.

Punishment: The aim is to make children hurt.

Quickening: The first fetal movement felt by the gestational parent.

Quiverfull movement (QF): A pronatalist belief that forgoes all forms of birth control.

Race-based traumatic stress theory: People who encounter racism and/or discrimination experience it as psychological trauma, provoking physical, social, and emotional responses similar to post-traumatic stress.

Racial/ethnic socialization: The way in which families teach children about the social meanings of their race/ethnicity.

Racism: A belief system which holds that race accounts for differences in human character and/or ability; it results in discrimination and prejudice based on someone's race or ethnic background.

Reciprocity: Positive or negative interactions.

Regulated couples: Use communication patterns and interpersonal behaviors that promote closeness and intimacy, such as using more positive comments than negative comments during times of tension.

Relationship stability: Factors that are indicators of a couple's proneness to divorce.

Remarriage: Instances when either one or both of the spouses have been previously married.

Remote grandparenting: The distant grandparent has little or no contact with grandchildren and is only involved on occasional holidays or birthdays.

Replacement fertility rate: The rate of live births at which the population of a society is replaced (typically 2.1).

Residual tasks: Bill paying, running errands, and other tasks which are more flexible.

Resigned acceptance: A family eventually accepts the situation.

Resilience-based interventions: Resources and programs that help parents and caregivers adapt well to psychological stress.

Resource dilution hypothesis: Parental time, energy, and resources are limited and become diluted when spread over many children.

Respeto: The respect of dependence and dutifulness to cultural, hierarchical relationships in Latinx cultures.

Responsivity: The degree to which a parent responds to the baby's cries.

Role: A system of cultural meanings.

Sandwich generation: The life phase when parenting adolescents or younger children while at the same time caring for aging parents.

Scapegoating: When anger and hostility are directed at one family member in particular, who always bears the brunt of everyone's frustration.

Second shift: Burden of taking on the dual responsibilities of wage-earner and housekeeper.

Second trimester: Weeks 13 to 26 of pregnancy.

Secondary aging: Physiological declines that are the result of environmental and behavioral influences that significantly impact how we age.

Secondary divorce stressors: The "fallout" associated with divorce, such as depression in adults or behavior problems in children.

Secondary sex characteristics: The physical sexual maturation changes in a child's body.

Secure: The infant is securely attached and uses the parent as a safe base.

Self-concept: A sense of belonging, worth, and competence.

Self-identity: How people define themselves in relation to family, friends, school, and other social environments.

Self-regulation: The child's ability to manage or direct his/her thoughts, emotions, and behaviors.

Self-regulation: An individual's ability to modulate emotional, cognitive, and behavioral arousal in the context of environmental demands.

Sensitive period: Experiences and environmental stimuli exert disproportionate influence on long-term developmental outcomes.

Sensitivity: The parent's ability to perceive the infant's signals and to respond appropriately.

Severely cost-burdened: Families who pay 50% of their total income on housing.

Sexual and gender minority youth (SGMY): Individuals who identify as gay, lesbian, bisexual, or transgender.

Sexual and reproductive health (SRH): Topics pertaining to an individual's sexual characteristics, values, behaviors, and communication.

Sexual minority youth (SMY): People who identify as gay, lesbian, or bisexual, who are romantically attracted to or enjoy sexual contact with people of the same sex.

Shift work: Varying hours of work rather than a typical workweek.

Social identity: Constructed by the culture in which people live.

Social model: Supports the idea that disability is determined by the ways in which a society accommodates or limits people's abilities to function in that society.

Socialization needs: Ensuring healthy emotional and mental development.

Socioeconomic status (SES): The government's measure of the family's relative economic and social ranking within a community.

Special education: A wide range of educational and social services for people with disabilities.

Specific learning disability: A disorder in which one or more learning processes (i.e., language, listening, thinking, speaking writing, etc.) is adversely impacted.

Speech disorder: An impairment of voice, articulation of speech sounds, and/or fluency.

Sperm banks: Donor sperm that is collected and stored.

Spina bifida: Occurs when the bones in the spine or the spinal cord do not close correctly in pregnancy.

Spontaneous abortion/miscarriage: The loss of an embryo or fetus during pregnancy.

Stepfamily: The presence of a stepparent, stepsibling, or half sibling designates a family as a stepfamily.

Sterility: The inability to reproduce.

Stillbirth: The death of a fetus after the 20th week of pregnancy.

Stimming: Ways in which children self-stimulate.

Stonewalling: When communication between partners completely shuts down.

Strange situation: An experiment designed to assess an infant's attachment type.

Structural-functionalist: A theory that accounts for gender-based role specializations in families.

Student loan debt: Money that is owed on a loan that was taken out by a student to pay for educational expenses.

Subsystems: The separate individuals within a family system.

Suicidality: Refers to the risk of suicide, and includes suicidal ideation and/or intent; suicide attempts; interrupted attempts; aborted attempts; and suicidal acts of preparation.

Survival needs: The basic needs of infants and children, including food, shelter, safety, security, and love.

Symbolic Interaction theory: The paradigm that asserts that human behavior is a continuous dialogue in which people watch the behaviors of other people and then react to those behaviors.

Symbols: Used to convey meanings among actors.

Synapse formation: The connections that form between brain neurons.

Synaptic pruning: The process by which the brain prunes away unused or unneeded synapses.

Synaptogenesis: The first wave of brain growth that occurs prenatally; the overproduction of connections.

Synchrony: Reciprocal, mutually rewarding interactions.

Systemic/institutional racism: Prevailing discrimination found in the criminal justice system, employment, housing, healthcare, and education in the United States.

Tactile stimming: Repetitive behaviors that help a child to connect to their sense of touch (such as tapping fingers).

Teen dating violence (TDV): A type of intimate partner violence that can include *physical violence* and *sexual violence.*

Temporal influences: The passage of time following a stressor, such as parents' divorce.

Teratogens: External agents that can cause prenatal damage.

Theory: A general principle that is used to understand or to explain certain events or family experiences.

Third trimester: Weeks 27 through 40 of pregnancy.

Time-based conflict: Demands from the work domain and the family domain vie for a parent's time and attention.

Timing: The age at which a transition takes place.

Tolerable stress response: The body's reactions are more severe and are the result of uncommon stressors.

Total fertility rate: The average number of live births per woman, in a given population, per year.

Toxic stress response: The most severe stress response a child experiences due to frequent and/or prolonged harsh and/or dangerous living environments and relationships, and other protracted stress that is outside of the child's control.

Transactional: A process in which we simultaneously affect and are affected by our intimate relations.

Traumatic brain injury (TBI): Occurs when a child's brain has experienced an injury because of some type of force; TBI does not apply to congenital or birth trauma brain injuries.

Trust versus Mistrust: Erikson's first stage of psychosocial development.

Turning point: A transition that entails a permanent, lasting shift in the direction of the lifecourse.

Uninvolved parenting: Parents are low in responsiveness, warmth, and affection.

Vernix: A white, waxy coating on the baby's skin; acts as a lubricant.

Vestibular stimming: Twirling or spinning.

Visual impairments: Includes blind and partially sighted children.

Vulnerability factors: Physical and cognitive factors that increase the risk of suicidality.

Wage discrimination: Discrimination shown in the payment of wages, salaries, and earnings to minority groups.

Warmth: A parent's emotional expressions of love.

white-collar professional occupations: Occupations with generally higher earnings (attorneys, bankers, doctors, etc.).

Whole/holistic child: The recognition that a child's development encompasses 4 domains; all 4 domains interact with one another.

Women's liberation: A feminist movement of the 1960s and 1970s that sought to end patriarchal oppression in society.

Work–family spillover/crossover: Occurs when a spouse brings the emotional events and tensions of one environment to the other.

***X* factor:** The end product of the stressor life event.

Zygote intrafallopian transfer (ZIFT): Fertilized eggs are placed directly into the fallopian tubes.

INDEX